THE LYLE OFFICIAL ANTIQUES REVIEW 1987

COMPILED & EDITED BY
TONY CURTIS

FRONT COVER

CHIPARUS BRONZE AND IVORY FIGURE. *(Christie's)*
AN AUSTRIAN WALNUT AND PARQUETRY TABLE CLOCK. *(Christie's)*
MINTON JARDINIERE WITH MOULDED DECORATION, 1858. *(Christie's)*
VICTORIAN KNIFE CLEANER. *(Lyle)*

SPINE

LOIE FULLER BRONZE LAMP, BY RAOUL LARCHE, CIRCA 1900. *(Lyle)*

BACK COVER

REGENCY BRASS BOUND MAHOGANY WINE COOLER. *(Christie's)*
SEVRES DESSERT PLATE, CIRCA 1823. *(Christie's)*
18th CENTURY CHERRYWOOD BUREAU. *(Christie's)*

While every care has been taken in the compiling of information contained in this volume the publishers cannot accept any liability for loss, financial or otherwise, incurred by reliance placed on the information herein.

All prices quoted in this book are obtained from a variety of auctions in various countries during the twelve months prior to publication and are converted to dollars at the rate of exchange prevalent at the time of sale.

The publishers wish to express their sincere thanks to the following for their involvement and assistance in the production of this volume:

KAREN DOUGLASS (Art Editor)
JANICE MONCRIEFF (Assistant Editor)
ANNETTE CURTIS
NICHOLA FAIRBURN
MARGARET ANDERSON
TANYA FAIRBAIRN
FRANK BURRELL
ROBERT NISBET
LYNN MARTIN
DAVID BOLAND
EILEEN BURRELL
SALLY DALGLIESH

British Library Cataloguing in Publication Data

The Lyle official antiques review. — 1987-
  1. Antiques — Prices — Periodicals
338.4'37451   NK1

ISBN 0-86248-056-6

SBN 0-86248-056-6

INTRODUCTION

This year over 100,000 Antique Dealers and Collectors will make full and profitable use of their Lyle Official Antiques Review. They know that only in this one volume will they find the widest possible variety of goods — illustrated, described and given a current market value to assist them to BUY RIGHT AND SELL RIGHT throughout the year of issue.

They know, too, that by building a collection of these immensely valuable volumes year by year, they will equip themselves with an unparalleled reference library of facts, figures and illustrations which, properly used, cannot fail to help them keep one step ahead of the market.

In its sixteen years of publication, Lyle has gone from strength to strength and has become without doubt the pre-eminent book of reference for the antique trade throughout the world. Each of its fact filled pages are packed with precisely the kind of profitable information the professional Dealer needs — including descriptions, illustrations and values of thousands and thousands of individual items carefully selected to give a representative picture of the current market in antiques and collectibles — and remember all values are prices actually paid, based on accurate sales records in the twelve months prior to publication from the best established and most highly respected auction houses and retail outlets in Europe and America.

This is THE book for the Professional Antiques Dealer. 'The Lyle Book' — we've even heard it called 'The Dealer's Bible'.

Compiled and published afresh each year, the Lyle Official Antiques Review is the most comprehensive up-to-date antiques price guide available. THIS COULD BE YOUR WISEST INVESTMENT OF THE YEAR!

Tony Curtis

Printed by Hazell Watson & Viney Limited, Aylesbury, Bucks.
Bound by Dorstel Press Limited, Harlow, Essex.

CONTENTS

Advertising Signs 66
Aeronautical 70
    Aircraft 72
    Paintings 73
Arms & Armour 74
    Badges 78
    Daggers 84
    Helmets 88
    Medals 94
    Pistols 99
    Powder Flasks 110
    Rifles 112
    Swords 118
    Tsubas 124
    Weapons 128
Automatons 129
Barometers 130
Books 134
Bronze 138
Buckets 153
Caddies & Boxes 154
Cameras 160
Chandeliers 163

China 164
    American 164
    Arita 166
    Belleek 167
    Berlin 168

Bow 169
Bristol 169
British 170
Caiger-Smith 175
Canton 175
Cardew, Michael 176
Carltonware 177
Chelsea 178
Chinese 179
Clarice Cliff 183
Coalport 184
Copeland 184
Coper, Hans 185
Delft 186
Della Robbia 188
De Morgan 188
Derby 188
Doulton 189
Dresden 191
Earthenware 191
European 192
Famille Rose 194
Famille Verte 195
French 196
German 198
Goldscheider 201
Goss 202
Grueby 203
Han 203

Imari	205	Stoneware	251
Italian	208	Tang	254
Japanese	210	Terracotta	256
Jones	212	Tournai	256
Kangxi	212	Vienna	257
Kutani	213	Vyse, Charles	257
Kyoto	213	Wedgwood	258
Leach, Bernard	214	Whieldon	262
Leach	214	Wood	262
Lenci	215	Worcester	263
Liverpool	215	Clocks & Watches	270
Longton Hall	216	Bracket Clocks	270
Lowestoft	216	Carriage Clocks	273
Lustre	216	Clock Sets	276
Martinware	217	Longcase Clocks	278
Mason's	218	Mantel Clocks	286
Meissen	219	Skeleton Clocks	294
Ming	226	Wall Clocks	295
Minton	227	Watches	298
Moorcroft	231	Wristwatches	304
Nantgarw	232	Cloisonne	308
Oriental	232	Copper & Brass	312
Parian	232	Costume	318
Paris	233	Decoys	323
Pilkington	234	Dolls	324
Prattware	234	Enamel	330
Redware	234	Fans	334
Lucie Rie	235	Furniture	336
Rookwood	236	Beds	336
Royal Dux	236	Bookcases	338
Ruskin	237	Bureau Bookcases	341
Satsuma	237	Bureaux	344
Sevres	239	Cabinets	350
Shelley	243	Canterburys	359
Song	244	Chairs, Dining	360
Spode	245	Easy	373
Staffordshire	246	Elbow	384

Chests of Drawers 393
Chests on Chests 400
Chests on Stands 402
Chiffoniers. 404
Clothes Presses 405
Commodes & Pot Cupboards 406
Commode Chests. 407
Corner Cupboards 410
Cupboards 412
Davenports. 414
Display Cabinets 416
Dressers. 420
Dumbwaiters 422
Kneehole Desks. 423
Lowboys 426
Screens 427
Secretaires 430
Secretaire Bookcases 432
Settees & Couches 436
Sideboards. 442
Stands. 446
Stools 453
Suites 456
Tables 458
    Card & Tea Tables 458
    Centre Tables 464
    Console Tables 468
    Dining Tables 470
    Dressing Tables 474
    Drop-Leaf Tables. 476
    Gateleg Tables 478
    Large Tables. 480
    Occasional Tables 482
    Pembroke Tables 492
    Side Tables. 494
    Sofa Tables 498
    Workboxes & Games Tables. 500

Writing Tables & Desks. 504
Trunks & Coffers. 509
Wardrobes & Armoires 512
Washstands. 514
Whatnots. 515
Wine Coolers 516
Glass. 518
    Beakers 518
    Bottles 519
    Bowls 520
    Boxes 521
    Candlesticks 522
    Decanters. 523
    Dishes 524
    Drinking Sets 525
    Flasks 526
    Goblets 527
    Jugs 532
    Miscellaneous Glass 533
    Paperweights 534
    Scent Bottles 540
    Shades. 540
    Tumblers. 541
    Vases 542
    Wine Glasses. 548
Gold. 552
Horn. 556
Indian Art 557
Inros. 560
Instruments 562
Iron & Steel 572
Ivory. 574
Jade 580
Jewellery 582
Lacquer. 586
Lamps. 587
Marble. 592

Mirrors	594	Cups	708
Miscellaneous	602	Dishes	709
Model Ships	606	Ewers	712
Model Trains	608	Flatware	713
Models	612	Frames	716
Motoring Items	614	Goblets	717
Musical Boxes & Polyphones	618	Inkstands	718
Musical Instruments	622	Jugs	719
Netsuke	626	Miscellaneous Silver	720
Paper Money	634	Models	722
Pewter	636	Mugs	723
Photographs	640	Mustards	724
Pianos	646	Nutmegs	725
Portrait Miniatures	648	Porringers	725
Posters	658	Salts	726
Prints	662	Sauceboats	727
Quilts	670	Snuff Boxes	728
Rugs	672	Tankards	730
Samplers	682	Tazzas	732
Silver	684	Tea & Coffee Sets	733
Baskets	684	Tea Caddies	738
Beakers	685	Tea Kettles	739
Bowls	686	Teapots	740
Boxes	688	Trays & Salvers	741
Candelabra	690	Tureens	744
Candlesticks	692	Urns	746
Casters	696	Vases	747
Centrepieces	697	Vinaigrettes	748
Chambersticks	698	Wine Coolers	749
Chocolate Pots	699	Snuff Boxes	750
Cigarette Boxes	699	Stone	752
Cigarette Cases	700	Tapestries	754
Claret Jugs	701	Textiles	757
Coasters	702	Toys	762
Coffee Pots	703	Transport	770
Cream Jugs	706	Weathervanes	776
Cruets	707	Wood	778

Acknowledgements

Abridge Auctions, *(Michael Yewman), Market Place, Abridge, Sussex*
Anderson & Garland, *Anderson House, Market Street, Newcastle*
Ball & Percival, *132 Lord Street, Southport*
Banks & Silvers, *66 Foregate Street, Worcester*
Barbers Fine Art Auctioneers, *(Chobham Ltd.), The Mayford Centre,*
  Smarts Heath Rd., Mayford, Woking
Bearnes, *Rainbow, Avenue Road, Torquay*
Bermondsey Antiques Market, *Tower Bridge Road, London*
Biddle & Webb, *Ladywood Middleway, Birmingham*
Bloomsbury Book Auctions, *3 & 4 Hardwick Street, London*
Boardman Fine Art Auctioneers, *Station Road Corner, Haverhill, Suffolk*
Bonham's, *Montpelier Gardens, Montpelier Street, London*
Bracketts, *27-29 High Street, Tunbridge Wells*
J. R. Bridgford & Sons, *1 Heyes Lane, Alderley Edge, Cheshire*
British Antique Exporters, *206 London Road, Burgess Hill, W. Sussex*
Wm. H. Brown, *Westgate Hall, Grantham, Lincs*
Butler & Hatch Waterman, *86 High Street, Hythe, Kent*
Capes, Dunn & Co., *The Auction Galleries, 38 Charles Street, Manchester*
Chancellors Hollingsworths, *31 High Street, Ascot*
Christie's, *8 King Street, St. James's, London*
Christie's, *502 Park Avenue, New York, N.Y. 10022*
Christie's (Monaco) S.A.N., *Park Palace, 98000 Monte Carlo*
Christie's (Hong Kong) Ltd., *3607 Edinburgh Tower, 15 Queen's Rd. Hong Kong*
Christie's, *Cornelis Schuytstraat 57, 1071 JG, Amsterdam*
Christie's East, *219 East 67th Street, New York, N.Y. 10021*
Christie's & Edmiston's, *164/166 Bath Street, Glasgow*
Christie's S. Kensington, *85 Old Brompton Road, London*
Coles, Knapp & Kennedy, *Georgian Rooms, Ross-on-Wye, Herefordshire*
Cooper Hirst, *Goldway House, Parkway, Chelmsford.*
Dacre, Son & Hartley, *1-5 The Grove, Ilkley, Yorkshire*
Dee & Atkinson, *The Exchange Saleroom, Driffield, Yorkshire*
Dreweatts, *Donnington Priory, Newbury, Berkshire*
Hy. Duke & Son, *Weymouth Avenue, Dorchester, Dorset*
Elliott & Green, *40 High Street, Lymington, Hants*
R. H. Ellis & Sons, *44-46 High Street, Worthing, Sussex*
Frank H. Fellows & Son, *Bedford House, 88 Hagley Road, Edgbaston, Birmingham*
Fox & Sons, *41 Chapel Road, Worthing*

ANTIQUES REVIEW

Geering & Colyer, *22-24 High Street, Tunbridge Wells*
Goss & Crested China, *(N. J. Pine), 62 Murray Road, Horndean*
Andrew Grant, *59-60 Foregate Street, Worcester*
Graves, Son & Pilcher, *71 Church Road, Hove, Sussex*
Hobbs & Chambers, *'At the Sign of the Bell', Market Place, Cirencester*
John Hogbin & Son, *8 Queen Street, Deal, Kent*
Edgar Horn, *46-50 South Street, Eastbourne, Sussex*
Jacobs & Hunt, *Lavant Street, Petersfield, Hants*
W. H. Lane & Son, *64 Morrab Road, Penzance, Cornwall*
Lawrence Fine Art, *South Street, Crewkerne, Somerset*
Locke & England, *Walton House, 11 The Parade, Leamington Spa*
Lots Road Chelsea Auction Galleries, *71 Lots Road, London*
Thomas Love & Son, *South St. John Street, Perth*
Mallams, *24 St. Michael's Street, Oxford*
May, Whetter & Grose, *Cornubia Hall, Par, Cornwall*
Morphets, *4-6 Albert Street, Harrogate, Yorkshire*
Neales of Nottingham, *192 Mansfield Road, Nottingham*
D. M. Nesbit & Co., *7 Clarendon Road, Southsea, Hants*
Onslows, *123 Hursley, Winchester, Hants*
Outhwaite & Litherland, *Kingsway Galleries, Fontenoy Street, Liverpool*
Parsons, Welch & Cowell, *49 London Road, Sevenoaks, Kent*
Phillips, *Marylebone Auction Rooms, Hayes Place, London*
Phillips, *65 George Street, Edinburgh*
Phillips, *98 Sauchiehall Street, Glasgow*
Phillips, *Blenstock House, 7 Blenheim Street, New Bond St., London*
Phillips, *The Old House, Station Road, Knowle, Solihull, W. Midlands*
Phillips & Jolly's, *The Auction Rooms, 1 Old King Street, Bath*
John H. Raby & Sons, *21 St. Mary's Road, Bradford*
Reeds Rains, *Trinity House, 114 Northenden Road, Sale, Cheshire*
Russell, Baldwin & Bright, *Ryelands Road, Leominster, Herefordshire*
Sandoe, Luce Panes, *Chipping Manor Salerooms, Wotton-under-Edge*
Robt. W. Skinner Inc., *Bolton Gallery, Route 117, Bolton, Mass*
H. Spencer & Sons Ltd., *20 The Square, Retford, Notts.*
Street Jewellery, *10 Summerhill Terrace, Newcastle-upon-Tyne*
Stride & Son, *Southdown House, St. John's Street, Chichester, Sussex*
G. E. Sworder's & Sons, *19 North Street, Bishops Stortford, Herts*
Vidler & Co., *Auction Offices, Cinque Ports St., Rye, Sussex*
Wallis & Wallis, *West Street Auction Galleries, Lewes, Sussex*
Ward & Partners, *16 High Street, Hythe, Kent*
Warner, Sheppard & Wade, *16-18 Halford Street, Leicester*
Peter Wilson & Co., *Market Street, Nantwich, Cheshire*
Woolley & Wallis, *The Castle Auction Mart, Castle Street, Salisbury*
Worsfolds Auction Galleries, *40 Station Road West, Canterbury*

PERIODS   MONARCHS

PERIODS		MONARCHS	
TUDOR PERIOD	1485 - 1603	HENRY IV	1399 - 1413
ELIZABETHAN PERIOD	1558 - 1603	HENRY V	1413 - 1422
INIGO JONES	1572 - 1652	HENRY VI	1422 - 1461
JACOBEAN PERIOD	1603 - 1688	EDWARD IV	1461 - 1483
STUART PERIOD	1603 - 1714	EDWARD V	1483 - 1483
A. C. BOULLE	1642 - 1732	RICHARD III	1483 - 1485
LOUIS XIV PERIOD	1643 - 1715	HENRY VII	1485 - 1509
GRINLING GIBBONS	1648 - 1726	HENRY VIII	1509 - 1547
CROMWELLIAN PERIOD	1649 - 1660	EDWARD VI	1547 - 1553
CAROLEAN PERIOD	1660 - 1685	MARY	1553 - 1558
WILLIAM KENT	1684 - 1748	ELIZABETH	1558 - 1603
WILLIAM & MARY PERIOD	1689 - 1702	JAMES I	1603 - 1625
QUEEN ANNE PERIOD	1702 - 1714	CHARLES I	1625 - 1649
GEORGIAN PERIOD	1714 - 1820	COMMONWEALTH	1649 - 1660
T. CHIPPENDALE	1715 - 1762	CHARLES II	1660 - 1685
LOUIS XV PERIOD	1723 - 1774	JAMES II	1685 - 1689
A. HEPPLEWHITE	1727 - 1788	WILLIAM & MARY	1689 - 1695
ADAM PERIOD	1728 - 1792	WILLIAM III	1695 - 1702
ANGELICA KAUFMANN	1741 - 1807	ANNE	1702 - 1714
T. SHERATON	1751 - 1806	GEORGE I	1714 - 1727
LOUIS XVI	1774 - 1793	GEORGE II	1727 - 1760
T. SHEARER	(circa) 1780	GEORGE III	1760 - 1820
REGENCY PERIOD	1800 - 1830	GEORGE IV	1820 - 1830
EMPIRE PERIOD	1804 - 1815	WILLIAM IV	1830 - 1837
VICTORIAN PERIOD	1837 - 1901	VICTORIA	1837 - 1901
EDWARDIAN PERIOD	1901 - 1910	EDWARD VII	1901 - 1910

SILVER MARKS

Birmingham
Chester
Dublin
Edinburgh
Exeter
Glasgow
London
Newcastle
Sheffield
York

Example for 1850

	B	C	D	Ed	Ex	G	L	N	S	Y
1700										
1701	A			A						B
1702	B	P		B			A			C
1703	C			C			B			D
1704	D						C			
1705	E		A	E			D			F
1706	F		B	F			E			G
1707	G		C	G		B	F			
1708	H		D	H			G			
1709	I		E	I		D				
1710	K		F	K						
1711	L		G	L						
1712	M		H	M						
1713	N		I	N						
1714	O		K	O						
1715	P		L	P						
1716	Q	Z	M	Q			A			
1717	R		N	R			B			
1718	S		O	S			C			
1719	T		P	T			D			
1720	U	A	Q	V			E			
1721	V	B	R	W			F			
1722	W	C	S	X			G			
1723	X	D	T	Y			H			
1724	Y	E	U	Z			I			
1725	Z	F	V				K			
1726	A	G	W				L			
1727	B	H	X	C			M			
1728	C	I	Y		S		N			
1729	D	K	Z				O			
1730	E	L	A				P			

	B	C	D	Ed	Ex	G	L	N	S	Y
1731	F		B				Q			
1732	G		C				R			
1733	H	N	D				S			
1734				K	S		T			
1735	K	P					V			
1736	L		G	m			a			
1737	M		K				b			
1738	N	S		o			C			
1739	O	T	K	p			d			
1740	P	U	L	q			e			A
1741	Q	W	M	r			f			B
1742	R	W	N	s			g			C
1743	S		O			S	h			D
1744	T		P	u			i			E
1745	U		Q	w			K			F
1746	V	Z	R				l			G
1747	W	A	S			S	m			H
1748	X	B		Z			n			I
1749	Y	C	U	A			o			K
1750	Z	D	V	B			P			L
1751	a	E	W	C			q			M
1752	b	F	X	D			r			N
1753	C	G	Y	E						O
1754	d	H	Z	F			t			P
1755	e			G			u			Q
1756	f		B	H	S					R
1757	G	I	C	II			B			S
1758	h	K	D	K	S		C			
1759	i	L	E	L						A
1760	k	M	F	M			E			B
1761	l	N	G	N			F			
1762	m	O	H	O			G			
1763	n	P	I	P	E		H			
1764	O	Q	k	Q			I			
1765	P	R	L	R			K			
1766	Q	S		S			L			
1767	R	T		T			M			
1768	S	U		U			N			
1769	T	W	P	W			O		6	
1770		X	Q	X			P		D	
1771	U	Y	R	Y			Q		E	
1772	V	Z	S	Z			R		F	
1773	A	W				S	S		G	E
1774	B	X			B		T		H	F

16

Hallmark date-letter chart

Year	B	C	D	Ed	Ex	G	L	N	S	Y
1775	C	Y	C	D	C		U		N	
1776	D	a	d	I	D	O		K	R	
1777	E	b	E	B	E		b	L	h	
1778	F	c	F	Z	F		C	M	S	C
1779	G	d	G	B	G		d	N	A	D
1780	H	e	H	A	H		e	O	Z	E
1781	I	f	I	B		U		f	P	F
1782	K	g	K	C			g	Q	G	G
1783	L	h	L	D	K	S	h	R	B	H
1784	M	i	M	E	L		i	S	I	J
1785	N	k	N	F	M	S	k	T	K	K
1786	O	l	O	G	N		l	U	R	L
1787	P	m	P		O		m	W	A	A
1788	Q	n	Q	H	P		n	X	M	B
1789	R	O	R	IJ	Q		o	Y	M	C
1790	S	P	S	K	r	S	p	Z	L	d
1791	T	q	T	L	f		q	A	P	e
1792	U	r	U	M	t		r	B	U	f
1793	V	S	W	N	U		S	C	G	g
1794	W	t	X	O	W		t	D	h	h
1795	X	U	Y	P	X	S	U	E	q	i
1796	Y	V	Z	Q	y		A	F	Z	k
1797	Z	A	A	R	A		B	G	X	L
1798	a	B	B	S	B		C	H	V	M
1799	b	C	C	T	C		D	I	E	N
1800	c	D	D	U	D	S	E	K	N	O
1801	d	E	E	V			F	L	H	P
1802	e	F	F	W	F		G	M	M	O
1803	f	G	G	X	G		H	N	P	R
1804	g	H	H	Y	H		I	O	B	S
1805	h	I	I	Z	I		K	P	B	T
1806	i	K	K	a	K		L	Q	A	U
1807	j	L	L	b	L		M	R	S	V
1808	k	M	M	M			N	S	B	W
1809	l	N	N	d	N		O	T	K	X
1810	m	O	o	e	O		P	U	L	Y
1811	n	P	p	f	P		Q	W	C	Z
1812	O	Q	q	g	Q		R	X	B	a
1813	P	R	R	h	R		S	Y	R	b
1814	q	S	S	i	S		T	Z	W	c
1815	r	T	T	j	T		U	A	O	d
1816	S	U	U	k	U		a	B	T	e
1817	t	V	W	l	a		b	C	X	f
1818	u	A	X	m	b		C	D	I	g
1819	V	B	Y	n	C	A	d	E	V	h

Year	B	C	D	Ed	Ex	G	L	N	S	Y
1820	W	C	Z	o	d	B	e	F	Q	i
1821	X	D	A	P	e	C	f	G	Y	k
1822	y	D	B	q	f	D	g	H	Z	l
1823	Z	E	C	r	g	E	h	I	U	m
1824	A	F	D	S	h	F	i	K	a	n
1825	B	G	E	t	i	G	k	L	b	o
1826	C	H	F	u	k	H	l	M	C	p
1827	D	I	G	V	l	I	m	N	d	q
1828	E	K	H	W	m	J	n	O	e	r
1829	F	L	I	X	n	K	O	P	f	S
1830	G	M	K	y	O	L	p	Q	h	t
1831	h	N	L	Z	p	M	q	R	h	u
1832	J	O	M	A	q	N	r	S	k	v
1833	K	P	N	B	r	O	S	T	l	w
1834	L	Q	O	C	S	P	t	U	m	x
1835	M	R	P	D	t	Q	u	W	P	y
1836	N	S	Q	E	u	R	A	X	q	z
1837	O	T	R	f	f	S	B	Y	r	A
1838	P	U	S	G	t	T	C	Z	S	B
1839	Q	A	T	H	u	U	C	A	t	C
1840	R	B	U	I	v	W	C	B	u	D
1841	S	C	V	K	w	f	C	V	E
1842	T	D	W	L	f	X	G	D	X	F
1843	U	E	X	M	G	Y	H	E	Z	G
1844	U	F	Y	n	D	Z	J	F	A	H
1845	W	G	Z	O	A	R	G	B	I
1846	X	h	a	P	K	S	L	H	C	K
1847	Y	i	b	q	L	T	M	I	D	L
1848	Z	K	C	R	M	U	N	J	E	M
1849	A	l	d	S	A	C	O	K	N
1850	B	m	e	t	f	P	L	O
1851	C	n	f	u	G	Q	M	H	P
1852	D	o	g	V	R	N	I	Q
1853	E	P	h	W	S	O	K	R
1854	F	q	j	X	S	T	P	L	S
1855	G	R	k	Y	R	Q	M	T
1856	H	S	l	Z	S	R	N	V
1857	I	T	m	A	A	S	h	A
1858	J	U	n	B	B	T	i	C	T	P
1859	K	V	o	C	C	U	j	D	U	R
1860	L	W	P	D	e	f	S
1861	M	X	Q	E	G	f	X	T
1862	N	Y	r	F	R	g	Y	U
1863	O	Z	S	G	S	h	Z	V
1864	P	a	t	H	H	T	i	a	W

17

Left half (1865–1909):

Year	B	C	D	Ed	Ex	G	L	N	S	Y
1865	Q	b	u	i	I	k	b		X	
1866	R	c	v	K	K	l	c		Y	
1867	S	d	w	L	L	m	d		Z	
1868	T	e	x	M	M	n	e		A	
1869	U	f	y	N	N	o	f		B	
1870	V	g	z	O	O	p	g		C	
1871	W	h	A	P	P	q	h		D	
1872	X	i	B	Q	B	r	i		E	
1873	Y	k	C	R	C	s	k		F	
1874	Z	l	D	S	D	t	l		G	
1875	a	m	E	T	E	u	m		H	
1876	b	n	F	U	F	A	n		J	
1877	c	o	G	V	G	B	o		K	
1878	d	p	H	W	H	C	p		L	
1879	e	q	I	X	I	D	q		M	
1880	f	r	K	Y	J	E	r		N	
1881	g	s	L	Z	K	F	s		O	
1882	h	t	M	a	L	G	t		P	
1883	i	u	N	b	U	H	u		Q	
1884	k	A	O	c		I	A		R	
1885	l	B	P	d		K	B		S	
1886	m	C	Q	e		L	C		T	
1887	n	D	R	f		M	D		U	
1888	o	E	S	g		N	E		V	
1889	p	F	T	h		O	F		W	
1890	q	G	U	i		P	G		X	
1891	r	H	V	k		Q	H		Y	
1892	s	I	W	l		R	I		Z	
1893	t	K	X	m		S	K		a	
1894	u	L	Y	n		T	L		b	
1895	v	M	Z	o		U	M		c	
1896	w	N	A	p			N		d	
1897	x	O	B	q			O		e	
1898	y	P	C	r			P		f	
1899	z	Q	D	s			Q		g	
1900	a	R	C	t			R		h	
1901	b	A	f	v			S		i	
1902	c	B	G	w			T		k	
1903	d	C	H	r			U		l	
1904	e	D	H	v			H		m	
1905	f	E	K	3			K		n	
1906	g	F	L	A			L		o	
1907	h	G	M	B			m		p	
1908	i	H	N	C			N		q	
1909	k	I	O	D			O		r	

Right half (1910–1954):

Year	B	C	D	Ed	Ex	G	L	N	S	Y
1910	l	K	P	E			N		p	S
1911	m	L	Q	F			O		q	t
1912	n	M	R	G			P		r	u
1913	o	N	S	H			Q		s	v
1914	p	O	T	I			R		t	w
1915	q	P	U	K			S		u	x
1916	r	Q	A	L			T		a	y
1917	S	R	b	M			U		b	z
1918	t	S	C	N			V		c	a
1919	u	T	D	O			W		d	b
1920	V	U	E	P			X		e	c
1921	W	V	F	Q			Y		f	d
1922	X	W	S	R			Z		g	e
1923	y	X	h	S			a		h	f
1924	Z	Y	I	T			b		i	g
1925	A	Z	U	U			C		k	h
1926	B	a	V	V			d		l	i
1927	C	b	m	W			e		m	k
1928	D	c	n	X			f		n	l
1929	E	d	O	Y			g		o	m
1930	F	e	p	Z			h		p	n
1931	G	ff	A	A			i		q	o
1932	H	g	B	B			j		r	p
1933	J	h	R	C			k		s	q
1934	K	i	S	D			l		t	r
1935	L	k	C	E			m		u	s
1936	M	l	U	F			N		a	t
1937	N	m	V	G			O		B	u
1938	O	n	W	H			P		C	v
1939	P	o	X	I			q		D	w
1940	Q	p	Y	K			r		E	x
1941	R	q	Z	L			s		F	y
1942	S	A	A	A			t		H	z
1943	T	B	B	N			u		H	A
1944	U	C	C	O			V		I	B
1945	V	D	D	P			W		K	C
1946	W	E	E	Q			X		L	D
1947	X	F	F	R			Y		M	E
1948	Y	G	G	S			Z		N	F
1949	Z	H	H	T			A		O	G
1950	A	I	I	U			B		P	h
1951	B	J	J	V			C		Q	i
1952	C	K	K	W			D		R	k
1953	D	L	L	X			E		S	L
1954	E	M	M	Y			F		T	M

REGISTRY OF DESIGNS

BELOW ARE ILLUSTRATED THE TWO FORM OF 'REGISTRY OF DESIGN' MARK USED BETWEEN THE YEARS OF 1842 to 1883.

EXAMPLE: An article produced between 1842 and 1867 would bear the following marks. (Example for the 12th of November 1852).

CLASS OF GOODS

YEAR

MONTH — DAY

BUNDLE

EXAMPLE: An article produced between 1868 and 1883 would bear the following marks. (Example the 22nd of October 1875).

CLASS OF GOODS

DAY

BUNDLE — YEAR

MONTH

DATE AND LETTER CODE USED 1842 to 1883

1842	X	63	G
43	H	64	N
44	C	65	W
45	A	66	Q
46	I	67	T
47	F	68	X
48	U	69	H
49	S	70	O
50	V	71	A
51	P	72	I
52	D	73	F
53	Y	74	U
54	J	75	S
55	E	76	V
56	L	77	P
57	K	78	D
58	B	79	Y
59	M	80	J
60	Z	81	E
61	R	82	L
62	O	83	K

January	C	July	I
February	G	August	R
March	W	September	D
April	H	October	B
May	E	November	K
June	M	December	A

CHINESE DYNASTIES

Shang	1766 – 1123BC
Zhou	1122 – 249BC
Warring States	403 – 221BC
Qin	221 – 207BC
Han	206BC – AD220
6 Dynasties	317 – 589
Sui	590 – 618
Tang	618 – 906
5 Dynasties	907 – 960
Liao	907 – 1125
Song	960 – 1279
Jin	1115 – 1234
Yuan	1260 – 1368
Ming	1368 – 1644
Qing	1644 – 1911

REIGN PERIODS

MING

Hongwu	1368 – 1398	Hongzhi	1488 – 1505
Jianwen	1399 – 1402	Zhengde	1506 – 1521
Yongle	1403 – 1424	Jiajing	1522 – 1566
Hongxi	1425	Longqing	1567 – 1572
Xuande	1426 – 1435	Wanli	1573 – 1620
Zhengtong	1436 – 1449	Taichang	1620
Jingtai	1450 – 1456	Tianqi	1621 – 1627
Tianshun	1457 – 1464	Chongzheng	1628 – 1644
Chenghua	1465 – 1487		

QING

Shunzhi	1644 – 1662	Daoguang	1821 – 1850
Kangxi	1662 – 1722	Xianfeng	1851 – 1861
Yongzheng	1723 – 1735	Tongzhi	1862 – 1874
Qianlong	1736 – 1795	Guangxu	1875 – 1908
Jiali	1796 – 1820	Xuantong	1908 – 1911

CHINA MARKS

BELLEEK
1857 onwards

BLOOR DERBY
1815-1840

BLOOR DERBY

BOW
1750-1776

1750   1760   1770

CAUGHLEY
1772-1814

imitation
Worcester   in blue   in blue   SALOPIAN impressed

CHELSEA
1745-1784

Chelfea 1745

incised   in relief   red   gold
1745-1749   1750-1753   1755   1758-1770

COLEBROOK DALE
1785-1820

CDale.   Coalport
1785-1820

COPELAND
1847

COPELAND & GARRETT
1833

1847   1847-1891   NEW FAYENCE
1833-1847

DAVENPORT
1793-1882

Davenport

DAVENPORT
LONGPORT
STAFFORDSHIRE

DAVENPORTS
STONE CHINA

DERBY
1745 onwards

1750   1760   1770-1780

DOULTON
1815

pre 1836   1872

FRANKENTHAL
1755-1800

blue   blue   blue   blue
1756   1756-1759   1762-1793   1771

HOCHST
1750-1798

red   blue   impressed
1750-1762   1762-1796   1765-1774   1760-1765

LEEDS
1760-1878

Hartley, Greens & Co
LEEDS POTTERY
1760-1783

LEEDS POTTERY
LEEDS POTTERY
impressed 1864

MARTIN BROS
1873-1915

Martin Bros
London & Southall
1873

R.W. MARTIN & BROS
1900

MASONS
1795-1854

MASONS
PATENT IRONSTONE CHINA

FENTON STONE WORKS

MEISSON
1713

1713-1724   1725-1750   modern

MENNECY
1734-1748

DV   .D.V.
incised   in blue

MINTON
1793 onwards

1800-1836   1851   1860-1880

MINTON B B New Stone   MINTONS
1861 onward   20th century

NANTGARW
1811-1820

Nantgarw
1811

NANTGARW
1813

SWANSEA
NANGARW
1814

NANT GARW
O.W.
1816-1820

NEWHALL
1782-1835

N 332

PETIT JACOB
1796-1862

J.P.
1800   1820

PLYMOUTH
1768-1772

ROCKINGHAM

ARD MELO
Rockingham
ROCKINGHAM
early 19th century

Baguley
Rockingham Works
red 1824

CHINA MARKS

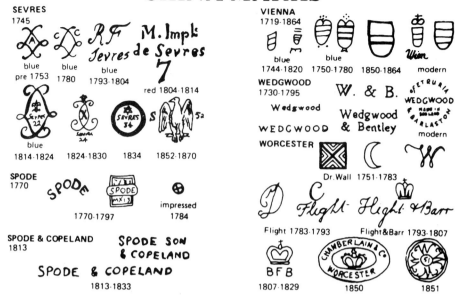

RECOGNITION & DATING

Obviously the task of committing every china mark to memory is one which will be outside the scope of most collectors and, indeed, most dealers too. For this reason, the following simple guides may prove to be of some assistance in determining the approximate date of a piece without having recourse to long, and frequently involved, lists of the marks used by various manufacturers over the years.

Any piece bearing the words 'English Bone China' or simply 'Bone China' is a product of the twentieth century and the words 'Made in England' also suggest twentieth century manufacture, though they could relate to pieces dating from 1875 onwards.

The word 'England' stamped on a piece suggests compliance with the McKinley Tariff Act of America, 1891 which required all imports to America to bear the name of the country of origin.

In 1862, the Trade Mark Act became law. Any piece bearing the words 'Trade Mark' therefore, can be assumed to date from 1862 onward.

Following the law relating to companies of limited liability, the word Limited or its abbreviations appears after 1860, though more commonly on pieces dating from 1885 onwards.

When a piece bears a pattern number or name, it can be assumed to date no earlier than about 1810.

Royal Arms incorporated into a small mark indicates a date after 1800.

During the mid 19th century the word 'Royal' was commonly added to the Manufacturer's name or trade name and, consequently, pieces bearing this word can usually be placed after 1850.

CHAIR BACKS

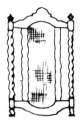

1660
Charles II.

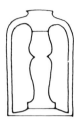

1705
Queen Anne.

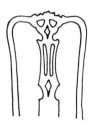

1745
Chippendale.

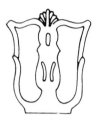

1745
Chippendale.

1750
Georgian.

1750
Hepplewhite.

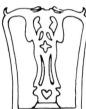

1750
Chippendale.

1760
French Rococo.

1760
Gothic.

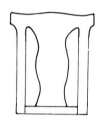

1760
Splat back.

1770
Chippendale
ladder back.

1785
Windsor
wheel back.

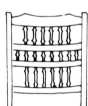

1785
Lancashire
spindle back.

1785
Lancashire
ladder back.

1790
Shield and
feathers.

1795
Shield back.

1795
Hepplewhite.

1795
Hepplewhite
camel back.

1795
Hepplewhite.

1810
Late Georgian
bar back.

CHAIR BACKS

1810
Thomas Hope
'X' frame.

1810
Regency
rope back.

1815
Regency.

1815
Regency
cane back.

1820
Regency.

1820
Empire.

1820
Regency
bar back.

1825
Regency
bar back.

1830
Regency
bar back.

1830
Bar back.

1830
William IV
bar back.

1830
William IV.

1835
Lath back.

1840
Victorian
balloon back.

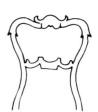

1845
Victorian.

1845
Victorian
bar back.

1850
Victorian.

1860
Victorian.

1870
Victorian.

1875
Cane back.

LEGS

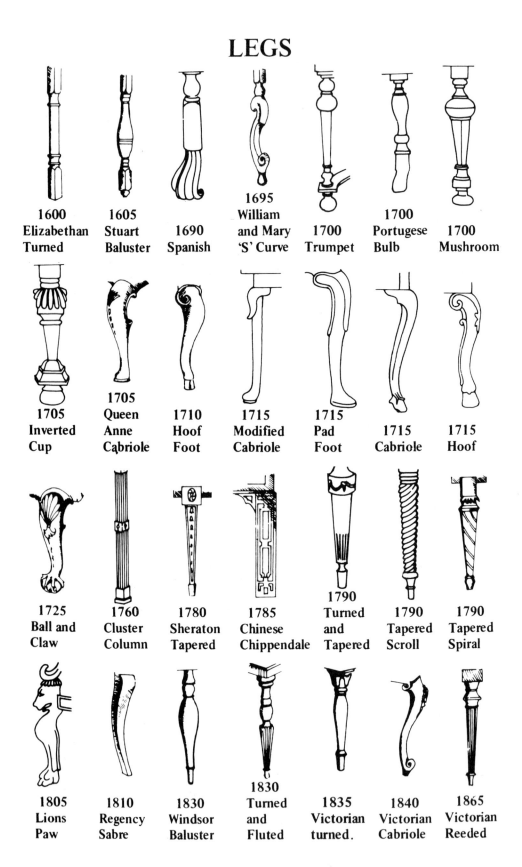

| 1600 Elizabethan Turned | 1605 Stuart Baluster | 1690 Spanish | 1695 William and Mary 'S' Curve | 1700 Trumpet | 1700 Portugese Bulb | 1700 Mushroom |

| 1705 Inverted Cup | 1705 Queen Anne Cabriole | 1710 Hoof Foot | 1715 Modified Cabriole | 1715 Pad Foot | 1715 Cabriole | 1715 Hoof |

| 1725 Ball and Claw | 1760 Cluster Column | 1780 Sheraton Tapered | 1785 Chinese Chippendale | 1790 Turned and Tapered | 1790 Tapered Scroll | 1790 Tapered Spiral |

| 1805 Lions Paw | 1810 Regency Sabre | 1830 Windsor Baluster | 1830 Turned and Fluted | 1835 Victorian turned. | 1840 Victorian Cabriole | 1865 Victorian Reeded |

FEET

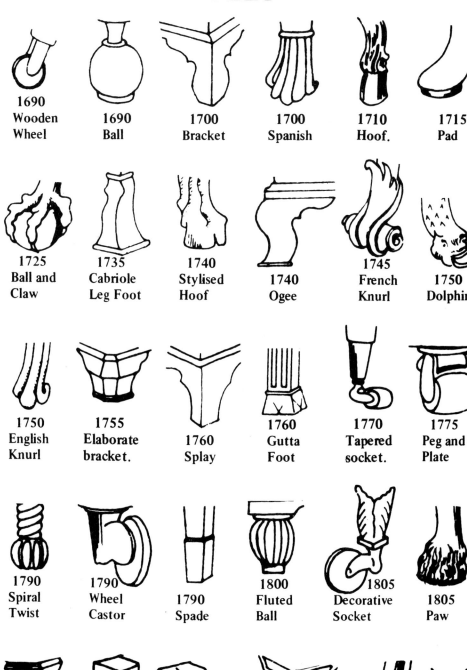

1690 Wooden Wheel

1690 Ball

1700 Bracket

1700 Spanish

1710 Hoof.

1715 Pad

1725 Ball and Claw

1735 Cabriole Leg Foot

1740 Stylised Hoof

1740 Ogee

1745 French Knurl

1750 Dolphin

1750 English Knurl

1755 Elaborate bracket.

1760 Splay

1760 Gutta Foot

1770 Tapered socket.

1775 Peg and Plate

1790 Spiral Twist

1790 Wheel Castor

1790 Spade

1800 Fluted Ball

1805 Decorative Socket

1805 Paw

1805 Regency

1810 Socket

1815 Lions Paw

1830 Regency

1830 Victorian Scroll

1860 Victorian Bun

HANDLES

1550
Tudor
drop.

1560
Early
Stuart
loop.

1570
Early
Stuart
loop.

1620
Early
Stuart
loop.

1660
Stuart
drop.

1680
Stuart
drop.

1690
William &
Mary solid
backplate.

1700
William &
Mary split
tail.

1700
Queen Anne
solid back-
plate.

1705
Queen Anne
ring.

1710
Queen Anne
loop.

1720
Early
Georgian
pierced.

1720
Early
Georgian
brass drop.

1730
Cut away
backplate.

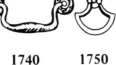

1740
Georgian
plain brass
loop.

1750
Georgian
shield drop.

1755
French
style.

1760
Rococo
style.

1765
Chinese
style.

1770
Georgian
ring.

1780
Late Georgian
stamped.

1790
Late Georgian
stamped.

1810
Regency
knob.

1820
Regency
lions mask.

1825
Campaign.

1840
Early
Victorian
porcelain.

1850
Victorian
reeded.

1880
Porcelain or
wood knob.

1890
Late Victorian
loop.

1910
Art
Nouveau.

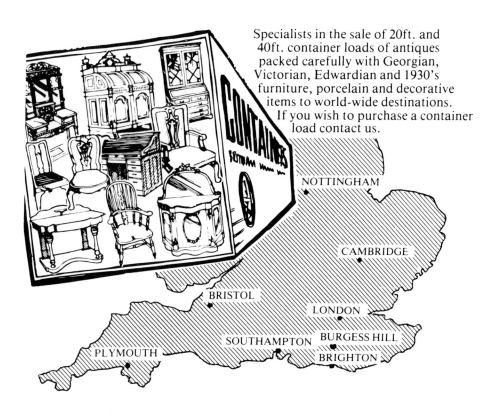

THERE ARE A GREAT MANY ANTIQUE SHIPPERS IN BRITAIN

but few, if any, who are as quality conscious as Norman Lefton, Chairman and Managing Director of British Antique Exporters Ltd. of Burgess Hill, Nr. Brighton, Sussex. Twenty-four years' experience of shipping goods to all parts of the globe have confirmed his original belief that the way to build clients' confidence in his services is to supply them only with goods which are in first class saleable condition. To this end, he employs a cottage industry staff of over 50, from highly skilled antique restorers, polishers and packers to representative buyers and executives. Through their knowledgeable hands passes each piece of furniture before it leaves the B.A.E. warehouses, ensuring that the overseas buyer will only receive the best and most saleable merchandise for their particular market. This attention to detail is obvious on a visit to the Burgess Hill showrooms where potential customers can view what must be the most varied assortment of Georgian, Victorian, Edwardian and 1930s furniture in the UK. One cannot fail to be impressed by, not only the varied range of merchandise, but also the fact that each piece is in showroom condition awaiting shipment.

BRITISH ANTIQUE EXPORTERS LTD

QUEEN ELIZABETH AVENUE
BURGESS HILL
WEST SUSSEX, RH15 9RX, ENGLAND
Telex 87688

Member of L.A.P.A.D.A.
Guild of Master Craftsmen

Telephone BURGESS HILL (04446) 45577

As one would expect, packing is considered somewhat of an art at B.A.E. and the manager in charge of the works ensures that each piece will reach its final destination in the condition a customer would wish. B.A.E. set a very high standard and, as a further means of improving each container load, their customer/container liaison dept. invites each customer to return detailed information on the saleability of each piece in the container, thereby ensuring successful future shipments. This feedback of information is the all important factor which guarantees the profitability of future containers. "By this method" Mr. Lefton explains, "we have established that an average £7000 container will immediately it is unpacked at its final destination realise in the region of £10000 to £14000 for our clients selling the goods on a quick wholesale turnover basis". When visiting the warehouses various container loads can be seen in the course of completion. The intending buyer can then judge for himself which type of container load would be best suited to his market. In an average 20-foot container B.A.E. put approximately 75 to 150 pieces carefully selected to suit the particular destination. There are always at least 10 outstanding or unusual items in each shipment, but every piece included looks as though it has something special about it.

Based at Burgess Hill, 7 miles from Brighton and 39 miles from London on a direct rail link, (only 40 minutes journey), the Company is ideally situated to ship containers to all parts of the world. The showrooms, restoration and packing departments are open to overseas buyers and no visit to purchase antiques for re-sale in other countries is complete without a visit to their Burgess Hill premises where a welcome is always found.

BRITISH ANTIQUE EXPORTERS LTD

QUEEN ELIZABETH AVENUE
BURGESS HILL
WEST SUSSEX, RH15 9RX, ENGLAND
Telex 87688

Member of L.A.P.A.D.A.
Guild of Master Craftsmen

Telephone BURGESS HILL (04446) 45577

29

INTERIOR DESIGN SERVICES

Due to expansion of our facilities, British Antique Furniture Co. are able to offer for the first time the services which have been available to their Export clients for over 25 YEARS. Everything from Brasswork and Marble Masonry to Restoration, French Polishing and Upholstering.

ALL THESE SERVICES ARE IN-HOUSE

HAND-DYED LEATHER
LINING SERVICE.

BRASS CLEANING &
REPAIRING

MARBLE CLEANING &
CUTTING SERVICE

UPHOLSTERY

RESTORATION

RESTORERS AT WORK

FRENCH POLISHING

BRITISH ANTIQUE FURNITURE CO.

SCHOOL CLOSE, QUEEN ELIZABETH AVENUE
BURGESS HILL, WEST SUSSEX RH15 9RX

Tel: Burgess Hill (04446) 45577

OFFICE FURNITURE

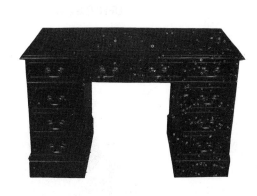

DESKS, DESK CHAIRS, FILE CABINETS, BOOKCASES, BOARD ROOM TABLES.

BRITISH ANTIQUE FURNITURE CO.
SCHOOL CLOSE, QUEEN ELIZABETH AVENUE
BURGESS HILL, WEST SUSSEX RH15 9RX
Tel: Burgess Hill (04446) 45577

ANTIQUES
REVIEW 1987

The 'Restless M' sailed into antiques history during 1986 carrying with it a cargo of porcelain which sold for more than £10 million. The owner of the ship is Michael Hatcher, an ex-Barnardo's boy, who dredged up more than 150,000 pieces of blue and white Chinese porcelain from the wreck of the Dutch East Indiaman 'Geldermalsen' in the depths of the South China Seas and made himself a multi millionaire as a result.

Part of the fabulous treasure salvaged from the Dutch East Indiaman 'Geldermalsen' in the South China Seas.

Captain Michael Hatcher preparing to dive.

The 'Nanking Cargo', as Hatcher's spectacular find is now called, was auctioned by Christie's in a five day sale at Amsterdam. Dealers and collectors flocked to the sale from all over the world and astounded the auctioneers by paying prices as much as five times above estimate for 18th century plates, cups, vomit bowls and cream jugs.

This is the second time that Mike Hatcher has thrown the antiques world into turmoil because in 1984 he discovered the wreck of a 17th century Chinese junk with more than 20,000 pieces of Ming porcelain in its hull.

An underglaze blue and enamelled vomit pot painted with a tree peony, circa 1750.

Because Hatcher was reticent about the details of the wreck and because the porcelain was not top quality, the antiques world was reluctant to buy but a few who did have been rewarded with a hefty profit. Sets of six plates made £400 in the sale but within weeks collectors were paying more than £150 each for them. Everyone now wants a piece of Hatcher's romantic find and even though pieces fetched more than double their intrinsic value in the auction, they were soon being sold on at twice as much again within days of the sale being over. 'Nanking Cargo' plates made a minimum of £100 each for the smallest; when offered for resale the prices are ranging between £150 and £250.

'Dulcinea', HN1343, designed by L. Harradine, issued 1929-1938, 5½in. high. £900

The shiver that swept the collecting world when the news of Hatcher's second find came out, now proves to have been unnecessary because the 'Nanking Cargo' has not depressed prices. They have in fact been elevated and are likely to stay that way. Today blue and white china is as popular as it was in the 17th century when rooms of royal palaces and prosperous private houses were covered with row upon row of the distinctive Chinese porcelain.

Another offspin of the Hatcher story is an upsurge in the already strong interest among collectors in all things Chinese. Not just blue and white china but also 'China Trade' porcelain of all sorts, especially crested china painted for European customers; Chinese textiles and furniture; silver; bronze and decorative items all look likely to increase in price.

Perhaps as a result of the 'Nanking Cargo' hysteria however, china has now nudged furniture out of the pre-eminent position with collectors.

One of the most bouyant areas is Doulton ware. In 1986 it was estimated that there were 15,000 serious collectors of Doulton all over the world and the figure continues to rise. What they buy are not only specialist items like the work of Hannah Barlow and Mark Marshall but, more surprisingly, character jugs and figures of very recent date

A massive Doulton & Co. faience baluster vase, by Florence Lewis, 193cm. high, circa 1893. (Phillips) £31,320

which all fetch high prices. This is a wonderful field for profit seekers because, since people who own Doulton are often not aware of the value of their mantlepiece ornaments, many pieces have not yet come onto the market.

What makes the search even more fascinating is that there is a comprehensive list of every recent Doulton figure or jug ever produced . . . the discoverer of one of the smaller ranges feels almost as lucky as Mike Hatcher because prices can be spectacular.

'Kate Hardcastle', HN1719, designed by L. Harradine, issued 1935-49, 8in. high. £185

George Washington Bicentenary Jug, designed by C. J. Noke and H. Fenton, issued 1932, 10¾in. high. £2,500

A flambe 'Leaping Salmon', Model 666, designed by C. J. Noke, introduced 1940, withdrawn 1950. £300

'Silks and Ribbons', HN2017, designed by L. Harradine, issued 1949, 6in. high. £63

Clark Gable Character Jug, D6709, designed by S. Taylor, issued 1984. £2,200

Smuts Character Jug, D6198, designed by H. Fenton, issued 1946-48. £800

'Miss Demure', HN1402, designed by L. Harradine, issued 1930-75, 7½in. high. £85

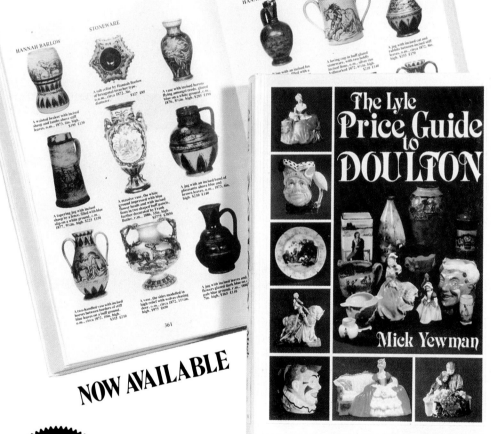

ANTIQUE DEALERS POCKET BOOK

At last! Instant recognition and dating of thousands of antiques is possible — with this clear and comprehensive pocket manual from the world's foremost publisher of antiques reference books. There is more information to the square inch in this book than in any you can buy, whether you are a dealer, collector, or merely interested in identifying your own family heirlooms. Here are over 3,500 clear illustrations, not only of expensive objects but especially of the day-to-day items (many less than 100 years old but still of value) which make up the bulk of the antiques market. The Antique Dealers Pocket Book is a must for everyone interested in antiques — and an education in itself.

ISBN 0-86248-062-0
256 Pages
Size 8 x 5½in. Hardback
Over 3,500 clear illustrations

JUST
£3·95

Monarchs, Chinese Dynasties, Periods, Registry of Designs, China Marks, Handles, Pediments, Legs, Feet, Chair Backs, Silver Marks, Barometers, Bronze, Caddies & Boxes, Cameras, Cane Handles, Carved Wood, China, Clocks, Cloisonne, Copper & Brass, Dolls, Enamel, Fans, Furniture, Glass, Gold, Horn, Inros, Instruments, Iron & Steel, Ivory, Jade, Jewellery, Lamps, Lead, Marble, Mirrors, Model Ships, Model Trains, Money Banks, Musical Boxes, Netsuke, Quilts, Rugs, Samplers, Seals, Shibayama, Tsubas.

For example a white character jug of Winston Churchill , produced during the 1939-45 war but quickly withdrawn because the great man felt the likeness to be unflattering, is now worth about £7,000. A 'George Robey' toby jug recently made £4,000, a red haired clown made £1,500 and the cockney 'pearlie' can demand four figure prices while a porcelain figure of a girl entitled 'Folly' sold for £550 at auction in the spring of 1986. Most astonishing of all is the portrait jug of a boy which Doulton's made as the result of a request to the 'Jim'll Fix It' television programme in which viewers ask for their dreams to be realised. The jug, 'Toby Gillette', was produced in an edition of only three and when one of them was sold at auction the price was £15,950.

George Robey Toby Jug, issued 1925, 10½in. high. (Phillips) £4,000

'Folly', HN1750, designed by L. Harradine, issued 1936-49, 9½in. high.

Churchill Character Jug, D6170, designed by C. Noke, issued 1940-41.

'Sleeping Beauty, The Fairies at the Christening', a good Doulton Lambeth faience tile panel, by Margaret Thompson, 105cm. high. (Phillips) £3,600

'Orange Lady', HN1953, designed by L. Harradine, issued 1940-75, 8½in. high. £90

A Goldscheider painted terracotta group, 57cm. high. (Phillips) £1,500

Minton majolica peacock, by Paul Comolera (1818-1897). (Phillips)

A large De Morgan two-handled amphora vase, attributed to Fred Passenger, 17½in. high. (Christie's) £2,100

The Doulton name means magic in the collecting world today. Even hitherto disregarded items like pottery tiles and advertising wares made by Doulton are soaring in price. Look out for Dr Scholl's advertising plaques showing 'bunion reducers' and 'arch binders' and for another plaque made for De Reszke cigarettes showing a smart couple lighting up together.

And of course Doulton is still producing. They recently brought out a Ronald Reagan jug that did not sell well so it too was withdrawn which means that anyone lucky enough to possess one will be onto a winner, sometime in the future.

The Art Pottery market is in fact booming and in the past year record prices have been made including £10,450 for an 1893 Doulton ewer by Mark Marshall and £12,100 for a 1900 William de Morgan vase. A Minton nine colours pâté sur pâté vase signed by Charles Toft and dated 1878 sold for £1,500 and a five foot tall Minton majolica ware peacock, one of only nine ever made, by French animalier sculptor Paul Comolera (1818-1897) made around £20,000 at Phillips in London.

Rising prices are also recorded for more recent pieces including items decorated by Clarice Cliff and her girls. The more Art Deco in style Clarice Cliff's work is, the more collectors will pay to secure it. An example is the coffee service 'Inspiration', sold in London by Christie's for £5,184, while her two sided plaque 'Age of Jazz' sold at Phillips for £4,000.

Price Guide to PRINTED COLLECTIBLES

* one paperback worth £100
* an American comic worth £7,500
* a licence for a male servant worth £2.50

Beer Bottle Labels . . . Bill Heads . . . Birthday Cards .
Blotters . . . Bonds & Share Certificates . . .
Bookmarks . . . Book Plates . . . Bubble Gum
Business Calendars . . .
Cheese Labels . . . C
Children's Annuals .
Cigar Box Labels .
Cigarette Packets . .
Comic Books . . . C
Crime & Detec'
Dressmak'
Fashi
F'

In
Inv
Labe
Letter
Magazi
Newspap
Novelty B
Ocean Line
Paperbacks .
Pop-Up Book:
Postcards . . . F
Radio Times . . .
Railway Tickets .
Royalty . . . Scien
Scraps . . . Seed Pack
Signed Photographs . .
Thea   rammes . .
V   . Vie
            Vomen's

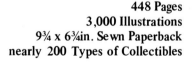

448 Pages
3,000 Illustrations
9¾ x 6¾in. Sewn Paperback
nearly 200 Types of Collectibles

ONLY £6·95

* FASCINATING — check out over 3000 more amazing money-making facts

44

A Clarice Cliff 'Inspiration' baluster vase and circular wall plaque, the vase £864 and the plaque £3,780. (Christie's)

A Clarice Cliff 'Age of Jazz', two sided plaque, 17.5cm. high. (Phillips) £4,000

The work of ceramic designer Charlotte Rhead who died in 1947 and is best known for her attractive tube line designs, also fetches record prices. She was a member of a vastly talented family of artists who worked in the Potteries for over a century. Her grandfather, father and uncles were all skilled pottery decorators and gilders and the brightly coloured work of her father Frederick Alfred Rhead is also highly regarded by collectors. The pieces he painted for the Foley 'Intarsio' ware range now vary in price from £300 to £1,000 each.

An Art Nouveau rectangular leaded glass panel, by Jacques Gruber, 256cm. high. (Christie's) £9,720

Stained glass of the 19th century is another area to watch in the future because collectors are becoming more aware of its decorative value. There is already one thriving company specialising in seeking out houses of substance which are about to be demolished. They take out the stained glass before the breakers set about their work.

Doulton was one of the producers of stained glass in the late 19th century when it was a popular means of decorating shops, public houses and churches. Religious themes are not too popular today but a glass panel with a landscape or a non religious subject sells for around £30 a square foot at the moment. This is likely to rise.

Furniture never loses its popularity in the collecting world but this year the bottom has dropped out of the market as far as mediocre quality is concerned. 'Tat' has zoomed down dramatically in price but good pieces of Georgian and Regency furniture, as well as high quality Victorian and Edwardian pieces, continue to command ever rising prices because these are becoming more difficult to find and their rarity ensures a steady growth in value.

An example is a pair of George III giltwood mirrors in the manner of Thomas Johnson which sold for over £20,000 at a sale in Scotland at the end of last year. Johnson, a Londoner who had a high reputation as a cabinet maker around 1750, was a specialist subcontractor to cabinet makers and upholsterers of his day.

At the same sale Christie's secured more than £12,000 for a set of 16 Victorian dining chairs of George III design. A decade ago it would have been surprising to get more than £2,000 for such a set. Phillips also sold a set of ten carved mahogany elbow chairs in the Hepplewhite style for £12,500. Good quality sets of chairs are in fact at a premium with, for example, an Edinburgh dealer advertising ten George III chairs and two serving chairs of later date for over £26,000.

A Regency mahogany concentric leaf extending table sold at Phillips' London

Two of a set of eight George III mahogany side chairs with arched rectangular backs and scroll-headed cabriole legs. (Christie's)
£7,560

rooms at £15,000 and a bid of more than £30,000 was secured for a rare George II mahogany commode which was sold from Glamis Castle in Scotland for less than three figures in the 1940's. An early Hepplewhite period marquetry bureau de dame attributed to John Linnell and Christopher Furlogh made £30,000 in Phillips' London auction rooms. A pair of ormolu mounted ebony torcheres sold at a house sale in Thame, Oxfordshire, for £28,000.

In Edwardian furniture rising prices are reported for good examples which a few years ago would have been scorned by serious collectors. An example was an inlaid rosewood ladies' writing desk sold by Phillips for £900.

One of a pair of George III giltwood mirrors, by Thomas Chippendale. (Christie's) £64,800

A Regency Anglo-Indian mahogany sofa with padded double scrolled back, arm supports and seat with moulded frame, the back centred by carved flowerheads, the arm supports with flowerheads and foliage on scrolling claw feet with anthemions and flowerheads, 90in. wide. (Christie's) £1,728

A Regency mahogany breakfront bookcase with moulded cornice, the frieze with fruitwood key-pattern ornament on an ebonised ground above two pairs of geometrically-glazed cupboard doors, the base with a pair of panelled cupboard doors enclosing two drawers flanked by a pair of glazed cupboard doors fitted with gilt metal trelliswork centred by flowerheads on spirally-turned ribbed feet, 122in. wide. (Christie's) £10,800

A FORTUNE in your ATTIC

* a Victorian milk bottle worth £150
* a model aeroplane worth £1,200
* a walking stick worth £4,000

Angling Books ... Animal Traps ... Ashtrays .
Autograph Letters & Documents ... Aviatio
Cards ... Badges ... Bairnsfatherware ...
Bakelite ... Barrel Ta
Beer Mats ... Blow L
Bottle Openers ... Bo
Bricks ... Bridle Bits
Buckles ... Buttons .
Carte De Visite .
Charity Boxe
Cheese Di
Cigare
C

E
Fire
Fishi
Handk
Inhalers
Key Rings
Lawnmowe
Model Aircra
Pen Nibs ... Pe
Playing Cards ...
Railwayana ... Rai
Scissors ... Shop Fi
Souvenirs ... Specta
Taxidermy ... Teddy
Tin Openers ... Tins ...
Transp   tcards ... Tra
Tre   form Butt
V   ures ... W

448 Pages
3,000 Illustrations
9¾ x 6¾in. Sewn Paperback

ONLY £6·95

* SURPRISED? – check out over 3000 more
  amazing money-making facts

Price Guide to COLLECTIBLES

❋ one light bulb worth £300
❋ a fire insurance mark worth £2,500
❋ 20th century French doll worth £24,000

Advertising Signs ... American Indianware ... Autom
Automatons ... Automobilia ... Amusement ...
Machines ... Anim
Badges ... Banknot
Beer Bottle Labels
Bus Tickets ... Rail
Railwayana ... Raz
Pin-Up Mags. ... Po
Rock n' Roll ... Sc
Seals ... Shells ..
Shoes ... Slag
Spoons
Staff

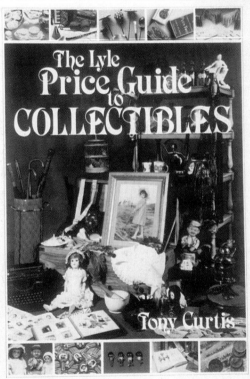

St
Spo
Shells
Slag Gla
Snuff Bo
Spoons
Staffordshire
Stevengraphs
Teapots ... Treen
Thimbles ... Telep
Tiles ... Tobacco
Tools ... Toys ... Ts
Treen ... Tsubas ...
Typewriters ... Valentin
Vinaigr ... Walking
W...... Watches
..........Whistles

448 Pages
3,000 Illustrations
9¾ x 6¾in. Sewn Paperback
nearly 200 Types of Collectibles

❋ AMAZED – then check out over 3000 more
amazing money-making facts

A stained oak cabinet designed by Charles Rennie Mackintosh, with beaten brass door panels signed by Margaret Macdonald and dated 1899, 182cm. wide. (Phillips)   £115,000

Furniture of more recent date has also been making considerable prices but items have to be unique. Some hopes for high prices in modern or Art Deco pieces have been disappointing especially in Monte Carlo but pieces of furniture by Charles Rennie Mackintosh, many of which are still emerging from obscurity, always do well. Phillips in Edinburgh had an international coup when their furniture expert was called in to value a rather battered cupboard which turned out to be the work of Mackintosh with panels by his artist wife Margaret Macdonald. It sold for £115,000 and then went on to the salerooms of Europe, gaining in value en route while a pair of mahogany ladderback chairs merely attributed to Mackintosh ensured that they made £6,000 at auction.

One of a pair of mahogany ladderback elbow chairs, attributed to Charles Rennie Mackintosh. (Phillips)   £6,000

American furniture is also securing increased prices in New York where a Federal mahogany and curly maple veneered square sofa made in New England around 1805 sold for $46,000.

As a tip for future investment time pieces would seem worthy of attention. Clocks have always had a strong following with big prices being paid in the past for longcase clocks, which however have been rather static of late, but it is more worthwhile looking out for good examples of Art Nouveau style clocks, particularly those sold by Liberty's and designed by artists such as Archibald Knox or Christopher Dresser. They are quite expensive now but will get even more pricey soon.

Watches are also worthy of attention. Recent dates are no drawback for a 1940 gold Rolex made more than £4,000 in auction in London recently while a modern Patek Philippe Nautilus watch sold for the equivalent of £5,000 at Phillips' New York rooms. Watches made in the 1920's and 30's are particularly highly prized and prices are on a rising graph for names like Cartier, Patek Philippe, Baume, Mercier and Piaget. Handcraftsmanship and the individuality of design as well as the mechanical quality of the movements make those watches of particular worth. Prices start around £300 but can go above £4,400.

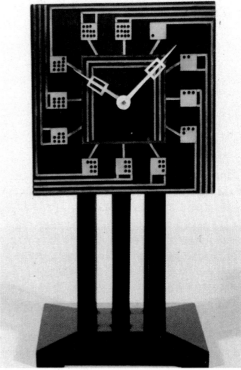

A Liberty & Co. 'Cymric' silver timepiece, designed by Archibald Knox. (Phillips) £3,200

An important Domino mantel clock, designed by Charles Rennie Mackintosh, circa 1917. (Phillips)

A fine selection of 20th century wristwatches by Rolex, Patek Philippe, Audemars Piguet and Vacheron Constantin. (Phillips)

Age is no criteria of value in cameras either. Very rare early examples are of course expensive and highly priced by collectors but interest is beginning to turn to Kodak and Agfa cameras produced in the 1940's and 1950's . . . and sometimes even later.

Jewellery has always been popular with collectors and while those who were investment minded used to concentrate exclusively on heavy and expensive diamond and emerald pieces, the more popular field was concerned with Victorian jewellery. In recent years the size and quality of the stones has not been the only determining factor and design now plays a part. Art Deco jewellery in particular has been making record prices, especially in Geneva, Monte Carlo and America. Van Cleef and Arpels duly paid £353,571 for a fan shaped brooch with nine cushion shaped rubies and Cartier paid £275,000 for a clip of their own making in rubies and diamonds shaped like a palm tree.

Cartier is the 'in' name among jewellery buyers at the moment and this trend was recognised at the Grosvenor House Antiques Fair where a room was devoted to Cartier jewellery. Their pieces were particularly admired by the late Duchess of Windsor who owned a vast private collection of jewellery including many Cartier items, some of which had been specially designed for her. The publicity given to the Duchess's pieces is sure to raise even higher the prices for Cartier and similar items of recent date.

A Cartier calendar table clock with adjustable day and date, 11 x 7cm. (Christie's) £3,024

Lady Docker, the daughter of a Derby car salesman, married three millionaires, and became famous in the 1960's through her third husband, Sir Bernard Docker, head of the Daimler car company. Lady Docker said that "while other girls would be satisfied with fur, I asked for mink or sable . . . ." and her magnificent Russian Kunchatka sable coat was sold for around £7,500.

A pair of emerald and diamond earrings by Cartier. (Phillips) £85,000

The most sought after precious stone at the moment is however the humble pearl. Already strings of pearls of the sort which were round every fashionable woman's neck in the 1930's are high fashion news for they are benefitting from the fondness for them of the trendsetting Princess of Wales. In the spring of 1986 a triple strand cultured Burmese pearl necklace sold in New York for an astonishing $286,000.

Other items of finery which are becoming collectors' items are furs. As wild life enthusiasts condemn the killing of animals for their skins, the value of old furs has been steadily rising. One of the pioneers of fur sales in Great Britain are Phillips in London and it was there that a collection of furs belonging to Lady Docker was sold during the year.

One of Lady Docker's furs, a fine quality Russian Kunchatka sable coat. (Phillips)

Popular ANTIQUES and their VALUES 1800~1875

The purpose of this publication, and its companion, is to make it easy for those either buying, selling, or merely interested in the value of the pieces in their own home to identify and have a knowledge of the price an Antique Dealer is likely to pay for a piece in average condition.

ISBN 0-86248-060-4
256 Pages
Size 8 x 5½in. Hardback
Over 2,000 photographs

Badges, Barometers, Bronze, Buckets, Caddies & Boxes, Card Cases, Carved Wood, Chandeliers, China, Clocks & Watches, Copper & Brass, Dolls, Enamel, Furniture, Glass, Gold, Helmets, Icons, Inros, Instruments, Iron & Steel, Ivory, Jade, Jewellery, Lacquer, Medals, Mirrors, Model Ships, Musical Instruments, Netsuke, Pewter, Photographs, Portrait Miniatures, Powder Flasks, Quilts, Samplers, Seals, Silhouettes, Silver, Snuff Bottles, Textiles, Toys,

Popular ANTIQUES and their VALUES 1875~1950

People with an eye for a bargain never move house, clear out an attic or pass a junk shop without consulting their Popular Antiques & Their Values books.

ISBN 0-86248-061-2
256 Pages
Size 8 x 5½in. Hardback
Over 2,000 photographs

Advertising Signs, Amusement Machines, Automatons, Bronze, Caddies & Boxes, Cameras, China, Clocks, Cloisonne, Copper & Brass, Dolls, Enamel, Furniture, Glass, Gold, Icons, Instruments, Ivory, Jewellery, Lamps, Model Ships, Model Trains, Money Banks, Musical Boxes, Netsuke, Pewter, Photographs, Posters, Rock'n' Roll, Rugs, Shibayama, Silver, Textiles, Toys, Transport, Weathervanes, Wood.

A fashion plate from 'Gazette Du Bon Temps', circa 1920. (Christie's)

Second hand clothes are no longer synonymous with poverty, quite the opposite in fact because the salerooms have realised the huge interest there is in period costume among the buying public. Some items are bought for wear again, particularly 'vogue' clothes like Edwardian dresses which had a boom in popularity after the success of the film 'A Room With A View'', but many of them are only collectors' items because the shape of women, particularly in the period between 1900 and the late 1920's means that their clothes cannot be worn today.

Buying old clothes in auction has proved to be a good investment and it looks as if there is a good deal of mileage in the market yet. For example, two dresses which Christie's sold in their South Kensington rooms in 1967 at 35 guineas for the pair went for £400 and £500 respectively less than 20 years later; a two piece suit bought for £600 in 1980 sold for £3,000 this year.

Interest now is concentrated either in Victorian clothing which is still reckoned to be cheap or in post war clothes. Even the clothes of the sixties are beginning to make their saleroom debut but remember to look for labels. A Balenciaga suit without a label could be worth £1,000 less than one with that precious scrap of material.

Paisley shawls are still making good prices but there seems to have been little increase for them over the past year. Perhaps they have reached the top of their market for the moment. They are however still very popular with many collectors, particularly with Americans and Continental Europeans. A keen British collector is Princess Margaret.

William IV silver tea tray, by Robert Garrard, London, 1835, engraved with the arms of Baron Nathan Meyer de Rothschild impaling those of his wife, Hannah Cohen, 82cm. long. (Christie's)

George II silver basket, by Paul de Lamerie, 1744, 35cm. long. (Christie's)

A George IV wine cooler, by Philip Rundell, 1821, together with a Victorian mirror plateau, by Wm. Bateman, 1838. (Christie's)
£97,200

Another old favourite which has recently gone through a time of depression is heavily decorated Victorian silver. From the early years of the century no one wanted the ornate presentation silver beloved of the Victorians except for its melt down value. In the 1970's however pieces began to be snapped up by wealthy Iranians but after the collapse of the Shah the market crashed again. In recent months there has been a significant renewal of interest from Middle Eastern buyers, especially from Arabs furnishing homes in Britain. It seems however that this is still a dicey market which may not last very long.

A safer bet than Victorian silver, though it may sound unlikely, are Carousel horses and decorative items for the garden − or as the auctioneers grandly call them, 'architectural garden fittings'. In the early summer of '86 Phillips of New York had a very successful sale of 48 Carousel animals including horses, tigers, goats and a stag. For some years interior decorators have been fond of buying these for the homes of rich clients but this was their first specialist sale and it was highly successful for a horse sold for $19,000 and a snarling tiger for $32,000.

A large Looff stander, outside-row Carousel Horse with cascading cut-through mane and conquistador's head at saddle cantle, 58in. high, 66in. long. (Phillips) $19,000

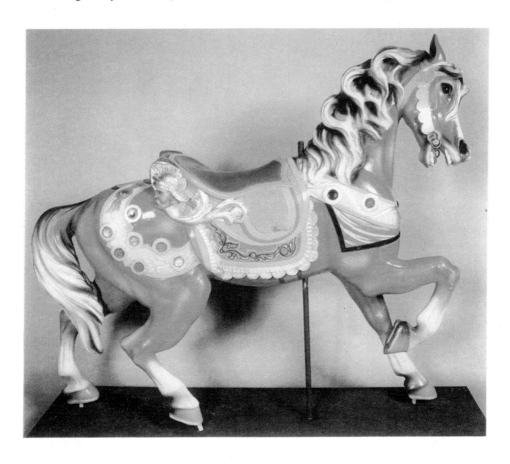

Cash-in on Collecting

✳ This book contains the stories of many fascinating and successful collectors. They are men and women of all ages and from all walks of life who have been bitten by the collecting bug. Their specialities range from old bank notes to cigarette lighters, from dolls to picture postcards.

ISBN 0-86248-055-8
448 Pages
Size 10 x 7in. Hardback
32 Pages in full colour

From their own experience they give first hand tips on collecting including how to start, where to go and, most interesting of all for the would be collector, what to start specialising in now so that your hobby can be turned into money.

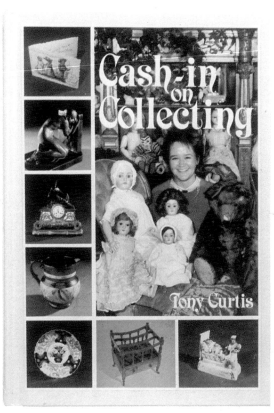

JUST £9·95

✳ Everything and anything can be collected from 18th century prints to today's throwaway beer cans. In this book you learn how to build up your collection and also how to add an unexpected pleasure to your life for collecting can not only be a cure for boredom and the blues but it carries with it the very real possibility of turning a modest outlay into a considerable nest egg.

A pair of terracotta jardinieres formed as sea horses supporting shells, 35in. wide. (Christie's) £3,200

A bronze fountain base formed as three putti pulling on drapes, 37in. high. (Christie's) £1,500

For the upper bracket garden, collectors are buying cherubs, naked ladies, fauns and Grecian urns that once decorated Victorian flower beds. They are being tipped as an area to invest in by several dealers and auction houses because people are becoming more garden conscious.

There has not been such an upsurge in buying for the garden since the middle Victorian period when a new rich lavished money on their gardens in the same way as they poured it into fancy furniture. Garden artefacts are highly popular with buyers from the Southern states of America where the all round year weather is more conducive to garden living than it is in Europe. Look out for cast iron chairs with fern and ivy backs (around £400 each); for stone putti (between £800 and £1,200 a pair) and elegant urns which can cost anything between £150 and £250 each. Female nudes cost more than male nudes and fountains are especially popular.

One of a pair of early 19th century lead garden urns, the bulbous bodies cast with putti handles and garlands of fruits on foliate capped square bases, 30in. high. (Christie's)

A rare Carette enamelled Mercedes two-seater open tourer with clockwork mechanism, German, circa 1907, 10¼in. long. (Christie's) £7,200

An extremely fine 2in. scale model of the Burrell 5 N.H.P. 'Gold Medal' tractor. (Christie's) £7,500

A Steiff gold plush teddy bear together with a Steiff black and white dog. (Phillips)

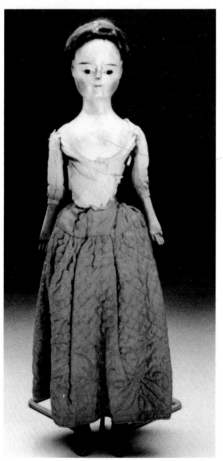

A turned and painted wooden doll with inset brown enamel eyes, 20in. high, circa 1760. (Christie's)

Toys continue to boom, especially Teddy Bears. To make real money bears have to be by the German house of Steiff with the ear button in situ. The 1985 record price of £3,740 was rapidly broken in the summer of 1986 by a bear selling in London for £5,280. He still had his original price label of eighteen shillings and ninepence.

Collectors looking out for a new area should abandon the pricey search for Britain's lead soldiers and look instead for Corgi toys of the 1950's which are making their saleroom debut at healthy and rising prices.

The past year has seen a seesaw in buying patterns. At the beginning of the period covered, American buyers were much in evidence both in the saleroom and going round city and provincial antique shops but the attack on Libya and the apprehension that affected Americans as a result meant they became almost as rare as roses in midwinter. This had two effects – the market hardened so that only good quality items held their price through the summer and also shipping dealers did very well because they were able to cater for the hungry market in the USA. At the time of going to press however a few brave Americans are beginning to trickle back and prices are on a rising graph again.

Liz Taylor

ANTIQUES REVIEW 1987

THE Lyle Official Antiques Review is compiled and published with completely fresh information annually, enabling you to begin each new year with an up-to-date knowledge of the current trends, together with the verified values of antiques of all descriptions.

We have endeavoured to obtain a balance between the more expensive collector's items and those which, although not in their true sense antiques, are handled daily by the antiques trade.

The illustrations and prices in the following sections have been arranged to make it easy for the reader to assess the period and value of all items with speed.

You will find illustrations for almost every category of antique and curio, together with a corresponding price collated during the last twelve months, from the auction rooms and retail outlets of the major trading countries.

When dealing with the more popular trade pieces, in some instances, a calculation of an average price has been estimated from the varying accounts researched.

As regards prices, when 'one of a pair' is given in the description the price quoted is for a pair and so that we can make maximum use of the available space it is generally considered that one illustration is sufficient.

It will be noted that in some descriptions taken directly from sales catalogues originating from many different countries, terms such as bureau, secretary and davenport are used in a broader sense than is customary, but in all cases the term used is self explanatory.

Ovaltine. (Street Jewellery)$120 £80

Jones' Sewing Machines. (Street Jewellery) $150 £100

His Master's Choice, Kenya Beer.(Street Jewellery) $150 £100

Singer Sewing Machines, 11 x 7½in. (Street Jewellery) $127 £85

Late 19th century American apothecary sign, 3ft. high. (Robt. W. Skinner Inc.) $1,200 £810

Patent Steam Carpet Beating Co, Ltd. (Street Jewellery) $375 £250

W. D. & H. O. Wills, 'Westward Ho!' Smoking Mixture. (Street Jewellery) $112 £75

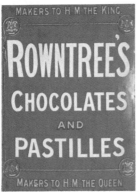

Morris Service. (Street Jewellery) $187 £125

Rowntree's Chocolates and Pastilles. (Street Jewellery) $67 £45

Raleigh, The All-Steel Bicycle. (Street Jewellery) $180 £120

An advertising plaque bearing
Rowland's Macassar Oil, the
reverse impressed T. J. & J.
Mayer, Longport, 16 x 22cm.
(Phillips) $675 £500

Henko, Maker Holzl, Vienna, 1920's,
28 x 18in. (Street Jewellery)
$150 £100

Wills's Star Cigarettes.
(Street Jewellery)
$120 £80

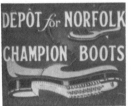

Depot for Norfolk Champion
Boots. (Street Jewellery)
$112 £75

Wills's Woodbines. (Street Jewellery)
$45 £30

United Kingdom Tea
Company's Delicious Teas.
(Street Jewellery)
$300 £200

Player's Please. (Street Jewellery) $75 £50

Chivers' Carpet Soap. (Street Jewellery) $300 £200

Reckitt's Blue. (Street Jewellery)
$450 £300

Churchman's 'Tortoiseshell' Smoking Mixture. (Street Jewellery) $262 £175

Ruberoid Roofing, made by Willings & Co., 1930's, 36 x 27in. (Street Jewellery) $112 £75

Depot for 'Swan' Ink. (Street Jewellery) $127 £85

Union Castle Line to South & East Africa. (Street Jewellery)$450 £300

Player's Navy Mixture. (Street Jewellery) $225 £150

An enamel sign, 'Hush!! He's Busy', a political cartoon of Lloyd George, 51 x 71cm. (Osmond Tricks) $244 £170

Rowntree's Elect Cocoa. (Street Jewellery) $60 £40

Blue Band Margarine. (Street Jewellery) $67 £45

Puritan Soap, Pure as the Breeze'. (Street Jewellery) $187 £125

Brasso Metal Polish. (Street Jewellery) $75 £50

Mitchells and Butlers' Ales. (Street Jewellery)
$300 £200

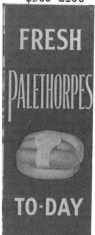

Persil, made by Ferro Email, 1930's, 23 x 15in. (Street Jewellery) $120 £80

John Sinclair's Rubicon Twist. (Street Jewellery) $60 £40

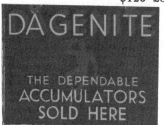

Dagenite, The Dependable Accumulators Sold Here. (Street Jewellery) $60 £40

Robin Starch. (Street Jewellery) $262 £175

Fresh Palethorpes Today. (Street Jewellery)$150 £100

Stephens Inks. (Street Jewellery) $127 £85

An advertising plaque bearing Rowland's Aqua D'Oro, the reverse impressed T. J. & J. Mayer, Longport, 16 x 22cm. (Phillips) $675 £500

Spratt's 'builds up' a dog! (Street Jewellery) $67 £45

Crow Bar Tobacco, 37 x 24½in., 1920's. (Street Jewellery)$150 £100

A sheepskin-lined U.S. Army flying jacket, type B-3, size 48. (Christie's) $231 £150

A model of an aeroplane constructed from leaves, matches and other items, made by a Belgian soldier, 1914-16, 5in. long. (Christie's) $42 £30

An openface pocket watch, the white face inscribed 'Shock proof lever, Swiss made' and depicting a mono-plane, 2in. diam. (Christie's) $84 £55

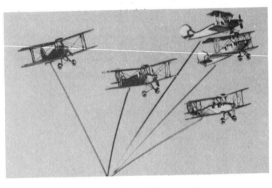

A silk Stevengraph depicting a balloon and entitled 'Many happy returns of the day, made by T. Stevens of Coventry on 28th Feb. 1874', 10in. long. (Christie's) $92 £65

A static display of five stain-less steel bi-planes, each plane approx. 2in. long, on a stand, 12in. high. (Christie's) $130 £90

An ivory paper knife, reputed to have been salvaged from Manfred von Richthofen's aircraft, 12in long. (Christie's) $539 £380

A blue enamel oval snuff box, the cover painted with a hot air balloon over the country-side, 2¼in. long. (Christie's) $646 £420

A complimentary Season Pass to the London Aero-drome, Hendon, 1914, issued to John F. Plummer, together with a collection of other related material. (Christie's) $200 £130

A pair of sheepskin-lined flying trousers, type B-1. (Christie's) $115 £75

A commemorative plate depicting Immelmann's Fokker III monoplane, by N. Roe, oil, signed, inscribed and dated 1981, 9in. diam. (Christie's) $241 £170

A silver lapel badge in the form of a gnome engine with propeller, 1¾in. long. (Christie's) $78 £55

One of four silver place-setting holders depicting a Wright flyer, 1½in. high, in presentation case. (Christie's) $589 £350

A colour lithograph poster inscribed 'Graceful Parachute Descent', published by H. Miller Junr. & Co., 28 x 18in. (Christie's) $184 £130

A polychrome wax bust of Montgolfier, inscribed 'Discovered Aerostation, 1784', 3¾in. (Christie's) $107 £70

A humorous cartoon by Brookbank, signed, water-colour, designer gouache and pastel, 12 x 10in. and a cover from Punch Magazine. (Christie's) $50 £35

A white metal souvenir spoon commemorating the journey of Norwegian airship 'Norge' in 1926, 5in. long. (Christie's) $61 £40

Two of a set of twenty-four coloured magic lantern slides depicting early ballooning and flying scenes, in original box. (Christie's) $213 £150

A German glider pilot's zinc badge, 2¼in. high, in presentation case. (Christie's) $75 £50

AERONAUTICAL

1939 De Havilland DH94 Moth Minor, Registration G-AFPN, engine de Havilland Gipsy Minor, all up weight 1,550 pounds. (Christie's) $21,560 £14,000

1943 Auster J/IN, Registration G-AGYD, engine de Havilland Gipsy Major I, all up weight 2,000 pounds. (Christie's) $5,852 £3,800

1956 Morane Saulnier MS 733 Alcyon, Registration F-BLXU, engine Potez 6D OOA, all up weight 3,680 pounds. (Christie's) $7,700 £5,000

1942 De Havilland DH 82A Tiger Moth, Registration G-AOGR, engine de Havilland Gipsy Major I, all up weight 1,825 pounds. (Christie's) $21,560 £14,000

1951 De Havilland DHC 1 Chipmunk, Registration G-BCYE (Military WG350), engine de Havilland Gipsy Major 10 MK2, all up weight 2,100 pounds. (Christie's) $21,560 £14,000

1941 North American T6G-NT (Harvard), Registration G-BKRA, engine Pratt and Whitney Wasp R-1340-AN-1, all up weight 5,300 pounds. (Christie's) $35,420 £23,000

1955 Morane Saulnier MS 733 Alcyon, Registration F-GDRO, engine Potez 6D OOA, all up weight 3,680 pounds. (Christie's) $6,468 £4,200

1935 British Aircraft BA Swallow 2, Registration G-ADPS, engine Pobjoy Cataract II, all up weight 1,500 pounds. (Christie's) $7,700 £5,000

Colour lithograph poster published by Masileau & Co., Paris, copyright 1910, Meeting d'Heliopolis, Rougier le Gagnant sur Biplane Voisin, 17¼ x 35in. (Christie's) $198 £140

Short Solent and P.R. Spitfire, by Norman Jones, signed, inscribed and dated 1951, watercolour, 10 x 15¾in. (Christie's) $170 £120

Fairy Firefly, by Davis, signed, gouache, 10 x 14½in. (Christie's) $142 £100

DH 60 'Gypsy Moth' G-AADS, by Stanley Orton Bradshaw, signed and dated '29, watercolour, 9¼ x 13in. (Christie's) $639 £450

Spitfires over Countryside, by Roy Nockolds, signed and dated 1940, watercolour and bodycolour, 19½ x 16in. (Christie's) $511 £360

Avro trainer, by Stanley Orton Bradshaw, signed and dated '30, gouache heightened with white, 10 x 15in. (Christie's) $397 £280

Fairy 111D three-seater reconnaissance aeroplane, by Coombe Richards, signed and dated 1927, watercolour, 10 x 14in. (Christie's) $142 £100

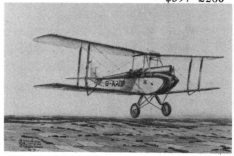

DH 60 'Gypsy Moth' G-AADP, by Stanley Orton Bradshaw, signed and dated '29, watercolour, 9 x 13¼in. (Christie's) $681 £480

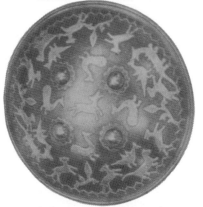

One of a pair of U.S. Army officer's full dress epaulettes, possibly of Civil War period. (Wallis & Wallis) $138 £105

A decorated Indian steel shield dahl, 14¼in. diam. (Wallis & Wallis) $92 £70

A Nazi period Field Marshal's epaulette with gold and silver embroidery. (Wallis & Wallis) $125 £85

An officer's full dress sporran of The Gordon Highlanders, white goat's hair and five bullion tassels. (Wallis & Wallis) $310 £210

A pair of 17th century iron stirrups decorated in silver and gilt with massed cherry-blossom and meyuimon, signed Kitamura. (Christie's) $1,698 £1,188

A Prussian officer's full dress sabretache of The 12th Hussars, circa 1890. (Wallis & Wallis) $325 £220

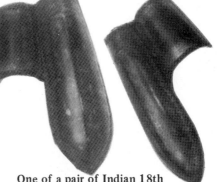

One of a pair of pre 1830 Light Company officer's wings of The 54th (West Norfolk) Regt. (Wallis & Wallis) $296 £200

One of a pair of Indian 18th century gold damascened arm defences, Bazu-Band, 12in. (Wallis & Wallis) $297 £225

A full dress waistbelt and slings for a mounted officer of The Royal Scots. (Wallis & Wallis) $240 £165

A pair of East India Company Light Company officer's wings of The 6th (Bengal?) Regt. (Wallis & Wallis) $251 £170

An Indo-Persian steel shield dahl with 4 steel bosses, gold and silver damascened. (Wallis & Wallis) $251 £170

A shakudo-nanakoji fuchi-kashira and kozuka, each decorated in takabori and gilt takazogan. (Christie's) $4,633 £3,240

An Imperial German Cavalry officer's full dress sabretache of The 2nd Hanoverian Hussars, circa 1850. (Wallis & Wallis) $458 £310

One of a pair of Georgian officer's full dress epau-lettes of The Royal East India Vol. (Wallis & Wallis) $58 £40

A breastplate struck with maker's mark and a musket ball proof test, circa 1600. (Wallis & Wallis) $567 £430

Prussian Regt. of Garde du Corps officer's parade cuir-ass. (Christie's)
            $6,525 £4,500

A lacquered saddle frame decorated in gold takamakie on a red ground, with a pair of stirrups, early 19th century. (Christie's) $5,287 £3,888

An officer's silver mounted shoulder belt and pouch of The 16th (The Queen's) Lancers, HM Birmingham 1890. (Wallis & Wallis)
            $467 £320

A Bandsman's full dress blue tunic of The First Cardigan Vol. Artillery, circa 1905. (Wallis & Wallis) $236 £160

A kebiki-laced kuchiba-iro-odoshi tosei-gusoku. (Christie's) $4,406 £3,240

A post 1902 Lt. Colonel's part uniform of The Prince of Wales's Own Royal Wiltshire Yeomanry. (Wallis & Wallis) $666 £450

Part of an extensive set of uniforms of The King's Own Regt. of Norfolk (Imperial) Yeomanry. (Christie's) $3,190 £2,200

The Imperial Russian uniform of Count A. Benckendorff, Ambassador to the Court of St. James's, together with British Court dress cocked hat. (Christie's) $2,465 £1,700

A suit of armour dated Tenmon gonen (1536). (Christie's) $3,706 £2,592

A World War II Italian Air Force officer's tunic of Air Rank. (Wallis & Wallis) $458 £310

A complete post 1902 trooper's full dress blue uniform of the City of London Yeomanry (Rough Riders). (Wallis & Wallis) $792 £600

A post 1902 uniform of Lt. Col. C. W. Bowle, Royal Army Medical Corps. (Wallis & Wallis) $666 £450

A South Australia Militia Lancers uniform. (Christie's) $5,510 £3,800

Part of an officer's 88th Connaught Rangers uniform. (Christie's) $7,250 £5,000

A uniform of the Gordon Highlanders 3rd (Militia) Bn. (Christie's) $1,160 £800

BADGES

A Victorian officer's gilt, silvered and enamel helmet plate of The Border Regt, type 2, worn 1891-1901. (Wallis & Wallis)$236 £160

An other rank's white metal Glengarry badge of The 4th Vol. Bn. The Black Watch, pair of matching collars and pair 4/V/RH shoulder titles. (Wallis & Wallis) $100 £70

An officer's silvered helmet plate of The West Yorkshire Regt. (Wallis & Wallis) $116 £80

An officer's pre 1881 gilt and silvered Glengarry badge of The 72nd (Duke of Albany's Own) Highlanders. (Wallis & Wallis) $525 £355

A Georgian other rank's brass bearskin plate, die-stamped 1801-16 Royal Arms and motto. (Wallis & Wallis) $592 £400

A Victorian other rank's white metal Maltese Cross helmet plate of The Rohilkund Vol. Rifle Corps. (Wallis & Wallis) $124 £85

An officer's silvered helmet plate of The 1st Northumberland Artillery Vols. (Wallis & Wallis) $131 £90

A Victorian officer's gilt, silvered and enamel helmet plate of The Border Regt., first pattern, worn 1881-91. (Wallis & Wallis) $458 £310

An officer's gilt and silvered Glengarry badge of The Prince of Wales's Own (W. Yorkshire) Regt. (Wallis & Wallis) $26 £20

A post 1902 officer's gilt
and silvered helmet plate
of The Norfolk Regt.
(Wallis & Wallis) $73 £50

A pre 1881 other rank's
Glengarry badge of The
73rd (Perthshire) Regt.
(Wallis & Wallis) $66 £46

A Victorian trooper's helmet
plate of The Hertfordshire
Yeomanry. (Wallis & Wallis)
$74 £50

An other rank's white metal
Glengarry of The Royal
Tyrone Fusiliers. (Wallis &
Wallis) $167 £115

An officer's shoulder belt
plate of The 21st Foot,
Royal North British Fusi-
liers. (Wallis & Wallis)
$236 £160

A Victorian officer's gilt
and silvered forage cap badge
of The South Wales Borderers.
(Wallis & Wallis) $79 £60

A trooper's helmet plate
of The 5th Dragoon
Guards. (Wallis & Wallis)
$67 £47

A U.S.A. gilt and enamelled
sterling silver badge of The
Joint Chiefs of Staff, by H.
S. Meyer Inc., New York.
(Wallis & Wallis) $46 £35

A Victorian officer's gilt
and silvered helmet plate
of The York & Lancaster
Regt. (Wallis & Wallis)
$131 £90

BADGES

A post 1902 officer's cast silvered cap badge of The Indian Army Service Corps. (Wallis & Wallis) $26 £20

An 1871 pattern other rank's helmet plate of The 7th Dragoon Guards. (Wallis & Wallis) $72 £55

A Victorian officer's gilt and silvered helmet plate of The Dorsetshire Regt. (Wallis & Wallis) $109 £75

An other rank's white metal Glengarry badge of The 5th Vol. Bn. Argyll & Sutherland Highlanders. (Wallis & Wallis) $80 £55

A Victorian hollow-cast gold plaid brooch of the Clan Mackinnon, 1.2oz. Troy. (Wallis & Wallis) $296 £200

A Victorian officer's gilt and silvered Glengarry badge of The Essex Regt. (Wallis & Wallis) $108 £75

An officer's silvered 1869 pattern shako plate, universal Militia pattern. (Wallis & Wallis) $47 £36

A post 1902 officer's gilt and silvered helmet plate of The 1st Vol. Bn. South Lancashire Regt. (Wallis & Wallis) $85 £65

An officer's silver Glengarry badge of The Argyll & Sutherland Highlanders, HM Edinburgh 1916, approx. 2½ Troy oz. (Wallis & Wallis) $214 £145

A Victorian officer's silvered helmet plate of The 1st Vol. Bn. South Staffordshire Regt. (Wallis & Wallis) $138 £105

A Victorian other rank's helmet plate of The Queensland Scottish. (Wallis & Wallis) $80 £55

A Victorian officer's gilt and silvered forage cap badge of The Devonshire Regt. (Wallis & Wallis) $65 £45

A Turkish Empire official's French silver gilt pin-back shield badge. (Wallis & Wallis) $133 £90

An other rank's white metal Glengarry badge of The 6th Vol. Bn. (Fifeshire) Black Watch. (Wallis & Wallis) $37 £22

An officer's silver Maltese Cross pouch belt badge of The King's Royal Rifle Corps, HM Birmingham 1917. (Wallis & Wallis) $79 £60

An Edward VII trooper's brass helmet plate of H.M. Reserve Regt. of Dragoon Guards. (Wallis & Wallis) $32 £22

An other rank's white metal Glengarry badge of The 2nd Vol. Bn. Border Regt. (Wallis & Wallis) $59 £45

An other rank's white metal Glengarry of The 5th Vol. Bn. Royal Scots. (Wallis & Wallis) $46 £32

BADGES

A Victorian officer's gilt and silvered Glengarry badge of The King's Own Light Infantry, (S. Yorks. Regt.). (Wallis & Wallis) $259 £180

A Georgian officer's silver gilt gorget of the East India Co., HM London 1798. (Wallis & Wallis) $370 £250

A Victorian other rank's brass Glengarry badge of The 1st Royal Lanark Militia. (Wallis & Wallis) $105 £80

An other rank's white metal Glengarry badge of The Dublin County Light Infantry. (Wallis & Wallis) $80 £55

A Georgian officer's silver rectangular shoulder belt plate of The 13th (1st Somersetshire) Regt., worn 1801-16. (Wallis & Wallis) $438 £300

A post 1902 officer's gilt and silvered helmet plate of The Royal Warwickshire Regt. (Wallis & Wallis) $87 £60

A white metal shako badge of The Eton Vol. Rifle Corps. (Wallis & Wallis) $39 £30

A Panzer troop's standard bearer's sleeve badge embroidered in silver bullion and black and pink thread. (Wallis & Wallis) $125 £85

A brass cap badge of The 1st V.A. Bn. Home Guard. (Wallis & Wallis) $58 £40

BADGES

An officer's silver cap badge of The Royal Tank Regt., HM Birmingham 1940. (Wallis & Wallis) $58 £40

A Victorian other rank's white metal Glengarry badge of The Buckingham Rifle Vol. (Wallis & Wallis) $58 £40

A trooper's brass and white metal helmet plate of The 4th (Royal Irish) Dragoon Guards. (Wallis & Wallis) $79 £55

A Georgian Grenadier Co. back badge of The 97th (Highland) Regt. or Strathspey Highlanders. (Wallis & Wallis) $198 £150

A Nazi Govt. Admin. official's field grey sleeve badge to the rank of Regierungsamtmann. (Wallis & Wallis) $185 £125

An other rank's white metal cap badge of The 1st. Vol. Bn. Royal Fusiliers. (Wallis & Wallis) $36 £25

A Victorian other rank's helmet plate of The Orkney Artillery Vols. (Wallis & Wallis) $88 £60

An officer's silvered plaid brooch of The 5th Vol. Bn. The Black Watch. (Wallis & Wallis) $122 £85

An N.C.O.'s copper gilt shoulder belt plate of The 96th (or Queen's Own) Regt., worn 1816-18. (Wallis & Wallis) $192 £130

DAGGERS

A Malayan kris, wavy laminated blade 15in., foliate chiselled brass cup, wooden garuda, in its two-piece wooden
sheath with carved top. (Wallis & Wallis) $85 £65

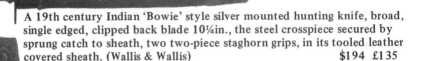

A 19th century Bowie type hunting knife, heavy single edged blade 12in.,
with spear point, oval steel guard, staghorn hilt with plain steel mounts.
(Wallis & Wallis) $50 £35

A 19th century Indian 'Bowie' style silver mounted hunting knife, broad,
single edged, clipped back blade 10¼in., the steel crosspiece secured by
sprung catch to sheath, two two-piece staghorn grips, in its tooled leather
covered sheath. (Wallis & Wallis) $194 £135

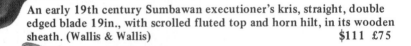

A Bali kris, wavy black and silver coloured pamir blade 15in., with fluted
scrolled top, ebonised hilt and sheath carved with a dancing figure.
(Wallis & Wallis) $108 £75

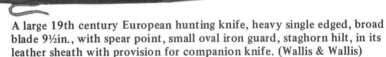

An early 19th century Sumbawan executioner's kris, straight, double
edged blade 19in., with scrolled fluted top and horn hilt, in its wooden
sheath. (Wallis & Wallis) $111 £75

A large 19th century European hunting knife, heavy single edged, broad
blade 9½in., with spear point, small oval iron guard, staghorn hilt, in its
leather sheath with provision for companion knife. (Wallis & Wallis)
                                                   $93 £65

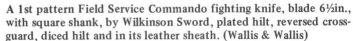

A Balkan jambiya, watered double edged blade 10½in., with raised central
rib. Black horn hilt, in silver covered wire and filigree ornamented sheath.
(Wallis & Wallis) $151 £105

A 1st pattern Field Service Commando fighting knife, blade 6½in.,
with square shank, by Wilkinson Sword, plated hilt, reversed cross-
guard, diced hilt and in its leather sheath. (Wallis & Wallis)
                                                   $458 £310

ARMS & ARMOUR

A late Spanish left-hand dagger, shallow diamond section blade 11in., with cage-shaped guard with octagonal quillons and wirebound grip. (Wallis & Wallis) $158 £110

A Bowie knife, straight, single edged blade 7in., with spear point, by Joseph Rodgers, Sheffield, white metal oval crosspiece and hilt with diced wood grips, in its leather sheath with belt loop. (Wallis & Wallis) $151 £105

A 19th century Tibetan silver mounted dagger, 16¾in., single edged blade 9in., hilt and sheath of embossed and pierced Tibetan silver. (Wallis & Wallis) $302 £210

A Nazi S.A. dagger by Eickhorn, the sheath with three plated mounts and covered in brown leather with plated suspension chains of gilt swastikas and alternating S.A. emblems. (Wallis & Wallis) $208 £145

A George V Scottish officer's dirk set of The Argyll & Sutherland Highlanders, scallop backed blade 12in., the corded wood hilt with cast plated mounts and piquet studs, in its leather covered metal sheath. (Wallis & Wallis) $576 £400

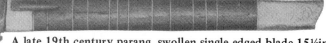

A Nazi N.S.K.K. dagger with plated mounts, in its black painted metal sheath. (Wallis & Wallis) $93 £65

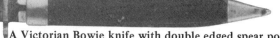

A late 19th century parang, swollen single edged blade 15½in., one-piece horn hilt carved with a stylised lion's head pommel, inlaid ivory eyes. In its palmwood scabbard with horn top and belthook. (Wallis & Wallis) $122 £85

A Victorian Bowie knife with double edged spear pointed 8in. blade, stamped at forte G. Woodhead, 6 Howard Street, Sheffield, nickel plated quillon and horn grips, in its tooled leather sheath. (Christie's) $260 £200

DAGGERS

A 19th century Malay kris, broad, wavy etched pamir blade 14in., with carved ivory garuda hilt, in its wooden sheath with bone tip. (Wallis & Wallis) $281 £190

A Scottish garter dirk, Skean Dhu, polished blade 4in., with strapwork carved ebony grip set with copper gilt figure of St. Andrew on his cross, in its copper gilt sheath. (Wallis & Wallis) $151 £115

A 19th century Caucasian silver mounted kindjal, double edged watered blade 15in., with deep fullers. Two-piece ivory grips and in its velvet covered sheath. (Wallis & Wallis) $1,188 £900

A Georgian Naval officer's dirk, circa 1812, double edged, tapering blade 6¾in., the turned baluster ivory hilt with turned pommel, in its copper gilt sheath. (Wallis & Wallis) $180 £125

A Naval officer's dirk, by Paul Weyersberg, with brass mounts and wire-bound white grip, in its brass sheath. (Wallis & Wallis) $182 £125

An Indian gold damascened pesh-kabz, blade 9½in., gold damascened with foliage at forte, en-suite with grip strap and back edge. Two-piece ivory grips, in its leather sheath with copper gilt finial. (Wallis & Wallis) $532 £370

ARMS & ARMOUR

A 19th century African Fang tribal knife, 18in., swollen blade 12in. In its wooden sheath covered with monitor skin. (Wallis & Wallis) $43 £30

An Indian dagger, bichwa, curved bi-furcated blade 8in., brass hilt with geometric pattern to guard, baluster inserts to grip. (Wallis & Wallis)
$72 £50

A silver mounted mid 17th century English plug bayonet, hollow ground, blade 9¾in., with false edge. Silver crosspiece and ribbed silver ferule. (Wallis & Wallis) $518 £350

A Nazi Luftwaffe 2nd pattern officer's dagger with grey metal mounts, wirebound white celluloid grip and original bullion dress knot, in its grey metal sheath with original hanging straps and belt clip. (Wallis & Wallis) $115 £80

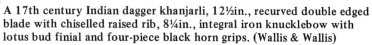

A 17th century Indian dagger khanjarli, 12½in., recurved double edged blade with chiselled raised rib, 8¼in., integral iron knucklebow with lotus bud finial and four-piece black horn grips. (Wallis & Wallis)
$158 £110

A Nazi S.A. dagger by F. Herder, with German silver mounts, in its metal sheath and single leather suspension strap and belt hook. (Wallis & Wallis) $148 £100

HELMETS

An 18-plate oboshi-hoshibachi, the rear plate signed Myochin Munenaga, 17th century. (Christie's) $1,395 £1,026

An Imperial German Hussar officer's busby of The 17th (Brunswick) Hussars. (Wallis & Wallis) $266 £180

A Nazi Army Desert issue pith helmet with original leather sweat band. (Wallis & Wallis) $96 £65

A Prussian Garde du Corps trooper's helmet, with parade eagle to crown. (Wallis & Wallis) $1,656 £1,150

A brass helmet much as for officers of the French Carabiniers, 1856-71. (Christie's) $652 £450

The 6th Dragoon Guards (The Carabiniers) officer's gilt helmet with chin-chain. (Christie's) $894 £600

A German burgonet, one-piece skull with tall comb and pierced hinged ear flaps, circa 1600. (Wallis & Wallis) $759 £575

The 17th (Duke of Cambridge's Own) Lancers officer's chapka. (Christie's) $1,639 £1,100

An officer's Albert pattern helmet of The Bombay Horse Artillery. (Wallis & Wallis) $657 £450

A 62-plate Japanese helmet, kabuto, signed Iye Mushi, with two feather gilt mon and printed doe skin covering. (Wallis & Wallis) $1,859 £1,300

An Artillery officer's busby by Hawkes & Co., the metal case inscribed Earl of Chester's Rifles. (Christie's) $261 £180

A Czech Army steel helmet, captured by the Nazis, with Nazi oval transfer badge. (Wallis & Wallis) $44 £30

An officer's composite metal eagle-topped helmet of the Prussian Regimental of Garde du Corps. (Christie's) $1,740 £1,200

A French Dragoons trumpeter's helmet, circa 1870. (Christie's) $696 £480

A British Grenadier's fur mitre cap of 1768 pattern. (Christie's) $2,682 £1,800

A composite metal helmet generally as for an officer of the Swedish Livregementel till haft but fitted with a painted plate. (Christie's) $377 £260

A 4-plate folding buff, top plate with roped border and pierced sights, circa 1600. (Wallis & Wallis) $825 £625

An embossed and parcel gilt helmet, together with two arm guards, Persia, 19th century. (Robt. W. Skinner Inc.) $700 £510

HELMETS

A Nazi Wehrmacht Russian Front fur-bodied officer's cap. (Wallis & Wallis) $81 £55

A German World War I officer's peaked cap of a Brunswick Infantry Regt., with silk lining. (Wallis & Wallis) $88 £60

A Nazi Panzer round cap with black felt crown and four breather holes. (Wallis & Wallis) $244 £165

An Edward VII helmet of The King's Own Norfolk Imperial Yeomanry. (Wallis & Wallis) $458 £310

An officer's 1855 (French) pattern shako of The Royal Lancashire Militia. (Wallis & Wallis) $370 £250

A blue cloth helmet similar to Royal Artillery but possibly Royal Military Academy, Woolwich. (Christie's) $290 £200

A Bavarian Infantry N.C.O.'s ersatz (pressed felt) pickelhaube with gilt helmet plate and mounts. (Wallis & Wallis) $208 £141

A Nazi Police officer's shako with bullion cockade and silk and leather lining. (Wallis & Wallis) $296 £200

A composite metal helmet generally as for officers of Prussian Line Cuirassier Regts. (Christie's) $696 £480

ARMS & ARMOUR

A Nazi Political Leader's cap. (Wallis & Wallis) $95 £72

A Waffen S.S. fez of The Handschar Division, with cloth eagle and death's head, and black tassel. (Wallis & Wallis) $592 £400

A World War I German officer's peaked cap of Mecklenburg, with scarlet cap band. (Wallis & Wallis) $81 £55

A Victorian officer's Albert pattern helmet of The 4th (Royal Irish) Dragoon Guards. (Wallis & Wallis) $504 £350

A Victorian officer's lance cap of The 17th (Duke of Cambridge's Own) Lancers. (Wallis & Wallis) $1,008 £700

A Victorian officer's helmet of The Royal Horse Guards (The Blues). (Wallis & Wallis) $2,072 £1,400

A Prussian Staff officer's pickelhaube with silvered 'Line Eagle' helmet plate. (Wallis & Wallis) $414 £280

A composite leather pickelhaube of 1842 pattern, bearing an eagle plate of Prussian Garde-Infanterie pattern. (Christie's) $464 £320

A Prussian Infantryman's ersatz pickelhaube with original leather lining and chinstrap. (Wallis & Wallis) $118 £80

HELMETS

An other rank's composite metal helmet of the Prussian Line Cuirassier Regts. (Christie's) $580 £400

A Bavarian Jager Regt. man's ersatz shako with brass helmet plate and cloth cockade. (Wallis & Wallis) $118 £80

A Baden Infantry N.C.O.'s pickelhaube with lacquered brass helmet plate and leather lining. (Wallis & Wallis) $185 £125

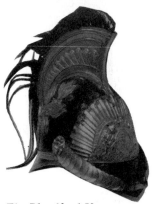

The Blandford Yeomanry Cavalry black japanned metal helmet of early 19th century Roman style. (Christie's) $968 £650

The helmet of Captain L. E. G. Oates, 6th (Inniskilling) Dragoons. (Christie's) $3,190 £2,200

A Victorian officer's shako of The Royal Dockyard Bn., contained in its original japanned tin. (Phillips) $625 £420

A Baden Infantryman's pickelhaube of The 109th Leib Regt., with German silver helmet plate. (Wallis & Wallis) $384 £260

A Nazi Police shako with white metal helmet plate and leather chinstrap. (Wallis & Wallis) $125 £85

A Prussian Artilleryman's ersatz pickelhaube with grey painted helmet plate and mounts. (Wallis & Wallis) $155 £105

A Prussian infantry Reservist officer's pickelhaube with gilt brass helmet plate. (Wallis & Wallis) $224 £170

A Nazi Fire Police steel helmet, black painted finish and aluminium comb. (Wallis & Wallis) $88 £60

An Army Veterinary Dept. officer's helmet (Victorian plate), in metal case. (Christie's) $319 £220

An 18th century Prussian mitre cap, Fusiliermutze, circa 1740-56. (Christie's) $2,831 £1,900

A post 1902 officer's helmet of The Royal Horse Guards. (Wallis & Wallis) $1,258 £850

The 1st Huntingdonshire Light Horse Volunteers (Duke of Manchester's), black leather helmet. (Christie's) $521 £350

A Hesse Infantryman's pickelhaube, with lacquered brass helmet plate and mounts. (Wallis & Wallis) $266 £180

A Prussian Military 1897 Guard infantryman's pickelhaube with lacquered brass helmet plate, brass spike and mounts. (Wallis & Wallis) $198 £150

A Prussian Artillery officer's pickelhaube, with gilt helmet plate with battle honours 'Peninsula, Waterloo, Gohrde, Colberg 1807'. (Wallis & Wallis) $444 £300

MEDALS

Meritorious Service Medal, George V issue. (Wallis & Wallis) $132 £100

Three: DCM George V, BWM and the Victory. (Wallis & Wallis) $321 £220

Naval General Service, 1790-1840, four clasps, Nymphe 1793, Indefatigable 1797, Arethusa 1806, Algiers. (Christie's) $514 £350

Five: DCM George V, M.M. George V, first type, Mons star, B.W.M. and Victory. (Wallis & Wallis) $452 £310

South Africa 1853. (Wallis & Wallis) $174 £120

Three: Queen's Sudan, L.S. & G.C., George V. Khedive's Sudan, 1 bar The Atbara. (Wallis & Wallis) $365 £250

Afghanistan 1878-80, no bar. (Wallis & Wallis) $36 £25

ARMS & ARMOUR

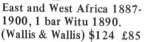

East and West Africa 1887-1900, 1 bar Witu 1890. (Wallis & Wallis) $124 £85

Three: I.G.S. 1854, China 1857, Naval L.S. & G.C. Victorian issue. (Wallis & Wallis) $162 £110

Indian Mutiny, 1 bar, Defence of Lucknow. (Wallis & Wallis) $1,221 £825

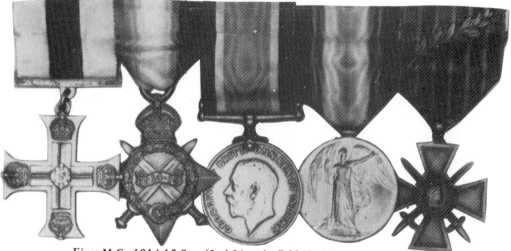

Five: M.C., 1914-15 Star (2nd Lieut.)., B.W.M., Victory, France Croix de Guerre with palm, with group of miniatures. (Wallis & Wallis) $251 £170

Seringapatam 1799, Silver Medal of the Calcutta mint. (Wallis & Wallis) $310 £210

Four: M.C. George V, 1914-15 star trio. (Wallis & Wallis) $189 £130

Waterloo 1815. (Wallis & Wallis) $1,406 £950

Candahar, Ghuznee, Cabul,
1842, (Lieut. A. MacQueen
42nd Reg. Bengal L.I.).
(Christie's) $294 £200

Five: D.S.M., George V, 1914-15 star trio, Naval L.S. and
G.C., George V, first type. (Wallis & Wallis) $219 £150

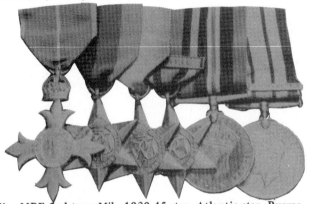

Six: MBE 2nd type Mil., 1939-45 star, Atlantic star, Burma
star with Pacific bar, War, N.G.S. 1915 1 bar S.E. Asia 1945-
46, together with a set of miniatures. (Wallis & Wallis)
                                    $204 £155

Pair: Q.S.A. 1 bar Defence of
Kimberley, Kimberley Star
1900. (Wallis & Wallis)
                $192 £130

Ten: Distinguished Conduct Medal Victorian issue, Q.S.A., K.S.A.,
I.G.S. 1908, B.W.M. Victory, L.S. and G.C. Edward VII issue,
M.S.M. George V, Prussia Order of the Red Eagle, bronze medal,
D.C.M. dated 21.10.99. (Wallis & Wallis) $1,517 £1,025

Six: Companion of the Order of the Bath, (22ct. gold, HM.London 1815), Crimea, four bars, China 1857, 1 bar, Turkey Order of Medjidieh, Turkish Crimea, France Legion of Honour. Together with three miniatures. (Wallis & Wallis) $1,314 £900

Naval General Service, 1793-1840, one clasp, 16 July Boat Service 1806.(Christie's) $514 £350

China 1857, 1 bar Taku Forts 1860. (Wallis & Wallis) $108 £75

Nine: DSM George V Admiral's bust, BEM George VI For Meritorious Service, 1914-15 star trio, 1939-45 star, Defence, War, R.N. George V Admiral's bust, together with a 'diary', press cuttings, photos etc. (Wallis & Wallis) $508 £385

Five: DCM George V, M.M., 1914-15 star trio. (Wallis & Wallis) $467 £320

MEDALS

The Royal Household Faithful Service medal, George V issue. (Wallis & Wallis) $226 £155

Four: Egypt, 1 bar Gemaizah 1888, I.G.S. 1895, Q.S.A., 1 bar C.C., Khedive's Star. (Wallis & Wallis) $204 £140

The Most Distinguished Order of St. Michael and St. George 1818, in original case from Garrard & Co. Ltd. (Lawrence Fine Art) $667 £451

Nine: 1939-45 star, France & Germany star, Defence and War, A.G.S. 1902 1 bar Kenya, G.S.M. 1918, G.S.M. 1962 and Indian Independence 1947. (Wallis & Wallis) $226 £155

Naval General Service Medal 1793, 1 bar Nile. (Wallis & Wallis) $473 £320

Nazi group of five: Iron Cross, 2nd Class, 4 Year Army Long Service medal, Rumanian gilt 1941 medal and Memel and Czech Annexation medals. (Wallis & Wallis) $399 £270

East & West Africa 1887-1900, 1 bar Sierra Leone, 1898-99. (Wallis & Wallis) $277 £190

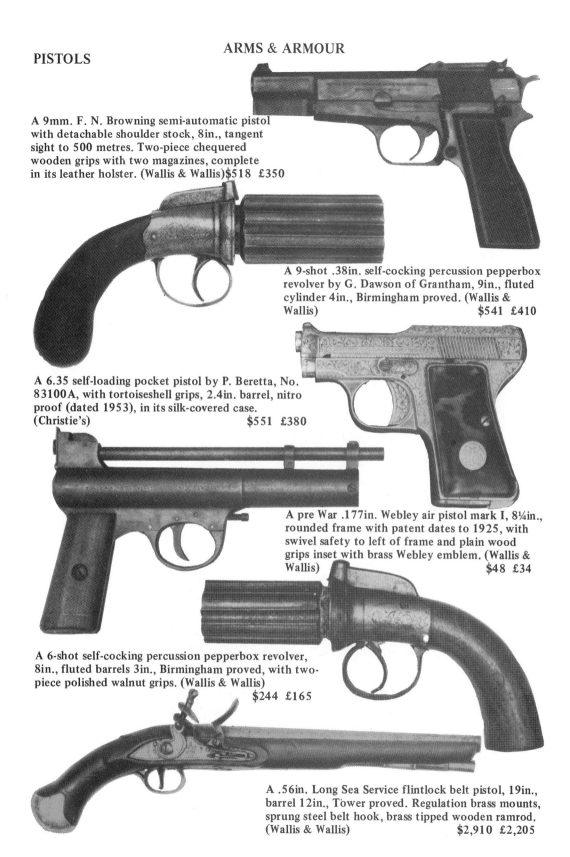

A 9mm. F. N. Browning semi-automatic pistol with detachable shoulder stock, 8in., tangent sight to 500 metres. Two-piece chequered wooden grips with two magazines, complete in its leather holster. (Wallis & Wallis)$518 £350

A 9-shot .38in. self-cocking percussion pepperbox revolver by G. Dawson of Grantham, 9in., fluted cylinder 4in., Birmingham proved. (Wallis & Wallis) $541 £410

A 6.35 self-loading pocket pistol by P. Beretta, No. 83100A, with tortoiseshell grips, 2.4in. barrel, nitro proof (dated 1953), in its silk-covered case. (Christie's) $551 £380

A pre War .177in. Webley air pistol mark I, 8¼in., rounded frame with patent dates to 1925, with swivel safety to left of frame and plain wood grips inset with brass Webley emblem. (Wallis & Wallis) $48 £34

A 6-shot self-cocking percussion pepperbox revolver, 8in., fluted barrels 3in., Birmingham proved, with two-piece polished walnut grips. (Wallis & Wallis)
$244 £165

A .56in. Long Sea Service flintlock belt pistol, 19in., barrel 12in., Tower proved. Regulation brass mounts, sprung steel belt hook, brass tipped wooden ramrod. (Wallis & Wallis) $2,910 £2,205

ARMS & ARMOUR

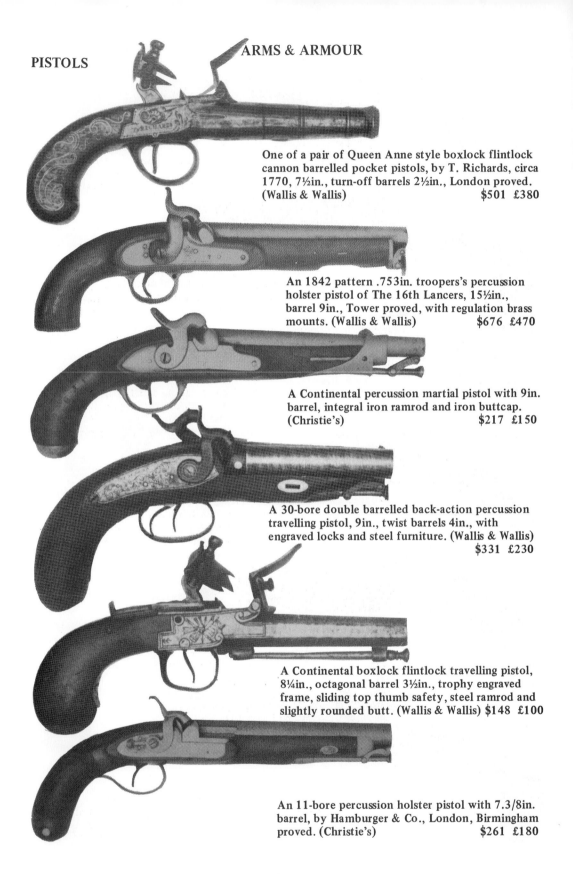

One of a pair of Queen Anne style boxlock flintlock cannon barrelled pocket pistols, by T. Richards, circa 1770, 7½in., turn-off barrels 2½in., London proved. (Wallis & Wallis) $501 £380

An 1842 pattern .753in. troopers's percussion holster pistol of The 16th Lancers, 15½in., barrel 9in., Tower proved, with regulation brass mounts. (Wallis & Wallis) $676 £470

A Continental percussion martial pistol with 9in. barrel, integral iron ramrod and iron buttcap. (Christie's) $217 £150

A 30-bore double barrelled back-action percussion travelling pistol, 9in., twist barrels 4in., with engraved locks and steel furniture. (Wallis & Wallis) $331 £230

A Continental boxlock flintlock travelling pistol, 8¼in., octagonal barrel 3½in., trophy engraved frame, sliding top thumb safety, steel ramrod and slightly rounded butt. (Wallis & Wallis) $148 £100

An 11-bore percussion holster pistol with 7.3/8in. barrel, by Hamburger & Co., London, Birmingham proved. (Christie's) $261 £180

ARMS & ARMOUR

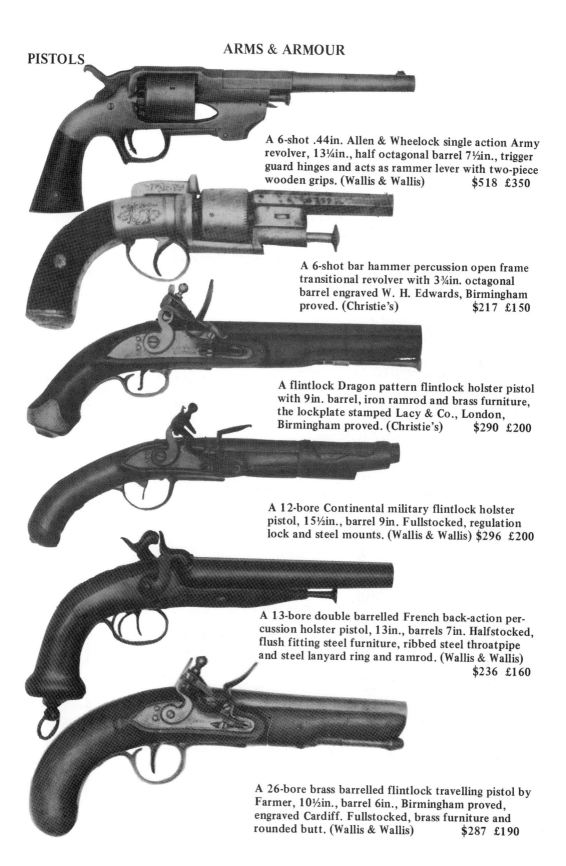

A 6-shot .44in. Allen & Wheelock single action Army revolver, 13¼in., half octagonal barrel 7½in., trigger guard hinges and acts as rammer lever with two-piece wooden grips. (Wallis & Wallis) $518 £350

A 6-shot bar hammer percussion open frame transitional revolver with 3¾in. octagonal barrel engraved W. H. Edwards, Birmingham proved. (Christie's) $217 £150

A flintlock Dragon pattern flintlock holster pistol with 9in. barrel, iron ramrod and brass furniture, the lockplate stamped Lacy & Co., London, Birmingham proved. (Christie's) $290 £200

A 12-bore Continental military flintlock holster pistol, 15½in., barrel 9in. Fullstocked, regulation lock and steel mounts. (Wallis & Wallis) $296 £200

A 13-bore double barrelled French back-action percussion holster pistol, 13in., barrels 7in. Halfstocked, flush fitting steel furniture, ribbed steel throatpipe and steel lanyard ring and ramrod. (Wallis & Wallis) $236 £160

A 26-bore brass barrelled flintlock travelling pistol by Farmer, 10½in., barrel 6in., Birmingham proved, engraved Cardiff. Fullstocked, brass furniture and rounded butt. (Wallis & Wallis) $287 £190

PISTOLS

A 6-shot .44in. Remington Army single action percussion revolver, 14in., octagonal barrel 8in., stamped Patented Sept. 14 1858, brass trigger guard and two-piece wooden grips. (Wallis & Wallis)
$754 £510

A 5-shot 54-bore Beaumont Adams double action percussion revolver 11½in., barrel 5½in., London proved., with side lever rammer and a one-piece chequered walnut grip. (Wallis & Wallis) $460 £320

A 5-shot .38in. bore model 1851 Adam's Patent self-cocking percussion Dragoon revolver, 13½in., barrel 7¾in., London proved, with one-piece chequered wooden grip. (Wallis & Wallis) $290 £220

A 6-shot .44in. Starr Arms Co. single action percussion Army revolver, 13½in., barrel 8in., underlever rammer and one-piece wooden grip. (Wallis & Wallis) $417 £290

A 5-shot 54-bore self-cocking 1851 model Adams percussion revolver, 12in., barrel 6¾in., London proved, with sprung hammer safety and chequered one-piece walnut grip. (Wallis & Wallis) $374 £260

A 6-shot .44in. Magnum Ruger Super Blackhawk single action revolver, 13½in., barrel 7½in., with sidegate loading and ejection. (Wallis & Wallis)
$132 £100

PISTOLS

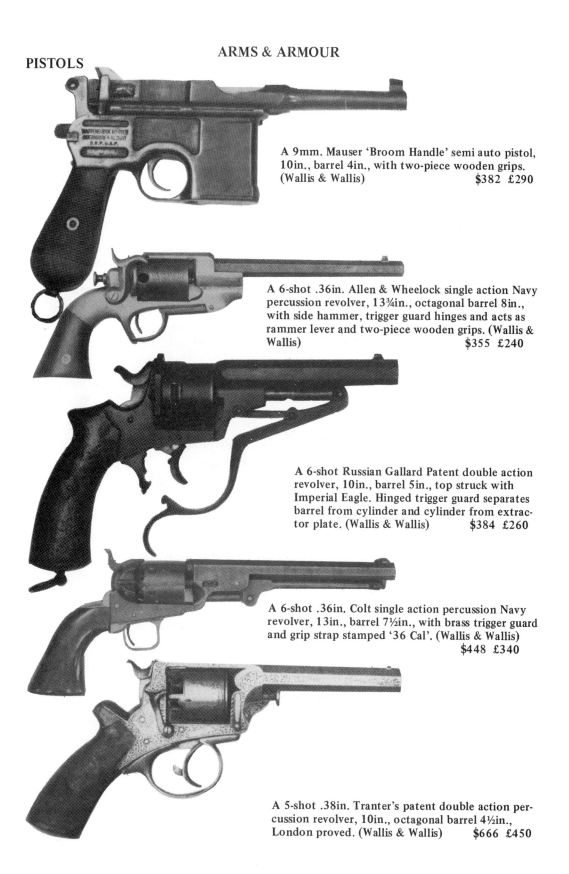

A 9mm. Mauser 'Broom Handle' semi auto pistol, 10in., barrel 4in., with two-piece wooden grips. (Wallis & Wallis) $382 £290

A 6-shot .36in. Allen & Wheelock single action Navy percussion revolver, 13¾in., octagonal barrel 8in., with side hammer, trigger guard hinges and acts as rammer lever and two-piece wooden grips. (Wallis & Wallis) $355 £240

A 6-shot Russian Gallard Patent double action revolver, 10in., barrel 5in., top struck with Imperial Eagle. Hinged trigger guard separates barrel from cylinder and cylinder from extractor plate. (Wallis & Wallis) $384 £260

A 6-shot .36in. Colt single action percussion Navy revolver, 13in., barrel 7½in., with brass trigger guard and grip strap stamped '36 Cal'. (Wallis & Wallis) $448 £340

A 5-shot .38in. Tranter's patent double action percussion revolver, 10in., octagonal barrel 4½in., London proved. (Wallis & Wallis) $666 £450

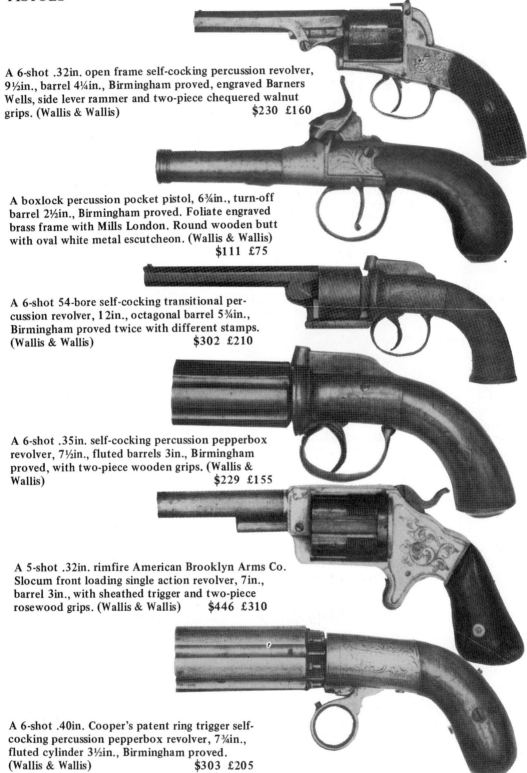

A 6-shot .32in. open frame self-cocking percussion revolver, 9½in., barrel 4¼in., Birmingham proved, engraved Barners Wells, side lever rammer and two-piece chequered walnut grips. (Wallis & Wallis) $230 £160

A boxlock percussion pocket pistol, 6¾in., turn-off barrel 2½in., Birmingham proved. Foliate engraved brass frame with Mills London. Round wooden butt with oval white metal escutcheon. (Wallis & Wallis) $111 £75

A 6-shot 54-bore self-cocking transitional percussion revolver, 12in., octagonal barrel 5¾in., Birmingham proved twice with different stamps. (Wallis & Wallis) $302 £210

A 6-shot .35in. self-cocking percussion pepperbox revolver, 7½in., fluted barrels 3in., Birmingham proved, with two-piece wooden grips. (Wallis & Wallis) $229 £155

A 5-shot .32in. rimfire American Brooklyn Arms Co. Slocum front loading single action revolver, 7in., barrel 3in., with sheathed trigger and two-piece rosewood grips. (Wallis & Wallis) $446 £310

A 6-shot .40in. Cooper's patent ring trigger self-cocking percussion pepperbox revolver, 7¾in., fluted cylinder 3½in., Birmingham proved. (Wallis & Wallis) $303 £205

PISTOLS

A 9mm. long barrelled Artillery Luger, 12½in.,
barrel 8in., stamped at breech 1917, with tan-.
gent sight, hinged safety and two-piece
wooden grips. (Wallis & Wallis) $1,512 £1,050

A 6-shot .36in. self-cocking percussion pepperbox
revolver, 8in., fluted barrels 3in., Birmingham proved,
with two-piece chequered wooden grip. (Wallis &
Wallis) $259 £180

A 6-shot .36in. Whitney Navy single action percussion
revolver, 13in., barrel 7¾in., with underlever rammer,
roll engraved cylinder, brass trigger guard and two-
piece wooden grips. (Wallis & Wallis) $458 £310

A double barrelled .45in. turnover boxlock
percussion travelling pistol, 7½in., blued octagonal barrels 3½in., Birmingham proved, with
dolphin hammer and one-piece chequered
walnut butt. (Wallis & Wallis) $230 £160

A 6-shot .38in. rimfire Allen & Wheelock single action
revolver, 10¾in., barrel 6in., trigger guard hinged to
act as ejector lever and with two-piece wooden grips.
(Wallis & Wallis) $429 £290

A 4-shot .36in. Mariette patent ring trigger self-
cocking Belgian percussion pepperbox revolver,
6½in., turn-off damascus barrels 2½in., Liege
proved with two-piece ebony grips. (Wallis &
Wallis) $199 £135

PISTOLS

A 5-shot 54-bore model 1851 Adam's Patent self-cocking percussion revolver, 12in., barrel 6in., London proved. Sliding cylinder locking bolt, sprung hammer safety, side lever rammer, chequered walnut butt. (Wallis & Wallis)
$740 £500

A 6-shot .31in. self-cocking transitional percussion revolver, 11in., barrel 5½in. Cylinder roll engraved with dogs and deer. Foliate engraved brass back-strap, one-piece chequered walnut grips. (Wallis & Wallis) $503 £340

A 5-shot 54-bore Tranter's Patent double trigger percussion revolver, 12in., barrel 6in., Birmingham proved. Foliate engraved frame, hardened cylinder and buttcap, sprung hammer safety, one-piece chequered walnut butt. (Wallis & Wallis) $592 £400

A 6-shot 54-bore self-cocking transitional percussion revolver, 12¼in., barrel 5¾in., Birmingham proved, plunger type rammer. Fluted cylinder, foliate engraved round steel frame, bar hammer and furniture. (Wallis & Wallis) $488 £330

A 5-shot 38-bore Deane Harding Patent double action percussion revolver, 12in., barrel 6in., London proved, underlever rammer, sliding cylinder locking catch. One-piece chequered grip. (Wallis & Wallis)
$547 £370

A 6-shot .45in. enclosed hammer single action percussion revolver by Devisme, No. 43, 13in., barrel 6¼in., swivel catch locks frame to barrel. (Wallis & Wallis) $725 £490

A 6-shot .44in. self-cocking transitional percussion revolver, 11¾in., mirror blued barrel 5¼in., Birmingham proved. Mirror blued cylinder, two-piece polished walnut grip. (Wallis & Wallis) $606 £410

ARMS & ARMOUR

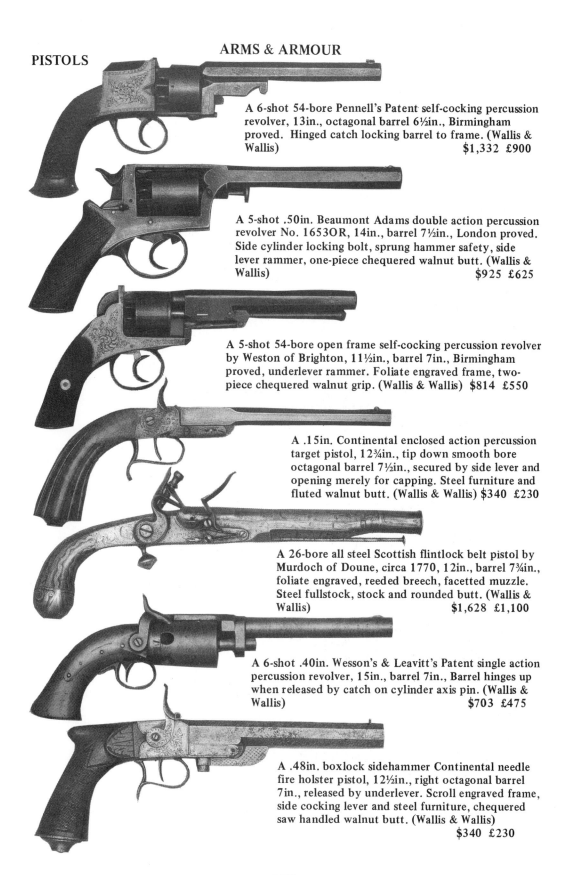

A 6-shot 54-bore Pennell's Patent self-cocking percussion revolver, 13in., octagonal barrel 6½in., Birmingham proved. Hinged catch locking barrel to frame. (Wallis & Wallis) $1,332 £900

A 5-shot .50in. Beaumont Adams double action percussion revolver No. 1653OR, 14in., barrel 7½in., London proved. Side cylinder locking bolt, sprung hammer safety, side lever rammer, one-piece chequered walnut butt. (Wallis & Wallis) $925 £625

A 5-shot 54-bore open frame self-cocking percussion revolver by Weston of Brighton, 11½in., barrel 7in., Birmingham proved, underlever rammer. Foliate engraved frame, two-piece chequered walnut grip. (Wallis & Wallis) $814 £550

A .15in. Continental enclosed action percussion target pistol, 12¾in., tip down smooth bore octagonal barrel 7½in., secured by side lever and opening merely for capping. Steel furniture and fluted walnut butt. (Wallis & Wallis) $340 £230

A 26-bore all steel Scottish flintlock belt pistol by Murdoch of Doune, circa 1770, 12in., barrel 7¾in., foliate engraved, reeded breech, facetted muzzle. Steel fullstock, stock and rounded butt. (Wallis & Wallis) $1,628 £1,100

A 6-shot .40in. Wesson's & Leavitt's Patent single action percussion revolver, 15in., barrel 7in., Barrel hinges up when released by catch on cylinder axis pin. (Wallis & Wallis) $703 £475

A .48in. boxlock sidehammer Continental needle fire holster pistol, 12½in., right octagonal barrel 7in., released by underlever. Scroll engraved frame, side cocking lever and steel furniture, chequered saw handled walnut butt. (Wallis & Wallis) $340 £230

ARMS & ARMOUR

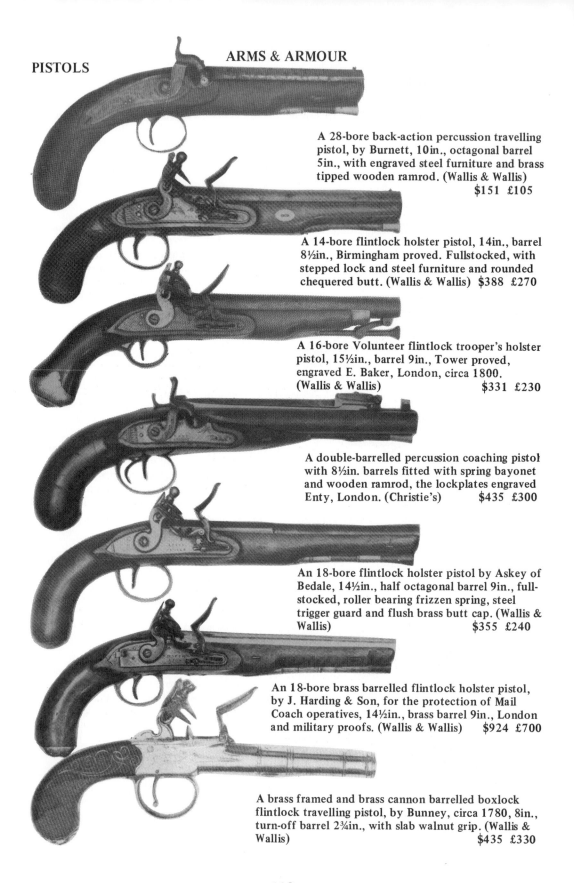

A 28-bore back-action percussion travelling pistol, by Burnett, 10 in., octagonal barrel 5 in., with engraved steel furniture and brass tipped wooden ramrod. (Wallis & Wallis) $151 £105

A 14-bore flintlock holster pistol, 14 in., barrel 8½ in., Birmingham proved. Fullstocked, with stepped lock and steel furniture and rounded chequered butt. (Wallis & Wallis) $388 £270

A 16-bore Volunteer flintlock trooper's holster pistol, 15½ in., barrel 9 in., Tower proved, engraved E. Baker, London, circa 1800. (Wallis & Wallis) $331 £230

A double-barrelled percussion coaching pistol with 8½ in. barrels fitted with spring bayonet and wooden ramrod, the lockplates engraved Enty, London. (Christie's) $435 £300

An 18-bore flintlock holster pistol by Askey of Bedale, 14½ in., half octagonal barrel 9 in., full-stocked, roller bearing frizzen spring, steel trigger guard and flush brass butt cap. (Wallis & Wallis) $355 £240

An 18-bore brass barrelled flintlock holster pistol, by J. Harding & Son, for the protection of Mail Coach operatives, 14½ in., brass barrel 9 in., London and military proofs. (Wallis & Wallis) $924 £700

A brass framed and brass cannon barrelled boxlock flintlock travelling pistol, by Bunney, circa 1780, 8 in., turn-off barrel 2¾ in., with slab walnut grip. (Wallis & Wallis) $435 £330

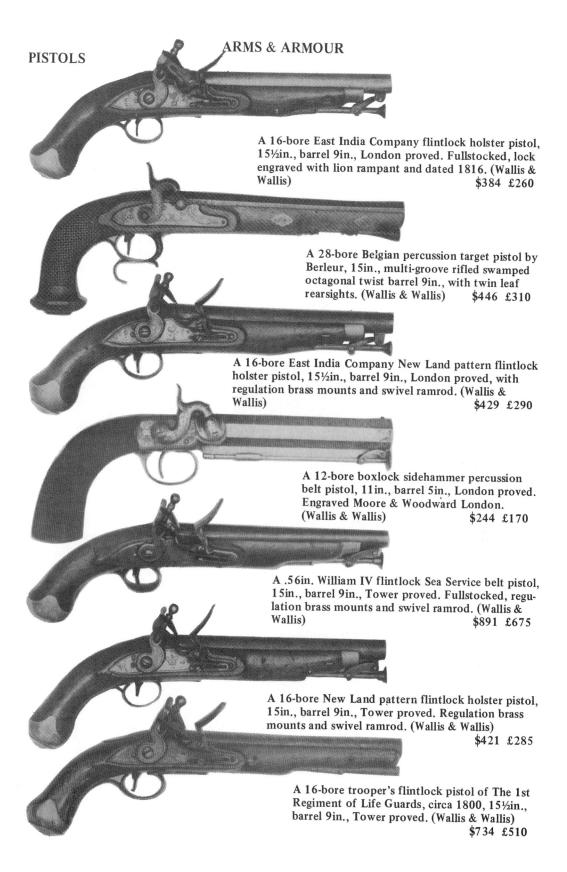

A 16-bore East India Company flintlock holster pistol, 15½in., barrel 9in., London proved. Fullstocked, lock engraved with lion rampant and dated 1816. (Wallis & Wallis) $384 £260

A 28-bore Belgian percussion target pistol by Berleur, 15in., multi-groove rifled swamped octagonal twist barrel 9in., with twin leaf rearsights. (Wallis & Wallis) $446 £310

A 16-bore East India Company New Land pattern flintlock holster pistol, 15½in., barrel 9in., London proved, with regulation brass mounts and swivel ramrod. (Wallis & Wallis) $429 £290

A 12-bore boxlock sidehammer percussion belt pistol, 11in., barrel 5in., London proved. Engraved Moore & Woodward London. (Wallis & Wallis) $244 £170

A .56in. William IV flintlock Sea Service belt pistol, 15in., barrel 9in., Tower proved. Fullstocked, regulation brass mounts and swivel ramrod. (Wallis & Wallis) $891 £675

A 16-bore New Land pattern flintlock holster pistol, 15in., barrel 9in., Tower proved. Regulation brass mounts and swivel ramrod. (Wallis & Wallis) $421 £285

A 16-bore trooper's flintlock pistol of The 1st Regiment of Life Guards, circa 1800, 15½in., barrel 9in., Tower proved. (Wallis & Wallis) $734 £510

POWDER FLASKS

A plain copper 3-way powder flask, brass mounts, swivel lid to shot compartment, containing lead shot. (Wallis & Wallis) $13 £10

A brass mounted priming horn, 7½in., charger with fixed nozzle and wrap around spring, twin brass hanging rings and brass end cap. (Wallis & Wallis) $50 £35

A shell embossed copper powder flask, 8in., common white metal top stamped Bartram & Co., with graduated nozzle. (Wallis & Wallis) $103 £70

A gun sized fluted copper powder flask, 7¾in., patent brass top stamped James Dixon & Sons, Sheffield. (Wallis & Wallis) $50 £35

A silver mounted tortoise-shell powder flask, 4in., with silver spout and sprung lever. (Wallis & Wallis) $103 £70

A foliate embossed copper powder flask, 8in., patent top stamped James Dixon & Sons, Sheffield. (Wallis & Wallis) $47 £32

A copper pistol sized powder flask, 4¼in., the common brass top with fixed nozzle. (Wallis & Wallis) $43 £30

A German flattened cowhorn powder flask with Boche charger, 13in., brass mounts and horn nozzle. (Wallis & Wallis) $118 £80

A copper three-way powder flask, 3½in., stamped Sykes, with common-brass top with blued spring. (Wallis & Wallis) $88 £60

POWDER FLASKS

A bag-shaped copper pistol flask, 5½in., brass top stamped James Dixon & Sons, Sheffield, graduated nozzle from 3/8 to 5/8 drams. (Wallis & Wallis) $110 £77

An Austrian powder flask of lanthorn, 8½in., pear shaped two-piece body with patent brass top. (Wallis & Wallis) $79 £60

An embossed copper powder flask, 8in., with woven design within acanthus borders, common top stamped G. & J. W. Hawksley. (Wallis & Wallis)
$81 £55

A pistol sized copper powder flask, 4½in., plain body with lacquered brass top, fixed nozzle and blued spring. (Wallis & Wallis) $37 £26

A brass mounted priming horn, 7½in., wrap around spring to fixed charger, with twin brass hanging rings, brass end cap and green hanging cord. (Wallis & Wallis) $28 £20

A copper powder flask of the type cased with Colts, 4in. (Wallis & Wallis)
$100 £70

A gun sized copper powder flask, 7in., of chamfered form, common brass top stamped Sykes Patent. (Wallis & Wallis) $79 £55

A late 17th century turned wooden powder flask of 'doughnut' form, 3in. diam., with steel suspension rings. (Wallis & Wallis) $158 £110

A copper three-way powder flask, 5.1/8in., common brass top with blued spring hinged ball cover to top. (Wallis & Wallis) $74 £50

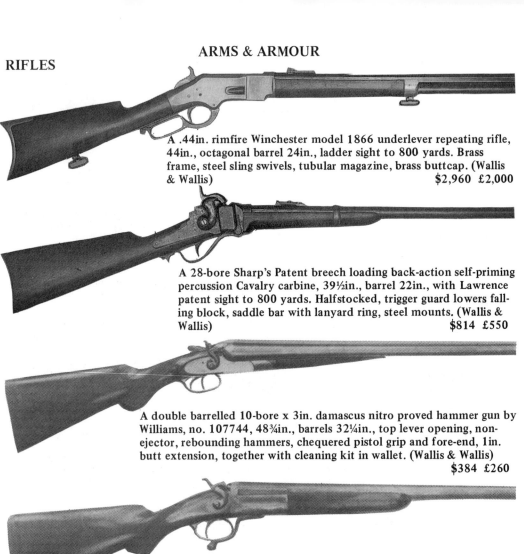

A .44in. rimfire Winchester model 1866 underlever repeating rifle, 44in., octagonal barrel 24in., ladder sight to 800 yards. Brass frame, steel sling swivels, tubular magazine, brass buttcap. (Wallis & Wallis) $2,960 £2,000

A 28-bore Sharp's Patent breech loading back-action self-priming percussion Cavalry carbine, 39½in., barrel 22in., with Lawrence patent sight to 800 yards. Halfstocked, trigger guard lowers falling block, saddle bar with lanyard ring, steel mounts. (Wallis & Wallis) $814 £550

A double barrelled 10-bore x 3in. damascus nitro proved hammer gun by Williams, no. 107744, 48¾in., barrels 32¼in., top lever opening, non-ejector, rebounding hammers, chequered pistol grip and fore-end, 1in. butt extension, together with cleaning kit in wallet. (Wallis & Wallis) $384 £260

A single barrelled 8-bore nitro proved back-action underlever hammer sporting gun, 52in., damascus barrel 35½in., engraved E. Cox, foliate engraved action and lock, chequered pistol grip, vacant escutcheon and rubber butt extension. (Wallis & Wallis) $620 £420

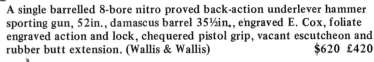

A 12-bore Belgian contract Brunswick back-action military percussion rifle, 46½in., barrel 30in., for the belted ball, with tangent rearsight. Regulation brass mounts with large butt trap. (Wallis & Wallis) $295 £205

A .44in. rimfire Winchester model 1866 factory engraved underlever repeating rifle, 44in., barrel 24in. Bronze frame. (Wallis & Wallis) $6,068 £4,100

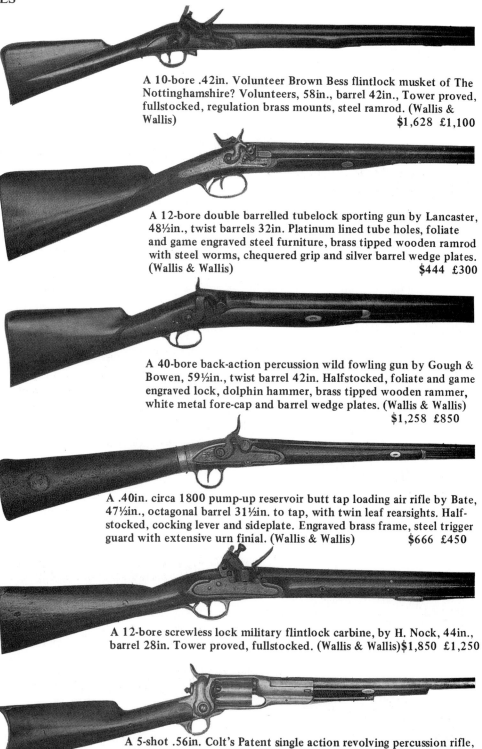

A 10-bore .42in. Volunteer Brown Bess flintlock musket of The Nottinghamshire? Volunteers, 58in., barrel 42in., Tower proved, fullstocked, regulation brass mounts, steel ramrod. (Wallis & Wallis) $1,628 £1,100

A 12-bore double barrelled tubelock sporting gun by Lancaster, 48½in., twist barrels 32in. Platinum lined tube holes, foliate and game engraved steel furniture, brass tipped wooden ramrod with steel worms, chequered grip and silver barrel wedge plates. (Wallis & Wallis) $444 £300

A 40-bore back-action percussion wild fowling gun by Gough & Bowen, 59½in., twist barrel 42in. Halfstocked, foliate and game engraved lock, dolphin hammer, brass tipped wooden rammer, white metal fore-cap and barrel wedge plates. (Wallis & Wallis) $1,258 £850

A .40in. circa 1800 pump-up reservoir butt tap loading air rifle by Bate, 47½in., octagonal barrel 31½in. to tap, with twin leaf rearsights. Halfstocked, cocking lever and sideplate. Engraved brass frame, steel trigger guard with extensive urn finial. (Wallis & Wallis) $666 £450

A 12-bore screwless lock military flintlock carbine, by H. Nock, 44in., barrel 28in. Tower proved, fullstocked. (Wallis & Wallis)$1,850 £1,250

A 5-shot .56in. Colt's Patent single action revolving percussion rifle, 43in., barrel 24in., underlever rammer. Fluted cylinder stamped Patented Sept. 10th 1850'. (Wallis & Wallis) $2,516 £1,700

ARMS & ARMOUR

A single barrelled 14-bore percussion sporting gun, 45½in., browned twist barrel 30in., with octagonal gold lined breech engraved J. Blanch & Son, figured walnut stock with chequered wrist. (Wallis & Wallis)
$384 £260

An Irish flintlock musketoon, 35in., half octagonal barrel 19in., with flared muzzle. Fullstocked, re-used Brown Bess lock, stamped Pattison. (Wallis & Wallis) $592 £400

A 16-bore double-barrelled French percussion sporting gun, breech converted from flintlock, 47in., barrels 31in. Fullstocked, plain steel furniture with French walnut stock. (Wallis & Wallis)
$488 £370

A 12-bore back-action percussion sporting gun by Simmons, 46in., twist barrel 30in., with gold breech lines, erased poincon and platinum safety plug. (Wallis & Wallis) $223 £155

A .177in. Militia Patent pre-war round frame air rifle, 39in., barrel 17½in., with octagonal breech. (Wallis & Wallis) $34 £26

A brass barrelled flintlock blunderbuss with spring bayonet, circa 1810, 30¼in., half octagonal barrel 14½in., Tower proved with thumb catch released spring bayonet. (Wallis & Wallis) $864 £600

A 16-bore and 6.5mm. snap action drilling combined hammer gun and rifle, 42½in., barrels 26½in., engraved Aug Luneburg Kile with sight mounts, back-action locks, underlever snap action, set right trigger and chequered pistol grip. (Wallis & Wallis) $310 £210

A 20-bore officer's flintlock fusil of The Herefordshire Militia, circa 1770, 47½in., half octagonal barrel 32in., London proved. Fullstocked with two-piece fore-end, steel furniture and acorn finialled trigger guard. (Wallis & Wallis) $432 £300

A 12-bore x 2½in. N.P. side lock ejector 'The Watts Gun' by London Sporting Park Ltd., no. 396, 46in., barrels 28in., top lever opening, gold inlaid auto safe and chequered fore and small, silver escutcheon, 1¾in. butt extension. (Wallis & Wallis) $777 £525

A 16-bore Belgian double barrelled flintlock sporting gun made for the Eastern market, 55½in., barrels 39½in., etched with Arabic inscription dated 1880. Halfstocked, foliate engraved locks and white metal furniture. (Wallis & Wallis) $504 £350

A 7mm. (.25in.) Britannia air rifle, no. 1137, 45in., barrel 18½in. to loading port with swivel cover. Hinged catch releases stock and action to cock cylinder. (Wallis & Wallis) $222 £150

A 10-bore E.I.C. New Land pattern sergeant's flintlock musket, 49in., barrel 33¼in., London proved, fixed sights with regulation brass mounts, steel sling swivels and ramrod. (Wallis & Wallis) $674 £510

A Turkish flintlock blunderbuss, 23in., flared barrel 12in. Fullstocked, with engraved steel furniture, the saddle bar with lanyard ring. (Wallis & Wallis) $604 £420

A 12-bore percussion sporting gun by Joseph Manton, No. 6964, 50in., half octagonal barrel 34in., with breech converter's poincon, barrel London proved. (Wallis & Wallis) $460 £320

ARMS & ARMOUR

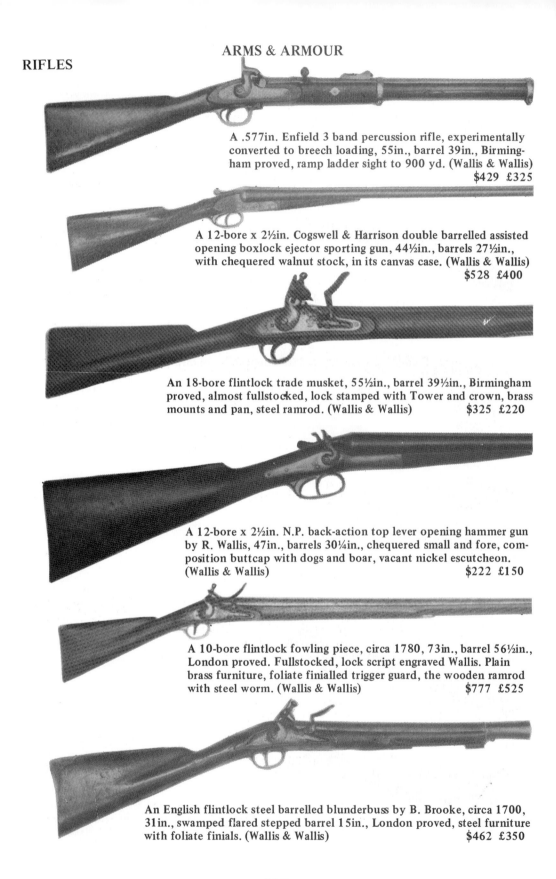

A .577in. Enfield 3 band percussion rifle, experimentally converted to breech loading, 55in., barrel 39in., Birmingham proved, ramp ladder sight to 900 yd. (Wallis & Wallis) $429 £325

A 12-bore x 2½in. Cogswell & Harrison double barrelled assisted opening boxlock ejector sporting gun, 44½in., barrels 27½in., with chequered walnut stock, in its canvas case. (Wallis & Wallis) $528 £400

An 18-bore flintlock trade musket, 55½in., barrel 39½in., Birmingham proved, almost fullstocked, lock stamped with Tower and crown, brass mounts and pan, steel ramrod. (Wallis & Wallis) $325 £220

A 12-bore x 2½in. N.P. back-action top lever opening hammer gun by R. Wallis, 47in., barrels 30¼in., chequered small and fore, composition buttcap with dogs and boar, vacant nickel escutcheon. (Wallis & Wallis) $222 £150

A 10-bore flintlock fowling piece, circa 1780, 73in., barrel 56½in., London proved. Fullstocked, lock script engraved Wallis. Plain brass furniture, foliate finialled trigger guard, the wooden ramrod with steel worm. (Wallis & Wallis) $777 £525

An English flintlock steel barrelled blunderbuss by B. Brooke, circa 1700, 31in., swamped flared stepped barrel 15in., London proved, steel furniture with foliate finials. (Wallis & Wallis) $462 £350

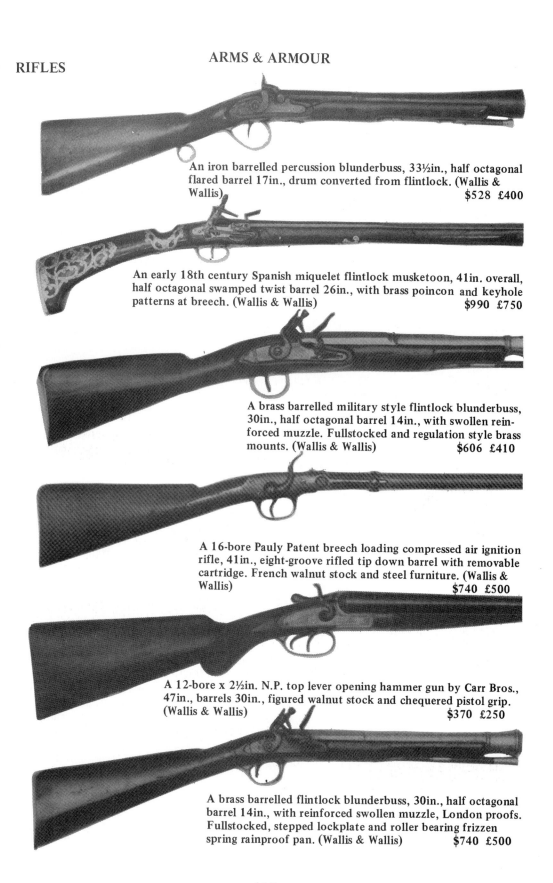

An iron barrelled percussion blunderbuss, 33½in., half octagonal flared barrel 17in., drum converted from flintlock. (Wallis & Wallis) $528 £400

An early 18th century Spanish miquelet flintlock musketoon, 41in. overall, half octagonal swamped twist barrel 26in., with brass poincon and keyhole patterns at breech. (Wallis & Wallis) $990 £750

A brass barrelled military style flintlock blunderbuss, 30in., half octagonal barrel 14in., with swollen reinforced muzzle. Fullstocked and regulation style brass mounts. (Wallis & Wallis) $606 £410

A 16-bore Pauly Patent breech loading compressed air ignition rifle, 41in., eight-groove rifled tip down barrel with removable cartridge. French walnut stock and steel furniture. (Wallis & Wallis) $740 £500

A 12-bore x 2½in. N.P. top lever opening hammer gun by Carr Bros., 47in., barrels 30in., figured walnut stock and chequered pistol grip. (Wallis & Wallis) $370 £250

A brass barrelled flintlock blunderbuss, 30in., half octagonal barrel 14in., with reinforced swollen muzzle, London proofs. Fullstocked, stepped lockplate and roller bearing frizzen spring rainproof pan. (Wallis & Wallis) $740 £500

SWORDS

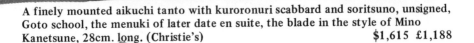

A finely mounted aikuchi tanto with kuroronuri scabbard and soritsuno, unsigned, Goto school, the menuki of later date en suite, the blade in the style of Mino Kanetsune, 28cm. long. (Christie's) $1,615 £1,188

A Georgian 1796 pattern Infantry officer's sword, blade 31in., etched at forte Craven & Co. Warranted, the copper gilt hilt with double shell guard and silver wirebound grip. (Wallis & Wallis) $145 £110

An Indian Army officer's mameluke hilted sword, broad curved fullered blade 31in., with steel crosspiece and grip strap and two-piece ivory grips, in its ass skin covered scabbard. (Wallis & Wallis) $340 £230

A mid 18th century European hunting sword, curved, single edged blade 18½in., with pronounced clipped back edge, brass half shell guard with eagle's head terminal and horn grip. (Wallis & Wallis) $79 £55

A Georgian 1796 pattern Infantry officer's sword, slim, tapering, double-edged blade 31½in., etched at forte J.J.R. Sohlingen and with the maker Bland & James, with silver wirebound grip, in its leather scabbard. (Wallis & Wallis) $105 £80

A Victorian 1821 pattern Artillery officer's sword, blade 34½in., by Hamburger Rogers, with triple bar steel guard and steel mounts. German silver wirebound fishskin covered grip, in its steel scabbard. (Wallis & Wallis) $93 £65

ARMS & ARMOUR

A wakizashi, the red lacquered scabbard simulating cherry bark, fitted with a gilt kogai and shakudo-nanakoji kozuka, the tsuba signed Kazuyoshi, Meiji period, the blade, unsigned, 16th century, 34.2cm. (Christie's)

$5,868 £4,104

A French smallsword, circa 1750, hollow ground triangular section blade 27in. Steel hilt, foliate chiselled quillon block, woven silver grip wire and iron tape with woven silver Turk's head. (Wallis & Wallis)

$198 £150

An Indian Army 1908 pattern Cavalry trooper's sword of Skinner's Horse, slim blade 34½in., by Wilkinson, issue mark for 1918, in its steel scabbard. (Wallis & Wallis)

$384 £260

A 19th century hunting sword, plain, single edged blade 13in., steel fluted shell guard, reversed hoof quillons, staghorn hilt with fluted steel pommel, in its leather sheath, with provision for companion knife. (Wallis & Wallis)

$86 £60

A William IV 1831 pattern General officer's mameluke sabre, curved, clipped back blade 30in., by W. Moore, in its leather scabbard with three copper gilt mounts. (Wallis & Wallis)

$396 £300

A George V Coldstream Guards officer's sword, blade 32in., by Johns & Pegg, London, with plated hilt and wirebound fish-skin covered grip, in its plated scabbard. (Wallis & Wallis)

$145 £110

119

An o-wakizashi, the scabbard covered with Dutch leather, a shibuichi kozuka and a copper kogai, the blade, signed and dated Eiroku ninen, 1559, 51.7cm. long. (Christie's) $1,853 £1,296

A daisho with mijingai-nuri scabbards decorated with gold hiramakie ho-o and kuroronuri kiri, with handashi style sahari-ishimeji fittings decorated with kiri, the blades both honzukuri and torii-zori, unsigned, 66.2cm. long, the wakizashi 47.4cm. long. (Christie's) $2,937 £2,160

A large katana, the scabbard with brown pine-needle design, the menuki formed as bats in flight, unsigned, the blade signed Kanesada (probably Kanesada III of Mino), 16th century, 76.5cm. long. (Christie's) $3,231 £2,376

An elaborately mounted tanto, the blade, wide takenokozori with sukashi kurikara horimono, fine mokume hada and komidare hamon of nie, ubu nakago, unsigned, 17th century, 28.8cm. long. (Christie's) $3,672 £2,700

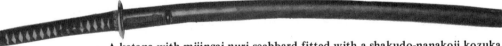

A katana with mijingai-nuri scabbard fitted with a shakudo-nanakoji kozuka, the tsuba decorated with a gilt rim and gilt and shakudo kiku, unsigned, Goto School, the blade, signed Kiyomitsu saku, circa 1573, 69.8cm. long. (Christie's) $1,698 £1,188

A late Japanese sword tachi, blade 66.4cm., inscribed Tadamitsu, muji hada, chu suguha hamon. Brass aoi tsuba, tsuka, dragon menuki, nashiji lacquered saya. (Wallis & Wallis) $1,702 £1,150

A well mounted katana with brown-sprinkled lacquer kizamisaya decorated with lightly punched mitsutomoemon with shibuichi basketwork kojiri, unsigned, 19th century, 59cm. long. (Christie's) $3,231 £2,376

A handachi katana, the mura-nashiji scabbard decorated in gold hiramakie, the fuchi signed Nakamura Haruhiro (Hirato school, mid 19th century), the blade signed Noshu Seki, circa 1644, 66.5cm. long. (Christie's)　　　　$2,643　£1,944

A large Shinto katana, broad blade 70.6cm., signed Rikouku Nokami Fujiwara Kanenobu, circa 1764. Bold sanbon sugi hamon, gunome hamon, distinct nie line. Tape bound tsuka, in its black lacquered saya. (Wallis & Wallis)　　　　$976　£660

A richly mounted handachi, the nashiji scabbard decorated with kotobuki and other seal characters in gold hiramakie, signed, circa 1800, the blade circa 1661, 69.6cm. long. (Christie's)　　　　$4,112　£3,024

A finely mounted hamidashi tanto with black ishime-nuri scabbard, signed Kitosai Terumitsu, circa 1800, the blade inscribed Yukimune, probably late 15th/early 16th century, Yamashiro School, 24.7cm. long. (Christie's)　　　　$1,101　£810

A Japanese World War II Army officer's sword katana, blade 66.5cm., signed Showato with dated Showa 16th year (1943), in shin gunto mounts with leather covered steel saya. (Wallis & Wallis) $171　£130

A late Japanese ito maki-no-tachi, blade 68.7cm., mumei, itame hada, gunome hamon. Tape bound tsuka, black lacquered saya. (Wallis & Wallis)　　　　$662　£460

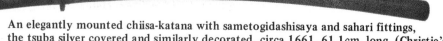

An elegantly mounted chiisa-katana with sametogidashisaya and sahari fittings, the tsuba silver covered and similarly decorated, circa 1661, 61.1cm. long. (Christie's)　　　　$3,672　£2,700

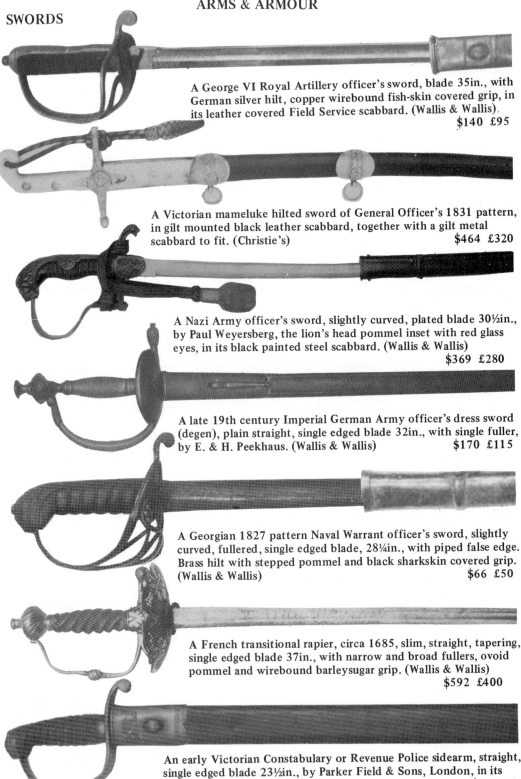

A George VI Royal Artillery officer's sword, blade 35in., with German silver hilt, copper wirebound fish-skin covered grip, in its leather covered Field Service scabbard. (Wallis & Wallis). **$140 £95**

A Victorian mameluke hilted sword of General Officer's 1831 pattern, in gilt mounted black leather scabbard, together with a gilt metal scabbard to fit. (Christie's) **$464 £320**

A Nazi Army officer's sword, slightly curved, plated blade 30½in., by Paul Weyersberg, the lion's head pommel inset with red glass eyes, in its black painted steel scabbard. (Wallis & Wallis) **$369 £280**

A late 19th century Imperial German Army officer's dress sword (degen), plain straight, single edged blade 32in., with single fuller, by E. & H. Peekhaus. (Wallis & Wallis) **$170 £115**

A Georgian 1827 pattern Naval Warrant officer's sword, slightly curved, fullered, single edged blade, 28¼in., with piped false edge. Brass hilt with stepped pommel and black sharkskin covered grip. (Wallis & Wallis) **$66 £50**

A French transitional rapier, circa 1685, slim, straight, tapering, single edged blade 37in., with narrow and broad fullers, ovoid pommel and wirebound barleysugar grip. (Wallis & Wallis) **$592 £400**

An early Victorian Constabulary or Revenue Police sidearm, straight, single edged blade 23½in., by Parker Field & Sons, London, in its brass mounted leather scabbard. (Wallis & Wallis) **$74 £50**

An Austrian Lorenz Jager carbine sword bayonet, blade 23½in., with broad fuller stamps to socket. (Wallis & Wallis) $66 £45

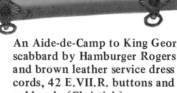

An Aide-de-Camp to King George V, mameluke hilted scimitar, the scabbard by Hamburger Rogers & Co., with undress steel scabbard and brown leather service dress scabbard, together with shoulder cords, 42 E.VII.R. buttons and two R.A. sabre tache slings and a gold sash. (Christie's) $464 £320

A transitional dish hilted rapier, circa 1630, slender blade 41½in., stamped Sebastian Hernantis in the fullers. Foliate chiselled hilt, pierced dish guard and wirebound grip. (Wallis & Wallis)
$488 £330

A late Victorian 'Lead Cutter' cutlass, broad, single edged, slightly curved blade 30½in., by Mole, Birmingham, issue stamps for '97, sheet steel guard and ribbed iron grip, in its leather scabbard. (Wallis & Wallis) $129 £90

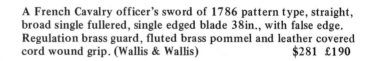

A French Cavalry officer's sword of 1786 pattern type, straight, broad single fullered, single edged blade 38in., with false edge. Regulation brass guard, fluted brass pommel and leather covered cord wound grip. (Wallis & Wallis) $281 £190

A mid 17th century Cavalry man's half basket hilted broadsword, straight, double edged blade 33in. Brass hilt, stepped bulbous pommel and leather covered grip. (Wallis & Wallis) $488 £330

An 1857 pattern Engineers officer's sword of The 2nd Gloucestershire Engineer Vols., polished fullered single edged blade 33in., with regulation pierced brass gilt hilt and wirebound sharkskin grip. (Wallis & Wallis) $177 £120

TSUBAS

A Japanese iron tsuba, 8.3cm., of mokko form, slightly raised rims with heart-shaped piercings. (Wallis & Wallis) $45 £31

A pierced iron Choshu tsuba, 7.5cm., chiselled with ears of rice in relief. (Wallis & Wallis) $115 £80

A Japanese pierced iron tsuba, 7.8cm., of circular form, pierced with geometric blossom. (Wallis & Wallis) $47 £32

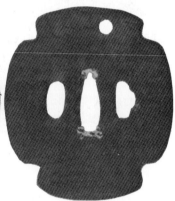

A squared iron tsuba, 6.7cm., chiselled with a prunus and inlaid soft metal flowers. (Wallis & Wallis) $79 £54

A circular iron tsuba, 7.3cm., signed Echizen noju kinai saku, pierced and chiselled with a dragon. (Wallis & Wallis) $100 £68

A Japanese pierced iron tsuba, 9cm., engraved with a stream, lilies, wheel, hexagonal devices and clouds. (Wallis & Wallis) $50 £34

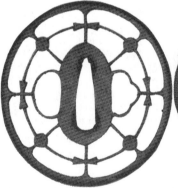

A Sado School tsuba, 7.3cm., signed Sashu no ju Toshioki, chiselled with a flower. (Wallis & Wallis) $79 £55

A Higo pierced iron tsuba, 7.5cm., pierced with a wheel of arrows. (Wallis & Wallis) $92 £64

A Japanese pierced iron tsuba, 8.6cm., of mokko form, pierced with a blossom. (Wallis & Wallis) $47 £32

A Japanese iron tsuba, 7cm., of mokko form with shaped lobes. (Wallis & Wallis)
$47 £32

A kyo-sukashi tsuba depicting five cranes, unsigned, Edo period, 8.7cm. (Christie's) $263 £194

A heavy Miochi iron mokko tsuba, 8.2cm., of mokume, with udenuki-an and sukashi stylised flower. (Wallis & Wallis) $50 £35

A Japanese pierced iron tsuba, 7.6cm., of eight lobed outline, pierced and chiselled in low relief with part flower heads. (Wallis & Wallis)
$47 £32

A circular iron tsuba, 7.1cm., signed Bushu noju kunihiro saku, pierced with waves. (Wallis & Wallis) $62 £42

An oval shibuichi tanto tsuba and associated fuchi-kashira, each signed Hosono Sozaemon Masamori, circa 1700. (Christie's) $440 £324

A Higo iron wakizashi tsuba, 6.8cm., chiselled with basket weave design, gold nunome to edge. (Wallis & Wallis)
$158 £110

A Japanese pierced iron tsuba, 7.1cm., thick squared plate with chidori joining various geometric devices. (Wallis & Wallis) $44 £30

A circular iron tsuba, 7.1cm., pierced and chiselled in low relief, two pieces of large flowering foliage. (Wallis & Wallis) $79 £55

One of a pair of circular iron tsuba for a Daisho, 6.9cm. and 7.3cm., signed Choshu-noju-Sakushinao Tomohisa. (Wallis & Wallis) $310 £210

A Higo pierced iron circular tsuba, 7.6cm., thick plate with crane and pine tree. (Wallis & Wallis) $79 £55

A circular iron tsuchimeji tsuba decorated with a gourdvine in copper and brass takazogan in Onin style, 8.2cm., and another. (Christie's) $263 £194

A shallow mokkogata shibuichi tsuba decorated in katakiribori and gilt, inscribed Joi, 6.5cm. (Christie's) $216 £160

A heavy pierced iron Owari tsuba of barbed mokko form, 7.4cm., pierced with bars. (Wallis & Wallis) $72 £50

A Japanese pierced iron tsuba, 7.4cm., of circular form, with a radial pattern of hammers. (Wallis & Wallis) $44 £30

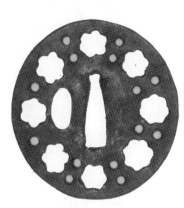

A Japanese pierced iron tsuba, 7.4cm., of circular form, pierced with geometric designs. (Wallis & Wallis) $44 £30

A circular iron tsuba, 7.3cm., signed Bushu noju nagamasa, depicting arrow heads in silhouette with engraved detail. (Wallis & Wallis) $59 £40

A circular iron tsuba, 7cm., inlaid in soft metals with a hanging basket of flowers. (Wallis & Wallis) $79 £55

126

TSUBAS

A circular copper tsuba, 6.7cm. tooled with the trails of snails and applied with five gilt snails, shakudo rim. (Wallis & Wallis) $116 £74

A Japanese pierced iron tsuba, 8cm., of irregular form, finely pierced with geometric devices. (Wallis & Wallis) $50 £34

A shibuichi tsuba in shakudo ishimeji with egrets among rushes in silver and gilt taka-zogan, unsigned, 19th century, 7.2cm. (Christie's) $202 £150

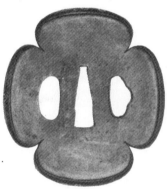

An iron mokko tsuba, 7.8cm., raised swollen rim inlaid with silver tendrils. (Wallis & Wallis) $100 £70

A Japanese pierced iron tsuba, 9.5cm., of mokko form, with geometric piercings and engraved detail. (Wallis & Wallis) $74 £50

A copper tsuba, 6.6cm., signed Hirochika, of rough hammered form. (Wallis & Wallis) $94 £64

A circular iron Soten tsuba, 7.3cm., signed Goshu ju Soheishi sei, details in gold nunome. (Wallis & Wallis) $151 £105

A Japanese pierced iron tsuba, 7.4cm., of irregular form, chiselled as an ear of corn in low relief with leaves. (Wallis & Wallis) $47 £32

A 19th century copper and sentoku hari-ishime hariawase tsuba, Mito Kinko School, 8.4cm. with fitted box. (Christie's) $2,625 £1,836

WEAPONS

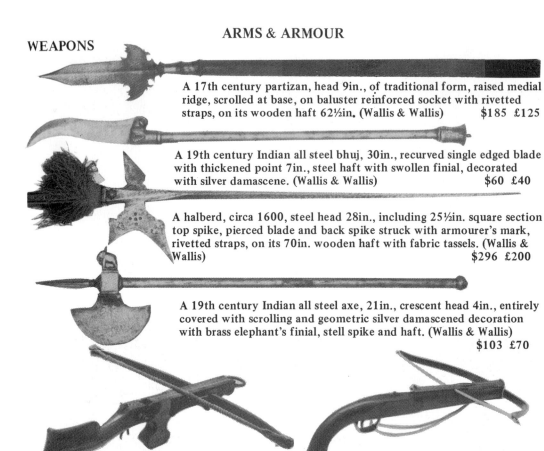

A 17th century partizan, head 9in., of traditional form, raised medial ridge, scrolled at base, on baluster reinforced socket with rivetted straps, on its wooden haft 62½in. (Wallis & Wallis) $185 £125

A 19th century Indian all steel bhuj, 30in., recurved single edged blade with thickened point 7in., steel haft with swollen finial, decorated with silver damascene. (Wallis & Wallis) $60 £40

A halberd, circa 1600, steel head 28in., including 25½in. square section top spike, pierced blade and back spike struck with armourer's mark, rivetted straps, on its 70in. wooden haft with fabric tassels. (Wallis & Wallis) $296 £200

A 19th century Indian all steel axe, 21in., crescent head 4in., entirely covered with scrolling and geometric silver damascened decoration with brass elephant's finial, stell spike and haft. (Wallis & Wallis) $103 £70

A late 19th century European target crossbow, 32in., span 31½in. Beech stock, brass lock sides, thumb lever sets action, double set triggers, bridled wheels for cocking lever and original cord and fore-sight. (Wallis & Wallis) $345 £240

An English pistol crossbow for use with darts at a target, 16in., span 15in., walnut stock, foliate engraved steel lock and brass furniture with urn finialled trigger guard. Octagonal brass 'barrel' 8¼in., circa 1800. (Wallis & Wallis) $288 £200

A Continental boar spear, 16th/17th century, diamond section shaped head 15in., with cylindrical socket and integral rivetted straps, on its octagonal wooden haft 73½in. (Wallis & Wallis) $138 £105

A 19th century Chinese polearm of glaive form, broad, curved, single edged blade 23 x 5in., with spiked back, on its 50in. hardwood haft. (Wallis & Wallis) $198 £150

A 17th century halberd, head 16in., with broad, shallow diamond section top blade, crescent cutting edge with back spike, on its 70in. wooden haft, silk covered with decorative brass studs. (Wallis & Wallis) $118 £90

An Armand Marseille musical/dancing bisque headed puppet doll, impressed 70·20,5. (Lawrence Fine Art) $777 £525

Late 19th century Continental singing bird automaton in repousse sterling silver gilt casket, 4¼in. wide. (Reeds Rains) $769 £520

A papier mache automaton of a clown, the head inset with fixed blue glass eyes, 18in. high. (Lawrence Fine Art) $843 £570

A German 19th century automaton of an organ grinder with miniature dancers, on a garden stage. (Phillips) $3,750 £2,500

An automaton mandolin player, with musical movement in base, stamped G. Vichy, Paris, 25½in. high. (Christie's) $2,160 £1,500

A musical automaton of a bisque headed doll beside a dressing table, marked Simon & Halbig S & H 6, the doll 15in. high. (Christie's) $3,000 £2,000

A composition headed automaton modelled as a standing Chinese man, 30in. high, French 1880. (Christie's) $9,000 £6,000

A mid 19th century German portable barrel organ automaton, 52cm. wide. (Phillips) $9,000 £6,000

A swivel headed clockwork musical walking doll, with a Parisienne type head, 21in. high. (Christie's) $1,500 £1,000

A mid 19th century wheel barometer, with 6in. silvered dial, 97cm. high. (Phillips) $387 £260

A 19th century mahogany marine barometer, with twin glazed ivory scales, 94cm. high. (Phillips) $2,235 £1,500

A mid 19th century mahogany wheel barometer, with level signed Pastorelli, 48¼in. high. (Christie's)
$1,323 £900

A 19th century mahogany stick barometer, the plate signed W. Harris & Co., London, 37in. high. (Christie's)
$675 £460

A 19th century mahogany stick barometer, the silvered brass plate signed Dollond, London, (Christie's)
$1,176 £800

An early 19th century mahogany wheel barometer, the 8in. dial signed J. Watkins, London, 39in. high. (Christie's)
$1,617 £1,100

A 19th century mahogany stick barometer, the silvered brass plate signed Palmer, London, 42¼in. high. (Christie's)
$2,205 £1,500

A George III mahogany clock barometer, 44in. high. (Christie's)
$4,116 £2,800

An early 19th century crossbanded mahogany and boxwood strung stick barometer, the scale signed P. Caminada, Fecit, 98cm. high. (Phillips) $596 £400

A Victorian mahogany banjo barometer. (Ball & Percival) $273 £190

A 19th century rosewood stick barometer, signed Trigg, Guildford, 36in. high. (Christie's) $382 £260

A 19th century wheel barometer, the 12in. dial inscribed Zuccani, London, 57in. high. (Parsons, Welch & Cowell) $651 £440

An early 19th century mahogany Sheraton shell wheel barometer, the 8in. dial signed M. Salmone, Oxford, 99cm. high.(Phillips) $521 £350

An early 19th century crossbanded mahogany stick barometer, the scale signed P. Manticha, London, 98cm. high. (Phillips) $521 £350

A late 19th century oak American Forecast or Royal Polytechnic bulb Cistern barometer, 107cm. high. (Phillips) $536 £360

A 19th century mahogany stick barometer, the silvered brass plate signed W., Foyne, 37¾in. high. (Christie's) $705 £480

BAROMETERS

A late 17th century walnut stick barometer, the engraved brass plates for Summer and Winter, 48in. high. (Christie's)
$2,499 £1,700

A 19th century oak Fisher or Sea Coast stick barometer, 99cm. high. (Phillips) $283 £190

A bird's-eye maple wheel barometer, the 8in. dial level signed J. Cetta, Stroudwater, 39in. high. (Christie's)
$705 £480

A late 17th century walnut stick barometer, unsigned, 39½in. high. (Christie's)
$3,234 £2,200

An early 18th century mahogany stick barometer, the brass plate signed J. Patrick, London, 39in. high. (Christie's)
$2,646 £1,800

Early 19th century aneroid barometer, thermometer and hydrometer, by J. Gricci, Liverpool. (Capes, Dunn & Co.) $415 £270

A George III figured mahogany stick barometer, the ivory register signed Gargory, 36in. long. (Reeds Rains)
$518 £350

An early Georgian mahogany pillar barometer signed A. Grimshaw fecit, 37in. high. (Christie's)
$1,428 £972

132

An early 19th century mahogany barometer, marked Pike & Son, 38in. long. (Robt. W. Skinner Inc.)
$1,300 £902

A George I walnut signal barometer, the brass plate inscribed Made by John Patrick in the Old Bailey London, 36¼ x 29½in. (Christie's) $9,266 £7,020

A 19th century mahogany stick barometer, the silvered brass plate signed N: Ortelli & Co: Fecit, 37½in. high. (Christie's) $441 £300

A George III mahogany stick barometer, by J. Somalvico & Son, London, 45in. high. (Christie's)
$825 £572

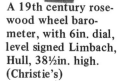

A Georgian mahogany stick barometer, the brass plate signed Wisker York, 36in. high. (Christie's)
$632 £430

A 19th century mahogany stick barometer, the silvered brass plate signed J. Hilliard, London, 43in. high. (Christie's)
$2,352 £1,600

A 19th century rosewood wheel barometer, with 6in. dial, level signed Limbach, Hull, 38½in. high. (Christie's)
$455 £310

A George III mahogany stick barometer, the brass plate signed J. Bird, London, 37in. high.(Christie's)
$1,102 £750

Jeu de la Giraffe, circa 1820.
(Phillips) $420 £280

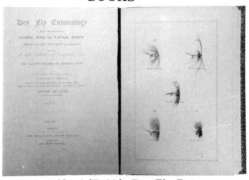

Halford (F. M.): Dry Fly Entomology, 2 vols., No. 22 of 75
copies signed by the author,
1897. (Phillips)
          $1,249 £850

The History of Guy, Earl
of Warwick, n.d. (Phillips)
          $240 £160

History and Topographical
Survey of the County of
Kent, by Edward Hasted,
First Edition, 4 vols.
(Parsons, Welch & Cowell)
          $1,480 £1,000

Grindlay (Capt. Robert Melville):
Scenery, Costumes and Architecture . . . on the Western Side
of India, col. vig. title, 36 hand-
col. plates, 1826. (Phillips)
          $2,682 £1,800

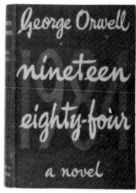

Orwell (G.): Nineteen Eight-
Four, First Edn., 1949.
(Phillips) $750 £500

Roscoe (William): Monandrian
Plants of the Order Scitamineae,
from Lord Derby's library with
his bookplate, 112 hand-col.
plates, 1828. (Phillips)
          $7,450 £5,000

Camden (W.): Britannia,
engraved title, 57 maps,
and 8 plates of coins,
London, folios, 1610.
(Phillips) $2,793 £1,900

Fowles (J.): The Collector,
First Edn., 1963. (Phillips)
          $135 £90

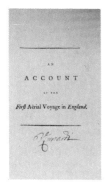

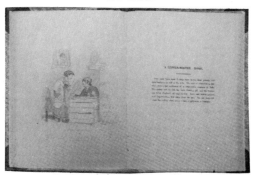

Lunardi (Vincent): An Account of the First Aerial Voyage in England, 2nd Edn., small 4to, 1784. (Phillips) $264 £180

Bridges (R): Sketches Illustrative of the Manners and Costumes of France, Switzerland and Italy, 49 col. plates, 4to, 1821. (Phillips) $447 £300

Philippes (Henry: The Advancement of the Art of Navigation, First Edn., 3 parts in 1 vol., illus. in text, 4to, 1657. (Phillips) $1,764 £1,200

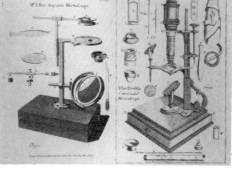

Hooker (Sir W. J.) and Lyons (J. C.): A Century of Orchidaceous Plants, from Lord Derby's library with his bookplate, 100 hand-col. plates, 4to, 1849. (Phillips) $3,129 £2,100

George Adams, Essays On The Microscope, with atlas of plates, First Edition, London 1787, 2 vols., 4to and oblong 4to (the atlas). (Christie's) $1,100 £759

Amis (K.): Lucky Jim, First Edn., 1953, and 19 others. (Phillips) $720 £480

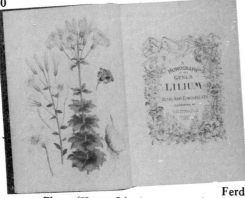

Spark (M.): The Prime of Miss Jean Brodie, First Edn., 1961, and 18 others. (Phillips) $210 £140

Elwes (Henry J.): A monograph of the Genus Lilium, Bookplate of Edmund Waller, 48 hand-col. plates by W. H. Fitch, 1880. (Phillips) $5,960 £4,000

Ferdinand Berthoud, L'Art De Conduire Et De Regler Les Pendules Et Les Montres, First Edition, Paris 1759, 12mo, modern calf. (Christie's) $550 £379

Pistofilo (Bonaventura): Il Torneo, engraved title, 114 (of 117) engraved plates of men in armour on 57 sheets, Bologna, 1627. (Phillips) $852 £580

Gerning (Johann Isaac von): A Picturesque Tour Along The Rhine from Mentz to Cologne, 24 hand-col. plates, folio, London, R. Ackermann, 1820. (Phillips) $1,690 £1,150

Legge (Capt. W. V.): A History of the Birds of Ceylon, 34 hand-col. litho plates, 4to, 1880. (Phillips) $1,564 £1,050

Buckskin gilt binding of Hours of the Virgin (Use of Chartres), printed text and miniatures on vellum, France, 1513. (Phillips)
$10,200 £6,800

Leybourn (William), Cursus Mathematics, Mathematical Sciences In Nine Books, London 1690. (Christie's)
$1,650 £1,138

The Iconography, by Sir Anthony van Dyck, seventeen plates, etchings with engravings, averaging 245 x 158mm. (Christie's) $4,505 £3,024

Fielding (T. H.) and Walton (J.): A Picturesque Tour of the English Lakes, hand-col. vig. title and 48 hand-col. plates, 4to, 1821. (Phillips)
$819 £550

Edwards (Sydenham): The New Flora Britannica, 61 hand-col. plates, 4to, 1812. (Phillips)
$1,564 £1,050

History of The Apple Pie and other stories, 1807-8. (Phillips) $660 £440

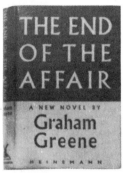

Greene (G.): The End of the Affair, First Edn., 1951. (Phillips) $52 £35

Idee Pittoresche Sopra La Fugga in Egitto di Giesu, Maria & Gioseppe, by Giovanni Domenico Tiepolo, etchings, frontispiece, title and set of 24 plates. (Christie's)
$16,092 £10,800

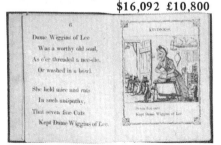

Dame Wiggins of Lee and Her Seven Wonderful Cats, circa 1850. (Phillips) $330 £220

Colden (Cadwallader): The History of the Five Indian Nations of Canada, First Edn., 2 parts in 1 vol., 1747. (Phillips) $470 £320

Binding — Dante Alighieri: La Divini Commedia, some col., green mor. gilt with black overlay abstract design and small gold stars, g.e. by D. Etherington, 4to, Bergamo, 1934. (Phillips) $441 £300

Daniell (W.) and Ayton (R.): A Voyage Round Great Britain, 8 vols. in 4 including 2 vols. of plates, 308 hand-col. aquatints, folio/Abbey 16/, 1814-26. (Phillips) $17,640 £12,000

Golding (W.): Lord of the Flies, First Edn., 1954. (Phillips) $225 £150

One of a pair of Regency bronze and ormolu tazzas, 8in. diam. (Christie's) $2,192 £1,512

A bronze model of a pug dog, signed Tsunemitsu, late Meiji/Taisho period, 13cm. high. (Christie's) $1,235 £864

A bronze bust of an Art Nouveau maiden cast after a model by van der Straeton, circa 1900, 31cm. high. (Christie's) $630 £432

A 16th/17th century Ming gilt lacquered bronze seated figure of Buddha, 11in. high. (Christie's) $609 £420

One of a pair of Regency ormolu urns, 10½in. high. (Christie's) $5,950 £4,104

A 19th century gilt bronze figure of a sporting hound, 'Tom', signed Barye Fils, 8½in. high. (Peter Wilson & Co.) $259 £180

A bronze and silver oviform incense burner and pierced domed cover, 5¼in. high. (Christie's) $3,045 £2,100

A 19th century bronze rounded rectangular koro and pierced domed cover, 96cm. high. (Christie's) $2,779 £1,944

One of a pair of bronze rabbits, signed Tsunemitsu saku, late Meiji/Taisho period, one 19cm. high, the other 21cm. long. (Christie's) $2,007 £1,404

A bronze bowl with swing handle cast after a model by G. Gurschner, signed and stamped with foundry mark K.K.K.F. Wien 1246, circa 1900. 15.5cm. (Christie's) $751 £518

A Japanese bronze figure on stand. (F. H. Fellows & Sons) $2,190 £1,500

A 19th century bronze model of a seated ape, unsigned, 16cm. high. (Christie's) $2,316 £1,620

An Austrian cold painted bronze figure of a bearded Arabian warrior sat on a horse, 9¼in. high. (Reeds Rains) $458 £310

A bronze relief of a negro, mounted on velvet in mahogany frame, 10½ x 10in. (Christie's) $469 £324

A 19th century bronze spelter model of a camel with saddle, 10½in. high. (Christie's) $861 £594

Late 19th century bronze sectional model of an eagle perched on rocks, 63cm. high. (Christie's) $1,003 £702

A bronze and marble tazza cast after a model by G. Gurschner, signed, circa 1915, 17.7cm. high. (Christie's) $939 £648

'Fisherman', a bronze vase cast from a model by J. Ofner, inscribed, 17.9cm. high. (Christie's) $783 £540

A bronze equestrian figure of Wellington modelled by Comte D'Orsay, dated 1848, 16in. high. (Christie's) $1,300 £1,000

An archaic bronze wine beaker, gu, Shang Dynasty, 25.5cm. high. (Christie's) $8,553 £6,480

A bronze figure of a stag, the oval base inscribed P. J. Mene, circa 1843, 8½in. high. (Anderson & Garland) $864 £600

A directoire bronze bust of a man on marble column, 7¼in. high. (Christie's) $783 £540

A pair of early 19th century bronze reliefs of King George III and Queen Caroline, 8½ x 6½in. (Christie's) $939 £648

One of a pair of early 19th century Italian bronze candlesticks in the style of G. B. Piranesi, 15¾in. high. (Christie's) $1,722 £1,188

A bronze relief of a Roman Emperor in gilt composition frame, Italian, 17th century, 7½ x 6in. (Christie's) $1,252 £864

A Regency bronze shell inkstand supported by a dolphin on marble plinth, 5in. high. (Christie's) $2,035 £1,404

A 19th century bronze conservatory fountain, 35in. high x 26in. wide, standing on an oak table. (Reeds Rains) $6,912 £4,800

A 19th century bronze figure of a man rowing a boat, signed Jobbagy and stamped F. Dunn & Co., 25¼in. long. (Dacre, Son & Hartley) $691 £480

A Jaeger bronze figure of a young woman on an oval marble base, inscribed, 13½in. high. (Christie's) $513 £380

A Regency bronze, ormolu and amboyna inkstand attributed to Weeks, 12¼in. wide, 7½in. deep. (Christie's) $4,989 £3,780

A French 19th century classical patinated bronze bust, 25½in. high. (Robt. W. Skinner Inc.) $550 £376

A pair of Regency bronze figures, each with a running figure in classical dress. (Christie's) $707 £540

'Nocturne', a bronze figure of a naked maiden cast after a model by Edward-Louis Collet, 45.7cm. high. (Christie's) $861 £594

A bronze portrait bust of Wellington modelled by H. Weigall, by Elkington Mason & Co., 1853, 16in. high. (Christie's) $416 £320

'Le Forgeron', a gilt bronze and glass lamp, signed Medcat and with foundry plaque, circa 1910, 29.5cm. high. (Christie's) $788 £540

An archaic bronze tripod libation vessel, jue, Western Zhou Dynasty, 18.5cm. high. (Christie's) $2,494 £1,890

A bronze figure of a recumbent tiger, Han Dynasty, 8cm. wide. (Christie's) $997 £756

A large bronze tripod censer, the shoulders applied with two S-shaped handles, with a Daoguang six-character mark, 54cm. wide. (Christie's) $712 £540

A bronze model of a rat, signed Muroe tancho saku, Meiji period, 14cm. long. (Christie's) $557 £410

A late 19th century bronze figure of Ebisu, unsigned but probably by Miyao, on wood stand, 58.5cm. high. (Christie's) $2,300 £1,728

A bronze cigarette box in the form of a girl in Middle Eastern dress, 4in. high. (Capes, Dunn & Co.) $504 £350

A mechanical bronze figure cast after a model by C. Kauba, on a square bronze base, circa 1920, 21cm. high. (Christie's) $1,103 £756

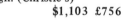

A Nepalese gilt bronze figure of Vajradhara seated in vajrasana on a double lotus base, late 15th/16th century, 20.2cm. high. (Christie's) $1,710 £1,296

A large bronze circular mirror cast with an inscription enclosing three human figures, Han Dynasty, 22.5cm. diam., fitted box. (Christie's) $1,349 £918

A large bronze tripod censer and pierced domed cover, six-character mark, Qing Dynasty, 55cm. high. (Christie's) $427 £324

BRONZE

A bronze dish cast after a model by Gazan Chiparus, circa 1920, 31.5cm. diam. (Christie's) $503 £345

A large bronze model of a hare, signed on the base Hisatoshi, 27cm. long. (Christie's) $2,056 £1,512

A bronze figure of a flamingo, the base signed Rochard, circa 1925, 47.5cm. high. (Christie's) $1,892 £1,296

One of a pair of ormolu wall brackets in the Regence style, circa 1740, possibly English, 9in. wide, 11½in. high. (Christie's) $12,830 £9,720

'Thoughts', a bronze figure cast after a model by M. Giraud Riviere, circa 1930, 17.8cm. high. (Christie's) $709 £486

One of a pair of 19th century bronze baluster vases decorated in iroe hirazogan and takazogan, 30.5cm. high. (Christie's) $2,203 £1,620

A late Ming gilt bronze figure of an Empress, late 16th/17th century, 32cm. high, with wood stand. (Christie's) $997 £756

A bronze model of a seated rabbit, signed Shosai chu, Meiji period, 17.3cm. long. (Christie's) $1,101 £810

An archaic bronze tripod cauldron, ding, with simple loop handles, Shang Dynasty, 23.6cm. high. (Christie's) $7,840 £5,940

BRONZE

A bronze group of a mother and two young toads, 7½in. wide. (Christie's)
$1,015 £700

A bronze figure, modelled as a discus thrower, mounted on a black marble base, 23cm. high. (Lawrence Fine Art) $96 £66

An early 20th century bronze, cast as a reclining female figure, after Aime Jules Dalou, 7in. long. (Lawrence Fine Art)
$944 £638

'Anagke', (Compulsion), a bronze figure cast after a model by Gilbert Bayes, signed and dated 1918, 59cm. high. (Christie's)
$15,660 £10,800

Pair of bronze figures of boy musicians on marble plinths, by Kessler, 9in. high. (Worsfolds)
$259 £180

One of a pair of bronze bottle shaped vases decorated in Nikubori and Takubori, 6in. high. (Christie's)
$275 £190

A large bronze figure of a girl wearing geta, signed Seiya, Meiji period, 78.5cm. high. (Christie's)
$2,162 £1,512

A Restoration bronze and ormolu encrier on scrolled base cast with foliage, 17in. wide. (Christie's)
$3,706 £2,808

Early 19th century bronze figure of Mercury, 14in. high, on ebonised socle. (Reeds Rains)
$13,024 £8,800

A bronze sculpture of Acteon by Emile Henri Laporte, 14in. high. (Worsfolds) $288 £200

One of a pair of Regency bronze and ormolu casso-lettes in the form of anti-que lamps, 8¾in. high. (Christie's)$2,662 £1,836

One of a set of four gilt metal three-light wall lights of Louis XV style with shaped back-plates, 23in. high.(Christie's) $2,423 £1,836

A bronze figure of a young woman, by S. Kinsburger, 25in. high. (Outhwaite & Litherland) $691 £480

Pair of 19th century Japanese bronze vases of onion shape, 27in. high. (Peter Wilson & Co.) $684 £475

A bronze model of a giraffe, 17in. high. (Christie's) $2,662 £1,836

A bronze figure cast after a model by Hugo Lederer, modelled as a naked maiden wearing a turban, signed, circa 1925, 43cm. high. (Christie's) $1,096 £756

An equestrian bronze group of Wellington, signed Boyer a Paris and stamped Regist-ered 9, Nov. 1852, 6in. high. (Christie's) $390 £300

A bronze figure of a harle-quin, cast after a model by St. Marceaux, signed and dated 1879 and with A. Collas foundry mark, 73cm. high. (Christie's) $1,644 £1,134

A 19th century French bronze model of a Shetland pony carrying a dead stag, signed I. Bonheur, 22.5 x 25.5cm. (Christie's) $690 £486

A silvered copper and bronze model of a snipe stepping over rocks, Meiji period, 49cm. long. (Christie's) $1,081 £756

Signed French bronze dog, circa 1875. (British Antique Exporters) $271 £201

A gilt bronze figure of Buddha standing, 13th/14th century, 19.2cm. high. (Christie's) $5,417 £4,104

An early 20th century French bronze statuette of a naked woman, known as 'La Verite Meconnue', after Aime Jules Dalou, 22.5cm. high.(Christie's) $1,456 £1,026

One of a pair of ormolu three-branch candelabra of Louis XVI design, 16½in. high. (Christie's) $3,888 £2,700

A late 19th/early 20th century French bronze group of St. Michael on horseback slaying the dragon, signed E. Fremiet, 58.5cm. high. (Christie's) $2,913 £2,052

A Lorenzl gilt and painted bronze figure of a lady holding the hem of her skirt, on onyx base, 10in. high. (Christie's) $650 £500

French bronze bust, circa 1850. (British Antique Exporters) $198 £147

BRONZE

One of a pair of large 19th century French bronze groups of a setter with a pheasant and a pointer with a hare, signed J. Moigniez, 42cm. high. (Christie's) $10,735 £7,560

One of a pair of 19th century bronze figural lamps, signed L. V. E. Robert, with milk glass shades, 24in. high without fixture. (Robt. W. Skinner Inc.) $1,100 £753

A 19th century French bronze group of a ten point stag brought down by two Scottish hounds, cast from a model by A. L. Barye, 39 x 57cm. (Christie's) $5,827 £4,104

One of a pair of 19th century ormolu and bronze nine-light candelabra on hexagonal boulle plinths, the candelabra 46in. high, the pedestals 57in. high.(Christie's) $16,329 £11,340

A late 19th century English bronze model of a wild cat crouching on a rocky promontory, cast from a model by J. Macallan Swan, 23.5cm. high. (Christie's) $2,453 £1,728

One of a pair of ormolu candlesticks in the style of the Slodtz brothers, 9½in. high. (Christie's) $2,280 £1,728

An early 20th century French bronze statuette of a seated nude drying herself, after Aime Jules Dalou, 34.5cm. high. (Christie's) $11,502 £8,100

An Art Deco bronze figure on a hexagonal base, inscribed Barbara MacDonald, 1936, 27in. high. (Christie's) $1,029 £780

A 19th century French gilt metal model of a seated Chinese fortune teller, 13in. high. (Christie's) $2,488 £1,728

One of a pair of bronze bears, cast three character mark, 6½in long. (Lawrence Fine Art) $1,116 £770

A gold splashed bronze censer of bucket shape with a flared rim, cast character mark of Hsuan-te, 4½in. diam. (Lawrence Fine Art) $733 £506

A bronze group of toads, 3½in. long. (Lawrence Fine Art) $542 £374

One of a pair of bronze vases cast in high relief with dragons among clouds, 14¾in. high. (Lawrence Fine Art) $446 £308

A bronze square mirror, Tang Dynasty, 10.7cm. square, fitted box. (Christie's) $7,144 £4,860

A bronze mounted stoneware vase designed by O. Eckmann, 50.5cm. high. (Christie's) $1,409 £972

Bronze figure of 'The Cossack's Adieu', by Eugene Lancere, 1848-86, 16in. high. (Robt. W. Skinner Inc.) $1,800 £1,313

'Exotic Dancer', a gilt bronze and ivory figure cast and carved from a model by A. Gori, 37.5cm. high. (Christie's) $1,722 £1,188

A miniature Nepalese gilt bronze figure of a Saviouress seated in lalitasana, 1½in. high. (Lawrence Fine Art) $478 £330

Late 19th century Russian bronze of a wolf, signed Lieberich Fabr. C.F. Woerffel, 5.7/8in. high. (Robt. W. Skinner Inc.) $592 £400

A Friedrich Gornik Viennese bronze casket, the handle modelled as Diana the huntress, circa 1925, 31.5 x 18.5cm. (Christie's) $626 £432

A 19th century bronze of a puppy, Japan, signed on base, 5¼in. high. (Robt. W. Skinner Inc.) $740 £500

A Regency bronze and ormolu inkstand modelled as a dolphin, 3½in. wide. (Christie's) $932 £626

A late Ming gilt lacquered bronze figure of Guandi, 16th/early 17th century, 70cm. high. (Christie's) $3,429 £2,376

'Dance of the Harlequinade', a gilt bronze and ivory figure, cast and carved after a model by Th. Ullmann, 30cm. high. (Christie's) $1,566 £1,080

One of a pair of late 19th century bronze incense burners, 14.5/8in. high. (Robt. W. Skinner Inc.) $550 £401

A bronze and champleve enamel duck incense burner, the wings forming the detachable cover, 8in. long. (Lawrence Fine Art) $271 £187

A bronze bell suspended by a dragon loop, ebonised wood frame, 14½in. high. (Lawrence Fine Art) $159 £110

A Godard patinated metal figure, 'Bubble Dance', 35cm. high. (Lawrence Fine Art) $578 £396

A bronze and champleve enamel winged horse incense burner, 12½in. long. (Lawrence Fine Art) $558 £385

A gilt metal figure of a dancing girl, mounted on a cylindrical marble base, 1930's. (Lawrence Fine Art) $146 £100

Late 19th century Japanese bronze vase with elephant head handles, 10½in. high. (Robt. W. Skinner Inc.) $740 £500

An Egyptian bronze cat's head, probably 6th century BC, 1¾in. high.(Lawrence Fine Art) $638 £440

A bronze hu of square baluster section and bracket handles, probably 18th century, 9in. high. (Lawrence Fine Art) $127 £88

'Flower Seller' a gilt bronze and ivory figure cast and carved from a model by A. Gori, 38.5cm. high. (Christie's) $4,071 £2,808

'The Fan Dancer', a bronze and ivory figure by Chiparus, on marble and onyx base, 15in. high. (Christie's) $6,615 £4,500

A bronze and champleve enamel group of an elephant and rider, 18in. high. (Lawrence Fine Art) $638 £440

An 18th century archaistic bronze jue, on three splayed triangular legs, 8in. high. (Lawrence Fine Art) $271 £187

A 19th century bronze Foo dog incense burner, China, 9in. high. (Robt. W. Skinner Inc.) $900 £656

A parcel gilt bronze vase cast after a model by Gustav Gurschner, stamped K.K.K.F. Wien 1411, 23cm. high. (Christie's) $500 £345

One of a pair of 19th century Faux bronze planters with gilt lion's head mask handles, 24in. high. (Christie's) $6,600 £4,583

A pair of 17th century bronze figures of dignitaries, 11in. high. (Lawrence Fine Art) $877 £605

An archaic bronze tripod libation vessel, jue, Western Zhou Dynasty, 20.5cm. high. (Christie's) $3,175 £2,160

'Dancing Girl', a silvered bronze and ivory figure cast from a model by Lorenzl, decorated by Crejo, 22.3cm. high. (Christie's) $939 £648

'Bat Dancer', a bronze and ivory figure cast and carved after a model by F. Preiss, 23.6cm. high. (Christie's) $5,324 £3,672

'Sunshade Girl', a gilt bronze and ivory figure cast and carved from a model by F. Preiss, 20.2cm. high. (Christie's) $2,035 £1,404

BRONZE

A bronze jue with single loop handle headed by an animal mask, 6½in. high. (Lawrence Fine Art) $223 £154

A bronze figure of a naked young lady dancing, by Karl Perl, 24½in. high. (Christie's)$1,584 £1,200

A Chinese bronze and parcel gilt maroon lacquer buddha, 9½in. high. (Lawrence Fine Art) $350 £242

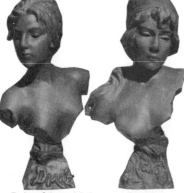

'Priestess', a gilt bronze and ivory figure cast and carved from a model by D. Chiparus, 43cm. high. (Christie's) $4,384 £3,024

Pair of late 19th or early 20th century French bronze busts of Mignon and Diana, signed on the shoulders E. Villanis, 36.5cm. high. (Christie's) $1,533 £1,080

A late 19th/early 20th century French parcel gilt bronze statuette of a seated Arab youth, signed E. Peynot, 67.5cm. high. (Christie's) $12,268 £8,640

A late 19th century French bronze statuette of Diana reclining on a crescent moon, signed Denecheau, revolving on a marble socle, 99cm. high overall. (Christie's) $18,403 £12,960

A 19th century French bronze statuette of a Turkish warrior, on a naturalistic base, 63cm. high. (Christie's) $9,201 £6,480

An early 20th century English bronze group of Salome and Herodias, cast from a model by Charles de Sousy Ricketts, 45cm. high. (Christie's) $9,968 £7,020

A George III mahogany peat bucket of cylindrical tapering form with two brass bands and handle, 15in. diam. (British Antique Exporters)$750 £500

Victorian leather bucket, circa 1860. (British Antique Exporters) $81 £60

A late 18th century brass bound mahogany plate bucket with brass swing handle, 17in. high. (Dacre, Son & Hartley) $979 £680

A George III brass bound mahogany plate bucket with copper liner, 11½in. diam. (Christie's) $1,496 £972

A George III brass bound mahogany plate bucket with later brass liner, 14½in. diam. (Christie's) $3,810 £2,592

A George III brass bound mahogany plate bucket with later circular liner, 11¼in. diam. (Christie's) $2,661 £1,728

Early 19th century Dutch brass bound fruitwood and ebonised bucket with carrying handle, 13in. high. (Christie's) $885 £594

A Victorian wooden fire bucket, 1860. (British Antique Exporters) $79 £59

An Irish mid Georgian brass bound mahogany peat bucket with carrying handle, 15in. diam. (Christie's) $3,132 £2,160

CADDIES & BOXES

Mahogany tea caddy with ivory key escutcheon, 1850. (British Antique Exporters) $87 £65

Early 19th century Palais Royale casket on four lion's paw feet with serpent handle to the hinged cover, 5in. long. (Christie's) $510 £345

Late 17th/early 18th century Continental tortoiseshell and mother-of-pearl mounted box, 18¼in. wide. (Lawrence Fine Art) $4,395 £2,970

Early 19th century carved pine watch hutch, 17in. high, 8½in. wide. (Robt. W. Skinner Inc.) $950 £659

A George III satinwood, rosewood and fruitwood tea caddy, the crossbanded lid with a silver plaque with initials J.E.R., 12¾in. wide. (Christie's) $1,676 £1,242

One of a pair of Regency mahogany knife boxes with turned finials and fitted interiors. (Christie's) $3,680 £2,592

Early 19th century rectangular document box, bunko, 43.1 x 33.9cm. (Christie's) $3,672 £2,700

A Victorian walnut brass bound letter box, 1850. (British Antique Exporters) $156 £116

Late 18th century Anglo-Indian ivory workbox with fitted interior, one drawer and a writing slide, 19in. wide. (Christie's) $1,367 £918

Northern Woodlands birch-bark container, Tetes-de-Boule, in the form of a trunk, 10¼in. wide. (Robt. W. Skinner Inc.) $300 £208

An 18th century Anglo-Indian vizagapatam casket with hinged lid and a drawer, 17in. wide. (Christie's) $2,662 £1,836

Victorian leather box, circa 1880. (British Antique Exporters) $41 £31

Victorian metal bound oak humidor. (British Antique Exporters) $133 £99

A rosewood fitted toilet case with eight glass bottles and boxes, five with Sheffield plated lids, 12½in. wide. (Capes, Dunn & Co.) $79 £55

Late 16th century Momoyama period Christian host box or pyx (seiheibako), 9.1cm. high. (Christie's) $27,993 £19,440

Victorian mahogany coal box, 1860. (British Antique Exporters) $67 £50

An early 19th century Anglo-Indian vizagapatam ivory and ebony games box, 18in. wide. (Christie's) $1,710 £1,296

Early 19th century Palais Royale rectangular jewel casket formed as a minia-ture dressing table, 5½in. long. (Christie's) $766 £518

Late 17th/early 18th century Indo-Portuguese tortoiseshell and mother-of-pearl portable box, 15¾in. wide. (Lawrence Fine Art) $2,035 £1,375

Victorian rosewood and maple lap desk, 1860. (British Antique Exporters) $251 £186

A Charles X cut steel mounted and maple casket of sarcophagus shape with carrying handles, 19½in. wide. (Christie's) $2,237 £1,512

One of a pair of George III mahogany cutlery boxes with silver key plates, 8¾in. wide. (Christie's) $1,065 £756

An early 19th century French Palais Royale musical jewel casket in the form of a miniature piano, 8¾in. long. (Christie's) $3,888 £2,700

A Regency parcel gilt and scarlet lacquer tea cannister, 17½in. high. (Christie's) $1,218 £864

A George III treen pear tea caddy, the lid with a stalk and enclosing a plain interior. (Christie's) $1,522 £1,080

A George IV rosewood and satinwood writing box, 15½in. wide. (Christie's) $349 £259

One of a pair of William IV black japanned coal boxes with domed oval lids, 20in. wide. (Christie's) $1,508 £1,026

A wood and lacquer box, the cover inset with a Komai panel decorated in Iroe Hira-zogan, 7¼in. wide. (Christie's) $246 £170

Victorian carved box with fitted interior, 1850. (British Antique Exporters) $164 £122

A black and gold lacquer two handled workbox opening to reveal a fitted interior with ivory accessories, 15½in. wide. (Christie's) $290 £200

A Victorian 12in. rectangular coromandel wood and brass bound vanity case, maker's mark J.V. (Parsons Welch & Cowell) $444 £300

A Regency brass inlaid mahogany writing box with leather lined sloping writing surface, and fitted with a Bramah lock, 20in. wide. (Christie's) $622 £475

One of a pair of George III mahogany cutlery boxes with boxwood stringing, 8¾in. wide. (Christie's) $1,065 £756

A rosewood and Tunbridge-ware tea caddy of waisted form, the domed top depicting Battle Abbey, 9in. wide. (Parsons, Welch & Cowell) $490 £350

A Sheraton period cross-banded tea caddy, having two division interior with Bristol blue glass blending bowl, 10¾in. wide. (Geering & Colyer) $431 £280

A Regency black and gilt japanned coal box with rounded rectangular domed lid, and another, 19in. wide. (Christie's) $6,350 £4,320

A mid 18th century painted pine trinket box, 7½in. wide. (Robt. W. Skinner Inc.) $1,900 £1,319

A George III mahogany decanter box, the divided interior with six bottles, an oval salver and two glasses, 10½in. wide. (Christie's) $843 £594

Early 19th century Palais Royale musical necessaire formed as a piano, 7½in. long. (Christie's) $2,877 £1,944

A George III mahogany cutlery box, the shaped top inlaid with the Prince of Wales's feathers, 9in. wide. with another, 9¾in. wide. (Christie's) $1,722 £1,188

An Anglo-Indian Regency calamander-wood box enclosing a fitted interior, 15½in. wide. (Christie's) $947 £702

One of a pair of Sheraton period knife boxes in inlaid mahogany, original interiors, 13in. high. (Hobbs & Chambers) $1,460 £1,000

Early 19th century suzuribako decorated in gold, silver and red hiramakie, takamakie, hirame and heidatsu on a nashiji ground, 22.2 x 20.2cm. (Christie's) $2,350 £1,728

One of a pair of George III mahogany vase-shaped cutlery boxes, 26in. high. (Christie's) $3,888 £2,700

A 19th century circular kogo decorated in gold hiramakie on a red ground, 7.9cm. diam. (Christie's) $1,101 £810

A Momoyama period rectangular black lacquered wood casket with hinged domed cover decorated in gold lacquer and shell inlay, circa 1600. (Christie's)
$2,488 £1,728

Antique cased set of three scent bottles with ormolu mounts and painted porcelain stoppers. (Worsfolds)
$230 £160

A brown and gold lacquer box with rounded corners on four winged dragon feet, 8½in. wide. (Christie's)
$493 £340

One of a pair of George III mahogany cutlery boxes with fitted interiors and silver key plates, 9in. wide. (Christie's) $3,067 £2,160

A William and Mary walnut table bureau, the leather-lined fall-flap enclosing a fitted interior, 22¼in. wide. (Christie's) $1,530 £1,134

A George III shagreen necessaire of shaped upright form, circa 1760, 2¾in. high. (Christie's) $1,555 £1,080

Late 19th century roironuri two-tiered covered box, unsigned, School of Zeshin, 24.2 x 19.7 x 19.2cm. (Christie's) $2,162 £1,512

A 17th century Flemish ebony and ivory table cabinet, on later bun feet, 21in. wide. (Christie's) $1,995 £1,512

A late 19th century rectangular tabako-bon decorated in gold and silver hiramakie, hirame and heidatsu on a yasuriko ground, 20.5cm. wide. (Christie's)$954 £702

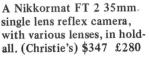

A Nikkormat FT 2 35mm. single lens reflex camera, with various lenses, in hold-all. (Christie's) $347 £280

A 45 x 107mm. Ernemann Reflex stereoscopic camera of Jumelle-form with Erne-mann Doppel Anastigmat 75mm. f 4.5 lenses, in leather case. (Christie's) $256 £190

A 6 x 9cm. Ontoflex twin-lens reflex camera, No. 8746, with a Tessar lens. (Christie's) $186 £150

A 9 x 12cm. Tropical Goerz Tenax folding plate camera with Xenar lens, in leather case. (Christie's)$270 £200

A 4.5 x 6cm. Ernemann Miniature-Ernoflex folding reflex camera with Ernon 7.5cm. f 3.5 lens in helical mount, in leather case. (Christie's) $675 £500

A quarter-plate Tropical Model Improved Artist Re-flex camera manufactured by The London Stereoscopic Co., with Tessar lens. (Christie's) $248 £200

A quarter-plate Gandolfi hand-and-stand camera in mahogany casing, with Aldis Anastigmat lens. (Christie's) $405 £300

A 6 x 9cm. Mentor folding reflex camera with Tessar lens. (Christie's) $198 £160

A 15 x 10cm. Ica Tropical folding plate camera in metal teak casing with Tessar lens in dial-set Compur shutter. (Christie's) $135 £100

An early brass mounted 35mm. hand-cranked cinematograph projector with R.R. lens, 15in. high. (Christie's)
$1,755 £1,300

An Alpa Reflex 35mm. s.l.r. camera, Mod. 6, No. 38996, with Kern Switar, Schneider and Alpa lenses. (Christie's)
$337 £250

A wide-angle Rolleiflex twin-lens Reflex camera, No. W 2490454 with Distagon lens, in carrying case. (Christie's)
$1,350 £1,000

A prototype V.P. mono-rail camera in aluminium casing, with Tessar lens. (Christie's)
$372 £300

A Stirn's Waistcoat detective camera, No. 5065, in nickel-plated brass casing, taking six circular exposures on circular plate. (Christie's) $696 £480

A four-lens multiple-exposure camera, probably by J. Lancaster & Sons, taking four 2 x 1½in. exposures on one quarter plate, in mahogany casing. (Christie's)
$1,740 £1,200

A Zeiss Contaflex 35mm. twin-lens reflex camera, No. Z 42268 with a Sonnar tak-ing lens and a Sucher-Objectiv lens, and an exposure meter. (Christie's) $558 £450

A 2¼ x 2¼ Redding's Luzo roll-film camera in brass re-inforced mahogany cas-ing, Patent No. 17328. (Christie's) $652 £450

A quarter-plate box-form mahogany survey camera by by J. H. Dallmeyer, London, in mahogany casing with lens, on brass tripod mount. (Christie's) $580 £400

A Leica M2 camera No. 938-006, with 3.5 Elmar 50mm. lens and Leica meter, in leather case. (Onslow's) $372 £250

A Houghton's 45 x 170mm. Royal Mail Stereolette camera in mahogany casing with box-comb joints. (Christie's) $742 £550

A London Stereoscopic Co.'s Stereoscopic changing box camera in mahogany casing, taking paired exposures on 6 x 5.5cm. plates. (Christie's) $551 £380

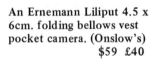

A tail board folding field camera by Stanley, with Ross 8¾in. wide angle Xpres f4 lens. (Onslow's) $119 £80

A Thornton-Pickard quarter-plate triple extension field camera. (Onslow's) $253 £170

An Ernemann Liliput 4.5 x 6cm. folding bellows vest pocket camera. (Onslow's) $59 £40

A quarter-plate Redding's Luzo box-form roll-film camera in ever-ready case. (Christie's) $797 £550

A Lancaster International field camera, with Busch Rapid Aplanat No. 3 10in. lens, in canvas carrying case. (Onslow's) $149 £100

A Kodak No. 1 Panoram camera Model A. (Onslow's) $111 £75

An ormolu and cut glass six-light chandelier, the boss hung with a profusion of pendant drops, 36in. high. (Christie's) $2,138 £1,620

A neo-classical giltwood eight-branch chandelier with foliate corona, 28in. high. (Christie's) $2,708 £2,052

A Regency cut glass and ormolu chandelier with spreading waterfall drops, 38in. high. (Christie's) $6,901 £4,860

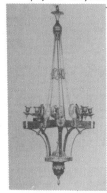

Venetian cut glass triple chandelier hung with cut glass drops, 31in. high. (Worsfolds) $770 £550

Victorian brass three-light chandelier, 1880. (British Antique Exporters) $139 £103

A Charles X ormolu and bronze chandelier, fitted for electricity, 45in. high. (Christie's) $1,140 £864

An Empire ormolu cut glass twelve-light chandelier, the nozzles fitted for electricity, 36in. high. (Christie's) $4,665 £3,240

A 19th century brass three-tiered chandelier, 47in. diam. (Christie's) $5,500 £3,819

An Empire ormolu and bronze ten-light lamp, 39in. high. (Christie's) $4,847 £3,672

AMERICAN

Late 19th century Dedham crackleware vase, incised CPUS, 7in. high. (Robt. W. Skinner Inc.) $1,600 £1,111

A Walrath pottery pitcher and five mugs, circa 1910, pitcher 6½in. high. (Robt. W. Skinner Inc.)
$1,300 £902

A Chelsea Keramic Art pottery vase with blue-green glossy glaze, circa 1885, 11¼in. high. (Robt. W. Skinner Inc.) $550 £387

A 19th century Santa Ana polychrome jar, 12in. diam. (Robt. W. Skinner Inc.) $2,800 £1,944

An early 20th century Walley Art pottery moulded vase, 6¾in. high. (Robt. W. Skinner Inc.) $625 £434

A Santa Clara blackware storage jar, 20½in. high. (Robt. W. Skinner Inc.)
$3,000 £2,083

A Marblehead vase decorated with blue floral trees on slate blue ground, circa 1915, 5¼in. high, 3¼in. diam. (Robt. W. Skinner Inc.) $700 £486

Saturday Evening Girls pottery motto plate, Mass., circa 1914, signed S.G. for Sara Galner, 7½in. diam. (Robt. W. Skinner Inc.)
$3,700 £2,569

A Walrath floral decorated vase, circa 1910, 7in. high. (Robt. W. Skinner Inc.)
$1,500 £1,041

AMERICAN

A majolica handled serving dish, by Griffen, Smith & Hill, Penn., 12.1/8in. long, 1876-90. (Robt. W. Skinner Inc.) $100 £72

A Dedham pottery crackle-ware vase, 8in. high, circa 1900. (Robt. W. Skinner Inc.) $2,100 £1,458

A majolica serving dish, by Griffen, Smith & Hill, Penn., 1876-90, 12¼in. long. (Robt. W. Skinner Inc.) $175 £127

A decorated Marblehead vase of squat bulbous form with incised leaves and berries, circa 1919, 3½in. high. (Robt. W. Skinner Inc.) $475 £329

A G. E. Ohr pottery vase, the concave-shaped mouth with elongated folded handles, circa 1900, 10in. high. (Robt. W. Skinner Inc.) $3,400 £2,361

A Marblehead pottery four-colour vase, signed H.T. for Hannah Tutt, circa 1915, 4½in. high, 4.1/8in. diam. (Robt. W. Skinner Inc.) $900 £625

A Weller Dickensware vase, circa 1900, 16in. high. (Robt. W. Skinner Inc.) $325 £225

A finely decorated Hopi Placca pottery bowl. (Robt. W. Skinner Inc.) $504 £350

A Losanti porcelain relief decorated vase by L. McLaughlin, circa 1901-04, 7½in. high. (Robt. W. Skinner Inc.) $10,500 £7,291

ARITA

Late 17th century Arita blue and white octagonal baluster jar with wood cover, 53cm. high. (Christie's)
$4,700 £3,456

An 18th century Arita blue and white deep bowl decorated with lobed panels, 17.5cm. diam. (Christie's)
$1,166 £810

An Arita blue and white broad oviform ewer with loop handle, circa 1670, .24cm. high. (Christie's)
$514 £378

Late 17th century Arita blue and white oviform vase, fitted with a silver cover and thumbpiece, probably 18th century, inset with a German thaler of 1660, 19.7cm. high. (Christie's) $699 £486

Late 17th century Arita oviform vase decorated in underglaze blue, 26cm. high. (Christie's) $926 £648

Late 17th century Arita blue and white baluster tankard with loop handle, 19.5cm. high. (Christie's)
$1,166 £810

Late 17th century Arita globular apothecary bottle decorated in underglaze blue, 20cm. high. (Christie's)
$1,010 £702

Late 19th century Arita model of a seated tiger decorated in iron-red and black enamels and gilt, signed, 15.5cm. high. (Christie's)
$926 £648

An Arita apothecary bottle painted in underglaze blue, circa 1665/80, 15½in. high. (Christie's) $6,960 £4,800

BELLEEK

A Belleek 'dolphin' candlestick, modelled as a putto seated on a dolphin, 19.5cm. high, no. D343. (Phillips) $1,078 £700

A pair of Belleek candlestick figures of a boy and girl basket bearer, 22cm. high. (Phillips) $5,328 £3,600

A Belleek figure of a cooper standing before two barrels forming vases, 21cm. high. (Christie's) $3,080 £2,000

A Belleek model of a lighthouse, impressed Belleek and black printed marks, registration mark for 1873, 23cm. high. (Christie's) $1,078 £700

A Belleek rectangular plaque painted by Horatio H. Calder, black printed Belleek mark, First Period, 17 x 11.3cm. (Christie's) $3,850 £2,500

A Belleek First Period figure of 'The Crouching Venus', 18¼in. high. (Christie's) $1,160 £800

A Belleek 'tulip' vase, standing in a circular basket base encrusted with leaves, 31cm. high, no. D93. (Phillips) $3,388 £2,200

A pair of Belleek figures of 'Meditation' and 'Affection', 35cm. high, nos. D1134 and D20. (Phillips) $2,772 £1,800

One of a pair of Belleek nautilus vases, naturally modelled and heightened in pink, 21cm. high. (Christie's) $1,540 £1,000

BERLIN

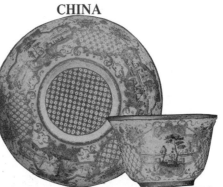

A Berlin two-handled oval ornithological soup tureen and domed cover, blue sceptre marks and Pressnummer 35, circa 1760-70, 36cm. wide. (Christie's) $2,478 £1,836

A Berlin enamel teabowl and matching saucer, workshop of Pierre Fromery, circa 1730, teabowl 2¾in. diam., saucer 4½in. diam. (Christie's) $6,713 £4,536

An 18th century Berlin faience red lacquered baluster vase and domed cover, mock Chinese seal mark, Funcke's factory, 71cm. high. (Christie's) $2,147 £1,512

Early 20th century KPM porcelain plaque, 'La Belle Chocolatiere', used as the trade mark for Baker's Cocoa and stamped Dresden, 8¾ x 6in. (Robt. W. Skinner Inc.) $1,400 £958

A Berlin plaque, The Madonna and Child, signed Wagner, 24 x 16cm., impressed sceptre and KPM. (Lawrence Fine Art) $638 £440

A 19th century Berlin porcelain KPM plaque, decorated at the Gebruder-Heubach factory, 10 x 7in. (Robt. W. Skinner Inc.) $1,800 £1,232

A Berlin white three-light candelabrum, blue clove mark and various incised and impressed marks, circa 1770, 28cm. high. (Christie's) $648 £432

A Berlin rectangular plaque painted after F. Sturm, impressed sceptre and KPM marks, circa 1880, 31.5 x 25.5cm. (Christie's) $933 £648

A Berlin white group emblematic of medicine from a set of the Sciences modelled by F. E. Meyer, late 18th century, 29cm. high. (Christie's) $729 £486

BOW

A Bow square dish painted in a pale Kakiemon palette with the Flaming Tortoise Pattern, circa 1754, about 18.5cm. square. (Christie's) $582 £410

A Bow white figure of an owl with moulded overlapping plumage, circa 1758, 19cm. high. (Christie's) $1,840 £1,296

A pair of Bow figures of a cock and hen, both on scroll moulded pad bases, circa 1758, 10cm. high. (Christie's) $5,214 £3,672

BRISTOL

A Bristol delft bowl, the interior painted in iron-red and the exterior in blue, circa 1740, 22.5cm. diam. (Christie's) $3,680 £2,592

Mid 18th century Bristol delft plate decorated in iron-red, blue and green, 13½in. diam. (Woolley & Wallis) $580 £400

A Bristol two-handled cup and trembleuse saucer of ogee outline, marked B6 in blue enamel. (Lawrence Fine Art) $957 £660

A Bristol delft blue-dash Adam and Eve charger, circa 1720, 34cm. diam. (Christie's) $1,005 £756

A Bristol globular teapot and cover with ear-shaped handle, Richard Champion's Factory, circa 1775, 16cm. high. (Christie's) $1,993 £1,404

A Bristol delft blue-dash tulip charger, the reverse with a tin glaze, circa 1720, 34.5cm. diam. (Christie's) $920 £648

Victorian white china foot bath, circa 1880. (British Antique Exporters) $87 £65

A signed Victorian pottery jardiniere, 1875. (British Antique Exporters) $43 £32

Victorian majolica serving plate, 1860. (British Antique Exporters) $21 £16

Victorian blue and white monogrammed slop pail, 1860. (British Antique Exporters) $75 £56

A finely decorated floral bowl and pitcher, circa 1860. (British Antique Exporters) $43 £32

An earthenware handbuilt coiled amphora vase with two loop handles, by Fiona Salazar, circa 1984, 28cm. high. (Christie's) $288 £200

A late 17th century Westerwald blue and grey baluster stoneware jug, the neck and foot within silver mounts, London, probably 1851, 20.5cm. high. (Christie's) $367 £259

Part of a Foley Art china coffee set designed by G. Logan, with printed stylised rose motif and a diamond-shape pattern. (Christie's) $551 £378

Saltglaze water jar, circa 1880. (British Antique Exporters) $74 £55

Victorian floral jug and basin, 1860. (British Antique Exporters) $68 £51

Victorian floral china salad bowl, 1880. (British Antique Exporters) $41 £31

Mid 19th century soup tureen and stand, 'Italian Scenery', by J. Meir & Son, 23in. diam. (Capes, Dunn & Co.) $72 £50

Victorian floral pitcher, circa 1860. (British Antique Exporters) $24 £18

A large Foley Intarsio circular pottery plate painted with sunflowers, 12½in. diam. (Christie's) $224 £170

Early 20th century jug and basin set, 1910. (British Antique Exporters) $29 £22

Victorian biscuit barrel with plated top. (British Antique Exporters) $51 £38

Four historical blue pieces, England, early 19th century, pitcher 6½in. high. (Robt. W. Skinner Inc.)$900 £625

A Yorkshire pearlware portrait bust of an officer, circa 1800, 30cm. high. (Christie's) $1,380 £972

BRITISH

CHINA

An H. & R. Daniel green ground crested dish from the Shrewsbury Service, circa 1827, 48cm. wide. (Christie's) $920 £648

A Parian bust of Wellington wearing military uniform, 14in. high. (Christie's) $234 £180

One of a pair of Caughley quatrefoil sauce tureens and covers, 14.5cm. wide. (Christie's)$1,723 £1,296

A Brownfield jug modelled as a goose, the handle modelled as a standing monkey pushing open its beak, circa 1860, 35.5cm. high. (Christie's) $393 £291

Ashworths ironstone part dessert service with picture panels in the Chinese taste, impressed and transfer marks to base. (Peter Wilson & Co.) $302 £210

A Burmantofts jardiniere and stand, 31in. overall, stamped marks. (Christie's) $390 £300

An English porcelain oviform jug with angular loop handle, circa 1821, 21.5cm. high. (Christie's) $460 £324

One of a pair of baskets and stands, the baskets with pierced trellis sides and the stands with pierced borders, 8¼in. diam. (Christie's) $1,160 £800

A 14th century English globular jug with grooved strap handle, covered in a greenish ochre iridescent glaze, 28.5cm. high. (Christie's) $613 £432

BRITISH

A Brownfield jug modelled as a cockatoo, standing on logs, his crest forming the spout, 24.6cm. high. (Christie's) $523 £388

A globular green glazed bowl designed by Dr. C. Dresser, 14.5cm. high. (Christie's) $819 £561

A Parian bust of Wellington wearing classical dress, after E. W. Wyon impressed mark, 16in. high. (Christie's) $130 £100

A Morrisware pear-shaped vase painted with mauve flowerheads and green foliage on a blue ground, 11in. high. (Christie's) $290 £220

Part of a set of twenty-five late 18th century English tinglaze tiles. (Woolley & Wallis) $493 £340

An H. J. Wood Bursley Ware vase, slip-trailed and coloured 'Seed-Poppy' design, circa 1930-5, 12in. high. (Capes, Dunn & Co.) $100 £70

A Linthorpe teapot, the design attributed to Dr. C. Dresser, 21.3cm. high. (Christie's) $172 £118

A porcelain thrown and laminated triangular spiral vase modelled in pale blue, by D. Feibleman, 14.4cm. high, 1983. (Christie's) $936 £650

A large Louis Wain pottery vase, modelled as a seated cat, 25.4cm. high. (Christie's) $1,734 £1,188

BRITISH

A porcelain wide bowl, by Mary Rich, painted in gold lustre, 1985, 24.3cm. diam. (Christie's) $281 £194

Floral china chamber pot, 1850. (British Antique Exporters) $43 £32

Victorian blue and white tureen by Norman, 1880. (British Antique Exporters) $64 £48

A Foley Intarsio tapering cylindrical vase with bulbous rim, 8½in. high. (Christie's) $294 £200

A Davenport part dinner service, decorated with Oriental flowers in Imari colours, pattern no. 51, circa 1850-70. (Woolley & Wallis) $1,238 £860

An R. Philippe white glazed pottery group, modelled as a naked lady holding a child, 15¼in. high. (Christie's) $64 £45

A Lowestoft square inkwell, the base inscribed in black, 'Eliz,th. Buckle 1775', 5cm. high. (Lawrence Fine Art) $4,306 £2,970

A Linthorpe flaring organic form bowl designed by Dr. C. Dresser, 4in. high. (Christie's) $617 £420

A majolica tazza, England, with Art Nouveau polychrome iris decoration, circa 1900, 9¼in. diam. (Robt. W. Skinner Inc.) $125 £91

CHINA

CAIGER-SMITH

A large tin glazed earthenware lustre bowl by A. Caiger-Smith, date cypher for 1985, 48.5cm. diam. (Christie's) $548 £378

A tin glazed earthenware ewer and two of eight goblets, by A. Caiger-Smith, date cypher for 1983, ewer 28.1cm. high. (Christie's) $218 £151

A tin glazed earthenware albarello by A. Caiger-Smith, date cypher for 1985, 27.3cm. high. (Christie's) $140 £97

CANTON

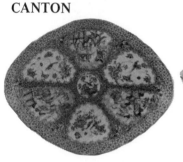

Late 19th century Oriental footed porcelain fruit bowl, China, 15in. long, 3½in. high. (Robt. W. Skinner Inc.) $850 £590

A 19th century Canton famille rose bowl, painted with birds and butterflies amongst fruit and flower sprays, 37cm. diam. (Christie's) $945 £626

A Canton enamel circular box and cover, painted Qianlong six character mark, 3in. diam. (Christie's) $261 £180

A Canton enamel saucer dish painted with figures standing by a pond, 6¼in. diam. (Christie's) $232 £160

A large Cantonese bowl, 22in. diam. (Edgar Horn) $6,935 £4,750

A 19th century Canton hexagonal garden seat of barrel shape, decorated in famille rose enamels, 47cm. high. (Lawrence Fine Art) $1,595 £1,100

MICHAEL CARDEW

A stoneware casserole and cover with strap handle, by Michael Cardew, impressed MC and Wenford Bridge seals, circa 1970, 29cm. diam. (Christie's)
$374 £260

An earthenware footed bowl by Michael Cardew, impressed MC and Winchcombe Pottery seals, circa 1935, 26cm. diam. (Christie's) $1,440 £1,000

A large stoneware wide bowl by Michael Cardew, covered in a khaki glaze over white slip, circa 1978, 38cm. diam. (Christie's) $500 £345

An earthenware oviform jug by Michael Cardew, impressed MC and Winchcombe Pottery seal, circa 1930, 22.6cm. high. (Christie's) $359 £248

An earthenware slip-decorated rhyme tankard by Michael Cardew, circa 1926, 13.7cm. high. (Christie's) $489 £340

A stoneware coffee pot and cover by Michael Cardew, impressed MC and Wenford Bridge seals, 25.3cm. high. (Christie's) $288 £200

A stoneware large bowl on shallow foot, attributed to Michael Cardew, Abuja seals obscured by glaze, 27cm. diam. (Christie's)$432 £300

An earthenware tankard, by Michael Cardew, covered in a pale yellow slip with brown base border, circa 1925; 12.8cm. high. (Christie's) $92 £64

An earthenware oval baking dish, decorated by Michael Cardew and moulded by E. Comfort, circa 1932, 31.9cm. wide. (Christie's)
$939 £648

MICHAEL CARDEW

CHINA

A large earthenware bowl on shallow foot by Michael Cardew, dated 1969, 35.4cm. diam. (Christie's) $375 £259

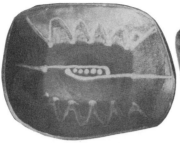

A stoneware dish with flared sides, attributed to Michael Cardew, impressed Wenford Bridge seal, 44cm. wide. (Christie's) $156 £108

A stoneware deep bowl, by Michael Cardew, impressed MC and Wenford Bridge seals, circa 1975, 30.5cm. diam. (Christie's)
$548 £378

CARLTONWARE

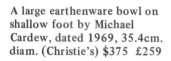

A Carltonware vase with polychrome decoration on a mottled purple and white ground, circa 1930, 26.7cm. high. (Christie's)$315 £216

A Carltonware service decorated in polychrome enamels, coffee pot 20.4cm. high. (Christie's) $1,174 £810

One of a pair of Carltonware vases, 21cm. high, and a tray, 25cm. wide. (Christie's)
$783 £540

A Carltonware rouge royale diamond-shaped dish with two 'fin' handles, 12in. wide. (Capes, Dunn & Co.) $21 £15

A Carltonware oviform ginger jar and cover, painted with clusters of stylised flowerheads and bold geometric bands, 31cm. high. (Christie's) $1,566 £1,080

A Carltonware plaque painted in gilt, orange, blue, green and white with wisteria and exotic plants, 15½in. diam. (Christie's)
$308 £200

One of a pair of Chelsea leaf dishes, moulded as cabbage leaves, red anchor marks, circa 1756, 29cm. and 29.5cm. wide. (Christie's) $2,298 £1,728

A Chelsea 'Hans Sloane' botanical plate, red anchor and 43 mark, circa 1755, 23.5cm. diam. (Christie's) $6,463 £4,860

A Chelsea fluted oviform teapot and cover painted in the Kakiemon palette, circa 1752, 12.6cm. high. (Christie's) $5,214 £3,672

A pair of Chelsea Derby figures of a youth and girl standing before a bocage supporting candle sconces, 29cm. high. (Lawrence Fine Art) $983 £660

A Chelsea lobed teaplant beaker painted in a vivid famille rose palette beneath a chocolate line rim. 1745-49, 7.5cm. high. (Christie's) $7,182 £5,400

A pair of Chelsea Derby figures, Neptune and Venus and Cupid, on high rocky bases, 24cm. and 25cm. high. (Lawrence Fine Art) $819 £550

A Chelsea silver shaped plate finely painted, circa 1752, 22.5cm. diam. (Christie's) $5,520 £3,888

A Chelsea apple tureen and cover naturally modelled and coloured in green and russet, the base with red 3 mark, circa 1755, 10.5cm. high. (Christie's) $6,134 £4,320

A Chelsea botanical plate, red anchor mark, circa 1756, 21.5cm. diam. (Christie's) $2,453 £1,728

CHINESE

One of a pair of biscuit figures of dogs of Fo, K'ang Hsi, 44cm. high. (Lawrence Fine Art)
$9,251 £6,380

A Cizhou brown-glazed oviform jar, Jin/Yuan Dynasty, 32.5cm. diam. (Christie's)
$1,140 £864

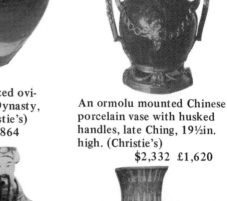

An ormolu mounted Chinese porcelain vase with husked handles, late Ching, 19½in. high. (Christie's)
$2,332 £1,620

A Cizhou oviform vase with four looped strap handles, Yuan Dynasty, 28cm. high. (Christie's) $784 £594

A pair of Chinese porcelain figures of Immortals, F'u Hsing and possibly Wen Chang, 18¼in. high. (Geering & Colyer)
$388 £270

A Yangshao Culture, 3rd/2nd Millennium B.C. Gansu neolithic pottery jar, 30.5cm. high. (Christie's)
$2,698 £1,836

A 1st Millennium B.C. tall red pottery jar, 31.5cm. high. (Christie's)
$1,031 £702

One of a pair of green dragon jars and covers, Qianlong six-character seal marks and of the period, 20cm. high. (Christie's) $11,113 £7,560

Late 18th century pair of Export porcelain covered urns, China, 17½in. high. (Robt. W. Skinner Inc.)
$6,250 £4,340

An 18th century large metallic brown-glazed bottle vase, 58cm. high. (Christie's)
$7,128 £5,400

A Longquan celadon broad globular jarlet under an even greyish green glossy glaze, 13th/14th century, 8cm. diam. (Christie's)
$784 £594

A Dehua blanc-de-chine figure of Guanyin seated on rockwork, 17th/18th century, 24cm. high, with fitted box. (Christie's)
$2,423 £1,836

A late 19th century Oriental Export porcelain garden seat, China, 19in. high. (Robt. W. Skinner Inc.) $1,700 £1,164

A Nankin blue and white porcelain stick stand, painted with prunus blossom, 1ft.11in. high. (Capes, Dunn & Co.) $100 £70

A neolithic pottery two-handled oviform jar, Gansu, Yangshao Culture, 3rd/2nd Millennium B.C., 31.5cm. high. (Christie's)
$7,413 £5,616

A He Chaozong Dehua blanc-de-chine figure of Wen Chang, late 18th/early 19th century, 30.2cm. high. (Christie's)
$2,851 £2,160

A Jun Yao two-handled globular jar with short cylindrical neck, Yuan Dynasty, 20.5cm. diam. (Christie's)
$2,708 £2,052

One of a pair of early 19th century Chinese vases with semi-domed covers, 14¼in. high. (Anderson & Garland)
$849 £590

CHINESE

A neolithic pottery horizontal oil bottle painted in black on a red ground, Gansu, Yangshao Culture, 3rd/2nd Millennium B.C., 12.5cm. long. (Christie's) $712 £540

An 18th century Chinese Export porcelain teapot with silver spout, Chien Lung, circa 1770. (Capes, Dunn & Co.) $54 £38

One of a pair of green and yellow dragon bowls, encircled Yongzheng six-character marks and of the period, 14cm. diam. (Christie's) $9,836 £7,452

A Transitional Wucai slender pear-shaped vase, circa 1660, 41cm. high. (Christie's) $2,566 £1,944

A pair of 18th century Chinese porcelain cockerels, 10½in. high. (Dacre, Son & Hartley) $1,440 £1,000

A green and yellow-glazed buff pottery pear-shaped bottle vase, Liao Dynasty, 23.5cm. high. (Christie's) $5,417 £4,104

Late 18th century Chinese Export porcelain cider jug with interwoven strap handle, 11½in. high. (Robt. W. Skinner Inc.) $425 £291

A Jizhou bowl decorated in deep chocolate-brown with three quatrefoil motifs on a russet ground, Southern Song Dynasty, 10.8cm. diam. (Christie's) $997 £756

An 18th century He Chaozong Dehua blanc-de-chine figure of a seated lady, impressed three-character seal mark, 13cm. high. (Christie's) $1,995 £1,512

CHINESE

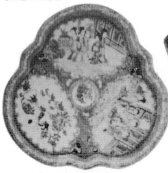

A 19th century trefoil rose medallion porcelain tray, China, 10½in. diam. (Robt. W. Skinner Inc.)
$350 £243

Mid 19th century rose Mandarin export porcelain bowl, China, polychrome decorated, 14½in. diam. (Robt. W. Skinner Inc.) $1,100 £774

A 6th century olive glazed oviform jar with four double loop handles, 25.5cm. high. (Christie's) $9,525 £6,480

A blue, red and white cylindrical vase painted in underglaze blue and copper-red, large Qianlong six-character seal mark and of the period, 47.5cm. high. (Christie's)
$15,876 £10,800

A 3rd/2nd Millennium B.C. Ma Jia Yao neolithic pottery two-handled jar, 26cm. diam. (Christie's)
$2,063 £1,404

One of a pair of K'ang Hsi baluster vases and domed covers, 52cm. and 53cm. high. (Lawrence Fine Art)
$1,116 £770

A barrel shaped mug decorated with a panel of figures on a basketwork ground, 5¼in. high. (Christie's)
$406 £280

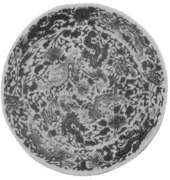

A blue and white dish enamelled in yellow, red, green and aubergine, encircled Xuande six character mark, 9¾in. diam. (Christie's)
$1,160 £800

A pear shaped mug painted with figures at various pastimes, 4¾in. high. (Christie's)
$65 £45

CLARICE CLIFF

A Clarice Cliff Bizarre 'Inspiration' baluster pottery vase, 12½in. high. (Christie's) $650 £500

A Clarice Cliff Bizarre vase, printed marks, moulded 370, 15.5cm. high. (Lawrence Fine Art) $321 £220

A Clarice Cliff 'Inspiration' vase of tall baluster shape, circa 1930, 41cm. high. (Christie's) $4,730 £3,240

A Clarice Cliff Bizarre Fantasque lotus vase, painted with red, orange and yellow leaves, 11¾in. high. (Christie's) $765 £580

A Clarice Cliff Bizarre oviform jug in the 'Snake Tree' pattern, 6¾in. high. (Christie's) $514 £350

A Clarice Cliff 'Fantasque' single-handled 'Isis' vase, printed marks, 24.6cm. high. (Lawrence Fine Art) $449 £308

A Clarice Cliff Fantasque baluster shaped vase, 16¼in. high. (Christie's) $1,617 £1,100

A Clarice Cliff Bizarre circular wall charger, 45.6cm. diam. (Christie's) $548 £378

A Bizarre Clarice Cliff hand-painted lotus vase with design of trees and houses on blue and white ground, 10½in. high. (Chelsea Auction Galleries) $680 £460

COALPORT

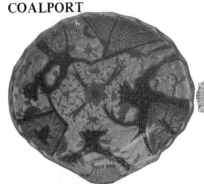

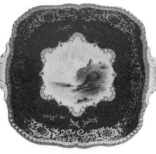

A Coalport (John Rose) part dessert service painted in the Imari style, circa 1805. (Christie's) $1,686 £1,188

A Coalport square-shaped dessert dish, painted with a view of Tantallon Castle, by A. Perry, 28.5cm., 1908. (Lawrence Fine Art) $287 £198

A Coalport (John Rose) part dessert service, circa 1810. (Christie's) $383 £270

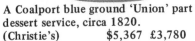

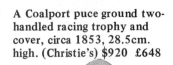

A Coalport goblet vase, 22.2cm. high, printed mark in green and impressed mark for January 1908. (Lawrence Fine Art) $398 £275

A Coalport blue ground 'Union' part dessert service, circa 1820. (Christie's) $5,367 £3,780

A Coalport puce ground two-handled racing trophy and cover, circa 1853, 28.5cm. high. (Christie's) $920 £648

COPELAND

A Copeland Spode Toby jug, blue printed diaper and floral coat and hat, 8in. high. (Capes, Dunn & Co.) $77 £55

Part of a Copeland & Garrett topographical dessert service, printed blue-green mark and pattern no. 6903, circa 1842. (Christie's) $3,725 £2,500

A Copeland Parian group, entitled 'Go To Sleep', impressed Art Union of London, J. Durham Sc 1862, 26in. high overall. (Anderson & Garland) $525 £370

HANS COPER

An early stoneware bowl, by Hans Coper, circa 1955, 27.8cm. diam. (Christie's)
$10,179 £7,020

A black stoneware stemmed cup form, by Hans Coper, circa 1965, 16.7cm. high. (Christie's) $5,184 £3,600

An early stoneware vase, by Hans Coper, the onion-shaped form with white sgraffito linear decoration, circa 1952, 33.2cm. diam. (Christie's)
$17,280 £12,000

A stoneware bulbous bottle, by Hans Coper, circa 1965, 16.9cm. high. (Christie's)
$3,758 £2,592

A stoneware 'Tripot', by Hans Coper, circa 1956, 27.5cm. high. (Christie's)
$7,203 £4,968

A stoneware buff spade-form vase, by Hans Coper, impressed HC seal, 1973, 28.3cm. high. (Christie's)
$6,336 £4,400

A stoneware 'thistle' vase, by Hans Coper, circa 1962, 24cm. high. (Christie's)
$7,830 £5,400

A stoneware shaped cylindrical bottle, by Hans Coper, circa 1966, 20.4cm. high. (Christie's) $2,975 £2,052

A monumental stoneware shouldered bottle, by Hans Coper, circa 1970, 43cm. high. (Christie's)
$12,528 £8,640

DELFT

A Bristol delft blue and white fluted hexagonal spoon tray, circa 1750, 15cm. wide. (Christie's) $315 £237

One of a pair of 18th century Dutch Delft polychrome chicken tureens and covers, 14cm. long. (Christie's) $11,502 £8,100

A Bristol delft blue and white documentary deep bowl, circa 1735, 35cm. diam. (Christie's)
$11,491 £8,640

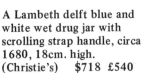
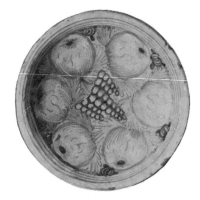

A Lambeth delft blue and white wet drug jar with scrolling strap handle, circa 1680, 18cm. high. (Christie's) $718 £540

A mid 17th century English delft charger, probably Southwark, 37cm. diam. (Christie's) $920 £648

A Lambeth delft blue and white drug jar for U:Sambuc, circa 1740, 17.5cm. high. (Christie's) $287 £216

A Lambeth delft blue-dash Royalist portrait charger, circa 1705, 35cm. diam. (Christie's) $3,734 £2,808

A London delft dated blue and white wet drug jar for S. Cichorei.Sympi with date 1659, 20cm. high. (Christie's)
$1,226 £864

A London delft Royalist blue and white plate, circa 1715, 22.2cm. diam. (Christie's) $1,380 £972

DELFT

Mid 17th century Southwark delft polychrome armorial salt of rectangular form, 13cm. wide. (Christie's)$6,441 £4,536

One of a pair of 18th century Dutch Delft polychrome cows with yellow horns, 21cm. long. (Christie's) $2,453 £1,728

One of a pair of Dutch Delft circular polychrome dishes, 14in. diam. (Anderson & Garland) $576 £400

A Dublin delft blue and white baluster vase, circa 1750, 32cm. high. (Christie's) $1,456 £1,026

A London delft blue-dash tulip charger, circa 1700, 35cm. diam. (Christie's) $1,993 £1,404

A massive London delft dated polychrome armorial drug jar of swelling form, circa 1656, 36cm. high. (Christie's) $25,855 £19,440

A Bristol delft blue and white barber's bowl, circa 1740, 25.5cm. diam. (Christie's) $1,292 £972

One of a pair of Dutch Delft blue and white gourd shaped vases, circa 1670, with metal covers. (Christie's) $729 £486

A Lambeth delft ballooning plate painted in blue, green, yellow and manganese, circa 1785, 30cm. diam. (Christie's) $1,867 £1,404

DELLA ROBBIA

CHINA

A Della Robbia pottery vase by Roseville Pottery, signed with Rozane Ware seal, circa 1906, 8¼in. high. (Robt. W. Skinner Inc.)
$850 £590

A Della Robbia wall charger, the base incised DR with a sailing ship and artist's monogram, 47.5cm. diam. (Christie's) $532 £378

A Della Robbia pottery vase, with marks of Chas. Collis, potter and sgraffito artist and G. Russell, Paintress, circa 1903/06, 11in. high. (Capes, Dunn & Co.)
$100 £70

DE MORGAN

A William de Morgan ruby lustre charger, decorated with a peacock, circa 1900, 36cm. diam. (Christie's)
$803 £550

A small William de Morgan lustre bowl, 5½in. diam. (Christie's) $297 £220

A William de Morgan wall plate designed by Chas. Passenger, 47cm. diam. (Christie's) $1,879 £1,296

DERBY

A Derby shepherdess in yellow-lined pink jacket, Wm. Duesbury & Co., circa 1765, 24.5cm. high. (Christie's) $582 £410

A pair of Derby figures emblematic of Summer painted in the London studio of Wm. Duesbury, Andrew Planche's period, circa 1753, 16.5cm. high. (Christie's)
$3,987 £2,808

A Derby white figure of John Wilkes, Wm. Duesbury & Co., circa 1765, 29.5cm. high. (Christie's) $489 £345

DOULTON

A Royal Doulton figure, 'Dinky Doo', designed by L. Harradine, HN1678, introduced 1934, 12cm. high. (Lawrence Fine Art) $59 £41

A Royal Doulton pottery character jug modelled as Santa Clause, D6690, 7½in. high. (Christie's) $60 £42

'The Mendicant', a Royal Doulton figure designed by L. Harradine, HN1365, introduced 1929, withdrawn 1969, 20.9cm. high. (Lawrence Fine Art) $208 £143

A Doulton Lambeth stoneware golfing jug, circa 1900, 8¾in. high. (Lawrence Fine Art) $947 £640

A Doulton Lambeth faience coffee service, P.O.D.R. mark for 29th May, 1879, coffee pot 26.9cm. high. (Lawrence Fine Art) $321 £220

A Faience oviform vase, by Emily Gillman, impressed Doulton, Lambeth Faience mark, 9¼in. high. (Christie's) $124 £85

'The Old Balloon Seller', Royal Doulton figure, designed by L. Harradine, HN 1315, introduced 1929, impressed date code for 1936, 19cm. high. (Lawrence Fine Art) $77 £53

A Royal Doulton two-handled loving cup commemorating King George V silver jubilee, 10in. high, No. 584 of a limited edition of 1,000. (Christie's) $338 £260

The 'Lily Maid', a Royal Doulton polychrome glazed stoneware fountain figure, designed by Gilbert Bayes, 61.5cm. high. (Christie's) $13,311 £9,180

DOULTON

A pottery character jug modelled as 'The Hatless Drake', with printed Royal Doulton marks, 6in. high. (Christie's) $3,105 £2,300

A Royal Doulton figure of 'Lucy Anne', HN 1502, 5½in. high. (Christie's) $91 £70

A Royal Doulton pottery character jug modelled as The Fortune Teller, D 6497, 6¾in. high. (Christie's) $390 £300

A slender oviform vase, by Hannah Barlow, impressed Doulton Lambeth, 1881, 10½in. high. (Christie's) $501 £380

Pair of Doulton saltglazed stoneware baluster vases, circa 1906/7, 12½in. high. (Capes, Dunn & Co.) $288 £200

One of a pair of Royal Doulton baluster shaped vases, by Francis C. Pope, 8¾in. high. (Christie's) $201 £140

A Royal Doulton character jug, St. George, 7½in. high. (Hobbs & Chambers) $73 £50

A Doulton Burslem figure designed by Chas. J. Noke, 33cm. high. (Lawrence Fine Art) $658 £451

A stoneware group modelled as two frogs attacking two mice, 'The Combat', by G. Tinworth, 4in. high. (Christie's) $864 £600

DRESDEN

One of a pair of 'Dresden' schneeballen vases and covers, 58cm. high, crossed swords mark in underglaze blue. (Lawrence Fine Art) $1,116 £770

A Dresden standing figure of a polar bear, 55cm. long, crossed swords mark in underglaze blue. (Lawrence Fine Art) $1,196 £825

One of a pair of Dresden yellow ground oviform vases and covers, 12½in. high. (Christie's) $325 £220

A pair of Dresden candelabra for five lights, on square bases with four scroll feet, 14cm., crossed swords mark in underglaze blue. (Lawrence Fine Art) $1,229 £825

A mantel clock in porcelain drum shaped case in Dresden style, 39cm. high, marked with monogram J.R. (Lawrence Fine Art) $655 £440

Pair of Dresden bulbous vases with covers and painted panels on yellow ground. (Worsfolds) $604 £420

EARTHENWARE

An earthenware circular charger by Ljerka Njers, 1985, 38.5cm. diam. (Christie's) $343 £237

One of a pair of earthenware boxes and covers of square shape, one with incised signature, 4¼in. high. (Lawrence Fine Art) $255 £176

A handbuilt, burnished and polished red clay vase by Magdalene A. N. Odundo, 1985, 34.7cm. high. (Christie's) $1,566 £1,080

EUROPEAN

CHINA

A Northern European faience asparagus tureen and cover naturally modelled, circa 1775, 34.5cm. long. (Christie's) $1,533 £1,080

A Continental faience figure of King Wenceslaus, mid 18th century, 18.5cm. high. (Christie's) $306 £216

European porcelain serving plate, 1810. (British Antique Exporters) $78 £58

Late 15th century Hispano Moresque albarello in blue and gold lustre, Valencia, 29cm. high. (Christie's) $8,748 £6,480

A School of Koloman Moser seven-piece porcelain tea service, designed by Jutta Sika, teapot 16.7cm. high. (Christie's) $2,818 £1,944

An early 20th century Art Nouveau porcelain vase, by Riessner, Stetmacher & Kessel, 13in. high. (Robt. W. Skinner Inc.)$370 £250

A Rozenburg egg-shell square-shaped vase painted with blue and green stylised foliage on a white ground, 11in. high. (Christie's) $950 £720

An ancient pottery hand grenade for 'Greek Fire', 3½in., wheel turned with red glaze. (Wallis & Wallis) $64 £45

A Georges de Feure porcelain figure of a woman in evening dress, inscribed, 30.2cm. high. (Christie's) $626 £432

EUROPEAN

CHINA

A Strasbourg oval dish with pierced border, blue H/860 mark, circa 1770, 30cm. wide. (Christie's) $324 £216

An Orchies pottery figure, designed by Dax, 13¼in. high, printed and painted marks. (Christie's) $139 £95

Late 18th century Spanish pottery, Alcora cockerel tureen, 23cm. high. (Christie's) $367 £259

An amphora vase of ovoid shape, impressed Amphora and printed Turn Teplitz R. St. K. with maker's device and D. 464, circa 1930, 18.5cm. high.(Christie's) $1,487 £1,026

A mid 18th century Brussels faience boar's head tureen, cover and stand, the stand 40cm. long. (Christie's) $7,668 £5,400

An ancient pottery hand grenade for 'Greek Fire', 4½in., of dense black stoneware. (Wallis & Wallis) $64 £45

An ancient pottery hand grenade for 'Greek Fire', 3¾in., wheel turned with green glaze. (Wallis & Wallis) $64 £45

A G. Riviere crackled white pottery figure of a kneeling naked woman, 22in. high. (Christie's) $514 £350

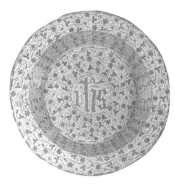

Mid 15th century Hispano Moresque blue and copper lustre deep dish, Valencia, 48cm. diam. (Christie's) $61,236 £45,360

FAMILLE ROSE

An 18th century famille rose bottle shaped vase, 9in. high. (Christie's) $159 £110

A large famille rose punch bowl painted with panels of figures at play, alternating with panels of flowers on a gilt scrolled ground, 15in. diam. (Christie's) $2,755 £1,900

A Canton famille rose oviform vase with buddhistic lion handles below a waved rim, 24½in. high. (Christie's) $348 £240

A famille rose cylindrical mug painted with figures in a fenced garden, with dragon handle, 5½in. high. (Christie's) $188 £130

One of a pair of Canton famille rose baluster vases, 15¼in. high. (Christie's) $1,740 £1,200

A famille rose cylindrical mug painted with a panel of figures in a garden by a pagoda, 5¼in. high. (Christie's) $275 £190

A famille rose oviform armorial tea caddy and odd cover painted with a coat-of-arms, 6in. high. (Christie's) $580 £400

A large famille rose fish bowl extensively decorated, 18in. high. (Edgar Horn) $2,409 £1,650

A famille rose turquoise-ground baluster vase, gilt incised Qianlong six-character mark and late in the period, 35cm. high. (Christie's) $4,276 £3,240

FAMILLE ROSE

One of a pair of Qianlong famille rose two-handled classical urn shaped vases and covers, 26½in. high. (Christie's)
$20,300 £14,000

A famille rose oviform vase, figure painted diaper borders with bird vignettes in reserve, 17½in. high. (Capes, Dunn & Co.) $387 £275

FAMILLE VERTE

A famille verte ginger jar and cover on hardwood stand, 9in. high. (Capes, Dunn & Co.) $91 £65

One of a pair of famille rose recumbent buddhistic lion joss stick holders, 4¼in. wide. (Christie's)
$1,812 £1,250

Part of a garniture of five famille rose armorial vases, comprising three baluster vases and two covers, 11¼in. high and two beaker vases, 9¼in. high. (Christie's) $1,421 £980

A famille verte fish bowl, the exterior painted with a scene of warriors proceeding to battle, 25in. diam. (Christie's) $5,510 £3,800

A Canton famille rose oviform vase with buddhistic lion handles, 35in. high. (Christie's) $1,595 £1,100

A Canton famille rose oviform vase with buddhistic lion handles, 24½in. high. (Christie's) $406 £280

One of a pair of famille verte porcelain vases of square section, 10in. high. (Capes, Dunn & Co.) $119 £85

FRENCH

Late 17th century Nevers bleu persan double gourd vase, 34.5cm. high. (Christie's) $407 £302

A late 19th century French rectangular plaque by Lucien Levy, 32 x 22cm. (Christie's) $714 £496

One of a pair of early 19th century ormolu mounted cobalt blue glazed porcelain urns, France, 16in. high. (Robt. W. Skinner Inc.) $2,500 £1,824

A large Strasbourg surtout-de-table, circa 1750, 52cm. high, the plateau 64cm. wide. (Christie's) $6,134 £4,320

A porcelain snuff box mounted in England en cage in gold, possibly Tournai, circa 1765, 7.5cm. wide. (Christie's) $8,434 £5,940

A Vincennes partly glazed white biscuit figure of a sleeping putto resting on a bale of hay, circa 1753, 11cm. high. (Christie's) $1,458 £972

A Rouen bleu persan shaped circular dish, decorated in the 'Gillibaud' style, circa 1700, 36cm. diam. (Christie's) $465 £345

A late 19th century Samson figure of a partridge, blue cross mark, 15cm. high. (Christie's) $123 £86

A French earthenware ornamental circular plaque, signed Belet, circa 1880-1900. (Capes, Dunn & Co.) $180 £125

196

FRENCH

CHINA

Late 19th century French porcelain figure group, 'L'Accordec du Village', after Greuze, 16in. long. (Capes, Dunn & Co.)
$244 £170

One of a pair of mid 18th century Tournai faience pug dogs, after the original Meissen models by J. J. Kandler, 15.5cm. high. (Christie's)$10,735 £7,560

A Samson figure of a white rhinoceros after the original by J. J. Kandler, blue cross mark, circa 1880, 22cm. wide. (Christie's)$714 £496

A Louis XVI travelling set, contained in a tulipwood and parquetry case lined with pink watered silk, 35.5cm. wide. (Christie's)
$3,240 £2,160

A large pair of Continental biscuit figures of a man and a woman in 18th century dress, impressed initial marks, probably France, circa 1900, 68cm. high. (Christie's)
$1,866 £1,296

An Aprey faience group, black AP p mark, circa 1770, 24cm. high. (Christie's)
$735 £518

Late 17th century Nevers bleu persan shallow bowl with everted rim, 23.5cm. diam. (Christie's)
$407 £302

A Limoges model of a leaping fish in pink, green and white glazes, designed by Sandoz, 7½in. high. (Christie's) $294 £200

One of a pair of Marseilles circular dishes painted en camaieu vert, Savy's factory, circa 1770, 28.5cm. diam. (Christie's)
$2,430 £1,620

GERMAN

CHINA

A mid 18th century Bayreuth two-handled oval basket, the pierced basket work sides with yellow lined lattice work, 25cm. wide. (Christie's) $2,300 £1,629

A Kloster Veilsdorf figure of Capitano Spavento modelled by Wenzel Neu, 1764-65, 16cm. high. (Christie's) $1,533 £1,080

A mid 18th century German faience asparagus tureen and cover, 17cm. long. (Christie's) $1,840 £1,296

A mid 18th century Fulda faience frog, 8cm. long. (Christie's) $4,294 £3,024

A Kloster Veilsdorf figure of Pierrot modelled by Wenzel Neu, 1764-65, 15.5cm. high. (Christie's) $7,668 £5,400

A Ludwigsburg miniature group of three figures rolling dice, blue interlaced C mark, circa 1775, 8cm. wide. (Christie's) $2,147 £1,512

A pair of Nymphenburg figures designed by Prof. J. Wackerle of stylised 18th century fops. (Christie's) $3,468 £2,376

A Thuringian figure of Provender for the Monastery, circa 1775, 11.5cm. high. (Christie's) $874 £648

A Volkstedt circular jagddose of compressed baluster form, the hinged silver gilt mount with waved decoration, blue hayfork and M mark, circa 1760, 9cm. diam. (Christie's) $8,748 £6,480

GERMAN

A Kloster Veilsdorf figure of a crouching leopard, probably modelled by Pfranger snr., circa 1775, 12cm. long. (Christie's) $611 £453

A Stralsund baluster vase with reticulated sides, circa 1770, 36.5cm. high. (Christie's) $1,226 £864

A Kloster Veilsdorf figure of Pantalone modelled by Wenzel Neu, 1764-65, 14.5cm. high. (Christie's) $3,067 £2,160

CHINA

A Potschappel two-handled vase and an armorial cover, the vase with crossed T mark, the stand with blue beehive mark, circa 1900, 84cm. high. (Christie's) $1,321 £918

A German lacquered earthenware baluster vase decorated with chinoiserie landscapes in black and red, 44½in. high. (Christie's) $1,409 £972

A stoneware tureen and cover attributed to Reinhold Merkelbach and the design to R. Riemerschmid, 33.5cm. high. (Christie's) $861 £594

A mid 18th century Erfurt faience cow tureen and cover, 20.5cm. long. (Christie's) $1,150 £810

A Rosenthal ceramic sculpture by Gerhard Schliepstein, circa 1930, 50.8cm. high. (Christie's) $2,035 £1,404

Mid 18th century Hannoversch-Munden faience cylindrical tankard with pewter cover, 21.5cm. high. (Christie's) $336 £237

GERMAN

A Limbach figure of St. Johannes Nepomuk, circa 1775, 21cm. high. (Christie's) $1,134 £756

One of a set of five Furstenberg shaped rectangular plaques painted by J. H. Eisentrager, with pastoral scenes after Nilson in landscape vignettes, circa 1765, 12 x 16cm. (Christie's) $29,160 £21,600

A Kloster Veilsdorf cane handle, formed as a bearded old man, circa 1770, 7.5cm. high. (Christie's) $810 £540

An 18th century German cylindrical pewter mounted tankard, perhaps Altenberg, 27cm. high. (Christie's) $210 £140

A Furstenberg figure of a young girl modelled by Carl G. Schubert, circa 1785, 19cm. high. (Christie's) $486 £324

A Furstenberg white biscuit oval plaque modelled with a portrait bust of J. H. C. v. Selchow, circa 1782, 7.5cm. high. (Christie's) $86 £64

'Winter', a Rosenthal white glazed porcelain figure designed by G. Schliepstein, 18.5cm. high. (Christie's) $343 £237

A German faience Hausmalerei circular dish painted en camaieu rose, early 18th century, 25cm. diam. (Christie's) $2,268 £1,512

A German blue and white cylindrical tankard, circa 1700, 25cm. high. (Christie's) $891 £594

GOLDSCHEIDER

A Goldscheider pottery figure modelled as a naked young lady holding a fan, and trailing a shawl behind, 13¾in. high. (Christie's) $514 £350

A Goldscheider Art Deco globular lamp base, decorated in white, orange, black and blue with banding, 25cm. high. (Phillips) $243 £180

A china Art Deco figure of a woman, by Goldscheider, Vienna, 15¼in. high. (Robt. W. Skinner Inc.) $222 £150

A china Art Deco figure of a woman by Goldscheider, Vienna, 12½in. high. (Robt. W. Skinner Inc.) $222 £150

A pair of Goldscheider pottery figures of a young girl and a young man, made in Austria, 15in. high. (Christie's) $528 £400

A Goldscheider pottery figure of a woman wearing a beaded costume, on a black oval base, 18in. high. (Christie's) $2,108 £1,700

A Goldscheider pottery figure modelled as naked young girl with her arms crossed in front of her, 14¼in. high. (Christie's) $617 £420

A Goldscheider pottery mask of a girl looking down, Made in Austria, circa 1925, 23cm. high. (Christie's) $473 £324

A Goldscheider pottery bust of a young woman in the Art Deco style, signed F. Donatello, 23½in. high. (Outhwaite & Litherland) $504 £350

GOSS

A Goss Parian bust of Queen Victoria, for Mortlock's of Oxford Street, 236mm. high. (Phillips) $235 £160

The Feathers Hotel, Ledbury, 114mm. long. (Goss & Crested China) $1,050 £700

Hastings kettle. (Goss & Crested China) $12 £8

Dr Samuel Johnson's House at Lichfield, 75mm. high. (Goss & Crested China) $210 £140

Little girl Goss doll with real hair, porcelain arms, head and legs. (Goss & Crested China) $600 £400

Shakespeare's Cottage, Stratford-on-Avon, 65mm. long. (Goss & Crested China) $97 £65

Flame colour pear-shaped vase with grapevine decoration. (Goss & Crested China) $262 £175

Hereford terracotta kettle and lid. (Goss & Crested China) $37 £25

1930's flower girl, 'Daisy', in yellow and green flapper dress. (Goss & Crested China) $270 £160

GRUEBY

A Grueby pottery two-colour vase, stamped and paper label, circa 1905, 7in. high. (Robt. W. Skinner Inc.) $550 £381

A Grueby two-colour pottery vase, circa 1905, 13in. high. (Robt. W. Skinner Inc.) $5,200 £3,611

A Grueby pottery vase, stamped and artist signed, circa 1905, 7.7/8in. high. (Robt. W. Skinner Inc.) $1,000 £694

HAN

A green-glazed red pottery table, 43.5cm. wide, and five related eared cups, Han Dynasty. (Christie's) $2,566 £1,944

A green glazed red pottery model of a house, areas of iridescence and earth encrustation, Han Dynasty, 41cm. wide. (Christie's) $5,397 £3,672

A green-glazed pottery model of a sheep and pig farm, Han Dynasty, 37cm. wide. (Christie's) $14,256 £10,800

A red painted pottery horse head, Han Dynasty, 15.5cm. high. (Christie's) $1,425 £1,080

A green glazed pottery model of a farm house tower in three sections, Han Dynasty, 58.5cm. high. (Christie's) $28,576 £19,440

A large proto-porcelain jar, the upper part under a semi-opaque olive-green glaze, Han Dynasty, 36.5cm. diam. (Christie's) $1,069 £810

A painted grey pottery
figure of a standing stallion,
Han Dynasty, 50cm. high.
(Christie's)
$20,638 £14,040

A green glazed red pottery
model of a tower, Han
Dynasty, 61.5cm. high.
(Christie's)
$53,978 £36,720

One of a pair of grey pottery
horse heads with bulbous eyes,
Han Dynasty, 15cm. high.
(Christie's) $1,587 £1,080

A green glazed red pottery
bird lamp, Han Dynasty,
64cm. high. (Christie's)
$11,907 £8,100

A green glazed red pottery
kidney shaped farm, Han
Dynasty, 28cm. wide.
(Christie's) $1,746 £1,188

A green glazed pottery
granary jar and related cover,
Han Dynasty, 33cm. high.
(Christie's) $855 £648

A green glazed pottery hill
jar and cover on three feet,
Han Dynasty, 21cm. high.
(Christie's) $2,423 £1,836

A green glazed pottery pear-
shaped vase, Han Dynasty,
31cm. high. (Christie's)
$2,423 £1,836

A red painted grey pottery
horse's head, Han Dynasty,
6in. high. (Lawrence Fine
Art) $1,595 £1,100

IMARI

An Imari model of a smiling courtesan decorated in underglaze blue, iron-red and gilt, Genroku period, 37.8cm. high. (Christie's) $1,544 £1,080

A 19th century Imari circular bowl decorated in underglaze blue, iron-red, green, yellow enamels and gilt, 40cm. diam. (Christie's) $1,698 £1,188

An 18th century Imari model of a roistering Dutchman seated astride a Dutch gin cask, 35.8cm. high. (Christie's) $18,662 £12,960

One of a pair of late 17th century Imari baluster vases and covers, 90cm. high. (Christie's) $18,532 £12,960

A Japanese Imari part dessert service, Edo period. (Christie's) $939 £648

One of a pair of early 19th century Imari porcelain and brass Temple jars, Japan, 16½in. high. (Robt. W. Skinner Inc.) $3,600 £2,500

One of a pair of late 19th century Imari slender oviform vases, 106cm. high. (Christie's) $19,305 £13,500

Late 19th century brass mounted Imari tureen, Japan, 16in. wide. (Robt. W. Skinner Inc.) $550 £401

Late 17th century Imari octagonal baluster vase and cover decorated in iron-red and gilt, 85cm. high. (Christie's) $8,494 £5,940

IMARI

An Imari shaving bowl decorated in iron-red, black enamels and gilt on underglaze
blue, Genroku period, 27.5cm.
diam. (Christie's) $734 £540

One of a set of five late
17th/early 18th century
Imari dishes, 9¼in. diam.
(Lawrence Fine Art)
$2,048 £1,375

An Imari shaving bowl decorated in iron-red, dark green
and light green, aubergine and
black enamels and gilt on a
blue ground, Genroku period,
26cm. diam. (Christie's)
$617 £432

An octagonal Imari vase
decorated in iron-red and
black enamels and gilt,
Genroku period, 59cm. high.
(Christie's) $2,780 £1,944

An Imari deep bowl and cover
decorated in iron-red, enamel
and gilt on an underglaze blue
ground, Genroku period,
21.5cm. diam. (Christie's)
$1,081 £756

Early 19th century Chinese
Imari design baluster shaped
vase with cover, 33in. high.
(Peter Wilson & Co.)
$1,728 £1,200

Late 17th century Imari
deep bowl and domed cover,
the brass acorn finial of later
date, 48.4cm. high. (Christie's)
$2,316 £1,620

An Imari circular plaque
painted with flowers, birds
and medallions, 18¾in. diam.
(Anderson & Garland)
$460 £320

A Ko-Imari baluster jar decorated in iron-red, green, yellow
and pale aubergine enamels in
Kakiemon style, circa 1660-80,
32.8cm. high. (Christie's)
$14,688 £10,800

IMARI

Late 19th century large Imari globular jardiniere painted in underglaze blue, iron-red, colours and gilt, 53cm. diam. (Christie's) $2,642 £1,944

An Imari ship's plate and cover decorated in iron-red, green and aubergine enamels and gilt on underglaze blue, Genroku period, 25.5cm. diam. (Christie's) $1,477 £1,026

A large Imari dish decorated in iron-red and black enamels and gilt on underglaze blue, Genroku period, 55cm. diam. (Christie's) $3,231 £2,376

A 19th century Imari porcelain vase decorated in underglaze blue, orange and ochre, 18½in. high. (Robt. W. Skinner Inc.) $600 £416

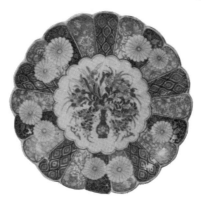

An Imari porcelain circular plaque, the border diaper panelled, 9¾in. diam. (Capes, Dunn & Co.) $60 £42

A Ko-Imari baluster jar decorated with three kirin among peony, circa 1660-80, 33.5cm. high. (Christie's) $13,219 £9,720

A large Imari dish painted in typical colours, circa 1700, 53.8cm. diam. (Christie's) $1,615 £1,188

Late 17th/early 18th century Imari oviform vase and cover, decorated in iron-red, enamel and gilt, 50cm. high. (Christie's) $2,316 £1,620

An Imari shaving dish decorated in underglaze blue, iron-red and gilt, Genroku period, 28cm. wide. (Christie's) $440 £324

ITALIAN

A Savona blue and white tankard with entwined handle, mid 18th century, 15.5cm. wide. (Christie's) $675 £450

Early 20th century majolica ewer with swan handle, 17½in. high. (Robt. W. Skinner Inc.) $375 £256

A Cantagalli majolica dish, ogival edged, bold floral design in blue, green and manganese, 15½in. diam. (Capes, Dunn & Co.) $119 £80

A Faenza wet drug jar of ovoid shape with an angled strap handle and straight spout, 22.5cm. high. (Phillips)$562 £380

A Castelli rectangular plaque painted with God appearing to Adam in the Garden of Eden, circa 1725, 21 x 28cm. (Christie's) $1,134 £756

A figure of Winter standing with his arms clasped around his chest, dated on the base 1779, 33.5cm. high. (Christie's) $2,478 £1,836

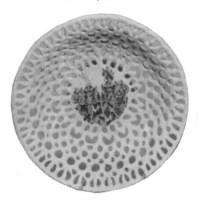

An early 18th century North Italian wet drug jar for Sy. Farfara, probably Savona, 19.5cm. high. (Christie's) $405 £270

A Faenza Compendiario armorial pierced circular tazza, circa 1570, 37.5cm. diam. (Christie's) $648 £432

A Faenza drug vase of compressed baluster form, the contents a. api, circa 1550, 21.5cm. high. (Christie's) $648 £432

ITALIAN

A Turin (Rossetti) shaped circular dish, circa 1760, 36cm. diam. (Christie's) $1,944 £1,296

An armorial wet drug jar painted in blue, the contents Mel.Ros. Solvtivo, circa 1600, possibly Faenza, 24cm. high. (Christie's) $648 £432

An Urbino Istoriato dish painted with the Rape of Proserpine, the reverse inscribed in blue Diplutto et Proserpina, circa 1555, 26cm. diam. (Christie's) $4,374 £3,240

An Orvieto ewer (brocca) of conventional form, circa 1470, 28cm. high. (Christie's) $17,496 £12,960

A Castelli rectangular plaque painted with Pan being comforted after the musical contest with Apollo seated, circa 1725, 28cm. square. (Christie's) $1,458 £972

A Castelli large vase of campana form painted in colours and gilt, circa 1720, 41cm. high. (Christie's) $2,250 £1,500

One of a pair of Faenza polychrome plates, Ferniani's factory, circa 1770, 24cm. diam. (Christie's) $420 £280

A Lenci figure of a rooster, painted marks Lenci 1936 S.P., 29cm. high.(Christie's) $1,566 £1,080

A Turin (Rossetti) shaped circular dish, blue cross mark, 1735-40, 32.5cm. diam. (Christie's) $486 £324

CHINA

A 17th century Kakiemon model of a dragon decorated in iron-red, blue, green and yellow enamels on a white glazed body, 19cm. high. (Christie's)
$13,899 £9,720

An 18th/19th century Kakiemon type mokkogata teapot with shallow domed cover and arch-shaped handle, 19cm. long. (Christie's)
$1,248 £918

Mid 19th century white glazed Hirado model of a stylised tiger, 20cm. long. (Christie's) $694 £486

A 19th century hexagonal Kyoto Satsuma vase, signed Kinkozan, 31cm. high. (Christie's) $1,081 £756

One of a pair of Kakiemon hexagonal jars and domed covers, Empo/Jokyo period (1673-87), 29.2cm. high. (Christie's)
$14,688 £10,800

An 18th/early 19th century Kakiemon type cylindrical sake bottle, tokkuri, fitted with a European gilt metal finial, 23cm. high.(Christie's)
$4,700 £3,456

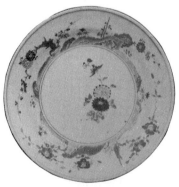

Late 19th century shaped and pierced baluster Kyoto vase decorated in coloured enamels and gilt, signed Donzan seizo, 17cm. high. (Christie's) $1,930 £1,350

Late 17th century Kakiemon figure of a standing bijin, 36.5cm. high. (Christie's)
$3,672 £2,700

Late 17th century Kakiemon shallow dish decorated in iron-red, blue, green, black and yellow enamels, 21cm. diam. (Christie's)
$2,779 £1,944

JAPANESE

Mid 19th century white glazed Hirado model of a recumbent goat, signed, 19cm. long. (Christie's) $586 £410

A raku wide and shallow footed bowl, by Keiko Hasegawa, covered in a thick shaded buff glaze, 30.3cm. diam.(Christie's) $751 £518

A Kakiemon hanging flower vase, kakehanaike, modelled as a dragon, circa 1660-80, 22cm. long. (Christie's) $6,609 £4,860

Late 19th century Kyoto vase decorated in coloured enamels and gilt, signed Ryozan, 21.5cm. high. (Christie's) $2,007 £1,404

A flattened rectangular press moulded bottle by Shoji Hamada covered in a rich khaki glaze, circa 1965, 22cm. high. (Christie's) $2,975 £2,052

A Kakiemon oviform vase decorated in blue, iron-red, green, yellow and black enamels, circa 1665, 26.5cm. high. (Christie's) $6,949 £4,860

A Kyoto type circular bowl with foliate rim, signed, Meiji period, 24.2cm. diam. (Christie's) $1,853 £1,296

A stoneware ewer with loop handle, overglazed in greyish white and blue enamels, Edo period, 20cm. high. (Christie's) $933 £648

A koro and cover on three bud feet, the cover signed in underglaze blue, 7in. high. (Lawrence Fine Art) $2,153 £1,485

211

A George Jones punch bowl with Mr. Punch lying on his back supporting the holly-decorated bowl in his arms, circa 1875, 36cm. diam. (Christie's) $4,228 £3,132

A George Jones tea-set, comprising a tea-pot, coffee-pot, milk-jug, sugar-basin with lid and a tray, circa 1873. (Christie's) $1,458 £1,080

A George Jones jardiniere, cobalt blue with turquoise interior and naturalistic colouring, 33cm. high. (Christie's) $874 £648

KANGXI

A Brinjal bowl with everted rim, 19cm. diam., Kangxi. (Christie's) $302 £200

A famille verte teapot and cover formed as a bunch of bamboo, 18cm. wide, Kangxi. (Christie's) $453 £300

A famille verte tazza, 22.5cm. diam., Kangxi. (Christie's) $453 £300

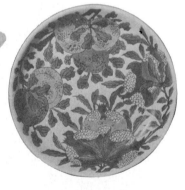

One of a pair of famille verte dishes with wide seeded green-ground border, 28.5cm. diam., Kangxi. (Christie's) $978 £648

A Kangxi blue and white cylindrical brush holder with slightly everted rim, 5in. high. (Christie's) $304 £210

A famille verte dish incised under the glaze with five-clawed dragons, encircled Kangxi six-character mark and of the period, 25cm. diam. (Christie's) $7,128 £5,400

KUTANI

CHINA

A 19th century Japanese Kutani porcelain punch bowl on teakwood stand, 14¾in. diam. (Robt. W. Skinner Inc.)$1,400 £972

One of a pair of 19th century Ao-Kutani baluster vases, signed Kyusekirin, 52cm. high. (Christie's)
· $1,762 £1,296

A 19th century Ao-Kutani saucer dish, signed Dai Nihon Kutani sei, Fukuriken, 59.3cm. diam. (Christie's) $881 £648

KYOTO

A Kyoto compressed globular koro, signed Kinzan, Meiji period, 8.2cm. diam. (Christie's) $1,175 £864

A Kyoto cylindrical vase decorated in colours and gilt on a royal blue ground, signed Kinkozan zo and Senzan, Meiji period, 11.8cm. high. (Christie's) $851 £626

Late 19th century Kyoto chrysanthemum-shaped deep bowl decorated in colours and gilt, signed Kizan kore o tsukuru, 29.8cm. diam. (Christie's) $1,248 £918

A Kyoto tapering rectangular vase painted with panels of a daimyo and his retainers, signed Nihon Yozan, Meiji period, 12.7cm. high. (Christie's) $909 £669

A Kyoto trumpet-shaped beaker vase decorated in coloured enamels and gilt, signed Kinkozan, Meiji period, 17.8cm. high. (Christie's) $1,395 £1,026

Late 19th century Kyoto hexagonal vase decorated in colours and gilt on a royal blue ground, signed Kinkozan zo, 43.6cm. high. (Christie's) $2,937 £2,160

LEACH, BERNARD

A stoneware rectangular slab bottle by Bernard Leach, covered in a rich iron-red glaze, circa 1955, 18.5cm. high. (Christie's)
$432 £300

A stoneware teapot with cane handle by Bernard Leach, circa 1920, 17.2cm. high. (Christie's)
$1,080 £750

A stoneware flattened rectangular slab bottle by B. Leach, impressed BL and St. Ives seals, circa 1960, 20.2cm. high.(Christie's)
$1,879 £1,296

A stoneware large oviform vase by Bernard Leach, impressed BL and St. Ives seals, circa 1958, 34.3cm. high. (Christie's) $1,008 £700

A slip-trailed soft raku bowl by Bernard Leach, impressed BL and St. Ives seals, circa 1920, 23.2cm. diam. (Christie's)
$1,152 £800

A stoneware barrel shaped bottle by Bernard Leach, impressed BL and St. Ives seals, circa 1970, 23.1cm. high. (Christie's)
$343 £237

LEACH

A stoneware cut decorated bottle by Janet Leach, impressed JL and St. Ives seals, circa 1958, 25.4cm. high. (Christie's) $288 £200

A stoneware tall pear shaped vase with two lugged handles, by John Leach, impressed JL seal and Muchelney, 1985, 29.8cm. high. (Christie's)
$218 £151

A black stoneware vase by Janet Leach, 1984, 27.3cm. high. (Christie's)$281 £194

CHINA

LENCI

A Lenci pottery wall mask modelled as a head of a young woman wearing a scarf, 12in. wide. (Christie's) $205 £140

A Lenci pottery figure modelled as a young girl standing beside a sledge, 13¼in. high. (Christie's) $661 £450

A Lenci pottery wall mask modelled as a young girl wearing a head scarf, 11½in. wide. (Christie's)$288 £200

LIVERPOOL

One of a pair of Liverpool delft plates, circa 1760-75, 13¼in. diam. (Woolley & Wallis) $435 £300

A Liverpool milk jug of spirally moulded helmet form with scroll handle, Philip Christian's Factory, circa 1770, 9cm. high. (Christie's) $428 £302

A Liverpool delft bowl decorated in blue and manganese purple, 18th century, 10½in. diam. (Woolley & Wallis) $609 £420

An early Chaffers Liverpool bell shape mug, with spurred handle, painted in blue, iron-red and gilt, 9cm. high. (Phillips) $858 £580

A Liverpool blue and white shell moulded pickle dish, perhaps Richard Chaffer's Factory, circa 1755, 9.5cm. wide. (Christie's) $214 £151

A Liverpool creamware inscribed and dated armorial oviform jug with loop handle, 1792, 14.5cm. high. (Christie's) $766 £540

215

LONGTON HALL

A Longton Hall blue and white coffee cup of flared form with split twig handle, circa 1755. (Christie's) $1,226 £864

A Longton Hall grape box and cover, circa 1755, 12cm. wide. (Christie's) $11,491 £8,640

A Longton Hall mug of flattened bell shape, with pointed 'broken' handle, 16cm. high. (Phillips) $592 £400

LOWESTOFT

A Lowestoft blue and white arched rectangular tea caddy, blue crescent mark, circa 1775, 10cm. high. (Christie's) $243 £183

A Lowestoft blue and white patty pan, blue crescent mark, circa 1768, 10.5cm. diam. (Christie's) $228 £172

A Lowestoft blue and white rectangular octagonal tea caddy, circa 1765, 13cm. high. (Christie's) $1,686 £1,188

LUSTRE

19th century Sunderland lustre ovoid jug, decorated with sailing ship, 5½in. high. (W. H. Lane & Son) $127 £85

A Maws red lustre circular plate outlined in gilt, 13in. diam. (Christie's) $108 £80

A large Bernard Moore lustre pottery jardiniere, 11½in. high. (Christie's) $892 £720

MARTINWARE

A Martin Bros. oviform single-handled pottery jug, in an uneven grey glaze with deeper brown patches, 9¼in. high. (Christie's) $250 £190

A Martin Bros. stoneware jug, the bulbous body suggesting a sea-creature, 21.8cm. high. (Christie's) $626 £432

A Martin Bros. stoneware 'judge' bird tobacco jar and cover, London & Southall 4-1889, 25.8cm. high. (Christie's) $3,445 £2,376

A Martin Bros. stoneware grotesque double-face jug, London and Southall G 1897, 17.3cm. high. (Christie's) $594 £410

A Martin Bros. stoneware slender oviform vase, London Southall, 1889, 13in. high. (Christie's) $405 £300

A Martinware gourd single-handled lobed pottery jug, London Southall, circa 1900, 10in. high. (Christie's) $513 £380

A Martin Brothers stoneware vase with incised decoration of flowering lilies and a dragon-fly, London & Southall 18.7.84, 20.5cm. high. (Christie's) $551 £378

A Martin Bros. face flask with two handles, incised marks dated 1901, 8in. high. (Christie's) $1,102 £750

A Martin Bros. stoneware tobacco jar and cover, modelled as a grotesque grinning cat, 1885, 22cm. high. (Christie's) $10,962 £7,560

MARTINWARE

CHINA

A Martin Bros stoneware spherical vase, London Southall, 1892, 9in. high. (Christie's) $472 £350

A Martinware flattened oviform pottery vase, London Southall, 1899, 12in. high. (Christie's) $229 £170

A Martin Bros. stoneware grotesque, double face jug with strap handle, 1897, 22.8cm. high. (Christie's) $1,879 £1,296

MASON'S

A Mason's ironstone part dinner service transfer-printed and painted in iron-red, blue, green and ochre in the Oriental style, pattern no. 1841, circa 1835. (Christie's) $2,115 £1,512

One of a pair of Mason's blue and gilt two handled vases and covers, 20in. high. (F. H. Fellows & Sons) $1,460 £1,000

Part of a Mason's patent ironstone china dessert service with a blue glaze, gilt and enamelled, circa 1820. (Lawrence Fine Art) $239 £165

A massive Mason's ironstone ewer of vase shape with double scroll handle, circa 1820, 67cm. high. (Christie's) $994 £700

A Meissen tau-shaped cane handle painted by Bonaventura G. Hauer, circa 1740, 12cm. long. (Christie's) $1,944 £1,296

A Meissen pipe bowl modelled as a recumbent sheep-dog with hinged neck, circa 1745, 8cm. long. (Christie's) $1,303 £918

A Meissen figure of a mallard duck, blue crossed swords mark at back, circa 1740, 28cm. high. (Christie's) $3,834 £2,700

A late Meissen pate-sur-pate baluster vase with cylindrical cover, 9¼in. high.(Christie's) $882 £600

Pair of 19th century Meissen vases and covers. (F. H. Fellows & Sons) $876 £600

A Meissen figure of Mezzetin, blue crossed swords mark under the base, circa 1742, 15.5cm. high. (Christie's) $5,367 £3,780

A Meissen shaped circular plate after the Chelsea original, circa 1770, 22cm. diam., blue crossed swords and dot mark. (Christie's) $611 £453

One of a pair of Meissen candlesticks, blue crossed swords marks, circa 1745, 23.5cm. high. (Christie's) $766 £540

A Meissen plate from the Swan service modelled by J. F. Eberlein & J. J. Kandler for Count Bruhl, circa 1738, 23.5cm. diam. (Christie's) $13,770 £9,180

MEISSEN

A Meissen baluster chinoiserie cream-pot and cover painted in the Horoldt workshop, gilt 10 mark, circa 1725, 12.5cm. wide. (Christie's) $2,106 £1,404

A Meissen miniature figure of a rabbit, circa 1750, on gilt metal base, the rabbit 3.5cm. long. (Christie's) $486 £324

One of a pair of Meissen coffee cups and saucers, blue crossed swords marks, Pressnummer 2 and 24, circa 1745. (Christie's) $1,749 £1,296

A Meissen figure of a cat, incised mark on base, circa 1740, 18.5cm. high. (Christie's) $3,373 £2,376

A pair of Meissen sweetmeat figures holding shaped oval baskets, moulded with ozier and painted with deutsche Blumen, circa 1750, 18cm. long. (Christie's) $1,020 £756

A Meissen hot water jug and cover, decorated in cisele gold, 17.5cm. high, red lustre mark 11, 1725. (Lawrence Fine Art) $9,889 £6,820

A Meissen figure of a shepherdess modelled by Meyer & Kandler, circa 1750, 23.5cm. high. (Christie's) $1,296 £864

A Meissen rectangular snuff box, the porcelain circa 1745, the silver London 1818, maker's mark of Chas. Rawlings, 9cm. wide. (Christie's) $1,166 £864

A Meissen rectangular tea caddy and cover, traces of blue crossed swords mark on base, circa 1770, 12.5cm. high. (Christie's) $1,539 £1,026

A Meissen pale turquoise ground circular bowl, blue crossed swords mark and gilder's mark 10, circa 1740, 15.5cm. diam. (Christie's) $1,296 £864

A Meissen inverted baluster teapot and cover, blue crossed swords mark and painter's mark 56 in puce, circa 1750, 14.5cm. wide. (Christie's) $810 £540

A Meissen compressed oviform cream-pot and shallow domed cover, gilder's mark 2 to each piece, circa 1730, 12.5cm. wide. (Christie's) $1,782 £1,188

A Meissen centrepiece, incised 1931, 42in. high. (F. H. Fellows & Sons) $2,336 £1,600

Pair of Louis XV ormolu mounted Meissen figures of a cockerel and hen, naturally modelled by J. J. Kandler, circa 1745. (Christie's) $10,735 £7,560

A Meissen figure of a pilgrim modelled by J. J. Kandler, blue crossed swords mark at back, circa 1745, 29cm. high. (Christie's) $1,150 £810

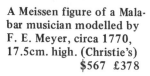

A Meissen figure of a Malabar musician modelled by F. E. Meyer, circa 1770, 17.5cm. high. (Christie's) $567 £378

A Meissen teapot and cover, decorated in cisele gold, 12cm. high, red lustre workman's cross mark, 1725. (Lawrence Fine Art) $8,772 £6,050

A Meissen Bergleute-shaped baluster jug and domed cover, blue crossed swords and dot mark, circa 1765, 28cm. high. (Christie's) $5,670 £3,780

MEISSEN

A Meissen bombe-shaped snuff box with contemporary silver mounts, scroll thumbpiece, circa 1745, 7cm. wide. (Christie's) $2,187 £1,620

A Meissen figure of a rhinoceros modelled by J. J. Kandler after Albrecht Durer, 1735-40, 17cm. long. (Christie's) $2,300 £1,620

A Meissen chinoiserie dish, the centre painted by C. F. Herold, blue crossed swords mark, circa 1734. (Christie's) $18,403 £12,960

A Meissen circular snuff box and cover painted by B. G. Hauer, the interior of the base solid gilt, 1725-30, 7.5cm. diam. (Christie's) $27,604 £19,440

A Meissen two-handled quatrefoil tray and four cups, blue crossed swords marks and Pressnummer 24 and 26, circa 1740. (Christie's) $9,968 £7,020

A Meissen figure of a jay modelled by J. J. Kandler, circa 1745, 39cm. high. (Christie's) $16,869 £11,880

A Meissen bullet-shaped vase and cover in blue with decorated panels, on stand. (F. H. Fellows & Sons) $613 £420

One of two Meissen figures of seated cats modelled by J. J. Kandler, circa 1740, 17.5cm. high. (Christie's) $9,201 £6,480

A Meissen oval bombeshaped snuff box and cover, 1725-28, 7cm. wide. (Christie's) $13,802 £9,720

MEISSEN

A Meissen oval bombe-shaped snuff box and cover painted en camaieu rose, 1730-40, 7.5cm. wide. (Christie's) $6,441 £4,536

A Meissen dolphin tureen and cover, blue crossed swords mark, circa 1750, 24cm. long. (Christie's) $2,147 £1,512

A Meissen KPM oblong sugar box and cover painted in the Horoldt workshop, 1723-25, 10.5cm. long. (Christie's) $13,035 £9,180

A Meissen rectangular snuff box and cover with contemporary two-colour gold mounts, circa 1750, 8.5cm. wide. (Christie's) $9,968 £7,020

A Meissen group of a scantily draped woman at her toilet, blue crossed swords marks and incised numerals, circa 1880, 15.5cm. high. (Christie's) $496 £345

A Meissen rectangular yellow-ground tea caddy painted in a Kakiemon palette, blue crossed swords mark and former's mark of Seidel, circa 1730, 10cm. high. (Christie's)$1,239 £918

A Meissen group of Die Polnische Verlobung modelled as a sultan with his Polish bride and Polish soldier servant, circa 1745, 15cm. high. (Christie's) $9,201 £6,480

One of a pair of Meissen pug dogs modelled by J. J. Kandler and P. Reinicke, one with blue crossed swords mark on base, circa 1745, 15cm. high. (Christie's) $4,600 £3,240

A Meissen model of a cottage modelled by J. J. Kandler for Count Bruhl, 1745-8, 15cm. wide. (Christie's) $9,201 £6,480

MEISSEN

A Meissen hot milk jug and cover with gilt side handle moulded with scrolls, circa 1745, 12cm. high. (Christie's) $1,458 £1,080

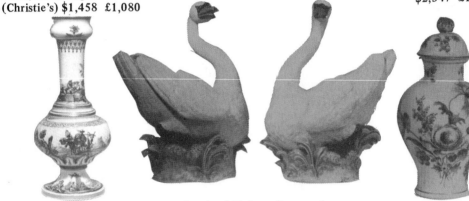

A Meissen (Marcolini) two-handled oval fruit basket with branch handles, circa 1785, blue crossed swords and star mark, 37cm. wide. (Christie's) $729 £540

A Meissen table centre, the two-handled tray with eight recesses painted with deutsche Blumen, circa 1750, 45cm. wide. (Christie's) $2,347 £1,836

A Meissen Hausmalerei tall baluster vase, the vase circa 1725, the base and decoration circa 1745, 29.5cm. high. (Christie's) $1,458 £1,080

A pair of Meissen figures of swans, blue crossed swords marks and incised numerals, circa 1880, 30.5cm. high. (Christie's) $2,099 £1,458

A Meissen baluster vase and domed cover with flower finial, circa 1745, 26.5cm. high. (Christie's) $1,458 £1,080

A Meissen clock case of shaped outline, circa 1880, the eight-day striking movement with enamel dial, 41.5cm. high. (Christie's) $1,555 £1,080

A Meissen Hausmalerei plate painted by F. F. Mayer von Pressnitz, the porcelain circa 1740, 22.5cm. diam. (Christie's) $729 £540

A Meissen baluster coffee pot and domed cover, blue crossed swords mark, Press-nummer 20 and gilder's no. 67, circa 1745, 22cm. high. (Christie's) $4,082 £3,024

CHINA

A Meissen Kakiemon fluted bowl, blue crossed swords mark, circa 1730, 19cm. diam. (Christie's) $1,458 £1,080

A Meissen group of dogs and a kennel, modelled by J. J. Kandler, blue crossed swords mark, circa 1750, 13cm. high. (Christie's) $6,123 £4,536

A Meissen baluster teapot and cover with pine-cone finial, blue crossed swords mark and gilder's mark H, circa 1745, 18cm. wide. (Christie's) $729 £540

A large Meissen white and gilt two-handled baluster vase, cancelled blue crossed swords and incised marks, circa 1880, 59cm. high. (Christie's) $1,399 £972

A pair of Meissen three-light candelabra emblematic of the Seasons, blue crossed swords mark and incised numerals, circa 1880, 34cm. high. (Christie's) $855 £594

A Meissen (Marcolini) figure of a chaffinch, blue crossed swords and star mark, circa 1790, 10cm. high. (Christie's) $522 £387

A Meissen group of two scantily draped putti counting money placed on the top of a wine barrel, circa 1880, 14.5cm. high. (Christie's) $434 £302

A Meissen Imari hexagonal plate, blue crossed swords mark and painter's mark for Kretzschmar, Pressnummer 22, circa 1740, 22.5cm. wide. (Christie's) $3,790 £2,808

A Meissen group of Count Bruhl's Tailor modelled by J. J. Kandler, circa 1740, about 25cm. high. (Christie's) $7,581 £5,616

A blue and white dragon bowl, encircled Kangxi six-character mark and of the period, 15.5cm. diam. (Christie's) $5,702 £4,320

A 16th century Ming green and black enamelled brush rest, 20cm. high. (Christie's) $1,905 £1,296

A blue and white saucer dish, encircled Yongzheng six-character mark and of the period, 17.4cm. diam. (Christie's) $2,138 £1,620

Late 17th/early 18th century shield-shaped Arita dish, the base with three spur marks and a Ming Chenghua mark, 12.4cm. (Christie's) $933 £648

One of a pair of blue and white late 18th century hexagonal barrel-shaped garden seats, 49cm. high. (Christie's) $4,847 £3,672

A Ming green dragon dish encircled Zhengde six-character mark and of the period, 23cm. diam., with fitted box. (Christie's) $5,987 £4,536

An early Ming blue and white saucer dish, Xuande, 27.4cm. diam. (Christie's) $23,814 £16,200

An early Ming blue and white vase, meiping, painted in a deep blue, Yongle, 28.5cm. high. (Christie's) $23,814 £16,200

A Ming blue and white broad oviform jar, encircled Jiajing six-character mark and of the period, 17.2cm. high. (Christie's) $2,280 £1,728

MING

A late Ming Wucai saucer dish, encircled Wanli six-character mark and of the period, 19cm. diam. (Christie's) $7,128 £5,400

A Ming Wucai square dish, unenclosed Jiajing six-character mark and of the period, 17cm. square. (Christie's) $2,423 £1,836

A late Ming Wucai barrel-shaped jar and cover, the base with Wanli six-character mark and of the period, 15cm. diam., fitted box. (Christie's) $50,803 £34,560

MINTON

A Minton turquoise ground pate-sur-pate part dessert service decorated by Desire Leroy, pattern no. G1859, circa 1878. (Christie's) $2,760 £1,944

A Minton vase and cover, painted by H. Boullemier, the reverse by W. Payne, 18cm. high, mark in gold. (Lawrence Fine Art) $95 £66

A Minton aquarium hexagonal plate, decorated in polychrome colours with three frogs resting, impressed date marks for 1882, 37.6cm. diam. (Christie's) $500 £345

One of a pair of Minton 'moon' vases with gilt loop handles, 26.5cm. high. (Lawrence Fine Art) $669 £462

MINTON

A Minton vase of classical shape on square pedestal base, impressed Minton 980 and with date code for 1864, 96.5cm. high. (Christie's)
$26,244   £19,440

A Minton double candle-snuffer, modelled as busts of a Medieval pair, the tray impressed Minton mark 427 and date code for 1865, 11cm. high. (Christie's)
$801 £594

A large Minton two-handled vase, amphora shape, impressed IA and with date code for 1859, 70cm. high. (Christie's)$11,664 £8,640

A Minton 'Amorini' fountain modelled as a pair of cherubs, impressed Minton 911 and with date code for 1868, 65cm. high. (Christie's) $5,832 £4,320

A Minton jardiniere and underdish with moulded decoration overall of rambling flowers, date code for 1858 on jardiniere, 37cm. high. (Christie's)
$2,478 £1,836

A Minton figure, 'Vintager with basket in each hand', impressed Minton. (Christie's) $874 £648

A Minton honeycomb dish modelled as a beehive, impressed Minton 1499 and date code for 1877, 18cm. high. (Christie's)
$2,916 £2,160

A Minton figural lamp stand, impressed Minton 1517 and with date code for 1881, 35.6cm. high. (Christie's)
$2,478 £1,836

A monkey 'match pot', impressed Minton 1692 and date code for 1873, 19.6cm. high. (Christie's)
$2,332 £1,728

MINTON

One of a pair of large Minton vases, the handles modelled as two writhing snakes, circa 1870, 62cm. high. (Christie's)
$5,103 £3,780

One of a pair of Minton flared rectangular spill vases with gilt fixed ring handles, circa 1880, 29cm. wide. (Christie's) $2,021 £1,404

A large amphora-shaped Minton vase on stand, impressed Minton and date code for 1866, 91cm. high. (Christie's) $1,749 £1,296

A Minton jardiniere and stand, designed by Albert Carrier de Belleuse, impressed Minton 990 and date code for 1882, 168cm. high. (Christie's)
$34,992   £25,920

A Minton 'Christmas Jug', the handle modelled as entwined holly branches, impressed Minton 580 (circa 1870), 22.5cm. high. (Christie's)
$1,166 £864

A Minton 'Perforated Garden Pedestal', impressed Minton 451 and date code for 1865, 80.5cm. high. (Christie's)
$729 £540

A Minton lidded 'Tower Jug', impressed Minton 1231 and date code for 1869, 34.5cm. high. (Christie's) $232 £172

A Minton figural group, 'Shell Carriers', impressed Minton 1296 and date code for 1862, 28cm. high. (Christie's)
$947 £702

A Minton 'Palissy' vase formed as a ewer, impressed Minton 900 and date code for 1872, 37cm. high. (Christie's) $437 £324

MINTON

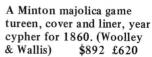

A Minton teapot modelled as a Chinaman holding a mask from which the spout projects, circa 1875, 14.4cm. high. (Christie's) $729 £540

A Minton majolica jardiniere embossed with foxgloves and ferns, 1ft.7in. wide over the handles, 13in. high, date marked for 1871. (Hobbs & Chambers) $876 £600

A Minton majolica game tureen, cover and liner, year cypher for 1860. (Woolley & Wallis) $892 £620

A large Minton 'moon flask' vase with two lug handles, circa 1890, 43.2cm. high. (Christie's) $551 £378

A pair of Minton full figure Toby jugs, impressed Minton 1104 and 1140 and with date stamps for 1867, restored, 28cm. and 28.4cm. high. (Christie's) $947 £702

A Minton figure, 'Seahorse with Shell', after Carrier-Belleuse, impressed Minton 326 and with date code for 1872, 41.5cm. high. (Christie's) $1,895 £1,404

A Minton blue-ground Wellington vase with gilt rams' mask handles, painted in the manner of Steel, circa 1835, 38cm. high. (Christie's) $616 £400

A Minton Parian group of a nude female figure seated on the back of a lion, circa 1847-48, 1ft.3½in. high. (Hobbs & Chambers) $73 £50

One of a pair of Minton 'Persian' pattern pottery vases decorated in the style of C. Dresser, 11in. high. (Christie's) $567 £420

MOORCROFT

A Moorcroft bowl with plated mount of squat bulbous form, 18.5cm. diam. (Lawrence Fine Art) $176 £121

A Moorcroft broad baluster pottery vase made for Liberty & Co., 8in. high. (Christie's) $594 £450

A Moorcroft squat shaped vase in the toadstool pattern, 7¾in. wide. (Christie's) $588 £400

A William Moorcroft grape pattern vase of ovoid form, 16in. high. (Capes, Dunn & Co.) $316 £220

A Moorcroft circular pottery dish painted in the Leaf and Berry pattern, 11½in. diam. (Christie's) $114 £85

One of a pair of Moorcroft Dawn pattern vases of ovoid form, 18.5cm. high. (Lawrence Fine Art) $610 £418

A Moorcroft globular pottery vase modelled with a swimming fish, outlined in blue on a pale green ground, 6½in. high. (Christie's) $189 £140

A Moorcroft Macintyre two-handled vase, design no. 360574, signed in green W. Moorcroft, 19cm. high. (Lawrence Fine Art) $449 £308

A Moorcroft pottery oviform vase made for Liberty & Co., in the Toadstool pattern, 10in. high, signed in green. (Christie's) $1,029 £715

NANTGARW

CHINA

A Nantgarw plate, London decorated with a branch and loose mulberries, 24.2cm. diam. (Lawrence Fine Art) $491 £330

A Nantgarw topographical plate, named in red script on the reverse, circa 1820, 21.5cm. diam. (Christie's) $1,686 £1,188

A Nantgarw plate, London decorated with a bouquet of flowers, 23.4cm. diam. (Lawrence Fine Art) $753 £506

ORIENTAL

Mid 19th century Oriental plate. (British Antique Exporters) $17 £13

A Safavid tile panel with a figure of Sagittarius surrounded by palmettes, 4ft. 1in. x 2ft.10in. (Christie's) $14,877 £10,260

One of a pair of earthenware bowls and covers of compressed circular shape, 7in. diam. (Lawrence Fine Art) $382 £264

PARIAN

A coloured Parian group modelled as a young girl on rockwork, entitled 'You can't read', 12¼in. high, possibly by Robinson & Leadbetter. (Christie's) $222 £150

A Parian standing female figure, probably Belleek but unmarked, 36.5cm. high. (Lawrence Fine Art) $159 £110

One of a pair of glazed Parian figure brackets, allegorical figures in rock-like niches, 9½in. high. (Capes, Dunn & Co.) $163 £110

PARIS

A Paris (Nast) ornithological part tea and coffee service, circa 1810.
(Christie's) $9,968 £7,020

A Paris matt blue ground part coffee service, circa 1815. (Christie's)
$766 £540

A Paris (Nast) ornithological part dessert service, circa 1810. (Christie's)
$10,735 £7,560

PILKINGTON

A Pilkington Lancastrian tall baluster vase with moulded strapwork at the neck decorated by Richard Joyce in bronze and ruby lustre, date code for 1908, 41.9cm. high. (Christie's) $315 £216

A Pilkington Lancastrian deep bowl designed by Walter Crane and decorated by Wm. S. Mycock, date code for 1913, 21.6cm. high.(Christie's) $1,261 £864

A Pilkington Lancastrian baluster vase decorated by Wm. S. Mycock in golden lustre, date code for 1910, 21.8cm. high. (Christie's) $598 £410

PRATTWARE

A Prattware pot lid depicting Strathfieldsay, 5in. diam. (Christie's) $71 £55

A large Prattware two-handled loving cup, bearing the Jolly Topers, malachite ground, gold line decoration. (Phillips) $661 £450

A Prattware pot lid depicting Wellington seated, 5in. diam. (Christie's) $117 £90

REDWARE

A 19th century Redware deep platter, with squiggle decoration, 17½in. long. (Robt. W. Skinner Inc.) $1,100 £774

A 19th century Redware covered jar, Gonic pottery, New Hampshire, 11½in. high. (Robt. W. Skinner Inc.) $550 £387

One of two 19th century Redware shallow circular dishes with crimped rims, 12¼in. diam. (Robt. W. Skinner Inc.)$350 £246

LUCIE RIE

A stoneware 'knitted' bowl, by Lucie Rie, inlaid and speckled with copper manganese, circa 1981, 25.2cm. diam. (Christie's)
$1,879 £1,206

A porcelain sgraffito and inlaid bottle by Lucie Rie, circa 1980, 21.4cm. high. (Christie's)
$1,008 £700

A stoneware bowl by Lucie Rie, covered in a shiny white glaze peppered with russet, circa 1956, 30.1cm. diam. (Christie's)
$1,331 £918

A porcelain sgraffito bottle covered in a bronze manganese glaze with sgraffito lines, by Lucie Rie, circa 1980, 25.3cm. high. (Christie's) $1,324 £920

A stoneware teapot and cover by Lucie Rie, covered in a matt manganese glaze, circa 1958, 15cm. high. (Christie's) $469 £324

A stoneware oviform bottle with wide scooped rim, by Lucie Rie, circa 1975, 27.9cm. high. (Christie's)
$1,368 £950

A stoneware bowl covered in a white glaze thickening to droplets, by Lucie Rie, circa 1960, 16.8cm. wide. (Christie's) $359 £248

A porcelain mallet shaped bottle, covered in a mottled pastel green glaze with pale coral spiral, by Lucie Rie, circa 1967, 29.8cm. high. (Christie's) $4,698 £3,240

A porcelain wide bowl covered in pastel green glaze, heightened with amber and coral, by Lucie Rie, circa 1967, 32.9cm. diam. (Christie's)
$6,890 £4,752

ROOKWOOD

A Rookwood pottery iris glaze vase, signed by F. D.H. Rothenbush, circa 1904, 9in. high. (Robt. W. Skinner Inc.) $300 £208

A Rookwood pottery vase with sterling silver overlay, circa 1899, signed by J. Zettel, 8½in. high. (Robt. W. Skinner Inc.)
$2,300 £1,597

A Rookwood pottery iris glaze vase, initialled by Olga G. Reed, circa 1902, 7¼in. high. (Robt. W. Skinner Inc.) $381 £264

A Rookwood pottery Indian squaw portrait vase, circa 1899, 11in. high. (Robt. W. Skinner Inc.) $650 £451

A Rookwood pottery standard glaze vase, initialled by Clara C. Linderman, 1904, 8¾in. high. (Robt. W. Skinner Inc.) $324 £225

A Rookwood standard glaze pottery Indian portrait vase, decorated by Grace Young, date cypher for 1905, 30.5cm. high. (Christie's) $4,620 £3,000

ROYAL DUX

Large Royal Dux group with camel and Bedouin seated on its back, 19¾in. high. (Reeds Rains) $835 £580

An Art Nouveau Royal Dux figural vase modelled as a tree trunk with a maiden climbing around the side, 46cm. high. (Phillips) $364 £270

A Royal Dux Art Nouveau conch shell group with three water nymphs in relief, 17½in. high. (Reeds Rains)
$676 £470

RUSKIN

A Ruskin high-fired transmutation glazed vase, 1911, 38cm. high. (Christie's) $594 £410

A Ruskin flambe vase, mallet-shaped with blue and red speckled glaze, 1909, 17.4cm. high. (Christie's) $236 £162

A large Ruskin high fired transmutation glaze vase and matching circular stepped stand, England, circa 1930, 36cm. high including stand. (Christie's) $346 £237

A Ruskin high fired shaped cylindrical vase, 1925, 23.6cm. high. (Christie's) $600 £400

A large Ruskin low-fired crystalline glaze vase of swollen cylindrical shape, England, 1926, 41.5cm. high. (Christie's) $283 £194

A Ruskin high fired transmutation glaze vase, England, 1933, 21cm. high. (Christie's) $283 £194

SATSUMA

A 19th century Satsuma broad oviform jar and domed cover with knob finial, signed Kintozan, 48cm. high. (Christie's) $660 £486

Pair of Japanese Satsuma pottery vases, 5in. high. (Hobbs & Chambers) $67 £45

A 19th century large Satsuma vase, Japan, signed on base, 15¼in. high. (Robt. W. Skinner Inc.) $1,000 £729

A Satsuma pottery cylindrical box, the cover painted and gilded with geishas, 3in. diam. (Reeds Rains) $288 £200

Late 19th century Satsuma model of a recumbent caparisoned elephant, signed, 25cm. long. (Christie's) $1,389 £972

A Satsuma pottery pot pourri bowl on three feet in the form of grotesque heads, 8½in. diam. (Capes, Dunn & Co.) $136 £95

A Satsuma oviform vase enamelled in black, red and green and gilt, 12in. high. (Christie's) $2,175 £1,500

A pair of Satsuma pottery vases, 9¼in. high, on carved wood bases. (Reeds Rains) $460 £320

Late 19th century Satsuma oviform vase decorated in colours and gilt, 62cm. high. (Christie's) $1,853 £1,296

A Satsuma miniature teapot, signed on base, 4in. high. (Reeds Rains) $460 £320

A 19th century Satsuma broad oviform jar on shallow tripod feet, 25cm. high. (Christie's) $2,496 £1,836

A 19th century large Satsuma oviform vase, signed Satsuma Tansai above an iron-red Shimazu mon, 50.2cm. high. (Christie's) $1,175 £864

CHINA

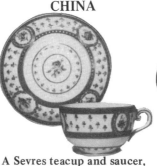

A Sevres pattern gilt bronze oval two-handled jardiniere, circa 1860, 44.5cm. wide. (Christie's) $1,380 £972

A Sevres teacup and saucer, blue interlaced L marks, enclosing the date letters ii for 1786 and painter's mark of J. Fontaine. (Christie's) $355 £237

A Sevres green ground deep bowl, blue interlaced L marks enclosing the date letter q for 1769, and painter's mark of Nicquet, 23.5cm. diam. (Christie's) $1,533 £1,080

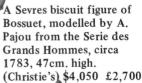

A large Sevres pattern royal-blue ground gilt bronze mounted two-handled vase, circa 1880, 90cm. high. (Christie's) $3,220 £2,268

A Sevres tete-a-tete service with Wittelsbach borders, blue interlaced L marks and HY, circa 1763, the tray 30cm. wide. (Christie's) $5,670 £3,780

A Sevres biscuit figure of Bossuet, modelled by A. Pajou from the Serie des Grands Hommes, circa 1783, 47cm. high. (Christie's) $4,050 £2,700

A Sevres Art Deco porcelain figure of a lady in evening dress designed by Odartchenko, 28cm. high. (Christie's) $548 £378

A Sevres ornithological cushion-shaped dish, blue interlaced L marks enclosing the date letter q for 1769 and painter's mark of Castel, 22cm. wide. (Christie's) $891 £594

A Sevres pattern pink ground gilt metal mounted tapering oviform two-handled vase and cover, late 19th century, 43.5cm. high. (Christie's) $460 £324

SEVRES

A Sevres porcelain shallow dish, 8½in. diam., the reverse with date mark for 1772, initials for Nicquet. (Hobbs & Chambers) $248 £170

A Sevres white biscuit group of Le Valet de Chien modelled by Blondeau after Oudry, circa 1776, 30.5cm. long.(Christie's) $1,749 £1,296

A Sevres bleu nouveau baluster milk jug, blue interlaced L mark enclosing the date letter q for 1769, and painter's mark B, 12cm. high. (Christie's)$613 £432

A Sevres-pattern porcelain and ormolu mounted mantel clock, imitation interlaced L and initial marks, circa 1880, 61.5cm. high. (Christie's) $3,732 £2,592

A pair of large documentary Sevres seaux a bouteille with gilt-edged shell and scroll handles, blue interlaced L marks and with incised marks 7, nu and C 6, 18.5cm. high. (Christie's) $20,412 £15,120

A Sevres bust of Napoleon as First Consul, dated 1802, 29cm. high. (Christie's) $1,093 £810

A Sevres ornithological circular sugar bowl and cover, blue interlaced L marks enclosing the date letter U for 1773 and painter's mark of Evans, 11.5cm. high. (Christie's) $766 £540

A pair of Sevres-pattern bleuceleste ground ormolu mounted baluster vases, circa 1860, 60cm. high. (Christie's) $3,110 £2,160

A Sevres ecuelle cover and stand, the stand with date letter K for 1763 and the ecuelle with small q for 1769, 20cm. diam. (Christie's) $2,624 £1,944

SEVRES

A Sevres bleu lapis two-handled seau a bouteille, blue interlaced L mark enclosing the date letter F for 1758 and with painter's mark of Jean Pierre Le Doux, 19cm. high. (Christie's) $13,122 £9,720

A Sevres biscuit group of The Judgement of Paris, circa 1781, 41cm. high. (Christie's) $1,895 £1,404

One of a pair of Sevres two-handled tureens and covers, incised marks, circa 1765. (Christie's) $1,993 £1,404

A Sevres bleu nouveau cylindrical cup and saucer, blue interlaced L marks, and painter's mark C.D. and incised 40, circa 1780. (Christie's) $613 £432

A pair of Sevres-pattern square bottles and stoppers decorated with portraits of Louis XIV and Me. de Lamballe, circa 1880, 15.5cm. high. (Christie's) $1,555 £1,080

A Sevres bleu nouveau cylindrical coffee cup and saucer, blue interlaced L marks enclosing the date letters EE for 1782. (Christie's) $766 £540

A Sevres soup plate from the Madame du Barry Service, blue interlaced L marks enclosing the date letter S for 1771, and painter's mark of Bulidon, 24cm. diam. (Christie's) $1,993 £1,404

A pair of Sevres-pattern turquoise ground gilt metal mounted vases and covers, circa 1860, 55cm. high. (Christie's) $3,732 £2,592

One of forty-four 18th century Sevres shaped circular plates, 25cm. diam. (Christie's) $3,207 £2,376

SEVRES

A Sevres circular sugar bowl and a cover painted en camaieu rose, circa 1765, 10cm. high. (Christie's) $420 £280

A Sevres bleu celeste cylindrical cup and saucer, blue interlaced L marks, the saucer with the date letter F for 1758. (Christie's) $324 £216

A Sevres bleu nouveau circular sugar bowl and cover, circa 1795, 12.5cm. high. (Christie's) $324 £216

One of a pair of late 19th century Sevres pattern metal mounted turquoise gound oviform vases, 84cm. high. (Christie's) $8,434 £5,940

A Sevres apple-green cup and saucer, blue interlaced L marks enclosing the date letter F for 1758, and painter's mark of Buteux aine. (Christie's) $1,686 £1,188

A Sevres biscuit standing figure of Marechal de Turenne modelled by A. Pajou from the Serie des Grands Hommes, circa 1783, 48cm. high. (Christie's) $4,860 £3,240

One of a pair of Sevres plates, blue interlaced L marks enclosing the date letters CC for 1780, 24cm. diam. (Christie's) $324 £216

A Sevres circular sugar bowl and cover, blue interlaced L marks enclosing the date letter S for 1771, 12cm. high. (Christie's) $517 £345

A jewelled Sevres cylindrical cup and saucer, gilt interlaced L marks and painter's marks LG of Le Guay, circa 1783. (Christie's) $12,150 £8,100

A Shelley bone china 'Tea for Two' service of eight pieces, Eric Slater's 'Mode' shape in orange and black enamels. (Capes, Dunn & Co.) $172 £120

A Shelley part tea service, comprising an octagonal milk jug, sugar bowl, sandwich plate, six side plates and six cups and saucers, registered no. 723404. (Lawrence Fine Art) $146 £100

A Shelley 'Mode' shape part teaset, comprising a milk jug, sugar bowl, six cups and saucers, six side plates and one sandwich plate, registered no. 756533. (Lawrence Fine Art) $321 £220

A Northern Celadon conical bowl moulded with two ladies reclining amongst clouds, Song Dynasty, 16.5cm. diam., fitted box. (Christie's) $9,525 £6,480

A Jun Yao globular jar with two looped straight handles, Song Dynasty, 15cm. diam. (Christie's) $2,381 £1,620

A Ding Yao lobed hexafoil dish, clear ivory glaze thinning towards the unglazed rim, Song Dynasty, 17.8cm. diam. (Christie's) $1,587 £1,080

A Cizhou painted pillow moulded from two parts as a lady recumbent, Song Dynasty, 33cm. wide. (Christie's) $12,117 £9,180,

A Northern Celadon bowl carved and combed with a continuous leaf scroll, Song Dynasty, 22cm. diam., fitted box. (Christie's) $2,540 £1,728

A Ding type stem bowl, ivory white glaze, Northern Song Dynasty, 8.9cm. diam. (Christie's) $1,031 £702

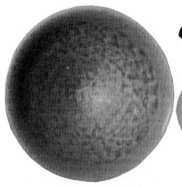  

A Northern Celadon conical bowl, Song Dynasty, 11.4cm. diam. (Christie's) $2,381 £1,620

A Jun Yao tripod censer under a rich lavender glaze thinning to an olive translucency at the rim, Song Dynasty, 6.5cm. diam. (Christie's) $1,428 £972

A large Northern Celadon bowl freely carved with a deer amongst scrolling foliage, Song Dynasty, 21cm. diam., fitted box. (Christie's) $5,556 £3,780

Part of a twenty-eight piece Spode tea service, painted with the 'Brocade' pattern, after Worcester. (Phillips) $1,361 £920

One of a pair of Spode urn-shaped pot pourri vases, pierced weights and covers, circa 1820, 13.5cm. high. (Christie's) $1,220 £918

Part of a thirty-four piece Spode tea service, painted with a Japan pattern of flowers and foliage, no. 2213. (Phillips) $1,036 £700

Part of a twenty piece Spode pottery dessert service, printed in brown with vases decorated with groups of classical figures on a marbled ground with fruiting vine, with yellow rims. (Lawrence Fine Art) $1,606 £1,078

A Spode pot pourri jar, cover and inner lid, with gilt loop handles, 23cm. high, marked Spode 2063 in red. (Lawrence Fine Art) $255 £176

Six Spode 'Old Concord' design coffee cups and saucers, date impressed for 1952. (Capes, Dunn & Co.) $72 £50

A Spode tulip cup with green stalk handle, script mark in red, circa 1820, 7cm. high. (Christie's) $766 £540

STAFFORDSHIRE

A Staffordshire soup tureen and undertray, by R. Hall, circa 1825, 12in. high. (Robt. W. Skinner Inc.) $950 £641

A Staffordshire saltglaze sauceboat with strap handle on three mask and paw feet, circa 1750, 20cm. wide. (Christie's) $1,292 £972

A Staffordshire jug depicting Wellington at Salamanca, 5½in. high. (Christie's) $117 £90

A Staffordshire pearlware box and cover modelled as a dog, the screw cover with the initials ET, circa 1815, 5cm. wide. (Christie's) $1,840 £1,296

A pair of Staffordshire pugilist figures modelled as the boxers Mollineux and Cribb, circa 1810, 22cm. high. (Christie's) $2,729 £2,052

An Obadiah Sherratt group of Polito's menagerie, circa 1830, 29.5cm. high. (Christie's) $21,546 £16,200

A Staffordshire salt-glazed stoneware cylindrical mug, circa 1750, 6in. high. (Capes, Dunn & Co.) $136 £95

One of a pair of late 18th century Staffordshire pottery cow creamers, 6¼in. long. (Dacre, Son & Hartley) $2,304 £1,600

A Staffordshire Toby jug of conventional type, seated holding a frothing jug of ale, circa 1780, 24.5cm. high. (Christie's) $613 £432

A Staffordshire slipware inscribed and dated two-handled loving cup, circa 1763, 17.5cm. high. (Christie's)$2,298 £1,728

A Staffordshire saltglaze tartan ground Royalist teapot and cover with loop handle, circa 1750, 14cm. high. (Christie's) $15,336 £10,800

A Staffordshire blue and white mug with moulded decoration depicting soldiers with trophies from Vittoria greeting Wellington, 5in. high. (Christie's) $78 £60

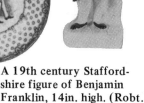

A Staffordshire full length standing figure of Wellington, 13in. high.(Christie's) $91 £70

A Staffordshire part tea-service printed in grey mono-chrome with bust and other portraits of Wellington. (Christie's) $364 £280

A 19th century Stafford-shire figure of Benjamin Franklin, 14in. high. (Robt. W. Skinner Inc.)$300 £211

A Staffordshire blue and white cylindrical mug prin-ted with equestrian figures of The Duke of Wellington and Lord Hill, 4¾in. high. (Christie's) $260 £200

A Staffordshire brown and white part glazed Parian jug with portraits of Wel-lington and Blucher, inscribed Jane Roberte, 7½in. high. (Christie's) $247 £190

A Staffordshire jug printed and coloured with an eques-trian portrait of the Duke of Wellington. (Christie's) $221 £170

STAFFORDSHIRE

A creamware model of a recumbent sheep, with brown markings, on oval shaped base, circa 1780, 3¼in. high. (Christie's) $193 £130

A pottery sauceboat in the form of a duck, circa 1785, 6½in. wide, perhaps Yorkshire. (Christie's) $819 £550

An early 19th century Staffordshire soup tureen with high domed cover, 12in. high. (Robt. W. Skinner Inc.) $900 £608

Part of a Staffordshire dinner service of ninety-two pieces, decorated in red, blue and yellow in Chinese style with vases and utensils in octagonal panels. (Lawrence Fine Art) $2,552 £1,760

A money box modelled as a chapel, inscribed Salley Harper Hougate March 16th 1845, 6¾in. high. (Christie's) $652 £450

A figure of George Parr, holding a cricket ball in his right hand, circa 1865, 14in. high. (Christie's) $819 £550

A pastille burner modelled as a cottage, on oval gilt lined base, 6in. high. (Christie's) $261 £180

CHINA

A creamware model of a recumbent sheep, facing to the right, 3¼in. high. (Christie's) $283 £190

A pair of rabbits with black markings, recumbent facing right and left, eating lettuce leaves, 5in. high. (Christie's) $2,900 £2,000

A blue Staffordshire sauce-boat, ladle and tray, by J. Stubbs, 1822-35, 6½in. high. (Christie's) $1,320 £963

A figure of a huntsman, holding a hunting horn in his right hand, circa 1795, 9¼in. high. (Christie's) $253 £170

A pair of well modelled spaniels with brown markings, wearing gilt collars, 10¼in. high. (Christie's) $1,740 £1,200

A figure of The Tichborne Claimant, holding a bird on his left hand, a rifle at his side, 14in. high. (Christie's) $406 £280

A figure of Peace, modelled as a woman wearing loose robes, the emblems of War at her side, circa 1810, 8¼in. high. (Christie's) $126 £85

A pair of spill vases modelled as horses with foals recumbent at their feet, 12½in. high. (Christie's) $348 £240

A white and gilt figure of Henry Joy McCracken, wearing a short coat, breeches and stockings, 13in. high. (Christie's) $232 £160

STAFFORDSHIRE

A group modelled as Hercules wrestling with a bull, circa 1810, 5½in. high. (Christie's) $1,266 £850

A well modelled group of a lion with a recumbent lamb at its feet, circa 1850, 7in. high. (Christie's) $417 £280

A pastille burner modelled as a cottage with an iron-red doorway flanked by flowers and trees, on an oval shaped base, 6in. high. (Christie's) $377 £260

A figure of Theobald Wolfe Tone holding two flags across his chest, the oval base named in gilt script, 13½in. high. (Christie's) $435 £300

A pair of figures of the Prince of Wales and Prince Alfred, circa 1858, 10¾in. high. (Christie's) $387 £260

A figure of Wellington standing, wearing full military uniform and full length cloak, on raised pink lustre marbled base, 13in. high. (Christie's) $261 £180

A group of Napoleon III and Empress Eugenie, the oval base named in gilt moulded capitals, circa 1854, 12in. high. (Christie's) $238 £160

An Obadiah Sherratt group, entitled 'Grecian and Daughter', 9in. high. (Christie's) $942 £650

A group of Victoria standing with her arm around The Princess Royal, circa 1842, 10in. high. (Christie's) $141 £95

STONEWARE

A salt-glazed stoneware two-gallon butter churn, circa 1840, probably New York, 13½in. high. (Christie's) $572 £417

A handbuilt stoneware bird bowl by Albert Diato, circa 1955, 36.3cm. wide. (Christie's) $500 £345

A handbuilt stoneware spout pot by Elizabeth Fritsch, circa 1974, 30.4cm. high. (Christie's) $5,324 £3,672

A stoneware press moulded rectangular bottle, by Kanjiro Kawai, covered in greyish-white glaze with khaki rims, circa 1952, 21.9cm. high. (Christie's) $1,096 £756

A slab built stoneware platter by Jacqueline Poncelet with cut rim, circa 1981, 47.9cm. wide. (Christie's) $469 £324

An early handbuilt vase by Elizabeth Fritsch, circa 1970, 12.6cm. high. (Christie's) $1,879 £1,296

A stoneware cylindrical vase by John Ward, circa 1983, 16.6cm. high. (Christie's) $171 £118

A stoneware tall flattened bottle by Joanna Constantinidis, covered in a semi-matt dark iron brown glaze, 1969, 43cm. high. (Christie's) $562 £388

A Nottingham type glazed red stoneware posset pot, dated 1791, 9½in. high. (Christie's) $1,650 £1,145

STONEWARE

A Westerwald grey stoneware spirit barrel, 33.5cm. high. (Christie's) $1,093 £810

A porcelain landscape plate textured and decorated with muslin and leaf indentation, by Ljerka Njers, 27.5cm. diam. (Christie's)$316 £220

A stoneware bowl with rounded sides, by Katharine Pleydell-Bouverie, circa 1930, 18.5cm. diam. (Christie's) $1,008 £700

A Bottger polished brown stoneware baluster coffee pot and domed cover, circa 1715, 17.5cm. high. (Christie's)$13,851 £10,260

Pair of tall salt-glazed stoneware vases, coloured grey-green with blue and ochre details, initials of Bessie Newbury, circa 1912-18, 12in. high. (Capes, Dunn & Co.) $79 £55

A 17th century Westerwald large oviform jug, 36cm. high. (Christie's) $874 £648

A large stoneware oviform vase by Margaret Rey, impressed seal, circa 1930, 30.2cm. high. (Christie's) $160 £110

A stoneware tall vase of oval rectangular section, by Joanna Constantinidis, 1971, 66.5cm. high. (Christie's) $547 £380

A Nottingham stoneware carved mug with grooved loop handle, circa 1700, 10.5cm. high. (Christie's) $1,220 £918

STONEWARE

A porcelain flask form vase by Wm. Marshall, circa 1983, 26.2cm. high. (Christie's) $403 £280

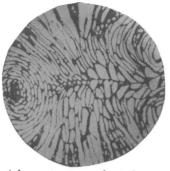

A large stoneware footed circular dish, incised James Tower 84 and with paper label inscribed James Tower No. 167 Reflections, 54.4cm. diam. (Christie's) $576 £400

A stoneware large grain jar and cover with two crescent shaped handles, by Audu Mugu Sokoto, circa 1960, 60.3cm. high. (Christie's) $403 £280

A large moulded stoneware vase of swelling rectangular section, incised James Tower 84, 54.3cm. high. (Christie's) $720 £500

Pair of inverted baluster form salt-glazed stoneware vases, initials of Florence E. Barlow, circa 1902-5, 10½in. high. (Capes, Dunn & Co.) $302 £210

An English brown glazed stoneware wall mask, modelled as Comedy, 24in. high. (Christie's) $172 £120

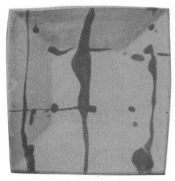

A stoneware press moulded rectangular dish by Wm. Marshall, impressed and incised WM, incised date 83, 31cm. wide. (Christie's) $72 £50

A Tapio Wirkkala stoneware vase of speckled stone colour, circa 1955, 15cm. high. (Christie's) $315 £216

A stoneware water pot by Ladi Kwali, made at Abuja, circa 1960, 29cm. high. (Christie's) $288 £200

A red pottery figure of a
mounted attendant, Tang
Dynasty, 31.5cm. high.
(Christie's) $1,746 £1,188

A blue splashed straw glazed
buff pottery bowl, Tang
Dynasty, 9.8cm. diam.
(Christie's) $1,349 £918

A painted red pottery figure
of a court lady, Tang Dynasty, 44.5cm. high.
(Christie's) $92,080 £62,640

A Sancai buff pottery figure
of a court attendant, Tang
Dynasty, 100.5cm. high.
(Christie's)
$38,102 £25,920

A phosphatic splashed brown
glazed oviform jar with two
strap handles, Tang Dynasty,
18cm. high. (Christie's)
$2,540 £1,728

An unglazed buff pottery
figure of a Western Asiatic
with curly hair, Tang
Dynasty, 26cm. high.
(Christie's) $2,063 £1,404

A red pottery figure of a
mounted lady attendant,
Tang Dynasty, 29.5cm. high.
(Christie's) $1,190 £810

A red pottery figure of a
standing camel, Tang Dynasty,
38cm. high. (Christie's)
$1,746 £1,188

An unglazed buff pottery
figure of a seated lady
musician, Tang Dynasty,
19.5cm. high.(Christie's)
$1,905 £1,296

TANG

An unglazed buff pottery figure of a court lady, Tang Dynasty, 10in. high. (Lawrence Fine Art)
$877 £605

A straw-glazed buff pottery figure of a standing ox, Tang Dynasty, 22cm. wide. (Christie's) $7,128 £5,400

An unglazed buff pottery figure of a court attendant, Tang Dynasty, 70cm. high. (Christie's) $1,568 £1,188

A Sancai pottery figure of a caparisoned horse, Tang Dynasty, 77cm. high. (Christie's)
$349,272 £237,600

A blue glazed tripod cylindrical jar standing on lion's paw feet, Tang Dynasty, 18cm. diam., with fitted box. (Christie's)
$20,638 £14,040

A red pottery figure of a tall standing horse, Tang Dynasty, 43.5cm. high. (Christie's)$4,127 £2,808

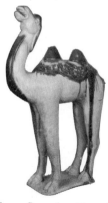

A large Sancai pottery figure of a standing Bactrian camel, Tang Dynasty, 65cm. high. (Christie's) $28,512 £21,600

A straw and ochre glazed standing pottery figure of a groom, Tang Dynasty, 29cm. high. (Christie's)
$1,587 £1,080

A straw-glazed buff pottery figure of a standing horse, Sui/early Tang Dynasty, 31.5cm. high. (Christie's)
$5,132 £3,888

TERRACOTTA

CHINA

A French terracotta bust of an 18th century lady with dressed hair, 16in. high. (Christie's) $2,505 £1,728

A pair of Regency painted terracotta figures modelled as Chinese ladies, 8½in. and 8in. high. (Christie's) $366 £280

A French terracotta bust of an 18th century boy, 18in. high. (Christie's) $3,288 £2,268

TOURNAI

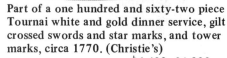

A Tournai spirally moulded, blue and white part coffee service, circa 1770. (Christie's) $567 £378

Part of a one hundred and sixty-two piece Tournai white and gold dinner service, gilt crossed swords and star marks, and tower marks, circa 1770. (Christie's) $6,480 £4,320

A Tournai ornithological oviform jar and cover from the Duc d'Orleans service, circa 1787, 18.5cm. high. (Christie's) $1,539 £1,026

One of seven Tournai shaped circular plates painted with sprays of fruit and flowers, circa 1770, 24cm. diam. (Christie's) $972 £648

One of a pair of Tournai two-handled seaux a glace covers and liners with moulded Ozier borders, circa 1770, 25cm. wide. (Christie's) $355 £237

VIENNA

A Vienna Du Paquier candle sconce or girandole, circa 1730, 39.5cm. high. (Christie's) $6,000 £4,000

A 19th century pair of Vienna vases and covers, 31.5cm. high, shield mark in underglaze blue. (Lawrence Fine Art)
$797 £550

A Du Paquier Vienna 'Schwarzlot' plate from the service made for Count Trivulzio of Milan, 21cm. diam. (Phillips)
$1,184 £800

A Vienna white figure of St. Paul, blue beehive mark, circa 1760, 47cm. high. (Christie's) $1,321 £918

A 'Vienna' gold-ground tete-a-tete, decorated with scénes from classical mythology, circa 1880, the tray 32.5cm. wide. (Christie's)
$1,710 £1,188

One of a pair of Vienna tea-cups and saucers painted in purple monochrome, blue beehive marks Pressnummer 5, circa 1750. (Christie's)
$590 £410

CHARLES VYSE

A Charles Vyse figure of a Shire horse, on rectangular base, 28.5cm. high. (Christie's) $423 £300

A Charles Vyse figure of a ribbon seller on a square plinth, circa 1925, 30.5cm. high, including plinth. (Christie's) $946 £648

A Charles Vyse pottery fig-ure of The Piccadilly Rose Woman, modelled as a plump lady, 10in. high. (Christie's) $742 £550

CHINA

A Wedgwood blue jasper dip cylindrical coffee cup and deep saucer, impressed mark. (Christie's) $444 £300

A Wedgwood Fairyland lustre circular footed bowl, printed Portland Vase mark and pattern no. Z5360/2, circa 1925, 23.5cm. diam. (Christie's) $718 £540

A Wedgwood 'Chintz' cream-ware teapot and cover of globular shape with baluster finial, 13cm. high. (Phillips) $1,386 £900

A Wedgwood black basalt bust of George II, circa 1790, 22.5cm. high. (Christie's) $1,150 £810

A pair of Wedgwood bronzed black basalt triton candlesticks of conventional type, impressed marks, circa 1880, 27cm. high. (Christie's) $996 £702

A Wedgwood & Bentley black basalt miniature bust of Aristophanes, circa 1775, 11cm. high. (Christie's) $1,993 £1,404

A 19th century Wedgwood blue and white jasper vase, 12in. high. (Christie's) $735 £500

A Wedgwood blue and white jasper plaque, portrait of Dr. Priestley, attributed to Hackwood, 10 x 8cm. (Lawrence Fine Art) $111 £77

A Wedgwood terracotta bust of Locke, impressed mark and inscribed on the reverse, circa 1785, 21.5cm. high. (Christie's)$287 £216

WEDGWOOD

A Wedgwood Whieldon pine-apple teapot and cover, 10cm. high. (Phillips)
$1,386 £900

A Wedgwood Fairyland lustre octagonal bowl, printed Portland Vase mark in gold and pattern no. Z4968T, circa 1925, 16cm. wide. (Christie's)
$1,149 £864

A Wedgwood creamware globular teapot and cover, painted in the manner of David Rhodes, circa 1768, 15cm. high. (Christie's)
$2,913 £2,052

A Wedgwood blue and white jasper portrait medallion of William Pitt The Younger, circa 1790, 9.5cm. high. (Christie's) $574 £432

A pair of Wedgwood black basalt griffin candlesticks, circa 1795, 34cm. high. (Christie's) $1,840 £1,296

A Wedgwood Fairyland lustre circular bowl, the exterior painted with birds in flight on a green ground, 11in. diam. (Christie's) $521 £350

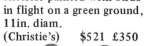

A black basalt tea kettle and cover, circa 1800, 23.5cm. high, (base cracked, rim to cover repaired). (Christie's)
$359 £270

A Wedgwood blue and white jasper oval plaque, portrait of J. Philip Elers, the potter, modelled by Wm. Hackwood, 10.7 x 7.4cm. (Lawrence Fine Art) $159 £110

A blue and white jasper two-handled oviform vase on black basalt base, probably Adams, circa 1800, 28cm. high. (Christie's)
$430 £324

WEDGWOOD

Part of a black basalt tea-service, comprising a teapot, milk jug, sugar bowl and slop basin, circa 1800.(Christie's) $344 £259

A Wedgwood Fairyland lustre octagonal bowl, the exterior decorated with panels of river scenes, 10¼in. wide. (Christie's) $1,160 £800

A Wedgwood creamware teapot and cover with flower finial, 11cm. high. (Phillips) $693 £450

One of a pair of Wedgwood & Bentley black basalt oviform ewers, circa 1775, 31cm. high. (Christie's) $996 £702

A pair of Wedgwood and Bentley black basalt oval portrait plaques of Vespasian and Nero, circa 1777, 20cm. high. (Christie's) $2,585 £1,944

One of a pair of Wedgwood three-colour jasper urn-shaped vases and covers, circa 1860, 33cm. high. (Christie's) $2,441 £1,836

A Wedgwood vase designed by Keith Murray, 16.5cm. high. (Christie's) $121 £86

A Wedgwood charger, the cobalt blue ground with raised polychrome decoration, 38.5cm. diam. (Christie's) $1,166 £864

A Wedgwood blue and white jasper bulb pot and cover, impressed mark and V, circa 1785, 24cm. high.(Christie's) $1,840 £1,296

WEDGWOOD

A Wedgwood black basalt Egyptian inkstand, impressed mark, circa 1810, 29.5cm. wide. (Christie's) $3,160 £2,376

A Wedgwood Whieldon cauliflower teapot and cover, 11.5cm. high. (Phillips) $924 £600

A Wedgwood three-colour jasper figure of a reclining child modelled by Wm. Hackwood after the Della Robbia original, circa 1785, 14.3cm. long. (Christie's) $15,336 £10,800

A Wedgwood pot pourri vase and pierced cover, the central area painted by H. Beardmore, signed, 34.5cm. high. (Phillips) $462 £300

Part of a Wedgwood coffee set, designed by Keith Murray, all with printed marks. (Christie's) $184 £120

A Wedgwood comport, oval base surmounted by a stem modelled as dolphins supporting a conch shell, date code for 1884, 42.5cm. high. (Christie's) $1,166 £864

A Wedgwood & Bentley black basalt hare's head stirrup cup, circa 1775, 16cm. high. (Christie's) $13,035 £9,180

A Wedgwood blue and white jasper plaque, portrait of T. Bentley, 11.5 x 8.5cm. (Lawrence Fine Art) $350 £242

A Wedgwood & Bentley black basalt compressed globular vase and cover, circa 1775, 16.5cm. high. (Christie's) $1,150 £810

WHIELDON

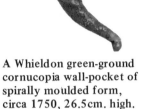

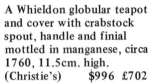

A Whieldon cow creamer and cover, 15cm. long. (Phillips) $3,108 £2,100

A Whieldon green-ground cornucopia wall-pocket of spirally moulded form, circa 1750, 26.5cm. high. (Christie's) $1,303 £918

A Whieldon globular teapot and cover with crabstock spout, handle and finial mottled in manganese, circa 1760, 11.5cm. high. (Christie's) $996 £702

WOOD

A Ralph Wood Bacchus mask jug, circa 1775, 23.5cm. high.(Christie's) $545 £410

An Enoch Wood model of a stag, circa 1800, 29cm. high. (Christie's) $2,441 £1,836

A Ralph Wood group of the Vicar and Moses of conventional type, circa 1770, 21.5cm. high. (Christie's) $643 £453

A Ralph Wood model of a polar bear wearing a collar, 9.5cm. wide. (Christie's) $1,150 £810

A Ralph Wood Toby jug of conventional type, circa 1770, 25cm. high. (Christie's) $888 £626

An Enoch Wood model of a lion, circa 1790, 29cm. wide. (Christie's) $790 £504

One of a pair of First Period Worcester circular butter tubs, covers and stands, 10.7cm. wide, square seal marks in underglaze blue. (Lawrence Fine Art)
$2,552   £1,760

A pair of Royal Worcester figures modelled as a lady and gentleman, 14in. high, circa 1887. (Christie's)
$1,480 £1,000

An oval Royal Worcester plaque, painted by John Stinton, signed, 16 x 24.5cm., printed mark in puce, 1906. (Lawrence Fine Art) $1,515 £1,045

One of a pair of First Period Worcester blue scale oviform vases and covers, 16cm. high, square seal marks in underglaze blue. (Lawrence Fine Art) $2,631 £1,815

A First Period Worcester apple-green teacup and saucer, crossed swords mark and 9 in underglaze blue. (Lawrence Fine Art)
$574 £396

A Hadley's Worcester lobed pear shaped jug with lion mask terminal and leaf moulded handle, 9in. high. (Christie's) $444 £300

A Royal Worcester pot pourri vase and pierced cover, with angular scroll handles, 24cm. high, printed mark in puce. (Lawrence Fine Art)
$701 £484

Pair of Royal Worcester vases and covers in Sevres style, signed J. Rushton, date letter for 1870, 39cm. high. (Lawrence Fine Art)
$3,030 £2,090

A Royal Worcester figure of Karan Singh, the trinket maker, 13cm. high, from the Indian Craftsman Series, shape 1204, 1884. (Lawrence Fine Art) $542 £374

CHINA

A Worcester yellow ground honeycomb moulded oval dish, circa 1770, 30.5cm. wide. (Christie's)
$7,668 £5,400

One of a pair of Royal Worcester vases painted by Stinton, signed, 6in. high. (Reeds Rains) $503 £340

A Worcester blue and white faceted oval creamboat painted with the Root Pattern, circa 1758, 10cm. wide. (Christie's)
$1,456 £1,026

A Worcester pink scale soup plate painted in the atelier of James Giles, circa 1770, 22.5cm. diam. (Christie's)
$2,760 £1,944

A Worcester blue and white baluster coffee pot and cover painted with an early version of the Plantation Pattern, circa 1754, 17cm. high. (Christie's) $1,456 £1,026

A Worcester yellow scale saucer dish painted with exotic birds and insects, circa 1765, 18.5cm. diam. (Christie's) $5,520 £3,888

A Worcester baluster mug with the monogram GG, circa 1770, 9cm. high. (Christie's) $1,380 £972

A Worcester plate painted in the atelier of James Giles in puce camaieu, circa 1770, 22.5cm. diam. (Christie's) $2,607 £1,836

A Worcester blue scale small jug with exotic birds among shrubs and trees, blue square seal mark, circa 1770, 9cm. high. (Christie's)
$1,533 £1,080

WORCESTER

A Worcester blue and white chamber candlestick with scroll handle, blue W mark, circa 1770, 14.5cm. wide. (Christie's) $2,872 £2,160

A Royal Worcester aesthetic teapot and cover, modelled as the upper part of a body, 15.5cm. high. (Christie's) $1,073 £756

A Worcester oval sauceboat of small size, circa 1754, 16.5cm. wide. (Christie's) $1,364 £1,026

A Worcester plate painted in the atelier of James Giles, circa 1770, 22.5cm. diam. (Christie's) $843 £594

A Royal Worcester three-light candelabrum, by J. Hadley, 19in. high. (Reeds Rains) $1,302 £880

A Worcester blue scale plate painted in the atelier of James Giles, circa 1770, 21cm. diam. (Christie's) $460 £324

A Worcester Imari pattern armorial mug, blue square seal mark, circa 1770, 9cm. high. (Christie's) $1,150 £810

A Worcester blue and white baluster cream jug painted with the Peony Pattern, circa 1758, 7.5cm. high. (Christie's) $428 £302

A Worcester blue and white small flared mug, painted with the Tambourine Pattern, circa 1756, 6cm. high. (Christie's) $766 £540

WORCESTER

One of a pair of Royal Worcester 'ivory' two-handled vases, pattern no. 1169, circa 1885, 30.5cm. high. (Christie's) $1,321 £918

A Chamberlain's Worcester rectangular two-handled tray, painted with Buckingham Palace, circa 1840, 33.5cm. wide. (Christie's)
$1,710 £1,188

A Royal Worcester 'ivory' mermaid and nautilus centrepiece, decorated by Callowhill, circa 1878. (Christie's)
$1,399 £972

A Worcester, Flight & Barr blue ground spill vase, circa 1805, 12cm. high. (Christie's) $544 £378

A Worcester blue and white foliage moulded dish, circa 1765, 27cm. wide. (Christie's) $1,149 £864

A Worcester, Flight & Barr, canary-yellow ground flared flower pot with fixed gilt ring handles, circa 1805, 16cm. high. (Christie's)
$2,021 £1,404

A Royal Worcester reticulated globular vase in the manner of George Owen, inscribed January 4th 1895, 11cm. high. (Christie's) $652 £453

A Royal Worcester bone china demi-tasse coffee set, with R.W. mark for 1923, and London import mark for 1908. (Capes, Dunn & Co.) $151 £105

A Chamberlain's Worcester globular vase and cover with gilt shell handles, painted by H. Chamberlain, circa 1810, 25cm. high. (Christie's)
$1,088 £756

WORCESTER

A Royal Worcester reticulated oviform vase by George Owen, pattern no. 1969, gilt marks and date code for 1912, 17cm. high. (Christie's) $2,799 £1,944

A Worcester quatrefoil two-handled chestnut basket, pierced cover and stand, circa 1770, the stand 25.5cm. wide. (Christie's)
$5,745 £4,320

A Worcester quatrefoil baluster vase painted in Kakiemon palette, circa 1758, 16cm. high. (Christie's)
$10,773 £8,100

A Worcester three-tier centrepiece on a pierced shell and coral encrusted base, circa 1770, 25.5cm. high. (Christie's) $1,867 £1,404

A pair of Royal Worcester glazed Parian figures of Paul and Virginia, circa 1865, 33cm. high. (Christie's) $684 £475

A Worcester flared wine funnel painted in a famille verte palette with an Oriental holding a fan, circa 1755, 13.5cm. high. (Christie's)
$17,236 £12,960

A Worcester, Flight & Barr, goblet, script mark and incised B, circa 1805, 12cm. high. (Christie's)
$1,399 £972

A Worcester plate of Grubbe type painted in the atelier of James Giles, circa 1770, 23cm. diam. (Christie's)
$4,021 £3,024

Part of a Chamberlain's Worcester apricot ground garniture, comprising a vase of urn shape and two beaker vases, circa 1805, 28cm. and 15.5cm. high. (Christie's)
$622 £432

WORCESTER

A Royal Worcester vase and cover with scroll handles, 40.5cm. high, printed mark in green, 1897. (Lawrence Fine Art) $877 £605

A Worcester fluted lozenge shaped dish painted in the Imari palette, circa 1770, 31.5cm. wide. (Christie's) $1,303 £918

One of a pair of Royal Worcester vases painted by Harry Stinton, signed, 12¾in. high. (Reeds Rains) $1,332 £900

A Royal Worcester standing figure of a lady, the base inscribed L'Allegro, 41.5cm. high. (Lawrence Fine Art) $478 £330

Part of a Worcester twenty-piece Imari pattern dessert service, Flight, Barr & Barr, 1807-40. (Robt. W. Skinner Inc.) $1,700 £1,240

A large Royal Worcester vase painted by J. Stinton, signed, 17½in. high. (Reeds Rains) $1,184 £800

A Royal Worcester vase and cover, painted by C. H. C. Baldwyn, signed, 43cm. high, printed mark in green, 1899. (Lawrence Fine Art) $2,312 £1,595

A pair of Worcester vases, painted by E. Raby, signed, 23.5cm. high, printed mark in puce. (Lawrence Fine Art) $557 £374

A Royal Worcester figure of Nazir Hassan, 20cm. high, from the Indian Craftsman Series, shape 1226, 1890. (Lawrence Fine Art) $574 £396

WORCESTER

A Royal Worcester figure of Bakshiran, the old potter, 19cm. high, from the Indian Craftsman Series, shape 1186, 1891. (Lawrence Fine Art) $462 £319

A Worcester blue-scale globular teapot and cover, blue square seal mark, circa 1770, 14.5cm. high. (Christie's) $766 £540

A Royal Worcester vase and cover by Grainger & Co., painted by J. Stinton, 36cm. high, printed shield mark in green. (Lawrence Fine Art) $988 £681

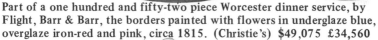

Part of a one hundred and fifty-two piece Worcester dinner service, by Flight, Barr & Barr, the borders painted with flowers in underglaze blue, overglaze iron-red and pink, circa 1815. (Christie's) $49,075 £34,560

A Royal Worcester vase and cover by George Owen, 26.5cm. high, with printed mark in gold. (Lawrence Fine Art) $2,552 £1,760

A Royal Worcester standing figure of Munnasall, in shaded ivory, painted in soft colours and gilt, 20.5cm. high, 1890. (Lawrence Fine Art) $510 £352

A First Period Worcester apple-green teapoy and cover with floral knop, 16.5cm. high. (Lawrence Fine Art) $1,116 £770

BRACKET CLOCKS

A George III ebonised musical bracket clock, dial signed Robt. Ramsey London, 24in. high. (Christie's)
$5,443   £3,780

A Charles II ebonised striking bracket clock, the square dial signed Hen. Jones London, 16in. high. (Christie's)
$4,600 £3,240

A George I ebonised striking bracket clock, the dial signed Ed. Bayley London, 19in. high. (Christie's)
$1,840 £1,296

An ebony veneered quarter repeating bracket clock, the dials signed Henry Fish, Royal Exchange London, 17½in. high. (Lawrence Fine Art) $4,232 £2,860

A mahogany veneered bracket clock, signed in the arch Richd. Ward, Winchester, 18½in. high. (Lawrence Fine Art) $2,523 £1,705

Late 18th century Austrian petite sonnerie bracket clock with carrying handle, 18½in. high. (Christie's)
$660 £455

A red walnut quarter repeating bracket clock, signed on the chapter ring Asselin, London, 19in. high.
(Lawrence Fine Art)
$1,383 £935

A George II ebonised grand sonnerie bracket clock, the dial signed Thos. Hughes, London, 9¾in. high.
(Christie's) $7,938 £5,400

A mid Georgian mahogany or red walnut striking bracket clock with brass handle, 19in. high. (Christie's)
$1,686 £1,188

BRACKET CLOCKS

A Chinese carved hardwood bracket clock on stand, the movement with twin chain fusees, 22½in. high. (Christie's) $1,399 £972

A James II ebonised Roman striking bracket clock of Phase III Type, signed Joseph Knibb, 12in. high. (Christie's) $16,869 £11,880

A George III mahogany striking bracket clock with brass handle, dial signed John Taylor London, 19½in. high. (Christie's) $1,944 £1,350

A George III mahogany striking bracket clock with brass handle, signed Benj. Ward London, 18½in. high. (Christie's) $3,987 £2,808

A George III ebonised bracket clock, the 7in. dial signed Alexdr. Cumming, London, 18½in. high. (Bermondsey) $1,400 £925

A George III ebonised striking bracket clock, the dial signed George Flashman London, 14in. high. (Christie's) $1,226 £964

A George III mahogany or red walnut striking bracket clock, the plaque signed Yeldrae Notron London 1053, 18in. high. (Christie's) $1,840 £1,296

A George III ebonised bracket clock, signed Eardley Norton, London, 19½in. high. (Christie's) $2,200 £1,518

A George II brown japanned bracket clock, dial signed Jn. Cotton London, 16¼in. high. (Christie's) $1,399 £972

BRACKET CLOCKS

An early George III ebonised striking bracket clock, the dial signed Robt. & Peter Higgs, London, 17½in. high. (Christie's)
$11,113 £7,560

A Regency boulle bracket clock, the dial signed Balthazar a Paris, with later movement, 39½in. high. (Christie's) $2,332 £1,620

A George III scarlet and gold japanned bracket clock, made for the Turkish market, the dial signed Wm. Dunant, London, 22½in. high. (Christie's)
$10,713 £8,640

A Regency boulle bracket clock, the dial signed Paliand a Besancon, 39½in. high. (Christie's)
$1,866 £1,296

A Regency period mahogany and brass bracket clock, dial signed Thomas Pace, London, 19in. high. (Reeds Rains)$1,053 £940

A French 18th century gilt brass mounted and inlaid rosewood bracket clock, signed Jean Tolly a Paris, 36in. high. (Lawrence Fine Art) $1,546 £1,045

A George II ebonised striking bracket clock, plaque signed Willm Morgan London, 21½in. high. (Christie's)
$1,380 £972

A George III satinwood 'balloon' bracket clock, the enamel dial signed Webster London, 24in. high. (Christie's) $6,220 £4,320

A mid-Georgian ebonised striking bracket clock, the dial signed John Fladgate London, 18½in. high. (Christie's) $2,021 £1,404

CARRIAGE CLOCKS

A brass grande sonnerie striking carriage clock, gorge case, stamp of Drocourt, 6in. high. (Christie's) $1,933 £1,404

Victorian carriage clock with cloisonne panels, 1860. (British Antique Exporters) $249 £185

A lacquered brass striking carriage clock, the movement with lever platform, 6½in. high. (Christie's) $714 £486

A brass one-piece striking carriage clock by Paul Garnier Hger. De La Marine A Paris, 6¼in. high. (Christie's) $1,840 £1,296

A silver gilt and enamel miniature 'carriage clock', 1¾in. high. (Christie's) $1,226 £864

An English chronometer carriage timepiece, by Dent, London, with mahogany carrying case, 8½in. high. (Lawrence Fine Art) $10,582 £7,150

A gilt brass striking carriage clock, stamp of Henri Jacot, 5½in. high. (Christie's) $920 £626

A satinwood four glass striking carriage clock, the dial signed Arnold & Dent London No 408, 8¾in. high. (Christie's) $4,976 £3,456

A French carriage clock with morocco travelling case and key, by F. A. Margaine, Paris, 6in. high. (Capes, Dunn & Co.) $568 £400

CARRIAGE CLOCKS

A French brass carriage timepiece with cylinder movement, in a plain pillared case, 6in. high. (Phillips) $352 £240

A 19th century French ormolu carriage clock, the lever movement striking on a gong with push repeat and alarm, 8½in. high. (Phillips) $1,012 £750

A 19th century French brass carriage clock, the lever movement with petite sonnerie, the dial signed for Dent London, 7in. high. (Phillips) $1,215 £900

A 19th century French brass carriage clock, signed on the backplate Bolviller A Paris, 7in. high.(Phillips) $764 £520

A gold mounted tortoiseshell miniature carriage timepiece, maker's mark CD, 1906, 9.5cm. high. (Lawrence Fine Art) $1,307 £902

Lacquered brass petite sonnerie small sized carriage clock with split bimetallic balance to silvered lever platform, 4¼in. high. (Christie's) $1,206 £810

A 19th century French gilt brass carriage clock, the lever movement striking on a bell with alarm, 6¼in. high. (Phillips) $323 £220

A silver and shagreen miniature travelling timepiece, the enamel dial signed W. Thornhill & Co., Paris, 3in. high. (Phillips) $367 £250

A 19th century French brass carriage clock, the lever movement with quarter striking on two gongs, 7in. high. (Phillips) $486 £360

CARRIAGE CLOCKS

A 19th century French gilt brass carriage clock, the backplate bearing the Drocourt trademark, 6½in. high. (Phillips)
$1,282 £950

A brass quarter striking carriage clock signed 7669 Leroy & Fils Palais Royal 13-15 Paris, 5¼in. high. (Christie's) $1,045 £702

An Austrian brass grande sonnerie carriage clock with calendar, 5½in. high. (Christie's) $2,413 £1,620

A French brass carriage clock, the lever movement striking on a gong, 4¾in. high. (Phillips) $220 £150

A 19th century French brass carriage clock, the lever movement striking on a gong with alarm and push repeat, 7½in. high. (Phillips) $1,911 £1,300

A 19th century French gilt brass carriage clock, signed on the back plate E. Dent, Paris, 944, 5½in. high. (Phillips) $2,719 £1,850

A 19th century French gilt brass carriage clock, bearing the Jacot trademark on the backplate, 6¾in. high. (Phillips) $1,146 £780

A gilt metal early multipiece carriage clock signed Leroy a Paris on backplate, 5in. high. (Christie's) $514 £345

Late 19th century French brass repeating alarm carriage clock, the dial signed E. Caldwell & Co., Philadelphia, 7½in. high. (Reeds Rains)
$1,154 £780

275

CLOCK SETS

A Sevres pattern pink-ground porcelain and gilt bronze composite garniture-du-cheminee, circa 1880, the clock 34cm. wide, the vases 26.5cm. high. (Christie's) $1,150 £810

A 19th century French ormolu clock garniture, 1ft.1½in. high, together with matching pair of two branch candelabra. (Phillips)
$1,470 £1,000

19th century Meissen blue and white clock set by Lund & Blockley, 39in. high. (Bermondsey) $1,300 £950

A pale Royal rouge marble and ormolu three-piece clock set, the lidded urn holding the clock, with two four-branch, four light candelabra, all 34in. high. (Andrew Grant) $8,928 £6,200

A 19th century French ormolu and porcelain clock garniture, the enamel dial signed Lenoir a Paris, 1ft.8½in. high, together with a matching pair of three branch candelabra. (Phillips)
$2,793 £1,900

A white marble and gilt metal three-piece clock set, by J. Marti & Cie., the clock 23in. high, the urns 17in. high.(Andrew Grant) $1,368 £950

CLOCK SETS

A 19th century French silver plated three-piece clock garniture, the striking movement by S. Marti & Cie, 16in. high, together with two five-light candelabra, 19in. high. (Parsons, Welch & Cowell) $670 £450

A Second Empire ormolu and green marble clock set on the theme of the Oath of the Horatii, the side pieces formed as ewers. (Christie's) $6,434 £4,377

19th century Sevres porcelain garniture de cheminee, by S. Wartenberg, Paris. (Bermondsey) $2,400 £1,800

An Empire ormolu mounted bronzed mantel clock with a seated figure of Ceres, and a pair of urn-shaped cassolettes, 41cm. high. (Christie's) $2,619 £1,782

A 19th century French ormolu clock garniture, the clock contained in a drum, 2ft.9in. high, together with matching pair of seven branch candelabra, 2ft.10in. high. (Phillips) $2,430 £1,800

A French ormolu and porcelain mounted three-piece clock garniture, the clock 13in. high, the side pieces 13¾in. high. (Parsons, Welch & Cowell) $465 £310

LONGCASE CLOCKS

Country Chippendale walnut tall case clock, by A. Hutchins, circa 1800, 86in. high. (Robt. W. Skinner Inc.) $3,200 £2,162

Federal mahogany inlaid tall case clock, circa 1790, 98in. high. (Robt. W. Skinner Inc.) $3,500 £2,430

A George II mahogany Yorkshire longcase clock, by Thos. Crofts, Halton, 94in. high. (Reeds Rains) $3,552 £2,400

A Federal mahogany tall case clock, inscribed O. Hopkins, 1756, 95in. high. (Christie's) $605 £441

A George III mahogany longcase clock, signed G. Forster, Sittingbourne, 7ft. 5in. high. (Phillips) $2,646 £1,800

A Queen Anne longcase clock movement with five ringed pillars; the dial signed Samuel Stevens London, 6ft. 8in. high. (Christie's) $4,762 £3,240

A Federal cherrywood tallcase clock, dial signed by Christian Winters, circa 1800, 97in. high. (Christie's) $4,400 £2,972

A Georgian mahogany longcase clock, signed on a cartouche John Hart, Yarmouth, 7ft.6in. high. (Phillips) $2,700 £2,000

LONGCASE CLOCKS

A Federal inlaid mahogany tallcase clock, dial signed Alex. J. Willard, early 19th century, 86¾in. high. (Christie's) $3,520 £2,378

A George II green japanned chiming longcase clock, the dial signed John Taylor London, 8ft. 3in. high.(Christie's) $3,810 £2,592

A Chippendale mahogany tallcase clock, dial signed by Joseph and John Hollingshead, circa 1780, 98in. high. (Christie's) $12,100 £8,174

A walnut longcase clock, signed W. Donald, Glasgow, 7ft.1½in. high. (Lawrence Fine Art) $1,302 £880

Late 18th century oak and brown oak banded eight-day longcase clock, the dial signed R. Street. (Peter Wilson & Co.) $936 £650

Federal inlaid mahogany tall clock, by E. Embree, circa 1790, 94½in. high. (Robt. W. Skinner Inc.) $14,000 £9,722

A mahogany cased three-weight Westminster chime grandfather clock, circa 1900.(British Antique Exporters) $760 £563

A Federal cherrywood tallcase clock, dial signed by Samuel Shourds, circa 1770, 89¼in. high. (Christie's) $2,420 £1,634

LONGCASE CLOCKS

An oak longcase
clock, signed J.
Green, Nantwich,
7ft. high.
(Lawrence Fine
Art)
  $1,546 £1,045

A Federal cherry
inlaid dwarf time-
piece, Mass., circa
1810, 43in. high.
(Robt. W. Skinner
Inc.) $3,250 £2,256

A George III maho-
gany eight-day strik-
ing longcase clock,
7ft.10in. high.
(Woolley & Wallis)
    $1,450 £980

A Regency mahogany
longcase regulator,
the 12in. dial signed
Grimalde London,
6ft.1in. high.
(Christie's)
    $9,208 £6,264

A Federal cherry-
wood tall case
clock, circa 1810-
30. (Christie's)
  $2,200 £1,527

A 19th century maho-
gany longcase clock,
the dial signed Brysons,
Edinburgh, 6ft.6in.
high. (Phillips)
      $1,176 £800

A Federal inlaid
mahogany tallcase
clock, dial signed
by Aaron Willard,
1805-10, 88½in.
high. (Christie's)
    $24,200 £16,349

A Queen Anne walnut
longcase clock, the
dial signed Jn. Motley
London, 7ft.1in. high.
(Christie's)
    $2,540 £1,728

LONGCASE CLOCKS

A week-going walnut longcase clock, the 12in. square dial signed at the base Geo. Graham, London, 7ft. 8½in. high. (Christie's) $43,545 £30,240

A late 17th century walnut longcase clock, by Daniel Quare, London, 6ft.8in. high. (Phillips) $16,170 £11,000

An early 18th century walnut quarter chiming longcase clock, by Claude Du Chesne, London, 8ft.1in. high. (Phillips) $12,495 £8,500

A late 18th century Irish eight-day, striking, mahogany longcase clock, 7ft.3in. high. (Woolley & Wallis) $1,324 £920

A late 17th century longcase clock, by R. Seignior, London, 6ft.8in. high. (Phillips) $5,586 £3,800

An early 18th century walnut and floral marquetry longcase clock, signed Cartwright, 7ft.2in. high. (Phillips) $7,938 £5,400

A Federal inlaid mahogany tallcase clock, dial signed by Aaron Willard, circa 1805-10, 94½in. high. (Christie's) $15,400 £10,404

Cherry tall case clock, by Jacob Hosteter, 94½in. high. (Robt. W. Skinner Inc.) $1,700 £1,148

LONGCASE CLOCKS

An 18th century
walnut longcase
clock, by Wind-
mills, London,
7ft.7in. high.
(Andrew Grant)
$1,224 £850

Early 19th century
painted pine tall
case clock by A.
Edwards, Mass.,
91in. high. (Robt.
W. Skinner Inc.)
$850 £582

A mahogany long-
case clock by
Nathaniel Brown,
Manchester, 95½in.
high. (Reeds Rains)
$3,816 £2,650

A Queen Anne green
japanned longcase
clock, dial signed
Markwick, London,
7ft.11in. high.
(Christie's)
$3,810 £2,592

A Federal cherry in-
laid tall case clock,
by J. Loring, Mass.,
circa 1800, 87in.
high. (Robt. W.
Skinner Inc.)
$6,250 £4,280

A 19th century burr
walnut and mahogany
longcase clock, maker's
name John Elliott,
London, 7ft.6in. high.
(Andrew Grant)
$3,024 £2,100

A mid Georgian
ormolu mounted
walnut clock by
Jno. Melling, Chester,
88½in. high.
(Christie's)
$12,117 £9,180

An 18th century
mahogany longcase
clock, maker John
Berry, London, 7ft.
high. (Andrew
Grant)
$3,168 £2,200

LONGCASE CLOCKS

A scarlet lacquer longcase clock, signed Micha. Shields, Aldgate, 96in. high. (Christie's) $3,520 £2,428

A George I green japanned longcase clock, signed Newman Cartwright, 105in. high. (Christie's) $4,687 £3,780

An ormolu mounted amaranth and tulipwood longcase regulator clock, dial signed Le Roy a Paris, 88in. high. (Christie's) $7,413 £5,616

A George III eight-day longcase clock by Wm. Carpenier, 7ft.10in. high. (Edgar Horn) $4,307 £2,950

A Federal cherry-wood inlaid tall-case clock, 1800/ 10, 93½in. high. (Christie's) $3,300 £2,275

A William III walnut and marquetry long-case clock, the 11in. dial signed Asselin London, 6ft.11in. high. (Christie's) $7,776 £5,400

A Federal eagle-inlaid mahogany tallcase clock, works signed by Effingham Embree, N.Y., 1790/95, 101in. high. (Christie's) $27,500 £18,965

A late Stuart Provincial burr walnut long-case clock, dial signed Tho. Power, 6ft. 6in. high. (Christie's) $4,762 £3,240

LONGCASE CLOCKS

A carved walnut musical clock with ten Symphonion metal discs, 7ft.5in. high. (Andrew Grant)
$6,912 £4,800

A Federal mahogany inlaid tall case clock, by Lebbeus Bailey, circa 1815, 91in. high. (Robt. W. Skinner Inc.)
$15,000 £10,416

Late 18th century oak and crossbanded longcase clock, by D. Collier, Gatley, 80in. high. (Reeds Rains)
$1,953 £1,320

A Dutch burr walnut musical longcase clock, signed N. Wyland, Amsterdam, mid 18th century, 113in. high. (Christie's)
$5,500 £3,795

A George III figured mahogany longcase clock with eight-day movement, by J. Lomax of Blackburn, 7ft.4in. high.(Capes, Dunn & Co.)
$1,411 £980

A Gustav Stickley oak tall case clock, circa 1902-04, 71in. high. (Robt. W. Skinner Inc.)
$7,750 £5,381

Federal walnut tall case clock, possibly Penn., circa 1820, 81in. high. (Robt. W. Skinner Inc.)
$1,800 £1,250

A 19th century style mahogany longcase clock, 8ft.4in. high. (Andrew Grant)
$5,472 £3,800

LONGCASE CLOCKS

A tallcase clock, dial signed S. Brenneiser, Penn., circa 1810. (Christie's) $5,500 £3,793

A gilt metal mounted marquetry longcase clock of Louis XV style, 90in. high. (Christie's) $3,421 £2,592

A Federal cherrywood tallcase clock, works signed by B. Willard, Mass., 87in. high. (Christie's) $7,150 £4,931

A Victorian mahogany eight-day striking longcase clock, circa 1850. (Peter Wilson & Co.) $828 £575

A Symphonion musical longcase clock with 'sublime harmony' twin comb 11.7/8in. movement, 78in. high.(Christie's) $3,828 £2,900

A George I Vernis Martin longcase clock, the 12½in. dial signed Wm. Stephens, Godalming, 7ft. high. (Christie's) $3,067 £2,160

A Victorian mahogany longcase regulator, the dial signed P. G. Dodd & Son, 6ft.3in. high. (Christie's)$2,857 £1,944

A George III dark green japanned longcase clock, dial signed Thomas A. Deptford, 7ft.6in. high. (Christie's) $2,760 £1,944

MANTEL CLOCKS

A 19th century French white marble and ormolu mounted lyre clock, 1ft.4in. high. (Phillips) $1,250 £850

An early 19th century ormolu mantel clock, 1ft.9in. high. (Phillips) $999 £680

A Federal inlaid mahogany shelf clock, by David Wood, Mass., circa 1800, 33¾in. high. (Christie's)
$55,000 £38,732

A Louis XVI white marble and ormolu mantel clock, the enamel dial inscribed A Paris, 1ft.10½in. high. (Phillips) $1,396 £950

A George III mahogany mantel timepiece, the dial signed Absolon, London, 10in. high. (Phillips)
$735 £500

A Germanic Renaissance gilt metal table clock case, the backplate signed Johannes Benner Aug., the case partly 16th/17th century, the movement 17th century, 17in. high. (Christie's) $4,773
£3,204

A Regency gilt bronze automaton mantel clock, the case in the form of a bird cage, signed Borrell, London, 1ft.7in. high. (Phillips) $8,085 £5,500

A fin de siecle 'bras en l'air' mantel clock with a gilt metal female figure against an enamel background, 17in. high. (Christie's)
$3,540 £2,376

A French 19th century ormolu mantel clock, on an oval rosewood plinth under a glass shade, 1ft.3in. high. (Phillips) $1,058 £720

MANTEL CLOCKS

A 19th century French ormolu and porcelain mounted mantel clock, the dial signed E. W. Streeter, 11in. high. (Phillips)
$793 £540

A French Louis XV style bronze and ormolu mantel clock, the enamel dial signed Thuillier A Paris, 1ft.3½in. high. (Phillips)
$2,058 £1,400

A 19th century gilt brass mantel timepiece, the enamel dial signed Ecole Horlogerie de Paris, 1ft.6½in. high. (Phillips) $955 £650

A French Louis XVI style black marble and ormolu mounted mantel clock, 1ft. 9in. high. (Phillips)
$1,396 £950

A Regency mahogany striking mantel clock, the dial signed Bateman, Great Tower Street, London, 13½in. diam.
(Christie's) $2,252 £1,512

A Louis XVI white marble and ormolu mounted mantel clock, the dial signed Hardy A Paris, 1ft.2in. high.
(Phillips) $1,250 £850

A Regency rosewood mantel timepiece, the dial signed Arnold & Dent, Strand, London, 10¼in. high.
(Phillips) $955 £650

A bronze and ormolu mantel clock of Louis XVI design with horizontal movement contained in an urn.
(Christie's) $4,276 £3,240

A mahogany mantel clock, by Breguet, 11¼in. high.
(Phillips) $6,174 £4,200

287

MANTEL CLOCKS

Victorian marble and malachite clock, 1880. (British Antique Exporters)
$108 £80

An early Victorian gilt metal carriage clock case, in the manner of T. Cole, 11½in. high. $3,373 (Christie's) £2,376

Victorian malachite and marble clock, 1860. (British Antique Exporters)
$294 £218

A French 'Rheims' cathedral clock, the movement with Brocot type suspension, 21½in. high. (Lawrence Fine Art) $1,953 £1,320

A French Empire striking clock, the movement with outside count wheel, 21in. high. (Andrew Grant)
$792 £550

A Foley 'Intarsio' earthenware clock case in the form of a miniature longcase clock, circa 1900, 33.8cm. high. (Lawrence Fine Art) $706 £484

A miniature enamel and gilt clock, Austria, the urn shape vase houses a Swiss movement, eight-day clock. (Robt. W. Skinner Inc.)
$1,776 £1,200

A Westminster chime Admiral's hat clock, circa 1900. (British Antique Exporters)
$24 £18

A lady's boudoir timepiece in the form of an ormolu mounted cut glass scent bottle, signed Jas. Watts, London, 6½in. high. (Lawrence Fine Art)
$1,139 £770

MANTEL CLOCKS

An ormolu mounted por-
phyry tripod vase clock of
Athenienne form, 20in. high.
(Christie's) $8,268 £6,264

Victorian black marble
mantel clock, 1880. (British
Antique Exporters)
$128 £95

A 19th century ormolu
mantel clock, marketed by
Bigelow Kennard & Co.,
Boston, 24in. high. (Robt.
W. Skinner Inc.)$850 £620

Orrery clock under glass
dome, Limited Edition
numbered 259.
(Worsfolds) $352 £250

An Art Deco green onyx
mantel clock with ivory figures carved after a model
by F. Preiss, 25.2cm. high.
(Christie's) $2,349 £1,620

An ebonised pendule reli-
gieuse, signed Nicolas
Brodon, Paris, circa 1680,
18in. high. (Christie's)
$4,400 £3,036

A French brass and enamel
four glass clock with singing
bird automaton, 30½in.
high. (Christie's)
$4,199 £2,916

A gilt bronze mantel clock
in the form of a pump with
white enamel face, 7¼in.
high. (Andrew Grant)
$1,160 £800

An American walnut framed
mantel clock, circa 1890.
(British Antique Exporters)
$83 £62

MANTEL CLOCKS

A mid 19th century gilt metal mantel clock in the form of a Gothic tower, 28in. high. (Andrew Grant) $936 £650

A bronze and ormolu clock, the dial signed Raingo Fres, Paris, 25in. wide.(Christie's) $2,423 £1,836

An Empire gilt metal and bronze mantel clock, the base shaped as an orange tub, 17in. high.(Christie's) $4,354 £3,024

A gilt metal calendar strut clock, the backplate stamped Thos. Cole, London, 5½in. high. (Christie's) $2,693 £1,836

A German gilt brass octagonal quarter striking table clock, the verge movement signed Christoph Forcker, Breslau, 3¾in. high. (Christie's)$3,175 £2,160

An Empire carved mahogany and veneer shelf clock, by Hotchkiss & Benedict, N.Y., circa 1825, 39in. high. (Robt. W. Skinner Inc.) $500 £347

A mid 19th century gilt metal striking mantel clock, 20½in. high. (Andrew Grant) $1,036 £720

A French red marble perpetual calendar mantel clock and barometer, 18½in. high. (Lawrence Fine Art) $1,139 £770

A Regency mahogany mantel timepiece signed Weeks Museum, Coventry St., on the enamel dial, 12in. high. (Christie's) $1,508 £1,026

290

MANTEL CLOCKS

A late Empire bronze ormolu and griotte marble mantel clock, 17½in. wide. (Christie's) $1,477 £1,026

An Empire ormolu mantel clock, the silk-suspended countwheel striking movement with enamel dial, 19in. wide. (Christie's) $2,332 £1,620

Early 17th century South German gilt metal tabernacle clock or turmuhr, 19¼in. high. (Christie's) $15,876 £10,800

A 19th century French porcelain mantel clock with eight-day striking movement, inscribed Raingo Freres, Paris, 15in. high. (Capes, Dunn & Co.) $302 £210

An ornate metal elephant clock with eight-day chiming movement, outside count wheel, 21in. high. (Andrew Grant) $864 £600

An Italian ormolu and cut glass portico mantel clock with chased dial, signed Ld Lacroix a Turin, 16½in. high. (Christie's) $1,568 £1,188

An early 19th century rosewood bracket clock by B. Lautier of Bath, 43cm. high. (Andrew Grant) $2,736 £1,900

A Louis XVI ormolu mantel clock, the dial signed Le Nepveu a Paris, 12in. wide. (Christie's) $997 £756

A Royal Presentation ormolu mounted ebony grande sonnerie spring clock by Thos. Tompion, London, No. 278, circa 1700, 28in. high. (Christie's) $365,148 £248,400

MANTEL CLOCKS

A Viennese silver, enamel and gemset desk clock on oval base with two dolphin supports, 4¼in. high. (Christie's) $777 £540

Early 18th century German gilt brass octagonal table clock, the top plate signed L. Petitot, Berlin, 4¼in. diam. (Christie's)
$4,445 £3,024

A mid 17th century South German negro automaton clock, 11½in. high. (Christie's) $5,715 £3,888

An Edwardian inlaid mahogany mantel or bracket clock, with silvered dial, 16¾in. high. (Capes, Dunn & Co.) $230 £160

A Victorian satinwood four glass mantel timepiece, dial signed Webster, Queen Victoria Street, London, 17273, 7¾in. high. (Christie's)
$2,566 £1,728

A Liberty & Co. Tudric pewter 'Architectural' mantel clock, circa 1920, 7¼in. high. (Robt. W. Skinner Inc.)
$750 £520

A Liberty pewter and enamel table clock designed by Archibald Knox, circa 1900, 14.2cm. high. (Christie's) $1,879 £1,296

A three-dimensional wood model picture clock showing a French Chateau, under glass dome, 21½in. high. (Andrew Grant)
$1,728 £1,200

An Empire carved mahogany shelf clock, by Riley Whiting, Conn., circa 1825, 29½in. high. (Robt. W. Skinner Inc.)
$250 £171

MANTEL CLOCKS

Late 19th century French champleve and ormolu desk timepiece, 8in. high. (Robt. W. Skinner Inc.)$475 £325

A mid 16th century South German gilt brass drum clock case, 2¾in. diam. (Christie's) $1,270 £864

A Meissen (Teichert) clock-case, blue Meissen mark, the movement by Lenzkirch, circa 1900, 51cm. high. (Christie's) $933 £648

A French gilt metal striking mantel clock with blue porcelain face, 28in. high. (Andrew Grant) $936 £650

A chiming and repeating dome top bracket clock, nine bells and one gong, 19½in. high. (Andrew Grant) $1,584 £1,100

A French rosewood regulateur de table, signed Breguet et Fils on the silvered dial, 25¼in. high. (Christie's)$9,350 £6,451

A South German silver fronted telleruhr, the circular movement signed Matthias Geill, on ebonised stand, 14in. high. (Christie's) $10,319 £7,020

A Regency ormolu mantel clock, the dial in drum-shaped case, 9½in. wide. (Christie's) $1,331 £918

A Liberty & Co. pewter, copper and turquoise enamel clock, marked Tudric 0150, circa 1900, 33cm. high. (Christie's) $867 £594

SKELETON CLOCKS

A 19th century English brass skeleton clock with steel chapter ring, on white marble oval base and under a glass dome, 18in. high. (Peter Wilson & Co.)$1,043 £700

15in. brass skeleton timepiece with strike and chain drive, under dome. (Worsfolds)
$326 £230

Mid Victorian brass skeleton timepiece with fretted silvered dial, 16in. high. (Bermondsey)
$450 £300

A 19th century brass skeleton clock, on an oval rosewood base, under a glass shade, 1ft. 11in. high. (Phillips)
$2,295 £1,700

A brass three-train 'Westminster Abbey' skeleton clock, striking on gong and nest of eight bells having mercury pendulum, 24in. high. (Andrew Grant)
$6,048 £4,200

A 19th century skeleton timepiece, the glass dial with visible motion work, 7½in. high. (Phillips) $702 £520

A Victorian brass chiming skeleton clock on rosewood base with replacement perspex gabled cover, 24in. high. (Christie's)
$3,701 £2,484

A Victorian brass skeleton chiming clock of York Minster type, 27½in. high overall. (Christie's) $4,827 £3,240

An English brass striking skeleton clock of York Minster type, on wood base with glass dome, 59cm. high. (Christie's)
$1,930 £1,313

294

A Federal mahogany gilt-wood and eglomise banjo clock, by Aaron Willard, 1820/25, 33¾in. high. (Christie's) $2,860 £1,972

A Louis XVI ormolu cartel clock, the enamel dial signed Charles Le Roy a Paris, 13in. high. (Christie's) $1,866 £1,296

A wall clock, by Sewill (maker to the Royal Navy), Liverpool, 40in. high. (Peter Wilson & Co.) $201 £140

A mid 19th century Bieder-meier mahogany Vienna regulator, 40½in. high. (Christie's) $7,144 £4,860

A George III eight-day wall clock, the dial inscribed Gray and Reynolds, Wimborne, 16in. high. (Woolley & Wallis) $1,872 £1,300

A mahogany Vienna regulator with satin birch line inlay to the glazed case, 19th century, 36½in. high. (Christie's) $2,853 £1,890

A Louis XVI cartel clock, the dial signed Charles Le Roy a Paris, 37in. high. (Christie's) $4,665 £3,240

Federal giltwood mahogany banjo timepiece, by Lemuel Curtis, Mass., circa 1820, 32in. high. (Robt. W. Skinner Inc.) $5,750 £3,993

A Continental striking cartel clock with white enamel face, overall length 25½in. (Andrew Grant) $892 £620

WALL CLOCKS

A massive walnut and ebonised single train weight-driven Vienna regulator, with 9.5in. enamel face. (Andrew Grant)
$2,880 £2,000

A French electrical wall regulator signed Systeme Campiche de Metz and Mees Nancy on the dial. (Christie's)
$1,226 £864

An early 19th century American mahogany cased wall clock, 30in. high. (Robt. W. Skinner Inc.) $775 £550

An early 19th century French ormolu cased wall clock with eight-day movement, 30in. high, overall. (Bermondsey)
$1,400   £1,000

A 19th century rosewood and ormolu mounted wall clock and barometer, the dial signed Aubert & Klaftenberger, London, 4ft.2in. high. (Phillips)
$4,704   £3,200

18th century German Zappler wall clock with brass and iron thirty-hour movement. (Christie's) $1,100 £750

A Continental eight-day mahogany weight driven two-train Vienna regulator, 58in. high. (Andrew Grant)
$489 £340

A Japanese gilt brass miniature lantern clock, 5¾in. high. (Christie's) $1,793 £1,188

A Federal giltwood banjo timepiece with painted dial and eight-day weight driven movement, circa 1820, 41in. high. (Robt. W. Skinner Inc.)
$1,200 £845

WALL CLOCKS

A late Biedermeier rosewood Vienna regulator stamped Crot Berlin 302 on the backplate of the weight driven movement, 39½in. high. (Christie's) $1,166 £810

An adapted George III brass mounted mahogany wall clock, the dial signed Mattw. & Willm. Dutton, London, 38in. high. (Christie's) $1,866 £1,296

A Federal mahogany and giltwood presentation banjo timepiece, Mass., circa 1820, 40in. high. (Robt. W. Skinner Inc.) $1,800 £1,232

A Federal mahogany and eglomise banjo clock, by Warren, Mass., 1815/30, 30in. high. (Christie's) $3,080 £2,124

A George III mahogany wall timepiece, the 12in. silvered dial signed Jefferys, London, 1ft.4½in. high. (Phillips) $1,764 £1,200

A Japanese pillar clock, the hood with glazed lift-up front, 19¾in. high. (Lawrence Fine Art) $846 £572

A Georgian mahogany wall timepiece, the 1ft.7in. diam. painted wood dial signed Field, Bath, 3ft.7in. high. (Phillips) $882 £600

A Federal mahogany and giltwood presentation banjo timepiece, Mass., 37in. long. (Robt. W. Skinner Inc.) $1,800 £1,232

A mid Georgian black japanned tavern or Act of Parliament clock signed Robert Allam, London, on the shaped 30in. dial, 59in. high. (Christie's) $5,827 £4,104

WATCHES

A gold quarter repeating duplex watch, the movement signed Rd. Webster, Cornhill, London, 5248, 53mm. diam. (Christie's) $949 £669

A Dutch enamel and silver pair cased verge watch with false pendulum, signed Martineau, London, 52mm. diam. (Christie's) $1,485 £1,024

A French gold and enamel pocket compass sundial, signed Armand a Paris, 50mm. diam. (Christie's) $690 £486

A chased and enamelled platinum openface watch, signed P. Philippe & Co., no. 200063, 43mm. diam. (Christie's) $1,320 £910

A French gold and enamel verge watch with wound through enamel dial, 57mm. diam. (Christie's)
$4,140   £2,916

A Swiss gold and enamel musical automaton verge watch, circa 1820, 60mm. diam. (Christie's)
$19,051 £12,960

A French quarter repeating cylinder watch, the gold cuvette signed Le Roy et fils Horogers Du Roi A Paris No. 4001, 45mm. diam. (Christie's)
$1,270 £864

A gold openface minute repeating chronograph with register, signed Touchon & Co., Geneva, 18ct. gold case, 52mm. diam. (Christie's)
$1,980 £1,366

A gold duplex watch, the full plate movement signed John Newton, London, No. 604, 54mm. diam. (Christie's) $766 £540

WATCHES

A Swiss gold openface split-second chronograph, retailed by Tiffany & Co., N.Y., 18ct. gold case, 51mm. diam. (Christie's) $1,650 £1,138

A gold and enamel reversible hunter or openface lever watch, the three-quarter plate movement signed Hamilton & Co., London, No. 35103, 41mm. diam. (Christie's) $1,042 £734

A gold pair cased watch, the full plate movement signed David Whitelaw, No. 120, and inscribed Edw Henderson, Edinburgh 1815, 55mm. diam. (Christie's) $489 £345

A French gold and enamel cylinder watch, the movement signed Breguet A Paris, 51mm. diam. (Christie's) $2,300 £1,620

A Swiss gold openface skeletonised quarter repeating verge watch with erotic automaton, circa 1820, 56mm. diam. (Christie's) $6,600 £4,554

A repousse gold pair-cased verge watch, signed J. Markham, London, no. 6828, 51mm. diam. (Christie's) $1,840 £1,296

A Swiss gold openface musical quarter repeating watch, circa 1820, 56mm. diam. (Christie's) $2,970 £2,049

A gold duplex watch, the movement signed Radford, Leeds, No. 2588, 53mm. diam. (Christie's) $1,380 £972

A multi-colour gold filled hunter cased pocket watch, signed Illinois Watch Co., fifteen jewel movement, 53mm. diam. (Christie's) $275 £189

WATCHES

A French gold and enamel
verge watch, the bridgecock
movement signed Chevalier
et Comp^e 1829, 50mm.
diam. (Christie's)
$1,150 £810

A verge watch, the movement
signed Daniel Delander,
London, 334, 55mm. diam.
(Christie's) $933 £648

A French gold and enamel
cylinder watch, the gold
cuvette signed J. A. Rossay
Palais Royal No 133 Paris,
No 2431, 40mm. diam.
(Christie's) $1,010 £702

A gold openface chrono-
graph with calendar and
moon phases, Swiss, circa
1885, 50mm. diam.
(Christie's) $1,540 £1,062

An enamelled gold cylinder
watch, signed F. delynne a
Paris, no. 206, 40mm. diam.
(Christie's) $3,680 £2,592

A silver pair cased verge
watch with automaton,
signed Sylvester, London,
no. 6788, 55mm. diam.
(Christie's) $880 £607

A small gold openface five-
minute repeating watch,
signed Fayette S. Giles,
36mm. diam. (Christie's)
$1,650 £1,138

An 18ct. gold open faced
keywind watch, the engraved
cock signed Margeret Wilson,
hallmarked 1845, 44mm.
diam. (Lawrence Fine Art)
$260 £176

A gold openface quarter
repeating watch with automaton, 18ct. gold case,
56mm. diam. (Christie's)
$2,640 £1,821

WATCHES

An 18ct. gold openface five-minute repeating watch, signed P. Philippe & Co., no. 97353, dial signed Tiffany & Co., 45mm. diam. (Christie's) $3,300 £2,277

A slim gold and enamel open faced keywind watch with Lepine calibre movement. (Lawrence Fine Art)
$1,058 £715

A French gold jump hour cylinder watch, the gold cuvette signed Leroy hger Du Roi Palais Royal No. 114 cof, No. 4780, 42mm. diam. (Christie's)
$2,332 £1,620

An 18ct. gold open faced keywind watch, signed Cooper, Colchester, hall-marked 1866, 45mm. diam. (Lawrence Fine Art)
$293 £198

An enamelled gold openface watch, signed P. Philippe & Co., nickel eighteen-jewel cal. 17-170 movement, 44mm. diam. (Christie's)
$1,430 £986

A gold quarter repeating jump hour ruby cylinder watch, inscribed Breguet No. 2097, 48mm. diam. (Christie's)
$4,445 £3,024

A Swiss gold openface quarter repeating musical watch, signed Breguet, 56mm. diam. (Christie's)
$2,640 £1,821

A gold jump seconds dual time cylinder watch, gold cuvette signed Breguet a Paris No 4275, 55mm. diam. (Christie's)
$3,110 £2,160

A gold openface quarter repeating duplex watch, signed Vulliamy, London, 18ct. gold case, 1835, 45mm. diam. (Christie's)
$1,430 £986

WATCHES

A gold hunter cased minute repeating watch, signed J. Jurgensen, Copenhagen, 18ct. gold case, 53mm. diam. (Christie's)
$6,050 £4,174

A gold hunter cased quarter repeating duplex watch, signed Courvoisier Freres, 18ct. gold case, 50mm. diam. (Christie's)
$1,100 £759

A Swiss gold hunter cased minute repeating keyless lever perpetual calendar watch, 57mm. diam. (Christie's) $14,152 £9,828

Mid 19th century Swiss three colour gold, pearl, turquoise and pink stone watch. (Robt. W. Skinner Inc.) $814 £550

A 9ct. gold combined cigarette lighter and watch by Dunhill, the base stamped Made in Switzerland, 5.3cm. high. (Lawrence Fine Art) $877 £605

An open faced keyless cylinder fob watch, the movement stamped Savoye Freres & Cie, signed on the cuvette Faucard a Dinard, 30mm. diam. (Lawrence Fine Art) $211 £143

A French gold skeletonised cylinder calendar watch, the dial plate signed Fleury A Nantes, 33mm. diam. (Christie's) $1,477 £1,026

A gold hunter cased lever watch, signed J. Jurgensen, Copenhagen, 18ct. gold case, 50mm. diam. (Christie's)
$1,430 £986

An 18ct. gold lever watch, the gold dial inscribed with twenty-four hour divisions, the case marked London 1860, 50mm. diam. (Phillips) $808 £550

WATCHES

A silver repousse pair cased striking coach clock watch, signed Johan, Georg Brodt, circa 1725, 126mm. diam. (Christie's)
$15,876 £10,800

A 19th century Austrian silver gilt, enamel and rock crystal verge watch, 68mm. across. (Phillips)
$2,940 £2,000

An 18ct. gold openface watch minute repeating on three gongs, signed P. Philippe & Co., Geneve, 48mm. diam. (Christie's) $13,200 £9,108

A 19th century French gold quarter repeating Jaquemart automaton watch, 56mm. diam. (Phillips) $5,585 £3,800

A gold pocket chronometer, the movement signed John Arnold & Son, 53mm. diam. (Christie's) $7,620 £5,184

A Swiss open faced keywind watch, stamped Stauffer, Ce. De-Fond, 38mm. diam. (Lawrence Fine Art)
$130 £88

An 18th century verge pocket watch with silver dial and case, by J. Hocker, Reading. (Capes, Dunn & Co.) $273 £190

A gold Karrusel lever watch, the movement signed John Dyson & Sons Leeds, 55mm. diam. (Christie's)
$5,080 £3,456

A 19th century Swiss three-colour gold, turquoise and pink stone watch. (Robt. W. Skinner Inc.) $703 £475

303

WRISTWATCHES

An 18ct. gold circular wrist-watch, the movement signed European Watch and Clock Co. Inc., the dial inscribed Cartier, 30mm. diam. (Phillips) $911 £620

An 18ct. gold self-winding wristwatch with perpetual calendar, signed P. Philippe & Co., Geneve, no. 1119138. (Christie's) $9,350 £6,451

A gent's gold wristwatch by Vacheron & Constantin, the signed gold dial inscribed Verga, 35mm. diam. (Phillips) $955 £650

A 14ct. gold self-winding wristwatch with centre seconds, signed Rolex Oyster Perpetual. (Christie's) $715 £476

A gold wristwatch, signed Patek Philippe & Co., Geneva, no. 1219325, with 18-jewel cal. 23-300 PM movement. (Christie's) $1,650 £1,100

An 18ct. gold self-winding calendar wristwatch with centre seconds, signed Rolex Oyster Perpetual, and a gold filled bracelet. (Christie's) $1,980 £1,320

A lady's Viennese gold wristwatch with square face, the bracelet formed from articulated rectangular plaques, total length 16.50cm. (Phillips) $710 £480

A 14ct. gold snake bracelet watch, 'Blancpain', 91gr. without movement. (Robt. W. Skinner Inc.) $1,700 £1,140

A gent's Swiss gold wristwatch by Movado, 34mm. diam. (Phillips) $1,764 £1,200

WRISTWATCHES

A lady's platinum wristwatch, set with 24 small brilliant-cut diamonds, on black silk cords. (Parsons, Welch & Cowell) $168 £120

A gold centre second wristwatch with perpetual calendar, signed Patek Philippe & Co., Geneva, no. 888001. (Christie's) $26,000 £17,333

A gold coin watch, 'Le Jour' Swiss movement, in a twenty dollar United States gold piece dated 1904. (Robt. W. Skinner Inc.) $1,400 £939

A gold wrist chronograph, signed P. Philippe & Co., Geneve, no. 868978, nickel twenty-three jewel cal. 13-130 movement. (Christie's) $7,920 £5,464

An 18ct. gold wristwatch, signed P. Philippe & Co., Geneve, nickel eighteen-jewel cal. 9'''-90 movement. (Christie's) $3,080 £2,125

A gold wristwatch with centre seconds, signed P. Philippe & Co., Geneve, nickel eighteen-jewel cal. 27-SC movement. (Christie's) $1,760 £1,214

A Concorde Watch Co. lady's watch, yellow metal set with peridots, topaz, diamonds and pearls. (Christie's) $3,132 £2,160

A Cartier gold wristwatch, rectangular face, hexagonal winder set with a sapphire. (Christie's) $8,672 £5,940

A lady's platinum and diamond wristwatch, signed P. Philippe & Co., Geneve, no. 199809. (Christie's) $1,100 £759

WRISTWATCHES

A lady's platinum wrist-
watch, signed P. Philippe &
Co., Geneve. (Christie's)
$715 £476

A Georg Jensen watch
designed by Torun Bulow-
Hube, round face with no
numerals. (Christie's)
$1,641 £1,080

A gold wristwatch and brace-
let, signed P. Philippe & Co.,
Geneve, no. 851446, 18ct.
(Christie's) $1,100 £759

A gold wristwatch, signed
P. Philippe & Co., Geneve,
nickel eighteen-jewel cal.
23-300PM movement.
(Christie's) $1,540 £1,062

A gold wristwatch, signed
Patek Philippe & Co., Geneva,
no. 794766, with 18-jewel
cal. 23-300 movement.
(Christie's) $1,980 £1,320

A gold World Time wristwatch,
signed Patek Philippe & Co.,
Geneva, no. 929572, the
leather strap with 18ct. gold
buckle. (Christie's)
$20,000 £13,333

A gentleman's 18ct. gold
wristwatch, Patek Philippe,
Geneva, with white dial.
(Robt. W. Skinner Inc.)
$1,100 £738

An 18ct. gold wristwatch,
signed P. Philippe & Co.,
Geneve, nickel eighteen-
jewel cal. 23-300 movement.
(Christie's) $2,640 £1,821

A lady's 18ct. yellow gold
wristwatch, Patek Philippe,
jewelled Swiss movement.
(Robt. W. Skinner Inc.)
$1,200 £805

WRISTWATCHES

An 18ct. gold wristwatch, signed Patek Philippe & Co., Geneva, no. 743586, with an 18ct. gold mesh bracelet. (Christie's) $1,210 £806

An 18ct. gold wristwatch, signed P. Philippe & Co., Geneve, nickel eighteen-jewel movement. (Christie's) $1,540 £1,062

A lady's rose gold wristwatch, signed Rolex, gold hands 17-jewel movement with an 18ct. gold bracelet. (Christie's) $990 £660

A gent's gold rectangular digital wristwatch, on a gold bracelet. (Phillips) $558 £380

A 14ct. gold, ruby and diamond watch, covered Swiss jewelled movement, circa 1940. (Robt. W. Skinner Inc.) $2,000 £1,342

A gold wristwatch within an 18ct. gold case, signed Audemars Piguet, with 14ct. mesh bracelet. (Christie's) $1,045 £696

An 18ct. gold wristwatch with fifteen jewel movement, signed Le Coultre Co., dated 1934. (Christie's) $1,540 £1,062

An 18ct. gold wristwatch with 21-jewel movement, signed Corum. (Christie's) $380 £253

A gentleman's 14ct. gold wristwatch, 'Le Coultre', automatic, Master Mariner, white dial and with a leather band. (Robt. W. Skinner Inc.) $150 £100

A cloisonne enamelled bowl with a design of dragons on black background, 12in. diam. (Capes, Dunn & Co.) $141 £98

A cloisonne enamel and gilt bronze censer and cover, modelled as a recumbent elephant, late Qianlong, 19.5cm. wide. (Christie's) $1,630 £1,080

A large 17th century cloisonne enamel two-handled censer, 41cm. wide. (Christie's) $2,954 £1,944

A 17th century cloisonne enamel shallow dish, the rim with cloud scrolls, 18.2cm. diam. (Christie's) $750 £500

An Ota Tameshiro slender pear-shaped cloisonne enamel vase, Meiji period, 24cm. high. and another. (Christie's) $1,184 £800

A 16th century cloisonne enamel tripod circular dish decorated on a pale-blue ground with a meander of peony and hibiscus, 19.8cm. diam. (Christie's) $1,050 £700

One of a pair of late 19th century cloisonne enamel oviform vases, with wood stands, 36cm. high. (Christie's) $1,028 £756

A cloisonne enamel and gilt bronze mounted censer and domed cover with large lotus finial, 18th century, 53cm. high. (Christie's) $4,200 £2,800

A 17th century cloisonne enamel pear-shaped vase with taotie and loose ring handles, 39cm. high. (Christie's) $855 £648

A small late 19th century cloisonne enamel vase and cover with ball finial, 11.5cm. high. (Christie's) $954 £702

A cloisonne enamel hand-warmer and pierced cover with hinged arched handle, Qianlong, 18.5cm. wide. (Christie's) $733 £486

A cloisonne enamel tripod censer and domed cover, circa 1880, 51cm. high. (Christie's) $3,283 £2,160

A large Ming cloisonne enamel deep dish, integral cloisonne enamel mark at the base centre, 50cm. diam. (Christie's) $25,401 £17,280

One of a pair of cloisonne enamelled vases, ovoid with waisted necks, 12in. high. (Capes, Dunn & Co.) $187 £130

A 16th century cloisonne enamel shallow dish, 16.3cm. diam. (Christie's) $4,800 £3,200

A tall tapering cloisonne vase decorated in coloured enamels, signed Daihei, Meiji period, 25.1cm. high. (Christie's) $647 £453

A pair of late 19th century cloisonne canted oviform vases in various coloured enamels, 31cm. high. (Christie's) $1,776 £1,200

A cloisonne enamel and gilt copper wig stand, Qianlong, 32cm. high. (Christie's) $952 £648

A cloisonne enamel and gilt bronze circular box and cover, Qianlong, 37.5cm. diam. (Christie's)
$8,268 £6,264

Late 19th century cloisonne cabinet decorated in various coloured enamels, 14.5 x 9 x 12cm. (Christie's)
$1,110 £750

A Japanese cloisonne shallow dish of octagonal form, 14in. diam. (W. H. Lane & Son) $288 £200

A large cloisonne oviform vase decorated on a royal blue ground, 25½in. high. (Christie's) $1,232 £850

Two 18th century cloisonne enamel and gilt bronze Ruyi sceptres, 31cm. long. (Christie's) $3,000 £2,000

A cloisonne enamel tapering hexagonal vase, signed Kyoto Namikawa, circa 1900, 24.5cm. high. (Christie's)
$3,231 £2,376

A cloisonne oviform vase decorated in various coloured enamels on a royal blue ground, Meiji/Taisho period, 19.5cm. high. (Christie's)
$710 £480

A rounded rectangular cloisonne enamel vase with trumpet-shaped neck, Meiji period, 44.6cm. high. (Christie's) $2,368 £1,600

A late Ming cloisonne enamel Hu-shaped vase, Wanli, 41.5cm. high. (Christie's) $1,149 £756

A late Ming cloisonne enamel tripod dish with everted rim, 16th century, 16.2cm. diam. (Christie's) $619 £410

One of a pair of cloisonne enamel vases and covers, 6in. high. (Lawrence Fine Art) $446 £308

A 16th century cloisonne enamel shallow tripod dish on three short feet, 16.5cm. diam. (Christie's) $1,125 £750

Late 19th century cloisonne enamel oviform vase with flaring neck, 61.5cm. high. (Christie's) $4,440 £3,000

A pair of 19th century cloisonne enamel and gilt bronze cockerels, 17½in. high. (Bermondsey) $2,100 £1,500

Late 19th century large cloisonne enamel hexagonal vase with flaring neck and spreading foot, 66.4cm. high. (Christie's) $4,440 £3,000

Late 19th century cloisonne lacquer on porcelain covered jar, Japan, 18in. high. (Robt. W. Skinner Inc.) $875 £638

A cloisonne enamel barrel shaped bowl on three small gilt metal lingzhi feet, 10cm. diam. (Christie's) $820 £540

An early 19th century cloisonne enamel vase with ring handles, 15¼in. high. (Bermondsey) $1,250 £850

Victorian pressed brass magazine rack, 1880. (British Antique Exporters) $32 £24

Victorian brass jardiniere, 1880. (British Antique Exporters) $48 £36

Victorian brass and oak letter rack, 1880. (British Antique Exporters) $67 £50

Victorian brass preserving pan, 1850. (British Antique Exporters) $59 £44

Victorian copper coal bin seat, circa 1880. (British Antique Exporters) $72 £54

Victorian copper kettle, circa 1850. (British Antique Exporters) $66 £49

Victorian copper firescreen with inset mirror, circa 1880. (British Antique Exporters) $43 £32

A Jean Dunand lacquered metal bowl, signed in red lacquer, circa 1925, 10cm. high. (Christie's) $1,252 £864

Late 19th century Art Nouveau style brass coal box. (British Antique Exporters) $82 £61

COPPER & BRASS

A gilt and inlaid copper cylindrical censer, six-character mark of Yun Wenming, 17th century, 11.7cm. diam. (Christie's) $1,853 £1,404

A pair of brass andirons, probably by R. Wittingham, N.Y., circa 1810, 25in. high. (Christie's) $1,430 £986

Victorian copper pan and lid, 1860. (British Antique Exporters) $70 £52

Late 19th century brass gong with hammer. (British Antique Exporters) $101 £75

A Victorian brass and wood paper rack, circa 1880. (British Antique Exporters) $24 £18

An early 20th century Arts & Crafts hammered copper umbrella stand, 25in. high. (Robt. W. Skinner Inc.) $400 £277

Mid 19th century copper electrotype model of the Vendome Column, 52in. high, the base 7¾in. square. (Christie's) $14,877 £10,260

A George III brass and steel fender of Adam style with vase finials, and a bowed fender, 48½in. wide. (Christie's) $12,117 £9,180

Victorian brass coal bucket, 1880. (British Antique Exporters) $72 £54

COPPER & BRASS

A George III brass serpentine fender of waved outline, 54in. wide.(Christie's) $1,331 £918

A brass framed ebony ultimatum brace by Robt. Marples, Sheffield, 13in. long. (Dacre, Son & Hartley) $155 £105

A Regency brass and steel fender on bun feet, 55in. wide. (Christie's) $3,057 £2,052

Pair of Victorian brass and onyx candelabra, 1875. (British Antique Exporters) $205 £152

One of a pair of brass bound mahogany jardinieres of ribbed outline, 10¼in. diam. (Christie's) $4,183 £2,808

Late 19th century mahogany and brass gong with hammer. (British Antique Exporters) $58 £43

A rosewood box plane with cast brass sole plate and steel blade by Hearnshaw Bros., 7½in. long. (Dacre, Son & Hartley) $96 £65

A Benham & Froud copper and brass kettle on wrought iron stand, designed by Dr. Christopher Dresser, 85cm. high. (Christie's) $459 £302

A pair of Federal brass andirons, 1800-10, 27in. high. (Christie's) $1,430 £993

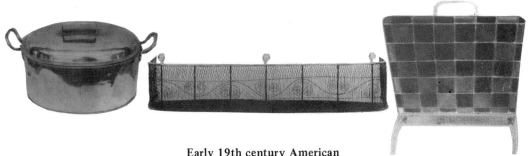

Copper fish kettle and lid, 1880. (British Antique Exporters) $93 £69

Early 19th century American brass and wire mesh fireplace fender, D-shaped, 15½in. wide. (Christie's) $825 £568

Victorian brass and leaded glass firescreen, 1880. (British Antique Exporters) $66 £49

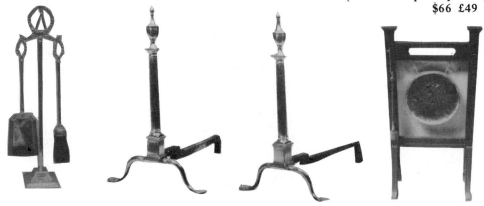

Late Victorian brass companion set, 1880. (British Antique Exporters) $29 £22

Chippendale brass andirons, the urn tops on turned tapering shafts, circa 1780, 22in. high. (Robt. W. Skinner Inc.) $1,600 £1,111

Victorian brass gong and stand, 1880. (British Antique Exporters) $81 £60

A pair of brass andirons with a shovel and poker, New York, 1800-15, 22in. high. (Christie's) $825 £573

A Siebe, Gorman & Co. brass and copper diver's helmet, English, circa 1920, 19in. high. (Lawrence Fine Art) $976 £660

A pair of Federal late 18th/early 19th century bell metal andirons, 24in. high. (Christie's) $1,320 £916

A seven-branch brass candle-stick, the design attributed to Bernhard Pankok, 29.8cm. high. (Christie's)
$2,035 £1,404

Victorian brass coal shovel. (British Antique Exporters)
$16 £12

A Georgian copper two-handled pan, circa 1800. (British Antique Exporters)
$74 £55

A Dutch brass octagonal lantern with segmented domed corona, fitted for electricity, 36in. high. (Christie's) $3,110 £2,160

Late 19th century brass coal bin with upholstered top. (British Antique Exporters) $64 £48

One of a pair of Anglo-Indian brass jardinieres on later stained oak bases, 41in. high. (Christie's)
$2,975 £2,052

Victorian brass firescreen, 1860. (British Antique Exporters) $43 £32

Large embossed brass jardiniere on claw feet. (Ball & Percival) $403 £280

Victorian brass jardiniere on paw feet, 1880. (British Antique Exporters) $55 £41

Victorian copper jardiniere, 1860. (British Antique Exporters) $51 £38

Late 19th century embossed brass ashtray. (British Antique Exporters) $16 £12

A Victorian copper kettle, 1860. (British Antique Exporters) $48 £36

Barlow's patent brass candlestick, Birmingham, England, circa 1839, 7.3/8in. high. (Robt. W. Skinner Inc.) $500 £347

A George III brass and steel basket grate, 34¼in. wide, 30½in. high. (Christie's) $7,047 £4,860

Victorian pressed brass bellows, circa 1880. (British Antique Exporters) $33 £25

A Benham & Froud brass kettle designed by Dr. C. Dresser, on three spiked feet, 24.5cm. high. (Christie's) $473 £324

A circular embossed brass double ended box, 1.7/8in. diam., with bust of Duke of Wellington on one side. (Wallis & Wallis) $29 £20

Copper milk churn with cover. (Ball & Percival) $95 £66

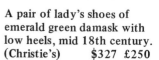

A pair of lady's shoes of emerald green damask with low heels, mid 18th century. (Christie's) $327 £250

A pair of lady's wedding shoes of ivory satin embroidered with silver thread, belonging to Margaret Gladstone, circa 1784. (Christie's) $589 £450

A child's or young lady's hat of ivory silk quilted with a scale design and trimmed with a rosette of ivory ribbons, circa 1820. (Christie's) $655 £500

A black satin bonnet trimmed with pleating, circa 1880. (Christie's) $26 £20

A pair of white kid gloves with deep cuffs of white satin embroidered in silver thread and sequins, mid 17th century. (Christie's) $3,744 £2,600

A muslin dress with an under-dress of saxe blue silk taffeta, circa 1880. (Christie's) $432 £300

A lady's glove of white kid, the deep cuff of ivory satin lined with pink silk, early 17th century. (Christie's) $366 £280

A pair of lady's high heeled shoes of ivory silk embroidered in silver thread, early 18th century. (Christie's) $628 £480

A straw bonnet with deep brim, trimmed later with satin with chine silk ribbon and artificial flowers, circa 1830. (Christie's) $340 £260

A pair of lady's flat heeled shoes of pink kid stencilled in black with a honeycomb design and bound with ivory satin, circa 1800-10. (Christie's)　　$419　£320

An apron of ivory silk embroidered in brightly coloured silks, circa 1730. (Christie's)　$379　£290

A pair of lady's high heeled shoes of black kid bound with black braid, circa 1785. (Christie's)　　　$248　£190

A lady's waistcoat of white cotton quilted in white silk and embroidered in yellow and red wools, English, circa 1730. (Christie's)　$4,032　£2,800

A pair of gloves of pale cream chamois leather, engraved under the thumb, F. Bull & Co., Jan 4th 1791, and a single glove of darker colour. (Christie's)　　　　　　　$288　£220

A boy's side fastening tunic of white pique embroidered in red cord with scrolling flowers. (Christie's)　　　　　　$201　£140

A pair of 19th century tin anniversary skates with adjustable strap at ankle and foot, 9in. long. (Robt. W. Skinner Inc.)　$550　£376

A bonnet of brown striped plaited straw trimmed with brown figured ribbons, edged with a fringe, circa 1850. (Christie's)　　　　$65　£50

A pair of lady's shoes of ivory silk brocaded with sprays of pale green and yellow flowers with kid rands and heels, circa 1750. (Christie's)　　　　　　$786　£600

A suit of rust-coloured wool with deep cuffs and wide skirts, circa 1760. (Christie's) $7,200 £5,000

A mid Victorian orange and purple flowered cream silk dress with boned bodice and slight train. (Dacre, Son & Hartley) $244 £170

An open robe of cotton printed overall with red and blue convolvulus with red stems against a grey ground, circa 1785. (Christie's) $2,882 £2,200

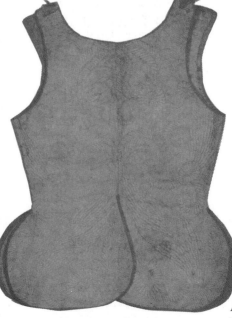

A cotton dress printed with sprigs of brown leaves, with a handkerchief front, circa 1810. (Christie's) $497 £380

A lady's waistcoat of linen finely quilted in yellow silk, English, circa 1730. (Christie's) $3,275 £2,500

A dress of pale pink silk figured with sprays of flowers, the sleeves, bodice and hem decorated with pink satin rouleaux, circa 1815. (Christie's) $547 £380

A gentleman's suit of deep blue satin, French, Lyons, circa 1770. (Christie's) $3,930 £3,000

A jacket and skirt of maroon figured silk brocaded with white stripes sprigged in pink and blue, circa 1770. (Christie's) $3,744 £2,600

A sleeved waistcoat of emerald green figured, voided silk, woven with sprays of flower heads, English, circa 1730. (Christie's) $1,179 £900

An open robe of pale yellow silk lustre, the neckline edged with 18th century Binche lace. (Christie's) $2,592 £1,800

A chasuble of bottle green velvet, the Flemish orphrey worked in gold thread and coloured silks, circa 1480, the velvet second half of the 15th century. (Christie's) $890 £680

A fine full length evening mantle of grey facecloth, by Rouff, 13 Boulevard Hausmann, Paris, 1900. (Christie's) $144 £110

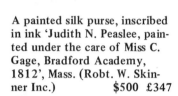

A painted silk purse, inscribed in ink 'Judith N. Peaslee, painted under the care of Miss C. Gage, Bradford Academy, 1812', Mass. (Robt. W. Skinner Inc.) $500 £347

A chasuble of crimson cut velvet woven with trailing stems and sprigs of leaves, 15th century. (Christie's) $1,179 £900

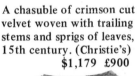

A gentleman's suit of voided velvet woven with pink and black sprigs against a pale blue silk ground, French, circa 1790, together with a waistcoat, circa 1770. (Christie's) $366 £280

A pair of lady's high-heeled shoes of royal blue velvet bound with blue braid, English, circa 1640. (Christie's) $11,520 £8,000

A dress of ivory silk woven with satin stripes, the bodice trimmed with ivory satin and with blond lace, lined with silk, circa 1830. (Christie's) $1,834 £1,400

A headdress of blue silk damask heavily embroidered with metal thread, artificial pearls and coloured glass, 1895. (Christie's) $37 £25

A dress of ivory satin printed in vertical bands of grey fleck design and a larger pink and grey chine design, circa 1834. (Christie's) $1,572 £1,200

A painted cedar hen canvas-back decoy, made by L. T. Ward Bros, 1936, 15in. long. (Christie's) $3,850 £2,655

A painted wooden Maine Flying Scoter decoy, by 'Gus' Aaron Wilson, circa 1880/1920, together with two black-painted wooden duck decoys. (Christie's) $4,620 £3,136

A Canada Goose decoy, by George Boyd, early 20th century, 29in. long. (Christie's) $1,760 £1,213

Two late 19th century painted wooden decoys, one 10in. long, the other 11½in. long. (Christie's) $330 £220

A pair of painted wooden American Merganser decoys, a hen and drake, by L. T. Holmes, circa 1855/65. (Christie's) $93,500 £64,482

Two late 19th century painted wooden decoys, 9½in. long. (Christie's) $300 £200

A painted wooden hollow constructed Canada Goose decoy, by Chas. H. Hart, Mass., circa 1890/1915, 20½in. long. (Christie's) $4,400 £3,034

A painted wooden Primitive Brant decoy, three-piece laminated construction, 18in. long. (Christie's) $242 £166

A painted wooden oversized Golden Eye decoy, by 'Gus' Aaron Wilson, circa 1880/ 1920, 20in. long.(Christie's) $1,760 £1,213

A poured-wax child doll with fixed pale blue eyes, 20in. high, in box. (Christie's) $497 £380

An early 19th century crudely carved wood doll with blue enamel and nail eyes and painted limbs, 15½in. high. (Anderson & Garland) $216 £150

A jointed wooden doll with painted features and real blond hair wig, circa 1845. (Christie's) $314 £240

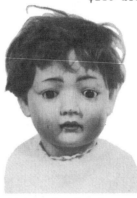

A bisque headed bebe with jointed wood and composition body, marked BRU Jner 4, 13in. high. (Christie's) $2,358 £1,800

A bisque headed character baby doll, marked K & W 13, Konig and Wernicke, 24in. high. (Christie's) $497 £380

A bisque headed bebe with jointed composition and wood body, by Steiner, 12in. high. (Christie's) $1,441 £1,100

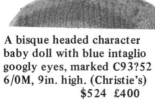

A bisque headed bebe with papier mache jointed body, marked 12 by Steiner, 29in. high. (Christie's) $3,144 £2,400

A bisque headed character baby doll with blue intaglio googly eyes, marked C93?52 6/0M, 9in. high. (Christie's) $524 £400

A poured-wax child doll with lace edged underclothes, circa 1851, 13in. high. (Christie's) $419 £320

A wax over composition headed doll with smiling painted face, circa 1878, 7in. high. (Christie's) $98 £75

A bisque headed clockwork walking, talking bebe petit pas, marked BRU Jne R 11, 24in. high. (Christie's) $3,275 £2,500

An all-bisque googly-eyed doll's house doll with smiling water-melon closed mouth, 4in. high. (Christie's) $288 £220

A poured-wax child doll with blue wired sleeping eyes, the stuffed body with bisque limbs in original nightgown, 21in. high. (Christie's) $419 £320

A bisque headed bebe with composition jointed body, marked FTE C 3/0 by Steiner, 10in. high. (Christie's) $1,572 £1,200

A bisque headed child doll with auburn wig and jointed composition body, 32in. high. (Christie's) $524 £400

A bisque headed autoperipatetikos doll with painted blue eyes and brown kid arms, 10in. high. (Christie's) $262 £200

A bisque swivel headed Parisienne, 17½in. high without stand, the head marked 3. (Christie's) $4,716 £3,600

A bisque two-faced doll with original blonde wig and with jointed composition body, 11in. high. (Christie's). $1,179 £900

A bisque headed character child doll with blue sleeping eyes, marked K*R SH115/A 42, 16½in. high. (Christie's) $3,243 £2,300

A cloth doll painted in oils with grey eyes and blonde painted short hair, 23in. high. (Christie's) $282 £200

A painted wooden Groden-thal type doll with grey curls, circa 1835, 12½in. high. (Christie's) $792 £550

A painted felt doll modelled as a young girl, marked on the feet Lenci, 25in. high. (Christie's) $239 £170

An early 19th century group of painted wooden headed dolls, 'There was an old woman who lived in a shoe', 5in. long. (Dacre, Son & Hartley) $178 £120

Late 19th century German bisque headed novelty doll, 13in. high. (Bermondsey) $450 £325

A waxed shoulder composition doll with painted closed mouth and fixed blue eyes, 30in. high. (Lawrence Fine Art) $458 £310

A bisque headed character baby doll with open closed mouth, marked 211 J.D.K., 17in. high. (Christie's) $535 £380

A fine German character doll by Kestner, with original clothes, 13in. high, circa 1915. (Bermondsey) $2,100 £1,500

A bisque shoulder headed doll with brown sleeping eyes, marked 309,5, 17in. high. (Christie's) $294 £200

A Bru Teteur bisque doll, French, circa 1875, 19in. high. (Lawrence Fine Art) $6,468 £4,400

A bisque shoulder headed doll with fixed blue eyes, marked Goss 18, 17in. high. (Christie's) $576 £400

An early Grodenthal type painted wooden doll with brown eyes, circa 1820, 18in. high. (Christie's) $2,058 £1,400

A Franz Schmidt bebe doll with sleeping brown eyes, open mouth and composition body, 9in. high. (Hobbs & Chambers) $187 £125

A Scottish boy doll in Highland dress, with bisque head, in original box marked 'Kelly Boy 306', 12in. high. (Lawrence Fine Art) $162 £110

A bisque headed doll with jointed composition body, marked Armand Marseille, Germany A9M, 24in. high. (Dacre, Son & Hartley) $283 £190

A bisque headed bebe, marked J. Steiner Paris, SreA.3, 11in. high. (Christie's) $1,152 £800

A bisque headed doll with glass eyes, open mouth and composition body, marked S.F.B.J. 60 Paris, 18in. high. (Dacre, Son & Hartley) $163 £110

A china doll of an Irish gentleman, with gusseted kid body and china lower limbs, 13in. high. (Lawrence Fine Art) $176 £120

A painted cloth doll with brown painted hair, the stuffed body jointed at hip and shoulder, by Kathe Kruse, 17in. high. (Christie's) $518 £360

A Jumeau bisque doll, French, circa 1880, 15in. high. (Lawrence Fine Art)
$1,940 £1,320

A bisque headed doll with moving eyes, marked on head A.M. 4DEP, Made in Germany, 19in. high. (Dacre, Son & Hartley) $268 £180

A clockwork toy of a bisque headed doll pulling a two-wheeled cart, marked 1079 Halbig S & H 7½, by Toullet Decamps. (Christie's)
$792 £550

Early 20th century German character doll by Kathe Kruse, 17in. high. (Bermondsey)
$425 £300

A bisque headed doll with composition body, marked Porzellan Fabrik Burggrub Daslachende Baby, 1930/3/ Made in Germany DRGM, 18in. high. (Dacre, Son & Hartley) $640 £430

A Dep Tete Jumeau bisque headed doll, impressed DEP 8, with jointed wood and composition body, 19in. high. (Lawrence Fine Art)
$518 £350

A wax over composition shoulder headed doll with short, blonde, curly wool wig, 1810-15, 14in. high. (Christie's) $345 £240

A bisque headed doll with tinted complexion and kid covered body, 21in. high. (Dacre, Son & Hartley) $372 £250

A wax over composition shoulder headed doll, the blue eyes wired from the waist. (Christie's) $432 £300

A bisque headed bebe with five upper teeth, fixed brown eyes and pierced ears, 18½in. high. (Christie's) $1,152 £800

An English mid 19th century vendor doll of wood and cloth, under glass dome with turned walnut base, 16in. high. (Robt. W. Skinner Inc.) $3,000 £2,112

An Armand Marseille '980' bisque headed doll with open and shut eyes, dressed, 22in. high. (Reeds Rains) $266 £180

An American 'Shirley Temple' personality doll, 21in. high, circa 1935. (Bermondsey) $675 £475

A wax composition doll, with sleeping blue eyes, fair wig and stuffed cloth body, 14in. long. (Lawrence Fine Art) $414 £280

A bisque headed child doll, marked SFBJ Paris 14, 32in. high, original box marked Bebe Francais. (Christie's) $1,128 £800

A fine French bisque headed doll by Emile Jumeau, circa 1885, 15in. high. (Bermondsey) $2,100 £1,500

A Battersea enamel plaque transfer printed and painted after Ravenet with The Gipsy Fortune-Teller, circa 1750, 4.1/8in. long. (Christie's) $1,198 £810

A 19th century Viennese silver gilt and enamel model of three gemset birds perched in a dead tree, 4.3/8in. high. (Christie's)
$622 £432

An English enamel plaque transfer printed and painted with Les Amours Pastorale after Boucher, 4.1/8in. long. (Christie's) $1,278 £864

Two Staffordshire white enamel tapersticks with gilt metal mounts, circa 1765, one 6.3/8in. and one 6½in. high. (Christie's)
$1,866 £1,296

A Viennese enamel sweetmeat dish with gilt metal mounts, circa 1900, 6.3/8in. high. (Christie's) $1,174 £810

A pair of Staffordshire white ground enamel column candlesticks, circa 1800, one 9¾in. and one 9.7/8in. high. (Christie's) $437 £302

An enamelled presentation snuff box, the cover with applied diamond set crowned initials for Tsar Nicholas II, 4in. long, 11oz.4dwt. (Christie's) $9,396 £6,480

A South German double enamel snuff box of waisted form with waved gilt metal mounts, circa 1740, 3in. high. (Christie's) $1,555 £1,080

A white metal and enamel box with parcel gilt interior, circa 1900, 10.3cm. diam. (Christie's) $861 £594

One of a pair of Birmingham rectangular white ground enamel caskets, with original gilt metal mounts, circa 1765, each 3½in. long. (Christie's) $5,637 £3,888

One of a pair of late 19th century Viennese silver mounted enamel cornucopiae, by Hermann Bohm, 8½in. long. (Christie's) $3,036 £1,944

An English enamel plaque transfer printed and painted after Boucher with La Toilette Pastorale, circa 1755, probably Birmingham, 4.1/8in. long. (Christie's) $2,077 £1,404

Pair of Staffordshire enamel mustard pots with gilt metal mounts, on three pad feet, circa 1770, probably Birmingham, each 5½in. high. (Christie's) $5,443 £3,780

Late 19th century Viennese silver and enamel mounted rock crystal tazza, 6½in. high. (Christie's) $2,877 £1,944

Two Staffordshire white ground enamel candlesticks, with gilt metal mounts, circa 1770, 9.5/8in. high. (Christie's) $656 £453

A Staffordshire enamel etui of upright form, with original gilt metal mounts, circa 1770, 4.1/8in. high. (Christie's) $1,399 £972

Two Staffordshire oval enamel portrait plaques, circa 1765, probably Birmingham, each 3¼in. (Christie's) $2,799 £1,944

One of three late 19th and 20th century enamel on copper religious plaques, 11¾in. wide. (Robt. W. Skinner Inc.) $425 £291

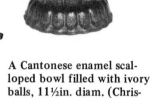

A Staffordshire enamel bonbonniere formed as a lemon, with gilt metal mounted hinged lid, 3in. long. (Christie's) $1,252 £864

Late 19th century Viennese silver mounted enamel horn, by Hermann Bohm, 27½in. long. (Christie's) $5,594 £3,780

A Cantonese enamel scalloped bowl filled with ivory balls, 11½in. diam. (Christie's) $4,071 £2,808

An 18th century Limoges style enamel on copper plate, 7.7/8in. diam. (Robt. W. Skinner Inc.) $600 £437

A 19th century German casket, with indented corners, 19cm. long. (Lawrence Fine Art) $797 £550

A Bilston enamel combined bonbonniere and patch box, 5cm. high. (Lawrence Fine Art) $1,116 £770

An early 19th century Swiss rectangular enamel plaque painted with a landscape, 2.5/8in. long. (Christie's) $901 £626

A 19th century champleve enamel and patinated brass oil burning floor lamp, China, 61¾in. high. (Robt. W. Skinner Inc.) $1,100 £802

A 19th century Naples casket, 26.5cm. long. (Lawrence Fine Art) $717 £495

An enamelled shaped hexa-gonal Freedom casket of Indian inspiration, Chester, 1888, maker's mark AP, 18ct., 8¼in. long. (Chris-tie's) $9,396 £6,480

A Staffordshire enamel snuff box in the form of a court shoe, circa 1780, 3¼in. long. (Christie's) $466 £324

A German oblong enamel snuff box painted on the cover with a peasant driving his mules in a landscape, circa 1760, 3.5/8in. long. (Christie's) $1,477 £1,026

A South Staffordshire enamel snuff box with gilt metal mount, 8cm. long. (Lawrence Fine Art) $1,499 £1,034

A Staffordshire white enamel combined bodkin case, scent bottle and thimble, circa 1765, 5.3/8in. long. (Christie's) $855 £594

An unrecorded Battersea enamel plaque, transfer printed and painted after Ravenet, 4.1/8in. long. (Christie's)$1,758 £1,188

A large oval snuff box with deep blue guilloche enamel panels, the cover with dia-mond set monogram, 3½in. long. (Christie's) $8,613 £5,940

A Swiss oblong enamel pla-que painted with a classical marriage ceremony, the ena-mel circa 1820, probably by Soiron, 2.5/8in. long. (Christie's) $1,166 £810

A Swiss circular gold and enamel snuff box, circa 1800, in fitted case, 3in. diam. (Christie's) $4,475 £3,024

An early 18th century Italian fan with carved ivory sticks decorated with silver pique and cloute with carved mother-of-pearl, 27cm. long. (Phillips) $355 £240

A late 19th century French fan with plain mother-of-pearl sticks, signed B. Bisson de Recy, 27cm. long. (Phillips) $192 £130

A fan, the leaf trompe l'oeil of watercolours and engravings lying on pink and mauve silk, strewn with lace, 11½in., Anglo-Italian, circa 1760. (Christie's) $1,249 £850

An English fan, the serpentine ivory sticks pique with silver and when closed the handle forms a serpent, circa 1730, 10in. (Christie's)
$261 £180

A late 18th century fan with wood sticks and carved guards, 29cm. long. (Phillips)
$592 £400

A French silk leaf fan, the ivory sticks pierced and silvered, 10½in., 1756. (Christie's)
$725 £500

An early 18th century bone brise fan painted with pairs of lovers, birds, flowers and chinoiserie, 20cm. long, probably Dutch. (Phillips) $236 £160

Mid 18th century fan, the leaf Italian, the sticks Flemish or English, 12in. (Christie's)
$841 £580

An Oriental ivory fan, gold takamakie lacquer landscape scenes with okibirame accents, with attached ojimi bead. (Robt. W. Skinner Inc.) $259 £175

A mid 18th century French fan with carved and pierced ivory sticks, 26cm. long. (Phillips) $888 £600

A mid 18th century French fan with carved, pierced silver and gilt mother-of-pearl sticks, 29cm. long. (Phillips) $148 £100

A fan, the leaf a hand-coloured etching with detailed Almanack for the year 1794, with plain wooden sticks, 11in. (Christie's) $264 £180

A fan, the leaf painted with shepherds and shepherdesses, the handle carved to show a vine when closed, 10in., English or Flemish, circa 1750. (Christie's) $588 £400

A mid 19th century fan with carved, pierced and gilded mother-of-pearl sticks, the printed leaf design by Johann Zoffany, 27cm. long. (Phillips) $140 £95

A fan, the chickenskin leaf painted with classical vignettes of slaves and satyrs, with plain ivory sticks, 10½in., Italian, circa 1780. (Christie's) $588 £400

A late 19th century French fan with gilded ivory sticks, 35cm. long. (Phillips) $444 £300

BEDS

Victorian brass and iron bed, 1875. (British Antique Exporters) **$182 £135**

An Empire mahogany lit en bateau with box spring, 54in. wide, 73in. long. (Christie's) **$4,276 £3,240**

Late 19th century Jacobean style oak bedstead. (British Antique Exporters) **$99 £74**

A late Federal carved mahogany bedstead, the footposts on brass ball feet, 57in. wide. (Christie's) **$8,800 £6,111**

Victorian mahogany bed head, circa 1880. (British Antique Exporters) **$82 £61**

A Federal carved maple high-post bedstead, Mass., 1790-1810, 57in. wide. (Christie's) **$7,150 £4,965**

A mahogany four-poster bed with box spring, 60in. wide. (Christie's) **$2,741 £1,944**

A Federal maple and birch tall post tester bed, New England, circa 1820, 57in. wide, 80in. long. (Robt. W. Skinner Inc.) **$3,500 £2,464**

A Georgian mahogany four-post bed, the canopy with breakfront cornice on reeded posts inlaid with satinwood panels, 72in. wide. (Christie's) **$6,320 £4,104**

Early 19th century Federal painted walnut pencil-post bedstead, North Carolina, 52½in. wide, overall. (Christie's) $4,180 £2,902

A Portuguese rosewood bed with pierced open headboard and with box spring, 18th century, 42in. wide. (Christie's) $3,078 £2,052

A late Federal figured maple bedstead, 62in. wide, overall. (Christie's) $1,870 £1,298

A 17th century oak four-poster bed with panelled headboard, 64in. wide, 93in. high. (Christie's) $3,537 £2,700

A Federal maple highpost bedstead, New England, 1800-20, 54in. wide. (Christie's) $4,180 £2,902

A mahogany four-poster bed with moulded canopy and floral chintz hangings, George III and later, 60in. wide. (Christie's)
$4,344 £2,916

A mahogany four-poster bed with plain headboard and square pillars, 61in. wide, 84in. high. (Christie's) $2,546 £1,944

A mahogany four-post bed with waved shaped and moulded cornice, 94in. wide. (Christie's)
$2,237 £1,512

A 17th century oak four-poster bed, the tester with moulded cornice and carved frieze, 156cm. wide. (Phillips) $3,014 £2,200

FURNITURE

A Regency mahogany open bookcase on turned feet, 34½in. wide. (Christie's) $2,263 £1,728

A Regency burr yew break-front bookcase supplied by Marsh & Tatham to the Prince of Wales at Carlton House, 73½in. wide. (Christie's) $211,410 £145,800

Victorian inlaid mahogany revolving bookcase, circa 1860. (British Antique Exporters) $463 £343

A George III mahogany breakfront library bookcase, 64in. wide. (Christie's) $25,056 £17,280

An oak book press of the Pepys model with glazed cupboard doors on bun feet. (Christie's) $5,376 £4,104

A George III mahogany breakfront bookcase with four plain glazed doors, 83in. wide. (Lawrence Fine Art) $11,396 £7,700

A George III mahogany breakfront bookcase with moulded dentilled cornice, 95½in. wide. (Christie's) $5,950 £4,104

A George III mahogany bookcase with two geo-metrically glazed doors, 59½in. wide, 98in. high. (Christie's) $2,916 £2,160

A Regency mahogany break-front bookcase on plinth base, 93in. wide. (Christie's) $18,792 £12,960

A George III mahogany bookcase of Gothic style, designed for an alcove, 36¾in. wide, 82½in. high. (Christie's)
$2,405 £1,836

A Regency rosewood dwarf bookcase, formerly with a superstructure, 42¼in. wide. (Christie's) $7,830 £5,400

An early 19th century Regency brass inlaid ebony open bookcase, 54in. wide. (Christie's) $13,311 £9,180

A 19th century mahogany breakfront library bookcase with four glazed doors, 11ft. wide. (Lawrence Fine Art)
$4,785 £3,300

A Victorian carved mahogany library bookcase on plinth base, 2ft.10in. wide. (Capes, Dunn & Co.)
$489 £340

A Regency mahogany breakfront bookcase in the manner of Gillows, with six glazed doors, 143½in. wide. (Christie's)
$34,732 £25,920

A 19th century copy of an Adams' style mahogany bookcase, 5ft.6in. wide. (Butler & Hatch Waterman)
$1,800 £1,250

Large stripped pine bookcase on cupboard, the two glazed doors enclosing three shaped shelves, 7ft. high. (Worsfolds)
$864 £600

A mahogany bookcase with six glazed doors over three compartments, circa 1920, 90in. high. (Peter Wilson & Co.) $792 £550

BOOKCASES

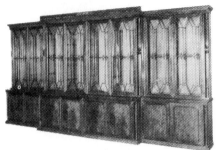

A Regency mahogany break-front bookcase in the manner of Gillows, 196in. wide. (Christie's) $15,660 £10,800

Six section Globe Wernicke cabinet, 1880. (British Antique Exporters) $394 £292

A Regency rosewood dwarf bookcase, the breakfront with grey marble top, 83in. wide. (Christie's) $17,226 £11,880

A mahogany breakfront bookcase with two pairs of glazed cupboard doors, 91in. wide. (Christie's) $4,344 £2,916

A George II mahogany book-case, the doors opening to a divided interior, circa 1730-50, 58¼in. wide. (Christie's) $7,700 £5,347

A Charles II oak bookcase with a pair of glazed and panelled cupboard doors, 55in. wide. (Christie's) $10,659 £7,560

A mahogany breakfront bookcase with moulded broken pediment, 80in. wide. (Christie's) $4,344 £2,916

A Simpoles chapter book-case of oak and leaded glass, 7ft.9in. wide. (J. R. Bridg-ford & Sons) $1,296 £900

One of a pair of mahogany breakfront bookcases with two pairs of glazed cupboard doors, 82in. wide.(Christie's) $11,309 £7,344

BUREAU BOOKCASES

A mid Georgian mahogany bureau cabinet with glazed cupboard doors, 45in. wide. (Christie's) $8,035 £6,480

A George I walnut bureau cabinet with later-glazed arched cupboard door, 21½in. wide. (Christie's) $22,809 £17,280

A mid-Georgian mahogany bureau cabinet, the glazed doors enclosing a partially fitted interior, 92in. high. (Christie's)$16,070 £12,960

A Queen Anne walnut bureau cabinet, the baize lined sloping flap enclosing a fitted interior, 43in. wide. (Christie's) $14,094 £9,720

Chippendale mahogany secretary desk on four ogee bracket feet, Rhode Island, circa 1780, 42in. wide. (Robt. W. Skinner Inc.) $17,000 £11,805

A Chippendale mahogany blockfront secretary desk, circa 1780, 42in. wide. (Robt. W. Skinner Inc.) $50,000 £34,722

A George II rosewood and walnut bureau cabinet with sloping flap enclosing a fitted interior, 38in. wide. (Christie's)$40,176 £32,400

A George I walnut desk and bookcase, circa 1720, 38in. wide. (Christie's) $4,180 £2,902

A George III mahogany desk and bookcase, the desk section with slant lid enclosing compartmented interior, 39¼in. wide. (Christie's) $4,400 £3,055

BUREAU BOOKCASES

A Queen Anne scarlet lacquer bureau cabinet, decorated overall in raised gilt with chinoiserie figures and birds, 37½in. wide. (Christie's)
$43,416 £32,400

Late 18th century George III mahogany secretary, 37¼in. wide. (Robt. W. Skinner Inc.)
$1,800 £1,313

A George II walnut bureau cabinet, the doors enclosing a fitted interior, 42in. wide. (Christie's) $37,497 £30,240

An early Georgian walnut bureau cabinet, the sloping flap enclosing a fitted interior, 37½in. wide. (Christie's)
$6,436 £4,320

A black and gold lacquer bureau cabinet, the mirrored cupboard doors enclosing a fitted interior, 40½in. wide. (Christie's)
$28,188 £19,440

A Georgian oak bureau bookcase, the doors with bands of mahogany and original brass handles, 42in. wide. (Lawrence Fine Art) $925 £638

A George III mahogany bureau bookcase on ogee bracket feet, 44in. wide. (Christie's) $3,353 £2,484

1930's oak bureau bookcase with glazed top. (British Antique Exporters)
$159 £118

A Chippendale cherrywood secretary bookcase, in two sections, circa 1765-80, 38in. wide. (Christie's)
$9,900 £6,875

BUREAU BOOKCASES

An early George III mahogany bureau bookcase, the bureau with fitted interior, 40in. wide. (Lawrence Fine Art) $4,232 £2,860

An early George III mahogany bureau cabinet with an arched mirror glazed cupboard door, 33in. wide. (Christie's) $9,396 £6,480

A George II walnut bureau cabinet, the fall-flap enclosing a fitted interior, 33in. wide. (Christie's) $4,687 £3,780

A Queen Anne walnut bureau cabinet, the fall-flap enclosing a fitted interior, 43½in. wide. (Christie's) $53,244 £36,720

A Queen Anne brown and gold lacquer bureau cabinet, the mirror cupboard doors enclosing a fitted interior, 40½in. wide. (Christie's) $52,099 £38,880

A Chippendale cherrywood desk and bookcase, in two sections, 1760-90, 41½in. wide. (Christie's) $17,600 £12,222

A Queen Anne walnut and burr walnut bureau cabinet, with two pairs of carrying handles, 41in. wide. (Christie's) $45,532 £36,720

A Chippendale transitional mahogany secretary, circa 1790, 46in. wide. (Robt. W. Skinner Inc.) $5,750 £3,993

A Queen Anne walnut bureau cabinet with two candle slides, 39in. wide. (Christie's) $8,046 £5,400

BUREAUX

An 18th century oak bureau with sloping fall front, fitted interior, 2ft.10in. wide. (Hobbs & Chambers)
$828 £560

A Chippendale tiger maple slant lid desk, New England, circa 1770, 35¼in. wide. (Robt. W. Skinner Inc.)
$5,750 £4,049

A Queen Anne scarlet lacquer bureau with fitted interior, on later bracket feet, 37½in. wide. (Christie's) $16,869 £11,880

A Chippendale walnut slant front desk, 1760/90, 43in. wide. (Christie's)
$3,300 £2,275

A Chippendale mahogany reverse serpentine slant front desk, 1760/80, 44in. wide. (Christie's)
$4,950 £3,413

An early Georgian oak bureau with double half round mouldings, 38in. wide. (Lawrence Fine Art)
$1,244 £858

Country Chippendale maple slant top desk, circa 1780, 36in. wide. (Robt. W. Skinner Inc.) $2,700 £1,875

A George III mahogany bureau, the baize lined fall-flap flanked by two hinged flaps enclosing a fitted interior, 57½in. wide. (Christie's)
$21,141 £14,580

A George III oak bureau with narrow mahogany crossbanding, 36in. wide. (Lawrence Fine Art)
$1,403 £968

BUREAUX

A Chippendale mahogany oxbow desk, circa 1780, 41¾in. wide. (Robt. W. Skinner Inc.)
$7,250 £5,034

A fine Victorian mahogany and marquetry cylinder bureau, 1875. (British Antique Exporters)
$1,132 £839

A walnut and other woods marquetry desk, Holland, circa 1760, 54in. wide. (Robt. W. Skinner Inc.)
$10,000 £7,042

A Chippendale mahogany slant top desk, Mass., circa 1780, 38in. wide. (Robt. W. Skinner Inc.) $4,750 £3,298

A Chippendale tiger maple and maple slant top desk, New England, circa 1780, 36in. wide. (Robt. W. Skinner Inc.) $2,700 £1,875

A William and Mary walnut bureau, the sloping flap enclosing a fitted interior, 38in. wide. (Christie's)
$4,228 £2,916

A Country Federal maple slant lid desk, New England, circa 1810, 40¼in. wide. (Robt. W. Skinner Inc.)
$1,200 £833

An early Georgian walnut bureau, the fall-flap enclosing a fitted interior, 39in. wide. (Christie's)
$4,384 £3,024

Early 20th century oak bureau. (British Antique Exporters) $275 £204

A William and Mary burr walnut bureau, the fall-flap enclosing a fitted interior with a well, 41in. wide. (Christie's)$12,830 £9,720

A Queen Anne cherry desk on frame, with fall-front, New England, circa 1760, 34in. wide. (Robt. W. Skinner Inc.) $3,500 £2,397

A William and Mary pollard oak bureau, the fall-flap enclosing a fitted interior, with a glass and marble recess dated 1698, 38in. wide. (Christie's) $18,532 £14,040

A Gustav Stickley dropfront desk, the doors opening to reveal a fitted interior, circa 1906, 38in. wide. (Robt. W. Skinner Inc.) $2,400 £1,666

A Country Federal cherrywood slant front desk, Mass., circa 1800, 40½in. wide. (Robt. W. Skinner Inc.) $1,600 £1,095

Early 20th century Jacobeanstyle oak secretary, 30½in. wide. (Robt. W. Skinner Inc.) $750 £513

A Country Federal cherry slant lid desk, New England, circa 1800, 40½in. wide. (Robt. W. Skinner Inc.) $1,800 £1,232

A William and Mary burr-yew bureau, the sloping flap enclosing a stepped fitted interior, 31½in. wide. (Christie's) $4,561 £3,456

A Federal birch, cherry and mahogany veneer slant lid desk, probably N. Hampshire, circa 1810, 39½in. wide. (Robt. W. Skinner Inc.) $1,000 £684

A late 18th century Italian marquetry bureau with crossbanded fall-flap inlaid with a landscape scene, 48in. wide. (Christie's)
$2,851 £2,160

A Louis XV kingwood and marquetry bureau de dame by A. M. Criaerd, 29½in. wide. (Christie's)
$3,421 £2,592

A Dutch walnut and marquetry bureau, the ogee sloping flap enclosing a fitted interior, 52in. wide. (Christie's)
$5,702 £4,320

A George II walnut and burr walnut bureau, the sloping flap enclosing a leather lined interior, 29in. wide. (Christie's) $10,044 £8,100

A George III satinwood cylinder bureau, the top with leather lined domed tambour shutter, 30½in. wide. (Christie's) $12,700 £8,640

A George III mahogany and sycamore bureau with leather lined shaped spreading fall-flap enclosing a fitted interior, 30in. wide. (Christie's) $3,790 £2,808

A William and Mary walnut bureau, the sloping flap enclosing a fitted interior, 36in. wide. (Christie's)
$6,415 £4,860

A George III mahogany and satinwood cylinder bureau, the solid cylinder enclosing a fitted interior, 45in. wide. (Christie's) $8,704 £7,020

A Chippendale maple and pine slant front desk, New England, circa 1780, 39in. wide. (Robt. W. Skinner Inc.) $2,100 £1,438

BUREAUX

An early Georgian walnut bureau, the crossbanded sloping flap with book-rest enclosing a fitted interior, 34½in. wide. (Christie's) $4,158 £2,700

A Queen Anne walnut bureau on later turned feet, 26in. wide. (Christie's) $3,862 £2,592

An 18th century Italian walnut marquetry and bone inlaid bureau, 43in. wide. (Christie's) $2,877 £1,944

An early Georgian walnut bureau, the crossbanded sloping flap enclosing a fitted interior, 36½in. wide. (Christie's) $5,149 £3,456

An early Georgian walnut bureau, the leather lined sloping flap enclosing a fitted interior, 37in. wide. (Christie's) $7,724 £5,184

An 18th century Italian walnut and bone inlaid bureau, the sloping flap enclosing a fitted interior, 50in. wide. (Christie's) $7,290 £4,860

A George III padoukwood bureau with moulded sloping lid enclosing a fitted interior, 31in. wide. (Christie's) $3,492 £2,376

An 18th century Continental walnut serpentine front bureau, 4ft.4in. wide. (Jacobs & Hunt) $5,180 £3,500

A Chippendale birch slant front desk, 1760-80, 39½in. wide. (Christie's) $4,840 £3,432

A Chippendale mahogany slant front desk, Mass., 1770-90. (Christie's) $2,420 £1,766

A Chippendale maple and tiger maple slant top desk, with fold down writing surface with cubbyholes and drawers in interior, circa 1760, 42in. wide. (Robt. W. Skinner Inc.) $3,200 £2,162

A George III mahogany bureau with leather lined sloping flap, 31½in. wide. (Christie's) $1,850 £1,242

An early Georgian walnut bureau, the sloping flap enclosing a fitted interior, 38½in. wide. (Christie's) $5,149 £3,456

Mid 18th century German walnut and oak bureau with crossbanded chamfered top, 46in. wide. (Christie's) $5,594 £3,780

Mid 18th century Dutch Colonial padoukwood bureau with fitted interior, 41½in. wide. (Christie's) $5,832 £3,888

A mahogany bureau, line inlaid and crossbanded in rosewood with fall flap, 31½in. wide. (Woolley & Wallis) $1,507 £1,100

A Chippendale cherry slant front desk on cut-out bracket feet, circa 1780, possibly New Jersey, 38.3/8in. wide. (Robt. W. Skinner Inc.) $6,200 £4,305

An early Georgian walnut bureau with crossbanded sloping flap enclosing a fitted interior, 36in. wide. (Christie's) $6,436 £4,320

A Regency satinwood side cabinet with an inset grey marble top, the door filled with pleated aquamarine silk, 21½in. wide.(Christie's) $5,659 £4,320

One of a pair of early George III rosewood cabinets on stands, each with pierced fretwork gallery, 37in. wide. (Christie's) $34,732 £25,920

An ormolu mounted king-wood cabinet on stand on turned tapering legs, 26½in. wide. (Christie's) $4,276 £3,240

An 18th century silver moun-ted Indo-Portuguese ivory inlaid hardwood cabinet on stand, 38in. wide.(Christie's) $14,256 £10,800

Mid 17th century ormolu mounted kingwood strong-box, possibly Flemish or German, 36in. wide, 48½in. high. (Christie's) $17,409 £14,040

An Art Deco wrought iron and zebra wood cabinet, carved signature J. Cayette, Nancy, circa 1925, 115cm. high. (Christie's) $2,049 £1,404

A 17th century Spanish ivory and tortoiseshell inlaid rose-wood and walnut cabinet on stand of papleira type, 43in. wide. (Christie's) $4,561 £3,456

A 19th century rectangular roironuri cabinet, the base fitted with a drawer below two hinged doors, 45.8 x 44 x 28.4cm. (Christie's) $1,726 £1,296

A Regency pollard oak and burr-yew dwarf cabinet, the top with ebony bandings, 26in. wide. (Christie's) $4,283 £3,456

CABINETS

FURNITURE

A William and Mary oyster-
veneered walnut cabinet on
stand, 36½in. wide.
(Christie's) $5,356 £4,320

A Sue et Mare rosewood,
ebonised and marquetry
music cabinet on elongated
ebonised legs, 95.2cm. wide.
(Christie's) $4,415 £3,024

A 17th century Flemish or
North German ebony cabinet
on stand, the frieze drawer
inlaid with a reversible backgammon and chess board,
33½in. wide. (Christie's)
$9,979 £7,560

A William and Mary oyster
veneered laburnum cabinet
on stand, 37in. wide.
(Christie's)
$25,660 £19,440

A late 18th century Anglo-
Indian engraved ivory and
tortoiseshell veneered table
cabinet, 19in. wide.
(Christie's) $4,561 £3,456

A Wm. Watt ebonised side
cabinet designed by E. W.
Godwin, 197.4cm. high by
128.6cm. wide. (Christie's)
$7,884 £5,400

A 19th century North Italian
ivory mounted ebony cabinet
on stand with stepped baluster gallery, stamped Pogliani,
32in. wide. (Christie's)
$2,708 £2,052

An oak bedside cabinet with
bronze drop handles, by P.
Waals assisted by P. Burchett,
1928, 78.9cm. high. (Christie's) $1,892 £1,296

A 19th century North
Italian ivory inlaid ebony
cabinet in the Renaissance
style, in two parts, 67in.
wide. (Christie's)
$16,394 £12,420

351

CABINETS

An 18th century Portuguese Colonial rosewood table cabinet, the front with various sized drawers, 13in. wide. (Christie's)$777 £540

An 18th century vizigatapam ivory inlaid hardwood table cabinet, with carrying handles, 17½in. wide. (Christie's) $3,421 £2,376

A Regency gilt metal mounted mahogany breakfront side cabinet, the doors filled with gilt trelliswork and mushroom silk pleats, 56in. wide. (Christie's) $5,214 £3,672

A Regency lacquer side cabinet, the ebonised top with pierced ormolu gallery, 43¼in. wide. (Christie's) $12,528 £8,640

A mid Victorian walnut and inlaid side cabinet with glazed door, 34½in. wide. (Dacre, Son & Hartley) $720 £500

A Victorian inlaid walnut and gilt metal mounted side cabinet, 32in. wide. (Reeds Rains)$633 £440

A Dutch walnut and marquetry cabinet on stand, 43in. wide. (Christie's)
$3,110 £2,160

A Regency ebonised and lacquer dwarf cabinet with Carrara marble top and cedar lined interior, 39½in. wide. (Christie's)
$10,962 £7,560

A Charles II black and gold lacquered cabinet on stand, 45in. wide. (Christie's)
$15,660 £10,800

CABINETS

A Regency parcel gilt, ebonised and simulated rosewood breakfront dwarf cabinet with inset moulded Carrara marble top, 47½in. wide. (Christie's)
$13,311 £9,180

A Dutch walnut child's bureau cabinet with fall-flap enclosing a fitted interior, 31in. wide. (Christie's) $4,199 £2,916

A Regency brass inlaid ebony and satinwood breakfront side cabinet, 36½in. wide. (Christie's) $2,607 £1,836

One of a pair of Empire gilt metal mounted mahogany pedestal cabinets with inset grey marble tops.(Christie's)
$9,331 £6,480

One of a pair of Regency rosewood side cabinets, 51in. wide. (Christie's)
$53,244 £36,720

A Gustav Stickley oak music cabinet, the ten pane single door with amber glass, circa 1912, 47¼in. high. (Robt. W. Skinner Inc.) $2,300 £1,597

A 17th century Flemish ebony, tortoiseshell and painted cabinet on stand, 38in. wide. (Christie's)
$13,996 £9,720

A William III walnut veneered cabinet on stand, the moulded frieze fitted with two drawers. (Woolley & Wallis)
$3,915 £2,700

A Flemish brass bound ebony coffre-port with carrying handles, the coffre 17th century, the stand early Georgian, 28in. wide.(Christie's)
$4,976 £3,456

CABINETS

Victorian oak hanging cabinet, 1880. (British Antique Exporters) $83 £62

An early Victorian ormolu mounted side cabinet with moulded shaped top, 75in. wide. (Christie's)
$4,140 £2,916

Victorian oak stationery cabinet, 1880. (British Antique Exporters)
$126 £94

A Chinese black and gold lacquer cabinet on Irish, George II, ebonised stand, the cabinet early 18th century, 39½in. wide. (Christie's)
$3,132 £2,160

Mid 18th century mahogany side cabinet with Verde Antico marble top, 46½in. wide. (Lawrence Fine Art)
$2,035 £1,375

Victorian mahogany filing cupboard, 1870. (British Antique Exporters)
$345 £256

A lacquered Japanese cherrywood cabinet with brass corner mounts and hinges, 48in. wide, 75in. high. (Reeds Rains) $1,224 £850

A Chinese black and gold lacquer cabinet on Charles II silvered wood stand, the cabinet 17th century, 40in. wide. (Christie's)
$21,925 £15,120

A North German parcel gilt and walnut cabinet on chest, circa 1730, 45in. wide. (Christie's) $9,331 £6,480

FURNITURE

Art Deco cabinet of various woods, 1930's. (British Antique Exporters) $810 £600

Victorian oak stationery cabinet. (British Antique Exporters) $114 £85

A marquetry vitrine cabinet with pate-sur-pate medallion mounts, Herter Bros., New York, circa 1870, 58in. wide. (Robt. W. Skinner Inc.) $13,000 £8,004

Late 19th century Japanese inlaid cabinet. (British Antique Exporters) $630 £467

A late 19th century lacquered Japanese cherry side cabinet fitted with sliding compartments, 38in. wide. (Reeds Rains) $1,008 £700

A Regency black and gold lacquered side cabinet, the legs probably added later, 45in. wide. (Christie's) $13,311 £9,180

An American mahogany filing cabinet, 1880. (British Antique Exporters) $372 £276

A Chinese Export black and gold lacquer cabinet, the cabinet late 18th century, the stand early 19th century, 37½in. wide. (Christie's) $9,396 £6,480

A Flemish tortoiseshell and ebony cabinet on stand, basically 17th century, 53in. wide. (Christie's) $4,976 £3,456

CABINETS

A Regency rosewood break-
front dwarf cabinet, the
Portor marble top with
ormolu gallery, 68in. wide.
(Christie's) $18,792 £12,960

A late 19th century satinwood and mahogany ven-
eered drawingroom side
cabinet, in Sheraton revival
style, 25in. wide. (Woolley
& Wallis) $1,644 £1,200

A Regency rosewood dwarf
cabinet, in the manner of S.
Jamar, with bowed break-
front grey marble top, 79½in.
wide. (Christie's)
$49,204 £36,720

An aesthetic movement
ebonised side cabinet, on
turned legs, 203cm. high.
(Lawrence Fine Art)
$578 £396

A Regency mahogany folio
cabinet, the top with twin
leather lined easels with
further easel beneath, 42in.
wide. (Christie's)
$5,149 £3,456

An early 19th century Chinese
Export black and gold lacquer
cabinet, 26½in. wide.
(Christie's) $1,609 £1,080

A William and Mary black
and gold lacquer cabinet-on-
chest, on later bun feet,
33½in. wide. (Christie's)
$12,052 £9,720

An early 20th century Louis
XVI style ormolu mounted
marble top music cabinet,
33½in. wide. (Robt. W. Skinner Inc.) $1,100 £802

Late 19th century red and
black lacquer cabinet on
stand fitted with stepped
shelves, 164.5cm. high.
(Christie's) $2,007 £1,404

CABINETS

A Regency mahogany side cabinet, the doors with gilt metal trelliswork and faded silk pleats, 26¾in. wide. (Christie's) $4,505 £3,024

A 17th century Flemish cabinet on stand, the lacquered front depicting riverside scene, on later Chinese hardwood base, 115cm. wide. (Phillips) $1,027 £750

An Ernest Gimson cedar wood cabinet, the interior fitted with sliding shelves, 116cm. high. (Lawrence Fine Art) $1,124 £770

Federal two-part mahogany and mahogany veneered cabinet, America, circa 1890, 19¼in. wide. (Robt. W. Skinner Inc.) $3,500 £2,430

A small Chinese lacquered cabinet, 1860. (British Antique Exporters) $43 £32

A 19th century German renaissance style architectural carved walnut cabinet, 62in. high. (Robt. W. Skinner Inc.) $650 £474

Late 19th century American filing cabinet. (British Antique Exporters) $382 £283

A Chinese black and gold lacquer double cabinet on stand, the cabinet 18th century, 21½in. wide. (Christie's) $26,622 £18,360

Victorian walnut Ambergs Patent cabinet, U.S.A. (British Antique Exporters) $409 £303

CABINETS

A Regency brass inlaid rosewood side cabinet with stepped green mottled scagliola marble top, 48½in. wide. (Christie's)
$5,632 £3,780

One of a pair of Biedermeier satin birch and ebonised side cabinets, 21in. wide. (Christie's) $1,944 £1,296

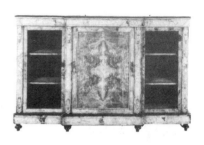

A Victorian boxwood banded walnut breakfront credenza with gilt metal mounts, 165cm. wide. (Phillips)
$1,027 £750

A William and Mary walnut cabinet on stand, the stand mid Georgian, 44½in. wide. (Christie's) $3,758 £2,592

An Edwardian mahogany pedestal filing cabinet with sliding trays, 20in. wide. (Christie's) $279 £190

A William and Mary burr walnut cabinet on chest., the doors with chased gilt lockplate and hinges, 44in. wide. (Christie's)
$19,958 £15,120

An early Georgian black and gold lacquer cabinet on a George III stand, 41in. wide. (Christie's)
$2,494 £1,620

A Goanese ivory inlaid ebony and hardwood cabinet on stand, the drawers with ivory studs, 42in. wide. (Christie's)
$15,184 £10,260

An Italian walnut and burr walnut 'Bambocci' cabinet on stand, the cabinet late 16th century, 34¼in. wide. (Christie's) $7,290 £4,860

CANTERBURYS

A Regency mahogany canterbury, trade label of 'Andw. Fleming & Co., Kirkaldy', 20in. wide. (Christie's) $3,283 £2,160

An early Victorian rosewood X-frame canterbury, 20in. wide. (Reeds Rains) $604 £420

A Victorian mahogany canterbury. (John Hogbin & Son) $793 £540

A Regency mahogany three-division canterbury with slatted sides and a drawer in the base, 19in. wide. (Christie's) $929 £650

Victorian walnut music canterbury/whatnot, 1860. (British Antique Exporters) $545 £404

A Victorian burr walnut music canterbury of three divisions with spindle turned columns, 1ft.9in. wide. (Capes, Dunn & Co.) $585 £380

Victorian walnut music canterbury, circa 1880. (British Antique Exporters) $341 £253

A Regency mahogany canterbury with frieze drawer, 20in. wide. (Christie's) $2,954 £2,052

A Victorian rosewood three division canterbury, 20¼in. wide. (Geering & Colyer) $769 £520

DINING CHAIRS

One of a set of six William IV rosewood dining chairs upholstered in buttoned orange suede. (Christie's) $3,218 £2,160

One of a set of six late 18th century Queen Anne walnut side chairs, Spain. (Robt. W. Skinner Inc.) $1,500 £1,027

One of a set of eight Victorian mahogany dining chairs with buttoned red leather upholstered seats. (Lawrence Fine Art) $2,279 £1,540

One of a set of four Chippendale cherrywood side chairs, 1780-1800. (Christie's) $4,950 £3,437

One of a set of six grain painted and stencilled fancy chairs, New England, 1820-30. (Christie's) $825 £572

A Chippendale mahogany side chair on cabriole legs ending in claw and ball feet, Mass., circa 1780. (Robt. W. Skinner Inc.) $1,850 £1,250

A Queen Anne maple side chair, Mass., circa 1770. (Robt. W. Skinner Inc.) $3,500 £2,364

One of a set of six Queen Anne walnut side chairs, 1740-60. (Christie's) $28,600 £19,861

One of a set of six mahogany and mahogany veneer Empire classical revival side chairs, Boston, circa 1830. (Robt. W. Skinner Inc.) $4,100 £2,847

DINING CHAIRS

Victorian mahogany turned leg chair, 1860. (British Antique Exporters) $63 £47

One of a set of eight Federal mahogany side chairs with shield backs, circa 1795. (Robt. W. Skinner Inc.) $7,500 £5,208

One of a set of four mahogany balloon back chairs, 1860. (British Antique Exporters) $681 £505

One of a set of eight late Georgian mahogany dining chairs, including two with arms. (Lawrence Fine Art) $8,140 £5,500

One of a set of early 19th century fancy painted side chairs, New England. (Christie's) $3,300 £2,291

A Chippendale mahogany side chair with slip seat, Phila., circa 1770. (Robt. W. Skinner Inc.) $3,600 £2,500

A Federal mahogany shield back side chair with upholstered bow front seat, circa 1800. (Robt. W. Skinner Inc.) $500 £347

One of a set of four Federal carved mahogany side chairs, 1790-1800. (Christie's) $3,520 £2,444

One of a set of six carved oak dining chairs, 1860. (British Antique Exporters) $487 £361

DINING CHAIRS

One of a set of five Queen
Anne maple side chairs
with rush seats, circa 1750.
(Robt. W. Skinner Inc.)
$8,250 £5,650

Two of a set of fourteen George III
mahogany ladder back dining chairs,
with leather upholstered seats.
(Christie's) $13,311 £9,180

One of a set of four Queen
Anne maple and ash side
chairs, New England, circa
1730. 42in. high. (Robt. W.
Skinner Inc.) $4,900 £3,450

One of a set of eight maho-
gany dining chairs in the
Georgian style. (Lawrence
Fine Art) $3,093 £2,090

Two of a set of eleven George III
mahogany dining chairs, including
an open armchair. (Christie's)
                    $21,924 £15,120

One of a set of six pine,
maple and ash bow-back
Windsor side chairs, New
England, circa 1770. (Robt.
W. Skinner Inc.)
          $8,700 £6,041

Queen Anne walnut side
chair, the yoke crest above
vase form splat, Mass., circa
1730. (Robt. W. Skinner
Inc.) $4,000 £2,777

A Federal carved mahogany
side chair and armchair,
possibly by John Carlile, Jr.,
Rhode Island. (Christie's)
          $3,080 £2,138

One of a set of six maple
turned side chairs, circa
1760, 39in. high. (Robt.
W. Skinner Inc.)
          $5,100 £3,541

DINING CHAIRS

One of a set of six Victorian mahogany chairs, 1870. (British Antique Exporters) $203 £151

Two of a set of eight mahogany ladder back chairs in the Chippendale manner. (Christie's) $2,466 £1,800

Queen Anne walnut side chair with yoke shaped crest above vase form splat, Boston, circa 1730. (Robt. W. Skinner Inc.) $3,400 £2,361

An ornate Victorian rosewood cabriole leg chair, 1840. (British Antique Exporters) $182 £135

Two of a set of ten mahogany dining chairs with X-shaped splats centred by flowerheads, the seats upholstered in point de hongerie needlework. (Christie's) $9,333 £6,264

One of a set of four Victorian mahogany dining chairs, 1860. (British Antique Exporters) $579 £429

One of a set of six Scottish Regency period mahogany side chairs, seats covered in striped material. (Woolley & Wallis) $3,425 £2,500

Two of a set of ten Regency rosewood dining chairs, the caned seats with velvet covered squab cushion. (Christie's) $9,968 £7,020

One of a pair of Country Chippendale walnut side chairs with square slip seats, Penn., circa 1780. (Robt. W. Skinner Inc.) $6,800 £4,722

DINING CHAIRS

One of a pair of George III yellow-painted chairs with gothic-arcaded backs. (Christie's) $6,577 £4,536

A Chippendale mahogany side chair, with a serpentine crest rail, circa 1760/85, 38in. high. (Christie's) $1,650 £1,137

One of a set of eight ebonised and parcel gilt dining chairs on sabre legs with drop-in seats, upholstered in pale yellow silk. (Christie's) $2,770 £2,052

A Regency cream and brown painted bamboo pattern chair, the caned seat with squab cushion, and another en suite. (Christie's) $5,637 £3,888

One of a set of thirteen Regency mahogany dining chairs, including a pair of armchairs. (Christie's) $12,268 £8,640

A Chippendale walnut side chair on cabriole legs with shell carved knees and claw and ball feet, 1760/80. (Christie's)$16,500 £11,379

One of a pair of Chippendale mahogany slipper chairs, 1750/80, 36½in. high. (Christie's) $1,100 £758

One of a set of six Regency simulated rosewood and parcel gilt dining chairs. (Christie's) $21,924 £15,120

A Queen Anne walnut side chair with balloon shaped seat, 1740/60, 41in. high. (Christie's) $13,200 £9,103

DINING CHAIRS

One of a set of eight George III stained beechwood dining chairs, the backs filled with trelliswork and pilasters, and a set of four en suite of a later date. (Christie's) $10,179 £7,020

One of a set of six Victorian walnut small chairs with button upholstered seats. (Lawrence Fine Art) $1,196 £825

One of a set of ten painted 'fancy' chairs, with balloon rush seats, New England, circa 1825, 33½in. high. (Robt. W. Skinner Inc.) $2,700 £1,849

One of a set of twelve Harlequin Dutch marquetry dining chairs. (Christie's) $7,776 £5,400

A Chippendale mahogany side chair, circa 1780, 37in. high. (Robt. W. Skinner Inc.) $2,300 £1,597

A Queen Anne walnut side chair with yoked crest, 1740/60, 40½in. high. (Christie's) $9,900 £6,827

One of a set of four Dutch marquetry inlaid dining chairs with drop-in seats. (Worsfolds) $1,296 £900

One of a set of eight George III mahogany dining chairs, including two armchairs. (Christie's) $8,143 £5,616

One of a set of four and a similar pair of Federal mahogany side chairs, N.Y., 1800/10, on moulded sabre legs. (Christie's) $3,030 £2,089

DINING CHAIRS

One of a set of six early Georgian walnut and oak dining chairs with drop-in seats. (Christie's) $10,044 £8,100

Two of a set of six Sheraton period mahogany dining chairs. (Woolley & Wallis) $4,608 £3,200

A Queen Anne mahogany side chair with balloon slip seat, Mass., circa 1770. (Robt. W. Skinner Inc.) $5,200 £3,561

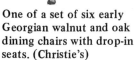
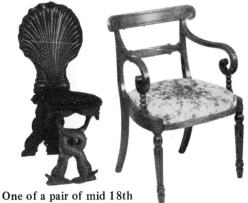

One of a pair of mid 18th century rococo walnut chairs, 17in. wide, 38in. high. (Christie's) $5,624 £4,536

Two of a set of three Irish Regency oak dining chairs, the drop-in seats covered with briar rose printed linen. (Christie's) $3,132 £2,160

One of a pair of Biedermeier walnut chairs with oval top-rails and waisted backs. (Christie's) $939 £648

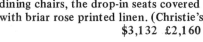

One of a pair of ash and maple fan-back Windsor side chairs, New. England, circa 1780. (Robt. W. Skinner Inc.) $1,600 £1,095

Two of a set of twenty-three Regency dining chairs, the seats covered in green striped horsehair (except one covered in green repp). (Christie's) $39,916 £30,240

One of a set of eight oak dining chairs of 17th century design. (Christie's) $3,288 £2,268

DINING CHAIRS

One of a pair of small mahogany and mahogany veneered Empire side chairs, New York, circa 1830. (Robt. W. Skinner Inc.) $850 £582

Two of a set of four single and one elbow 19th century Chippendale style mahogany dining chairs. (Dacre, Son & Hartley) $1,080 £750

One of a set of four black and gilt Empire chairs, in Grecian style, circa 1840, Eastern United States. (Robt. W. Skinner Inc.) $275 £188

One of a set of six carved hardwood chairs. (F. H. Fellows & Sons) $3,066 £2,100

Two of a set of six early 19th century rope twist and sabre leg dining chairs. (J. R. Bridgford & Sons) $2,520 £1,750

One of a set of four Victorian walnut side chairs on French cabriole front supports. (Reeds Rains) $835 £580

One of a set of six Regency mahogany hall chairs with solid seats and ring-turned tapering legs. (Christie's) $2,041 £1,512

Two of a set of twelve mahogany dining chairs, including a pair of armchairs, of George III style. (Christie's) $26,784 £21,600

One of eight late 19th century rococo Revival rosewood chairs, 37½in. high. (Robt. W. Skinner Inc.) $750 £513

DINING CHAIRS

One of four spindle back single chairs with rush seats and loose seat cushions in floral tapestry. (Capes, Dunn & Co.) $936 £650

One of a set of four Swiss oak hall chairs with pierced, shaped moulded backs carved with wolves' heads. (Christie's) $777 £540

One of a set of seven Regency mahogany chairs with solid seats, one stamped KL, one H, one S, one KL and H and one KL and S. (Christie's) $8,613 £5,940

A George II mahogany dining chair with interlaced gothic pattern and figure of eight splat. (Christie's) $1,879 £1,296

One of a set of eight Regency simulated rosewood dining chairs in beech. (Hobbs & Chambers) $633 £440

One of a set of late 19th century Queen Anne-style mahogany side chairs, England. (Robt. W. Skinner Inc.) $1,900 £1,301

One of a set of six George III mahogany dining chairs with bowed padded seats. (Christie's) $3,834 £2,700

One of a set of five Chippendale-style mahogany dining chairs. (Hobbs & Chambers) $1,944 £1,350

One of a set of six mahogany dining chairs, in the Georgian style with shield shaped backs. (Lawrence Fine Art) $1,435 £990

DINING CHAIRS

One of a set of eight Regency mahogany dining chairs of Gothic style with padded seats and moulded square legs. (Christie's) $5,214 £3,572

Late 18th century Windsor ash and maple fan back side chair, New England, 36in. high. (Robt. W. Skinner Inc.) $900 £633

One of a set of four George III grained hall chairs with solid bowed seats. (Christie's) $1,989 £1,404

One of a set of five George I red walnut dining chairs, including a pair of armchairs. (Christie's) $7,830 £5,400

One of a set of eight mahogany dining chairs with drop-in upholstered seats. (Christie's) $3,265 £2,268

One of a set of four Victorian rosewood dining chairs with pierced balloon backs carved with foliage. (Christie's) $3,834 £2,700

One of a set of four Macclesfield ladder back chairs with rush seats. (Peter Wilson & Co.) $1,008 £700

A William and Mary carved maple side chair, Mass., circa 1700, 48in. high. (Robt. W. Skinner Inc.) $4,250 £2,910

One of a set of six Regency ebonised dining chairs with bowed seats, four stamped SG. (Christie's) $2,607 £1,836

DINING CHAIRS

One of a set of six Regency mahogany dining chairs with tablet toprails. (Christie's) $3,395 £2,592

One of a pair of early 18th century Italian walnut side chairs with padded backs and seats covered in floral-decorated leather. (Christie's) $926 £702

One of a set of eight early George III mahogany dining chairs with pierced vase-shaped splats. (Christie's)
$37,497 £30,240

One of a set of six George III mahogany side chairs with shield-shaped backs. (Christie's) $6,026 £4,860

One of a set of four George III mahogany dining chairs, stamped E, together with a pair of armchairs and a pair of side chairs of later date. (Christie's)
$7,128 £5,400

One of a set of eight Regency cream painted simulated bamboo side chairs, the cane filled seats with pink silk cushions. (Christie's) $5,093 £3,888

One of a set of four George II mahogany chairs with bowed drop-in seats. (Christie's)
$18,748 £15,120

One of a set of twelve George IV oak dining chairs in the manner of Morel & Seddon. (Christie's) $19,958 £15,120

A George I walnut dining chair, the cartouche-shaped padded back and seat on cabriole legs. (Christie's)
$1,968 £1,458

DINING CHAIRS

One of a set of four George III mahogany side chairs with moulded oval pierced 'umbrella' backs. (Christie's) $6,026 £4,860

One of a set of six mid-Georgian mahogany dining chairs with drop-in needle-work-upholstered seats. (Christie's) $7,840 £5,940

A George III mahogany chair with oval padded back and serpentine seat covered in cafe-au-lait silk. (Christie's) $729 £540

One of a set of eight late 18th century Dutch neo-classical mahogany dining chairs with bowed uphol-stered seats. (Christie's) $6,415 £4,860

One of a set of twelve Regency mahogany dining chairs with panelled backs and X-shaped splats. (Christie's) $9,196 £7,020

A Serrurier-Bovy 'Silex' dismantling mahogany chair, circa 1905. (Christie's) $315 £216

One of a set of four George III cream and green painted dining chairs with shield-shaped backs. (Christie's) $1,607 £1,296

A George II walnut chair in the manner of Grendey, with drop-in seat.(Christie's) $1,697 £1,296

One of a pair of Regency mahogany hall chairs, the sabre back legs joined by ring-turned stretchers. (Christie's) $6,026 £4,860

DINING CHAIRS

One of a pair of George I walnut chairs with drop-in needlework seats, one missing. (Dreweatts) $2,475 £1,650

Two of a set of six painted ash bamboo fancy chairs, New England, 1800/15. (Christie's) $2,200 £1,517

One of a set of four 1920's oak chairs. (British Antique Exporters) $47 £35

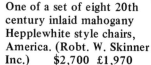

A Chippendale walnut side chair with square slip seat, circa 1760. (Robt. W. Skinner Inc.) $5,000 £3,472

One of a set of eight 20th century inlaid mahogany Hepplewhite style chairs, America. (Robt. W. Skinner Inc.) $2,700 £1,970

William and Mary maple side chair with rush seat on vase and block turned legs, New England, circa 1700. (Robt. W. Skinner Inc.) $6,100 £4,234

  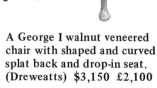

One of a set of eight Victorian mahogany framed balloon back dining chairs. (Lots Road Chelsea Auction Galleries) $1,117 £750

Two of a set of eight Regency mahogany dining chairs with aquamarine linen covered seats. (Christie's) $4,989 £3,240

A George I walnut veneered chair with shaped and curved splat back and drop-in seat. (Dreweatts) $3,150 £2,100

EASY CHAIRS

A George II walnut easy chair on carved cabriole legs with pad and disc feet. (Christie's) $2,420 £1,680

Victorian upholstered wing armchair, 1880. (British Antique Exporters) $113 £84

Victorian mahogany parlour chair, 1860. (British Antique Exporters) $120 £89

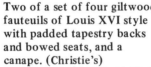

A 19th century carved mahogany side chair, with spoon shaped back, India, 48½in. high. (Robt. W. Skinner Inc.) $475 £346

Two of a set of four giltwood fauteuils of Louis XVI style with padded tapestry backs and bowed seats, and a canape. (Christie's) $2,423 £1,836

Victorian mahogany parlour chair, 1845. (British Antique Exporters) $349 £259

A George III mahogany armchair with arched padded back, arm supports and seat. (Christie's) $1,287 £864

Victorian parlour armchair, 1860. (British Antique Exporters) $310 £230

A George III mahogany library armchair with waved back, arm supports and seat upholstered in black leather. (Christie's) $3,132 £2,160

EASY CHAIRS

A Regency beechwood tub armchair, the back filled with cane and with green leather squab cushion. (Christie's) $1,528 £1,026

Tecno 'P 45' adjustable reclining wing armchair, designed by O. Borsani. (Christie's) $234 £162

An early George III mahogany library armchair, covered in gros and petit point needlework in wool and silk, 28in. wide. (Christie's) $15,660 £10,800

A Federal mahogany easy chair, on square tapering legs joined by a box stretcher, New England, 1790-1800. (Christie's) $2,640 £1,833

One of a pair of George III stained beechwood bergeres of Louis XV style with buttoned leather backs and bowed seats. (Christie's) $9,201 £6,480

A Queen Anne walnut wing armchair upholstered in olive leather. (Christie's) $7,241 £4,860

A Queen Anne walnut armchair, upholstered in lime green silk. (Christie's) $3,915 £2,700

A Charles II walnut open armchair, the upholstered seat covered in floral gros point needlework. (Christie's) $2,035 £1,404

A George I walnut wing armchair with out-scrolled arm supports and shell cabriole legs. (Christie's) $3,218 £2,160

EASY CHAIRS

One of a pair of painted beech frame armchairs in the French manner, English, circa 1775. (Woolley & Wallis) $5,754 £4,200

One of a pair of mid 19th century walnut folding armchairs with suede backs and seats, the frames carved to simulate bamboo. (Christie's) $3,862 £2,592

One of a set of three George III giltwood open armchairs covered in coral silk. (Christie's) $11,745 £8,100

One of a pair of George II giltwood open armchairs, the backs and seats covered with contemporary tapestry woven in wool and silk, 41½in. high. (Christie's) $133,110 £91,800

One of a pair of Regency mahogany bergeres, with distressed upholstery in ribbed frames. (Christie's) $5,481 £3,780

A George I mahogany easy chair on cabriole legs with slipper feet, 1720-30. (Christie's) $3,080 £2,138

A Federal upholstered mahogany lolling chair, circa 1775-95. (Christie's) $3,300 £2,291

A William IV mahogany library armchair with cane filled back, arms and seat, with leather squab cushions. (Christie's) $1,609 £1,080

A 17th century walnut and beechwood armchair, the seat covered in floral gros and petit point needlework. (Christie's) $1,331 £918

EASY CHAIRS

A George III parcel gilt and cream painted open armchair of Louis XV style, stamped WC. (Christie's) $1,409 £972

A mahogany carved chair in the form of a hand. (Christie's) $626 £432

One of a pair of George III polished beechwood open armchairs with the backs and seats covered in gros and petit point needlework, 39in. high. (Christie's) $2,818 £1,944

A George I walnut wing armchair covered in green material. (Christie's) $7,047 £4,860

A George III mahogany open armchair, lacking upholstery, (Christie's) $2,177 £1,512

One of a pair of giltwood fauteuils of Louis XV style, with cartouche shaped backs and serpentine seats. (Christie's) $1,244 £864

A Federal mahogany inlaid lolling chair, New England, circa 1815, 47in. high. (Robt. W. Skinner Inc.) $3,300 £2,323

A Regency brass mounted mahogany tub bergere with leather upholstered back, arms and squab cushion. (Christie's) $7,830 £5,400

One of a pair of William and Mary walnut and beechwood side chairs, upholstered in gold cut-velvet. (Christie's) $7,047 £4,860

EASY CHAIRS

A mid Georgian elm wing armchair with arched back and leather upholstery. (Christie's) $3,421 £2,376

A 17th century and later Flemish walnut open armchair with arched padded back and seat. (Christie's) $1,244 £864

One of a pair of mahogany library armchairs of early George III design. (Christie's) $6,134 £4,320

One of a pair of Regency rosewood tub bergeres with arched padded backs. (Christie's) $5,481 £3,780

Early 18th century parcel gilt and cream painted fauteuil with cartouche shaped back. (Christie's) $1,166 £810

A George II walnut wing armchair with padded back, arms and seat covered in green material, on cabriole legs and hairy-paw feet. (Christie's) $3,915 £2,700

A George II mahogany upright chair with padded back and seat on foliate cabriole legs. (Christie's) $1,331 £918

A George I walnut wing armchair with eared padded back and down-scrolled arms, covered in brown leather. (Christie's) $3,915 £2,700

A Regency mahogany tub bergere with cane-filled back and button drop-in seat, stamped HW. (Christie's) $1,150 £810

EASY CHAIRS

A beechwood fauteuil of Louis XV style with seat covered in 18th century gros and petit point needlework. (Christie's) $4,134 £3,132

A Venetian silver and painted grotto chair, the shaped back pierced with a dolphin, also bearing a paper trade label Frateli Rotali, Venezia. (Christie's) $1,995 £1,512

A William IV rosewood armchair with button-upholstered tub back and armrests. (Christie's) $2,546 £1,944

A George III mahogany library armchair, the back and seat upholstered in green floral silk. (Christie's) $4,687 £3,780

One of a pair of large mid 19th century ormolu mounted bergeres in the Empire style, the backs and seats covered in yellow silk. (Christie's) $12,830 £9,720

One of a pair of open armchairs, the backs and seats upholstered in gros point foliate needlework, late 17th century. (Christie's) $2,971 £2,268

One of a pair of mahogany open armchairs with upholstered shield-shaped backs and bowed seats. (Christie's) $5,356 £4,320

A George III giltwood bergere in the manner of J. Linnell, inscribed 'Roberts 1784' on the frame under the upholstery. (Christie's) $4,631 £3,456

One of a pair of Louis XV beechwood fauteuils with cartouche-shaped padded backs and serpentine upholstered seats. (Christie's) $3,421 £2,592

EASY CHAIRS

A 17th century beechwood X-framed open armchair covered in fragments of contemporary associated tapestry. (Christie's)
$5,702 £4,320

One of a pair of mid 19th century ormolu mounted mahogany bergeres in the Empire style. (Christie's)
$9,979 £7,560

A mid 18th century Venetian parcel gilt and aquamarine open armchair, the padded back and seat upholstered in point d'hongerie velvet. (Christie's) $1,425 £1,080

A Regency mahogany bergere with moulded arm supports and fluted tapering legs, the seat re-caned. (Christie's) $1,131 £864

A William IV mahogany armchair with scrolled shaped leather upholstered back and seat and ring-turned tapering legs. (Christie's)
$3,207 £2,376

A William and Mary walnut open armchair, the back and seat upholstered in yellow damask.(Christie's)
$2,280 £1,728

A Louis XV walnut bergere a oreilles with cushion seat covered in gros and petit point needlework. (Christie's)
$6,557 £4,968

A George III mahogany library armchair with padded back and seat. (Christie's)
$5,093 £3,888

A Louis XV beige-painted bergere, by J. B. Boulard, with shaped back and padded seat. (Christie's)
$2,280 £1,728

EASY CHAIRS

A Charles II oak sleeping armchair, the hinged back, wings and seat upholstered in raspberry damask. (Christie's) $4,134 £3,132

One of a pair of George IV giltwood open armchairs in the rococo style, attributed to Gillows of Lancaster. (Christie's) $17,107 £12,960

One of a pair of George III mahogany library armchairs upholstered in pale grey floral silk. (Christie's) $34,819 £28,080

One of a pair of early George III mahogany library armchairs with padded backs, arm supports and seats. (Christie's) $8,704 £7,020

One of a pair of William and Mary scarlet and gold lacquer X-frame open armchairs, 26½in. wide. (Christie's) $40,176 £32,400

A George III mahogany wing armchair upholstered in green leather. (Christie's) $2,544 £2,052

A Charles II walnut open armchair, the back and seat upholstered in green velvet damask. (Christie's) $3,421 £2,592

A Regency mahogany tub armchair, the back and seat upholstered in tan leather. (Christie's) $4,553 £3,672

A Regency mahogany open armchair with railed simulated bamboo back and padded arm supports and seat with leather cushion. (Christie's) $1,239 £918

EASY CHAIRS

An early George III parcel gilt and cream painted open armchair upholstered in floral needlework. (Christie's) $4,285 £3,456

A walnut open armchair with arched padded back and seat covered in floral tapestry woven with fables. (Christie's) $6,160 £4,968

A Regency giltwood throne armchair, attributed to Morel & Hughes. (Christie's) $28,512 £21,600

A George III mahogany armchair upholstered in blue velvet, partly re-railed. (Christie's) $3,961 £3,024

A Queen Anne walnut wing armchair with eared padded back, 36½in. wide. (Christie's) $45,532 £36,720

One of a pair of mid-Georgian mahogany library armchairs with padded backs, armrests and seats.(Christie's) $22,766 £18,360

A Charles I beech open armchair, the back and seat upholstered in gold and crimson velvet damask. (Christie's) $1,999 £1,512

A William and Mary walnut wing armchair upholstered in fruiting and floral tapestry. (Christie's) $14,256 £10,800

A Queen Anne walnut wing armchair upholstered in gros point needlework. (Christie's) $9,266 £7,020

EASY CHAIRS

A Renaissance Revival carved rosewood armchair, attributed to J. Jelliff, N.J., circa 1865, 29in. wide. (Robt. W. Skinner Inc.)
$1,900 £1,301

A Louis XV carved and gilded wood fauteuil upholstered in contemporary tapestry. (Dacre, Son & Hartley) $756 £525

One of a pair of George III giltwood open armchairs with serpentine seats. (Christie's) $5,011 £3,456

One of a set of six George II giltwood side chairs, the back and seat upholstered in crimson cut velvet, 27in. wide. (Christie's)
$166,428 £124,200

A mid Victorian easy armchair with buttoned back and seat upholstered in floral cut velvet and green velvet. (Christie's)
$5,950 £4,104

A George III mahogany side chair upholstered in gros point floral needlework. (Christie's) $1,566 £1,080

One of a pair of Victorian ebonised low chairs covered in blue felt applique with foliage and scrolls. (Christie's) $2,349 £1,620

A child's mahogany rocking chair commode, 2ft. high. (Capes, Dunn & Co.)
$79 £55

An early George III design mahogany open armchair upholstered in maroon velvet, 25in. wide. (Christie's)
$1,722 £1,188

EASY CHAIRS

A Regency mahogany correction chair upholstered in floral needlework on a caramel ground. (Christie's) $729 £540

A rococo Revival laminated rosewood upholstered armchair, attributed to J. H. Belter, New York, circa 1865. (Robt. W. Skinner Inc.) $7,500 £5,136

A mid Victorian mahogany armchair, upholstered in oxblood buttoned leather. (Christie's) $2,975 £2,052

One of a pair of laminated rosewood chairs, attributed to J. H. Belter, circa 1855, 38in. high. (Robt. W. Skinner Inc.) $2,700 £1,849

A mid Georgian Cuban mahogany Gainsborough armchair on cabriole legs, upholstered in yellow damask. (Dacre, Son & Hartley)$3,168 £2,200

A late 17th century beechwood side chair upholstered with sections of floral gros point needlework. (Christie's) $1,644 £1,134

A giltwood bergere with shaped back and sides ending in dolphin heads, circa 1840. (Christie's) $3,915 £2,700

A child's miniature mahogany rocking commode with hinged seat, 18th century. (Christie's) $510 £378

A Gustav Stickley willow armchair, circa 1907, 39in. high, 31in. wide. (Robt. W. Skinner Inc.) $400 £277

ELBOW CHAIRS

One of six Regency painted elbow chairs, the beech frames with rectangular and canted openwork backs and cane seats. (Lawrence Fine Art) $5,535 £3,740

Early 19th century comb-back rocker, New England, 39in. high. (Christie's)
$495 £361

A Chippendale walnut armchair on Marlborough legs, 1760-90, 42in. high. (Christie's) $2,200 £1,527

A Chippendale mahogany open armchair, circa 1770-85. (Christie's)
$12,100 £8,402

One of a set of eight Regency mahogany dining chairs with cane filled seats and sabre legs. (Christie's)
$5,793 £3,888

One of a pair of George III green-painted beechwood open armchairs with shaped drop-in seats. (Christie's)
$4,183 £2,808

An 18th century turned and painted bannister back armchair, New England. (Robt. W. Skinner Inc.)
$1,500 £1,013

One of a pair of satinwood open armchairs of Regency design, the caned seats with squab cushions. (Christie's)
$6,894 £4,536

One of a pair of early 19th century Gothic open armchairs with later solid seats. (Christie's) $8,367 £5,616

ELBOW CHAIRS

A mid 19th century Windsor writing armchair on rockers, 43½in. high. (Christie's) $1,100 £802

Victorian oak revolving office chair. (British Antique Exporters) $94 £70

Windsor maple, ash and pine bowback armchair, New England, circa 1780. (Robt. W. Skinner Inc.)
$1,600 £1,081

A Chippendale mahogany open armchair on Marlborough legs. (Christie's) $1,320 £916

A George III mahogany open armchair with padded serpentine seat. (Christie's)
$3,175 £2,160

A Regency mahogany open armchair of gothic style with pierced arcaded back. (Christie's) $1,931 £1,296

One of a pair of George III mahogany open armchairs, the seats upholstered with yellow floral damask. (Christie's) $2,790 £1,836

A Queen Anne maple corner chair with stepped horseshoe shaped back, 1735-65. (Christie's) $880 £611

An early Georgian walnut open armchair with drop-in needlework seat. (Christie's) $965 £648

ELBOW CHAIRS

One of a pair of Regency cream painted and gilded open armchairs with caned backs and seats. (Christie's) $1,722 £1,188

A Charles II walnut open armchair with cane-filled back and seat. (Christie's) $2,818 £1,944

One of a set of five George III mahogany dining chairs, with bowed padded seats. (Christie's) $2,975 £2,052

A William and Mary bannister back armchair, circa 1730, Conn., 49¾in. high. (Robt. W. Skinner Inc.) $1,700 £1,180

One of two late 18th century brace-back continuous arm Windsors, 38in. high. (Christie's) $3,850 £2,655

A Pilgrim Century turned oak armchair, with a rush seat, circa 1670/1710, 42½in. high. (Christie's) $330 £227

A gilt gesso open armchair of George I design, the drop-in seat covered with gros and petit point needlework. (Christie's) $1,566 £1,080

A grain painted rocker, circa 1840, 45in. high. (Robt. W. Skinner Inc.) $850 £590

A green painted bowback Windsor armchair, circa 1780. (Robt. W. Skinner Inc.) $3,000 £2,083

One of a set of six Wallace Nutting ash, pine and maple bowback Windsor chairs, Mass., circa 1920, 41in. high. (Robt. W. Skinner Inc.)
$5,000 £3,424

One of a pair of late George III mahogany shield-back armchairs, circa 1790/1810, 39in. high. (Christie's)
$1,870 £1,289

A Windsor ash and maple writing armchair, America, circa 1800, 43in. high. (Robt. W. Skinner Inc.)
$1,900 £1,338

A George III green painted open armchair, the shaped caned seat with squab cushion. (Christie's)
$548 £378

A Queen Anne walnut armchair with arched back and bowed seat, on pad feet. (Christie's) $7,365 £5,940

Early 19th century mahogany open armchair with leather padded seat. (Christie's) $3,265 £2,268

One of a pair of George III cream and green painted open armchairs, with bowed cane-filled seats. (Christie's) $1,722 £1,188

One of a pair of early 19th century yewwood Windsor elbow chairs with bow backs and pierced splats. (Lawrence Fine Art)
$1,515 £1,045

One of a pair of Regency painted open armchairs, the later solid seats with squab cusions. (Christie's)
$3,288 £2,268

ELBOW CHAIRS

One of a pair of George III mahogany open armchairs with tapering beaded railed backs. (Christie's)
$1,556 £1,188

One of a pair of Regency mahogany metamorphic library armchairs, the seat opening to reveal four treads, 23in. wide. (Christie's)
$16,070 £12,960

One of a set of four parcel gilt and green painted side chairs with cane-filled backs and seats, mid 18th century. (Christie's) $3,749 £3,024

One of a pair of Regency painted satinwood open armchairs with heart-shaped backs. (Christie's)
$9,979 £7,560

One of a pair of mid 18th century Dutch walnut burgomaster's chairs, the pierced tub backs with carved head finials. (Christie's) $9,979 £7,560

One of a set of nine satinwood and cream-painted open armchairs with U-shaped cane-filled toprails. (Christie's)
$64,152 £48,600

One of a set of six parcel gilt and simulated rosewood open armchairs of Regency style. (Christie's)
$8,488 £6,480

A Regency metamorphic library armchair attributed to Morgan & Saunders, the seat opening to reveal four treads. (Christie's) $4,989 £3,780

One of a pair of mahogany, Mason's open armchairs, with hinged foot rests, possibly Irish. (Christie's)
$3,537 £2,700

ELBOW CHAIRS

One of a set of eight walnut and mahogany dining chairs and two open armchairs by J. Henry Sellers. (Christie's) $4,730 £3,240

One of a pair of Regency parcel gilt and black painted open armchairs, the seats upholstered in aquamarine silk. (Christie's) $5,376 £4,104

One of a pair of Italian Empire parcel gilt and cream painted fauteuils with padded backs and seats. (Christie's) $4,561 £3,456

One of a set of three late George III painted open armchairs with caned seats, two with squab cushions, and a chair and triple-backed sofa en suite. (Christie's) $3,214 £2,592

One of a pair of George II mahogany hall armchairs, and a settee, 49in. wide. (Christie's) $19,958 £15,120

One of a set of eight George III painted open armchairs with shield-shaped backs, 21½in. wide. (Christie's) $14,256 £10,800

A late 18th century Italian walnut open armchair with upholstered seat. (Christie's) $997 £756

A George III green and gold lacquer open armchair with pierced oval wheelback. (Christie's) $3,749 £3,024

A Regency beechwood fauteuil with arched caned back and serpentine seat in moulded frame. (Christie's) $1,639 £1,242

ELBOW CHAIRS

A Windsor open armchair with yewwood hoop back, rails and arms, and elm seat. (Capes, Dunn & Co.)
$201 £140

One of a pair of Regency mahogany open armchairs, the later caned seats with leather squab cushions. (Christie's) $7,516 £5,184

A George I walnut open armchair, with shepherd's crook arms and drop-in padded seat. (Christie's)
$18,009 £12,420

A George IV mahogany reading chair attributed to Morgan & Saunders. (Christie's) $3,445 £2,376

A George I walnut open armchair with shell and husk cabriole legs and pad feet. (Christie's)
$6,264 £4,320

A George III mahogany folding campaign chair with arched and hinged leather covered back. (Christie's)
$1,088 £756

A Windsor comb-back rocking armchair, the saddle seat resting on bamboo turned legs, circa 1800, 48in. high. (Robt. W. Skinner Inc.)
$400 £281

One of a pair of Victorian open arm dining chairs with cane seats. (Butler & Hatch Waterman) $2,664 £1,850

A turned maple and ash ladder back armchair, New England, circa 1720, 47½in. high. (Robt. W. Skinner Inc.)
$2,000 £1,369

ELBOW CHAIRS

A Windsor bowback brace-back armchair, New England, circa 1780, 37½in. high. (Robt. W. Skinner Inc.) $3,200 £2,253

A 19th century Dutch walnut and marquetry elbow chair with spoon back, needlework upholstered drop-in seat and cabriole legs. (Dacre, Son & Hartley) $432 £300

One of a set of six George III painted open armchairs with later caned seats and ivory damask squab cushions. (Christie's) $26,622 £18,360

A William and Mary walnut open armchair, with shaped railed splats and padded seat. (Christie's) $1,174 £810

A George III parcel gilt and pale blue painted open arm-chair, upholstered in rose velvet. (Christie's) $2,035 £1,404

One of a pair of late 18th century black and gold lacquer open armchairs with upholstered seats. (Christie's) $5,481 £3,780

A William and Mary maple and ash slat back turned armchair, New England, circa 1710. (Robt. W. Skinner Inc.) $1,400 £972

One of a pair of early George III mahogany open armchairs with drop-in circular seats. (Christie's) $5,950 £4,104

One of a pair of painted beechwood open armchairs, the shield shaped backs with Prince of Wales plumes. (Christie's) $2,505 £1,728

One of a pair of early 19th century French Empire mahogany elbow chairs with bowed upholstered seats. (Lawrence Fine Art) $3,093 £2,090

Cromwellian style oak hall chair, circa 1870. (British Antique Exporters) $164 £122

One of a set of six George III cream painted open armchairs with cane filled backs and seats. (Christie's) $7,724 £5,184

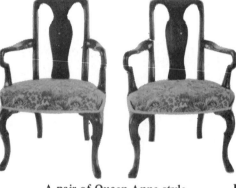

A Gothic oak stall with hinged seat and linenfold panelled sides, with silk and metal thread squab cushion, 26in. wide, 96in. high.(Christie's) $1,866 £1,296

A pair of Queen Anne style walnut armchairs, 35in. high. (Robt. W. Skinner Inc.) $3,000 £2,112

Late 19th century child's Windsor highchair. (British Antique Exporters) $157 £117

A walnut open armchair of George II style with paperscroll toprail. (Christie's) $3,540 £2,376

Chinese carved hardwood chair, circa 1860. (British Antique Exporters) $355 £263

One of a pair of George III mahogany open armchairs, with padded seats and partly-filled turned fluted tapering legs. (Christie's) $4,907 £3,456

FURNITURE

Chippendale mahogany ser-
pentine chest of drawers
with four graduated drawers,
Mass., circa 1780, 32in. high.
(Robt. W. Skinner Inc.)
$21,000 £14,583

Georgian oak chest of drawers,
1790. (British Antique Exporters)
$400 £297

A Chippendale cherrywood
chest of drawers on ogee
bracket feet, Penn., 1760-
80. (Christie's)
$2,090 £1,525

A Federal inlaid mahogany
bowfront chest of drawers,
1790-1810, 42in. wide.
(Christie's) $2,860 £2,087

A set of Victorian oak
filing drawers, 1880. (British
Antique Exporters)
$627 £465

A Federal mahogany and
mahogany veneer bureau,
possibly carved by Samuel
F. McIntire, circa 1810,
42½in. wide. (Robt. W.
Skinner Inc.)
$2,400 £1,621

A Federal mahogany and
mahogany veneer bowfront
bureau, circa 1800, 35½in.
wide. (Robt. W. Skinner Inc.)
$3,900 £2,708

A Chippendale mahogany bowfront chest of drawers, Mass.,
1760-80, 40½in. wide.
(Christie's) $2,200 £1,527

A Federal inlaid mahogany
bowfront dressing bureau,
the top drawer fitted with
a mirror, 38in. wide.
(Christie's) $3,410 £2,368

CHESTS OF DRAWERS

A William and Mary oyster veneered walnut and olive-wood chest, 34½in. wide. (Christie's) $6,696 £5,400

A Federal mahogany inlaid butler's desk on French feet, with replaced oval brass pulls, 44in. wide. (Robt. W. Skinner Inc.) $1,600 £1,095

A mid Georgian mahogany dressing chest with a fitted drawer and a baize-lined slide above three graduated long drawers, 36in. wide. (Christie's) $4,957 £3,672

A Georgian walnut veneered dwarf chest with writing slide, fitted with brass plate handles and escutcheons, 32in. wide. (Morphets) $6,248 £4,400

A Country pine grain painted blanket chest, New England, circa 1820, 39in. wide. (Robt. W. Skinner Inc.)$1,300 £890

A Deerfield-type pine blanket chest with brass engraved escutcheons and teardrop pulls, circa 1730, 39in. wide. (Robt. W. Skinner Inc.) $1,600 £1,095

A Country Chippendale maple chest of drawers, circa 1780, 36in. wide. (Robt. W. Skinner Inc.) $1,800 £1,232

A Federal mahogany inlaid bowfront bureau, circa 1811, 39in. wide. (Robt. W. Skinner Inc.) $1,700 £1,164

A Chippendale cherry chest of drawers, Conn., circa 1780, 40in. wide. (Robt. W. Skinner Inc.) $1,200 £821

FURNITURE

An early Georgian walnut
chest with two short and
three graduated long drawers,
40½in. wide. (Christie's)
$2,829 £2,160

A Queen Anne burr walnut
chest with a slide above four
graduated long drawers, 30in.
wide. (Christie's)
$5,376 £4,104

A William and Mary walnut
chest, the drawers with brass
drop handles, 3ft.1½in. x 2ft.
11in. x 21¾in. (Woolley &
Wallis) $5,800 £4,000

A walnut bachelor's chest
with hinged top and four
graduated long drawers,
30½in. wide. (Christie's)
$4,957 £3,672

A Queen Anne walnut and
burr walnut bachelor's
chest with crossbanded
folding top, 26in. wide.
(Christie's)
$26,049 £19,440

A mahogany Georgian chest
of drawers, original handles
missing and replaced with
Victorian style wooden
knobs. (Ball & Percival)
$1,008 £700

An early Georgian walnut
chest with four graduated
long drawers on later bracket feet, 33in. wide.
(Christie's) $6,123 £4,536

A Queen Anne burr walnut
bachelor's chest with crossbanded hinged top and four
graduated long drawers,
26¾in. wide. (Christie's)
$21,427 £17,280

A Queen Anne period walnut
chest, the drawers with brass
plates and escutcheons, 33½in.
wide. (Woolley & Wallis)
$7,250 £5,000

CHESTS OF DRAWERS

A mid Georgian mahogany chest with four graduated drawers on bracket feet, 30in. wide. (Christie's) $2,662 £1,836

A late Federal mahogany veneer bowfront chest of drawers, 1800/20, 43½in. wide. (Christie's) $935 £644

A Chippendale cherrywood chest of drawers, 1760/90, 40in. wide. (Christie's) $1,760 £1,213

A Queen Anne tiger maple chest of drawers, New England, circa 1750, 36in. wide. (Robt. W. Skinner Inc.) $2,900 £2,042

A Chippendale maple chest of drawers on bracket feet, New England, circa 1770, 34in. wide. (Robt. W. Skinner Inc.) $3,300 £2,323

A walnut bachelor's chest with crossbanded folding top, 31½in. wide. (Christie's) $21,924 £15,120

A Queen Anne walnut bachelor's chest with hinged top, on bracket feet, 29½in. wide. (Christie's) $37,584 £25,920

A late Federal inlaid mahogany bowfront chest of drawers, Mass., 1800/20, 44¾in. wide. (Christie's) $4,400 £3,034

A Chippendale mahogany chest of drawers, circa 1780, 40in. long. (Robt. W. Skinner Inc.) $6,100 £4,236

CHESTS OF DRAWERS

A Louis XV French Provincial walnut chest of serpentine and swelling shape, 49½in. wide. (Lawrence Fine Art)
$6,512 £4,400

A George III mahogany chest with four graduated long drawers, 49in. wide. (Christie's)$13,311 £9,180

A walnut bachelor's chest with crossbanded hinged top, the sides with carrying handles, 30in. wide. (Christie's)
$9,979 £7,560

A George III satinwood and mahogany serpentine chest, 41¼in. wide. (Christie's)
$7,464 £5,184

A Country Chippendale cherry grain painted tall chest, New England, circa 1800, 37in. wide. (Robt. W. Skinner Inc.)
$2,600 £1,805

A Federal cherry and bird's-eye maple veneered bow-front bureau, Mass., circa 1800, 39in. wide. (Robt. W. Skinner Inc.) $5,000 £3,521

A George III mahogany chest with crossbanded serpentine top, the fitted top drawer with baize lined slide and easel mirror, 36in. wide. (Christie's)
$13,311 £9,180

A Queen Anne mahogany block-front chest of drawers, Mass., 1750/80, 33½in. wide. (Christie's)
$38,500 £26,551

A George III mahogany chest with four graduated long drawers, mounted with gilt metal rococo handles, 37in. wide. (Christie's)
$5,950 £4,104

CHESTS OF DRAWERS

A Chippendale fruitwood reverse serpentine chest of drawers, Mass., circa 1780, 38in. wide. (Robt. W. Skinner Inc.) $14,000 £9,859

A George III mahogany chest with moulded serpentine top, baize lined writing slide and four graduated long drawers, 48in. wide. (Christie's) $4,071 £2,808

A George III mahogany chest with moulded serpentine top, 42in. wide. (Christie's) $5,481 £3,780

A Federal inlaid cherrywood chest of drawers, circa 1780/1810, 39in. wide. (Christie's) $2,860 £1,972

A Queen Anne maple chest of drawers with replaced Queen Anne style brasses, Rhode Island, circa 1750, 35in. wide. (Robt. W. Skinner Inc.) $1,600 £1,111

A Queen Anne walnut chest with three short and three long drawers, 29½in. wide. (Christie's) $28,188 £19,440

A Federal mahogany veneer bowfront chest of drawers, 1800-20, 35½in. wide. (Christie's) $1,870 £1,364

A Chippendale cherrywood reverse serpentine front chest of drawers, 1760-90, 42¼in. wide. (Christie's) $2,860 £2,087

A Queen Anne painted pine blanket chest, circa 1740, 37¼in. wide. (Robt. W. Skinner Inc.) $850 £590

CHESTS OF DRAWERS

A Chippendale mahogany reverse serpentine chest of drawers, 1760-90, 38in. wide. (Christie's)
$8,800 £6,111

A Chippendale birch chest of drawers on bracket feet, 38½in. wide. (Christie's)
$1,870 £1,298

A Chippendale mahogany and mahogany veneered bowfront chest with ball handles, Mass., circa 1790, 42¼in. wide. (Robt. W. Skinner Inc.)
$3,750 £2,604

A Queen Anne oyster veneered walnut chest, the top with geometric fruitwood stringing, on later bun feet. (Christie's)
$7,241 £4,860

A Chippendale maple tall chest of drawers, New England, circa 1760, 36in. wide. (Robt. W. Skinner Inc.)
$2,200 £1,486

A small George III mahogany chest with a caddy top, the front inset slide with brass knob handles, 31½in. wide. (Woolley & Wallis)
$2,055 £1,500

Victorian mahogany baronial chest of drawers, 1860. (British Antique Exporters)
$363 £269

A mahogany bachelor's chest, the hinged rectangular top with writing slide and four graduated long drawers, 31in. wide. (Christie's)
$3,057 £2,052

A Chippendale mahogany chest of drawers, 1765-85, 40in. wide. (Christie's)
$3,080 £2,138

CHESTS ON CHESTS

A Charles II walnut and marquetry cabinet on chest, on later bracket feet, 49½in. wide. (Christie's)
$12,528 £8,640

A James Bartram Chippendale mahogany chest on chest, in two sections, circa 1750/70, 44½in. wide. (Christie's)
$110,000 £75,862

An early Georgian walnut tallboy with moulded concave cornice, 43¼in. wide. (Christie's) $6,706 £4,968

A Chippendale cherrywood chest on chest, in two sections, 1760/80, 41in. wide. (Christie's) $4,950 £3,413

A Chippendale tiger maple tall chest with six graduated thumb moulded drawers, circa 1770, 36in. wide. (Robt. W. Skinner Inc.)
$4,000 £2,702

A Queen Anne walnut tallboy with chamfered cavetto cornice, 44in. wide. (Christie's) $5,481 £3,780

A mid Georgian oak tallboy, the base with two long drawers, 46in. wide. (Christie's)
$1,566 £1,080

Georgian mahogany chest on chest, 1780. (British Antique Exporters)
$1,080 £800

A George III mahogany tallboy with figured front and original brass handles, 47in. wide. (Lawrence Fine Art) $8,954 £6,050

A Queen Anne walnut and burr walnut tallboy, the lower part with a secretaire drawer, 43in. wide. (Christie's) $18,792 £12,960

A Chippendale walnut chest on chest on ogee bracket feet, 44in. wide, 1760-90. (Christie's)$37,400 £25,972

A Chippendale cherrywood chest on chest, in two sections, 1765-85, 38½in. wide. (Christie's) $8,250 £5,729

A Chippendale maple chest on chest, circa 1770-85, 38in. wide. (Christie's) $4,180 £2,902

A Queen Anne walnut cabinet-on-chest on later bracket feet, 39½in. wide. (Christie's) $7,959 £5,940

A George III mahogany tallboy with key-patterned cornice, 44½in. wide. (Christie's) $3,207 £2,376

A George III mahogany tallboy, the base fitted with a secretaire drawer, 44in. wide. (Christie's) $3,758 £2,592

A Chippendale maple tall chest, Rhode Island, circa 1780, 35.3/8in. wide. (Robt. W. Skinner Inc.) $3,000 £2,054

A George III mahogany tallboy with three short and six long drawers, 49in. wide. (Christie's) $6,114 £4,104

CHESTS ON STANDS

A Queen Anne maple high-boy, New Jersey, circa 1730, 37in. wide. (Robt. W. Skinner Inc.)
$8,500 £5,902

A Queen Anne cherrywood bonnet top high chest, circa 1740-70, 41in. wide. (Christie's)
$26,400 £19,270

A Chippendale maple highboy with original brasses, circa 1760, 38in. wide. (Robt. W. Skinner Inc.)
$10,000 £6,944

A William and Mary maple and burl walnut veneer high-boy, Mass., circa 1730, 39½in. wide. (Robt. W. Skinner Inc.)
$3,900 £2,746

A walnut chest-on-stand, the base with six various sized drawers, 42in. wide. (Christie's) $3,218 £2,160

A Queen Anne walnut veneer high chest of drawers, 1735-50, 40in. wide. (Christie's) $5,280 £3,666

A Queen Anne walnut chest-on-stand with two short and three graduated long drawers on the upper chest, 43in. wide. (Christie's) $2,263 £1,728

A Queen Anne walnut chest on frame, in two sections, Penn., 1750-80, 69in. high. (Christie's) $6,600 £4,583

A Queen Anne maple high chest of drawers, in two sections, Mass., 1740/60, 36in. wide. (Christie's)
$10,450 £7,206

CHESTS ON STANDS

A Queen Anne walnut high chest on frame, 1750-70, 40½in. wide. (Christie's) $10,450 £7,256

A Queen Anne cherrywood highboy, probably Wethersfield, Conn., circa 1740-65, 37½in. wide. (Christie's) $15,400 £10,694

Queen Anne maple highboy with five graduated drawers, one long drawer and three split drawers, circa 1740, 75¼in. high. (Robt. W. Skinner Inc.) $23,000 £15,972

A Queen Anne cherrywood high chest of drawers, in two sections, circa 1740-70, 39in. wide. (Christie's) $8,800 £6,111

A Queen Anne oyster veneered walnut chest-on-stand, 36in. wide. (Christie's) $10,459 £7,020

A William and Mary walnut and oak chest-on-stand, 40½in. wide. (Christie's) $1,770 £1,188

A William and Mary birch high chest of drawers, in two sections, 1710-20, 44in. wide. (Christie's) $10,450 £7,256

A Queen Anne oak grain painted chest on frame, England, circa 1730, 38in. wide. (Robt. W. Skinner Inc.) $3,000 £2,112

A Queen Anne burl and walnut veneer highboy, Mass., circa 1740, 61¼in. high. (Robt. W. Skinner Inc.) $16,000 £11,267

CHIFFONIERS

An early Victorian rosewood chiffonier, stamped W. Stratford, 50in. wide. (Christie's) $900 £600

A William IV rosewood and parcel gilt breakfront chiffonier, the doors filled with lime-green silk pleats, 70in. wide. (Christie's) $4,183 £2,808

A Regency ebonised maplewood and bois clair chiffonier with two open shelves, 34in. wide. (Christie's) $4,071 £2,808

A William IV figured mahogany chiffonier with scroll carved bracket supports, 3ft. 10in. wide. (Capes, Dunn & Co.) $950 £660

A Victorian walnut inlaid chiffonier with triple arched mirror back, 5ft. wide. (Peter Wilson & Co.) $782 £525

A Regency rosewood chiffonier with small canopy back and on four bun feet, 36in. wide. (Reeds Rains) $1,036 £700

An early Victorian mahogany chiffonier, the top with a three-quarter galleried superstructure, 40in. wide. (Christie's) $1,192 £800

A William IV mahogany chiffonier, the base with two recessed mirror panelled doors, 42in. wide. (Christie's) $1,837 £1,250

One of a pair of mid Victorian satinwood, purpleheart and gilt metal mounted chiffoniers applied with blue Wedgwood plaques, 42in. wide. (Christie's) $9,201 £6,480

An early George III sycamore clothes press on re-inforced ogee bracket feet, 45½in. wide. (Christie's) $2,624 £1,944

A George II mahogany clothes press, the cornice with foliate and egg-and-dart border, 53in. wide. (Christie's) $35,640 £27,000

A Federal mahogany linen press, in two sections, New York, 1800-15, 46¼in. wide. (Christie's) $4,400 £3,055

A Chippendale mahogany and mahogany veneer linen press, circa 1780, 48in. wide. (Robt. W. Skinner Inc.) $16,000 £11,111

A Federal inlaid mahogany linen press, in two sections, probably New York, circa 1785-1805, 45in. wide. (Christie's) $6,050 £4,201

A Federal mahogany linen press, signed by I. Bailey, New Jersey, 1807, 48in. wide. (Christie's) $8,250 £5,729

A George III satinwood clothes press, the cupboard doors enclosing five slides, 49½in. wide. (Christie's) $5,637 £3,888

A George III fiddleback mahogany serpentine clothes press, 54in. wide. (Christie's) $28,576 £19,440

A small Regency mahogany clothes press on sabre feet with square toes, 36¼in. wide. (Christie's) $7,241 £4,860

A late 18th century mahogany commode with tambour front and tray top, 20½in. wide. (Bermondsey)
$450 £300

Victorian mahogany pot cupboard with marble top. (British Antique Exporters)
$148 £110

A fine quality late 18th century mahogany tray top commode, complete with bowl, 20½in. wide. (Bermondsey) $1,000 £700

An early 19th century flame mahogany pot cupboard with a figured marble top. (Bermondsey) $175 £125

Victorian walnut pot cupboard, circa 1860. (British Antique Exporters)
$114 £85

One of a pair of Biedermeier mahogany bedside cupboards with hinged tops, 22in. wide. (Christie's) $26,622 £18,360

A George III mahogany bow front bedside commode, 21in. wide. (Christie's)
$1,350 £900

A Georgian mahogany enclosed washstand/commode with fold-over top, rising mirror and fitted compartments and basin, 18in. wide. (Lawrence Fine Art)
$877 £605

George III mahogany tray top commode with cupboard above sliding drawer, 20in. wide. (Reeds Rains)
$403 £280

COMMODE CHESTS

A directoire gilt metal mounted mahogany commode on turned tapering feet, 50in. wide. (Christie's)
$3,706 £2,808

An Italian walnut and marquetry commode in the style of Maggiolini, 45in. wide. (Christie's) $2,799 £1,944

One of a pair of South German walnut and fruitwood parquetry commodes, late 18th century, 51½in. wide. (Christie's)$22,680 £15,120

A George III satinwood commode crossbanded with rosewood and inlaid with amaranth bands, 47¼in. wide. (Christie's)
$11,421 £8,100

A Louis XV kingwood and marquetry miniature commode, the serpentine top inlaid with a musical trophy, 19½in. wide. (Christie's)
$1,910 £1,296

A George III cream and black painted commode on parcel gilt square tapering fluted legs, 62in. wide. (Christie's)
$23,490 £16,200

An Edwardian painted satinwood commode with D-shaped top inlaid with a halved bat's wing motif, 51in. wide. (Christie's)
$5,149 £3,456

A George III satinwood and marquetry commode in the French style, 45in. wide. (Christie's)
$41,277 £28,080

One of a pair of satinwood commodes crossbanded in rosewood with serpentine tops, 33½in. wide. (Christie's) $8,648 £5,616

COMMODE CHESTS

A Louis XV ormolu mounted kingwood and rosewood commode, with moulded serpentine breche violette marble top, 52½in. wide. (Christie's) $6,220 £4,320

An early 19th century German walnut parquetry commode, 50½in. wide. (Robt. W. Skinner Inc.) $2,200 £1,506

An 18th century Italian walnut serpentine commode, fitted with three long drawers outlined in fruitwood, 51½in. wide. (Christie's)$2,851 £2,160

A George III satinwood commode with eared oval top, 43in. wide. (Christie's) $14,094 £9,720

A 19th century Louis XV-style commode with moulded breccia marble top, 40¼in. wide. (Robt. W. Skinner Inc.) $1,200 £821

A mid 18th century French provincial carved, painted and gilded wood commode, 37½in. wide. (Dacre, Son & Hartley) $403 £280

A mid 18th century Venetian parcel gilt and painted commode with serpentine marble-ised top, 37in. wide. (Christie's) $2,488 £1,728

An 18th century French provincial oak commode with waved apron and shaped feet, 47in. wide. (Christie's) $4,665 £3,240

An ormolu mounted kingwood and tulipwood breakfront commode with moulded breccia marble top, 38in. wide. (Christie's) $3,136 £2,376

COMMODE CHESTS

A George III mahogany commode with crossbanded hinged rectangular top, 50in. wide. (Christie's)
$5,356 £4,320

A sycamore and marquetry serpentine commode on stepped ormolu feet, 71½in. wide. (Christie's)
$4,665 £3,456

An early George I mahogany commode of concave bombe outline, 39in. wide. (Christie's)$37,497 £30,240

A George III mahogany commode with serpentine top above a slide, 45in. wide. (Christie's) $12,722 £10,260

One of a pair of George III satinwood, sycamore and marquetry commodes, 46in. wide. (Christie's)
$28,944 £21,600

An ormolu mounted kingwood and floral marquetry bombe commode of Louis XV style, 51½in. wide. (Christie's) $2,954 £2,052

A George III mahogany serpentine commode with four graduated long drawers, 46½in. wide. (Christie's)
$13,024 £9,720

Mid 18th century Danish rosewood and parcel gilt commode with white marble top, 28in. wide. (Christie's) $2,954 £2,052

A George II mahogany dressing commode with lobed serpentine top and a drawer above a central cupboard door, 55½in. wide. (Christie's)
$15,919 £11,880

CORNER CUPBOARDS

A late Georgian oak barrel back corner cupboard, the upper part 89½in. high, the lower part 31in. high, top illustrated. (Lawrence Fine Art) $877 £605

A Federal cherrywood corner cupboard, American, 1790/ 1810, 50½in. wide. (Christie's) $2,640 £1,820

A Chippendale pine corner cupboard, 1760-90, 78½in. high. (Christie's) $5,280 £3,666

Mid 18th century German ormolu mounted walnut corner cabinet, 33in. wide. (Christie's) $1,866 £1,296

A George I black and gold lacquer corner cupboard, 22in. wide. (Christie's) $1,367 £918

A Federal pine corner cupboard on straight bracket feet, 50¾in. wide, 1780-1800. (Christie's) $3,740 £2,597

A carved oak corner cabinet with pentagonal bevelled glass front, Mass., circa 1900, 80¼in. high. (Robt. W. Skinner Inc.) $2,400 £1,751

A Federal cherrywood corner cupboard in two sections, circa 1820-60, 42in. wide. (Christie's) $2,860 £2,087

A pine corner cupboard with three shaped open shelves, New England, circa 1750, 37in. wide. (Robt. W. Skinner Inc.) $1,300 £878

CORNER CUPBOARDS

An early 18th century Dutch black japanned corner cupboard with a single panelled door, 21in. wide. (Christie's) $997 £756

A mahogany bow-fronted corner cupboard inlaid with Prince of Wales Feathers. (Ball & Percival) $864 £600

A George I scarlet and gold lacquer corner cupboard with arched bevelled glazed cupboard door, 24in. wide. (Christie's) $7,241 £4,860

Victorian inlaid mahogany swan neck corner cupboard. (British Antique Exporters) $1,452 £1,076

A painted cherry and pine hanging corner cupboard, circa 1790, New Jersey, 36½in. wide. (Robt. W. Skinner Inc.) $2,200 £1,486

A Dutch walnut and marquetry corner cupboard, the top inset with a clock, 30in. wide, 99in. high. (Christie's) $3,732 £2,592

A cherry corner cupboard with clock, Penn., circa 1815, 83in. high. (Robt. W. Skinner Inc.) $2,500 £1,689

A late Chippendale cherrywood corner cupboard, American, circa 1785/1810, 45in. wide. (Christie's) $3,300 £2,275

A Country Federal cherry corner cupboard, Penn., circa 1820, 56½in. wide. (Robt. W. Skinner Inc.) $1,200 £821

CUPBOARDS

A butternut and pine cupboard on tall bracket feet, New England or Canada, 49in. wide. (Robt. W. Skinner Inc.) $850 £574

A George III mahogany side cabinet of D-shape, the front with two panel doors enclosing four small drawers and two long drawers, 60in. wide. (Lawrence Fine Art) $2,930 £1,980

A 17th century Flemish oak cupboard, the lower part with a drawer with lion mask corbels, 55in. wide. (Lawrence Fine Art) $3,349 £2,310

An early George III mahogany cupboard with original brass handles, 44in. wide. (Lawrence Fine Art) $2,442 £1,650

An early 17th century James I inlaid oak court cupboard, 49in. wide. (Robt. W. Skinner Inc.) $4,750 £3,345

Mid 18th century French provincial oak cupboard, the doors partly filled with wire, 47in. wide. (Christie's) $3,110 £2,160

A partly 18th century oak cupboard on bracket feet, 62in. wide. (Lawrence Fine Art) $2,767 £1,870

A small painted pine cupboard with four interior shelves, circa 1810, 25¼in. wide. (Robt. W. Skinner Inc.) $2,300 £1,554

A green painted pine blanket chest/cupboard with lift top, probably Long Island, circa 1785/1825, 43½in. wide. (Christie's) $2,970 £2,048

CUPBOARDS

Late 18th century pine pewter cupboard, America, 41in. wide. (Robt. W. Skinner Inc.)
$6,750 £4,753

An early 17th century oak food cupboard on turned legs and platform stretcher, 50¼in. wide. (Christie's)
$5,322 £3,456

A grain painted walnut cupboard, Penn., circa 1820, 82½in. wide. (Robt. W. Skinner Inc.)
$1,200 £810

A Federal tiger maple cupboard with two glazed doors, 1800-10, 54½in. wide. (Christie's)
$4,180 £2,902

A 17th century Flemish rosewood, oak, ebonised and tortoiseshell cupboard, 64½in. wide.(Christie's)
$3,888 £2,700

A Federal pine step back cupboard, New England, circa 1810, 51in. wide. (Robt. W. Skinner Inc.) $1,800 £1,460

An 18th century oak livery cupboard with brass drop handles, 5ft.6in. x 6ft.9in. high. (Capes, Dunn & Co.)
$1,224 £850

An English oak corner buffet, circa 1900, 111cm. wide. (Christie's)
$313 £216

A pine step back cupboard, New England, circa 1800, 58½in. wide. (Robt. W. Skinner Inc.)
$2,000 £1,351

413

A Victorian walnut davenport with ebony inlay and hinged lid to stationery compartment, 21in. wide. (Butler & Hatch Waterman) $504 £350

A Victorian figured walnut davenport with hinged top, the base with four short and four dummy drawers, 1ft.9in. wide. (Capes, Dunn & Co.) $1,008 £700

An early Victorian figured walnut davenport, the surprise pop-up top with three-quarter gallery, 22½in. wide. (Christie's) $2,250 £1,500

A Victorian walnut davenport, the rectangular coffered top fitted with a sprung stationery compartment. (Christie's) $2,499 £1,700

Victorian inlaid walnut davenport, 1880. (British Antique Exporters) $579 £429

An early Victorian oak davenport, with hinged leather lined writing panel and four long graduated drawers, 21½in. wide. (Christie's) $750 £500

A Victorian rosewood davenport, the rectangular top with a three-quarter gallery, 24in. wide. (Christie's) $1,162 £780

A George III mahogany davenport with carrying handle and leather lined swivelling sloping flap, 15½in. wide. (Christie's) $9,201 £6,480

A Victorian burr walnut davenport with a sliding hinged writing slope, 33in. high. (Anderson & Garland) $1,065 £740

DAVENPORTS

Victorian walnut davenport with shaped legs, 1860. (British Antique Exporters) $1,264 £937

Victorian mahogany davenport with galleried stationery box, 22in. wide. (Coles, Knapp & Kennedy) $558 £380

A Regency davenport with gilt metal three-quarter pierced gallery, 20½in. wide. (Christie's) $2,954 £1,944

A mid Victorian gilt and mother-of-pearl, black japanned, papier mache davenport on bun feet, 27in. wide. (Christie's) $2,954 £1,944

A rosewood davenport with balustrade gallery, 23in. wide. (Outhwaite & Litherland) $1,232 £850

A Killarney arbutus wood davenport inlaid with architectural subject ovals, 31½in. wide. (Christie's) $5,920 £4,000

An inlaid burr walnut davenport with sycamore interior, late 19th century. (Peter Wilson & Co.) $1,188 £825

A Regency calamander wood davenport, the turned feet with brass castors, 21¼in. wide, circa 1820. (Woolley & Wallis) $1,562 £1,100

An inlaid burr walnut davenport with three-quarter pierced gallery, 24¾in. wide. (Christie's) $2,760 £1,944

An Edwardian satinwood display cabinet, the front with central glazed panel flanked by bowed glazed doors, 42in. wide. (Lawrence Fine Art)
$1,435 £990

Art Nouveau style oak display cabinet. (British Antique Exporters)
$383 £284

Late 19th century Louis XVI style ormolu mounted marquetry vitrine, America, 38in. wide. (Robt. W. Skinner Inc.) $3,000 £2,189

An Edwardian mahogany inlaid bow front corner display case with low gallery. (Peter Wilson & Co.)
$432 £300

An Edwardian mahogany display cabinet crossbanded in satinwood, 57½in. wide. (Christie's) $1,984 £1,350

An Edwardian satinwood display cabinet painted with flowers, ribbon-tied foliate scrolls and grisaille panels, 41in. wide. (Christie's)
$3,384 £2,400

Victorian walnut and ormolu display cabinet, 1860. (British Antique Exporters)
$1,944 £1,440

A figured walnut veneered display cabinet with shaped cresting above the glazed doors, 214cm. wide. (Christie's) $8,731 £5,940

A Dutch walnut and marquetry veneered display cabinet, 46in. wide. (Butler & Hatch Waterman) $3,550 £2,500

DISPLAY CABINETS

Gustav Stickley one door china closet, circa 1907, no. 820, 36in. wide. (Robt. W. Skinner Inc.) $1,300 £902

A Dutch walnut and marquetry display cabinet on later bun feet, 73in. wide. (Christie's) $6,998 £4,860

A Colonial calamander display cabinet, the drawers with silver plated handles, early 19th century, 57in. wide. (Christie's) $2,430 £1,620

A Regency mahogany cabinet of small size, 20½in. wide. (Lawrence Fine Art) $3,011 £2,035

A Victorian ebonised and brass inlaid side cabinet with glazed bow-fronted doors, 4ft.6in. wide. (Capes, Dunn & Co.) $710 £480

Late 19th century mahogany Chinese Chippendale design display cabinet on stand, 49 x 26 x 84in. high. (Peter Wilson & Co.) $4,752 £3,300

Late Victorian mahogany china display cabinet with carved surmount, 4ft. wide. (Hobbs & Chambers) $1,258 £850

A Dutch walnut and marquetry display cabinet with a pair of glazed doors, 59in. wide. (Christie's) $4,155 £2,808

An Edwardian satinwood breakfront china cabinet in Sheraton revival style, 4ft.9in. wide. (Woolley & Wallis) $3,456 £2,400

An Art Nouveau mahogany breakfront cabinet, probably made by Liberty, circa 1898, 139cm. wide. (Lawrence Fine Art) $803 £550

A Victorian rococo style mahogany side cabinet with arch top oblong mirror panel back, 5ft. wide. (Capes, Dunn & Co.) $1,562 £1,100

An Edwardian George III style satinwood display cabinet banded in ebony, 48in. wide. (Christie's) $2,205 £1,500

A shaped Dutch marquetry, domed top, display cabinet with brass handles, 4ft.0½in. wide. (Geering & Colyer) $2,736 £1,900

A 19th century Dutch walnut veneered showcase cabinet, 225cm. high. (Christie's) $4,595 £3,126

A walnut showcase cabinet, the single door and sides with glass panels, probably Dutch, 18th/19th century, 218cm. high. (Christie's) $4,136 £2,814

A 19th century French mahogany and brass cabinet with brass borders and ·mounts, 52in. wide. (Lawrence Fine Art) $1,953 £1,320

A figured walnut veneered display cabinet, 233cm. high. (Christie's) $4,365 £2,970

An Edwardian inlaid mahogany display cabinet with centre serpentine shaped drawer, 50in. wide. (Reeds Rains) $1,656 £1,150

DISPLAY CABINETS

Late 19th century Japanese lacquer display cabinet, 70in. high. (Robt. W. Skinner Inc.) $5,700 £3,904

An Edwardian Art Nouveau mahogany side cabinet with boxwood, satinwood and harewood stylised floral inlay, 4ft. wide. (Capes, Dunn & Co.) $624 £440

Late 18th century Netherlands rococo mahogany marquetry cabinet, 56in. wide. (Robt. W. Skinner Inc.) $7,700 £5,422

A Georgian style carved mahogany display side cabinet of serpentine outline, 4ft.4in. wide. (Capes, Dunn & Co.) $1,512 £1,050

Art Nouveau style oak china cabinet, 1920. (British Antique Exporters) $98 £73

A Wylie & Lochhead mahogany display cabinet, designed by E. A. Taylor, 88cm. wide. (Christie's) $2,505 £1,728

An Edwardian mahogany china display cabinet with Gothic style astragal glazing, 4ft.6in. wide. (Capes, Dunn & Co.) $748 £520

A black and gold lacquer display cabinet with two brass mounted oval panelled glazed doors, 50½in. wide. (Christie's) $4,698 £3,240

An Edwardian mahogany display cabinet, inlaid with chequered boxwood lines and harewood, 52in. wide. (Christie's) $1,800 £1,200

DRESSERS

A mid 18th century oak dresser with brass drop handles and escutcheons, 98in. long. (Dacre, Son & Hartley) $3,744 £2,600

An early Georgian low oak dresser with rectangular top, 65in. wide. Lawrence Fine Art) $797 £550

An early Georgian oak dresser with moulded rectangular top, the frieze with three drawers, 73½in. wide. (Christie's) $3,353 £2,484

A Georgian oak dresser with plate rack. (F. H. Fellows & Sons) $2,920 £2,000

An oak dresser on square cabriole legs and pad feet, mid 18th century, 78in. wide. (Christie's) $5,322 £3,456

A George III oak dresser with mahogany crossbanding throughout, 85½in. wide. (Lawrence Fine Art) $2,930 £1,980

An 18th century low oak dresser with a moulded top above three frieze drawers, 90 x 32in. high. (Lawrence Fine Art) $2,711 £1,870

A Georgian oak dresser, the upper part fitted with open shelves flanked by two spice cupboards, 6ft.4in. wide. (Geering & Colyer) $3,150 £2,100

An early 19th century oak and fruitwood dresser base with three drawers, on cabriole legs, 79in. wide. (Christie's) $4,344 £2,916 .

DRESSERS

Georgian oak dresser base of two deep drawers on slightly shaped legs. (Lots Road Chelsea Auction Galleries) $1,092 £780

An oak three-drawer dresser with three baluster turned front legs, circa 1700, 6ft. 3in. long. (Peter Wilson & Co.) $5,760 £4,000

An 18th century oak dresser of fine patina and colour, 86½in. wide. (Christie's) $5,942 £4,536

An early 18th century Southern Welsh oak enclosed dresser raised on stump feet, 158cm. wide. (Osmond Tricks) $1,859 £1,300

A George III oak dresser with three drawers to the base and open shelves above, 63in. wide. (Chelsea Auction Galleries) $2,664 £1,800

A mid 18th century oak dresser, the three drawers with brass knobs, 69in. wide.(Dacre, Son & Hartley) $1,500 £1,000

A George III low oak dresser with three frieze drawers, 82in. wide. (Lawrence Fine Art) $1,355 £935

Victorian oak Welsh dresser, circa 1880. (British Antique Exporters) $675 £500

A Georgian low oak dresser fitted with three frieze drawers, 80in. wide. (Lawrence Fine Art) $2,392 £1,650

DUMBWAITERS

A George III mahogany three-tier dumbwaiter on vase-shaped shaft, foliate cabriole legs and pad feet, 42in. wide. (Christie's) $2,588 £1,836

A mid Georgian mahogany two-tier dumb waiter with circular trays and turned vase-shaped shaft. (Christie's) $2,147 £1,512

A George III mahogany three-tier dumbwaiter, 46in. high. (Christie's) $2,192 £1,512

A late Georgian mahogany two-tier dumb waiter, each circular tier with two flaps, 36in. high. (Lawrence Fine Art) $1,790 £1,210

A Georgian mahogany three-tier dumbwaiter, 48in. high. (Outhwaite & Litherland) $609 £420

A George III two-tier mahogany dumbwaiter with moulded circular shelves, 37in. high. (Christie's) $1,218 £864

A Regency mahogany three-tier dumbwaiter with graduated twin-flap shelves, 23½in. wide, 45½in. high.(Christie's) $919 £702

A George III mahogany two-tier dumbwaiter, 20½in. wide, 36in. high. (Christie's) $7,840 £5,940

A mid Georgian mahogany dumb waiter with two turned tiers, 20in. diam. (Christie's) $2,574 £1,728

A George III mahogany partner's desk with leather lined top and nine drawers on both sides. 60¼in. wide. (Christie's) $6,577 £4,536

A 20th century mahogany partner's desk, Steven Smith, Boston, with brass pulls and escutcheons, 58in. long. (Robt. W. Skinner Inc.) $3,000 £2,054

A George III mahogany pedestal desk with moulded, scarlet leather lined rectangular top, 54in. wide. (Christie's) $1,496 £972

An early Georgian pollard elm kneehole desk, 37½in. wide. (Christie's) $3,540 £2,376

A Queen Anne walnut kneehole desk on bracket feet, the sides with gilt metal carrying handles, 27¾in. wide. (Christie's) $17,463 £11,880

An early George III mahogany serpentine kneehole desk with gadrooned top and a fitted secretaire drawer, 44½in. wide. (Christie's) $12,873 £8,640

A Queen Anne walnut kneehole desk with folding top, enclosing an oak lined interior, 46in. wide. (Christie's) $10,179 £7,020

Oak twin pedestal roll-top desk, 1900. (British Antique Exporters) $984 £729

A Regency mahogany partner's desk with leather lined top, four slides and three frieze drawers, 66in. wide. (Christie's) $4,158 £2,700

FURNITURE

A Regency mahogany part-
ner's desk with leather lined
top, 77½in. wide.
(Christie's) $5,103 £3,780

A George III mahogany
partner's desk with leather
lined top, 59½in. wide.
(Christie's) $4,527 £3,456

A mid 18th century Italian
walnut and marquetry kneehole desk on cabriole legs
and square pad feet.
(Christie's) $7,413 £5,616

An early Georgian walnut
kneehole desk with one long
and eight short drawers,
32in. wide. (Christie's)
$5,443 £3,780

A Queen Anne walnut knee-
hole desk of golden colour,
32in. wide. (Christie's)
$15,919 £11,880

A Queen Anne pollard elm
kneehole desk, the top
crossbanded with oak her-
ringbone bands, 33in. wide.
(Christie's) $4,553 £3,672

A Country Federal cherry
partner's desk, circa 1820,
53½in. wide. (Robt. W.
Skinner Inc.)
$3,000 £2,083

A George III mahogany kneehole secretaire in the manner
of Gillows, with leather lined
top, 49½in. wide. (Christie's)
$3,991 £3,024

A George III mahogany
partner's desk, the kneehole
flanked by six graduated
drawers, 55in. wide. (Christie's) $10,179 £7,020

George III mahogany tambour pedestal desk. (Hobbs & Chambers) $2,160 £1,500

An English Arts & Crafts brass mounted mahogany, sycamore and walnut marquetry partner's desk, 129.6cm. wide. (Christie's) $3,626 £2,484

Twin pedestal oak roll-top desk, 1880. (British Antique Exporters) $1,588 £1,177

A mahogany partner's desk with leather lined top and thirteen drawers, 46½in. wide. (Christie's) $3,288 £2,268

An early Georgian walnut and burr walnut kneehole desk on ogee bracket feet, 34in. wide. (Christie's) $5,950 £4,104

A late 18th century Italian walnut and marquetry kneehole desk, the top inlaid with a musical trophy, 36in. wide. (Christie's) $1,140 £864

A George III mahogany kneehole desk with seven various sized drawers, 33in. wide. (Christie's) $2,505 £1,728

An oyster veneered kingwood kneehole desk of Mazarin form, late 17th century, 33½in. wide. (Christie's) $10,179 £7,020

A Queen Anne walnut kneehole desk on later bun feet, 36½in. wide. (Christie's) $3,395 £2,592

LOWBOYS

A Chippendale style carved
walnut dressing table on
acanthus carved cabriole
legs, 36in. wide.(Christie's)
$2,090 £1,525

George I oak lowboy.
(Hobbs & Chambers)
$1,123 £780

A George II mahogany
rectangular lowboy, the
drawers with wooden handles,
32in. wide. (Dreweatts)
$3,750 £2,500

A Queen Anne maple dress-
ing table on four cabriole
legs ending in pad feet, circa
1760, 33in. wide. (Robt. W.
Skinner Inc.)
$9,500 £6,418

A Queen Anne maple dressing
table with one long and three
short drawers, 31¾in. wide.
(Christie's) $1,540 £1,124

An early Georgian walnut
lowboy with three drawers
above the waved apron, 32in.
wide. (Christie's)
$2,091 £1,404

A walnut lowboy, the shaped
frieze with three drawers on
shell and husk cabriole legs,
30½in. wide. (Christie's)
$67,050 £45,000

A Dutch burr walnut lowboy
with moulded waved top,
early 18th century, 30in.
wide. (Christie's)
$4,568 £3,240

A Queen Anne walnut dressing table on tapering cylindrical legs with disc feet,
33in. wide, 1735-50.
(Christie's) $8,800 £6,111

FURNITURE

Victorian mahogany three-fold screen, 1880. (British Antique Exporters) $194 £144

Late 18th century coromandel twelve-fold screen, China, 99½in. high, panel width 19½in. (Robt. W. Skinner Inc.) $18,000 £12,500

One of a pair of Regency parcel gilt and cream painted firescreens with later glazed adjustable panels, 18in. wide. (Christie's) $578 £388

A mahogany polescreen with rectangular petit point needlework panel worked with the parable of the Prodigal Son, 60in. high. (Christie's) $5,471 £3,672

A four-leaf screen decorated with 18th century Chinese wallpaper, each leaf 86 x 21½in. (Christie's) $5,065 £3,780

Regency rosewood pole screen, circa 1830. (British Antique Exporters) $232 £172

Chinese two-fold inlaid screen, 1860. (British Antique Exporters) $344 £255

Victorian bamboo fire-screen, 1880. (British Antique Exporters)$55 £41

A late 19th century black and gold lacquer four-leaf screen, 77 x 26in. (Christie's) $2,413 £1,620

SCREENS

A Chinese Export black and gold lacquer eight-leaf screen depicting the history of tea-making, 18th century, each leaf 84 x 21½in. (Christie's) $27,496 £20,520

One of a pair of George III mahogany polescreens, the adjustable panels with later silk floral sprays, 14½in. wide. (Christie's) $466 £324

A late 18th/early 19th century Chinese painted six-leaf screen decorated in colours with an extensive view, each leaf 23½in. wide, 83in. high. (Christie's) $17,409 £14,040

Late 19th century ivory mounted two-leaf table screen, signed Shizan (for the Shibayama inlay) and Shinko (for the lacquer decoration). (Christie's) $3,231 £2,376

A Victorian wooden fencing, Maine, circa 1850, 39½in. high, total length 172in. (Robt. W. Skinner Inc.) $475 £325

A six-leaf Japanese screen, sumi and colour on gold paper, signed, 26 x 80in. each leaf. (Edgar Horn) $3,285 £2,250

An 18th century Chinese Export black and gold lacquer eight-leaf screen, each leaf 22in. wide, 76½in. high. (Christie's) $9,201 £6,480

One of a pair of Regency giltwood screens, with glazed Beauvais tapestry panels, 24½in. wide. (Christie's) $1,409 £972

Late 19th century ivory mounted two-leaf lacquer table screen decorated in Shibayama style, signed Masayuki, each panel 30 x 16.5cm. (Christie's) $2,056 £1,512

An 18th century Dutch six-leaf canvas screen painted with rustic scenes, each leaf 21¼in. wide, 65¼in. high. (Christie's) $4,600 £3,240

One of a pair of William IV rosewood polescreens, the brass shafts with faded crimson silk banners, 19in. wide. (Christie's) $939 £648

An 18th century Chinese black and gold lacquer eight-leaf screen, each leaf 81in. high, 21in. wide. (Christie's) $29,462 £23,760

An 18th century coromandel lacquer eight-leaf screen incised and decorated in colours, each leaf 15¾in. wide, 83in. high. (Christie's) $6,026 £4,860

A Victorian mahogany polescreen with oval framed adjustable screen, circa 1870. (Peter Wilson & Co.) $374 £260

A Japanese Export lacquer and Shibayama inlaid two-fold screen, decorated in bone, mother-of-pearl, ivory and hardwood, each fold 2ft.5½in. wide, 5ft.7in. high. (Capes, Dunn & Co.) $878 £610

An 18th century Dutch painted and gilded leather six-leaf screen, each leaf 108in. high, 21in. wide. (Christie's) $5,598 £3,888

A Charles X fruitwood and ebonised firescreen with glazed needlework panel, 53½in. high. (Christie's) $2,192 £1,512

A late 19th century four-fold low screen in maroon velvet and bands of Berlin woolwork, 41in. high, each fold 18in. (Christie's) $3,445 £2,376

Late 18th/early 19th century gilt metal mounted mahogany secretaire a abattant, 37½in. wide. (Christie's)$2,332 £1,620

A George III mahogany secretaire chest, the top with hinged flap, 60in. wide. (Christie's) $5,788 £4,320

A late George III mahogany secretaire cabinet, the doors enclosing sliding tray shelves, 46in. wide. (Lawrence Fine Art) $1,953 £1,320

A George III mahogany secretaire cabinet, 30in. wide, 63½in. high. (Christie's) $10,962 £7,560

A Federal inlaid mahogany bureau desk, possibly by M. Allison, 1790/1810, N.Y., 46½in. wide. (Christie's) $4,400 £3,034

A Regency rosewood secretaire cabinet, the baize-lined drawer with fitted interior, 23in. wide. (Christie's) $16,443 £11,340

A pale mahogany Campaign chest with central secretaire drawer. (Worsfolds) $1,440 £1,000

A late George III mahogany and partridgewood secretaire, 30½in. wide. (Christie's) $2,091 £1,404

An Empire painted bureau with original brass pulls, New England, circa 1825, 41in. wide. (Robt. W. Skinner Inc.) $3,200 £2,163

A 19th century German
(Ludwig II) ormolu moun-
ted Japanese black and
gold lacquer cartonnier,
46½in. wide. (Christie's)
$29,548 £20,520

A George III mahogany
secretaire on ogee bracket
feet, 32½in. wide.
(Christie's)
$43,416 £32,400

A George III mahogany
secretaire cabinet on fluted
square legs and block feet,
43in. wide. (Christie's)
$100,440 £81,000

A Louis XV kingwood
semainier of bombe outline,
the seven drawers inlaid a
deux faces, stamped F. C.
Franc JME, 26in. wide.
(Christie's) $4,354 £3,024

A Chippendale mahogany
bureau with four drawers,
Boston, circa 1790, 36½in.
wide. (Robt. W. Skinner
Inc.) $18,000 £12,500

A George III satinwood
secretaire, with fitted secretaire drawer above two long
and one deep drawer, 32½in.
wide. (Christie's)
$8,850 £5,940

An 18th century walnut
secretaire a abattant with
fall front, 36in. wide.
(Worsfolds) $4,320 £3,000

A Louis XVI kingwood and
tulipwood semainier by J.
J. Kirschenbach, 56in. high.
(Christie's) $4,276 £3,240

Late 19th century marque-
try secretaire with pull-out
secretary drawer, Holland,
41½in. wide. (Robt. W.
Skinner Inc.)
$1,200 £875

One of a pair of Regency mahogany secretaire book-cases, 47½in. wide. (Christie's)$11,491 £7,560

A Regency mahogany secre-taire bookcase on plinth base, 37½in. wide. (Christie's) $4,082 £3,024

A Federal inlaid mahogany secretary, Mass., 1800-20, 36in. wide. (Christie's) $4,620 £3,372

An Empire stencilled maho-gany secretary in two parts, New York, 1820-30, 42¼in. wide. (Christie's) $7,480 £5,459

A Federal mahogany secre-tary bookcase, in two parts, circa 1805/25, 39½in. wide. (Christie's) $3,300 £2,275

An Irish mid-Georgian mahogany kneehole secre-taire bookcase, 40in. wide. (Christie's) $9,477 £7,020

A Regency mahogany secre-taire cabinet with two gothic pattern glazed cupboard doors, 43in. wide. (Chris-tie's) $5,211 £3,594

A Federal inlaid mahogany and bird's-eye maple desk and bookcase, 1790/1810, 41in. wide. (Christie's) $19,800 £13,655

A George III mahogany secre-taire cabinet with later silver lined interior, 36½in. wide. (Christie's) $10,179 £7,020

432

SECRETAIRE BOOKCASES

A Federal mahogany veneered secretary, Mass., 1800-1810, 41¾in. wide.
(Christie's) $7,700 £5,347

A Regency mahogany secretaire bookcase, 48½in. wide.
(Lacy Scott) $4,205 £2,900

Federal mahogany butler's secretary, with high French feet, circa 1810, 41in. wide.
(Robt. W. Skinner Inc.)
$7,750 £5,381

A 19th century oak twin pedestal cylinder top desk bookcase, 3ft.8in. wide.
(Bridgfords) $803 £590

A George III mahogany secretaire cabinet with moulded tear-drop cornice, 49in. wide.
(Christie's)$4,957 £3,672

A Federal mahogany secretary with two glazed panel doors with crosshatching, circa 1795, 41in. wide.
(Robt. W. Skinner Inc.)
$4,750 £3,209

An early 19th century Regency mahogany secretary with adjustable shelves, 47in. wide. (Robt. W. Skinner Inc.)
$2,700 £1,824

A Victorian Arts & Crafts carved walnut Masonic secretaire, 4ft.2in. wide.
(Capes, Dunn & Co.)
$864 £600

An Edwardian mahogany secretaire bookcase in the Sheraton revival manner, 240 x 127cm. (Phillips)
$2,192 £1,600

SECRETAIRE BOOKCASES

A George III mahogany and satinwood secretaire cabinet, 49in. wide. (Christie's) $9,201 £6,480

A mahogany secretaire bookcase with four glazed doors enclosing adjustable shelves, 55in. wide. (Christie's) $2,384 £1,600

A Federal mahogany and mahogany veneer inlaid secretary, Mass., circa 1815, 39in. wide. (Robt. W. Skinner Inc.) $4,500 £3,082

A late George III mahogany secretaire bookcase, the glazed panel doors enclosing adjustable shelves, 43in. wide. (Anderson & Garland) $5,040 £3,500

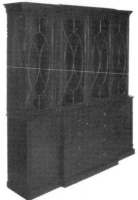

A George III mahogany secretaire bookcase, the frieze inlaid with fruitwood foliate ovals, 102in. wide. (Christie's) $8,613 £5,940

A George III mahogany secretaire cabinet with two glazed doors, 49in. wide. (Christie's) $4,827 £3,240

A George III satinwood secretaire cabinet with geometrically-glazed doors, 31½in. wide. (Christie's) $27,496 £20,520

A George III mahogany secretaire bookcase, the interior with adjustable shelves, 3ft.7in. wide. (Woolley & Wallis) $3,425 £2,500

A George III mahogany secretaire cabinet, the secretaire drawer with fruitwood and maple veneers, 43½in. wide. (Christie's) $4,344 £2,916

SECRETAIRE BOOKCASES

A George III mahogany secretaire cabinet with a pair of glazed cupboard doors, 43½in. wide. (Christie's) $6,436 £4,320

A Federal mahogany secretary with glazed panel doors above a fold-down writing surface, circa 1795, 40in. wide. (Robt. W. Skinner Inc.) $7,500 £5,281

A Regency mahogany secretaire cabinet, the doors flanked by ebony mouldings, 49in. wide. (Christie's) $6,512 £4,860

A George III mahogany and satinwood secretaire bookcase with baize lined fitted secretaire drawer, 39½in. wide. (Christie's) $3,680 £2,592

An English 19th century Chippendale style mahogany secretaire cabinet, 86in. long. (Robt. W. Skinner Inc.) $22,000 £15,277

A George III satinwood and rosewood secretaire cabinet, the baize-lined fall-flap enclosing a fitted interior, 36in. wide. (Christie's) $12,052 £9,720

A George III mahogany secretaire cabinet with a pair of glazed cupboard doors, 45½in. wide. (Christie's) $3,395 £2,592

A Georgian secretaire bookcase with glazed doors enclosing brocade lined shelves. (Worsfolds) $1,820 £1,300

A satinwood secretaire bookcase, late 18th century, possibly Anglo-Indian, 31½in. wide. (Christie's) $5,786 £4,104

SETTEES & COUCHES

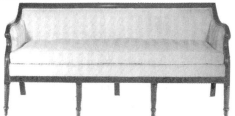

A Federal upholstered mahogany sofa on ring turned and reeded legs, circa 1800-15, 75½in. long. (Christie's) $4,950 £3,437

A Federal mahogany sofa, the padded back with arched crest, 1790-1810, 80¼in. wide. (Christie's) $4,400 £3,055

A Regency mahogany hall bench, the scrolled sabre legs with turned baluster carrying handles, stamped James Winter 101 Wardour St., 47in. wide. (Christie's) $7,959 £5,940

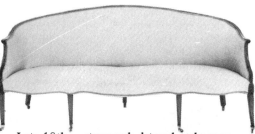

Late 18th century upholstered mahogany Sheraton sofa, 79in. long. (Robt. W. Skinner Inc.) $1,500 £1,094

A 19th century Netherlands rococo style mahogany and marquetry inlaid settee, overall exotic wood and mother-of-pearl floral and bird inlay, 49in. wide. (Robt. W. Skinner Inc.) $1,200 £845

A 19th century Jacobean-style carved oak hall settle with lift-up seat, 66¾in. wide. (Robt. W. Skinner Inc.) $650 £445

A Federal carved mahogany sofa, Phila., 1805-20, 75¾in. long. (Christie's) $4,950 £3,437

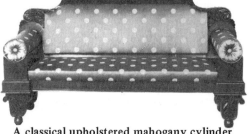

A classical upholstered mahogany cylinder arm sofa, circa 1810-30, 72in. long. (Christie's) $990 £687

SETTEES & COUCHES

A Federal mahogany carved sofa, the arched crest rail with grape and vine decoration, 75in. wide. (Robt. W. Skinner Inc.)
$2,000 £1,351

One of a pair of grain painted 'fancy' settees, each with a back of four sections, 74in. wide, 1800-10. (Christie's) $4,950 £3,437

19th century oak settle, circa 1890. (British Antique Exporters) $162 £120

A Victorian mahogany framed settee, circa 1860. (British Antique Exporters)
$453 £336

A Regency simulated bamboo sofa with pierced triple chairback, cane filled seat and squab cushion, 54in. wide. (Christie's)$2,413 £1,620

Georgian pine settle, circa 1770. (British Antique Exporters) $346 £257

A George III mahogany sofa with serpentine back, Irish, late 18th century, 86in. wide. (Christie's) $3,300 £2,291

A Federal mahogany sofa, the upholstered back and seat with beaded bow front, probably Mass., circa 1810, 73in. wide. (Robt. W. Skinner Inc.) $3,700 £2,500

FURNITURE

'Anfibio', a white leather upholstered sofa bed designed by Alessandro Becchi, 240cm. wide. (Christie's) $867 £594

A laminated birchwood chaise longue designed by Bruno Mathsson, Made in Sweden, 151cm. long. (Christie's) $709 £486

A George III mahogany humpback sofa with plum-coloured floral damask loose cover, squab and four cushions, 85in. wide. (Christie's) $6,696 £5,400

One of a pair of Regency rosewood sofas with triple cushion backs and cushion seats covered in green velvet, 77in. wide. (Christie's) $16,070 £12,960

A small, George III, mahogany humpback sofa with upholstered back, scrolled arms and waved seat on square tapering legs, 63in. wide. (Christie's) $8,268 £6,264

A walnut sofa with padded back and seat, with outscrolled arm supports, on shell and husk cabriole legs and pad feet, 62in. wide. (Christie's) $4,631 £3,456

One of a pair of George II mahogany hall settles with solid seats, on turned tapering foliate legs and stepped turned feet, 49in. wide. (Christie's) $64,281 £51,840

A George III mahogany sofa upholstered in apricot silk, 66in. wide. (Christie's)
                    $2,678 £2,160

FURNITURE

'Djinn series', an upholstered chaise longue designed by Olivier Mourgue, in green nylon stretch jersey, circa 1965, 170cm. long.
(Christie's) $1,103 £756

One of a pair of George II carved pine sofas with waved drop-in seats, 144in. wide.
(Christie's) $40,176
£32,400

A Regency mahogany sofa with double-scrolled padded back and squab cushion upholstered in green watered silk stripes, 78in. wide. (Christie's)
$2,546
£1,944

A George III mahogany sofa, the arched padded back, out-scrolled arms and bowed seat on moulded square legs, 77in. wide.
(Christie's) $5,942 £4,536

A George I walnut twin-back settee with drop-in bowed seat, the arm supports carved with eagle's heads, on shell and husk cabriole legs, 55½in. wide.   (Christie's) $12,117
£9,180

One of a set of four parcel gilt and grey painted corner chairs, forming a sociable, with yellow silk backs and seats.
(Christie's) $4,385 £3,348

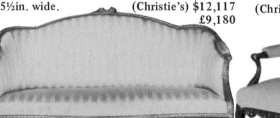

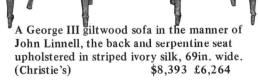

A George III giltwood sofa in the manner of John Linnell, the back and serpentine seat upholstered in striped ivory silk, 69in. wide.
(Christie's) $8,393 £6,264

An early George II mahogany sofa in the French taste, the serpentine seat covered in green silk repp, 61in. wide.
(Christie's) $4,341 £3,240

SETTEES & COUCHES

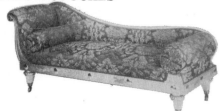

A William IV giltwood chaise longue with scrolled upholstered back, seat and footrest, 92in. wide. (Christie's) $1,456 £1,026

One of a pair of George II mahogany twin chairback settees, with arms ending in eagles' masks, 64in. wide. (Christie's)
$24,105 £19,440

Part of a carved mahogany bergere lounge suite of five pieces, the settee with three-panel back and padded seat. (Capes, Dunn & Co.) $2,016 £1,400

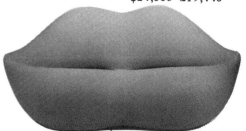

A 'Lip' sofa after a design by Salvador Dali, upholstered in red nylon stretch fabric, 209cm. wide. (Christie's) $2,192 £1,512

A George III giltwood small sofa in the manner of Thos. Chippendale, the back and seat covered in blue and white floral printed cotton, 58in. wide. (Christie's) $3,132 £2,160

A Regency satinwood chaise longue, the scrolled back crossbanded with rosewood and framed by ebonised and boxwood lines, 67in. wide. (Christie's)
$6,531 £4,536

An L. & J. G. Stickley slat-back settle, style no. 281, with spring cushion seat, circa 1912, 76in. wide. (Robt. W. Skinner Inc.)
$1,600 £1,111

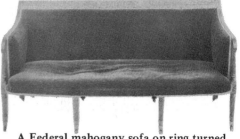

A Federal mahogany sofa on ring turned reeded legs and brass castors, 75in. long, circa 1815. (Robt. W. Skinner Inc.)
$5,750 £3,993

An early Georgian walnut settee, the arched padded back and seat upholstered in blue-grey patterned silk, on cabriole legs and pad feet, 58in. wide. (Christie's) $3,790 £2,808

Late 19th century rococo Revival rosewood settee, N. Schott, America, 65in. wide. (Robt. W. Skinner Inc.) $250 £171

A Louis XVI giltwood canape with curved and arched padded back and bowed seat covered in floral gros point needlework, 93in. wide. (Christie's) $4,384 £3,024

A late 19th century rococo Revival rosewood sofa, impressed Gentso?, America, 84in. wide. (Robt. W. Skinner Inc.) $300 £205

A Chippendale upholstered sofa, the serpentine back flanked by outward flaring arms, circa 1780, 80in. long. (Robt. W. Skinner Inc.) $3,400 £2,361

A George III mahogany humpback sofa upholstered in raspberry floral damask, 82in. wide. (Christie's) $4,384 £3,024

A 19th century Netherlands rococo style mahogany and marquetry settee, overall inlay of exotic woods, ivory and mother-of-pearl with bird and floral motifs, 71in. long. (Robt. W. Skinner Inc.) $2,000 £1,408

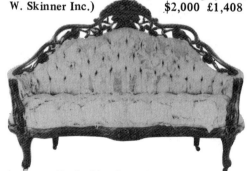

A rococo Revival laminated rosewood settee, attributed to John Henry Belter, New York, circa 1855, 66in. wide. (Robt. W. Skinner Inc.) $8,000 £5,479

FURNITURE

A Federal mahogany sideboard on turned and reeded legs, 1800-10, 96in. long. (Christie's) $3,080 £2,138

A late Federal mahogany sideboard on tapering leaf carved feet, Mass., 1800-10, 78in. wide. (Christie's) $330 £240

Small Federal cherry inlaid sideboard, New England, circa 1815, 44in. wide. (Robt. W. Skinner Inc.) $1,400 £945

A Federal mahogany sideboard with serpentine top, Maryland, 1790-1810, 72in. wide. (Christie's) $11,000 £7,638

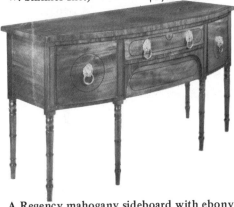

A Regency mahogany sideboard with ebony stringing and bowed top, 69½in. wide. (Christie's) $5,149 £3,456

A Louis XVI style ebonised sideboard with bronze and ormolu mountings, America, 1865-70, approx. 69in. wide. (Robt. W. Skinner Inc.) $1,800 £1,313

A Federal mahogany sideboard with D-shaped top, Rhode Island, 1790-1810, 67in. long. (Christie's) $7,700 £5,347

A Federal mahogany veneer sideboard with bowed rectangular top, 1790-1815, 70in. wide. (Christie's) $4,400 £3,055

SIDEBOARDS

A Federal mahogany sideboard, the top shaped to fit a curved recess, circa 1790, 7.3in. wide. (Christie's) $7,150 £4,965

A Federal mahogany inlaid sideboard, the four square tapering legs with tiger maple banded burl panels, stringing and bellflower inlay, circa 1790, 72in. wide. (Robt. W. Skinner Inc.) $8,500 £5,743

Late 19th century carved teak sideboard, China, 48in. wide. (Robt. W. Skinner Inc.) $1,200 £875

A Federal mahogany sideboard, the top with broad ovolo corners, circa 1795, 69in. wide. (Robt. W. Skinner Inc.) $7,250 £5,034

A classical mahogany sideboard with marble top, New York, 1815-25, 75in. long. (Christie's) $3,300 £2,291

A George III mahogany sideboard with serpentine top, with one frieze drawer, flanked by two deep drawers, one a cellarette drawer, 79in. wide. (Christie's) $2,896 £1,944

A Federal mahogany sideboard, the front with a pair of cockbeaded short drawers centred by a bowed long drawer, 69½in. long, circa 1785-1800. (Christie's) $4,950 £3,437

A Federal mahogany inlaid sideboard with bow front, Mass., circa 1815, 70in. wide. (Robt. W. Skinner Inc.) $9,000 £6,081

SIDEBOARDS

A late Georgian mahogany sweep front sideboard on six turned supports, 54¼in. wide. (Lawrence Fine Art) $2,233 £1,540

A George III mahogany sideboard with bowed concave centred top, the drawer crossbanded with rosewood in the arched centre, 72in. wide. (Christie's) $14,877 £10,260

A George III mahogany and satinwood sideboard with crossbanded D-shaped top, 48in. wide. (Christie's) $8,704 £7,020

A Victorian rococo style flame mahogany pedestal sideboard with two central serpentine drawers, 7ft. wide. (Capes, Dunn & Co.) $568 £400

A Federal inlaid mahogany serpentine front sideboard, circa 1780/1800, 74½in. wide. (Christie's) $9,350 £6,448

A George III mahogany serpentine sideboard with a central drawer above an arch, flanked by deep drawers, 67in. wide. (Lawrence Fine Art) $11,396 £7,700

A Victorian mahogany mirror back sideboard outlined in simulated malachite, the lower section with six snakewood panels, 198cm. high. (Osmond Tricks) $648 £450

A George III mahogany demi-lune sideboard, the ormolu backrail with vase finials, 90in. wide. (Christie's) $2,916 £2,160

SIDEBOARDS

A Regency mahogany breakfront sideboard on square tapering legs and spade feet, 76in. wide. (Christie's) $5,214 £3,672

A George III mahogany and satinwood sideboard with gilt metal and enamel handles, Scottish, 103in. wide. (Christie's) $13,311 £9,180

Victorian oak sideboard with pediment, 1895. (British Antique Exporters) $144 £107

Georgian mahogany four-door sideboard, 1840. (British Antique Exporters) $1,286 £953

A Federal mahogany sideboard, the top with bowed front edge, circa 1795/1815, 75½in. wide. (Christie's) $3,960 £2,731

A George III mahogany sideboard with crossbanded serpentine top, 65½in. wide. (Christie's) $8,613 £5,940

A Sheraton period mahogany sideboard inlaid with satinwood and ebony herringbone stringing, 68in. wide. (Morphets) $1,944 £1,350

A George III mahogany and satinwood bow fronted sideboard with a cellarette drawer to the right and a cupboard to the left, 72in. wide. (Christie's) $5,093 £3,888

Victorian brass bound oak
jardiniere, circa 1880.
(British Antique Exporters)
$72 £54

Victorian inlaid mahogany
towel rail, circa 1880.
(British Antique Exporters)
$93 £69

An ormolu mounted
amboyna gueridon in the
manner of Weisweiler, the
top with turquoise ground
saucer inscribed Sevres RF
Sc, 30in. high. (Christie's)
$3,288 £2,268

Victorian oak tiled back
hall stand, 1860. (British
Antique Exporters)
$264 £196

A George III mahogany
library steps table with
moulded hinged top, 48in.
high, extended. (Christie's)
$3,132 £2,160

An 18th century style mahogany urn stand with tray top,
11in. wide. (Capes, Dunn &
Co.) $273 £190

A tripod cherry candlestand
with candle drawer, Mass.,
circa 1760, 25½in. high.
(Robt. W. Skinner Inc.)
$5,000 £3,521

A Regency brass music stand with
blue painted and gilded rest pierced
with oak leaves and acorns, 60½in.
high. (Christie's) $1,473 £1,188

Victorian brass banded
oak fern stand, 1880.
(British Antique Exporters)
$105 £78

A William and Mary walnut torchere with moulded circular top, spirally-turned shaft and scrolled tripartite base, 12in. diam. (Christie's) $801 £594

One of a set of George III mahogany library steps, with carrying handles, 30in. wide. (Christie's) $4,071 £2,808

Victorian oak barley twist cakestand, 1860. (British Antique Exporters) $52 £39

A Regency rosewood duet music stand, the pierced top filled with lyres. (Christie's) $947 £702

A Regency mahogany reading stand, the sloping writing surface lined with tooled green leather, 23½in. wide. (Christie's) $21,924 £15,120

A Regency burr walnut and giltwood torchere with concave-sided triangular top, 17in. wide. (Christie's) $4,285 £3,456

A Regency brass inlaid rosewood teapoy with Bramah lock and carrying handles, 17½in. wide. (Christie's) $3,207 £2,376

Victorian mahogany butler's tray, 1850. (British Antique Exporters) $180 £134

Victorian oak double-shelf cakestand, 1880. (British Antique Exporters) $112 £83

STANDS

One of a pair of William and Mary walnut and marquetry torcheres, 10¾in. diam., 35½in. high. (Christie's) $3,421 £2,592

A George III green painted and gilded jardiniere after a design by Robert Adam, 36in. wide. (Christie's) $50,652 £37,800

Victorian mahogany shaving stand, 1880. (British Antique Exporters) $260 £193

An Emile Galle walnut and marquetry music stand, 90.4cm. high when not extended. (Christie's) $1,419 £972

Victorian mahogany hall stand, 1860. (British Antique Exporters) $102 £76

A Gustav Stickley three-drawer bedside stand, style no. 842, copper hardware with loop handles, circa 1907, 29½in. high. (Robt. W. Skinner Inc.) $1,100 £763

French marble and ormolu pedestal, 1860. (British Antique Exporters) $400 £297

Victorian mahogany butler's tray with stand, 1860. (British Antique Exporters) $209 £155

One of two Regency rosewood tripod jardinieres, one bearing the label of Richard Henry Masters, possibly Anglo-Indian, 34½in. high. (Christie's) $6,998 £4,860

An ormolu mounted amboyna gueridon in the manner of Weisweiler with circular brocatello marble top, stamped Henry Dasson, 1885, 30¼in. high. (Christie's) $5,011 £3,456

A Regency mahogany teapoy, the hinged top enclosing a divided interior with later tin liners, 20in. wide.(Christie's) $3,136 £2,376

Victorian mahogany and brass cakestand, 1875. (British Antique Exporters) $82 £61

Victorian mahogany tiled top plant stand, 1860. (British Antique Exporters) $95 £71

Pair of mid 19th century gilt metal mounted mahogany torcheres, 11in. diam. (Christie's) $2,122 £1,620

Victorian walnut pedestal, 1860. (British Antique Exporters) $336 £249

A Japanese carved padouk-wood urn stand with circular inset marble top, 10in. diam. (Capes, Dunn & Co.) $244 £170

A classical mahogany tilt-top candlestand, N.Y., circa 1820/40, 30¾in. high. (Christie's) $990 £682

A Regency maple and ebony collector's cabinet with panelled doors enclosing fourteen various sized drawers, 19in. wide, 47½in. high. (Christie's) $1,749 £1,296

STANDS

A mid Victorian black, gilt and mother-of-pearl japanned papier mache music stand, 50¼in. high. (Christie's) $820 £540

A Regency mahogany three-tier etagere, the grey marble shelves with ormolu galleries, 24½in. wide. (Christie's) $14,094 £9,720

A polished chromium hat stand made for Bazzi in Milan, 51.6cm. high. (Christie's) $656 £453

A Federal mahogany candlestand with octagonal top, New England, 1790-1810, 21¼in. wide. (Christie's) $550 £381

A William and Mary walnut stand, Penn., 1700-40, 25¼in. wide. (Christie's) $1,870 £1,364

A Chippendale mahogany birdcage candlestand with a dished and moulded circular tilt top, 1760-90, 23½in. diam. (Christie's) $4,620 £3,208

A Chippendale mahogany candlestand with tilt top, the legs terminating in padded snake feet, circa 1770, 27in. high. (Robt. W. Skinner Inc.) $3,200 £2,222

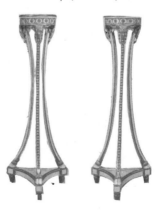

A pair of white painted and gilded tripod torcheres, the tops 13in. diam. (Christie's) $5,080 £3,456

One of a pair of classical Revival carved and gilt pedestals with marble tops, circa 1835, 36½in. high. (Robt. W. Skinner Inc.) $4,600 £3,194

FURNITURE

A Federal inlaid mahogany candlestand on a vase-turned pedestal, 1790-1810, 29½in. high. (Christie's)
$1,760 £1,222

A pine easel, adjustable, on a trestle base, with castors, 29in. wide. (Christie's)
$715 £496

A Country Federal painted candlestand with oval top, circa 1810, 20in. wide. (Robt. W. Skinner Inc.)
$1,500 £1,013

A Chippendale mahogany candlestand with circular tilt top, 1760-80, 22in. diam. (Christie's)
$1,045 £725

An early Victorian walnut coal bin of sarcophagus form with coffered top and hinged front with metal liner, 21in. wide.(Christie's)
$1,533 £1,080

Chippendale cherry candle-stand, the square top on vase turned post and tripod cabriole leg base, 26in. high, circa 1780. (Robt. W. Skinner Inc.) $1,200 £810

Victorian oak bookstand, 1880. (British Antique Exporters) $87 £65

A Federal mahogany tilt top candlestand, 1790-1810, 26in. wide. (Christie's)
$825 £572

One of a pair of giltwood stands with stepped circular white marble tops, 19in. wide. (Christie's)
$4,860 £3,240

STANDS

An ormolu mounted mahogany gueridon in the manner of Weisweiler, 30½in. high. (Christie's)
$5,637 £3,888

Victorian pine and cast iron butter maker, 1860. (British Antique Exporters)
$290 £215

A Chippendale mahogany bird cage candlestand, Phila., circa 1760, 27½in. high. (Robt. W. Skinner Inc.)
$4,500 £3,125

Victorian oak hall stand, 1860. (British Antique Exporters) $186 £138

Victorian oak three-tiered buffet, circa 1870. (British Antique Exporters)
$166 £123

A Japonnaiserie bamboo and porcelain hat and coat stand, 51in. wide, 84in. high. (Christie's)
$1,879 £1,296

A painted pine candlestand, New England, circa 1780, 27in. high, 20in. diam. (Robt. W. Skinner Inc.)$900 £625

A late Federal pine stand, with single drawer above two cupboard doors, 1810-30, 22½in. wide.(Christie's)
$528 £385

One of a pair of George III giltwood torcheres on cloven hoof feet, 49½in. high. (Christie's)
$16,070 £12,960

A mahogany fender stool, the seat covered in floral gros and petit point needlework on mid 18th century cabriole legs, 45½in. wide. (Christie's)$20,358 £14,040

Victorian footstool with beaded cover, 1850. (British Antique Exporters) $75 £56

A George III mahogany stool with button-upholstered crimson velvet seat, 36in. long. (Christie's) $3,132 £2,160

Victorian mahogany revolving piano stool, 1860. (British Antique Exporters) $110 £82

Late 19th century mahogany piano stool. (British Antique Exporters) $20 £15

A walnut stool, the oval padded seat on splayed club legs and pad feet, 20in. wide. (Christie's) $1,686 £1,188

An early 17th century oak joint stool on fluted tapering legs joined by plain stretchers, 17in. wide. (Christie's) $926 £702

One of a pair of George III pine window seats with differently upholstered bowed seats and double-scrolled ends, 48½in. wide. (Christie's) £7,840 £5,940

A Middle Eastern hardwood stool with saddle seat, inlaid with ivory stylised flowerheads, 17in. wide. (Christie's) $626 £432

A Queen Anne walnut stool, the rectangular seat covered in floral tapestry woven with a fable, 18¾in. wide. (Christie's) $5,088 £4,104

One of a pair of George III simulated rosewood window seats with bowed seats and double scroll ends upholstered in rose velvet, 46in. wide. (Christie's) $14,094 £9,720

A George I walnut stool with drop-in seat covered with floral petit point needlework, 22in. wide. (Christie's) $17,226 £11,880

A George II mahogany stool with bowed rectangular needlework upholstered drop-in seat, possibly Irish, 20½in. wide. (Christie's) $2,332 £1,728

One of a set of six 17th century oak joint stools, 18in. wide. (Christie's) $37,584 £25,920

One of a pair of George III mahogany stools, one branded VR BP N22224 1866, 23½in. wide. (Christie's) $17,366 £12,960

A Derby & Co. oak window seat, the cut-out armrests with spindle supports, circa 1910, 28in. high. (Robt. W. Skinner Inc.) $375 £260

An early Victorian mahogany octagonal seat, the hinged lid upholstered in floral needlework, 20¼in. wide. (Christie's) $4,071 £2,808

A William and Mary walnut stool upholstered with a fragment of early 17th century tapestry, 17in. wide. (Christie's) $2,851 £2,160

A George I gilt gesso stool with drop-in seat, 24½in. wide. (Christie's)
$32,886 £22,680

A Regency mahogany window seat of horseshoe shape with caned seat and leather squab cushion, 63in. wide. (Christie's) $10,179 £7,020

A 17th century oak joint stool with ring-turned legs joined by plain stretchers, 17¼in. wide. (Christie's) $1,354 £1,026

A walnut and parcel gilt stool of George I style, the drop-in seat painted in gilt and scarlet with a coat-of-arms, 26in. wide. (Christie's) $2,678 £2,160

One of a pair of Regency mahogany music stools with lyre-shaped carved splat backs. (Reeds Rains) $2,592 £1,800

A George I walnut stool with rectangular needlework drop-in seat, on shell and foliate cabriole legs, 22in. wide. (Christie's) $3,132 £2,160

A Chinese scarlet and gold lacquer circular panel, now associated with a chinoiserie bamboo pattern parcel gilt stool, 17in. diam. (Christie's) $1,252 £864

Late 19th century pottery garden seat, probably France, whimsically depicting a cushion resting on a basket, 20in. high. (Robt. W. Skinner Inc.) $750 £528

Late 17th/early 18th century oak and elm joint stool, 18½in. wide. (Christie's) $2,280 £1,728

SUITES

Two of a set of six 18th century German walnut fauteuils and canape, upholstered in gros and petit point needlework, the canape 51in. wide. (Christie's) $7,452 £4,968

An Edwardian mahogany drawingroom suite of seven pieces, with satinwood panel and boxwood string inlay. (Capes, Dunn & Co.) $648 £450

Part of a suite of early George IH mahogany seat furniture, the sofa with serpentine back and seat, 84in. long. (Dreweatts) $54,000 £36,000

SUITES

A suite of George III mahogany seat furniture comprising a set of four
library armchairs, upholstered in gros and petit-point needlework, a
window seat and a sofa, the window seat 51in. wide, the sofa 84in.
wide. (Christie's) $46,980 £32,400

Two of a set of eight open armchairs, one of three window seats and a sofa
all with caned seats with squab cushions, the sofa 72½in. wide.
(Christie's) $63,027 £42,876

Two of a set of six early George III mahogany dining chairs, the seats covered
in gros point floral needlework and a humpback sofa , 78in. wide. (Christie's)
$34,133 £23,220

CARD & TEA TABLES

A Federal mahogany card table, attributed to Chas. H. Lannvier, circa 1800-15, 36in. wide. (Christie's) $3,080 £2,138

Victorian walnut card table, 1850. (British Antique Exporters) $1,147 £850

Federal mahogany and mahogany veneer card table, with serpentine shaped folding top, Mass., circa 1790, 37in. wide. (Robt. W. Skinner Inc.) $6,250 £4,340

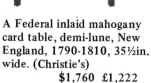

Late 18th century George III mahogany demi-lune card table, England, 36in. wide. (Robt. W. Skinner Inc.) $450 £328

A George II mahogany tea table with shaped fold-over top, the drawer with brass drop handle, 28½in. wide. (Dacre, Son & Hartley) $1,628 £1,100

A Federal inlaid mahogany card table, demi-lune, New England, 1790-1810, 35½in. wide. (Christie's) $1,760 £1,222

A Federal inlaid mahogany card table, 1790/1810, 35¼in. wide. (Christie's) $1,430 £986

A George III satinwood and calamander card table, the top with fan inlay, 35½in. wide. (Christie's) $5,793 £3,888

A Federal inlaid mahogany card table, Mass., 1800/20, 34¼in. wide. (Christie's) $2,200 £1,517

FURNITURE

A Federal mahogany inlaid card table, circa 1800, 36in. wide. (Robt. W. Skinner Inc.) $1,400 £972

A classical Revival mahogany and mahogany veneered card table with D-shaped top, N.Y., circa 1810, 36in. wide. (Robt. W. Skinner Inc.) $4,500 £3,125

A George III satinwood and fruitwood card table with baize-lined crossbanded D-shaped top, 36in. wide. (Christie's) $2,913 £2,052

A Federal mahogany circular card table with demi-lune hinged top, N.Y., 1790-1810, 36in. wide. (Christie's) $1,760 £1,222

A Federal mahogany card table, the lift top with D-shaped front and sides, Boston, circa 1795, 35in. wide. (Robt. W. Skinner Inc.) $4,100 £2,887

A Georgian mahogany double fold-over tea/games table fitted with two small drawers. (Worsfolds) $2,448 £1,700

Federal mahogany and mahogany veneer card table, the lift top with ovolo corners, circa 1795, top 36 x 34½in. (Robt. W. Skinner Inc.) $2,200 £1,527

An early Georgian calamander wood and walnut card table, the top with candle sconces and guinea wells, 34in. wide. (Christie's) $10,459 £7,020

A late Federal mahogany card table with hinged D-shaped top, Mass., 1820-30, 36in. wide.(Christie's) $1,870 £1,364

CARD & TEA TABLES

A George III mahogany
card table with baize lined
serpentine top, 39½in. wide.
(Christie's) $5,637 £3,888

A Regency rosewood card
table with baize lined top
inlaid with brass lines,
36in. wide. (Christie's)
$10,962 £7,560

One of a pair of classical
mahogany card tables,
N.Y. or Baltimore, 1810/
70, 35¾in. wide. (Christie's)
$7,150 £4,931

A Regency rosewood card
table with leather lined
swivelling top inlaid with
brass lines and ivory foliage,
37in. wide. (Christie's)
$12,528 £8,640

A George II walnut card
table with lobed folding top
and baize lined interior, 34in.
wide. (Christie's)
$15,660 £10,800

A Regency brass inlaid and
rosewood tea table with
twin-flap swivelling top,
35½in. wide. (Christie's)
$3,067 £2,160

A late Federal mahogany
card table with serpentine
top, 1810/20, 35¾in. wide.
(Christie's) $825 £568

A Regency ormolu mounted
calamander card table with
baize lined D-shaped folding
top, 38in. wide. (Christie's)
$10,962 £7,560

A Federal mahogany and
mahogany veneer card table
with lift top, circa 1795,
34½in. wide. (Robt. W.
Skinner Inc.)
$4,400 £3,055

CARD & TEA TABLES

An early Victorian mahogany tea table with swivel and flap top, 3ft. wide. (Capes, Dunn & Co.)
$426 £300

A Federal mahogany sofa card table, the top with shaped leaves, circa 1810/30, 51½in. wide, open. (Christie's) $1,100 £758

A George III kingwood and satinwood card table, with baize lined crossbanded top, 36½in. wide. (Christie's)
$1,566 £1,080

A Regency rosewood card table, the baize lined top with boxwood stringing, 36in. wide. (Christie's)
$2,975 £2,052

A mid Georgian mahogany combined card and tea table with candle sconces, possibly Irish, 35in. wide. (Christie's)
$4,600 £3,240

A Regency penwork card table with swivelling top, 36in. wide. (Christie's)
$1,096 £756

A George I walnut tea/games table with lobed triple-flap top, 33in. wide. (Christie's)
$7,516 £5,184

One of a pair of early 19th century mahogany card tables, 34¾in. wide. (Christie's)
$17,226 £11,880

A mid Georgian mahogany tea table with D-shaped hinged top and three frieze drawers, possibly Irish, 32½in. wide. (Christie's)
$2,624 £1,944

CARD & TEA TABLES

A Regency D-shaped card table banded and inlaid with satinwood lines, 35in. wide. (Christie's) $2,818 £1,944

One of a pair of Regency rosewood card tables with hinged D-shaped baize lined tops, 35¾in. wide. (Christie's) $4,561 £3,456

A George II mahogany card table, the baize lined rectangular top with ribbon-and-rosette border, 35½in. wide. (Christie's) $14,472 £10,800

An early Georgian mahogany combined tea, card and writing table, possibly Irish, 32½in. wide. (Christie's) $6,366 £4,860

An early George III mahogany tea and games table with serpentine triple-flap top, 32½in. wide. (Christie's) $9,374 £7,560

One of a pair of satinwood and rosewood card tables, the D-shaped tops inlaid with fan motifs, 36in. wide. (Christie's) $10,713 £8,640

A George III satinwood card table with baize lined top and the drawer with chased silvered handles, 38½in. wide. (Christie's) $3,762 £2,808

A Sheraton revival style inlaid mahogany demi-lune folding card table with green baize and tooled leather lined interior. (Capes, Dunn & Co.) $1,224 £850

A George III mahogany card table, the back with a secret drawer, 33in. wide. (Christie's) $2,187 £1,620

One of a pair of George III mahogany tea tables on square tapering legs, 36in. wide. (Christie's)
$7,290 £5,400

A Regency crossbanded mahogany card table with fold-over top, 36in. wide. (Dacre, Son & Hartley)
$720 £500

An ormolu mounted kingwood and parquetry card table, the top inlaid with floral sprays with rockwork clasps and baize lined interior, 33½in. wide. (Christie's) $3,136 £2,376

A William and Mary burr walnut card table fitted with two candle slides, 30¼in. wide. (Christie's)
$22,809 £17,280

A mid 18th century Italian walnut tea table on scrolled cabriole legs and hoof feet, 33½in. wide. (Christie's)
$4,561 £3,456

A Sheraton period mahogany veneered half round tea table, 3ft. wide. (Woolley & Wallis)
$576 £400

A George II mahogany tea table with shaped eared top and concertina action, 33in. wide. (Christie's)
$2,829 £2,160

A Federal mahogany inlaid card table, Mass., circa 1800, 35¾in. wide. (Robt. W. Skinner Inc.) $1,750 £1,198

A George II mahogany tea table with eared folding top, 32in. wide.(Christie's)
$3,749 £3,024

A William and Mary birch and pine tavern table, New England, circa 1750, 46in. wide. (Robt. W. Skinner Inc.) $2,750 £1,858

A 17th century Spanish walnut centre table with rectangular top and pierced shaped trestle ends, 51in. wide. (Christie's) $2,799 £1,944

A William and Mary maple and pine tavern table, New England, circa 1700, top 47 x 29½in. (Robt. W. Skinner Inc.) $3,400 £2,394

An 18th century Queen Anne maple centre table, with a single walnut drawer, 42in. wide. (Christie's) $1,650 £1,137

A rosewood centre table, the top inlaid with specimen marbles and semi-precious stones, 23in. wide. (Christie's) $5,011 £3,456

A Regency parcel gilt and maple centre table with circular top, 51½in. diam. (Christie's) $12,268 £8,640

A 17th century and later Spanish walnut centre table, 46½in. wide. (Christie's) $2,488 £1,728

An 18th century North Italian kingwood centre table with leather lined top, 58¼in. wide. (Christie's) $1,788 £1,242

An Italian walnut centre table, the top inset with a panel of specimen marbles, 37½in. wide. (Christie's) $2,177 £1,512

FURNITURE

A Regency brass inlaid rosewood centre table with tipup top, 49½in. wide. (Christie's) $10,962 £7,560

Late 19th century Renaissance Revival inlaid mahogany centre table, America, 45½in. wide. (Robt. W. Skinner Inc.)
$850 £620

A mid Victorian ormolu mounted thuya and marquetry centre table attributed to Holland & Sons, 51½in. diam. (Christie's) $11,745 £8,100

An ormolu and mahogany centre table of Louis XVI style, on twinned simulated bamboo legs, 27in. diam. (Christie's) $1,710 £1,188

An early 18th century boulle gilt metal and ebony centre table, the top inlaid with a berainesque scene, 37in. wide. (Christie's)
$2,488 £1,728

One of a pair of gilt gesso centre tables with later inset honey-coloured marble tops, 21in. wide. (Christie's)
$7,830 £5,400

A George III satinwood centre table, the tip-up top crossbanded with rosewood, 41in. diam. (Christie's) $10,179 £7,020

A grained and parcel gilt centre table in the early Georgian style with massive breche violette top, 69in. wide. (Christie's)
$3,996 £2,700

A Regency brass inlaid rosewood centre table with tipup top, 50in. diam. (Christie's) $7,516 £5,184

CENTRE TABLES

A Regency and parcel gilt plum-pudding mahogany centre table, 50½in. diam. (Christie's) $6,696 £5,400

A Victorian satinwood, ebony and marquetry centre table with waved frieze, 42in. wide. (Christie's)
$3,481 £2,808

A Regency mahogany centre table with tip-up top on a ring-turned baluster shaft and quadrapartite base, 50in. diam. (Christie's)
$2,332 £1,782

A rosewood centre table, the square top inset with specimen marble, 15½in. square. (Christie's) $1,768 £1,350

An oak centre table framed by chequered inlaid lines executed by Peter Waals assisted by P. Burchett, 1928, 68.3cm. wide. (Christie's)
$2,207 £1,512

A Victorian mahogany centre table with marble and semi-precious stone top, 27in. diam. (Christie's) $6,026 £4,860

An early 19th century Tyrolean parquetry centre table on a scrolled tripartite base, 31½in. diam. (Christie's)
$1,283 £972

A Renaissance Revival marble top parlour table, by T. Brooks Cabinet & Upholstery Warehouse, circa 1865, the white oval top 37in. long. (Robt. W. Skinner Inc.)
$1,100 £753

A Regency parcel gilt, mahogany and ebony centre table, the circular black fossil marble top with pierced brass border, 25in. diam. (Christie's) $12,830 £9,720

FURNITURE

A Regency brass inlaid rosewood centre table with tip-up top, 50½in. diam. (Christie's) $3,645 £2,700

A Regency rosewood centre table, the top inlaid with brass banding, 45in. wide. (Christie's) $3,112 £2,376

A Regency parcel gilt and burr-maple centre table, the top inlaid with ebony banding, 52in. diam. (Christie's)
$12,301 £9,180

A Biedermeier mahogany centre table with circular marble tray top, 36in. diam. (Christie's) $2,851 £2,160

A Queen Anne giltwood centre table, the top with geometric strapwork foliage and shells, 30in. wide. (Christie's) $4,687 £3,780

Early 19th century fruit-wood centre table, Austrian or North Italian, 37in. diam. (Christie's) $1,096 £756

  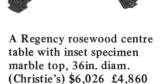

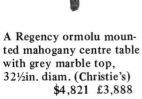

A Regency ormolu mounted mahogany centre table with grey marble top, 32½in. diam. (Christie's)
$4,821 £3,888

A black and gold lacquer centre table of early Georgian design, 34in. wide. (Christie's)
$2,192 £1,512

A Regency rosewood centre table with inset specimen marble top, 36in. diam. (Christie's) $6,026 £4,860

CONSOLE TABLES

An Irish giltwood console table, the top with inset serpentine marble slab, 58½in. wide. (Christie's) $3,218 £2,160

One of a pair of Regency rosewood and parcel gilt console tables with white marble tops, 54in. wide. (Christie's) $9,020 £6,264

A George II giltwood console table with later, eared serpentine, mottled grey marble top, 46¼in. wide. (Christie's) $6,696 £5,400

A Louis XVI mahogany console desserte with brass mounts and grey veined marble top, 34in. wide. (Lawrence Fine Art) $2,116 £1,430

One of a pair of grained pine console tables with marble tops on carved eagle supports, 42¼in. wide. (Christie's) $2,946 £2,376

A classical brass inlaid mahogany marble top pier table, N.Y., circa 1810/30, 41½in. wide. (Christie's) $2,640 £1,820

A George II stained pine console table with serpentine marble top, 53in. wide. (Christie's) $11,577 £8,640

An 18th century Italian parcel gilt and painted corner console, 23in. wide. (Christie's) $1,088 £756

A mid 18th century giltwood console table, sold with another en suite of a later date, 41½in. wide. (Christie's) $6,415 £4,860

FURNITURE

A Regency walnut console table with serpentine breccho-litto marble top, 52in. wide. (Christie's)　$3,706　£2,808

An Irish pine console table with shaped rectangular serpentine marble top, 69in. wide. (Christie's)
$11,264　£7,560

A George II white-painted and gilded pier table, after a design by T. Langley, with mottled grey and white marble top, 56¼in. wide. (Christie's) $26,049　£19,440

A Louis XV Provincial walnut console table with later breccia marble top, 34½in. wide. (Christie's)　$1,555　£1,080

One of a pair of giltwood console tables with serpentine moulded white tops, 40in. wide. (Christie's)
$3,706　£2,808

A George II grained pine console table with later onyx marble top, 59½in. wide. (Christie's) $2,896　£1,944

One of a pair of Italian pine pier tables, the serpentine tops with gadrooned borders, 35½in. high. (Christie's)
$4,665　£3,240

One of a pair of Louis XV giltwood console tables with shaped breccia marble tops, 23½in. wide. (Christie's)
$4,043　£2,808

One of a pair of George II giltwood pier tables, each with D-shaped white marble top, 35in. wide. (Christie's)
$159,192　£118,800

DINING TABLES

A William IV rosewood dining table with circular tilt-top , 55in. diam. (Christie's) $1,350 £900

A Flemish oak dining table with draw leaf top on cup and cover legs, partly late 16th century, 100in. long open. (Christie's) $1,069 £810

A large carved oak dining table. (John Hogbin & Son) $888 £600

A George III satinwood and rosewood breakfast table with tip-up top, 49½in. wide. (Christie's) $13,862 £9,560

A William IV rosewood veneered circular snap-top breakfast table, 4ft.3½in. diam. (Woolley & Wallis) $994 £700

A George III satinwood and mahogany breakfast table with tip-up top, 53in. wide. (Christie's) $7,516 £5,184

A William IV twin pedestal mahogany dining table with rounded rectangular top, 69in. long, including one extra leaf. (Christie's) $2,235 £1,500

A Federal mahogany dining table, circa 1815, 47in. wide. (Robt. W. Skinner Inc.) $800 £555

A Regency mahogany breakfast table with circular tip-up top, 66½in. diam. (Christie's) $10,962 £7,560

FURNITURE

A William and Mary oak side or refectory table with a three plank top, 83½in. wide. (Lawrence Fine Art)
$2,360 £1,595

An oyster veneered yewwood, marquetry and parcel gilt draw-leaf dining table, 97½in. wide, open. (Christie's)
$1,073 £756

A Regency mahogany patent dining table, the handles inscribed G. Oakley, Maker, 57 x 147in. (Christie's)
$20,412 £15,120

A Regency mahogany breakfast table with moulded oval tip-up top, vase-shaped shaft and quadripartite base, 64in. wide. (Christie's)
$3,218 £2,160

A mid Victorian walnut and inlaid loo table, 48in. wide. (Dacre, Son & Hartley)
$529 £360

A George III rosewood and satinwood breakfast table with oval crossbanded tip-up top, 57in. wide. (Christie's)
$10,854 £8,100

A late Georgian circular mahogany breakfast table centred by an inlaid floral medallion, 55in. diam. (Anderson & Garland)
$1,164 £820

An early Regency period, faded mahogany, circular snap-top breakfast table, 3ft.10in. diam. (Woolley & Wallis)
$3,358 £2,300

An early Victorian mahogany breakfast table, on heavy gun barrel turned column, with curvilinear platform base, 4ft. 9in. x 3ft.7in. (Capes, Dunn & Co.)
$568 £400

DINING TABLES

A William IV mahogany library table with four frieze drawers flanked by dummies, 59in. diam. (Christie's) $5,103 £3,780

1920's oak dining table. (British Antique Exporters) $270 £200

A Regency rosewood breakfast table, the top with burr-elm banding on ring-turned ebonised shaft, 59½in. wide. (Christie's) $2,829 £2,160

A 19th century circular mahogany tip-top dining table with lion's paw feet, 52in. diam. (W. H. Lane & Son) $489 £340

Victorian oak draw-leaf table, circa 1900. (British Antique Exporters) $97 £72

Regency rosewood loo table with scroll feet, 1830. (British Antique Exporters) $1,140 £845

A George III ormolu mounted rosewood library table with leather lined circular top, 44in. diam. (Christie's) $8,035 £6,480

A William IV mahogany library table with leather lined circular top, possibly Irish, 35½in. diam. (Christie's) $3,395 £2,592

A George III mahogany drum table with revolving octagonal top, 43½in. wide. (Christie's) $11,577 £8,640

DINING TABLES

A Restoration mahogany breakfast table with circular top, 45¼in. diam. (Christie's) $2,662 £1,836

A Victorian mahogany extending dining table with concave-sided plinth bases, 58 x 166in. including four leaves. (Christie's) $13,122 £9,720

A Regency mahogany library table with circular leather lined top on a tripartite base and claw feet, 47½in. diam. (Christie's) $2,624 £1,944

A Gustav Stickley round library table, no. 633, circa 1904, 48in. diam. (Robt. W. Skinner Inc.) $1,700 £1,180

Regency rosewood centre pedestal table, circa 1830. (British Antique Exporters) $1,236 £916

Victorian walnut dining table, 1880. (British Antique Exporters) $103 £77

A George IV oak octagonal library table with leather lined top, 42½in. wide. (Christie's) $2,505 £1,728

A Federal mahogany and veneer drum table on a tripod cabriole leg base, 31in. diam, circa 1820. (Robt. W. Skinner Inc.) $600 £410

A George III mahogany drum table with leather lined revolving circular top, 38½in. diam. (Christie's) $6,561 £4,860

DRESSING TABLES

Victorian walnut and ebony dressing table, 1860. (British Antique Exporters) $569 £422

Late Victorian walnut dressing table, 1880. (British Antique Exporters) $334 £248

Victorian oak dressing table, 1880. (British Antique Exporters) $202 £150

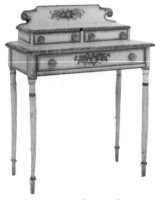

A yellow painted pine dressing table with stencil and foliate designs, New England, circa 1825, 34in. wide. (Robt. W. Skinner Inc.) $800 £547

A green and gold lacquer, serpentine top, dressing table with chinoiserie decoration and pull-out writing slide, 31½in. wide. (Christie's) $1,840 £1,296

A George III mahogany dressing chest, the hinged top enclosing a fitted interior with an easel mirror, 24½in. wide. (Christie's) $4,773 £3,204

A Country Queen Anne cherry dressing table, central Mass., circa 1800, 24in. wide. (Robt. W. Skinner Inc.) $4,750 £3,298

An Italian Empire gilt metal mounted walnut and fruit-wood dressing table, 49in. wide. (Christie's) $1,555 £1,080

A Regency mahogany dressing table by Gillows of Lancaster, 41½in. wide. (Christie's) $3,395 £2,592

DRESSING TABLES

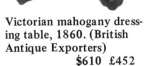

A Chippendale walnut dressing table with scalloped front skirt, circa 1765-80, 35¼in. wide. (Christie's)
$4,400 £3,055

Victorian mahogany dressing table, 1860. (British Antique Exporters)
$610 £452

A Regency mahogany dressing table, the top with three-quarter gallery, stamped Gillows of Lancaster, 52in. wide. (Christie's)
$2,488 £1,728

American mahogany dressing table, 1900. (British Antique Exporters)
$112 £83

A Louis XV amaranth, tulipwood and floral marquetry table de toilette by G. Peridiez, 35in. wide. (Christie's)
$5,987 £4,536

A George III mahogany and satinwood dressing chest, the fitted interior with easel mirror, 28in. wide. (Christie's)
$4,023 £2,700

A Federal mahogany and mahogany veneered dressing table, circa 1810, 35in. wide. (Robt. W. Skinner Inc.) $750 £520

A small Victorian Duchess dressing table, 1860. (British Antique Exporters)
$1,309 £970

Edwardian mahogany dressing table with cabriole shaped legs, circa 1910. (British Antique Exporters)
$487 £325

475

A Chippendale walnut drop-leaf table, with two gate legs, 1760-80, 48in. long. (Christie's) $5,280 £3,666

A Chippendale carved mahogany and cherrywood drop-leaf table, on cabriole legs, 1750-75, 54in. long. (Christie's) $20,900 £14,513

A Chippendale mahogany drop-leaf table on four stationary and two swing square legs, 47¾in. long, 1770-90. (Christie's) $715 £496

A Chippendale mahogany dining table with two drop-leaves, Phila., 1765-85, 55in. long. (Christie's) $1,320 £916

A Queen Anne maple dining table with circular drop-leaf, circa 1760, 41¾in. wide. (Robt. W. Skinner Inc.) $8,000 £5,405

A Federal mahogany breakfast table, New York, circa 1815, top 38¾ x 48¾in., open. (Robt. W. Skinner Inc.) $1,500 £1,027

A Chippendale walnut drop-leaf dining table on Marlborough legs, 1765-85, 56in. long, extended. (Christie's) $3,190 £2,215

A late George II mahogany two flap table with oval top, 49 x 59in. extended. (Lawrence Fine Art) $2,930 £1,980

A Chippendale walnut dining table, circa 1770, 48½in. long. (Robt. W. Skinner Inc.) $6,000 £4,166

DROP-LEAF TABLES

A Chippendale mahogany drop-leaf dining table on six shaped legs with claw and ball feet, New York, 1760-80, 57½in. wide. (Christie's) $1,650 £1,204

A Federal mahogany drop-leaf table, 1790/1810, 57in. long, open. (Christie's) $3,300 £2,275

A mid Georgian mahogany gateleg dining table, the adapted oval twin flap top on club legs and pad feet, 60½in. wide open. (Christie's) $1,409 £972

A Queen Anne maple dining table with oval drop-leaf top, New England, circa 1760, 40½in. wide. (Robt. W. Skinner Inc.) $1,200 £810

A Chippendale mahogany card table with scalloped front skirt, Mass., circa 1770, 31½in. wide, open. (Robt. W. Skinner Inc.) $6,100 £4,236

A late Federal mahogany drop-leaf table, the top clover shaped, N.Y., 1800/20, 37in. wide. (Christie's) $352 £242

A George III mahogany gateleg dining table with twin flap top, 56in. wide open. (Christie's) $3,680 £2,592

A classical carved mahogany drop-leaf table, circa 1815, 38in. wide. (Christie's) $935 £649

A Queen Anne walnut drop-leaf table with square top, circa 1750, 34in. wide, open. (Christie's) $2,860 £1,986

GATELEG TABLES

A William and Mary maple gateleg table, the top flanked by semi-circular drop leaves, New England, 1710-45, the top 55 x 48in. (Christie's) $3,300 £2,408

A Georgian mahogany gateleg dining table, 5ft. wide. (Worsfolds) $5,550 £3,750

A 17th century oak gateleg dining table with oval twin-flap top and baluster supports, 67in. wide, open. (Christie's) $7,309 £5,184

A mid Georgian mahogany gateleg table with oval twin-flap top on turned legs, 48½in. wide, open. (Christie's) $4,976 £3,456

A William and Mary fruitwood gateleg table on baluster legs, joined by moulded stretchers, and scrolled feet, 29in. wide. (Christie's)
$9,646 £6,264

A George III mahogany gateleg dining table with oval twin-flap top and two fielded frieze drawers, 53in. diam., open. (Christie's) $19,958 £15,120

An early Georgian mahogany gateleg table with twin-flap top, on turned tapering legs and claw and ball feet, 54in. wide, open. (Christie's) $2,187 £1,620

A William and Mary mahogany gateleg table, the drop leaves opening to form an oval, N.Y., circa 1710/40, top 67 x 53in. open. (Christie's) $38,500 £26,551

GATELEG TABLES

An oak gateleg dining table with oval twin-flap top, 17th century, 75in. wide. (Christie's)
$2,829 £2,160

A large oak gateleg dining table with twin-flap rectangular top, 66in. wide, open. (Christie's)
$2,546 £1,944

A William and Mary maple gateleg table, the bowed top with oval drop leaves, New England, 1720-30, 44in. long. (Christie's)
$3,960 £2,750

A George III mahogany gateleg table with oval twin-flap top and a frieze drawer, on cabriole legs, 59in. wide, open. (Christie's)
$6,696 £5,400

An Irish mid Georgian mahogany gateleg table with oval twin-flap top on cabriole legs, 58½in. wide. (Christie's)
$8,613 £5,940

A William and Mary walnut gateleg table with moulded twin-flap sixteen-sided top and bobbin-turned frame, 42½in. wide. (Christie's)
$9,979 £7,560

A William and Mary padoukwood and oak gateleg dining table with oval twin-flap top, 56in. wide, open. (Christie's) $4,561 £3,456

An oak gateleg dining table with oval twin-flap top and bobbin-turned frame, 17th century, 70in. wide, open. (Christie's)
$3,678 £2,808

LARGE TABLES

A George III mahogany serving table, the serpentine top with chamfered corners, 70in. wide. (Christie's) $3,987 £2,808

A Regency mahogany patent dining table with D-shaped ends, 53 x 123in. (Christie's)
$17,409 £14,040

An Empire carved mahogany three-part dining table, 1825-35, 111½in. long, top extended. (Christie's) $4,400 £3,211

A Regency mahogany patent dining table with D-shaped end-sections, 45¾ x 113½in. (Christie's) $3,987 £2,808

A mid 19th century Shaker Community table, possibly New Hampshire, 21ft.3in. long. (Robt. W. Skinner Inc.)
$38,000 £26,760

A mahogany dining table with D-shaped end-sections, 54 x 98in., including two extra leaves. (Christie's) $4,023 £2,700

A 16th century and later Italian walnut refectory table with solid rectangular top and ring-turned baluster trestle ends, 85½in. wide. (Christie's) $3,110 £2,160

Late 19th century 'Monarch' marquetry and cast iron pool table, by Brunswick & Balke-Collender Co., Buffalo, 9ft. x 4½ft. (Robt. W. Skinner Inc.) $15,000 £10,948

LARGE TABLES

A Regency three-pedestal mahogany dining table, on ring turned baluster shafts and splayed tripartite bases, 45½ x 93in. (Christie's) $10,735 £7,560

A Regency mahogany patent Imperial dining table in the manner of Gillows, 66in. wide, 174½in. extended. (Christie's) $12,722 £10,260

A George III mahogany serpentine serving table with brass rail at the back, 97in. long. (Lawrence Fine Art) $13,024 £8,800

A George III mahogany dining table with five pillar supports, 183in., fully extended, the two extra leaves and pillars unillustrated. (Lawrence Fine Art) $56,980 £38,500

A Regency mahogany three-pedestal dining table with rounded rectangular end-sections on baluster shafts and splayed bases, 53½ x 196in. (Christie's) $11,113 £7,560

An early 17th century oak refectory table, 18ft.2in. x 3ft.5in. (Woolley & Wallis) $8,700 £6,000

A Regency padoukwood and mahogany patent dining table, 154in. long, including four leaves. (Christie's) $20,638 £14,040

A Regency mahogany dining table with ring-turned baluster shafts and quadripartite bases, 52½ x 125in. (Christie's) $11,664 £8,100

FURNITURE

A Chippendale mahogany tilt-top tea table, Penn., 1760-80, 29in. high. (Christie's)
$2,090 £1,525

A Chippendale mahogany tilt-top tea table, Mass., 1760-80, 29in. wide. (Christie's) $1,540 £1,069

A mahogany tripod table, the legs carved with lion mask shoulders on paw feet, 32½in. wide. (Christie's)
$1,931 £1,296

A Queen Anne maple tea table, the skirt with crenelated edge, 28½in. wide. (Christie's) $1,045 £762

A Federal mahogany tilt-top table, circa 1800-20, top 34 x 22½in. (Christie's) $1,045 £725

A Federal carved mahogany serving table with D-shaped top, 1810-15, 36in. wide. (Christie's) $2,640 £1,833

A Regency ebony and mahogany side table, the turned tapering legs with ribbed collars, 20in. wide. (Christie's)
$5,520 £3,888

A Chippendale mahogany birdcage tea table with circular tilt-top, 1760-80, 33in. diam. (Christie's)
$3,520 £2,444

Chippendale mahogany tip tea table on three cabriole legs, Phila., circa 1770, 28¾in. high. (Robt. W. Skinner Inc.) $3,800 £2,638

Mid 18th century Queen Anne maple, rectangular top, tea table with outset porringer corners, 36in. wide. (Christie's) $1,210 £883

A parcel gilt, grained and specimen marble low table, the top inset with a mosaic of doves drinking, 28½in. diam. (Christie's) $6,114 £4,104

A Chippendale cherrywood serpentine-top tea table on three cabriole legs, 33½in. wide. (Christie's) $1,045 £725

A Galle mahogany and marquetry two-tier etagere, signed in the marquetry Galle, 59.3cm. wide. (Christie's) $2,662 £1,836

A Chippendale mahogany tilt-top tea table, circa 1770-85, top 34 x 33½in. (Christie's) $3,080 £2,138

A Chippendale mahogany tip table on a vase turned post and tripod cabriole leg base, circa 1780, 29in. high. (Robt. W. Skinner Inc.) $1,400 £945

A Chippendale cherrywood birdcage tea table, 1760-90, 36in. diam. (Christie's) $990 £687

A Federal birch and maple stand on tripod arched spider legs, 1790-1810, 16in. wide. (Christie's) $1,210 £840

A Chippendale carved mahogany tea table with circular top, Mass., 1765-85, 29½in. diam. (Christie's) $2,090 £1,451

OCCASIONAL TABLES

A George II mahogany tripod table with piecrust top, 9¾in. diam., 22in. high. (Christie's)
$2,349 £1,620

A green and white painted bamboo low table, the top covered with a Chinese 18th century painting, 51½in. wide. (Christie's)
$10,179 £7,020

A Victorian octagonal table inlaid with various woods, 1880. (British Antique Exporters) $704 £522

A padoukwood and mother-of-pearl inlaid tripod table with tip-up top, 38in. diam. (Christie's) $696 £480

A Regency mahogany library table with leather lined swivelling circular top, 35¾in. diam. (Christie's) $14,094 £9,720

One of a pair of Regency rosewood and parcel gilt lamp tables, 15½in. wide. (Christie's) $6,264 £4,320

Early 20th century oak occasional table. (British Antique Exporters)
$47 £35

A George II mahogany tripod table, the top with pierced fretwork gallery, 15in. diam., 24½in. high. (Christie's) $2,349 £1,620

Late 19th century Moorish inlaid occasional table. (British Antique Exporters)
$54 £40

OCCASIONAL TABLES

A cast iron pub table, 1869. (British Antique Exporters) $143 £106

One of a pair of early 19th century black and gold lacquer low tables, 49½in. wide. (Christie's) $3,445 £2,376

Late 19th century oak occasional table. (British Antique Exporters) $125 £93

Victorian octagonal table inlaid with various woods, 1860. (British Antique Exporters) $337 £250

Victorian inlaid walnut octagonal table, 1850. (British Antique Exporters) $217 £161

A Regency ebonised lamp table with rectangular hinged lacquer top, 18¼in. wide. (Christie's) $1,566 £1,080

Victorian mahogany occasional table, circa 1880. (British Antique Exporters) $48 £36

One of a pair of brass mounted satinwood tripod tables with octagonal tops, 15¾in. wide. (Christie's) $6,577 £4,536

Victorian brass tray on folding stand, 1875. (British Antique Exporters) $74 £55

FURNITURE

A William and Mary pine and maple tavern table, New England, circa 1730, 30½in. wide. (Robt. W. Skinner Inc.) $850 £590

A Regency faded rosewood drum table, the frieze with three drawers, 35¾in. diam. (Christie's) $9,082 £6,264

An early 19th century white marble circular conservatory table, probably Italian, 61in. diam. (Peter Wilson & Co.) $24,480 £17,000

A revolving mahogany tip-up, tray top table on turned tripod base, 32in. diam. (Butler & Hatch Waterman) $1,704 £1,200

A Queen Anne maple and pine tea table, New England, circa 1770, 25½in. wide. (Robt. W. Skinner Inc.) $1,700 £1,164

A Georgian style walnut wine table with two tiers of revolving book racks, 30in. high. (Anderson & Garland) $695 £490

A mid Georgian burr yew tripod table with circular tray tip-up top, 23in. diam. (Christie's) $4,447 £3,132

A table with glazed, brass framed, hide top supported on elephant feet, 27in. wide. (Christie's) $704 £486

A Federal cherry inlaid tip table, circa 1790, 28½in. high. (Robt. W. Skinner Inc.) $2,300 £1,597

OCCASIONAL TABLES

Late 19th century Centennial Chippendale Philadelphia mahogany birdcage tea table, 27½in. diam. (Robt. W. Skinner Inc.) $2,200 £1,504

An early 19th century Chinese Export bamboo low table with later square top, 15¾in. square. (Christie's) $783 £540

A mahogany tripod table, the tip-up top with pierced balustrade gallery, 35½in. wide. (Christie's) $2,021 £1,404

A transitional parquetry, kingwood and bois-satine table a ecrire, by J. P. Dustantoy, 15½in. diam. (Christie's) $5,443 £3,780

A Victorian papier mache tray on stand, with deep waved outline, 31½ x 24 x 10½in. high. (Lawrence Fine Art) $683 £462

A 19th century carved Chippendale mahogany tea table with hinged top, 30in. diam. (Robt. W. Skinner Inc.) $575 £393

A Chippendale mahogany tilt-top tea table, on three cabriole legs, Rhode Islànd, circa 1760, 35in. diam. (Robt. W. Skinner Inc.) $2,700 £1,901

A rococo Revival laminated rosewood lamp table, by J. B. Belter, New York, circa 1855, 26in. diam. (Robt. W. Skinner Inc.) $23,000 £15,753

A Regency rosewood pedestal table, the octagonal top with an Italian inlaid marble panel, 24½in. wide. (Christie's) $1,686 £1,188

A Regency painted satinwood tripod table with tip-up top, 35½in. wide. (Christie's)
$7,128 £5,400

A George III mahogany tripod table, the tray top on triple-scrolled shaft, 10½in. diam. (Christie's) $1,603 £1,188

A mid 18th century rococo walnut table with twin-scalloped top, 60in. wide. (Christie's)
$16,070 £12,960

A George III yewwood occasional table, the top inlaid with squares of specimen woods, 20½in. wide. (Christie's) $4,017 £3,240

A George III mahogany architect's table with double easel top and a frieze drawer, 35½in. wide. (Christie's)
$3,961 £3,024

A boulle jardiniere, the lift-out tin liner with milled edge, on cabriole legs, 17in. wide. (Christie's)
$2,851 £2,160

A mid Georgian mahogany tripod table with tip-up piecrust top, 27½in. diam. (Christie's) $8,019 £5,940

A set of four satinwood quartetto tables, the tops with ebony stringing, 14in. to 19½in. (Christie's)
$4,527 £3,456

A Regency rosewood tripod table with marble top, 20½in. wide. (Christie's)
$4,285 £3,456

A mahogany tripod table, the tip-up top with a needle-work panel worked in gros and petit point, 34in. wide. (Christie's) $1,339 £1,080

A mahogany and beechwood small table with circular tray top and baluster shaft with leather foot rest on four legs carved as boots, 15in. diam. (Christie's) $583 £432

A mid Georgian walnut archi-tect's table, the frieze drawer with leather lined slide and swivelling ink drawer, 33in. wide. (Christie's) $5,540 £4,104

An Emile Galle oak and mar-quetry table a deux plateaux, 60.2cm. wide. (Christie's) $630 £432

Early 19th century Anglo-Indian ebony and specimen wood table with hexagonal top, 23in. diam. (Christie's) $2,041 £1,512

A mahogany, ebonised and marquetry jardiniere in the style of Charles Bevan, 77.6cm. high. (Christie's) $3,942 £2,700

A George III mahogany tripod table with webbed claw and ball feet, 16½in. diam. (Christie's) $1,697 £1,296

A Queen Anne giltwood table on foliate cabriole legs and pad feet, 22in. wide. (Christie's) $3,348 £2,700

An early George III maho-gany tripod table with scrolling scalloped top, birdcage action, 29¾in. wide. (Christie's) $2,041 £1,512

A Regency rosewood occasional table, the top inlaid with an Italian octangular panel of specimen marbles, 31in. wide. (Christie's) $4,541 £3,132

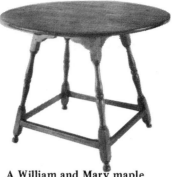

A William and Mary maple tavern table, New England, circa 1730, 34in. diam. (Robt. W. Skinner Inc.) $4,100 £3,887

Late 18th century Italian fruitwood tripod table with four frieze drawers. (Christie's) $1,866 £1,296

A George IV ebonised and gilded pedestal table, 24in. wide. (Christie's) $1,174 £810

Early 19th century Chinese Export bamboo tray table, 29in. wide, 26¼in. high. (Christie's) $6,557 £4,536

A George III satinwood and rosewood tripod table, in the manner of Thos. Chippendale, 26½in. wide. (Christie's) $12,528 £8,640

A Georgian mahogany tripod table, the circular top with marquetry pattern of birds and flowers, 28in. diam. (Lawrence Fine Art) $638 £440

A George III mahogany architect's table with adjustable top above a pull-out front section fitted with compartments, 37½in. wide. (Lawrence Fine Art) $4,232 £2,860

A walnut and beechwood tripod table, the tip-up top with a floral gros and petit point needlework panel, 33in. wide. (Christie's) $1,409 £972

A walnut draw-leaf table, Switzerland, circa 1700, top 43 x 30in. (Robt. W. Skinner Inc.) $4,250 £2,992

A George IV ormolu mounted parcel gilt and fruitwood library table, 56in. diam. (Christie's) $14,569 £10,260

A bamboo pattern centre table, the glazed top inset with a panel of 18th century Chinese painting on silk, 37¾in. wide. (Christie's) $4,698 £3,240

A mahogany urn table, the top with pierced fretwork gallery, 13in. square. (Christie's) $2,349 £1,620

A set of four Regency rosewood quartetto tables on twinned, shaped and turned supports, 26½in. to 13in. wide. (Christie's) $3,834 £2,700

A Sheraton design satinwood drum table on a turned, fluted and writhen column, 23in. diam. (Morphets) $1,224 £850

A George III mahogany tripod table on a baluster stem with cabriole shape supports, 34in. diam. (Lawrence Fine Art) $1,790 £1,210

A Regency circular tripod table with parquetry inlay. (F. H. Fellows & Sons) $1,095 £750

A Victorian circular top table, inset with specimen marbles and hardstones, 34in. diam. (Lawrence Fine Art) $8,294 £5,720

PEMBROKE TABLES

A George III mahogany Pembroke table, the twin-flap top with one bowed frieze drawer, 42½in. wide. (Christie's) $5,011 £3,456

A Country Chippendale cherry Pembroke table, with drop leaves and serpentine ends, circa 1780, 33 x 35in. (Robt. W. Skinner Inc.) $1,400 £985

A George III burr walnut and mahogany Pembroke table, the twin-flap top with a wide satinwood band, 43½in. wide. (Christie's) $4,384 £3,024

A George III satinwood and fruitwood Pembroke table, on square tapering legs, 37½in. wide. (Christie's) $6,508 £4,968

A Federal cherry, inlaid Pembroke table, circa 1810, 36in. wide. (Robt. W. Skinner Inc.) $900 £625

A George III mahogany Pembroke table with oval twin-flap top crossbanded in faded rosewood, 38in. wide, open. (Christie's) $2,574 £1,728

A Federal mahogany Pembroke table with two drop leaves, Penn., 1800-10, 49¾in. wide, open. (Christie's) $1,650 £1,145

A late Regency mahogany Pembroke table with a rosewood crossbanded two-flap top, 20 x 32in. extended. (Lawrence Fine Art) $1,790 £1,210

A George III satinwood and maplewood Pembroke table, the twin-flap top inlaid with stained and natural fruitwoods, 37½in. wide, open.(Christie's) $4,698 £3,240

PEMBROKE TABLES

A George III satinwood and fruitwood Pembroke table on square tapering legs, 40in. wide. (Christie's)
$15,660 £10,800

A George III Pembroke table with twin-flap rectangular top, the legs joined by an X-shaped stretcher, 44½in. wide open. (Christie's)
$1,749 £1,296

A Sheraton design mahogany and satinwood Pembroke table with shaped flaps, 36in. wide. (Morphets)
$1,633 £1,150

A Federal mahogany Pembroke table with two drop leaves, 1790-1810, 35in. wide. (Christie's)
$2,860 £1,986

An early Victorian mahogany Pembroke work table with fall leaves, 1ft.7in. wide. (Capes, Dunn & Co.)
$460 £320

An Hepplewhite satinwood veneer Pembroke table with drop leaves, circa 1800, top 32 x 37in. (Robt. W. Skinner Inc.) $4,500 £3,125

A late Federal mahogany Pembroke table with clover shaped top, 1815-25, 40¾in. long, top extended. (Christie's) $1,210 £840

A George III satinwood Pembroke table with harewood, kingwood and other crossbanding and stringing decoration, 32in. wide. (Chancellors Hollingsworths)
$2,499 £1,700

A Federal inlaid mahogany Pembroke table, Mass., 1790/1810, 31in. wide. (Christie's) $1,980 £1,365

One of a pair of Dutch walnut and marquetry side tables, each with one frieze drawer, 41½in. wide. (Christie's) $5,443 £3,780

A giltwood side table with sienna marble top, 53in. wide. (Christie's)　$2,557 £1,728

One of a pair of satinwood and marquetry side tables, 36in. wide. (Christie's)　$19,575 £13,500

A Dutch walnut and marquetry side table on cabriole legs and pointed pad feet, 34in. wide. (Christie's)　$2,954 £2,052

A George III parcel gilt and painted side table with distressed D-shaped white marble top, 32in. wide. (Christie's)　$2,147 £1,512

A scarlet and gold lacquer side table, basically late 17th century, 32½in. wide. (Christie's) $2,035 £1,404

One of a pair of parcel gilt and bronzed side tables with mottled green marble tops, 34½in. wide. (Christie's)　$10,179 £7,020

A Dutch walnut and marquetry side table on cabriole legs and ball and claw feet, 35½in. wide. (Christie's)　$3,110 £2,160

A Louis XVI ormolu mounted side table with inset grey marble, eared rectangular, concave sided top, 41½in. wide. (Christie's)　$3,421 £2,376

SIDE TABLES

An Irish, George III satinwood and fruitwood side table, the D-shaped top crossbanded in faded rosewood, 60in. wide. (Christie's) $8,613 £5,940

One of a pair of copies of 16th century French walnut hall side tables, 3ft.3in. wide. (Woolley & Wallis)
$1,178 £860

19th century carved oak side table, 1860. (British Antique Exporters)
$194 £144

A mid 17th century oak side table with brass drop handles, 30in. wide. (Woolley & Wallis)
$2,466 £1,800

A mahogany and satinwood side table with D-shaped top, 39½in. wide. (Christie's) $2,413 £1,620

An early George III mahogany side table with bowed serpentine top, 30½in. wide. (Christie's) $3,758 £2,592

One of a pair of Queen Anne gilt gesso side tables, 27½in. wide. (Christie's)
$56,376 £38,880

Victorian carved oak side table, 1860. (British Antique Exporters) $623 £462

An early Georgian walnut side table with carved border, formerly a card table, 33in. wide. (Christie's)
$1,456 £1,026

FURNITURE

A George II cream painted parcel gilt side table with grey marble top, 80½in. wide. (Christie's) $32,140 £25,920

A Charles II walnut side table on bobbin-turned legs joined by conforming stretchers with later oak feet, 35in. wide. (Christie's) $3,353 £2,484

A Regency mahogany serving table with breakfront top and brass gallery with vase finials, 84in. wide.(Christie's) $10,611 £8,100

A mid 17th century oak side table with chamfered top, 27½in. wide. (Christie's) $17,107 £12,960

An early Georgian red walnut side table, the triangular hinged top enclosing a compartment, with later base, 36½in. wide, open. (Christie's) $2,332 £1,728

One of a pair of George III satinwood pier tables with crossbanded D-shaped tops and ebonised spade feet, 23in. wide. (Christie's) $14,472 £10,800

A grain painted serving table, New England, circa 1825, 32in. wide. (Robt. W. Skinner Inc.) $4,100 £2,805

A William and Mary oak side table on slender turned baluster and knopped legs with bun feet, 18½in. wide. (Christie's) $3,991 £3,024

A Gustav Stickley three-drawer server, no. 818, circa 1910, 48in. wide. (Robt. W. Skinner Inc.) $950 £659

SIDE TABLES

A George II walnut side table with breccia marble top, on hairy claw and ball feet, 56½in. wide.(Christie's) $24,105 £19,440

A George II giltwood side table with brown jasper veneered top, 52½in. wide. (Christie's) $18,792 £12,960

A George II mahogany side table with Portor marble top, 43½in. wide. (Christie's) $15,919 £11,880

A neo-classical giltwood side table with moulded D-shaped mottled pink marble top, possibly Scandinavian, 41in. wide. (Christie's) $3,706 £2,808

One of a pair of gilt gesso side tables with breccia marble tops, on cabriole legs and pad feet, 17½in. wide. (Christie's) $9,266 £7,020

A 17th century oak side table, the D-shaped top with a flap at the back, 37¼in. wide. (Christie's) $5,702 £4,320

Late 18th century painted and gilded pier table with Portor marble top, 46¼in. wide. (Christie's) $7,047 £4,860

A Federal mahogany and mahogany veneer server, New England, circa 1815, 37¾in. wide. (Robt. W. Skinner Inc.)$700 £479

A green and white painted and gilded side table with verde antico top, 53in. wide. (Christie's) $2,818 £1,944

SOFA TABLES

A Regency yewwood sofa table with twin-flap top, on reeded splayed legs, 64½in. wide, open. (Christie's) $4,071 £2,808

A George IV painted elm and marquetry sofa table with twin-flap top, 57in. wide, open. (Christie's) $5,556 £3,780

A Regency rosewood and satinwood sofa table with trestle ends and splayed feet, 58in. wide, open. (Christie's)$8,046 £5,400

A Regency rosewood sofa table with brass stringing, on reel turned baluster column and quartette supports, 5ft. x 2ft.3in. (Capes, Dunn & Co.) $864 £600

Classical revival mahogany and mahogany veneer sofa table with shaped leaves, circa 1825, 35½in. wide. (Robt. W. Skinner Inc.) · $425 £287

Victorian mahogany sofa table on lyre supports with turned stretchers and with two fitted drawers. (Worsfolds) $547 £380

A Scottish George III mahogany sofa table, stamped Bruce EdinH, 63in. wide, open. (Christie's) $8,208 £5,400

A Regency rosewood sofa table, inlaid with brass in stylised foliate design, 36½ x 59in. extended. (Lawrence Fine Art) $2,711 £1,870

A George III rosewood sofa table with twin-flap top and two cedar lined frieze drawers, 54in. wide. (Christie's) $5,637 £3,888

SOFA TABLES

A Regency black and gold lacquer sofa table with brass bordered twin-flap top, 61½in. wide, open. (Christie's) $8,683 £6,480

A Regency maplewood sofa table with twin-flap top, the tapering feet with claw castors, 63in. wide. (Christie's) $12,025 £9,180

A Regency calamander sofa table, the twin-flap top crossbanded in satinwood, 59in. long. (Christie's) $7,047 £4,860

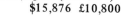

A Regency mahogany sofa table with twin-flap top and one frieze drawer, 53in. wide, open. (Christie's) $3,987 £2,808

A classical mahogany sofa table, the working drawer with a brass lion head pull, circa 1810/20, Phila., 42in. wide. (Christie's) $3,850 £2,655

A Regency rosewood sofa table with twin-flap top and frieze drawers, 58in. wide, open. (Christie's) $15,876 £10,800

A George IV mahogany sofa table with twin-flap top and two frieze drawers, the trade label R. Snowdon, Cabinet Maker and Appraiser, Northallerton., 62in. wide, open. (Christie's) $2,913 £2,052

A Regency calamander sofa table with twin-flap top, 58in. wide. (Christie's) $15,660 £10,800

A Regency rosewood sofa table, the solid trestle ends with scrolling bases, 58in. wide, open. (Christie's) $8,731 £5,940

An early Victorian black and mother-of-pearl japanned papier mache pedestal sewing box with hinged top, 32½in. high. (Christie's) **$1,805 £1,188**

Mid 19th century Regency inlaid mahogany and mahogany veneer work table, 36in. wide. (Robt. W. Skinner Inc.) **$600 £405**

A Federal mahogany and mahogany veneer work table with two drawers and one work bag pull out, Mass., circa 1795, top 21 x 17in. (Robt. W. Skinner Inc.) **$6,750 £4,687**

A William IV mahogany pedestal work table, the boxed top enclosed by a hinged canted lid, 19in. wide. (Christie's) **$570 £380**

A Chippendale mahogany and cherrywood sewing table, New England, 1815-25, 70½in. wide. (Christie's) **$660 £458**

A mid Victorian black, gilt and mother-of-pearl, japanned papier mache pedestal sewing box, 15in. wide. (Christie's) **$2,298 £1,512**

A Federal mahogany work table on water-leaf carved and scrolled sabre legs, 29in. high. (Christie's) **$1,430 £993**

An Edwardian Sheraton style inlaid and figured mahogany work table on tapering supports, 1ft.4in. wide. (Bridgfords) **$616 £450**

A Federal mahogany work table with octagonal top, the bottom drawer fitted with bag, New England, circa 1810, 28in. high. (Robt. W. Skinner Inc.) **$1,900 £1,283**

WORKBOXES & GAMES TABLES

An early Victorian rosewood work and games table with folding swivel top, 20in. wide. (Dreweatts)
$975 £650

A George II mahogany triple folding top games table on cabriole legs, 34in. wide. (Dreweatts) $9,300 £6,200

A George IV satinwood and fruitwood work table, possibly Scottish, 17¾in. wide. (Christie's) $2,035 £1,404

A Regency rosewood work table by Gillows of Lancaster, 35½in. wide, open. (Christie's) $1,126 £756

A George II mahogany, triple fold-over, shaped top tea/games table, 2ft.7½in. wide. (Edgar Horn) $7,592 £5,200

An Edwardian painted maple work table, the top with hinged flap, on square tapering legs, 21in. wide. (Christie's) $1,995 £1,296

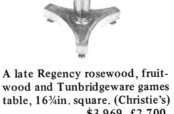

A parcel gilt and calamander games table on twinned simulated bamboo trestles, 28½in. wide. (Christie's)
$3,045 £2,160

A late Regency rosewood, fruitwood and Tunbridgeware games table, 16¾in. square. (Christie's)
$3,969 £2,700

A Victorian rectangular inlaid burr walnut needlework table with hinged top, 24in. wide. (Parsons, Welch & Cowell) $784 £530

A Regency rosewood games/
work table on a U-shape
support, 26in. wide.
(Lawrence Fine Art)
$3,581 £2,420

A 19th century Netherlands
rococo style mahogany in-
laid games table, top 34 x
31in. (Robt. W. Skinner Inc.)
$700 £492

Victorian maple and rose-
wood workbox, 1840.
(British Antique Exporters)
$603 £447

A late Federal inlaid mahogany work table with a
single drawer, Mass., 1800/
20, 17¼in. wide. (Christie's)
$825 £568

A classical gilt stencilled
rosewood sewing table,
probably N.Y., circa 1815/
30, 24¾in. wide.
(Christie's) $4,400 £3,034

A Federal inlaid mahogany
and bird's-eye maple sewing
table, attributed to John
and/or Thos. Seymour,
circa 1800/10, 20in. wide.
(Christie's)
$52,800 £36,413

A Regency period mahogany
work table with two fall
leaves and on lyre shaped
refectory supports. (Mor-
phets) $766 £540

A Country Federal tiger maple
work table, New England, circa
1820, on simulated bamboo
legs, 17½in. wide. (Robt. W.
Skinner Inc.) $2,800 £1,971

A classical Revival mahogany
work table, possibly Baltimore, circa 1810, 27.3/8in.
wide. (Robt. W. Skinner Inc.)
$2,500 £1,712

WORKBOXES & GAMES TABLES

Victorian padoukwood games table, 1850. (British Antique Exporters) $228 £169

A George II mahogany games table, the hinged top enclosing a backgammon well, 36in. wide.(Christie's) $2,624 £1,944

Victorian mahogany work table, circa 1860. (British Antique Exporters) $369 £274

A Victorian tole workbox, the glazed octangular lid decorated with a winter scene, 19½in. wide. (Christie's) $1,331 £918

A Federal carved mahogany work table, probably New York, circa 1810, 22in. wide. (Robt. W. Skinner Inc.) $15,000 £10,273

A Regency mahogany combined games and work table, the sides with candle-slides, 19in. wide. (Christie's) $5,499 £4,104

A George III satinwood and fruitwood work table, the top crossbanded with maplewood and tulipwood, 22in. wide. (Christie's) $5,702 £4,320

Late 19th century lady's work table in Japanese gold lacquer, 25 x 17in. (Peter Wilson & Co.) $748 £520

A Federal maple inlaid work table, New England, circa 1810, 18¾in. wide. (Robt. W. Skinner Inc.) $2,600 £1,830

WRITING TABLES & DESKS

A Chippendale pine standing desk, New England, 1780-1810, 30½in. wide. (Christie's) $1,100 £763

A 19th century George III style inlaid mahogany writing desk, America, 46in. wide. (Robt. W. Skinner Inc.) $900 £656

A Federal carved mahogany lady's writing table, N.Y., 1805-15, 20½in. wide. (Christie's) $3,080 £2,138

A lady's Federal mahogany tambour front writing desk, 32¾in. wide. (Christie's) $660 £481

A Queen Anne walnut desk with hinged slant lid, 1740-60, 30½in. wide. (Christie's) $3,300 £2,291

Victorian oak desk with leather top, 1880. (British Antique Exporters) $206 £153

A late Regency mahogany writing table, the top with fluted edge and inset tooled leather panel, 41in. wide. (Lawrence Fine Art) $1,465 £990

Edwardian oak fall front desk cabinet, 1910. (British Antique Exporters) $121 £90

A George III mahogany writing table with rectangular red leather-lined top and three frieze drawers, 48½in. wide. (Christie's) $4,490 £2,916

WRITING TABLES & DESKS

A Federal cherrywood writing desk, 1800-15, 30½in. wide. (Christie's)
$1,320 £963

A Regency ormolu mounted mahogany writing table, the top with pierced quatrefoil three-quarter gallery, 45in. wide. (Christie's)
$11,907 £8,100

Victorian oak fall front desk, 1880. (British Antique Exporters)
$125 £93

A Regency mahogany Carlton House desk, in the manner of Gillows, 55½in. wide. (Christie's)$23,155 £17,280

A mahogany and satinwood crossbanded bonheur du jour by T. Willson, London, 45in. wide. (Reeds Rains)
$1,094 £760

A Regency writing desk in the manner of Gillows, the drawer with Bramah lock. (Christie's) $4,666 £3,132

A George III mahogany writing table with rectangular faded scarlet leather-lined top, 51in. wide. (Christie's)
$5,322 £3,456

A George III mahogany writing table with revolving easel top, 25in. wide. (Christie's) $4,071 £2,808

A Renaissance Revival burled walnut library table, labelled by Alex. Roux, N.Y., circa 1860, 48in. wide.(Christie's)
$2,090 £1,451

WRITING TABLES & DESKS

A satinwood writing table with leather lined top and two cedar-lined frieze drawers, 39in. wide. (Christie's) $12,117 £9,180

An Edwardian satinwood, rosewood and marquetry Carlton House desk with leather lined easel, 49in. wide. (Christie's) $8,488 £6,480

A Regency rosewood writing table with leather lined crossbanded top, 43in. wide. (Christie's) $10,044 £8,100

An ormolu mounted kingwood bonheur du jour, the superstructure with inset mottled grey marble top, 28¾in. wide. (Christie's) $2,423 £1,836

A George III burr-yew and satinwood bonheur du jour with a recessed central cupboard door, 35½in. wide. (Christie's) $5,499 £4,104

An early 18th century walnut and mahogany writing cabinet on stand with folding leather lined top, 19¾in. wide. (Christie's) $3,499 £2,592

A George III mahogany bonheur du jour, the superstructure with two oval-inlaid doors, 36¼in. wide. (Christie's) $4,687 £3,780

An early Victorian bird's-eye maple writing table, 36½in. wide. (Christie's) $2,505 £1,728

A Victorian mahogany writing table with spindle galleried top, 45½in. wide. (Christie's) $1,174 £810

WRITING TABLES & DESKS

A Regency mahogany writing-table with leather lined top, 55in. wide. (Christie's) $8,704 £7,020

A late George III mahogany library desk with pierced gallery and Vitruvian scroll frieze, the plinth base 72in. diam. (Christie's) $33,285 £24,840

A contrepartie boulle bureau mazarin, the top inlaid with a Berainesque scene within strapwork, 53in. wide. (Christie's) $5,417 £4,104

A mid 18th century German ormolu mounted black lacquer bureau cabinet, 53in. wide. (Christie's) $10,692 £8,100

A 19th century Dutch walnut and marquetry cylinder top bombe-shaped bureau, 36in. wide. (Dacre, Son & Hartley) $2,088 £1,450

A William and Mary walnut writing or card table, the top lined with crimson velvet, 30in. wide.(Christie's) $9,979 £7,560

An ormolu mounted mahogany bureau plat of Louis XVI style with five panelled drawers, 42in. wide. (Christie's) $2,851 £2,160

One of a pair of Regency ormolu mounted rosewood writing tables, the drawers with leopard mask handles, 35½in. wide. (Christie's) $42,854 £34,560

An Empire mahogany desk with ten leathered compartments and leather lined easel writing surface, 57in. wide.(Christie's) $4,989 £3,780

WRITING TABLES & DESKS

A George III mahogany and satinwood bonheur du jour with leather lined writing slide, 26¼in. wide. (Christie's) $2,349   £1,620

A Regency mahogany writing table with leather lined top and two frieze drawers, 54in. wide. (Christie's)
$4,023   £2,700

A sailor made ship's desk, constructed by a sailor on the Bark Messenger, circa 1850, 23½in. wide. (Robt. W. Skinner Inc.)
$2,000   £1,388

Victorian walnut writing table, 1870. (British Antique Exporters) $329   £244

A Louis XV kingwood and parquetry writing table on cabriole legs, 26in. wide. (Christie's) $8,791   £5,940

A Regency calamander writing table with ormolu bordered crossbanded top inlaid with brass stars, 48in. wide. (Christie's)
$23,490   £16,200

A George IV ebony inlaid mahogany library table, on trestle ends and bar feet, 57½in. long. (Christie's)
$14,094   £9,720

Late 19th century oak tambour top desk. (British Antique Exporters)
$236   £175

A Maurice Dufrene semi-circular wooden desk, 31in. high, and a chair upholstered in red velvet, 32in. high, signed and dated 1935. (Christie's) $3,472   £2,800

TRUNKS & COFFERS

A Chippendale painted pine and poplar blanket chest with lift top, probably Penn., 1750-1800, 50½in. wide. (Christie's) $1,650 £1,204

Victorian pine trunk with brass carrying handles, 1850. (British Antique Exporters) $180 £120

An 18th century oak six plank chest, 38in. wide. (Peter Wilson & Co.) $506 £340

A red pine painted joined blanket chest, America, circa 1820, 37½in. wide. (Robt. W. Skinner Inc.) $500 £347

An 18th century Chinese black and gold lacquered coffer with hinged lid, 57¼in. wide. (Christie's) $2,741 £1,944

One of two early 19th century Chinese Export black and gold lacquer coffers on stands, 30¼in. wide. (Christie's) $6,577 £4,536

A William and Mary painted blanket chest with thumb moulded hinged lid, 46in. wide. (Christie's) $286 £208

A basically 16th century Florentine painted walnut cassone, 56in. wide. (Christie's) $3,356 £2,268

One of a pair of early 18th century Chinese Export black and gold lacquer coffers, 53½in. wide. (Christie's) $8,683 £6,480

TRUNKS & COFFERS

A grain painted pine blanket chest with turned brass pulls on cut-out base, 36in. wide, circa 1810. (Robt. W. Skinner Inc.) $1,500 £1,041

A George I oyster veneered walnut and kingwood coffer with a drawer, the sides with brass carrying handles, 47in. wide. (Christie's) $10,962 £7,560

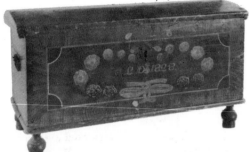

A Scandinavian painted dower chest with slightly domed, hinged top, dated 1828, 51in. wide. (Robt. W. Skinner Inc.) $800 £563

A Queen Anne walnut coffer on spirally turned legs, waved stretchers and bun feet, 38in. wide. (Christie's) $5,832 £4,320

A 17th century oak coffer with plain cover, panel sides and front with an arcaded frieze, 55in. wide, with repairs. (Lawrence Fine Art) $3,093 £2,090

A 17th century Spanish walnut coffer with plank top, 66½in. wide. (Christie's) $855 £594

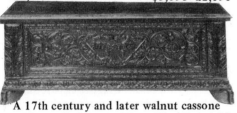

A 17th century and later walnut cassone with panelled front, 67in. wide.(Christie's) $4,043 £2,808

A 16th century Italian walnut cassone, the spreading panelled lid with foliate and scalloped banding, 73in. long. (Christie's) $9,331 £6,480

TRUNKS & COFFERS

A Kuwaiti Dowry chest richly decorated with ornate brass overlay. (Butler & Hatch Waterman) $1,917 £1,350

A 16th century Continental oak coffer, the top formed of three planks and with strap hinges, 5ft.10in. wide. (Woolley & Wallis) $3,045 £2,100

A partly 17th century walnut coffer on bun feet, 73in. wide. (Christie's) $1,321 £918

A late 17th century Swiss painted pine coffer with panelled rectangular top, 64in. wide. (Christie's) $997 £756

An 18th century oak dower chest with swan neck loop handles, 5ft.1in. wide. (Capes, Dunn & Co.) $460 £320

An 18th century Dutch Colonial padoukwood blanket chest with pierced brass clasps and carrying handles, on bun feet, 67in. wide. (Christie's) $1,425 £1,086

A 17th century Spanish oak and walnut coffer with rectangular top, on block feet, 61in. wide. (Christie's) $1,010 £702

An 18th century oak dower chest with brass swan neck handles and pierced back plates, 5ft.4in. wide. (Capes, Dunn & Co.) $482 £340

WARDROBES & ARMOIRES

A Federal walnut linen press on French feet, 1800-10, 43¾in. wide.(Christie's) $8,250 £5,729

A mid Victorian mahogany cylinder wardrobe, the drawers with turned handles, 255cm. wide. (Phillips) $890 £650

A mid 18th century French provincial cherrywood armoire with moulded cornice, 56in. wide.(Christie's) $2,138 £1,620

A French gold and parcel gilt armoire on squat cabriole feet. (Christie's) $2,352 £1,600

A George III satinwood breakfront wardrobe inlaid with narrow bands and stringing, 104in. wide. (Lawrence Fine Art) $4,884 £3,300

A Chippendale carved mahogany wardrobe, in two sections, New York, 1760-80, 53in. wide. (Christie's) $4,180 £2,902

One of a pair of Louis XVI kingwood armoires with two pairs of cupboards filled with gilt wire, 70in. wide. (Christie's) $22,377 £15,120

A Louis XVI amaranth, tulipwood and parquetry armoire, possibly Dutch, 41in. wide. (Christie's) $4,860 £3,240

A South African stinkwood armoire on claw and ball feet, with silver handles stamped IB, 64in. wide. (Christie's) $2,280 £1,728

WARDROBES & ARMOIRES

A Dutch hardwood armoire, possibly Colonial, 64in. wide. (Christie's) $926 £702

A 17th century South German walnut armoire, 79in. wide. (Christie's) $9,642 £6,696

A classical mahogany armoire, attributed to Chas. H. Lannvier, circa 1800-15, 55in. wide. (Christie's) $24,200 £16,805

Late 18th/early 19th century oak armoire with moulded cornice, 69½in. wide. (Reeds Rains) $1,238 £860

A Regency period mahogany breakfront wardrobe/linen press, 8ft.2in. long. (Woolley & Wallis) $2,740 £2,000

A Louis XVI oak armoire with moulded foliate cornice, 61½in. wide. (Christie's) $2,799 £1,944

Victorian carved walnut armoire, 1860. (British Antique Exporters) $253 £188

An Empire Gothic mahogany wardrobe, signed by Joseph Stewart Jr., New York, and dated 1831, 69in. wide. (Christie's) $3,850 £2,810

An 18th century Scandinavian walnut armoire, 57in. wide. (Christie's) $5,443 £3,780

WASHSTANDS

Late 18th century mahogany bow fronted corner wash-stand on splay feet, 2ft.3½in. wide. (Bermondsey)
$485 £325

Victorian mahogany marble top washstand, 1860. (British Antique Exporters)
$247 £183

Federal mahogany corner washstand on splay feet, 21½in. wide, circa 1800. (Robt. W. Skinner Inc.)
$1,000 £700

A Federal mahogany carved washstand, probably Mass., circa 1815, 20in. wide. (Robt. W. Skinner Inc.)
$2,100 £1,418

Victorian marble top oak washstand, 1860. (British Antique Exporters)
$35 £25

A late Georgian mahogany washstand with gallery back, shelf and single drawer, 18in. wide. (Peter Wilson & Co.)
$149 £100

Victorian marble top wash-stand, 1860. (British Antique Exporters) $249 £185

A George III mahogany pedestal washstand with hinged coffered folding top, 13in. wide. (Christie's)
$1,176 £800

Victorian tiled back marble top washstand, 1860. (British Antique Exporters)
$279 £207

FURNITURE

Victorian walnut four-tier whatnot, 1840. (British Antique Exporters)
$521 £386

A mid 19th century parquetry three tier etagere, 19½in. wide. (Christie's)
$1,879 £1,296

Victorian marble top whatnot, 1860. (British Antique Exporters) $396 £294

An early 19th century three-tier mahogany whatnot, 45in. high. (W. H. Lane & Son) $403 £280

An ebonised four tier etagere with galleried top, circa 1830, 29in. wide, 49½in. high. (Christie's) $2,818 £1,944

Victorian walnut whatnot, 1860. (British Antique Exporters) $249 £185

One of a pair of Regency mahogany whatnots with vase finials, 17¾in. square. (Christie's) $2,818 £1,944

A late Georgian bird's-eye maple four tier etagere, 24in. wide, 31in. high. (Christie's) $4,228 £2,916

An early 19th century mahogany whatnot, 1ft.6in. square. (J. R. Bridgford & Sons)
$648 £450

WINE COOLERS

A Regency mahogany wine cooler with lead lined interior, 34in. wide. (Christie's) $3,445 £2,376

A Regency mahogany wine cooler with tin liner, 34in. wide. (Christie's) $3,701 £2,484

A Regency mahogany wine cooler with detachable liner, carrying handles and hairy paw feet, 27½in. wide. (Christie's) $2,946 £2,376

A late 18th century Sheraton style mahogany crossbanded and inlaid octagonal cellarette, 19in. wide. (Dacre, Son & Hartley) $3,600 £2,500

A Regency carved mahogany wine cooler with lion mask brass ring handles, 26½in. wide. (Dacre, Son & Hartley) $1,728 £1,200

A Federal inlaid cherrywood cellarette and stand, 1790-1810, 36in. high. (Christie's) $7,150 £4,965

A George III mahogany wine cooler, the tapering brass bound body with carrying handles, 19½in. wide. (Christie's) $2,177 £1,512

A Federal inlaid mahogany wine cooler with lift top, 22in. wide. (Christie's) $3,080 £2,138

A mid Georgian brass bound mahogany wine cooler with detachable tin liner, 23½in. wide. (Christie's) $2,770 £2,052

WINE COOLERS

A Regency mahogany oval wine cooler in the manner of Gillows with lead-lined interior, 27¼in. wide. (Christie's) $5,540 £4,104

A Regency mahogany wine cooler with lead-lined body, on ebonised claw feet, 28in. wide. (Christie's) $4,631 £3,456

A Regency mahogany wine cooler in the manner of Gillows, with oval tin liner, 29in. wide. (Christie's) $6,264 £4,320

A George III brass bound mahogany cellarette with lead lined interior retaining tap beneath, 19in. wide. (Christie's) $3,481 £2,808

One of a pair of George III brass bound wine coolers with detachable tin liners, 27in. wide. (Christie's) $7,668 £5,400

A George III mahogany, crossbanded and inlaid cellarette on brass castored feet. (Dacre, Son & Hartley) $864 £600

One of two George III brass bound mahogany wine coolers with detachable liners, 25in. and 24in. wide. (Christie's) $10,713 £8,640

A Regency ormolu mounted mahogany wine cooler with hinged oval domed fan-shaped top, 29in. wide, 27in. high, 23in. deep. (Christie's) $14,731 £11,880

A George III mahogany brass bound wine cooler with carrying handles, 25in. wide. (Christie's) $2,971 £2,268

BEAKERS

An engraved spa glass, the bowl cut with panels, circa 1840, 5½in. high. (Bermondsey) $215 £110

A Bohemian amethyst-overlay, cylindrical beaker, 4½in. high. (Christie's) $195 £130

A Bohemian amber flash, fluted cylindrical beaker cut with oval panels engraved with named buildings, 5¼in. high. (Christie's) $300 £200

A Bohemian lithyalin, flaring cylindrical beaker, 4¾in. high. (Christie's) $330 £220

A German Ochsenkopf flared beaker, the sides enamelled in colours with the usual symbols, 1708, 11.8cm. high. (Christie's) $1,866 £1,296

A Silesian armorial flared beaker, the ogee bowl with moulded and cut flutes to the lower part, circa 1745, 11cm. high. (Christie's) $1,296 £864

A mid 19th century Austrian enamel and clear glass beaker decorated with a scenic band. (Bermondsey) $525 £350

An enamelled milchglas beaker of cylindrical form, circa 1780, 3½in. high. (Bermondsey) $210 £140

A Bohemian transparent-enamelled chinoiserie beaker, circa 1835, 12.5cm. high. (Christie's) $1,480 £1,000

A late 17th century Netherlandish blue serving bottle, 17cm. high. (Christie's) $1,866 £1,296

A large Roman green glass bottle with globular bowl, cylindrical neck and everted lip, swirling iridescence, 16.5cm. high. (Phillips) $191 £130

'Figurines Avec Bouchon', a Lalique frosted glass bottle and stopper, 11½in. high. (Christie's) $1,368 £950

A 17th century Facon-De-Venise bottle in vetro a fili, 30.5cm. high. (Christie's) $289 £193

A set of four Bristol blue sauce bottles and stoppers, the bases incised W. R. & Co., and one with a dated 1788?, 11cm. high. (Lawrence Fine Art) $214 £143

A Dimple Haig clear glass bottle, decorated with pierced plated mounts depicting Chinese dragons, original stopper, 10½in. high. (Peter Wilson & Co.) $120 £80

A sealed and dated green glass wine bottle of mallet shape with conical neck, the seal inscribed IOS Dalyzell and dated 1738, 8¾in. high. (Christie's) $588 £400

An oak bottle box with thirteen blown glass bottles, late 18th/early 19th century, 13½in. wide. (Christie's) $1,100 £763

A Galle oviform clear and enamelled glass bottle decanter with moulded flutes, 7¾in. high. (Christie's) $273 £180

519

BOWLS

A marriage bowl inscribed I. Davyz E. Hannaford Maryd. Oct. 30 1769, 21cm. diam. (Christie's) $891 £594

A Lalique clear and frosted two-handled oval bowl, 'Jardiniere Saint—Hubert', 19in. long, inscribed. (Christie's) $403 £280

A Lalique deep circular bowl, 'Saint-Vincent', the blue opalescent satin finished glass moulded with bands of fruit laden vines, circa 1930, 34.5cm. wide. (Christie's)
$1,576 £1,080

 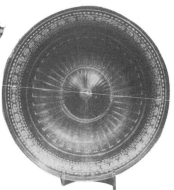 

One of a set of four cut glass cylindrical bowls, with silver gilt mounts, the glass circa 1820, the handles with maker's mark of John Bridge, 1824, 16cm. wide. (Christie's) $2,268 £1,512

A Venetian shallow bowl with everted folded rim, enamelled in colours, circa 1500, 22.5cm. diam. (Christie's)
$972 £648

A Steuben crystal-footed bowl and cover, 'The Plains', designed by Lloyd Atkins, 33cm. high. (Christie's)
$2,365 £1,620

A Lalique opalescent deep circular bowl, 'Ondine Ouverte', 12in. diam. (Christie's) $864 £600

A Decorchment pate-de-verre bowl, green and brown marbled glass, circa 1940, 25.7cm. wide. (Christie's)
$2,349 £1,620

A Lalique bowl, the opalescent blue satin finished glass moulded with budgerigars, 23.7cm. diam. (Christie's)
$1,879 £1,296

A clear and brown stained rectangular box, by Rene Lalique, 4in. wide. (Bermondsey) $450 £300

An early 20th century Galle glass box and cover, 3in. diam., signed. (Bermondsey) $1,200 £900

Mid 19th century Bohemian enamelled and ruby glass casket, 6in. square. (Bermondsey) $600 £400

'Dahlia', a Lalique circular box and cover in clear and satin finished glass, 13.6cm. diam. (Christie's) $626 £432

A Guild of Handicrafts silver and glass box and cover, designed by C. R. Ashbee, with London hallmarks for 1900, 21cm. high, 16oz. 15dwt. gross weight without cover. (Christie's) $6,894 £4,536

A Bohemian dated, double overlay, gilt metal mounted, rectangular casket for the Persian market, circa 1848, 15cm. wide. (Christie's) $3,240 £2,160

A Baccarat gilt metal mounted rectangular casket, circa 1830, 13.5cm. wide. (Christie's) $403 £280

'Three Dahlias', a Lalique blue opalescent circular box and cover of clear and satin finished glass, 20.9cm. diam. (Christie's) $469 £324

Mid 19th century Bohemian overlay and enamelled casket, the body in opaque white, 5¼in. wide. (Bermondsey) $600 £400

CANDLESTICKS

A baluster stemmed glass candlestick with three graduated knops, circa 1750, 9¼in. high. (Bermondsey) $675 £450

One of a pair of Georgian ormolu mounted, cut and coloured glass candlesticks, 13½in. high. (Christie's) $2,138 £1,620

A Sandwich Clambroth and blue glass dolphin candlestick, circa 1820, 10in. high. (Robt. W. Skinner Inc.) $250 £176

A baluster candlestick the cylindrical nozzle with everted folded rim, circa 1745, 20cm. high. (Christie's) $839 £583

A pair of Charles X ormolu and cut glass candlesticks with faceted, hobnail-cut stems, 16½in. high. (Christie's) $3,136 £2,376

An airtwist candlestick on a domed and terraced foot, circa 1750, 20cm. high. (Christie's) $807 £561

A baluster candlestick, the stem with true baluster section above a beaded knop and triple annulated basal knop, circa 1745, 19.5cm. high. (Christie's) $901 £626

One of a pair of cut glass five-light wall lights, the nozzles with silver plated liners, 25in. high. (Christie's) $2,349 £1,620

Mid 18th century pedestal stemmed candlestick, on a domed foot, 20.5cm. high. (Christie's) $648 £432

GLASS

DECANTERS

A green baluster decanter with lozenge stopper, 9½in. high, and a blue decanter, 9in. high. (Christie's) $236 £160

A Victorian electroplate decanter stand, by Elkington & Co., with design registration mark for 2nd October 1868, 29.4cm. high overall. (Lawrence Fine Art) $485 £330

A Lalique glass decanter, the broadly shouldered tapering body with stepped serrated bands to the base, 24.3cm. high. (Lawrence Fine Art) $112 £77

One of a pair of cut glass decanters and stoppers of club shape, circa 1820. (Christie's) $648 £432

A Hukin & Heath 'Crow's foot' decanter, designed by Dr. C. Dresser, electroplate and glass, with registration lozenge for 1879, 24cm. high. (Christie's) $11,275 £7,776

A Guild of Handicraft hammered silver and green glass decanter, the design attributed to C. R. Ashbee, with London hallmarks for 1903, 22.5cm. high. (Christie's) $1,892 £1,296

A cylindrical file-cut decanter and stopper, cut with three rings to the neck, 10in. high. (Christie's) $88 £60

A pair of Georgian wine decanters, one with disc stopper, the other with replacement faceted ball stopper, 14½in. high. (Capes, Dunn & Co.) $374 £260

Victorian glass decanter, 1870. (British Antique Exporters) $70 £52

523

DISHES

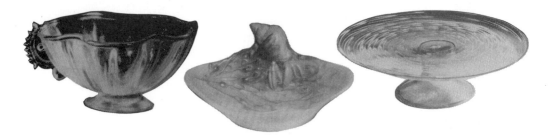

Late 17th century Facon-De-Venise shallow cup with applied pincered scroll handle, 11.5cm. wide. (Christie's) $388 £270

An Almaric Walter pate-de-verre dish of lozenge shape, designed by H. Berge, 24.6cm. wide. (Christie's)
$1,879 £1,296

Mid 17th century Facon-De-Venise filigree tazza, 31cm. diam. (Christie's)
$1,056 £734

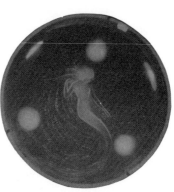

A sweetmeat glass, the shallow flared bucket bowl with gad-rooned underside and folded rim, circa 1730, 9.5cm. high. (Christie's) $528 £367

A Lalique opalescent glass dish, 'Sirene', signed, circa 1925, 14½in. diam. (W. H. Lane & Son) $936 £650

One of a pair of Portland clear overshot glass compotes, late 19th century, 8¾in. high. (Robt. W. Skinner Inc.)
$500 £335

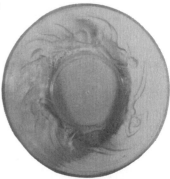

A glass dish attributed to H. P. Glashutte with enamel painted decoration of a purple clematis bloom, circa 1900, 23.5cm. diam. (Christie's) $249 £172

A Baccarat close millefiori wafer dish, the base with a cane inscribed 'B1848', 10cm. high. (Christie's)
$1,533 £1,080

An opalescent 'Ondines' dish, engraved R. Lalique, France, 8in. diam. (Capes, Dunn & Co.)
$465 £310

DRINKING SETS

A WMF electroplated liqueur set and tray, the decanters 9in. high, the tray 16in. wide, all with stamped marks. (Christie's)
$705 £480

'Coquelicot', a Lalique globular decanter and stopper, 6¾in. high, and five glasses en suite. (Christie's) $187 £130

A Patriz Huber liqueur set, white metal and glass, stamped with 935 German silver mark and PH, circa 1900, decanter 18.4cm. high. (Christie's) $4,099 £2,808

A Gabriel Argy-Rousseau pate-de-verre eight-piece liqueur service, the tray 40.1cm. wide. (Christie's) $3,132 £2,160

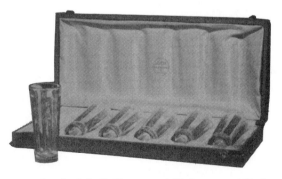

A Lalique oviform clear and frosted glass decanter and stopper, 7in. high, and eight glasses en suite. (Christie's) $288 £200

A set of six Lalique aperitif glasses moulded in clear glass with amethyst tinted panels of Grecian maidens, circa 1930, 9.8cm. high. (Christie's) $1,644 £1,134

FLASKS

A vertically ribbed chestnut flask, golden amber, sheared mouth-pontil scar, 4½in. high, 1820-40. (Robt. W. Skinner Inc.) $160 £112

A Heath & Middleton silver topped glass flask, possibly designed by C. Dresser, Birmingham 1891, 10in. high. (Christie's)$705 £480

A scroll pint flask, GIX-11, golden amber, sheared mouth-pontil scar, 1845-60. (Robt. W. Skinner Inc.) $200 £140

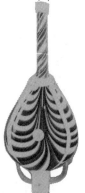

A mid 19th century Nailsea red, white and blue bellows flask, 12½in. high. (Robt. W. Skinner Inc.) $225 £158

One of two half pint Adams-Jefferson portrait flasks, GI-114, olive amber, sheared mouth-pontil scars, 1830-50. (Robt. W. Skinner Inc.) $210 £147

A gimmel flask in ruby glass with a wavy combed design in red and opaque white, 24cm. long. (Lawrence Fine Art) $90 £60

A Masonic eagle historical pint flask, golden amber, White Glass Works, 1820-40. (Robt. W. Skinner Inc.) $275 £193

Late 18th century amethyst flask, the globular body moulded with 'nipt diamond waves', 20cm. high. (Christie's) $1,053 £702

A double eagle historical pint flask, GII-40, bright green, sheared mouth-pontil scar, Kensington Glass Works, 1830-38. (Robt. W. Skinner Inc.) $275 £193

GLASS

An engraved light baluster goblet, the stem with beaded dumb-bell section, circa 1755, 21cm. high. (Christie's) $2,643 £1,836

A composite stemmed engraved goblet with round funnel bowl with fruiting vinestock, 19cm. high. (Christie's) $403 £280

A Dutch Friendship goblet with funnel bowl, circa 1755, 18cm. high. (Christie's) $372 £259

A baluster goblet, the thistle bowl supported on a cushion above a drop knopped section, circa 1700, 15.5cm. high. (Christie's) $1,088 £756

An armorial light baluster goblet, on a multi-knopped stem and domed foot, circa 1755, 19cm. high. (Christie's) $588 £388

A baluster goblet, the funnel bowl supported on an inverted baluster stem, circa 1720, 20.5cm. high. (Christie's) $372 £259

A baluster goblet with a slender thistle-shaped bowl, circa 1705, 17.5cm. high. (Christie's) $1,166 £810

A composite stemmed goblet by Jacob Sang, on a conical foot, circa 1760, 19.5cm. high. (Christie's) $5,499 £4,104

A baluster goblet, the funnel bowl supported on an inverted baluster stem above a folded conical foot, circa 1720, 18cm. high. (Christie's) $466 £324

GLASS

A baluster goblet, the stem with a wide angular knop, circa 1715, 16.5cm. high. (Christie's) $403 £280

A Bohemian hyalith goblet with gilt interior, Count Buquoy's Glassworks, circa 1835, 12.5cm. high. (Christie's) $963 £669

A Silesian engraved goblet with fluted oviform bowl, circa 1760, 16cm. high. (Christie's) $855 £594

A baluster goblet on a folded conical foot, circa 1700, 17.5cm. high. (Christie's) $496 £345

A pair of topographical goblets with bell bowls, circa 1765, 22cm. high. (Christie's) $5,065 £3,780

A baluster goblet with bell bowl supported on a triple annulated knop, circa 1720, 18cm. high. (Christie's) $466 £324

A mid 18th century German armorial goblet with funnel bowl, 19cm. high. (Christie's) $434 £302

A Vienna Secession glass goblet attributed to Moser and the design to J. Hoffmann, circa 1915, 12.8cm. high. (Christie's) $391 £270

An engraved light baluster goblet, the bowl with seven arrows tied by ribbon representing the Seven Provinces of the Netherlands, circa 1760, 18.5cm. high. (Christie's) $1,088 £756

GLASS

A baluster goblet with a funnel bowl, circa 1700, 17.5cm. high. (Christie's) $466 £324

One of six large Vedar goblets, enamel painted with a continuous frieze of dancing putti with floral garlands, 19.4cm. high. (Christie's) $1,892 £1,296

A baluster goblet, the funnel bowl supported on an inverted baluster stem, circa 1720, 17cm. high. (Christie's) $466 £324

A Royal armorial light baluster goblet, the bowl engraved with the crowned arms of William V, circa 1760, 21cm. high. (Christie's) $933 £648

Pair of 19th century overlaid and cut Bohemian covered goblets, 19in. high. (J. R. Bridgford & Sons) $2,736 £1,900

A baluster goblet, the funnel bowl supported on a cushion knop, circa 1710, 20.5cm. high. (Christie's) $652 £453

A baluster goblet with straight-sided funnel bowl, circa 1705, 18cm. high. (Christie's) $714 £496

A Bohemian transparentemail goblet, decorated in transparent enamels in shades of pink and amber with fish, circa 1840, 14.5cm. high. (Christie's) $777 £540

A mid 18th century light baluster Royal armorial goblet with multi-knopped stem, 20.5cm. high. (Christie's) $2,170 £1,620

A calligraphic baluster goblet, attributed to Bastiaan Boers or Francois Crama, the rim engraved in diamond-point, circa 1700, 17.8cm. high. (Christie's) $7,959   £5,940

A betrothal goblet by Jacob Sang, supported on a waist-knopped section above a beaded inverted baluster stem, 1755-60, 18.5cm. high. (Christie's) $2,604 £1,944

An opaque twist shipping goblet attributed to Jacob Sang, circa 1785, 19.5cm. high. (Christie's) $4,631 £3,456

A pedestal stemmed Alliance goblet in the manner of Robart, 1735-40, 19cm. high. (Christie's) $1,519 £1,134

A pedestal stemmed armorial goblet engraved by Willem O. Robart, 1735-45, 20cm. high. (Christie's) $2,098 £1,566

A facet cut shipping goblet attributed to Simon J. Sang, 1770-80, 23.5cm. high. (Christie's) $3,473 £2,592

A light baluster betrothal goblet, the funnel bowl decorated in the manner of David Wolff, late 18th century, 19.2cm. high. (Christie's) $4,052 £3,024

A large armorial goblet, the funnel bowl engraved with the arms of Delfland, circa 1780, 23cm. high.(Christie's) $868 £648

A stipple engraved goblet on a 19th century replacement parcel gilt lower section, by Frans Greenwood, circa 1744, 24.3cm. high overall. (Christie's) $43,416 £32,400

A light baluster goblet by Jacob Sang, supported on a waist-knopped section above a beaded inverted baluster stem, 1755-65, 19cm. high. (Christie's) $2,026 £1,512

An armorial baluster goblet with bucket bowl, circa 1760, 16cm. high. (Christie's) $1,736 £1,296

A light baluster armorial goblet by Jacob Sang, the funnel bowl engraved with the crowned arms of Prussia, circa 1765, 19.5cm. high. (Christie's) $1,881 £1,404

A composite stemmed marriage goblet by Jacob Sang, on a conical foot, circa 1760, 19.5cm. high. (Christie's) $2,894 £2,160

A composite stemmed goblet by Jacob Sang, supported on a beaded dumb-bell section above an inverted baluster stem, 1759, 18.3cm. high. (Christie's) $6,946 £5,184

A mid 18th century hunting goblet, the engraving perhaps by a German hand, 22.5cm. high. (Christie's) $4,341 £3,240

A composite stemmed shipping goblet by Jacob Sang, supported on a knopped section filled with airtwist spirals, 1760-70, 19.5cm. high. (Christie's) $6,512 £4,860

A light baluster friendship goblet by Jacob Sang, on a conical foot, 1755-60, 19.5cm. high. (Christie's) $2,894 £2,160

A light baluster armorial goblet engraved by the monogrammist JB, circa 1750, 22.3cm. high. (Christie's) $4,341 £3,240

A Galle oviform single-
handled ewer, the silver
mount modelled with styl-
ised flowers, signed, 10¼in.
high. (Christie's) $1,066 £820

A Nailsea jug, pale green,
with strap handle, the neck
with white enamel rim,
19.5cm. high. (Lawrence
Fine Art) $313 £209

A Victorian electroplated
claret jug, by Elkington &
Co., with date letter code
for 1883, 36cm. high.
(Lawrence Fine Art)
                   $358 £242

A Nailsea jug, dark green
splashed with white, with
flared neck, 23cm. high.
(Lawrence Fine Art)
                $115 £77

One of two late 17th century
Venetian small jugs with
applied blue rims, 10cm. high.
(Christie's) $453 £302

A Galle enamelled and green
oviform single-handled glass
jug, 8½in. high, inscribed.
(Christie's) $288 £200

A Hukin & Heath electro-
plated metal mounted glass
claret jug, designed by Dr.
C. Dresser, with registration
lozenge for 12th November
1879, 23.7cm. high.
(Christie's) $9,460 £6,480

An engraved claret jug with
plated mounts and hinged
cover, circa 1880, 27.5cm.
high. (Christie's) $388 £259

A Hukin & Heath silver
mounted claret jug designed
by Dr. C. Dresser, with
London hallmarks for 1884,
23cm. high. (Christie's)
                 $1,182 £810

GLASS

A 19th century clear and cranberry glass bell, 13in. high, and a red, white and blue Nailsea float, 5in. long. (Robt. W. Skinner Inc.) $200 £140

A decalcomania rolling pin, profusely decorated with soldiers, sailors, policemen, female figures and animals, 43.5cm. long. (Lawrence Fine Art) $90 £60

A Whitefriar's paperweight inkwell, from the Bacchus period, circa 1840, 7in. high. (Robt. W. Skinner Inc.) $400 £281

A Daum limited edition pate-de-verre and fibre glass surrealist sculpture by Salvador Dali, depicting a soft clock slumped on a coat hanger. (Christie's) $2,975 £2,052

A 19th century glass drug jar with a lid, 24in. high. (Lots Road Chelsea Auction Galleries) $210 £140

Early 20th century dimpled glass firescreen with an oak frame. (British Antique Exporters) $51 £38

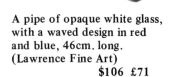

An Etling opalescent figure of a semi naked woman, 11in. high. (Christie's) $691 £480

Part of a Bohemian ruby and white overlay glass dessert service, three compotiers 18cm. high, two 16.5cm. high and ten plates, 25cm. diam. (Lawrence Fine Art) $2,552 £1,760

A pipe of opaque white glass, with a waved design in red and blue, 46cm. long. (Lawrence Fine Art) $106 £71

GLASS

A St. Louis panelled close millefiori weight, 7.7cm. diam. (Christie's)
$5,443 £3,780

A St. Louis concentric millefiori mushroom weight, on a star-cut base, 7.8cm. diam. (Christie's)
$1,321 £918

A French scramble paper-weight with blue, green, white and red canes, 3in. diam. (Robt. W. Skinner Inc.) $425 £291

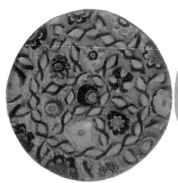

A Clichy pink and white 'barber's pole' chequer weight, 6.5cm. diam. (Christie's) $1,477 £1,026

A Paul Ysart bouquet weight, the centre to one flower with PY initials, 7.6cm. diam. (Christie's)
$466 £324

A Baccarat mushroom weight on a star-cut base, 8cm. diam. (Christie's)
$2,488 £1,728

A Clichy moss ground flower weight, 6.5cm. diam. (Christie's) $6,531 £4,536

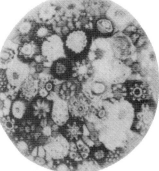

A Clichy miniature close millefiori weight, 4.7cm. diam. (Christie's)
$777 £540

A St. Louis pink ground pompom weight, 7cm. diam. (Christie's)
$1,866 £1,296

GLASS

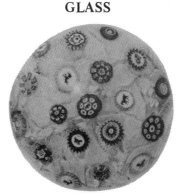

A Paul Ysart double-fish
weight on a translucent
amethyst base, signed PY
on a cane, 7.5cm. diam.
(Christie's) $590 £410

A Baccarat dated scattered
millefiori weight, 7.8cm.
diam. (Christie's)
$1,010 £702

A Baccarat garlanded white
double clematis weight, on
a star-cut base, 7.3cm. diam.
(Christie's) $933 £648

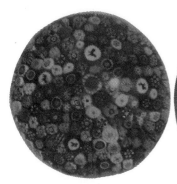

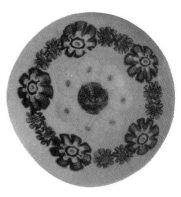

A Baccarat dated close mille-
fiori weight, a cane inscribed
'B 1848', 6.6cm. diam.
(Christie's) $933 £648

A Clichy pansy weight,
6.3cm. diam. (Christie's)
$1,399 £972

A Clichy patterned concentric millefiori weight, 5.5cm.
diam. (Christie's) $496 £345

A Clichy blue and white
dahlia weight, 7.2cm. diam.
(Christie's) $9,331 £6,480

A Clichy garlanded patterned millefiori weight,
7.5cm. diam. (Christie's)
$5,443 £3,780

A Baccarat miniature col-
oured sulphide pansy weight,
4.7cm. diam. (Christie's)
$1,166 £810

GLASS

A Clichy faceted posy weight, on a star-cut base, 6.5cm. diam. (Christie's) $466 £324

A Paul Ysart garlanded bouquet weight, with PY initials included in the bouquet, 7.5cm. diam. (Christie's) $466 £324

A St. Louis faceted concentric millefiori mushroom weight, 8cm. diam. (Christie's) $558 £388

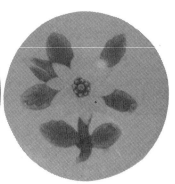

A St. Louis blue dahlia weight, 6.1cm. diam. (Christie's) $1,244 £864

A large Paul Ysart garlanded flat bouquet weight, 9.5cm. diam. (Christie's) $933 £648

A Baccarat white double clematis weight, on star-cut base, 6.4cm. diam. (Christie's) $777 £540

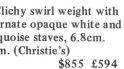

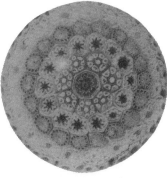

A Clichy garlanded patterned millefiori weight, 7.5cm. diam. (Christie's) $1,710 £1,188

A Clichy swirl weight with alternate opaque white and turquoise staves, 6.8cm. diam. (Christie's) $855 £594

A Bacchus close concentric millefiori weight, 9.2cm. diam. (Christie's) $777 £540

GLASS

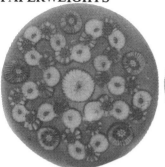

A Clichy pink ground patterned millefiori weight, 8cm. diam. (Christie's) $855 £594

A Paul Stankard St. Anthony's fire spray weight, signed on a cane with the initial S and engraved script number 39776, 7.6cm. diam. (Christie's) $622 £432

A Baccarat pink and white dog-rose weight, on a star-cut base, 6.7cm. diam. (Christie's) $1,010 £702

A St. Louis fruit weight, 6.2cm. diam. (Christie's) $622 £432

A Clichy red ground concentric millefiori weight, 6.1cm. diam. (Christie's) $590 £410

A Clichy blue and white 'barber's pole' concentric millefiori weight, 6.5cm. diam. (Christie's) $1,710 £1,188

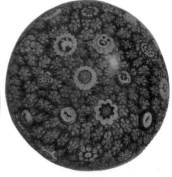

A Clichy blue ground patterned millefiori weight, 6.8cm. diam. (Christie's) $652 £453

A St. Louis miniature daisy weight, 4.5cm. diam. (Christie's) $933 £648

A Baccarat dated red carpet ground weight, a cane inscribed 'B 1848', 8cm. diam. (Christie's) $5,443 £3,780

A Clichy turquoise ground concentric millefiori weight, 6.2cm. diam. (Christie's) $699 £496

A St. Louis crown weight, 7cm. diam. (Christie's) $777 £540

A Baccarat cobalt ground millefiori paperweight, 3in. diam. (Robt. W. Skinner Inc.) $1,200 £821

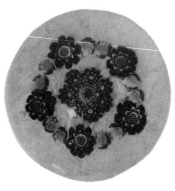

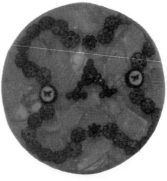

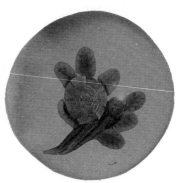

A Clichy patterned concentric millefiori weight, 5.5cm. diam. (Christie's) $652 £453

A Baccarat millefiori initialled weight, the letter A in blue canes, 6.2cm. diam. (Christie's) $1,010 £702

A Clichy rose weight, 6.7cm. diam. (Christie's) $5,909 £4,104

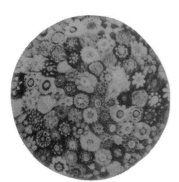

A Clichy close millefiori weight, 6.5cm. diam. (Christie's) $1,166 £810

A Baccarat close millefiori mushroom weight on a star-cut base, 8cm. diam. (Christie's) $745 £518

A Clichy blue ground scattered millefiori weight, 6.5cm. diam. (Christie's) $466 £324

A St. Louis small crown weight, 5.5cm. diam. (Christie's) $855 £594

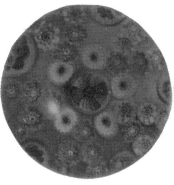

A Clichy green ground patterned millefiori weight, 7.3cm. diam. (Christie's) $855 £594

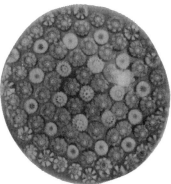

A Clichy blue ground scattered millefiori weight, 8.5cm. diam. (Christie's) $855 £594

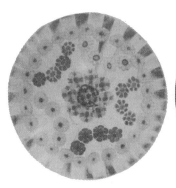

A Baccarat patterned millefiori weight, on a sunray-cut base, 7.8cm. diam. (Christie's) $311 £216

A Clichy flat bouquet weight, 7cm. diam. (Christie's) $13,996 £9,720

A Clichy faceted patterned concentric millefiori weight, 6.7cm. diam. (Christie's) $699 £486

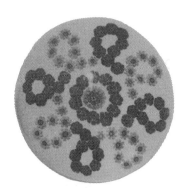

A Baccarat patterned millefiori weight, 7.7cm. diam. (Christie's) $247 £172

A Clichy swirl weight, with alternate turquoise and white staves radiating from a central claret, green and white cane, 8.2cm. diam. (Christie's) $855 £594

A Baccarat mushroom weight with star-cut base, 7.3cm. diam. (Christie's) $933 £648

An Apsley Pellatt sulphide and cut glass scent bottle and a stopper, 9.5cm. high. (Christie's) $486 £324

A Franchini silver gilt mounted millefiori scent bottle, the base with a cane dated 1847, 7.2cm. long. (Christie's) $383 £270

One of a pair of Edwardian cut glass cologne bottles, by Wm. Comyns, London, 1905, 5½in. high. (Christie's) $1,036 £700

A Clichy cut glass and patterned millefiori scent bottle and stopper, 18cm. high. (Christie's) $1,533 £1,080

A glass scent bottle and stopper, inscribed 'Cigalia, Roger et Gallet, Paris', 13cm. high, in original box. (Phillips) $378 £280

A Marinot scent bottle and stopper, with enamel painted decoration, circa 1920, 17cm. high. (Christie's)
              $1,734 £1,188

A Baccarat enamelled cut glass scent bottle with gilt metal screw cover, 9.5cm. long. (Christie's)
          $1,296 £864

19th century cameo glass salts bottle with silver screw top, in case, 4in. long. (Capes, Dunn & Co.)
              $280 £195

A Franchini gilt metal mounted scent bottle, the hinged cover with ring and bead chain attachment, 7.5cm. long. (Christie's)
              $367 £259

SCENT BOTTLES

GLASS

'Amphyrite', a Lalique perfume bottle and stopper, the blue tinted frosted glass moulded as a snail shell, 9.5cm. high. (Lawrence Fine Art)$626 £429

Late 18th century Spanish opaque opaline scent flask, in the form of a bird, painted in colours and enriched in gilding with flower sprays, 20cm. wide. (Christie's) $1,088 £756

'Worth', a Lalique glass scent bottle, with original Worth paper label, 24.5cm. high. (Christie's) $406 £280

SHADES

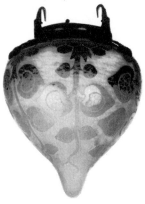

One of a set of four Tiffany Favrile electric light shades, N.Y., circa 1920, 3½in. high, 4¾in. diam. (Robt. W. Skinner Inc.) $525 £350

A pair of 19th century, blown, colourless glass hanging lamps, approx. 15in. high. (Christie's) $1,320 £916

A Le Verre Francais cameo glass hanging lamp shade in the form of a strawberry overlaid in orange and blue, 30.9cm. high. (Christie's) $1,174 £810

TUMBLERS

A Continental blue pressed glass, Royal portrait tumbler, perhaps Bercy, Paris, circa 1840, 11cm. high. (Christie's) $388 £270

A Bohemian ruby overlay engraved tumbler of flared form, circa 1860, 12.5cm. high. (Christie's) $622 £432

A Baccarat moulded enamelled cylindrical tumbler, decorated in colours on gilt foil, 9cm. high. (Christie's) $372 £259

VASES

A tall vase attributed to Ercole Barovier, with turquoise patchwork decoration, circa 1955, 34.6cm. high. (Christie's)
$1,340 £918

A Venini handkerchief vase in blue with a white interior, 9½in. high. (Christie's)
$145 £110

A brass mounted iridescent glass vase attributed to Loetz and the design in the manner of Hans Christiansen, circa 1900, 37cm. high. (Christie's) $788 £540

One of a pair of small Galle enamelled glass vases with bulbous base, 5½in. high. (Christie's) $248 £200

A Lalique opalescent glass vase, 'Bacchantes', 9½in. high. (Christie's)
$3,472 £2,800

A Richard cameo glass vase overlaid in brown and red, 13½in. high. (Christie's)
$520 £400

A Daum double overlay cameo glass and acid-etched vase, engraved with cross of Lorraine, 50.3cm. high. (Christie's) $3,153 £2,160

A Lalique conical flower vase with intaglio moulded rose design, signed, 9¼in. high. (Capes, Dunn & Co.)
$172 £120

An Aldo Nasson double-neck organic-form glass vase, inscribed Nasson, 14½in. high. (Christie's) $260 £200

VASES

A Delatte cameo glass landscape vase, broad baluster shape with cylindrical neck, 33.1cm. high. (Christie's) $788 £540

A Lalique globular vase, 'Gui', the opalescent glass moulded with intertwined fruiting mistletoe, circa 1930, 16.9cm. high. (Christie's) $503 £345

A Muller Croismaire cameo glass vase, the shaded orange and amber ground overlaid with darker orange, circa 1900, 35.3cm. high. (Christie's) $946 £648

A Lalique opalescent tapering cylindrical glass vase, 'Rampillon', 5in. high. (Christie's) $434 £350

A large Galle cameo glass vase, blue glass over a frosted base with stylised floral and foliate decoration, circa 1900, 72.2cm. high. (Christie's) $2,522 £1,728

A Lalique clear and frosted glass vase, 'Aigrettes', inscribed, 10in. high. (Christie's) $1,122 £850

A large Galle cameo glass vase, pale amber over a ground shading from blue to yellow, circa 1900, 48.6cm. high. (Christie's) $6,307 £4,320

A Lalique cylindrical glass vase, 'Coqs et Plumes', circa 1930, 15.4cm. high. (Christie's) $503 £345

A glass vase and cover attributed to Fachschule Haida, circa 1910, 32cm. high. (Christie's) $315 £216

VASES

A Loetz vase, the body with four dimples and the rim and shoulders with deep blue pulled loop decoration, 13.8cm. high. (Christie's) $2,349 £1,620

A Daum cameo landscape vase, the tapering cylindrical body with swollen collar, 27cm. high. (Christie's) $783 £540

A free-hand ware vase by the Imperial Glass Co., Ohio, 1920's, 5.7/8in. high. (Robt. W. Skinner Inc.) $300 £205

'Aras', a Lalique opalescent globular vase , engraved France No. 919, 22.7cm. high. (Christie's) $1,096 £756

A Galle cameo glass vase, overlaid in deep mauve with sprays of laburnum, circa 1900, 31.3cm. high. (Lawrence Fine Art) $995 £682

'Formose', a Lalique opalescent vase, moulded with a shoal of goldfish, 17cm. high. (Christie's) $626 £432

A Galle double overlay cameo oviform vase with cylindrical neck, overlaid in lilac and green, 18.4cm. high. (Christie's) $783 £540

Victorian red overlay glass vase, 1860. (British Antique Exporters) $59 £44

A Galle cameo vase, the flattened globular body on splayed foot, 23.5cm. high. (Christie's) $1,722 £1,188

VASES

A large Regency ormolu and cut glass vase, the urn-shaped body set with faceted cabochons in latticework frame, 22in. high. (Christie's)
$14,968 £11,340

A Nuutajarvi Notsjo vase, designed by Gunnel Nyman, clear glass over amber with asymmetrical design of air bubbles, 33.8cm. high. (Christie's) $283 £194

A Lalique opalescent glass vase, 'Lievres', 15.8cm. high. (Lawrence Fine Art) $401 £275

'Poivre', a Lalique smoked glass vase modelled with fruiting vine, 10in. high. (Christie's) $835 £580

An iridescent tear vase, attributed to Meyr's Neffe, the pinkish-green glass with silvery blue streak decoration, 22.3cm. high. (Christie's) $1,252 £864

'Vaso a valve', an Italian glass vase, attributed to Seguso and the design to F. Poli, 23.5cm. high. (Christie's) $783 £540

A Ver Centre vase, elongated ovoid shape enamel painted in various colours over a green ground, signature Ver Centre 1927, 29cm. high. (Christie's) $1,576 £1,080

A glass vase designed by Koloman Moser, the clear glass with gilt loop decoration and iridescent red tears, 17.1cm. high. (Christie's) $2,035 £1,404

A Galle cameo vase overlaid with brown glass etched with orchid spray against a mottled green, blue and opaque ground, 18.5cm. high. (Christie's) $626 £432

A Lalique vase, 'Yvelines', grey tinted clear and satin finished glass moulded with lug handles, circa 1930, 20cm. high. (Christie's) $661 £453

A Galle fire polished cameo glass vase of squat oviform with flaring stem, 17in. high, inscribed. (Christie's) $845 £650

A Wiener Werkstatte amethyst glass vase and cover designed by Josef Hoffmann, 17cm. high. (Christie's) $1,017 £702

'Perruches', a blue Lalique oviform vase, 25.9cm. high. (Christie's) $4,698 £3,240

One of a pair of pink-flash narrow tapering two-handled vases, 16½in. high. (Christie's) $1,036 £700

A campana shaped vase, star and stud cut with faceted knop to stem, 10½in. high. (Capes, Dunn & Co.) $57 £40

'Danaides', a Lalique blue opalescent cylindrical vase, the clear and satin finished glass moulded with naked maidens, 18cm. high. (Christie's) $1,252 £864

A Venini 'Pezzato' vase designed by F. Bianconi, cigar shaped with patchwork decoration, circa 1960, 27.2cm. high. (Christie's) $6,264 £4,320

An Argy Rousseau pate-de-verre vase, France, circa 1925, 15.2cm. high. (Christie's) $3,915 £2,700

GLASS

A yellow ground cameo vase of compressed form, circa 1890, 22cm. high. (Christie's) $1,321 £918

A Galle marqueterie de verre vase, bun foot with body shaped like a crocus bloom, circa 1900, 35cm. high. (Christie's) $13,311 £9,180

A white opaline baluster vase with flaring neck, 12in. high. (Christie's) $266 £180

'Formose', a green Lalique vase, the clear and satin glass moulded with goldfish, 17cm. high. (Christie's) $1,722 £1,188

A blue opaline tapering oviform vase with two gilt metal scrolling foliage handles, 20½in. high. (Christie's) $429 £300

A Stourbridge olive-green opaline vase on four gilt feet detailed in white and black enamel, 12¾in. high. (Christie's) $228 £160

A Venini 'Occhi' vase designed by Carlo Scarpa, the cased red, black and clear glass pressed together to form 'windows', circa 1955, 15.5cm. high. (Christie's) $5,011 £3,456

A Ferdinand Poschinger Glasshuten vase, the pale green glass with combed deep red 'peacock feather' design, 25cm. high. (Christie's) $1,566 £1,080

An Arsale overlay glass vase, the flattened slender pear shaped body overlaid with russet-coloured glass, 31.6cm. high. (Christie's) $437 £302

547

WINE GLASSES

A 'Lynn' opaque twist glass with horizontally ribbed ogee bowl, circa 1770, 14cm. high. (Christie's) $714 £496

An incised twist wine glass with generous funnel bowl, on a conical foot, circa 1760, 14cm. high. (Christie's) $233 £162

An engraved opaque twist wine glass, the stem with opaque corkscrew core entwined by two spiral threads, circa 1770, 15cm. high. (Christie's) $777 £540

A wine glass by David Wolff, the stem cut with diamond facets, 1790-95, 15cm. high. (Christie's) $5,065 £3,780

A colour twist firing glass with ogee bowl, on a terraced foot, circa 1770, 10.5cm. high. (Christie's) $2,643 £1,836

A plain stemmed wine glass with ovoid bowl decorated with a nude putto, by D. Wolff, The Hague, circa 1790, 14cm. high. (Christie's) $4,341 £3,240

A colour twist wine glass with waisted bucket bowl, circa 1760, 17cm. high. (Christie's) $2,799 £1,944

A baluster deceptive wine glass, the thick-walled flared funnel bowl set on a cushion knop above a plain stem, circa 1705, 11.5cm. high. (Christie's) $558 £388

An opaque twist wine glass with octagonally moulded ogee bowl, circa 1770, 14.5cm. high. (Christie's) $388 £270

WINE GLASSES

A Beilby opaque twist wine glass, the funnel bowl decorated in white with a border of fruiting vine, circa 1770, 15cm. high. (Christie's) $1,306 £907

A plain stemmed Jacobite wine glass, the funnel bowl with a seven-petalled rose and a bud, circa 1750, 15cm. high. (Christie's) $434 £302

A facet stemmed friendship wine glass by Jacob Sang, 1761, 17.8cm. high. (Christie's) $10,854 £8,100

A Beilby enamelled opaque twist wine glass, circa 1770, 15.5cm. high. (Christie's) $901 £626

A wine glass with ovoid bowl, by David Wolff, The Hague, 1780-90, 15.3cm. high. (Christie's) $3,473 £2,592

A Jacobite airtwist wine glass, the stem with swelling waist knop filled with airtwist spirals, 16.5cm. high. (Christie's) $745 £518

A faceted stemmed portrait wine glass, by David Wolff, The Hague, 1780-85, 15.8cm. high. (Christie's) $6,946 £5,184

A Jacobite airtwist wine glass, the funnel bowl engraved with a rose and bud, circa 1750, 15cm. high. (Christie's) $777 £540

A plain stemmed landscape wine glass by David Wolff, on a plain stem and conical foot, The Hague, 1790, 15cm. high. (Christie's) $7,959 £5,940

GLASS

An engraved airtwist wine glass of Jacobite significance, circa 1750, 14.5cm. high. (Christie's) $466 £324

A colour twist wine glass with bell bowl, circa 1760, 16.5cm. high. (Christie's) $1,088 £756

A colour twist wine glass with bell bowl, circa 1760, 17cm. high. (Christie's) $1,056 £734

An engraved mixed twist ale flute, the flared funnel bowl with a hop-spray and two ears of barley, circa 1760, 18cm. high. (Christie's) $434 £302

An armorial light baluster wine glass, the funnel bowl engraved with the arms of Schieland, circa 1760, 18.2cm. high. (Christie's) $1,399 £972

An incised twist wine glass, the bell bowl with honey-comb-moulded lower part, circa 1760, 17.5cm. high. (Christie's) $372 £259

A canary twist wine glass with pan-topped funnel bowl, circa 1760, 14.5cm. high. (Christie's) $3,732 £2,592

An opaque twist deceptive cordial glass with thick-walled ogee bowl, circa 1770, 14cm. high. (Christie's) $652 £453

A composite stemmed wine glass of drawn trumpet shape, circa 1750, 18cm. high. (Christie's) $185 £129

An engraved colour twist wine glass of Jacobite significance, the rounded bowl with a rosebud, circa 1765, 13cm. high. (Christie's) $652 £453

A composite stemmed wine glass of drawn trumpet shape, the stem filled with airtwist spirals set into a beaded inverted baluster section, circa 1750, 17.5cm. high. (Christie's) $247 £172

A 'Lynn' opaque twist wine glass with horizontally ribbed ogee bowl, circa 1775, 14cm. high. (Christie's) $496 £345

A Jacobite airtwist wine glass, the stem with a twisted air core entwined by spiral threads, circa 1750, 14.5cm. high. (Christie's) $434 £302

An opaque twist ale or ratafia glass, the slender funnel bowl with hammered flutes, circa 1765, 18cm. high. (Christie's) $434 £302

A baluster wine glass, the bell bowl with a small tear to the solid lower part, circa 1715, 14cm. high. (Christie's) $403 £280

A Williamite baluster wine glass with trumpet-shaped bowl, 18th century, 17.5cm. high. (Christie's) $2,021 £1,404

A colour twist wine glass with generous bell bowl, circa 1760, 17.5cm. high. (Christie's) $1,866 £1,296

A light baluster dated betrothal wine glass by the monogrammist ICL, 1753, 19.7cm. high. (Christie's) $2,894 £2,160

A George II gold and mocha-agate snuff box of cartouche shape, circa 1745, 2¾in. long. (Christie's)
$5,114 £3,456

A Louis XV small gold mounted blonde tortoise-shell snuff box, circa 1750, 2in. diam. (Christie's)
$2,077 £1,404

An early 19th century Scottish octagonal gold mounted presentation snuff box, 2.7/8in. long. (Christie's)
$2,643 £1,836

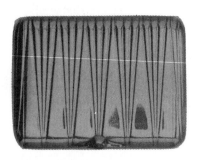

An oblong gold coloured cigarette case with cabochon bluestone pushpiece, with Swedish control marks, 3¼in. long. (Christie's)
$1,166 £810

A 19th century gold mounted walking stick, the pommel with Japanese ivory okimono of a snake entwined on top of a human skull, 18ct. (Christie's)
$544 £378

A George II gold mounted shell-shaped amethystine quartz snuff box, circa 1750, 1¾in. high. (Christie's) $3,265 £2,268

A shallow gold snuff box of cartouche shape, London, 1824, maker's initials IN probably for John Northam, 2¾in. long. (Christie's)
$3,996 £2,700

A George III oval gold mounted mottled agate snuff box, circa 1760, 2.3/8in. long. (Christie's)
$1,358 £918

A French gold presentation snuff box, the interior with gold standard mark for 1798 -1809 and warranty mark for 1819-38, 4in. long. (Christie's) $8,553 £5,940

A Swiss oval gold and enamel presentation snuff box, circa 1800, with French prestige marks, 3¼in. long. (Christie's) $4,199 £2,916

A gold mounted mauve agate sweetmeat dish in the 16th century style, the oval foot en suite to the bowl, 19th century, 5in. high.(Christie's) $7,776 £5,400

A shallow octagonal gold snuff box, the cover hinged, circa 1725, 2¾in. long. (Christie's) $3,516 £2,376

Late 18th century circular gold mounted figured white quartz snuff box, with French import marks, 2¼in. diam. (Christie's) $3,356 £2,268

Charles II cylindrical gold counter-case of upright form, circa 1685, 1.3/8in. high. (Christie's) $12,787 £8,640

A George III gold and enamel scent bottle of shaped flask form, circa 1755, 2.3/8in. high. (Christie's) $5,287 £3,672

A vari-coloured gold snuff box, Swiss or Austrian, with maker's initial B between two rosettes, the flange with inventory no. 14301, circa 1810, 3.3/8in. long. (Christie's) $2,397 £1,620

A 19th century Continental oblong gold snuff box with engine-turned body, 3½in. long. (Christie's) $2,021 £1,404

A 17th century gold and polychrome enamel devotional reliquary of arched form, possibly French, in 18th century red leather case, 1.5/8in. high. (Christie's) $5,909 £4,104

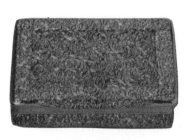

An Irish gold and silver gilt oblong Masonic snuff box, the base inscribed Dublin, 1819, maker's initials E.(?), 3½in. long. (Christie's) $1,772 £1,188

A 19th century gold mounted striated agate scent bottle of flattened flask form, 1¾in. long.(Christie's) $391 £270

An oblong gold presentation snuff box with slightly bombe sides, by J. Willmore, Birmingham, 1826, 18ct., 3.5/8in. long. (Christie's) $10,886 £7,560

'Mondain', a Dunhill 9ct. plain gold petrol lighter, Pat. No. 143752, gold marks for 1929, 4.3cm. high. (Christie's) $315 £216

One of a pair of gemset gold lorgnettes in the Russian taste, 5½in. long.(Christie's) $939 £648

A Furstenburg shaped rectangular snuff box and cover with contemporary gold mounts, circa 1770, 8cm. wide.) (Christie's) $12,268 £8,640

A Dunhill 'Bijou' lady's 18ct. plain gold petrol lighter, Pat. 143752 Fab. Suisse, 3.2cm. high. (Christie's) $473 £324

A gold mounted wooden reliquary crucifix made from the 'Waterloo Tree', the mounts engraved June 18, 1815. (Christie's)$221 £170

A French oblong gold coloured cigarette case with cabochon redstone thumbpieces, retailer's name Tonnel, Paris, in case, 3in. long. (Christie's) $1,088 £756

A Swiss diamond set, gold and enamel, oval snuff box with scalloped rims, circa 1840, 3in. long. (Christie's) $2,954 £2,052

A gold desk seal with handle modelled in ivory as a hand clasping a baton with bloodstone or cornelian seal ends, circa 1830, 2¾in. long. (Christie's) $2,557 £1,728

A Louis XVI oblong gold and enamel toothpick case, by Nicolas Marguerit, Paris, 1778, 3¼in. long. (Christie's) $4,475 £3,024

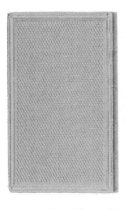

A George III gold snuff box formed as a book, by A. J. Strachan, London, 1802, 18ct., 2¾in. long. (Christie's) $1,166 £810

George III gold christening font, by Paul Storr, Figure of Faith 7¼in. high, Figure of Hope 4½in. high, Figure of Charity 4¼in. high, bowl 4½in. high, 220oz.16dwt. gross excluding Hope's foot rest, 22ct. (Christie's) $1,368,576 £950,400

A Tiffany & Co. Douglass petrol lighter, patterned yellow metal, stamped 14 Karat Solid gold, 5cm. high. (Christie's)$220 £151

'Mondain', a Dunhill patterned 9ct. gold petrol lighter, gold marks for 1950, 4.7cm. high. (Christie's) $378 £259

A French vari-coloured gold and enamel mounted parasol handle, with Paris restricted gold warranty mark in use from 1838, 3¼in. long. (Christie's)$2,877 £1,944

A French gold, silver and translucent enamel mounted photograph frame in the Faberge style, the gold mounts with warranty mark in use from 1838, 7¼in. high. (Christie's) $6,264 £4,320

A 17th/18th century large rhinoceros horn libation cup, 18.5cm. wide, wood stand. (Christie's) $2,310 £1,750

A 17th/18th century rhinoceros horn libation cup, 13cm. wide. (Christie's) $1,320 £1,000

A rhinoceros horn libation cup, 17th/18th century, 14.3cm. wide. (Christie's) $2,138 £1,620

A Bohemian carved staghorn powder flask decorated with three deer moving through a forest, with silver mounts. (Bermondsey) $1,200 £800

An 18th century stag antler netsuke of a standing bow-legged Dutchman holding a long-tailed cockerel, unsigned. (Christie's) $694 £486

A late 18th century Scottish horn snuff mull carved with the profile of the Old Pretender, 4¼in. high. (Christie's) $466 £324

Victorian horn and brass gong. (British Antique Exporters) $101 £75

17th century flattened cow horn powder flask decorated overall with geometric circles, scallops and foliate patterns, 12in. long. (Bermondsey) $450 £300

Early 18th century rhinoceros horn libation cup, 6½in. wide. (Christie's) $2,250 £1,500

'Long Hair Dancer', by Bruce Timeche, tempera, signed, 10 x 13in. (Robt. W. Skinner Inc.) $275 £187

Southwestern pottery dough bowl, Cochiti, the interior painted over a cream slip in black foliate motifs, 14in. diam. (Robt. W. Skinner Inc.) $1,200 £816

'Warrior', by Velino Shije Herrera, signed 'Ma-Pe-Wi '45', tempera on white paper, 9½ x 12½in. (Robt. W. Skinner Inc.) $700 £476

A Southwestern basketry tray, Apache, woven in devil's claw on a dark golden field, 19in. diam. (Robt. W. Skinner Inc.) $1,400 £952

Two Plains paint decorated parfleche containers, Crow, a shoulder bag, 12 x 13in. and a case 12 x 23½in. (Robt. W. Skinner Inc.) $500 £347

A Southwestern polychrome basketry tray, Yavapai, woven in red and dark brown designs on a golden field, 14½in. diam. (Robt. W. Skinner Inc.) $950 £646

Navajo Germantown weaving, woven on a red ground in black and white, 41 x 69in. (Robt. W. Skinner Inc.)$1,300 £884

'Eagle Dancer', by Raymond Chavez, signed, 13 x 17¼in. (Robt. W. Skinner Inc.) $300 £204

'Rattle for Germination', by Fred Kabotie, tempera, signed, 15 x 22½in. (Robt. W. Skinner Inc.) $900 £612

INDIAN ART

Southwestern pottery jar, Zia, painted over a pinky cream slip in black and red, 12¾in. diam. (Robt. W. Skinner Inc.)
$1,000 £680

'Untitled', by Gerda Christofferson, pastel portrait, signed and dated '57, 18½ x 24in. (Robt. W. Skinner Inc.)
$260 £176

A Hopi polychrome pottery canteen, painted over a creamy yellow slip in dark brown linear and 'Koshare' figural decoration, 3¼in. high. (Robt. W. Skinner Inc.)
$200 £136

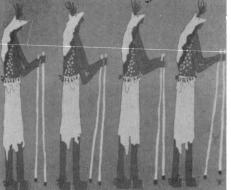

'Owl Kachina', by Peter Shelton, acrylic on paper, signed 'Hoyewva '64', 14 x 21in. (Robt. W. Skinner Inc.) $500 £340

'Deer Dancers', by Harry Fonseca, signed in interlocking initials, dated 1975 on back, acrylic on canvas board, 20 x 23in. (Robt. W. Skinner Inc.) $450 £306

Southern Plains painted buffalo fur robe, 92in. long, 67in. wide. (Robt. W. Skinner Inc.) $500 £347

Large Navajo pictorial weaving, woven on a red field in mustard, white and navy, 61 x 88in. (Robt. W. Skinner Inc.) $2,300 £1,564

Northwest coast mask, Bella/Bella Coola, of polychrome cedar wood, 12.5/8in. high. (Robt. W. Skinner Inc.)
$49,000 £33,333

'King of the Herd', by Quincy Tahoma, tempera, signed and dated '53, 6½ x 10in. (Robt. W. Skinner Inc.) $650 £442

A Southwestern polychrome canteen, Zia, 19th century, painted over a cream slip in black and red, 10¾in. deep. (Robt. W. Skinner Inc.)
$1,200 £816

'Sioux Maiden', by Gerda Christofferson, pastel portrait, signed and dated '57, 19 x 24in. (Robt. W. Skinner Inc.)
$375 £255

A Southwestern polychrome jar, Zia, with indented base, flaring sides and tapering rim, 12½in. diam. (Robt. W. Skinner Inc.) $1,000 £680

Yuma polychromed female figure with traditional horsehair coiffure, inscribed 'Yuma, Arizona Indian 1931', 8in. high. (Robt. W. Skinner Inc.) $375 £255

'Apache Mountain Spirit Dance', by Carl Nelson Gorman, signed 'Kin-Ya-Onny-Beyeh', oil on canvas, 19½ x 23½in. (Robt. W. Skinner Inc.)
$900 £612

A Hopi wood Kachina doll, 'Mahuu' (locust), with black, mustard and rose decoration over a white painted body, 15¾in. high. (Robt. W. Skinner Inc.) $1,200 £816

Basket Maker, by Patrick Robt. Desjarlait, tempera, signed, 14 x 17in. (Robt. W. Skinner Inc.)
$1,300 £884

A Southwestern polychrome storage jar, San Ildefonso, of tall rounded form, 12½in. high. (Robt. W. Skinner Inc.)
$700 £476

Navajo Germantown serape, finely woven on a red ground, 47 x 68in. (Robt. W. Skinner Inc.) $2,300 £1,597

A 19th century three-case Kinji inro, with attached black lacquer bead ojime and red lacquered mokko-gata netsuke. (Christie's) $4,800 £3,200

A 19th century three-case silver inro, with attached silver filigree bead ojime and lightly stained ivory netsuke. (Christie's) $9,750 £6,500

Early 19th century three-case inro decorated in gold hiramakie, takamakie, heid-atsu and togidashi on a yas-uriko ground. (Christie's) $772 £540

A 19th century Tamenuri three-case inro, with cornelian glass bead ojime. (Christie's) $720 £480

A small three-case Ginji inro, decorated in gold hiramakie, with wakasa-nuri bead ojime. (Christie's) $2,100 £1,400

Late 19th century three-case hirame inro decorated in takamakie and raden, ivory and other inlay, signed Jushuhan Chohei. (Christie's) $1,312 £918

A 19th century three-case Kinji inro, with attached copper and gilt ojime, and a stained ivory netsuke. (Christie's) $5,250 £3,500

A 19th century three-case Kinji inro, with attached gold and silver lacquer ojime and an ivory netsuke. (Christie's) $3,450 £2,300

19th century three-case Kinji inro, with attached ojime and stained ivory netsuke. (Christie's) $2,850 £1,900

Early 19th century three-case gold sprinkled roironuri inro, with attached pink coral bead ojime. (Christie's) $1,145 £842

A 19th century four-case fundame inro decorated on each side with a hawk on a perch, signed Nikkosai. (Christie's) $1,081 £756

A 19th century three-case ivory inro, with attached ivory bead ojime and ivory manju netsuke. (Christie's) $2,250 £1,500

Late 18th/early 19th century four-case Kinji inro, decorated in gold, black and red hiramakie, takamakie, hirame and nashiji. (Christie's) $1,275 £850

An 18th century four-case Nashiji inro, decorated in gold hiramakie, takamakie and hirame, unsigned. (Christie's) $1,050 £700

Early 19th century four-case inro, signed Kakosai. (Christie's) $825 £550

A 19th century five-case silver ground, ginji, inro, with attached silver, shakudo and copper ojime. (Christie's) $4,112 £3,024

A 19th century four-case Kinji inro, signed Hasegawa saku above a red tsubo seal and Shibayama on a shell tablet. (Christie's) $1,321 £972

Early 19th century five-case Kinji inro, signed Shoryusai Kogyoku saku. (Christie's) $1,909 £1,404

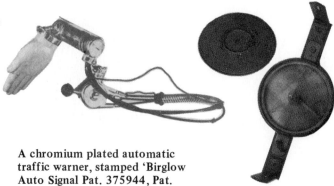

Late 18th century brass 3in. reflecting telescope, on folding tripod base with scroll feet, body tube 46.5cm. long. (Christie's) $770 £531

A chromium plated automatic traffic warner, stamped 'Birglow Auto Signal Pat. 375944, Pat. 376564, Reg. design 767816', 42in. long. (Christie's) $198 £160

An 18th century brass surveyor's compass, signed Gab. Stoak, Dublin fecit, 28.5cm. long. (Christie's) $242 £166

A brass transit on tripod foot with three levelling screws, signed Stanley, London, No. 11013, 42cm. high. (Christie's) $825 £569

An English Withering type botanical microscope and case, circa 1800, with box, 10.5cm. high. (Christie's) $495 £341

A rosewood pedestal stereoscope with turned wood eye pieces with brass lens. (Christie's) $1,147 £850

A small one-day marine chronometer by John Roger Arnold, the dial 64mm. diam. (Christie's) $3,732 £2,592

A 17th century engraved silver and gilt brass geared astronomical dial, signed Ph. Dagoneau, Grenoble, 13.8cm. diam. (Christie's) $5,500 £3,793

A brass and mahogany 4in. refracting telescope, signed Steinheil in Munchen, no. 2811, the sighting telescope, no. 2886, 171cm. long. (Christie's) $1,650 £1,137

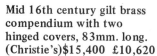

A chromium plated automatic traffic warner, bulb and mounting bracket labelled Rolph's Patents. (Christie's) $62 £50

Mid 16th century gilt brass compendium with two hinged covers, 83mm. long. (Christie's) $15,400 £10,620

A French 19th century universal dial, signed Bordi, Ing. Cons. Optician, Paris, 18.5cm. high. (Christie's) $660 £455

A gilt brass pedometer, German, possibly Augsburg, circa 1700, 65mm. long. (Christie's) $1,100 £759

A Henry Crouch brass binocular microscope, No. 2092, of Lister limb construction. (Lawrence Fine Art) $814 £550

A brass transit on circular foot with focus levelling screws, signed Troughton & Simms, London, 39cm. high. (Christie's) $715 £493

A two-day marine chronometer, the silvered dial signed James Muirhead, Glasgow, No. 2169, 100mm. diam. of dial. (Christie's) $7,668 £5,400

A brass astrolabe, signed Georgivs Hartman Norenberge Faciebat Anno MD XXX11, 137mm. diam. (Christie's) $26,400 £18,206

A watchmaker's wheel-cutting engine, signed Cibert & Cie, no. 53, 24cm. long. (Christie's) $1,045 £721

A chased silver universal equatorial dial with perpetual calendar, signed Jean-David Beyser, Augsburg, ·circa 1750, 80mm. long. (Christie's) $1,100 £758

A Lambert typewriter No. 2908, by The Lambert Typewriter Co., New York. (Christie's) $259 £180

An early 19th century small brass circumferentor, signed Harris, London, 10.5cm. diam. (Christie's) $495 £341

A London Stereoscopic Co. Brewster-pattern stereoscope with brass mounted eye pieces, in fitted rosewood box, 13in. wide. (Christie's) $513 £380

A French clockwork globe, signed Empire Clock, highlighting in red the British Empire, 16in. high. (Christie's) $2,310 £1,593

An 18th century brass horizontal dial, signed Butterfield a Paris, 16.5cm. long. (Christie's) $880 £606

A cradle-mounted stereographoscope in black ebonised finish with lens panel, 16in. high. (Christie's) $248 £200

An American brass and plated brass compound monocular microscope, signed E. Gundlach, pat. Sept. 14, 1878, 29cm. high approx. (Christie's) $418 £288

A silver and gilt brass universal dial, signed 'Cadran Universel et a Meridienne. Fait et invenie par Julien le Roy de la Societe des Arts', 80mm. long. (Christie's) $3,300 £2,275

A Grover & Baker hand-sewing machine, the brass Patent plaque with patents to 1863. (Christie's) $1,584 £1,100

A 19th century English brass universal equatorial dial with three levelling screws, 11.5cm. diam. (Christie's) $605 £417

A Baird televisor, No. 204, in typical arched brown painted aluminium case with disc, valve and plaque on front. (Christie's) $1,848 £1,400

Late 16th century gilt and silvered brass astrolabe, probably German, 172mm. diam. (Christie's) $11,000 £7,586

A brass Martin type orrery with tellurium of American interest, signed T. Blunt, London, 22cm. diam. (Christie's) $15,400 £10,620

A cast iron sundial by E. T. Hurley, circa 1900, 10¼in. diam. (Robt. W. Skinner Inc.) $425 £295

A mahogany folding Cumino-scope concave mirror photo-graph/print viewer, by The Cuminoscope Patent Brevetes, S.G.D.G. (Christie's) $223 £180

A small Zoetrope optical toy on wood stand with several picture strips, diam. of drum 5¼in. (Christie's) $124 £100

A small brass sextant of T-frame style signed Berge, London, in fitted shaped mahogany case, circa 1800. (Reeds Rains) $1,944 £1,350

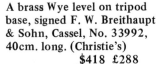

A brass graphometer, signed Canivet a la Sphere a Paris, dated 1765, 13.5cm. radius. (Christie's)　$715　£493

A goldsmith's steel scale and set of weights, with the label of Joh. Pet. Poppenberg, dated 1776, 17.5cm. long. (Christie's)　$528　£364

A brass Wye level on tripod base, signed F. W. Breithaupt & Sohn, Cassel, No. 33992, 40cm. long. (Christie's)
$418　£288

A Regency mahogany library globe, 28in. diam. (Christie's)
$23,490　£16,200

Mid 19th century drum microscope, signed F. Cox, London, within fitted mahogany box, 25.5cm. high. (Christie's)　$385　£265

Late 18th century brass protractor, signed Lenoir a Paris, 13cm. radius. (Christie's)　$209　£144

A mariner's brass astrolable, the scale divided from 0° to 90°, with rising loop handle, 23.5cm. diam. (Christie's)
$1,430　£986

A German cube dial, the wooden cube with five printed scales, signed D. Beringer, 7in. high. (Lawrence Fine Art)
$814　£550

An early 17th century Roman terrestrial table globe, signed by M. Greuter Romae 1630, 27½in. (Christie's)
$1,088　£756

A 19th century brass draining level, signed Newton & Co., London, 35.5cm. long. (Christie's) $550 £379

An 18th century brass combined analemmatic and inclining dial, signed M:Semah Aboab tot Amsterdam, 185mm. long. (Christie's) $6,600 £4,551

A brass gimbal mounted dumpy level with compass, signed on the body tube Elliot Bros., London, the mount signed Doerings Patent level, No. 16, 39cm. long. (Christie's) $286 £197

A silver pseudo astrolabe, signature of Abd al-A-imma and the date 1127AH (=1715), 15cm. diam. (Christie's) $3,520 £2,427

A pair of W. & T. Avery snuff scales, to weigh 1lb., class B. No. A189 with brass pans, together with a set of 5 weights. (Osmond Tricks) $172 £120

Late 18th century brass transit instrument, signed Lenoir (Paris), on circular base with three levelling screws, the telescope 53.5cm. long. (Christie's) $3,080 £2,124

A 16th century gilt brass miniature armillary sphere, probably German, 55mm. diam. (Christie's) $4,180 £2,882

A small 2½in. reflecting telescope, signed J. Watson, London, circa 1800, on folding tripod base, 235mm. long. (Christie's) $1,320 £910

A 19th/20th century brass noon cannon on a circular marble base, diam. of base 16cm. (Christie's) $990 £682

An 18th century brass and steel Hahn type geared universal dial, German, 37cm. high. (Christie's)
$8,800 £6,068

A 17th/18th century brass graduated circle, probably French, 13.7cm. diam. (Christie's) $880 £607

An enamel clock globe, signed Redier a Paris, 1873, on octagonal onyx base, 20cm. high. (Christie's)
$3,850 £2,655

A Lahore brass astrolabe, 1666, 25cm. diam. (Christie's)
$26,400 £18,206

A 19th century walnut thunder house, the chimney carrying electrical wire, 19.5cm. long. (Christie's)
$770 £531

A large brass mounted lodestone with bail handle, 20.5cm. high. (Christie's)
$3,850 £2,656

An 18th century brass Butterfield type dial, signed LeMaire fils, Paris, 94mm. long. (Christie's)
$1,045 £720

Early 19th century brass compound monocular microscope, probably English, length of tube 17.3cm. (Christie's)
$605 £417

Late 18th century brass Culpeper type microscope, on circular brass base, with central pivot mirror, 25cm. high. (Christie's) $825 £568

An English 18th century brass universal ring dial, 10.5cm. diam. (Christie's) $605 £417

Late 19th century brass watchmaker's lathe, driven by cranked gear, 38cm. long. (Christie's) $990 £683

One of a pair of Regency Cary's terrestrial and celestial library globes, the terrestrial dated 1815, the celestial adapted to the year 1800, 27in. diam. (Christie's) $32,886 £22,680

A brass circular protractor with box, signed Blunt, London, circa 1800, 78mm. radius. (Christie's) $418 £288

A 19th century German silver pocket terrestrial globe, engraved with Zodiacal calendar, 60mm. diam. (Christie's) $2,090 £1,441

An 18th century brass analemmatic and horizontal inclining dial, signed J. Deens, Vienae, 113mm. long. (Christie's) $880 £606

A French 19th century brass orrery on stand depicting the asteroids, 23cm. diam. (Christie's) $1,320 £910

An Ive's Kromskop colour stereoscopic viewer, in wood carrying case. (Christie's) $868 £700

A two-day marine chronometer, the dial signed by Dobbie McInnes Ltd., Glasgow, no. 9615, dial 10cm. diam. (Christie's) $880 £607

A Hall typewriter with rubber type sheet (defective), in walnut case with instructions in lid. (Christie's) $273 £190

Early 19th century wooden cube dial, signed D. Beringer, 24cm. high. (Christie's) $528 £364

An 18th century brass geared universal ring dial, probably from the workshop of T. Heath, London, 36cm. high. (Christie's) $26,400 £18,206

Victorian oak cased sewing machine, 1880. (British Antique Exporters) $66 £49

Late 18th century brass drum microscope, possibly from the workshop of G. F. Brander, Augsburg, 28cm. high. (Christie's) $1,980 £1,365

Late 19th century oak and iron sewing machine. (British Antique Exporters) $40 £30

Late 19th century Turkish turned wood pillar dial, 17cm. high. (Christie's) $2,860 £1,972

A brass and nickel plated yacht timepiece modelled as a turret with simulated cannons, 4½in. high, and a matching barometer. (Christie's) $107 £70

An 18th century brass sector, signed Briere a Paris, 170mm. long. (Christie's) $209 £144

A Victorian lacquered brass binocular microscope, probably by Smith & Beck, 23in. high, circa 1890. (Reeds Rains) $769 £520

Early 19th century brass refracting telescope, signed Dollond, London, body tube 46cm. long. (Christie's) $715 £493

A brass compound microscope, signed E. Hartnack & A. Prazmowski, Paris, length of body tube 16.5cm. (Christie's) $220 £151

Victorian brass and iron scales, circa 1880. (British Antique Exporters) $58 £43

A Marconiphone V-2 two-valve receiver with BBC transfer, two wavelength plates and regenerator unit. (Christie's) $547 £380

A terrestrial globe on a mahogany stand, globe printed by J. & W. Cary, London, 1818, 24¾in. high. (Christie's) $1,650 £1,145

A Walmore crystal set in oak case with BBC transfer, glazed cover and two pairs of headphones. (Christie's) $79 £55

An early 19th century American set of brass parallel rules with protractor, signed S. Dod, Newark, 30.5cm. long. (Christie's) $880 £607

Brass ship's barometer, circa 1860. (British Antique Exporters) $71 £53

A late 19th century cast iron Newfoundland figure dog, 65in. long. (Robt. W. Skinner Inc.)
$10,500 £7,094

An early 19th century cast iron ship's bulwark swivel cannon, 22in., bore 1in., with turned reinforces, swollen muzzle and curved iron tiller for aiming. (Wallis & Wallis)
$518 £360

A George III polished steel and cast iron basket grate, 35in. wide, and a fender 46in. wide. (Christie's)
$3,288 £2,268

One of a pair of late 19th century russet iron Komai style oviform vases, 20.5cm. high. (Christie's)
$1,003 £702

Late 18th century pair of iron and brass 'knifeblade' andirons, 20¼in. high. (Christie's) $1,430 £986

A hollow cast iron 19th century explosive ball for a mortar, 10in. diam., with cast lifting lugs and hole for fuse. (Wallis & Wallis)
$93 £65

One of two decorated 19th century steel sipars, Persia, 14in. diam. (Robt. W. Skinner Inc.) $600 £437

A George III paktong and cast iron fire grate with bowed front, 33½in. wide. (Christie's)
$27,086 £20,520

Late 19th century moulded iron and zinc jeweller's trade sign, America. (Robt. W. Skinner Inc.) $600 £405

A Degue wrought-iron mounted circular, mauve to orange glass bowl, the branches forming the central handle, 9½in. high. (Christie's)
$175 £130

Late 19th century American cast iron elk figure, 49in. wide. (Robt. W. Skinner Inc.)
$2,900 £1,959

A part 16th century steel composite triptych, 40 x 24cm. (Phillips)
$2,250 £1,500

One of a pair of iron Komai baluster vases decorated in two shades of gilt, signed Moriyama, circa 1890, 13.7cm. high. (Christie's)
$1,264 £885

A Regency Gothic wrought iron three-seater garden bench, 57¼in. wide. (Christie's)
$1,200 £800

A cast iron pedestal with marble top, 1860. (British Antique Exporters)
$230 £171

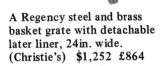

One of a pair of Regency coal boxes on gilt paw feet, 20½in. wide. (Christie's)
$1,770 £1,188

An early 19th century iron cannon barrel, 32in., with 1¾in. diam. bore, swollen muzzle and cascabel. (Wallis & Wallis) $367 £255

A Regency steel and brass basket grate with detachable later liner, 24in. wide. (Christie's) $1,252 £864

Late 19th century ivory okimono of a girl and a little boy, signed Kogyoku to, 10.8cm. high. (Christie's) $440 £324

Late 19th century sectional ivory okimono of a basket weaver and his wife, signed Eitoku, 10cm. high. (Christie's) $762 £561

A stained ivory censer and fluted cover, signed Tamayuki, Meiji period, 29.8cm. high. (Christie's)
                $1,321 £972

A two-handled metal gilt mounted ivory cup and cover, the ivory barrel Augsburg, late 17th century, the mounts circa 1800, 17¾in. high. (Christie's)
            $12,441 £8,640

A tall ivory group of the Hehe Erxian, the laughing twins, 18th century, 37.5cm. high. (Christie's)
            $3,706 £2,808

A large, late 19th century, Continental silver mounted ivory tankard and cover, 16in. high. (Christie's)
            $10,108 £7,020

A Ming ivory figure of a bearded scholar, 17th century, 12.5cm. high, with wood stand. (Christie's) $1,568 £1,188

A wood and ivory carving of a woodcutter, signed Ryukai, Meiji period, 42.5cm. long, 39cm. high. (Christie's) $2,203 £1,620

A 19th century Tokyo School ivory carving of a lady, signed Koraku, 25.5cm. high. (Christie's) $1,175 £864

Large ivory figure of a hunter holding a musket, on natural base with dead hares, 19½in. high. (Reeds Rains) $2,160 £1,500

One of a set of five ivory groups of musicians, 5¾in. high. (Reeds Rains) $835 £580

Late 19th century ivory carving of a fisherman, signed Shinsai(?), 14.5cm. high. (Christie's) $278 £205

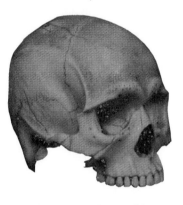

Late 19th century ivory carving of a woodcutter, signed Shunjuken Tadaomi and kao, 28.5cm. high. (Christie's) $881 £648

A 19th century ivory okimono of a human skull, signed Shosai to, 13cm. long. (Christie's) $4,993 £3,672

Late 19th century wood and ivory carving of a drum seller, signed Kazuyuki, 26cm. high. (Christie's) $1,468 £1,080

A Tokyo School ivory carving of Fudo Myo-o, signed Shinmei saku, Meiji period, 34cm. high. (Christie's) $2,643 £1,944

Late 19th century ivory carving of Kannon, signed Shunyosai Nobuyuki, 13.9cm. high. (Christie's) $734 £540

Carved ivory figure of a fisherman with basket of fish around his waist, 15½in. high. (Reeds Rains) $1,440 £1,000

An ivory carving of Guan-yin standing on a cart among waves, 7½in. high. (Christie's) $942 £650

A sectional ivory group of a kneeling basket maker and his son, signed Toshimasa, Meiji period, 20.5cm. wide. (Christie's) $2,315 £1,620

Late 19th century ivory carving of a fisherman returning with his catch, signed Gyokudo, 24cm. high. (Christie's) $1,003 £702

One of a pair of ivory bottle shaped vases carved all over with children at play in a garden, 5¼in. high. (Christie's) $870 £600

A late 19th century Chinese ivory carving of a bearded scholar, 20.5cm. high, together with another pair, 23cm. high. (Christie's) $926 £648

One of a pair of ivory tusks carved in relief with figures and animals by a stream, on wood and lacquer stands, 11½in. high. (Christie's) $870 £600

A stained ivory okimono of a standing priest, signed Hozan, late Meiji period, 19.8cm. high. (Christie's) $617 £432

Early 19th century Anglo-Indian ivory sewing box shaped as a cottage, 6in. wide. (Christie's) $4,384 £3,024

An ivory carving of a girl holding a small boy in her arms, signed Chikayoshi, Meiji period, 21.5cm. high. (Christie's) $1,312 £918

Late 19th century ivory okimono of a girl walking, unsigned, 11.4cm. high. (Christie's) $647 £453

Late 19th century ivory okimono of a kneeling grape seller, signed Gyokuzan, 7.5cm. high. (Christie's) $617 £432

Late 19th century ivory carving of a weaver spinning her yarn, signed Tadaomi to, 20cm. high. (Christie's) $1,467 £1,026

An oviform vase carved with birds in flight, 3½in. high, together with an ivory group of eight turtles, 4in. high. (Christie's) $551 £380

Late 19th century sectional ivory carving of the Shichi-fukujin in the Takarabune, 46cm. long. (Christie's) $2,316 £1,620

Late 19th century oval ivory box and cover, signed on a pearl tablet Tohekido Yoshi-kazu, 18cm. high. (Christie's) $2,626 £1,836

Late 19th century ivory carving of one of the Chinese handmaidens, signed Seiso, 21cm. high. (Christie's) $338 £237

Late 19th century ivory carving of a basket seller, signed Jogyoku, 25cm. high. (Christie's) $1,930 £1,350

Late 19th century ivory carving of Jurojin, signed Nagamitsu, 18.5cm. high. (Christie's) $1,930 £1,350

An articulated ivory model of a crab, 13½in. wide. (Christie's) $1,595 £1,100

A 19th century carved ivory figure of a medieval knight, Europe, 10.1/8in. high. (Robt. W. Skinner Inc.) $900 £656

Late 19th century ivory carving of Yokhi and the Emperor Meiko, signed Gyoku, 25cm. high. (Christie's) $1,158 £810

A German 17th century ivory plaque carved with half length figures, 11.5 x 9.7cm. (Lawrence Fine Art) $574 £396

A 19th century carved ivory farmer, Japan, signed on base, 7.1/8in. high. (Christie's) $225 £164

An ivory model of a warrior, his hands held to his chest, 9¼in. high. (Lawrence Fine Art) $574 £396

An ivory carving of a monkey trainer, signed Tamahide, Meiji period, 28.8cm. high. (Christie's) $1,835 £1,296

A pair of ivory figures of Lohands, one carrying a bell, the other a parasol, 9in. high. (Lawrence Fine Art) $638 £440

Late 19th century ivory carving of a fisherman and a small boy, signed Shunpu, 34cm. high. (Christie's) $2,471 £1,728

An ivory medical figure of a maiden, signed, 7¼in. long. (Lawrence Fine Art) $797 £550

Late 19th century ivory tusk vase inlaid in Shibayama style, signed Masamitsu, 89cm. overall. (Christie's) $3,088 £2,160

Late 19th century ivory carving of a Rakan, signed Kozan, 29cm. high. (Christie's) $1,235 £864

A 19th century carved ivory fisherman and child, Japan, signed on base, 10¼in. high. (Robt. W. Skinner Inc.) $425 £310

A mid 19th century decorated ivory ink stand, Europe, 3in. high, 5in. diam. (Robt. W. Skinner Inc.) $259 £175

Late 19th century ivory carving of a woodcutter, signature tablet missing, 20cm. high. (Christie's) $1,003 £702

'Nude', an ivory figure carved after a model by F. Preiss, on a green marble base, 43.9cm. high. (Christie's) $12,528 £8,640

Late 19th century ivory tusk vase inlaid in Shibayama style, signed, overall height 42.7cm. (Christie's) $772 £540

A 19th century carved ivory ewer with nude woman handle, Europe, 17½in. high. (Robt. W. Skinner Inc.) $1,300 £948

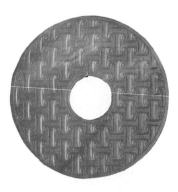

A pale celadon jade figure of a recumbent horse, Yuan Dynasty, 4.6cm. long. (Christie's) $2,143 £1,458

A jade figure of a recumbent horse, Tang/Song Dynasty, 6.5cm. long. (Christie's) $1,140 £864

A celadon jade brush washer modelled as a pressed hollowed melon, 3in. wide. (Christie's) $986 £680

An 18th century flecked celadon and russet jade box and cover, 8cm. wide, with fitted box. (Christie's) $641 £486

A pale celadon and brown jade vase, 17th/18th century, 12.5cm. high, with wood stand. (Christie's) $7,128 £5,400

An early celadon jade circular disc, bi, Han Dynasty, 10.7cm. diam., in fitted box. (Christie's) $3,564 £2,700

An archaic jade pierced circular disc, bi, Zhou Dynasty, 16cm. diam. (Christie's) $1,111 £756

A Longquan celadon yanyan vase, early 14th century, 26.5cm. high. (Christie's) $3,991 £3,024

A small Longquan celadon jarlet and lotus-moulded cover, 13th/14th century, 7.5cm. high. (Christie's) $1,568 £1,188

An 18th century flecked celadon jade group formed as a slender bodied recumbent deer, 15cm. wide, wood stand. (Christie's) $1,905 £1,296

An 18th century white jade group of a recumbent horse, 6.5cm. high, with wood stand. (Christie's) $1,140 £864

A large celadon jade peach-shaped brushwasher, late Qing Dynasty, 19.5cm. wide. (Christie's) $2,138 £1,620

A Mogul dark celadon jade ewer of oval octafoil cross-section, 17th/18th century, 15.5cm. high. (Christie's) $7,840 £5,940

An early celadon and russet jade burial cicada, Han Dynasty or earlier, 5cm. wide. (Christie's) $570 £432

A celadon lobed hexafoil dish, Northern Song Dynasty, 17.4cm. diam. (Christie's) $8,553 £6,480

A pale celadon jade model of two mythical birds feeding from a branch of peaches, 6¾in. wide, on wood stand. (Christie's) $3,480 £2,400

A pale celadon jade tripod libation vessel carved with a single bracket handle, Qianlong seal mark, 13.4cm. high. (Christie's) $6,032 £4,104

A jade figure of a crouching Buddhistic lion, probably Han/Six Dynasties, 6.8cm. wide. (Christie's) $1,140 £864

A diamond pendant roundel brooch set with collets and rose cut stones. (Lawrence Fine Art) $510 £352

A fish brooch designed by Henning Koppel, stamped HK Georg Jensen, 306, circa 1950. (Christie's) $406 £280

A diamond target brooch, the central diamond calculated as weighing 1.24ct. (Lawrence Fine Art) $3,744 £2,530

A pair of Victorian gold earrings, each of pear shape with raised oval centres. (Lawrence Fine Art) $423 £286

A diamond and pearl brooch of rectangular form. (Lawrence Fine Art) $7,488 £5,060

An Art Nouveau circular mirror pendant, set with small rose diamonds. (Christie's) $1,096 £756

A tortoiseshell necklace carved with eleven female heads, divided by a graduating ram's mask, with a similar pair of earrings. (Lawrence Fine Art) $1,269 £858

A peridot, diamond and pearl pendant, the central peridot measuring 19.6 x 14.3mm. (Lawrence Fine Art) $1,674 £1,155

A Victorian diamond Indian star brooch. (Lawrence Fine Art) $748 £506

An emerald and diamond ring, the square cut emerald flanked by three old cut diamonds on an 18ct. gold shank. (Lawrence Fine Art)
$1,914 £1,320

A brooch, pierced and engraved with a fawn among foliage, stamped Georg Jensen 925 S 256. (Christie's) $124 £86

An emerald and diamond cluster ring on a plain shank with bifurcated shoulders. (Lawrence Fine Art)
$1,036 £715

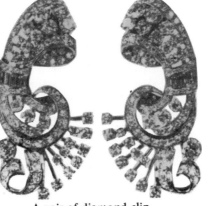

A pendant, white metal, designed by P. Wolfers, stamped Wolfers Freres 80, P.W. 1903. (Christie's)
$375 £259

A pair of diamond clip brooches, each of open scroll form set with various brilliant and eight-cut stones. (Lawrence Fine Art)
$3,828 £2,640

A Van Cleef & Arpels ruby, diamond and cultured pearl circle and twin rosette and tassel brooch, stamped Paris 34220. (Christie's)
$2,049 £1,404

A Victorian brooch formed of interwoven gold scrolls set with chrysoberyls and amethysts. (Lawrence Fine Art) $733 £506

An emerald and diamond ring, the central emerald within a surround of forty-two diamonds, on a plain shank. (Lawrence Fine Art)
$1,116 £770

An emerald, gold and enamel brooch, together with a pair of emerald cluster earrings. (Lawrence Fine Art)
$1,244 £858

A diamond three-stone ring, claw set on an 18ct. gold shank. (Lawrence Fine Art) $1,709 £1,155

A 9ct. gold, diamond and ruby bar brooch, in the form of a diamond set fox mask with ruby eyes. (Lawrence Fine Art) $227 £154

A ruby and diamond ring, the central ruby calculated as weighing 2.37ct. (Lawrence Fine Art) $3,581 £2,420

A jade pendant carved with three geese amongst lotus and rockwork, with white gold clip and chain attachment, approx. 46 x 17 x 6mm. (Christie's) $3,166 £2,229

A sapphire and diamond ring, the central sapphire weighing 14.61ct. on a plain shank. (Lawrence Fine Art) $1,754 £1,210

A jade cylindrical section mounted as a ring in gold, approx. 20 x 12.3 x 2.5mm. (Christie's) $1,333 £938

A sapphire and pearl star pendant brooch, one blue stone is a synthetic sapphire replacement. (Lawrence Fine Art) $651 £440

A tree brooch designed by Henning Koppel, stamped HK Georg Jensen, 323, circa 1950. (Christie's) $375 £259

One of a pair of jade bangles, overall diam. approx. 74mm., the thickness 9mm. (Christie's) $2,916 £2,053

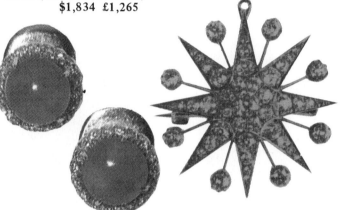

An emerald five-stone ring, the stones graduating from the centre, on a plain gold shank. (Lawrence Fine Art) $1,834 £1,265

An enamel and scarab bracelet, yellow metal, the scarab in oval mount, stamped 585.(Christie's) $1,409 £972

A diamond five-stone ring, the central stone calculated as weighing 1.01ct., on a gold shank. (Lawrence Fine Art) $2,197 £1,485

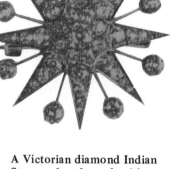

A pair of jade circular cabochons, mounted as earrings in white gold, each with a border of nineteen diamonds. (Christie's) $458 £322

A Victorian diamond Indian Star pendant brooch with detachable brooch pin. (Lawrence Fine Art) $1,595 £1,100

A pair of earrings, yellow metal, design attributed to H. Koppel, stamped Georg Jensen 1119. (Christie's) $437 £302

A Victorian diamond and turquoise bangle, centred 'by five old cut diamonds on a Maltese Cross. (Lawrence Fine Art) $1,302 £880

A jade oval cabochon mounted as a ring in white gold, the cabochon approx. 25.2 x 16.2 x 6mm. (Christie's) $4,166 £2,933

A gold and blue enamel memorial reliquary brooch enclosing a lock of Wellington's hair, engraved on reverse 'Died 14 Sept 1852'. (Christie's) $546 £420

A red lacquer circular box and cover, Qianlong, 21.5cm. diam., in fitted box. (Christie's) $997 £756

An 18th century Korean inlaid silver flecked brown lacquer box and cover, 65.5cm. wide. (Christie's) $4,127 £2,808

A red lacquer peach-shaped box and cover, Qianlong, 37cm. wide. (Christie's) $2,851 £2,160

A Momoyama period lacquer Christian shrine (seigan), 49.3cm. high. (Christie's) $101,088 £70,200

A late Ming gilt lacquered wood figure of a seated dignitary, 16th/17th century, 80cm. high, with wood stand. (Christie's) $1,995 £1,512

A 19th century rectangular lacquer kashibako, unsigned, 15 x 10cm., with hinoki box. (Christie's) $1,698 £1,188

A carved red lacquer square centre table, Qianlong, 87cm. high, 105cm. wide. (Christie's) $4,989 £3,780

A 19th century lacquer sake ewer with black and gold lacquer handle, 13.5cm. diam. (Christie's) $277 £194

A rectangular black lacquered chest, nagamochi, with carrying handles, late Edo period, 146.3cm. wide. (Christie's) $7,344 £5,400

Late 19th century boule student lamp with lithophane shades, Germany, 23½in. high. (Robt. W. Skinner Inc.)
$1,600 £1,167

Victorian brass coach lamp, 1880. (British Antique Exporters) $52 £39

A Regency ormolu hall lantern with glazed hexagonal body and foliate corona, 31½in. high. (Christie's) $5,011 £3,456

A 19th century gilt metal hall lantern with bevelled glazed hexagonal body with scrolled corona, 37in. high. (Christie's) $1,722 £1,188

A Tiffany Studios favrile glass and bronze ten-light lily lamp, 19½in. high. (Woolley & Wallis)
$6,576 £4,800

Early 20th century Tiffany blue iridescent candle lamp, signed, 1924, New York, 12¼in. high. (Robt. W. Skinner Inc.)
$950 £693

A Legras etched and enamelled glass table lamp with mushroom shaped shade, 50.6cm. high. (Christie's)
$2,349 £1,620

'Nymph among the bullrushes', a bronze table lamp cast after a model by Louis Convers, 28.1cm. high. (Christie's)
$751 £518

A Tiffany Studios gilt bronze and glass table lamp, stamped Tiffany Studios New York 590, 48cm. high.(Christie's)
$2,505 £1,728

An early 20th century Handel lamp on Hampshire pottery base, with Mosserine shade, 20in. high. (Robt. W. Skinner Inc.) $900 £625

A Victorian iron lamp with green tole shaft, stamped Palmer & Co. Patent, 32in. high. (Christie's) $2,035 £1,404

An early 20th century pairpoint table lamp with blownout shade, New Bedford, 14in. diam. (Robt. W. Skinner Inc.) $1,400 £958

A George III ormolu hall lantern with arched glazed cylindrical body, 20in. diam. (Christie's) $6,428 £5,184

A Fulper pottery 'Vase-Kraft' table lamp, circa 1915, 18in. high, 16½in. diam. (Robt. W. Skinner Inc.) $5,600 £3,888

A plique a jour and metal lantern, each panel depicting a female figure in the manner of Robt. A. Bell, 34.5cm. high. (Christie's) $2,522 £1,728

An Art Nouveau bronze oil lamp base with jewelled glass shade and glass funnel, cast after a model by G. Leleu, circa 1900, 57cm. without funnel. (Christie's) $867 £594

One of a pair of brass electric headlamps, stamped 'Carl Zeiss Jena', 10½in. diam. (Christie's) $124 £100

One of a pair of mid 19th century French ormolu mounted turquoise glazed baluster vase lamps of Louis XVI design, 25in. high. (Christie's) $4,276 £3,240

LAMPS

An Empire ormolu lamp bouillotte with tole shade and two adjustable branches, 23½in. high. (Christie's) $2,280 £1,728

A mid 19th century overlay kerosene lamp, probably Sandwich, 11¾in. high. (Robt. W. Skinner Inc.) $600 £410

A Restoration bronze and ormolu candlestick lamp with tripod base and fringed green silk shade, 21in. high, including shade. (Christie's) $861 £594

One of a pair of black painted and brass carriage lamps, stamped 'Howes & Burley patent No. 2070', 17¼in. high. (Christie's) $86 £70

A Gustav Stickley hammered copper lamp with willow shade, circa 1905, signed, 22in. high, 20in. diam. (Robt. W. Skinner Inc.) $1,500 £1,041

A carved cameo helmet shell lamp, probably Italy, depicting Homer and nine muses dancing, 11½in. high. (Robt. W. Skinner Inc.) $250 £171

A late Georgian silver plated Corinthian column lamp, 30½in. high, including shade. (Christie's) $1,566 £1,080

One of a pair of brass Lucas 'King of the Road' paraffin side lamps, inscribed No. 624, 10½in. high. (Christie's) $186 £150

A tole urn decorated in lacquer with flowers and with pleated silk shade, 27½in. high, including shade. (Christie's) $1,800 £1,242

LAMPS

A Doulton Flambe figure by Noke, modelled as a seated Buddha, mounted as a lamp, circa 1930, 57.5cm. high. (Christie's) $1,252 £864

A lampe bouillotte with green silk shade, fitted for electricity, 26in. high. (Christie's) $2,035 £1,404

A Daum Art Deco table lamp, frosted glass with wrought iron, engraved with cross of Lorraine, circa 1925, 46cm. high. (Christie's) $4,698 £3,240

An Art Deco bronzed electric table lamp on oval base with onyx stand, 20in. high. (Anderson & Garland) $397 £280

A Galle blowout lamp, varying shades of red on an amber ground, signed, circa 1900, 44.5cm. high. (Christie's) $59,508 £41,040

A Galle triple overlay cameo glass lamp, blue and green over a pale amber ground, circa 1900, 61cm. high. (Christie's) $14,094 £9,720

A Galle double overlay and wheel-carved glass table lamp, the matt-yellow ground overlaid in brown, blue and purple, circa 1900, 52.5cm. high. (Christie's) $9,396 £6,480

A plated two-branch student's oil lamp with green tinted shades. (Peter Wilson & Co.) $244 £170

Victorian spelter lamp, signed Louis Moreau, 1880. (British Antique Exporters) $399 £296

A Victorian three-branch brass light fitting, 1880. (British Antique Exporters) $210 £156

A 1950's French floor lamp, the black painted stand in the form of a stylised praying mantis, 162.4cm. high. (Christie's) $503 £345

A lampe bouillotte with three candlebranches and pleated green silk shade, 20in. high. (Christie's) $2,114 £1,458

A patinated bronze and ormolu baluster vase, with ivory silk shade, 24½in. high. (Christie's) $2,349 £1,620

A Galle double overlay cameo glass lamp, circa 1900, 32.4cm. high. (Christie's) $10,962 £7,560

A bronze, marble and glass lamp cast after a model by M. Le Verrier, signed, circa 1925, 86.2cm. high. (Christie's) $2,035 £1,404

A Regency gilt metal hanging lantern, fitted for electricity, 19in. wide, 42in. high. (Christie's) $7,356 £5,616

Victorian brass desk lamp, 1900. (British Antique Exporters) $87 £65

A Louis Comfort Tiffany bronze leaded glass and favrile glass two-light table lamp, 56cm. high. (Christie's) $6,264 £4,320

Fine French marble bust, 1870. (British Antique Exporters) $441 £327

One of a pair of Verde di Prato models of lions, 21¼in. wide, 16½in. high. (Christie's) $4,071 £2,808

A white marble bust of a bearded gentleman, with draped shoulders, 30in. high. (Christie's) $330 £220

A white marble relief of a Roman Emperor in white and gold oval frame, 7½in. high. (Christie's)
$626 £432

An early 19th century Italian white marble reduction of a sarcophagus, 9½in. wide. (Christie's)
$1,174 £810

A Bilbao looking glass with pink marble rectangular frame with gilt beaded borders, 30in. high. (Robt. W. Skinner Inc.)
$2,200 £1,549

Late 17th/early 18th century Roman white marble bust of the head of Laocoon, 27in. high. (Christie's)
$10,962 £7,560

A marble relief of a Roman Emperor on a blue ground, in giltwood frame, 8½ x 7in., and another similar. (Christie's) $2,662 £1,836

A marble statuette of a maiden in classical dress, signed P. Barzanti Florence, 44in. high. (Worsfolds)
$2,736 £1,900

A white marble bust of an elderly man with draped head and shoulders, 28in. high. (Christie's)
$225 £150

A white marble sculpture of a standing naked Venus, 26in. high. (Lots Road Chelsea Auction Galleries) $562 £380

A white marble group of a mother and child with a deer, inscribed G. Geefs Premier, Statuaire de S.M. le Roi, 42in. high. (Christie's) $1,200 £800

A white marble classical female torso, Greco-Roman, circa 200 B.C., torso 8½in. (Robt. W. Skinner Inc.)
$1,300 £915

A 19th century Indian, Jaipur, white marble bench, the back and sides pierced with trellis and foliage, 60in. wide. (Christie's) $2,250 £1,500

A white marble figure of Venus seated on a fountain with cupids embracing below, 55in. high, the cylindrical plinth 28in. high.(Christie's)
$5,250 £3,500

A pair of Breccia and black marble obelisks, 15in. high. (Christie's) $643 £432

A marble rectangular relief of a man with a laurel wreath, in giltwood frame, 6¼ x 5½in. (Christie's)
$265 £183

Sienna marble column, circa 1860. (British Antique Exporters) $257 £191

A George III giltwood mirror with later shaped rectangular plate, 46 x 24½in. (Christie's) $6,114 £4,104

A late Federal gilt convex mirror, 1815-25, 26½in. diam. (Christie's) $8,800 £6,111

One of a pair of giltwood mirrors of Queen Anne style, 52 x 27in. (Christie's) $14,094 £9,720

A Meissen rococo dressing table mirror, circa 1750, 67.5cm. high. (Christie's) $3,564 £2,376

Early Victorian mahogany swan base cheval mirror, 1840. (British Antique Exporters) $575 £426

A 19th century American carved and giltwood dressing mirror, 19in. wide. (Christie's) $1,540 £1,069

A Queen Anne walnut looking glass with two-part mirror plate, 1740-60, 47½in. high. (Christie's) $2,090 £1,451

A George III mahogany and parcel gilt mirror, 37 x 22½in. (Christie's) $1,448 £972

A Federal giltwood looking glass, 48in. high. (Christie's) $1,760 £1,222

One of a pair of Regency convex mirrors with circular plates and ebonised slips, 34½ x 18in. (Christie's) $9,977 £6,696

One of a pair of Georgian rococo mirrors, attributed to M. Darley, England, circa 1765, 64 x 42½in. (Robt. W. Skinner Inc.) $34,000 £23,611

A gilt convex mirror surmounted by a spread-wing eagle, 35¼in. diam., circa 1815. (Christie's) $1,540 £1,069

A Chippendale gilt looking glass, England, circa 1760, 32½ x 13in. (Robt. W. Skinner Inc.) $2,300 £1,597

A Chippendale mahogany looking glass, England, circa 1760, 35 x 16½in. (Robt. W. Skinner Inc.) $1,500 £1,041

Queen Anne walnut mirror, possibly America, circa 1750, 32¾in. high. (Robt. W. Skinner Inc.) $900 £633

A George II giltwood pier glass with rectangular plate, 59½ x 33½in. (Christie's) $6,901 £4,860

A mid 18th century Queen Anne mahogany and mahogany veneer mirror, probably England, 16in. high. (Robt. W. Skinner Inc.) $550 £371

An Irish giltwood mirror, fitted as a toilet mirror with later easel, 37 x 18in. (Christie's) $939 £648

A Chippendale mahogany looking glass, New England, circa 1800, 30in. high. (Robt. W. Skinner Inc.) $800 £555

Late 18th century George III dressing mirror with desk, 19in. wide. (Christie's) $830 £572

Late 18th century courting mirror, North Europe, 23in. high. (Robt. W. Skinner Inc.) $3,100 £2,183

A Federal gilt gesso looking glass, circa 1815. (Robt. W. Skinner Inc.) $2,700 £1,901

A walnut and marquetry mirror with later bevelled rectangular plate, 32½ x 37in. (Christie's) $2,035 £1,404

A walnut and parcel gilt mirror with waved arched cresting, 63 x 32in. (Christie's) $3,527 £2,484

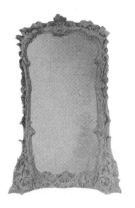

A mid 18th century German stained oak mirror, 62 x 41in. (Christie's) $3,110 £2,160

Victorian inlaid rosewood overmantel, 1860. (British Antique Exporters) $392 £291

A giltwood mirror of Regency design, the sides with ho-ho birds, 72 x 48in. (Christie's) $4,665 £3,240

Late 18th century Oriental lacquered dressing stand, China, 17in. wide. (Robt. W. Skinner Inc.)
$1,100 £763

An 18th century Chippendale carved giltwood oval wall mirror, 122cm. high. (Andrew Grant)$8,352 £5,800

A Queen Anne scarlet lacquer toilet mirror with fitted interior, 18½in. wide. (Christie's) $2,818 £1,944

A 17th century Spanish parcel gilt and grained mirror, 40½ x 28½in. (Christie's) $544 £378

A Chippendale curly maple mirror, New Hampshire, circa 1773, 18¼in. long. (Robt. W. Skinner Inc.)
$2,900 £2,042

One of a pair of George II cream painted mirrors, 68 x 33½in. (Christie's)
$11,745 £8,100

An Irish, George III giltwood mirror with oval plate, 32¼ x 20½in. (Christie's)
$5,011 £3,456

A George III giltwood mirror with shaped rectangular plate, 49 x 27in. (Christie's)
$4,071 £2,808

An 18th century giltwood mirror with oval bevelled plate, 49 x 36in.(Christie's)
$3,421 £2,376

A Regency giltwood convex mirror with two candle-branches, 31½ x 32in. (Christie's) $5,637 £3,888

A Chippendale mahogany and giltwood mirror, circa 1770, 55in. high. (Robt. W. Skinner Inc.) $3,000 £2,054

A mid 18th century Chippendale rococo style carved and gilded wood wall mirror, 65in. high. (Dacre, Son & Hartley) $7,200 £5,000

Victorian mahogany marble top toilet mirror, 1860. (British Antique Exporters) $230 £171

An early George II walnut toilet mirror, the box base with three drawers with brass knob handles, 17in. high. (Woolley & Wallis) $648 £450

An ornate Victorian mahogany toilet mirror, 1860. (British Antique Exporters) $210 £156

A gilt gesso mirror with scrolling candle-branches with turned nozzles, 45½in. x 26½in. (Christie's) $7,074 £5,400

A late 18th century Anglo-Indian vizagapatam toilet service veneered with engraved ivory. (Christie's) $6,026 £4,860

A giltwood pier glass with arched plate, possibly Scandinavian, 72 x 31in. (Christie's) $2,505 £1,728

A George I walnut and parcel gilt mirror, 37 x 17in. (Christie's) $4,374 £3,240

A George III giltwood mirror, the oval plate with rope-twist slip, 48 x 28in. (Christie's) $3,991 £3,024

A German Art Nouveau bronze domed mirror, 21in. high. (Christie's) $604 £420

A mid Georgian giltwood mirror with shaped divided plates, 63 x 32in. (Christie's) $8,553 £6,480

A 19th century birchwood toilet mirror, the oval plate in Gothic arched frame, 29in. wide. (Christie's) $1,096 £756

A giltwood mirror in the mid Georgian style, second quarter 18th century, 95 x 49in. (Christie's) $9,477 £7,020

An Irish, George III, giltwood architectural pier glass by J. & W. Booker of Dublin, 78 x 45½in. (Christie's) $8,683 £6,480

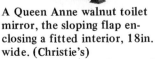

A Queen Anne walnut toilet mirror, the sloping flap enclosing a fitted interior, 18in. wide. (Christie's) $2,263 £1,728

A George II giltwood mirror with rectangular bevelled plate, 46 x 25in.(Christie's) $5,132 £3,888

A Regency giltwood and
ebonised overmantel in the
manner of Thos. Hope,
58½ x 50in. (Christie's)
$9,396 £6,480

A Chippendale mahogany
veneer and giltwood looking
glass, England or America,
circa 1770, 39½in. high.
(Robt. W. Skinner Inc.)
$2,100 £1,418

A Federal gilt convex mirror,
circa 1820, 27½in. high.
(Robt. W. Skinner Inc.)
$500 £347

An Irish, George III mirror,
with later oval plate, 25½
x 17½in. (Christie's)
$3,834 £2,700

A 17th century Flemish
ebony and tortoiseshell
mirror, 34½ x 28¾in.
(Christie's) $1,710 £1,188

A George III giltwood
mirror, the pierced rockwork
frame with foliate C-scroll
cresting, 44 x 25in. (Christie's) $7,516 £5,184

An early 18th century
William and Mary walnut
veneered mirror, 20in. wide.
(Robt. W. Skinner Inc.)
$1,400 £972

A giltwood overmantel of
George III style, 78 x 72in.
(Christie's) $10,179 £7,020

A George III giltwood mirror
with later rectangular plate,
64 x 42in. (Christie's)
$14,877 £10,260

One of a pair of George III giltwood mirrors, 45 x 24½in. (Christie's) $8,990 £6,200

A William and Mary marquetry and oyster-veneered walnut mirror, 48 x 30½in. (Christie's) $11,745 £8,100

Late 18th century courting mirror, Northern Europe, 21 x 10in. (Robt. W. Skinner Inc.) $1,600 £1,126

A Queen Anne gilt gesso mirror, fitted with a pair of late Regency gilt brass candlebranches, 47 x 21½in. (Christie's) $5,011 £3,456

A mirror attributed to Bugatti, various woods decorated with beaten copperwork and copper and pewter inlay, circa 1900, 66 x 61.8cm. (Christie's) $2,035 £1,404

A Queen Anne giltwood mirror, 47 x 27½in. (Christie's) $3,132 £2,160

A Chippendale inlaid mahogany mirror, possibly N.Y., 1760/80, 43½in. high. (Christie's) $1,320 £910

A Irish, George III giltwood overmantel with shaped divided plates, the upper panel painted with a Venetian scene. (Christie's) $23,490 £16,200

A George II gilt gesso mirror with bevelled rectangular plate, 42½ x 23in. (Christie's) $2,662 £1,836

A Victorian quillwork basket, circa 1880.(British Antique Exporters)$55 £41

A miniature Federal painted and decorated pine blanket chest, Penn., circa 1810/30, 26½in. wide. (Christie's) $24,200 £16,689

An early 19th century rectangular Roman micromosaic panel, 2¾in. long. (Christie's) $2,975 £2,052

Two fragments of early George III printed wallpaper, after C. N. Cochin the Younger, 44½ x 22½in. and 47½ x 22¾in. (Christie's) $482 £324

An Empire mahogany miniature sofa, American, circa 1840, 19in. wide. (Christie's) $1,430 £986

One of two sheets of Chinese wallpaper painted in fresh colours, 18th century, 92 x 38in. (Christie's) $1,749 £1,296

 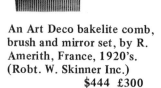 

A papier mache model of Nipper with electrically operated wagging tail, 17in. high, in EMI wooden dispatch case. (Christie's) $682 £550

An Art Deco bakelite comb, brush and mirror set, by R. Amerith, France, 1920's. (Robt. W. Skinner Inc.) $444 £300

A 19th century reddish-brown agate bust of a male carved in the antique manner, 3½in. high.(Christie's) $388 £270

Early 19th century micro-mosaic plaque, depicting the Temple of Vesta at Tivoli, 2½in. long. (Christie's) $1,174 £810

A smoked crystal figure of a hawk, perched on a rocky outcrop, 9in. high. (Lawrence Fine Art) $303 £209

Late 19th century Oriental carved coral figural group, 8in. long. (Robt. W. Skinner Inc.) $296 £200

Late 18th century George III mahogany inlaid miniature chest of drawers, 12in. wide. (Christie's) $1,540 £1,062

An ivory staff, the knob and handle carved with swarming and entwined rats, 9¾in. long. (Reeds Rains) $460 £320

An early 19th century miniature Dutch marquetry and mahogany bureau. (Woolley & Wallis) $580 £400

A 19th century Italian mosaic picture panel, four pigeons drinking from a bronze bowl, 5½ x 4in. (Peter Wilson & Co.) $417 £290

A Victorian mahogany miniature work table with silk covered base, 12in. high. (Christie's) $524 £400

A 19th century large papier mache tray with raised rim, 30½ x 22in. (Lawrence Fine Art) $2,472 £1,705

A Roman rectangular micro-mosaic box top depicting Pliny's Doves of Venus, circa 1840, 3in. long. (Christie's) $1,487 £1,026

Mid 19th century soapstone group. (British Antique Exporters) $22 £17

An early 19th century American hooked rug, 34in. deep, 53in. wide. (Christie's) $660 £481

A group of yacht 'Gore' sail design books, by the Ratseys and Lapthorn sailmaking firm, New York, 1902-60. (Christie's) $8,250 £6,021

A group of late 18th century cream-coloured wax bust-length profile medallions, each 2¼in. high.(Christie's) $622 £432

A pair of Regency gilt plaster candlesticks, the base inscribed G. Bullock Pub Jan 1804, 24in. high. (Christie's) $3,288 £2,268

A chromium plated and enamelled Brooklands Aero-Club badge inscribed 21, 3¾in. high. (Christie's) $520 £420

A percussion trap gun with 12in. barrel, combined external spring hammer and rod trigger on swivel pivot mount. (Christie's) $139 £95

One of a pair of glazed waxed octagonal reliefs of Robt. Adam after Tassie, 6 x 4½in. (Christie's) $1,331 £918

MISCELLANEOUS

A pair of Victorian wax reliefs of Queen Victoria and Prince Albert, in mahogany frame, 6 x 8½in. (Christie's) $187 £129

An Eley 'Sporting and Military' cartridge board, including brass rifle and pistol cartridge cases and tins of primers etc., in its oak frame. (Christie's)
$205 £140

A Spanish Colonial dress saddle with white leather seat and pommel, also a pair of 'Botas' leggings, 30in. long. (Robt. W. Skinner Inc.)
$925 £642

Late 19th century American moulded zinc mastiff figure, 48in. high, 48in. wide. (Robt. W. Skinner Inc.)
$1,400 £945

Pair of Georgian straw-work pictures of the Church at Chilton, Wiltshire, and the Parsonage, 7 x 9½in. (Christie's) $1,331 £918

A refrigerator decorated by Piero Fornasetti, on black painted tubular steel framed base, 70cm. wide. (Christie's)
$861 £594

Early 19th century cabinet of geological specimens, by M. le Prof. Jurine et M. Brard. (Christie's)
$1,320 £910

A silhouette of a young woman in original gold leaf frame, America, circa 1830, image 7¼ x 5in. (Robt. W. Skinner Inc.)
$2,600 £1,780

One of twenty sheets of Chinese wallpaper painted in fresh colours.(Christie's)
$78,408 £59,400

A 20th century American model of the
extreme clippership 'Cutty Sark', on a
walnut base, fitted in a glass case. (Christie's)
$1,320 £964

A contemporary early 19th century French
prisoner of war bone and horn model man of
war reputed to be the French ship of the line
'Redoubtable' of 74 guns, 20½ x 26¾in.
(Christie's) $11,600 £8,000

Late 18th century prisoner-of-war carved
ivory ship, with rigging and thirty-four gun
ports, Europe, 13½in. long. (Robt. W.
Skinner Inc.) $800 £583

A planked and rigged model of a Royal Naval
Cutter built by I. H. Wilkie, Sleaford, 36 x
42in. (Christie's) $507 £350

A planked and framed fully rigged model of
the Royal Naval armed brig H.M.S. 'Grasshopper'
of circa 1806, built by R. Cartwright, Plymouth,
32 x 41in. (Christie's) $942 £650

Early 19th century prisoner-of-war bone
model of a ship-of-the-line, 7¾in. long.
(Christie's) $3,190 £2,328

A 20th century American model of a fishing schooner, 'Kearsar', fitted in a glass case, 33½in. long. (Christie's) $935 £682

A 19th century three-masted ship model, sails furled, approx. 36in. long. (Robt. W. Skinner Inc.) $500 £364

A detailed ¼in.:1ft. model of a twelve gun brig of circa 1840 built to the plans of H. A. Underhill by M. J. Gebhard, Tottenham, 36 x 47in. (Christie's) $4,350 £3,000

A 19th century carved bone model of a frigate, probably French, 16½in. long. (Christie's) $3,080 £2,248

An early 19th century French prisoner-of-war bone model of a ship-of-the-line, 8½in. long. (Christie's) $2,530 £1,846

Early 19th century prisoner-of-war bone model of a First Class ship-of-the-line, 21in. long. (Christie's) $9,900 £7,226

A rake of three fine gauge 1 Great Western Railway twin bogie passenger coaches, by G. Carrette. (Christie's) $435 £300

A rake of three gauge 1 Midland Railway twin bogie passenger cars, including two first class coaches and a 3rd class brake car, by Bing for Bassett-Lowke, circa 1927. (Christie's) $532 £360

A gauge 1 clockwork model of the London and and North Western Railway 4-6-2 'Bowen-Cooke' tank locomotive No. 2663, in black livery, by Marklin for Bassett-Lowke, circa 1913. (Christie's) $1,258 £850

Two gauge 1 Great Northern Railway, teak, 1st/3rd class twin bogie passenger cars, Nos. 2875, by Marklin, circa 1925. (Christie's) $384 £260

An early Bing 2½in. gauge II live steam spirit fired Midland Railway 4-4-0 locomotive, with a six-wheel tender and a six-wheel carriage, the locomotive 14in. long, circa 1902-06. (Lawrence Fine Art) $976 £660

A gauge 3 live- steam spirit-fired model of the London and South Western Railway 4-4-0 locomotive and tender, by Bing for Bassett-Lowke, circa 1904. (Christie's) $4,144 £2,800

A gauge 0 clockwork model of the North Boarder Railway 4-4-0 pannier tank locomotive, by Bing for Bassett-Lowke, and a Bassett-Lowke clockwork mechanism. (Christie's) $217 £150

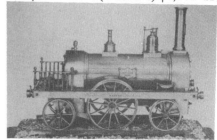

A contemporary mid 19th century 4½in. gauge brass model of the 2-2-2 locomotive 'Apollo' of 1844 built by Franklin & Co., Manchester, 9¾ x 14¼in. (Christie's) $4,640 £3,200

A fine gauge 1 clockwork model of the London and North Western Railway 4-4-2 'Precursor Tank' locomotive No. 44, in black livery, by Bing for Bassett-Lowke, circa 1810. (Christie's) $562 £380

A Marklin 3RE 20 volts 4-4-0 LMS locomotive and four wheeler tender, the first/third class carriages and brake van, Bing controller. (Phillips) $653 £460

Two gauge 0 C.I.W.L. twin bogie passenger coaches, restaurant car, Ref. No. 1746/GJ1, and sleeping car, Ref. No. 1747/GJ1, by Marklin. (Christie's) $98 £75

A 3½in. gauge model of the London and North Eastern Railway Class V2 2-6-2 locomotive and tender 'Green Arrow' built by A. Ficker, Radlett, 10½ x 53in. (Christie's) $2,175 £1,500

A 5in. gauge model of the London and North Eastern Railway Class J39 0-6-0 locomotive and tender No. 2934, built by K. Edge, Peterborough, 13¾ x 59in. (Christie's)
$3,625 £2,500

A Bing spirit fired 0-4-0 LNWR locomotive and tender No. 1942 with separated lamps and a Bing gauge 1 signal. (Phillips) $397 £280

A gauge 1 (3-rail) electric model of a Continental 4-4-0 locomotive and tender, by Bing, circa 1910. (Christie's) $464 £320

A gauge 0 (3-rail) electric model of the 0-4-0 locomotive, Ref. No. RF66/12920, by Marklin. (Christie's) $314 £240

A 7¼in. gauge model of the Hunslet 0-4-0 contractor's locomotive designed by M. R. Harrison and modelled by J. Maxted, Ramsgate, measurements overall 33½ x 98in. (Christie's)
$4,060 £2,800

'Juliet', a 3½in. gauge live steam coal fired 0-4-0 tank locomotive, together with a trailer, 20in. long overall. (Lawrence Fine Art)
$296 £200

A gauge 1 London and North Western Railway twin bogie 3rd class brake car, by Bing for Bassett-Lowke, circa 1922. (Christie's)
$192 £130

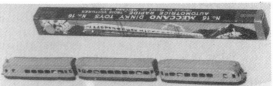

Pre-war French Factory 16Z diesel streamlined train by Dinky. (Phillips) $499 £340

609

A 7¼in. gauge model of the Great Western Railway 15XX Class 0-6-0 Pannier tank locomotive No. 1500, rebuilt by F. West, Lee Green, 21 x 55in. (Christie's) $7,250 £5,000

A gauge 0 live steam spirit-fired model of the S.E.C.R. steam railcar, by Carette, circa 1908. (Christie's) $1,450 £1,000

A collection of the Great Western Railway coaching stock including the twin bogie full brake No. 188, the six wheel full brake No. 95 and the four wheel horsebox No. 88, painted by L. Goddard. (Christie's) $362 £250

A 7¼in. gauge model of the Great Western Railway 4-6-0 locomotive and tender No. 1011 'County of Chester' rebuilt and reboilered by F. West, 21¾ x 10in. (Christie's) $17,400 £12,000

A 5in. model of the London and North Eastern Railway Class A3 4-6-2 locomotive and tender No. 2568 'Sceptre' built by K. Edge, 1975, 15 x 75in. (Christie's) $4,640 £3,200

A gauge 0 (3-rail) electric model of a Continental 4-6-2 'Pacific' locomotive and twin bogie tender, Ref. No. HR64/13020, by Marklin, circa 1930. (Christie's) $1,965 £1,500

A 3½in. gauge model of the 4-4-0 locomotive and tender No. 573 built to the designs of 'Virginia', 11½ x 45in. (Christie's) $1,305 £900

A 7mm. finescale two rail electric model of the London Midland and Scottish Railway Class 7P 4-6-2 locomotive and tender No. 6231 'Duchess of Athol' as built in 1938, the model by D. Jenkinson and painted by L. Goddard, 3¾ x 20½in. (Christie's) $1,087 £750

A gauge 0 (3-rail) electric model of a Continental Doll BLS electric engine, with overhead pantograph, by Bing, circa 1930. (Christie's) $262 £200

An exhibition standard 5in. gauge model of the William Dean diagram 21 Brake Composite twin bogie passenger coach No. 3391 of 1897, 13 x 57in. (Christie's) $2,610 £1,800

A detailed exhibition standard 5in. gauge model of the British Railways Class 7 4-6-2 locomotive and tender No. 70000 'Britannia', 14 x 76in. (Christie's) $8,700 £6,000

A 5in. gauge model of the Great Western Railway 4-6-0 locomotive and tender No. 6011 'King James I' built by K. Edge, 15 x 73in. (Christie's) $7,540 £5,200

A 3½in. gauge model of the London and North Eastern Railway Class B1 4-6-0 locomotive and tender No. 8301 'Springbok' built by T. Dyche, York, 10¼ x 47in. (Christie's) $2,465 £1,700

A 5in. gauge model of the Great Western Railway 0-6-0 Pannier tank locomotive No. 9716 built to the designs of Pansy, 13½ x 34in. (Christie's) $2,030 £1,400

A gauge 0 clockwork model of the London Midland and Scottish Railway 4-4-0 locomotive and six-wheel tender No. 5320 'George V', by Bing for Bassett-Lowke. (Christie's) $217 £150

A 7mm. finescale two rail electric model of the London Brighton and South Coast Railway Stroudley Class D1 0-4-2 side tank locomotive No. 351, built by B. Miller, 3¾ x 8¾in. (Christie's) $609 £420

A 5in. gauge model of the Great Northern Railway Stirling Single 4-2-2 locomotive and tender No. 9 built by H. Bannister, Burton-on-Trent, 15 x 58in. (Christie's) $4,060 £2,800

A 5in. gauge model of the London Midland and Scottish Railway re-built Scot Class 4-6-0 locomotive and tender No. 6154 'The Hussar' built by K. Edge, Peterborough, 15½ x 70in. (Christie's) $4,350 £3,000

A 7mm. finescale two rail electric model of the British Railways (ex L.M.S.) 0-6-0 'Jinty' side tank locomotive No. 47469, built by M. H. C. Models, Bolton, 3½ x 8½in.(Christie's) $609 £420

An exhibition standard 5in. gauge model of the Great Western Railway Dean Single 4-2-2 locomotive and tender No. 3012 'Great Western', 14 x 61in. (Christie's) $10,150 £7,000

A 1½in. scale model of a spirit-fired Shand-Mason horsedrawn fire engine of 1894. (Phillips) $1,176 £800

A scale model of a Ferguson TE20 tractor and plough, 15¾in. long overall. (Lawrence Fine Art) $421 £285

An exhibition standard model of the three cylinder compound surface condensing vertical reversing marine engine fitted to the Cunard Liner S.S. 'Servia' and modelled by Thos. Lowe, 1907, 14½ x 12½in. (Christie's) $5,075 £3,500

A fine contemporary late 19th century small, full size, single cylinder horizontal mill engine, measurements overall 18 x 25in. (Christie's) $968 £650

A well engineered 3in. scale model of a Suffolk Dredging tractor, built by C. E. Thorn, 27 x 30in. (Christie's) $705 £480

A 2in. scale model of a single cylinder three shaft two speed Davey-Paxman general purpose agricultural traction engine built by A. R. Dyer & Sons, Wantage, 23½ x 38in. (Christie's) $2,610 £1,800

A finely engineered, exhibition standard 1in. scale model of the single cylinder two speed four shaft general purpose agricultural traction engine 'Doreen', built to the designs of 'Minnie', by H. A. Taylor, 1980, 11½ x 18in. (Christie's)
$1,617 £1,100

A 1½in. scale model of a Burrell single crank compound two speed three shaft general purpose agricultural traction engine, built by J. B. Harris, Solihull, 15½ x 25in. (Christie's)
$3,190 £2,200

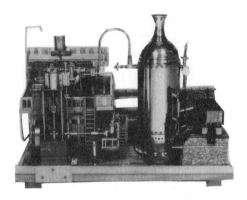

A finely engineered and well presented model 'M E', centre pillar beam engine, built by K. R. F. Kenworthy, measurements overall 13 x 17½in. (Christie's) $1,192 £800

A detailed steam driven model of a Bengali Die Mixing plant, built by A. Sare, Northleach, measurements overall 18½ x 24in. (Christie's)
$1,043 £700

An exhibition standard 2in. scale model of the Burrell 5 n.h.p. double crank compound two speed three shaft 'Gold Medal' tractor, engine No. 3846, Registration No. AD7782 'Pouss-nouk-nouk', built from works drawings by P. Penn-Sayers, Laughton, 19¾ x 27¼in. (Christie's)
$10,875 £7,500

An early 20th century model single cylinder surface condensing 'A' frame beam engine, 19½ x 24in. (Christie's) $2,465 £1,700

MOTORING ITEMS

A chromium plated Goddess of Sport, inscribed A.E.L., 5in. high. (Christie's) $176 £120

A brass buckle depicting a copulating couple, incorporating a chassis, 4in. long. (Christie's) $220 £150

A chromium plated and enamelled Brooklands B.A.R.C. badge inscribed 100, 3¾in. high.(Christie's) $210 £170

The Spirit of Triumph, a chromium plated figure, 6½in. high, on mahogany base. (Christie's) $68 £55

Six Brooklands Official Race Cards and Programmes for 1937. (Onslows) $60 £40

A nickel plated brass car mascot, caricature figure of an airman with printed porcelain head and moveable helmet, inscribed Hassall, 4¼in. high. (Christie's) $620 £500

A chromium plated and gilt desk timepiece modelled as an Edwardian tourer, 8½in. high. (Christie's) $661 £450

A chromium plated decanter in the form of a Bugatti radiator, by Classic Stable Ltd., 6¾in. high. (Onslows) $390 £260

The Brooklands Gazette, Vol. 1 no. 3, September 1924. (Onslows) $82 £55

A spelter smoker's compendium modelled as a sports roadster, 9in. long. (Christie's) $441 £300

'Cinq Chevaux', a Lalique car mascot moulded in clear glass, etched France No. 1122, 11.5cm. high. (Christie's) $3,445 £2,376

'Levrier', a Lalique car mascot, clear and satin finished glass moulded in intaglio with a racing greyhound, 7.5cm. high. (Christie's) $406 £280

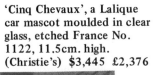

A brass nymph holding a torch in front with leg raised and trailing scarf, 5¾in. high. (Christie's) $74 £60

Official Programme for the 200 Miles Race, October 1927 and the Brooklands Lagonda 2nd Annual Fete Programme, 1928. (Onslows) $84 £56

'Grenouille', a Lalique car mascot in clear and satin finished glass moulded as a seated frog, 6.3cm. high. (Christie's) $5,011 £3,456

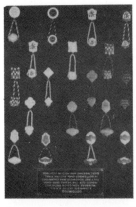

Part of a collection of 62 members' badges and guest brooches, in mahogany display case. (Onslows) $4,800 £3,200

A chromium plated stylised eagle perched on a globe, inscribed 'C. Brau', 8½in. high. (Christie's) $73 £50

Five Brooklands Official Race Cards and Programmes for 1938 and 1939. (Onslows) $48 £32

A nickel plated Milegal 'Meter', 4¼in. diam. (Onslows) $75 £50

A chromium plated Boa-Constrictor horn with mounting brackets and extension, 45in. long. (Christie's) $80 £55

A chromium plated stylised cat, stamped Nikolsky No. 14, 6in. long. (Christie's) $117 £95

A brass bust of Minerva, stamped, 6in. high, on circular plinth.(Christie's) $173 £140

An A. T. Speedometer Co. Ltd. Bentley 6½ or 8 litre speedometer, and a rev counter. (Onslows) $300 £200

A nickel plated speed nymph clutching a scarf, by Lejeune, stamped Reg. AEL, 6in. high. (Christie's) $186 £150

One of two photographs of Leyland-Thomas No. 1 Babs, signed by Parry Thomas. (Onslows) $180 £120

A chromium plated stork, 7in. long. (Christie's) $68 £55

Harrods Ltd. Automobiles, Petrol Steam Electric Cars, Motorcycles Accessories of All Descriptions, catalogue with prices and text, circa 1903. (Onslows)$195 £130

Souvenir of the Brooklands Automobile Racing Club, July 6th 1907. (Onslows) $150 £100

A glass mascot in the form of two leaping Borzoi dogs, possibly Red Ashay, 7½in. long. (Christie's) $588 £400

A chromium plated stylised Jaguar Mascot, No. 7100911 WBB, 7½in. long, mounted on circular ashtray. (Christie's) $173 £140

A chromium plated A.A. badge inscribed 'Stenson Cooke, Secretary, No. 12162', 5½in. high. (Christie's) $66 £45

The Austin Magazine, original artwork for the Christmas Number, December 1937, signed, watercolour, 21½ x 17in. (Christie's) $161 £110

A chromium plated charging Red Indian, 6in. long. (Christie's) $74 £60

Six Brooklands Official Race Cards and Programmes for 1936. (Onslows) $69 £46

'Mother', a corning glass female head with flowing hair, 6½in. long. (Christie's) $99 £80

Motor Sport, Vol. 5 no. 1, October-November 1928. (Onslows) $210 £140

A 19th century Swiss musical box, the movement playing twelve airs, striking on six bells and a drum, 25½in. long. (Woolley & Wallis) $1,315 £960

A Gramophone & Typewriter Ltd. New Style No. 3 gramophone, with 7in. turntable and concert soundbox, circa 1904. (Onslows) $834 £560

A Columbia type BS coin-operated graphophone with floating reproducer and glazed oak case. (Christie's) $1,224 £850

A Spanish 32-note miniature barrel piano with castanet and triangle, playing six tunes, 24in. wide, on wood handcart. (Christie's) $554 £420

An Edison Diamond disc phonograph in walnut case of Louis XV design, 50in. high, and 46 Edison discs. (Christie's) $1,188 £900

A Gramophone & Typewriter Ltd. single-spring Monarch, with Kayophone soundbox and original Morning Glory horn. (Onslows) $447 £300

A fairground organ with 58-note paper roll reed-organ action, in covered trolley, 100in. wide, with 63 Angelus/Symphony rolls. (Christie's) $2,376 £1,800

An Edison Fireside combination type phonograph, Model B No. 89443, with four minute gearing. (Onslows) $700 £470

A buffet style musical box playing eight airs accompanied by drum and six bells with tune indicator, 28in. wide. (Christie's) $2,160 £1,500

A harp mandolin musical box playing 16 airs (2 per turn), by J. H. Heller, Bern, No. 4534, with zither attachment, 28½in. wide. (Christie's) $1,984 £1,600

An Edison Standard phonograph, Model C No. 660275, with combination gear and Bettini reproducer. (Onslows) $357 £240

Late 19th century singing bird music box, Switzerland, with bird-shaped key, 4in. wide. (Robt. W. Skinner Inc.) $2,220 £1,500

An Edison Red Gem phonograph, Model D No. 316478D, with K combination reproducer, maroon fireside octagonal horn and crane. (Onslows) $491 £330

A 19th century square section bird cage of wire and turned wood, the base containing a musical box, 17in. high. (Peter Wilson & Co.) $201 £140

A Decca Dulcephone horn gramophone with fine tin flower horn. (Onslows) $268 £180

A Viel-O-Phone horn gramophone, with light oak case applied with company transfer, and fluted brass horn. (Onslows) $447 £300

A 26-key barrel organ by Willm. Hubt. Van Kamp, Holborn, with two eleven-air barrels and four pipe ranks with stops, 89in. high. (Christie's) $1,860 £1,500

An HMV horn gramophone, the square oak base with 10in. diam. turntable, with plywood horn, 17½in. diam, circa 1920. (Lawrence Fine Art) $503 £340

A changeable cylinder overture box by Nicole Freres, with five cylinders each playing four tunes, 38in. wide. (Christie's)
$5,760 £4,000

An early Kammer & Reinhardt Berliner gramophone with gilt-lined japanned cast iron base. (Christie's)
$691 £480

A gilt metal and enamel singing bird box, decorated with Watteauesque scenes. (Christie's) $990 £750

An 11.7/8in. Symphonion disc musical box with twin comb movement in rococo simulated case, with 15 discs. (Christie's)
$1,364 £1,100

An oak HMV Monarch gramophone, 1911 model, with double-spring motor and fluted oak horn. (Christie's)
$691 £480

A 15.5/8in. Polyphon in panelled walnut case with double combs and forty-seven discs in circular wood box. (Christie's)
$2,304 £1,600

A portable street reed barrel organ by Chiappa, playing seven tunes, on thirty-one notes, 22in. wide. (Christie's) $4,032 £2,800

A 15-key chamber barrel organ by H. Bryceson, 38 Long Acre, in mahogany case, 59¾in. high. (Christie's)
$1,612 £1,300

A musical box playing 12 sacredains accompanied by 9 bells with bee strikers, 31in. wide. (Christie's)
$2,108 £1,700

Late 19th century French key-wind singing bird automaton, 4in. wide. (Reeds Rains) $604 £420

A lever wind musical box, by Nicole Freres, No. 51725, playing 4 overtures, with tune sheet and rose-wood veneered case, 27½in. wide. (Christie's) $3,300 £2,500

An HMV Model 29 horn gramophone with single-spring motor in oak case, the horn 18½in. diam., circa 1928. (Christie's) $259 £180

A 14in. Stella disc musical box with twin-comb move-ment in walnut case with disc storage drawer, and 13 discs. (Christie's) $1,736 £1,400

A 19.1/8in. upright Symphonion disc musical box with 'Sublime Harmony' combs, and six discs. (Christie's) $2,448 £1,700

A horn gramophone with mahogany case of HMV Model 7 design, double spring motor and brass flower horn. (Christie's) $547 £380

A horn gramophone with oak case, Big Ben No. 1 sound-box and blue flower horn of early Morning Glory pattern. (Christie's) $259 £180

A 19th century German Symphonion having walnut case inlaid with ivory, 11 x 13in., also a collection of eight discs. (Peter Wilson & Co.) $561 £390

An HMV Junior Monarch oak horn gramophone with panelled oak case, soundbox replaced. (Christie's) $744 £600

An Italian violin,
by Joseph Rocca,
1850, length of
back 13.15/16in.,
in oak case.
(Christie's)
$40,154 £28,080

A violin by Ernest
L. Holder, dated
1913, length of
back 14in.
(Phillips)
$2,072 £1,400

An English violin,
by Arthur Richard-
son, 1928, length
of back 13.15/16in.,
with bow. (Chris-
tie's)
$2,007 £1,404

A French violin by
Jean-Baptiste
Vuillaume, length
of back 14½in., in
case. (Christie's)
$15,876 £10,800

An English violin, by
Lockey Hill, length
of back 13.7/8in.,
in case. (Christie's)
$5,556 £3,780

Early 20th century
violoncello, length
of back 30in., with
two bows. (Reeds
Rains) $518 £360

An Italian violin by
Giulio & Eugenio
Degani, the length
of back 14in., in
case with two bows.
(Christie's)
$6,123 £4,536

An Italian violin by
Eugenio Degani,
1896, the length of
back 14.1/8in.
(Christie's)
$6,123 £4,536

A violin by Vincenzo Carcassi, Florence, dated 1763, length of back 13.7/8in. (Phillips)
$13,320 £9,000

An Italian violin by Ferdinando Gagliano, length of back 13.7/8in. (Christie's)
$23,133 £15,120

A French violin, by Joseph Hel, 1878, length of back 14.3/16in., in case. (Christie's)
$4,533 £3,240

An Italian violin by Joseph Rocca, length of back 14in., in case with bow. (Christie's)
$38,102 £25,920

An Italian violin by Nicola Gagliano, 1761, the length of back 14in., in case. (Christie's)
$13,122 £9,720

A French violin by Jean-Baptiste Vuillaume, length of back 14.1/16in. (Christie's)
$28,576 £19,440

A violin by Richard Duke, London, circa 1770, length of back 14in., with a bow in shaped case. (Phillips)
$3,700 £2,500

A French violin by Caressa & Francais, 1903, the length of back 14.1/16in., in case with two bows. (Christie's)
$3,645 £2,700

An Italian violin by R. Antoniazzi, 1910, the length of back 13.14/16in., in double violin case with two silver mounted bows. (Christie's) $4,374 £3,240

An Italian violin, by H. Fagnola, 1893, length of back 14.3/16in., in case. (Christie's) $13,899 £9,720

An Italian violoncello by Romeo Antoniazzi, 1910, length of back 29. 13/16in., in case with bow. (Christie's) $14,580 £10,800

An Italian viola labelled Antoniazzi Romeo Cremonese/ fece a Cremona l'anno 1910, length of back 15.11/16in. (Christie's) $6,998 £5,184

An Italian violin, by G. Gagliano, 1765, length of back 13.15/16in., in case. (Christie's) $30,888 £21,600

An Italian violin by A. Orlandini, 1976, the length of back 14.1/16in., in case with bow.(Christie's) $1,458 £1,080

A French viola, labelled Bennettini Milano 1881, length of back 15¾in. (Christie's) $2,625 £1,836

A violin ascribed to Bernard Calcanus, 1749, the length of back 14in., in case. (Christie's) $6,561 £4,860

A violin, possibly
Neapolitan School,
length of back 14.
3/16in., in case.
(Christie's)
$2,625 £1,836

A French violin by
Jean-Baptiste Vuil-
laume, the length
of back 14in., in
case. (Christie's)
$18,954 £14,040

A French viola by
Justin Derazey,
the length of back 16.
1/16in., in case.
(Christie's)
$3,790 £2,808

An Italian violin by
R. Antoniazzi, 1910,
the length of back
14in. (Christie's)
$4,665 £3,456

An Italian violin,
labelled Leandro
Bisiach, Milano
1895, length of
back 14.1/16in.,
in case. (Christie's)
$9,266 £6,480

A violin ascribed
to Giovanni Gaida,
length of back
13.15/16in., in
case. (Christie's)
$4,015 £2,808

An English violin,
by John Lott,
length of back
14in., in case.
(Christie's)
$23,166 £16,200

An English violin,
by Wm. Atkinson,
1905, length of
back 14in. (Chris-
tie's)
$1,158 £870

Late 18th/early 19th century
ivory netsuke of a crouching
wolf, inscribed Rantei.
(Christie's) $734 £540

Mid 19th century boxwood
netsuke of Ono No Komachi,
unsigned. (Christie's)
                $704 £518

Late 19th century inlaid
wood and ivory netsuke
formed as Daikoku's hammer
of wealth, signed Meikei.
(Christie's) $1,101 £810

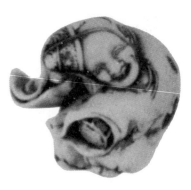

A 19th century stag-antler
style manju netsuke of
Raiden, signed with the seal
of Hoshunsai Masayuki.
(Christie's) $1,468 £1,080

Late 18th century ivory
netsuke of a stylised goose
preening, unsigned.
(Christie's) $1,175 £864

A 19th century ivory net-
suke of a Manzai dancer,
signed Sekiran. (Christie's)
                $587 £432

An ivory netsuke of a seated
tiger looking down his long
tail, unsigned, Kyoto School,
circa 1800. (Christie's)
                $527 £388

Late 18th century stained
ivory seal-type netsuke of
a kirin, unsigned.(Christie's)
                $440 £324

A 19th century ivory netsuke
of three karako playing beside a tsuitate, unsigned.
(Christie's) $322 £237

Late 19th century ivory net-suke of a group of seven rats entwined, signed Tomo-chika. (Christie's)
$954 £702

A late 19th century ivory netsuke of a coiled snake, inscribed Toshitsugu. (Christie's) $616 £453

An ivory netsuke of a recum-bent cat with inlaid ebony eye pupils, unsigned. (Christie's) $881 £648

Early 19th century wood netsuke of a rat, eyes inset in translucent horn. (Christie's) $1,028 £756

A 19th century ivory net-suke of a tańuki, signed Kog-yokusai. (Christie's)
$704 £518

Early 19th century stained wood netsuke of a snail, signed Shigemasa. (Christie's)
$1,909 £1,404

A carved ivory netsuke of two playful Karashishi, signed Shoko, 18th cen-tury, with an ivory ojime signed Naokazu.(Christie's)
$1,762 £1,296

A 19th century ivory net-suke of a monkey, his young perched on his head, unsigned. (Christie's) $514 £378

Mid 19th century stained ivory netsuke of the Sambo Kojin, signed Ono Ryomin, Edo School. (Christie's)
$881 £648

Late 18th century ivory
netsuke of a dragon coiled
around a wave-beaten rock,
unsigned. (Christie's)
$881 £648

A 19th century ivory netsuke
of a Temple horse being
groomed, signed Kigyoku,
Edo School. (Christie's)
$660 £486

Early 19th century ivory
netsuke of a green frog
sitting on an awabi shell,
unsigned. (Christie's)
$499 £367

Early 19th century well-
carved boxwood netsuke of
a snail, signed Shigemasa.
(Christie's) $1,909 £1,404

A 19th century boxwood
netsuke of a monkey, un-
signed. (Christie's)
$395 £291

Early 19th century ivory
netsuke of Hotei holding an
uchiwa, inscribed Okakoto.
(Christie's) $233 £172

Early 19th century ivory
netsuke of Kanzan and
Jittoku reading a makimono,
unsigned. (Christie's)
$514 £378

Early 20th century stained
ivory netsuke of a partly
open chestnut, signed Yazan.
(Christie's) $660 £486

An 18th century ivory netsuke of a Chinese sage,
signed Yoshitomo (Boku-
saisai), Kyoto School.
(Christie's) $1,762 £1,296

Late 18th century wood netsuke carved as a group of five clam shells, signed Sari, Iwashiro School. (Christie's) $734 £540

A 19th century wood netsuke of a cicada on half a walnut, unsigned. (Christie's) $527 £388

A 19th century ivory netsuke of a dove on a group of three lotus leaves, the eyes inset in dark horn. (Christie's) $674 £496

A 19th century ivory netsuke of a large rat gnawing at a sheaf of millet, inscribed Okatomo. (Christie's) $1,028 £756

A 19th century ivory netsuke of a cicada, signed Masatsugu. (Christie's) $5,875 £4,320

Late 19th century ivory netsuke of a monkey and her two young, signed Masatami (Shomin), Yamada School. (Christie's) $1,395 £1,026

Late 19th century boxwood okimono-style netsuke of the Sennin Shiyei, signed Kogyoku (Anrakusai). (Christie's) $660 £486

A 19th century wood and ivory manju-type netsuke in the form of a gourd, signed Yamahiko. (Christie's) $514 £378

An ivory netsuke of Nitta No Shiro Tadatsune about to stab the boar, inscribed Masakazu. (Christie's) $1,028 £756

A wood and ivory netsuke of a kneeling fox priest, signed Kaigyokusai. (Christie's) $4,324 £3,024

An ivory netsuke of a catfish, inscribed Masanao, probably Meiji-Taisho period. (Christie's) $1,111 £777

Early 19th century carved kurogaki netsuke of a squatting toad, signed Yoshitada(?), Echigo School. (Christie's) $617 £432

A 19th century marine ivory netsuke of a seated puppy playing with an awabi shell, unsigned. (Christie's) $261 £183

Late 19th century ebony and ivory netsuke of a standing karako, unsigned. (Christie's) $849 £594

Late 19th century ivory okimono style netsuke of two seated Manzai dancers, signed Fujiyuki. (Christie's) $308 £216

Late 19th century lacquered netsuke of a monkey dressed as a Sambaso dancer, unsigned. (Christie's) $540 £378

A 19th century boxwood netsuke of a dragon coiled inside a pumpkin, style of Toyomasa, Tamba School. (Christie's) $400 £280

Late 19th century ivory netsuke of Daikoku, signed Masatamo. (Christie's) $308 £216

A 19th century ivory net-
suke of a shrimp, unsigned.
(Christie's) $1,698 £1,188

Mid 19th century ivory netsuke of a tigress seated with
her cubs, signed Hakuryu,
Kyoto School. (Christie's)
$2,625 £1,836

A 19th century pale boxwood
netsuke of a cicada, signed
Issai. (Christie's) $1,028 £756

A late 18th century wood
netsuke of a seated tigress
licking her cub, signed Kokei,
Tsu School. (Christie's)
$1,248 £918

A marine ivory netsuke of a
faceless female ghost rising
from her grave, unsigned,
circa 1800, 10cm. high.
(Christie's) $4,406 £3,240

Mid 19th century circular
ivory manju netsuke carved
in shishiaibori, signed Ono
Ryomin. (Christie's)
$849 £594

Late 19th century ivory
okimono-style netsuke of a
monkey, signed Masatami
(Shomin), Yamada School.
(Christie's) $734 £540

A 19th century okimono
style ivory netsuke of the
Annamese tribute elephant,
signed Shibayama. (Chris-
tie's) $1,389 £972

Late 19th century ivory
netsuke of Ebisu, signed
Eishin. (Christie's)
$386 £270

Mid 19th century ivory netsuke of a karako stooping to lift Hotei's tasselled bag, signed Komin, and kao. (Christie's) $308 £216

An ivory netsuke modelled as a flatfish, signed Hodo, probably Neiji-Taisho period. (Christie's) $647 £453

Late 18th century ivory netsuke of a karashishi lying down, unsigned. (Christie's) $694 £486

An ivory netsuke of a maddened bull about to charge, unsigned, probably Taisho-Showa period. (Christie's) $617 £432

An early/mid 19th century well-carved ivory netsuke of a Chinese festival boat, signed Ryukosai. (Christie's) $386 £270

An ivory netsuke of a seated ape munching a persimmon (kaki), signed Kaiguoku. (Christie's) $15,444 £10,800

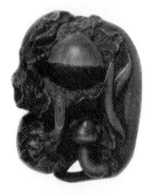

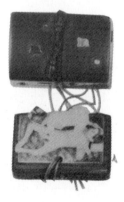

A 19th century well carved boxwood netsuke of a group of vegetables and fruits, signed Shuji. (Christie's) $849 £594

Late 19th century ivory manju netsuke decorated in Shibayama style, signed Nobuyuki. (Christie's) $463 £324

Late 19th century pale boxwood netsuke of a chest tied with a tasselled rope, signed Tomoyuki. (Christie's) $1,028 £756

A 20th century boxwood netsuke of the 'Miraculous Tea Kettle' Legend, unsigned. (Christie's) $734 £540

Late 18th/early 19th century wood netsuke of The Great Wanderer Saigyo Hoshi contemplating Mount Fuji. (Christie's) $514 £378

Early 19th century ivory netsuke of a quail on a sheaf of millet, inscribed Okatomo, Kyoto School. (Christie's) $1,028 £756

An early/mid 19th century ivory netsuke of a professional sneezer, signed Ryuko, and kao. (Christie's) $679 £475

Early 19th century ivory netsuke of a sumo wrestler, unsigned. (Christie's) $2,162 £1,512

A 19th century stained boxwood netsuke of the Bodhidharma, signed Minko, (probably Juntoku). (Christie's) $1,544 £1,080

Late 19th century ivory okimono style netsuke of a group of five terrapins, signed Chuichi. (Christie's) $617 £432

A 19th century dark wood manju netsuke decorated in Shibayama style, unsigned. (Christie's) $431 £302

Early 19th century ivory netsuke of a monkey cradling one of its young, unsigned. (Christie's) $540 £378

Bahamas: 1937 4/-, plus Bermuda 1937 5/- and 1957 5/-. (Phillips) $75 £50

Cyprus: 1955-57 Queen Elizabeth II set of 250 mils—£5. (Phillips) $255 £170

Lincoln & Lindsey Banking Co: £5 proof on card, plus a letter dated 1839, instructing Perkins, Bacon & Petch to print and deliver 4,000 £5 notes. (Phillips) $56 £40

C. P. Mahon: Bank of England £5, 10 October 1925 issued at Leeds. (Phillips) $138 £92

South Africa: 1864 Durban Bank £25. (Phillips) $184 £130

1927 50 tomans Pick Plate Note, some pieces missing top edge. (Phillips) $568 £400

Ireland, Northern Bank: £5 proof on paper 1850, plus Ulster Bank £5 1942 and 1943. (Phillips) $93 £62

Provincial Bank: £1 and £3 1881 plus £1 1882, all proofs on paper with signature area cut out. (Phillips) $191 £135

Costa Rica: 1928 Banco Internacional 2 colones plus 1925 10 colones. (Phillips) $150 £100

Bolivia: 1911 El Banco Mercantil 10 bolivares. (Phillips) $90 £60

New Zealand: 1916 Bank of Australasia £1 issued at Wellington. (Phillips) $300 £200

Newmarket Bank: £5 1899, overstamped 'Cancelled' twice. (Phillips) $56 £40

Russia: 1819 10 roubles State Assignat. (Phillips) $71 £50

National Bank: £1 Specimen 1870. (Phillips) $149 £105

Argentina: 1880 Banco Otero & Ca. 20 pesos proof, engraved by Bradbury Wilkinson. (Phillips) $130 £92

Bury & Suffolk Bank: (Oakes, Bevan & Co.), £5 un-issued. (Phillips) $67 £45

Mid 19th century pewter flagon, the cast handle with heart-shaped end drop, base marked James Dixon, 13in. high. (Robt. W. Skinner Inc.) $350 £246

A pyriform teapot, by Thos. Danforth, Conn., 1805-50, marked on bottom, 7in. high. (Christie's) $935 £658

A pewter porringer, by Samuel or Samuel E. Harbeson, Providence R.I., circa 1780-1820, marked on handle with Laughlin touch 337, 4in. diam. (Christie's) $605 £426

One of two pewter beakers, by James Weekes, New York City, 1820-35, 3.1/8in. high. (Christie's) $308 £216

A Kayersinn pewter jardiniere, stamped Kayersinn 4093, 29.8cm. high. (Christie's) $375 £250

A Liberty pewter and enamel clock, designed by A. Knox, stamped 0608 Rd, 426015, 14cm. high. (Christie's) $1,446 £1,026

A pewter porringer, by Wm. Billings, Providence R.I., circa 1791-1806, marked on handle with Laughlin touch 346, 4.1/8in. diam. (Christie's) $330 £232

A WMF rectangular shaped pewter mirror, 14in. high, stamped marks. (Christie's) $691 £480

A pewter covered flagon, the flat lid with ball finial and cast C-scroll handle, 9½in. high. (Robt. W. Skinner Inc.) $300 £211

PEWTER

Early 19th century unmarked pewter porringer, with Rhode Ialand flowered handle. (Robt. W. Skinner Inc.) $200 £140

A teapot, the domed lid with finial, by Morey & Ober, Boston, 1852-55, 7½in. high. (Christie's) $275 £193

One of a pair of late 18th/ early 19th century, German, pewter flagons, 17¼in. high. (Christie's) $440 £309

A water pitcher, by Roswell Gleason, circa 1830, 11½in. high, together with a coffee pot and a water cooler. (Christie's) $418 £305

A WMF silvered pewter jardiniere cast as a conch shell with a salamander, 32cm. high. (Christie's) $702 £486

A lighthouse shaped flagon, by Thos. D. Boardman, marked with eagle touch, name touch and Hartford touch on base, 13¼in. high. (Christie's) $1,870 £1,316

A Liberty pewter and Clutha glass bowl on stand, designed by Archibald Knox, stamped Tudric 0276, circa 1900, 16.3cm. high. (Christie's) $656 £453

A 17th century pewter charger with reeded rim, 22in. diam. (Woolley & Wallis) $1,957 £1,350

A pewter tankard, by Henry Will, New York, marked on inside with Laughlin touch 491, 7.1/8in. high. (Christie's) $3,300 £2,323

An apple-shaped teapot, by Roswell Gleason, Mass., 1821-71, 7½in. high. (Christie's) $176 £123

A Liberty pewter and green glass bowl, designed by A. Knox, stamped Tudric 0320 Rd, 426933, 20.3cm. diam. (Christie's) $532 £378

A pewter bedpan, by Thos. D. and S. Boardman, Hartford, 1810-50, initial touch struck once on base, 17½in. long, overall. (Christie's)$385 £271

A 19th century pewter leech jar, the pierced lid with carrying handle, 7in. high. (Christie's) $382 £260

A Jugendstil polished pewter triptych mirror in the style of P. Huber, 32.2 x 53.4cm. (Christie's) $626 £432

A covered pitcher, by Boardman, Boardman & Hart, 1828-53, marked on bottom, 7¾in. high. (Christie's) $660 £464

One of two similar Italian, late 18th/early 19th century, pewter flagons, 14¼in. high. (Christie's) $528 £371

A pair of pewter fluid lamps, by James H. Puttnam, Mass., 1830-55, 7¾in. high. (Christie's) $660 £464

A tankard with a domed lid and scrolling thumbpiece, late 18th/early 19th century, unmarked, 6¼in. high. (Christie's) $1,540 £1,084

PEWTER

A pewter covered Church tankard of lighthouse shape with C-scroll handle, circa 1766. (Robt. W. Skinner Inc.) $550 £387

A pyriform teapot, by Wm. Calder, Providence R.I., 1817-56, marked on base, 7in. high. (Christie's) $2,640 £1,859

A pewter porringer, by J. Danforth, Jnr., Virginia, circa 1807-1812, 5in. diam. (Christie's) $1,760 £1,239

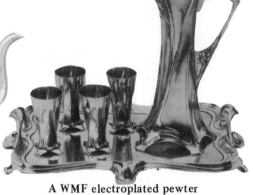

A lighthouse coffee pot, by Israel Trask, Mass., circa 1813-56, marked on base, 10½in. high. (Christie's) $605 £426

A WMF electroplated pewter drinking set with shaped rectangular tray, circa 1900, tray 48 x 34cm. (Christie's) $946 £648

One of a pair of mid 19th century pewter lanterns. (Robt. W. Skinner Inc.) $500 £352

An electroplated pewter mirror frame attributed to WMF, circa 1900, 50cm. high. (Christie's) $630 £432

A pair of early 19th century English pewter candlesticks, 9in. high. (Christie's) $75 £50

A tapering, cylindrical cann, by Robt. Palethorp, Phila., 1817-22, marked inside, 4.1/8in. high. (Christie's) $1,980 £1,394

Eight mammoth albumen prints of the classical architecture of Rome, 16 x 12½in. to 21in., early 1860's, photographer unknown. (Christie's) $691 £480

Royal Engineers album of 84 photographs , comprising ten salt prints, the remainder albumen, 1862-64. (Christie's)
                                                 $1,584 £1,100

A whole plate cased daguerreotype of a riverside mansion, the oval mat stamped 'Electrotypo', 'Fredricks e Weeks', 1850's. (Phillips)
                                 $4,116 £2,800

Still-life with game, stereoscopic daguerreotype, paper label in image reading 'Mr T. R. Williams, 35 West Square, Lambeth', paper cased, 1850's. (Christie's) $547 £380

Ten waxed paper negatives, five 10¼ x 12in., five 7 x 9in., by William Robert Baker, early 1850's. (Christie's) $1,152 £800

'Princess Alice, 1854', by Roger Fenton, albumen print, 5 x 6¾in. (Christie's)
                                               $562 £420

A half plate cased daguerreotype of riverside houses, the oval mat stamped 'Electrotypo', 'Fredricks e Weeks', 1850's. (Phillips)
                                 $4,410 £3,000

A leather bound album, embossed 'Jerusalem, 1865' and titled on flyleaf 'Ordnance Survey of Jerusalem . . . by Capt. Charles W. Wilson, R.E. . . . 1865'. (Phillips) $2,499 £1,700

'Camera Work', Nos. XXIV and XL, original wrappers, 4to., New York: Alfred Stieglitz, October 1908 and October 1912. (Christie's) $1,170 £900

A half plate part cased daguerreotype of a riverside mansion, 1850's. (Phillips) $1,323 £900

A gelatin silver print of 'Mary, Santa Marta', by D. Lyon, ref. no. '11/78/2' on reverse, 8½ x 12½in. (Christie's) $80 £60

Standing female nude, stereoscopic daguerreotype, gilt painted passe-partout, paper cased, re-bound, 1850's. (Christie's) $864 £600

Album of 79 albumen prints and one two-print panorama, of Ceylon, Burma and Singapore, by W. L. H. Skeen & Co., Scowen and others. (Christie's) $936 £650

Northern British Locomotive Co. Ltd., approx. 120 gelatin silver prints, from 4½ x 6in. to 10 x 15in., majority 1900-20, all captioned and documented on the reverse. (Christie's) $234 £180

A whole plate cased daguerreotype of a harbour, the oval mat stamped 'Electrotype', 'Fredricks e Weeks', 1850's. (Phillips) $6,615 £4,500

An 1850's scrap album, including twelve salt prints from paper negatives, various sizes up to 23 x 19cm. (Phillips) $235 £160

PHOTOGRAPHS

An albumen print of a man and woman, mounted on paper, 1870's or early '80's, 5¾ x 4¼in. (Christie's) $33 £25

An albumen print of two men, mounted on paper, 1870's or early '80's, 5¾ x 4¼in. (Christie's) $113 £85

Profile portrait of a young woman, albumen print, by O. G. Rejlander, circa 1860, 7¼ x 5¾in. (Christie's) $134 £100

An albumen print of a young woman in studio setting, 5¾ x 4¼in., 1870's or early '80's. (Christie's) $87 £65

A gelatin silver print of 'Peruvian Women', by Robt. Frank, 13½ x 11in. (Christie's) $241 £180

A gelatin silver print of Cecil Beaton, by E. Blumenfeld, 1940's, 13 x 10in. (Christie's) $643 £480

'Cathedral de Mollins', albumen print, by Chas. Marville, 1860's, 14 x 9¾in. (Christie's) $536 £400

'Princess Royal & Prince Arthur as Summer', by Roger Fenton, albumen print, 1854, 6 x 6¼in. (Christie's) $348 £260

Cathedrale de Mayence, facade sud-est', Blanquart-Evrard salt print, by Chas. Marville, early 1850's, 13½ x 10in. (Christie's) $938 £700

A gelatin silver print of 'London, Two Gentlemen', by Robert Frank, 9½ x 6¼in. (Christie's) $402 £300

Palais du Louvre and Palais des Tuilleries, four albumen prints, approx. 10¼ x 13¼in., 1850's or early 1860's. (Christie's) $214 £160

An autotype print of Chas. Hay Cameron, by Julia Margt. Cameron, 1869, 12½ x 9¾in. (Christie's) $402 £300

An album of 168 albumen prints of India and Ceylon, by Bourne, Shepherd and Bourne & Shepherd, 1890's, 9 x 11in. (Christie's) $1,072 £800

A gelatin silver print of 'NYC 1949', by Robert F. Frank, signed in ink in margin, 1949, 10½ x 14in. (Christie's) $737 £550

An albumen print of Nguni-speaking women, 5¾ x 4¼in., mounted on paper, 1870's or early '80's. (Christie's) $201 £150

A collection of 53 waxed paper negatives, 29 approx. 13 x 9in., the others 7½ x 9in., by G. Shepherd, 1853 and 1854. (Christie's) $1,340 £1,000

A gelatin silver print of 'Mohandas Gandhi', by Margt. Bourke-White, 13½ x 10¼in. (Christie's) $562 £420

A glossy gelatin silver print of 'Carnival Girls', by Robt. Doisneau, 12 x 9½in. (Christie's) $134 £100

PHOTOGRAPHS

Portfolio, 'Idylls of the Norfolk Broads', by Peter Henry Emerson, cover design by T. F. Goodall, oblong folio, London, 1886. (Christie's) $1,820 £1,400

A glossy gelatin silver print of Backstage Ballet Girls by Gotthard Schuh, 1950's, 11½ x 9½in. (Christie's)
$67 £50

Spring Morning, Busbridge, by Henry Taylor, salt print, 8¼ x 6½in. (Christie's)
$241 £180

An albumen print of Julia Jackson, by Julia Margt. Cameron, 1860's, 10¼ x 8¾in. (Christie's) $402 £300

Prince Albert, albumen print, mounted on card, 6¾ x 6in., 1854, by Roger Fenton. (Christie's)
$804 £600

A gelatin silver print of 'A New Way to Look at the Statue of Liberty', by Margt. Bourke-White, 13½ x 10½in. (Christie's) $402 £300

'Illustrations to Tennyson's Idylls of the King, and other poems', by Julia Margaret Cameron, publ. Henry S. King & Co., London, 1875.(Phillips) $3,234 £2,200

A Scottish Pictorial album of 69 photographs and six loose prints, platinum and gelatin silver prints, early 1900's to 1920's. (Christie's) $172 £120

'The Hairy Family of Mandalay', albumen print, 8½ x 7.1/8in., mounted on card, 1860/70, photographer unknown. (Christie's) $338 £260

PHOTOGRAPHS

Three cased quarter plate daguerreotype of two brothers, with a cased plate ambrotype of one brother alone. (Phillips) $352 £240

A gelatin silver print of Marilyn Monroe, by Cecil Beaton, 1940's, image size 7¼ x 7¼in. (Christie's) $174 £130

An albumen print of Chas. Darwin, by Julia Margt. Cameron, 1868, 12½ x 10½in. (Christie's)$113 £85

A half calf gilt album, 'Photographs from Abyssinia', with printed list of contents. (Phillips) $882 £600

A gelatin silver print of 'Cyril Ray in Islington', titled in ink on the reverse, by Bill Brandt, 9 x 7.5/8in. (Christie's) $294 £220

A 4¼ x 5¾in. daguerreotype with rounded top, of three little sisters in matching dresses, the front of the case embossed 'Prof. Highschool Daguerreotype Institution, 433 West Strand'. (Phillips) $191 £130

A gelatin silver print of Ava Gardner, by Man Ray, 13¾ x 10¾in., signed and dated in pencil on image, 1950. (Christie's) $720 £500

A gelatin silver print of an 'East End Girl, Dancing The Lambeth Walk', dated in ink on the reverse 1939, by Bill Brandt. (Christie's) $670 £500

Portrait album of 48 albumen prints, approx. 7½ x 6in. to 13½ x 10½in., by R. T. Crawshay, 1870's. (Christie's) $1,728 £1,200

A Federal mahogany pianoforte, label G. Gilfert, N.Y., circa 1805, 63in. long. (Robt. W. Skinner Inc.) $3,400 £2,361

An English spinet by Baker Harris, 1766, in a mahogany case, on a stand of Virginia walnut, 74in. wide. (Christie's) $19,828 £12,960

A 4ft. overstrung baby grand piano with steel frame and mahogany case, by A. Ramsden, Leeds. (Peter Wilson & Co.) $1,656 £1,150

An upright grand pianoforte, iron framed, overstrung and underdamped movement, by R. Gors & Kallmann. (Capes, Dunn & Co.) $1,008 £700

An English spinet by Thos. Hitchcock, in a case of Virginia walnut, on a later oak stand, circa 1725, 74in. wide. (Christie's) $8,019 £5,940

A marquetry boudoir grand piano by Steinway & Sons, the case by C. Mellier & Co., 57 x 86in. (Christie's) $11,502 £8,100

PIANOS

A classical mahogany pianoforte, labelled by P. & W. Geib, 68in. wide. (Christie's) $2,200 £1,527

An Eavestaff Art Deco mahogany and satinwood baby grand piano, inlaid metal inscription Healy, circa 1930, 151.2cm. wide. (Christie's) $3,468 £2,376

A concert grand pianoforte, by C. Bechstein, the rosewood case with square section trestle type supports, 8ft. x 5ft.2in. (Parsons, Welch & Cowell) $2,625 £1,750

A pianoforte by Wm. Southwell of Dublin, in the form of a semi-elliptical side table, 32½in. high, circa 1785. (Christie's) $34,992 £25,920

A classical carved mahogany pianoforte, by James L. Hewitt & Co., Boston, 1820-30, 67in. wide. (Christie's) $1,650 £1,145

An overstrung grand pianoforte, seven and a quarter octaves, by T. H. Steinway, no. 10625, in a painted satinwood case, 65in. wide. (Christie's) $13,500 £9,000

A gentleman facing right in black coat and waistcoat, by Alexander Gallaway, oval, 3in. high. (Christie's) $652 £453

A gentleman facing right in powder-blue coat, by Gervase Spencer, enamel, signed with initials and dated 1753, oval, 1½in. high. (Christie's) $1,010 £702

Edward Salmond in blue coat, by William Bone, signed on the reverse and dated 1821, oval, 3.1/8in. high. (Christie's) $466 £324

A gentleman full face in green coat, by Charles A. Claude Berny d'Ouville, signed, oval, 3in. high. (Christie's) $466 £324

A gentleman full face in black coat and waistcoat, by T. or J. Wheeler, locks of hair reverse, oval, 1½in. high. (Christie's) $201 £140

The Revolutionary Chaumette full face in grey coat, by Claude Alexandre Belin, oval, 2½in. high. (Christie's) $544 £378

A gentleman full face in blue coat, by Christian F. Zincke, enamel, oval 1.5/8in. high. (Christie's) $1,010 £702

A fine portrait of Mrs. Charles Edward Smith, by Richard Crosse, oval, 6.1/8in. high. (Christie's) $185 £129

The Hon. Francis Bowes Lyon as a child, by Miss Annie Dixon, oval, 4in. high. (Christie's) $1,166 £810

Abdul Mejid, Sultan of Turkey during the Crimean War, by Jean Portet, oval 1.3/8in. high. (Christie's) $434 £302

Miss Sharp facing left in blue dress, by Samuel Shelley, oval, 1¾in. high. (Christie's)
$933 £648

A gentleman facing left in blue coat, by Charles Shirreff, oval, 1¾in. high. (Christie's)
$1,010 £702

Captain Sir J. Wheate, R.N., by John Ramage, plaited hair reverse, oval, 1½in. high. (Christie's) $1,244 £864

A gentleman facing left in blue coat, by Thos. Hazle-hurst, oval 1.3/8in. high. (Christie's) $434 £302

Lieutenant Charles Howard, by Sir Wm. John Newton, oval, 2½in. high.(Christie's)
$247 £172

One of two children in white shifts, by Henry Burch, oval, 1½in. high.(Christie's)
$777 £540

Mrs. Siddons in brown dress with white edges, by Samuel Shelley, signed with initials and dated 1783, oval, 3.3/8in. high. (Christie's)
$1,710 £1,188

The Countess of Rochester, by D.M., circa 1660, oval, 2½in. high. (Christie's)
$372 £259

William Pitt (the Younger), plaited hair on reverse, by Michael Keene, oval, 1½in. high. (Christie's)$652 £453

A gentleman in red coat, by Horace Hone, signed and dated 1783, oval, 2¾in. high. (Christie's)
$1,866 £1,296

A gentleman facing right, by Wm. Marshall Craig, the reverse with gold monogram HW on plaited hair, oval 2.5/8in. high. (Christie's) $699 £486

A boy full face in blue coat, by Aimee Thibault, signed, oval, 2½in. high. (Christie's) $544 £378

A child full face in white shift, English School, circa 1830, oval, 2½in. high. (Christie's) $777 £540

A gentleman in brown coat, by Gervase Spencer, enamel, signed with initials and dated 1755, oval, 1.5/8in. high. (Christie's) $777 £540

Captain Salmond in blue coat with black collar, by George Engleheart, oval, 3¼in. high. (Christie's)
$1,166 £810

A gentleman facing right in black coat, by Simon J. Rochard, oval, 1¼in. high. (Christie's) $699 £486

A gentleman facing right in black coat, by Thos. Day, signed with initials and dated 178(1), oval, 1½in. high. (Christie's) $544 £378

Napoleon III, by Jean Baptiste Fortune de Fournier, signed and dated 1857, oval, 1.5/8in. high. (Christie's) $745 £518

A miniature of a young man by Francois Ferriere, signed and dated 1800, oval, 3½in. high. (Christie's) $1,088 £756

Francois Courtier, later Madame Navarre, by Jean Marie Voille, signed and dated l'an 1e (1793), oval, 2.5/8in. high. (Christie's) $4,043 £2,808

The Hon. Mrs. Stewart facing left in white dress, by John Bogle, signed with initials and dated 1801, oval, 2½in. high. (Christie's) $1,710 £1,188

Lady Emily Hervey, by Nathaniel Hone, signed with initials and dated 1760, oval, 1½in. high. (Christie's) $1,244 £864

A gentleman facing left in blue coat, by Sampson T. Roche, signed and dated 1811, oval, 3in. high. (Christie's) $313 £218

A gentleman facing left in blue coat, by Richard Conway, oval, 3¼in. high. (Christie's) $1,944 £1,350

A fine portrait of a gentleman called George Frederick Handel (1685-1759), by Christian F. Zincke, enamel, oval, 1.5/8in. high. (Christie's) $1,710 £1,188

A girl facing left in a white dress, the reverse with locks of hair, by Andrew Plimer, oval, 3in. high. (Christie's) $1,866 £1,206

Edward Maria Lichnowsky
in grey coat, by Christian
Tangermann, signed and
dated 1812, 3¼in. high.
(Christie's) $5,594 £3,780

A lady called Princess Amelia,
by Richard Cosway, dated
1801, 3¼in. high.(Christie's)
$2,237 £1,512

A nobleman in crimson
coat and lace jabot, by
Christian F. Zincke, 1.5/8in.
high. (Christie's)
$1,118 £756

A lady facing right in decollete white dress, Circle of
Engleheart, signed with
monogram, 3in. high.
(Christie's) $719 £486

A gentleman full face in blue
coat, School of Daubigny,
3in. diam. (Christie's)
$434 £302

Maria Pavlovna, by Alois G.
Rockstuhl, after Lampi,
signed and dated 1864, 4in.
high. (Christie's)
$3,036 £2,052

Frederick V, Elector Palatine,
King of Bohemia, enamel,
by Henry Pierce Bone, 3.5/8in.
high. (Christie's) $670 £453

A lady holding a rose, by
Castor, Gonzalex Velazquez,
signed, 2¼in. diam.
(Christie's) $544 £378

Alexander, 6th Earl of Galloway, by James Reily, signed
with initials and dated 1773,
oval, 1¾in. high. (Christie's)
$341 £237

Charles II facing right in lace jabot, by David des Granges, oval, 1in. high. (Christie's) $622 £432

Christiane Lichnowsky in white dress and pink stole, by Heinrich F. Fuger, 3in. high. (Christie's) $14,385 £9,720

General Ernest Frederick Gascoigne, as a child, by Andrew Plimer, signed with initials and dated 1787, gold frame, 2.1/8in. high. (Christie's) $2,397 £1,620

A Don facing right in black gown and white bands, by Samuel Collins, oval, 1.3/8in. high. (Christie's) $155 £108

The Stolen Kiss, Circle of Claude Jean Baptiste Hoin, oval, 2¾in. high.(Christie's) $933 £648

Master James Parke, by Andrew Plimer, gold frame with split pearl border, 3in. high. (Christie's) $6,713 £4,536

A portrait miniature of a gentleman in armour, by John Hoskins, signed with initials and dated 1657, 2½in. high. (Christie's) $6,713 £4,536

Charles James Fox and Lord North, enamel, oval, 1.7/8in. high. (Christie's) $622 £432

A Lady called Elizabeth, Lady Willoughby D'Eresby, by Isaac Oliver, 2.1/8in. high. (Christie's) $6,393 £4,320

A gentleman called William Augustus, Duke of Cumberland, by Henry Spicer, oval, 1¾in. high. (Christie's) $622 £432

The Duke of Penthievre, by Joseph Boze, 2in. diam. (Christie's) $855 £594

A gentleman facing right in brown coat, by Richard Crosse, oval, 1½in. high. (Christie's) $544 £378

A boy facing right in blue coat with lace-edged collar, by Richard Cosway, oval, 1.3/8in. high. (Christie's) $434 £302

A gentleman in blue coat and white cravat, by George Engleheart, oval, 1½in. high. (Christie's) $466 £324

The Rev. Chas. Roberts in black gown, by Wm. Singleton, signed with initial and dated (17)77, oval, 1½in. high. (Christie's) $233 £162

The Hon. G. Stewart in blue coat, by Cornelius Hoyer, oval, 2¼in. high. (Christie's) $622 £432

Frederick Louis, Prince of Wales, by Christian F. Zincke, enamel, oval, 2in. high. (Christie's) $7,464 £5,184

George Stewart as a child, English School, circa 1770, oval, 1½in. high. (Christie's) $311 £216

A gentleman facing left in brown coat, by Christian F. Zincke, enamel, oval 1¾in. high. (Christie's) $901 £626

A lady and gentleman dressed as pilgrims of love, French School, circa 1720, oval, 3.1/8in. wide. (Christie's) $2,332 £1,620

The Hon. Montgomery Stewart, by Andrew Plimer, with monogram M.G.S. on plaited hair reverse, oval 3¼in. high. (Christie's) $2,177 £1,512

A lady in decollete blue dress, by Claude Lefevre, on card, oval, 1¼in. high. (Christie's) $466 £324

James Hannen full face in dark grey coat and waistcoat, by Stephen Poyntz Denning, oval, 5½in. high. (Christie's) $1,477 £1,026

Prince James Stuart, James III, 'The Old Pretender', on card, by Louise Bourdin, oval, 2.1/8in. high. (Christie's) $3,421 £2,376

James II, signed on reverse James 2nd/London, June 1845/painted by H. P. Bone/ enamel painter to Her Majesty H.R.H. Prince/Albert, after Lely, oval 1.7/8in. high. (Christie's) $434 £302

Prince Augustus Frederick, Duke of Sussex, by Joseph Lee, oval, ¾in. high. (Christie's) $279 £194

Fanny Elssler facing left in white off the shoulder dress, by Aime Zoe Lizinka de Mirbel, signed and dated 1838, oval, 3¾in. high. (Christie's) $4,665 £3,240

A lady full face in decollete,
by Christian F. Zincke,
enamel, oval, 1¾in. high.
(Christie's) $1,555 £1,080

A German nobleman in
armour, by Anton F. Konig,
rectangular, 2.1/8in. high.
(Christie's) $434 £302

Maria Leczinska in red damask
dress with lace collar, by Pierre
Pasquier, 1.7/8in. diam.
(Christie's) $1,555 £1,080

A lady facing right in white
dress with laced bodice, by
John Cox Dillman Engle-
heart, signed and dated 1814,
rectangular, 3½in. high.
(Christie's) $777 £540

The Countess of Feversham
in black dress, by Mrs. Anne
Mee, rectangular, 5.1/8in.
high. (Christie's) $466 £324

A gentleman facing right,
by Nicolas Pinet, signed and
dated 1803, rectangular,
2½in. high. (Christie's)
               $933 £648

Le Comte D'Arlay, by Louis
Marie Autissier, circa 1805,
signed, rectangular, 2½in.
high. (Christie's)
               $622 £432

A lady facing left, by Madame
Terroux, enamel, oval, 1¾in.
high. (Christie's)
               $1,010 £702

A descendant of Andrew
Hamilton, by T. Carlyle,
signed and dated 1835,
rectangular, 3½in. high.
(Christie's) $247 £172

A gentleman facing left in brown coat, by John Barry, oval, 1½in. high. (Christie's) $434 £302

Frederick the Great of Prussia in blue coat, by Anton F. Konig, rectangular, 2½in. high. (Christie's) $2,177 £1,512

Jean Baptiste Poquelin Moliere (1622-1673), actor and dramatist, by Samuel Bernard, oval, 1in. high. (Christie's) $1,166 £810

Harriet Blanche facing left in decollete, by Sir Wm. Charles Ross, hexagonal, 2in. high. (Christie's) $622 £432

One of six Asiatic Heads, rectangular, 3.5/8in. to 4½in. high. (Christie's) $2,177 £1,512

Randolph, 9th Earl of Galloway, by Sir Wm. Charles Ross, hexagonal, 1¾in. high. (Christie's) $466 £324

Jane, Duchess of Marlborough, by Sir George Hayter, rectangular, 7in. high. (Christie's) $1,477 £1,026

Queen Charlotte raising the genius of Fine Arts with Cupid by her side, by Johann Heinrich Hurter, after A. Kauffman, enamel, signed on the reverse, oval 2¼in. high. (Christie's) $933 £648

Louisa, Countess of Feversham, by Sir Wm. Charles Ross, rectangular, 3½in. high. (Christie's) $933 £648

Camp Romain, Vin Rouge, Rose, Blanc, by L. Gadoud, lithograph in colours, on wove paper, 1600 x 1200mm. (Christie's) $240 £160

Laren, Tentoonstelling 1916, Hotel Hamdorff, Zunki Joska, by Willy Sluiter, lithograph in colours, printed by Senefelder, Amsterdam, 1086 x 778mm. (Christie's) $420 £280

For Real Comfort, New Statendam, Holland-America Line, by Adolphe Mouron Cassandre, lithograph in colours, 1928, 1050 x 806mm. (Christie's) $1,500 £1,000

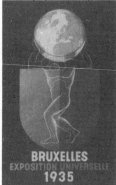

Rhum Charleston, by Leon D'Ylem, lithograph in colours, published by Vercassou, Paris, 1982 x 1275mm. (Christie's) $112 £75

Steinhardt, Unter Den Linden, by Hans Lindenstaedt, lithograph in colours, 1912, on wove paper, 710 x 945mm. (Christie's) $450 £300

Bruxelles, Exposition Universelle, 1935, by Marfurt, lithograph in colours, printed by Les Creations, Publicitaires, Bruxelles, 1000 x 620mm. (Christie's) $105 £70

Etoile Du Nord, by Adolphe Mouron Cassandre, lithograph in colours, on wove paper, 1048 x 752mm. (Christie's) $1,275 £850

Alcazar Royal, by Adolphe Crespin and Edouard Duych, lithograph in colours, 1894, 1010 x 775mm. (Christie's) $420 £280

David Hockney at the Tate Gallery, lithograph in colour, 1980, on wove paper, signed in pencil, 760 x 505mm. (Christie's) $67 £45

Pousset Spatenbrau, by Jean Carlu, lithograph in colours, on wove paper, printed by J. E. Goosens, Lille, 795 x 508mm. (Christie's) $330 £220

S. V. U. Manes, 150 Vystava, Clenska, lithograph in colours, 1929, printed by Melantrich Praha, Smichov, 1250 x 950mm. (Christie's) $180 £120

'Lenin's Push Into The Business Generation', by K. Poliarkova and R. Mozchaeva, lithograph in colours, 965 x 650mm. (Christie's) $142 £95

L'Oiseau Bleu, by Adolphe Mouron Cassandre, lithograph in colours, 1929, on wove paper, 996 x 616mm. (Christie's) $1,170 £780

Peugeot, by Rene Vincent, lithograph in colours, printed by Draeger, 1170 x 1540mm. (Christie's) $1,200 £800

Poster, 'P & O Cruises'. (Onslows) $139 £95

Opera, Bal Des Petits Lits Blancs, L'Intran, by Marie Laurencin, lithograph in colours, 1931, 1600 x 1196mm. (Christie's) $1,500 £1,000

G. Marconi, Le Maitre De La Radio, by Paul Colin, lithograph in colours, printed by Bedos & Cie, Paris, 1578 x 1130mm. (Christie's) $330 £220

Soiree De Paris, Spectacles, Choregraphiques et Dramatiques, by Marie Laurencin, lithograph in colours, signed in pencil and dated 1924, 796 x 578mm. (Christie's) $255 £170

Jane Renouardt, by Pierre Stephen, lithograph in colours, printed by M. Picard, Paris, 1538 x 1175mm. (Christie's) $150 £100

F. S. N. Van Hauteghem Freres, Liege, by Milo Martinet, lithograph in colours, printed by Benard, Liege, 1190 x 800mm. (Christie's) $480 £320

Job, by Alphonse Mucha, lithograph in colours, 1898, on wove paper, printed by F. Champenoise, Paris, 1500 x 1010mm. (Christie's) $5,250 £3,500

Wilhelm Mozer Munchen-Nord Adalbertstr, by Ludwig Hohlwein, lithograph in colours, 1909, on wove paper, 1250 x 911mm. (Christie's) $270 £180

XXVI Ausstellung Secession, by Ferdinand Andri, lithograph in colours, circa 1904, on wove paper, 920 x 602mm. (Christie's) $13,050 £8,700

Raphael Tuck, Celebrated Posters No. 1501, Ogden's Guinea Gold Cigarettes and another. (Christie's) $47 £35

Exposition Des Peintres Lithographes, by Fernand Louis Gottlob, lithograph in colours, 1899, printed by Lemercier, Paris, 1195 x 790mm. (Christie's) $450 £300

G. B. Borsalino Fu Lazzaro & C, by Marcello Dudovich, lithograph in colours, 1932, printed by R. Questura, Milano, 1390 x 1000mm. (Christie's) $375 £250

Nord Express, by Adolphe Mouron Cassandre, lithograph in colours, 1927, on wove paper, 1048 x 752mm. (Christie's) $1,950 £1,300

Raden Van Arbeid, by R. N. Roland Holst, lithograph in colours, on wove paper, 1084 x 794mm. (Christie's) $600 £400

Pierre Stephen, lithograph in colours, on wove paper, printed by Bauduin, Paris, 1538 x 1175mm. (Christie's) $630 £420

La Revue Des Folies Bergere, by Jules Alexandre Grun, lithograph in colours, 1905, printed by Ch. Verneau, Paris, 1246 x 880mm. (Christie's) $225 £150

Raphael Tuck, Celebrated Posters No. 1501, Rowntree's Elect Cocoa, and two others. (Christie's) $60 £45

Summer; Spring; Autumn; Winter, by Alphonse Mucha, lithograph in colours, 1896, on wove paper, 1040 x 530mm. (Christie's) $10,200 £6,800

Chemin De Fer, Martigny-Orsieres, by Albert Muret, lithograph in colours, 1913, on wove paper, printed by Sonor, 1000 x 700mm. (Christie's) $525 £350

Ein Rausch In Rot, Maskenball Wilder Mann, by C.M.I., lithograph in colours, 1928, on wove paper, 920 x 612mm. (Christie's) $225 £150

Absinthe Robette, by Privat Livemont, lithograph in colours, 1896, on wove paper, printed by J. L. Goffart, Bruxelles, 1105 x 806mm. (Christie's) $1,125 £750

Poster, 'Dolomiten Ski-Schule Val Gardena (Grodental) m.1300-2200'. (Onslows) $110 £75

Kupplerin, by Otto Dix, lithograph printed in red, yellow and blue, 1923, 597 x 465mm. (Christie's) $13,678 £9,180

Tiger, by Franz Marc, woodcut, 1912, on Japan, early proof before the edition, 249 x 332mm. (Christie's) $1,367 £918

Zinnie in un Vaso, by Giorgio Morandi, etching, 1932, on wove paper, first state (of two), 204 x 195mm. (Christie's) $4,023 £2,700

A nude seated on a red stool, entitled 'Asa', Morning, from the series Rajo Jusshu, 48.8 x 37.7cm. (Christie's) $493 £345

Plakat Muim Institut, by Ernst Ludwig Kirchner, woodcut printed in blue and black, 1911, on rose laid paper, 728 x 492mm. (Christie's) $7,241 £4,860

Saint Jerome in his Study, by Albrecht Durer, engraving 244 x 186mm. (Christie's) $5,909 £4,104

Okubi-e of the actor Ganjiro Nakamura in the role of Kamiya Jihei, signed Kamp, 42 x 27.3cm. (Christie's) $463 £324

Der Kuss, by Edvard Munch, etching with drypoint, 1895, on firm wove paper, signed in pencil, 346 x 277mm. (Christie's) $16,092 £10,800

Oban tate-e, a partly disrobed woman leaning against a pillar, signed Utamaro hitsu. (Christie's) $4,633 £3,240

L'Artisan Moderne, by Henri de Toulouse-Lautrec, lithograph printed in colours, 1894, on cream wove paper, 923 x 648mm. (Christie's) $10,459 £7,020

Selbstbildnis mit Frau, by Conrad Felixmuller, woodcut printed in colours, 1921, on soft Japan, 582 x 451mm. (Christie's) $9,655 £6,480

Campbell's Soup, by Andy Warhol, screenprints in colours, 1969, on wove paper, 907 x 657mm., and album. (Christie's) $5,443 £3,780

Melancholisches Madchen, by Ernst Ludwig Kirchner, woodcut printed in three colours from one block, 1922, on soft Japan, 752 x 445mm. (Christie's)$64,368 £43,200

Yvette Guilbert, by Henri de Toulouse-Lautrec, lithographs printed in olive green, 1894, on Arches, album, 410 x 393mm. (Christie's) $11,264 £7,560

From the Meisho Edo Hakkei series, Sudden Shower at Atake, signed Hiroshige ga. (Christie's) $6,949 £4,860

A nude woman seated, entitled 'Dokusho', from the series Rajo Jusshu, 48.6 x 37.5cm. (Christie's) $493 £345

Sun, from the Weather Series, by David Hockney, lithograph printed in colours, 1973, on Arjomari mould made wove paper, 750 x 645mm. (Christie's) $9,331 £6,480

The actor Nakamura Kichiemon in the role of Mitsuhide, signed and sealed Shunsen. (Christie's) $386 £270

'The Champion in Luck', published by Currier & Ives, 1882, small folio. (Robt. W. Skinner Inc.) $95 £54

'The Trotting Mare Goldsmith Maid, Driven By Budd Doble', published by Currier & Ives, 1870, large folio. (Robt. W. Skinner Inc.) $1,200 £810

'The Great Fire at Boston', published by Currier & Ives, 1872, small folio. (Robt. W. Skinner Inc.) $425 £287

'The Accommodation Train', published by Currier & Ives, 1876, small folio. (Robt. W. Skinner Inc.) $300 £202

'The Celebrated Horse Dexter, 'The King Of The World' Driven By Budd Doble'', publi-shed by Currier & Ives, 1867, large folio. (Robt. W. Skinner Inc.) $2,100 £1,418

'Rysdyk's Hambletonian', published by Currier & Ives, 1876, large folio. (Robt. W. Skinner Inc.) $1,700 £1,148

'The Darktown Yacht Club — On The Winning Tack', published by Currier & Ives, 1885, small folio. (Robt. W. Skinner Inc.) $250 £168

'The Four Seasons Of Life: Middle Age', published by Currier & Ives, 1868, large folio. (Robt. W. Skinner Inc.)
$1,200 £810

'Pigeon Shooting, 'Playing The Decoy'', published by Currier & Ives, 1862, large folio. (Robt. W. Skinner Inc.)$1,500 £1,013

'Camping in the Woods, 'Laying Off'', published by Currier & Ives, 1863, large folio. (Robt. W. Skinner Inc.) $3,200 £2,162

'Notice To Smokers And Chewers', published by N. Currier, 1854, small folio. (Robt. W. Skinner Inc.) $800 £540

'Maple Sugaring', published by Currier & Ives, 1872, small folio. (Robt. W. Skinner Inc.) $650 £439

The Pieta, by Hendrik Goltzius, engraving, second (final) state, 188 x 131mm. (Christie's) $2,896 £1,944

Oban tate-e, the courtesan Kisegawa of Matsubaya accompanied by two kamuro, signed and sealed Utamaro. (Christie's) $5,559 £3,888

Les Oranges renverses, by Louis Icart, drypoint with aquatint printed in colours, 1921, on wove paper, 398 x 297mm., and another. (Christie's) $933 £648

Frau in der Nacht, by Max Beckmann, drypoint, 1920, on soft Japan, 368 x 528mm. (Christie's) $9,655 £6,480

Femme au Corsage a Fleurs, by Pablo Picasso, lithograph, 1958, on Arches, third (final) state, one of six proof impressions, 635 x 483mm. (Christie's) $25,747 £17,280

Hommage a Marcel Duchamp, Pris, Editions Georges Visat, 1971, etchings, aquatints or lithographs, most printed in colours, overall size 390 x 295mm. (Christie's) $1,770 £1,188

La Baie des Anges, by Marc Chagall, lithograph printed in colours, 1962, on wove paper, 777 x 575mm. (Christie's) $388 £270

Joseph telling his Dreams, by Rembrandt Harmensz. van Rijn, etching, third (final) state, 112 x 84mm. (Christie's) $4,505 £3,024

Vor dem Spiegel, by Max Beckmann, drypoint, 1923, on laid paper, 227 x 172mm. (Christie's) $2,413 £1,620

Danseuse au Tabouret, from Dix Danseuses, by Henri Matisse, lithograph, 1927, on Arches, 455 x 277mm. (Christie's) $7,724 £5,184

Persuasion, by Claude Flight, linocut printed in colours, on Japan, signed in pencil, 340 x 297mm. (Christie's) $1,166 £810

Der Ritter und seine Schone, by Israhel van Meckenem, engraving, 162 x 112mm. (Christie's) $34,597 £23,220

Ein Handschuh, by Max Klinger, etchings, 1878-81, on Chine applique, set of ten plates, 255 x 347mm. and smaller. (Christie's) $5,632 £3,780

Tanzerin im Variete, by Erich Heckel, drypoint, 1911, on wove paper, signed and dated in pencil, 143 x 134mm. (Christie's) $3,057 £2,052

'The Great Bartholdi Statue, Liberty Enlightening The World', published by Currier & Ives, 1885. (Robt. W. Skinner) $1,200 £810

A young beauty, entitled Yuki Moyoi, Imminence of Snow, signed Shuho. (Christie's) $647 £453

Clement de Jonghe, Print-seller, by Rembrandt Harmensz. van Rijn, etching with drypoint and engraving, 209 x 162mm. (Christie's) $5,149 £3,456

The actor Asao Gakujuro as Mashiba Hisatsugu, a poem by Enjyaku above. (Christie's) $1,835 £1,296

Jahresgabe fur die Kandinsky-Gesellschaft, by Wassily Kandinsky, lithograph with extensive handcolouring, 1925, on Japan Imperial, 355 x 255mm. (Christie's) $27,356 £18,360

'The Celebrated Horse Lexington (5 years old), by 'Boston' out of 'Alice Carneal'', published by N. Currier, 1855, large folio. (Robt. W. Skinner Inc.) $600 £405

Le gros Pigeon, by Pablo Picasso, lithograph, 1947, on Arches, signed and no. 29/50, 400 x 510mm. (Christie's) $5,632 £3,790

Le Repos du Modele, by Henri Matisse, lithograph, 1922, on Chine volant, signed in pencil, 223 x 304mm. (Christie's) $2,735 £1,836

'Ethan Allen and Mate and Dexter', published by Currier & Ives, 1867, large folio. (Robt. W. Skinner Inc.) $1,200 £810

The Battle of the Sea Gods, the left half, by Andrea Mantegna, engraving, a clear but later impression, 296 x 413mm. (Christie's)
$2,954 £2,052

'Autumn Fruits', published by Currier & Ives, 1861, medium folio. (Robt. W. Skinner Inc.) $225 £152

'The Celebrated Trotting Stallion George Wilkes, Formerly 'Robert Fillingham'', published by Currier & Ives, 1866, large folio. (Robt. W. Skinner Inc.) $1,600 £1,081

Femme nue an Repos avec un Chat, by Tsuguji Foujita, etching on laid paper, signed in pencil, 355 x 455mm. (Christie's) $2,413 £1,620

Adonis in Y fronts, by Richard Hamilton, screenprint in colours, 1963, signed and dated in pencil, from the edition of 40, printed by Kelpra Studio, 604 x 815mm. (Christie's) $5,909 £4,104

The Portico with the Lantern, by Antonio Canal, II Canaletto, etching, third (final) state, 302 x 431mm. (Christie's) $1,710 £1,188

Nature Morte, by Gino Severini, lithograph printed in colours, 1958, on BFK Rives, signed in pencil, 391 x 564mm. (Christie's) $1,609 £1,080

Late 19th century crazy quilt with The Lord's Prayer, America, consisting of velvets, brocades and cottons of varying shapes, 69in. wide. (Robt. W. Skinner Inc.) $375 £256

An appliqued coverlet with pineapple pattern, America, circa 1840, 82 x 98in. (Robt. W. Skinner Inc.) $2,000 £1,388

A patchwork cover worked with hexagonal pieces of mid/late 19th century printed and plain coloured cotton, 2.50 x 2.34m., lined. (Phillips) $367 £250

Early 19th century red and blue patchwork Calamanco coverlet, America, 108 x 100in. (Robt. W. Skinner Inc.) $1,200 £833

An appliqued quilt with attached label 'Made by Mrs. J. Walter Marshall of Old Frankport Rd., Lexington, Kentucky', circa 1860. (Robt. W. Skinner Inc.) $2,000 £1,388

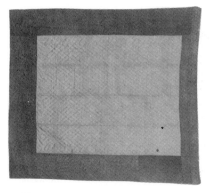

Late 18th century American Linsey-Woolsey coverlet with red centre area enclosed by a green border, 85 x 93in. (Christie's)
$1,210 £834

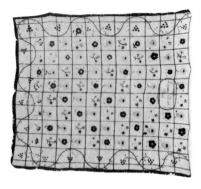

An embroidered blanket, probably New York,
'Lucretia Brush(?) Busti, 1831', large blue
and white check, 6ft.4in. x 7ft.4in. (Robt. W.
Skinner Inc.) $5,800 £3,918

A patchwork quilt, Penn., signed and dated
in ink on the back, 'Phebeann H. Salem's(?)
Presented by her Mother 1848', 8ft.11in. x 9ft.
(Robt. W. Skinner Inc.) $1,900 £1,319

A wool bed rug, worked with a darning stitch
in a tree-of-life pattern on a natural wool
foundation, dated 1773, 84 x 85in.
(Christie's) $11,000 £7,586

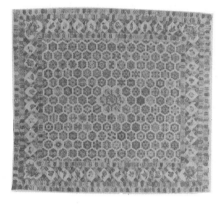

An early 19th century patchwork coverlet in
plain and coloured printed glazed cotton,
circa 1830, 2.70 x 2.24m. (Christie's)$911 £620

A 19th century American appliqued quilt,
7ft.1in. x 6ft.2in. (Robt. W. Skinner Inc.)
                        $1,200 £833

A pieced and quilted cotton coverlet, lily
pattern, American, circa 1900, approx. 84in.
long, 80in. wide. (Christie's) $715 £493

Early 20th century Heriz
Area carpet, 9ft.8in. x 13ft.
(Robt. W. Skinner Inc.)
$4,250 £3,219

Late 19th/early 20th century
S.W. Persian Qashqai bag face,
1ft.1in. x 1ft.3in. (Robt. W.
Skinner Inc.) $325 £246

Late 19th/early 20th cen-
tury Kazak rug, the red field
with concentric hooked
medallions, 4ft.6in. x 7ft.
(Robt. W. Skinner Inc.)
$2,200 £1,666

Early 20th century Kurdish
Kelim rug, the ivory field
with red and blue forked
medallions, 6ft.1in. x 8ft.4in.
(Robt. W. Skinner Inc.)
$275 £208

Late 19th/early 20th cen-
tury N.W. Persia, Soumak
bag face, the dark blue field
with medallions of various
colours, 2ft.1in. x 2ft. (Robt.
W. Skinner Inc.)
$1,500 £1,136

A Kashan embossed part
silk pictorial rug, 35½ x
24½in. (Capes, Dunn & Co.)
$864 £600

A J. J. Adnet wool pile
carpet in tones of russet,
black, brown and beige,
circa 1930, 156.5 x
144.4cm. (Christie's)
$1,340 £918

Late 19th century Caucasian
Kelim, red, blue, green, yellow, black and ivory rows of
stepped medallions, 5ft.5in.
x 10ft.5in. (Robt. W. Skinner Inc.) $1,100 £833

Late 19th century Kuba mat,
E. Caucasus, the blue field
with flowerheads of blue and
red, 2ft.8in. x 2ft.9in. (Robt.
W. Skinner Inc.) $800 £606

Late18th/early 19th century Tekke main carpet, Turkestan, with five rows of ten guls. (Robt. W. Skinner Inc.) $2,300 £1,742

Early 20th century Khamseh rug, S.W. Persian, with ivory, red, gold, blue, green and aubergine all over pattern, 4ft. x 6ft.3in. (Robt. W. Skinner Inc.) $550 £416

Late 19th/early 20th century Tekke Ensi, with maroon centre panel with dark blue 'candelabra' motif, 4ft. x 5ft.1in. (Robt. W. Skinner Inc.) $900 £681

Late 19th century Eastern Caucasian/Kuba rug, woven in the afshan or 'crab-kuba' design, 3ft.5in. x 4ft.10in. (Robt. W. Skinner Inc.) $500 £378

Late 19th/early 20th century Chi-Chi prayer rug with dark blue field, 4ft.3in. x 4ft.7in. (Robt. W. Skinner Inc.) $950 £715

Late 19th/early 20th century Kazak rug with madder red field, 4ft.5in. x 6ft.9in. (Robt. W. Skinner Inc.) $400 £273

Late 19th century Bergama Village rug, 3ft. x 3ft.9in. (Robt. W. Skinner Inc.) $750 £568

A silk Kashan rug, the ivory field with a column of palmettes, 6ft.8in. x 4ft.3in. (Christie's) $5,065 £3,780

Early 20th century N.W. Persia, Soumak bag face with white field, 1ft.8in. x 1ft.8in. (Robt. W. Skinner Inc.) $175 £132

Late 19th century 'Cloud-Band' Kazak rug, 5ft.9in. x 8ft.4in. (Robt. W. Skinner Inc.) $1,900 £1,310

A Soumac rug with shaded brick-red field, 10ft.5in. x 4ft.8in. (Christie's) $983 £734

A Bessarabian Kilim, the mottled ivory field with two large floral sprays, 6ft.6in. x 5ft. (Christie's) $548 £378

Late 19th century Eastern Caucasus Kuba rug, the blue-green centre field with ivory medallion, 4ft. x 6ft. (Robt. W. Skinner Inc.) $1,200 £827

Late 19th/early 20th century Anatolian Kelim with all over diamond shaped medallions, 4ft.9in. x 12ft. 6in. (Robt. W. Skinner Inc.) $500 £378

Late 19th century Kazak rug, the double niche ivory centre with green and red centre medallion, 3ft.5in. x 4ft.10in. (Robt. W. Skinner Inc.) $3,300 £2,275

Late 19th century Northwest Persian landscape carpet, 10ft.8in. x 13ft.3in. (Robt. W. Skinner Inc.) $17,000 £11,724

Late 19th century Baluch rug, East Persia, the corroded black field woven in all over star-like flowerheads, 3ft.11in. x 7ft.10in. (Robt. W. Skinner Inc.) $650 £492

A Perepedile rug, the red field woven with blue and white ram's horn motifs, 5ft.4in. x 3ft.5in. (Lawrence Fine Art) $2,116 £1,430

A Charles X Aubusson
carpet woven in pastel
shades, 10ft.8in. x 9ft.5in.
(Christie's) $2,799 £1,944

A Caucasian runner, possibly
Mogan, the brown black
field woven with six octa-
gons, 10ft.4in. x 3ft.4in.
(Lawrence Fine Art)
$1,465 £990

A Southwestern Caucasus
Kazak rug, 8ft. x 5ft.
(Robt. W. Skinner Inc.)
$8,000 £5,517

Late 19th century Serapi
carpet, North Central
Persia, 9ft.6in. x 13ft.3in.
(Robt. W. Skinner Inc.)
$7,000 £4,861

A Talish runner, the dark
blue field woven with small
red florets, 7ft.9in. x 3ft.
3in. (Lawrence Fine Art)
$2,604 £1,760

Late 19th/early 20th century
Shahsavan Kelim/South Caucasus, the horizontal bands
of dark blue with madder red
dumb-bell medallions, 3ft.9in.
x 4ft.3in. (Robt. W. Skinner
Inc.) $300 £207

Late 19th century Karachoph
Kazak, the red field with ivory
octagonal centre medallion,
8ft. x 5ft. (Robt. W. Skinner
Inc.) $2,500 £1,724

Late 19th/early 20th cen-
tury Anatolian Kelim with
diamond medallions of
various colours, 5ft.4in. x
11ft.6in. (Robt. W. Skinner
Inc.) $650 £492

An antique Beshir carpet,
the brick-red field with rows
of stylised palmettes and
plants, 15ft.10in. x 7ft.3in.
(Christie's) $1,409 £972

Mid to late 19th century
Kazak rug, S.W. Caucasus,
4ft.10in. x 7ft.2in. (Robt.
W. Skinner Inc.)
$2,800 £2,121

An early 19th century English pile
carpet, rebacked, 27ft. x 17ft.
(Christie's) $42,854 £34,560

Late 19th/early 20th cen-
tury Karabagh, S.W. Cauc-
asus, 5ft.2in. x 9ft. (Robt.
W. Skinner Inc.)
$1,100 £833

A Kirman Laver prayer rug
with burgundy field, 6ft.
10in. x 4ft.2in. (Christie's)
$1,447 £1,080

A Persian carpet sampler,
3ft.2in. x 3ft.10in. (Robt.
W. Skinner Inc.)
$1,300 £984

Late 19th/early 20th cen-
tury Kuba rug, with a brown-
black 'wine-cup' border, 4ft.
x 6ft.1in. (Robt. W. Skinner
Inc.) $1,000 £757

An Isfahan rug, the ivory
field with three flower vases
and flowering trees, 6ft.11in.
x 4ft.10in. (Christie's)
$4,052 £3,024

Late 19th century Soumak
bag, 1ft.8in. x 1ft.9in. (Robt.
W. Skinner Inc.)
$2,000 £1,515

A silk Kashan rug with yellow
gold field, 7ft.2in. x 4ft.5in.
(Christie's) $5,788 £4,320

Late 19th century Yomud main carpet, W. Turkestan, featuring Dynak and 'spread eagle' guls, 5ft.4in. x 10ft.1in. (Robt. W. Skinner Inc.) $10,500 £7,954

Late 19th/early 20th century Tabriz carpet, 25ft.9in. x 13ft.10in. (Robt. W. Skinner Inc.) $8,500 £6,439

Late 19th/early 20th century Marasali prayer rug, E. Caucasian, with light yellow field, 3ft.7in. x 4ft.9in. (Robt. W. Skinner Inc.) $600 £454

An early 20th century Mahal carpet with blue field of green, red, pink and light blue flowering vines, within a red floral border. (Robt. W. Skinner Inc.) $350 £239

Late 19th/early 20th century Soumak rug, E. Caucasus, with rust-red field, 4ft.8in. 6ft.9in. (Robt. W. Skinner Inc.) $600 £454

Early 20th century Hamadan Area rug, 4ft.10in. x 7ft.6in. (Robt. W. Skinner Inc.) $1,250 £946

Early to mid 19th century Konya Kelim, Central Anatolia, 5ft.4in. x 10ft. (Robt. W. Skinner Inc.) $550 £416

One of a pair of silk Kashan rugs, the ivory field with palmettes and floral sprays, 7ft. x 4ft.1in. (Christie's) $10,130 £7,560

A silk Kashan rug with pistachio-green field, 6ft.8in. x 4ft.3in. (Christie's) $7,959 £5,940

677

Late 19th century Persian Serapi carpet, 10ft. x 11ft. 9in. (Robt. W. Skinner Inc.) $13,000 £9,848

Late 19th/early 20th century Kurdish Soumak salt bag, 1ft.1½in. x 1ft.6in. (Robt. W. Skinner Inc.) $350 £265

Late 19th century Ziegler Mahal carpet, 10ft.9in. x 14ft.1in. (Robt. W. Skinner Inc.) $5,250 £3,977

A Heriz carpet, the dark red field with dark blue centre medallion, circa 1930's, 6ft. 10in. x 9ft.1in. (Robt. W. Skinner Inc.) $800 £547

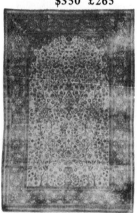

A silk Kashan prayer rug, the ivory field with central flower vase, 6ft.8in. x 4ft. 3in. (Christie's) $4,920 £3,672

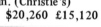

A Qum silk carpet, the ivory field with palmettes and floral sprays around a blood-red cusped panel, 12ft.11in. x 9ft.7in. (Christie's) $20,260 £15,120

A Shirvan rug the centre with six star medallions on a blue field and dated 1894, 6ft.5in. x 4ft.1in. (Woolley & Wallis) $1,450 £1,000

Early 20th century Heriz carpet with rust-red field, 8ft. x 11ft.2in. (Robt. W. Skinner Inc.) $3,750 £2,568

A Senneh rug, the indigo field divided into panels of flowering plants, wreaths and prayer arches, 6ft.8in. x 4ft. 4in. (Christie's) $4,052 £3,024

Early 20th century Kashan carpet, 13ft.4in. x 9ft.9in. (Robt. W. Skinner Inc.) $3,300 £2,500

An early 20th century reverse Soumak animal trapping, one bag, 1ft.3in. x 1ft. 4in., flanked by two small bags, 7 x 8in. (Robt. W. Skinner Inc.) $850 £643

Early 20th century Tekke Main carpet, W. Turkestan, 7ft. x 9ft.10in. (Robt. W. Skinner Inc.) $2,100 £1,590

A Mashad carpet with maroon field, circa 1930, 8ft.4in. x 12ft. (Robt. W. Skinner Inc.) $625 £428

Late 19th century Bergama Village rug, W. Anatolian, 3ft.2in. x 3ft.8in. (Robt. W. Skinner Inc.) $375 £284

A Souf silk and metal thread Kashan prayer rug, 6ft.9in. x 4ft.3in. (Christie's) $4,631 £3,456

Early 20th century Afshar rug, the dark blue field with rows of large boteh, 4ft. x 6ft. (Robt. W. Skinner Inc.) $750 £568

Late 19th/early 20th century Qashqai bag face with dark blue field. (Robt. W. Skinner Inc.) $350 £265

Early 20th century Kazak prayer rug, S.W. Caucasus, a red field with ivory medallion, 4ft.2in. x 6ft.11in. (Robt. W. Skinner Inc.) $1,600 £1,212

A Fetjiye rug in the Bessarabian style with a central medallion of roses and the date 1915, 86 x 55¾in. (Christie's) $1,566 £1,080

Late 19th century Mahal carpet, 13ft.9in. x 20ft. (Robt. W. Skinner Inc.) $10,000 £7,575

Late 19th century Karabagh long rug, S.W. Caucasus, 3ft.8in. x 11in. (Robt. W. Skinner Inc.) $1,300 £984

Late 19th century Northwest Persia, Heriz-Area carpet, 11ft. x 8ft.6in. (Robt. W. Skinner Inc.) $13,000 £8,965

Late 19th century Central Persian, Sultanabad carpet, the ivory field woven in all over flower filled trellis, 8ft.4in. x 10ft.5in. (Robt. W. Skinner Inc.) $2,900 £2,000

Late 19th/early 20th century 'Eagle' Kazak rug, Southwest Caucasus, 5ft. 11in. x 7ft.7in. (Robt. W. Skinner Inc.) $2,100 £1,448

A Kashan rug, the blue field woven with floral arabesques and centred by a brick red medallion, 6ft.10in. x 4ft. 10in. (Lawrence Fine Art) $1,530 £1,034

An antique Shirvan rug with indigo field, 8ft.1in. x 3ft. 8in. (Christie's) $2,192 £1,512

A Shirvan rug with multiple floral decoration on indigo field, 80 x 51½in. (Reeds Rains) $720 £500

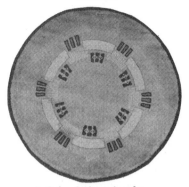

Late 19th century South Caucasian Karabagh rug, 4ft. 4in. x 7ft.11in. (Robt. W. Skinner Inc.)
$3,300 £2,500

A Jules Leleu circular woollen rug, 188cm. diam. (Christie's) $1,252 £864

A Ziegler carpet, 17ft.10in. x 12ft. (Christie's)
$10,962 £7,560

Late 19th century North-west Persian carpet, the yellow field woven in all over Mina Khani floral trellis, 10ft.5in. x 14ft. 7in. (Robt. W. Skinner Inc.) $4,100 £2,827

Late 19th century Karachoph rug, 5ft.2in. x 6ft.4in. (Robt. W. Skinner Inc.) $425 £293

Late 19th century North-west Persia, Serapi carpet, with a 'turtle' border, 9ft. 6in. x 13ft.4in. (Robt. W. Skinner Inc.)
$4,200 £2,896

A Navajo pictorial rug, 9ft.11½in. x 5ft.5½in. (Robt. W. Skinner Inc.)
$2,500 £1,736

A 19th century Serapi carpet, the red field with large ivory and pale blue green medallion, 10ft.10in. x 13ft.11in. (Robt. W. Skinner Inc.)$6,500 £4,482

A Kashan carpet, the light blue field with palmettes, trees and floral sprays, 11ft. 3in. x 6ft.4in. (Christie's)
$5,637 £3,888

A sampler by Mary-Ann Hayter, aged 8 years, 1823, worked in coloured silks, 15 x 13in. (Christie's) $482 £340

Early 19th century woolwork sampler, worked by Elizabeth Shufflebottoms 1841, 23½ x 23¾in. (Reeds Rains) $432 £300

An early 19th century American needlework sampler, 19½ x 21in. (Robt. W. Skinner Inc.) $2,750 £1,909

A sampler by Julia Matild Paisey, 1845, worked in dark silks, 16 x 12½in. (Christie's) $738 £520

A George IV needlework sampler, by E.H., 1826, 17 x 12½in. (Graves, Son & Pilcher) $465 £340

A needlework sampler by Mary Anne Hunter aged 14 years 1844, 26 x 16½in. (Anderson & Garland) $454 £320

Needlework sampler, marked 'Elizabeth C. Engle's work done in the 12th year of her age, August 23th, 1837', 17½ x 17½in. (Robt. W. Skinner Inc.) $600 £416

An American needlework sampler, signed Jane Littlefield, circa 1810, worked in silk threads on a dark green canvas, 24in. high, 15½in. wide. (Christie's) $3,740 £2,729

An early 19th century needlework sampler, 'Hannah L. Slessor aged 13 years', New England, 16½ x 15½in. (Robt. W. Skinner Inc.) $850 £590

A needlework sampler, 'Emily Furber her sampler aged 10, wrought March 16, 1827', 23 x 26in. (Robt. W. Skinner Inc.) $2,400 £1,666

A needlework family register worked by Lucia A. Daniels in 1832, 16 x 18in. (Robt. W. Skinner Inc.) $1,000 £694

A needlework sampler, 'Anna Fowler born March 2, 1739, this sampler I did the year 1754', 13 x 19½in. (Robt. W. Skinner Inc.) $2,300 £1,597

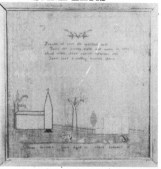

An early 19th century needlework sampler, 'Jane Slessors work aged 13 years January 16', New England, 17 x 17½in. (Robt. W. Skinner Inc.) $500 £347

An 18th century needlework sampler well decorated in coloured silks, 17 x 12½in. (Graves, Son & Pilcher) $712 £520

Early 19th century needlework sampler, 'Phebe L. Slessor work aged 11 years', New England, 16 x 16in. (Robt. W. Skinner Inc.) $900 £625

Needlework sampler marked 'Wrought by Sally Alden June 14 1811', Mass., 16 x 21in. (Robt. W. Skinner Inc.) $3,750 £2,604

A sampler by Charlotte Way, Portland, 1841, worked in pale brown silk, 14 x 11½in. (Christie's) $198 £140

Late 18th century needlework sampler family record, 10½ x 16in. (Robt. W. Skinner Inc.) $3,100 £2,152

A George II shaped oval cake basket, by Edward Aldridge, probably 1746, 14½in. long, 56oz. (Christie's)
$2,397 £1,620

One of a pair of George III oval dessert baskets, by Wm. Pitts & J. Preedy, 1799, 11in. long, 119oz. (Christie's) $5,594 £3,780

A George II shaped oval cake basket, by Edward Wakelin, 1749, 14½in. long, 59oz. (Christie's)
$4,475 £3,024

A George II shaped oval bread basket, by Paul Crespin, 1753, with later Russian marks, 14½in. long, 62oz. (Christie's)
$21,772 £15,120

A George III sugar basket, by Abraham Peterson, 1795, 17cm. across. (Lawrence Fine Art) $510 £352

A George III Irish cake basket, by J. Graham, Dublin, circa 1765, 35.2cm. long, 38oz. (Lawrence Fine Art)
$3,581 £2,420

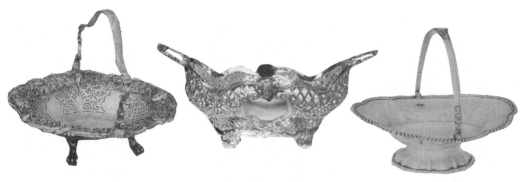

A George II cake basket, by Eliz. Godfrey, 1743, 35.3cm. across, 64.2oz. (Lawrence Fine Art)
$8,140 £5,500

One of a set of seven Victorian two-handled baskets, by Carrington & Co., 1899 and 1900, one 17¾in. long, two 14in. long and two 12in. long, 212oz. (Christie's)
$16,416 £10,800

A George IV shaped oval cake basket, by Rebecca Emes and E. Barnard, 1827, 33.5cm. wide, 34oz. (Lawrence Fine Art) $846 £572

A Continental beaker, possibly 17th century, punched only with an Augsburg pineapple and an assay scrape, 17cm. high, 10oz. (Phillips) $1,198 £850

A Latvian parcel gilt beaker, by J. D. Rehwald, Riga, circa 1740, 7in. high, 10oz. (Christie's) $1,395 £918

A Dutch tapering cylindrical beaker, by Agge Jelles Reinalda, Franeker, 1669, 6¾in. high, 9oz.17dwt. (Christie's) $6,073 £4,104

A 17th century Friesland beaker, by Paulus Sakes, Dokkum, 1649, 16.2cm. high, 10.25oz. (Phillips) $4,512 £3,200

One of a set of six George III small silver gilt cylindrical beakers, by Wm. Burwash & R. Sibley, 1809, 2.1/8in. high, 8oz.13dwt. (Christie's) $2,717 £1,836

A German parcel gilt beaker, late 17th/early 18th century, maker's mark only DL struck twice, 3¾in. high, 4oz.17dwt. (Christie's) $1,231 £810

A Commonwealth tapering cylindrical beaker, 1658, maker's mark RF between pellets, 4in. high, 5oz. (Christie's) $3,888 £2,700

A German silver gilt beaker, Strasbourg, circa 1700, maker's mark perhaps EB, 3¾in. high, 4oz.18dwt. (Christie's) $2,332 £1,620

A German silver gilt beaker, by J. P. Hofler, Nuremberg, circa 1690, 3¾in. high, 4oz. 17dwt. (Christie's) $1,313 £864

685

A Victorian two-handled circular punch bowl, by F. B. Thomas, 1878, 10½in. high, 86oz. (Christie's)
$2,626 £1,728

A 19th century Indian bowl, heavily chased in the usual manner, 24cm. diam., 37oz. (Lawrence Fine Art)
$472 £319

A Dutch two-handled octagonal brandy bowl, Bolsward, circa 1685, maker's mark indistinct, 8oz.12dwt. (Christie's) $4,698 £3,240

A 19th century Indian silver deep bowl, 8½in. diam., 33 troy oz. approx. (Robt. W. Skinner Inc.)$400 £291

Late 19th century Viennese circular jewelled and silver gilt mounted striated agate bowl, 5½in. high. (Christie's) $3,132 £2,160

A George III Irish bowl, maker's mark script IL for John Laughlin Jnr., J. Lloyd Snr., or J. Locker, Dublin, 1784, 23.5cm. diam., 19.8oz. (Lawrence Fine Art)
$814 £550

A punch bowl, the hemispherical body divided into arched panels, maker's mark probably that of Chas. S. Harris & Sons, 1929, 28.2cm. diam., 37.5oz. (Lawrence Fine Art) $748 £506

A Victorian fluted shell design bowl on reeded supports, by George Unite, Birmingham, 1870, 6¼in. high, 11oz. (Christie's) $444 £300

A footed bowl designed by J. Rohde, stamped Dessin J.R. 925 S Georg Jensen 242, circa 1920, 12.6cm. high, 16oz. (Christie's)
$1,722 £1,188

SILVER

A Victorian partly fluted two-handled circular punch bowl, by Elkington & Co., Birmingham, 1889, 12½in. high, 109oz. (Christie's) $2,557 £1,728

An Edwardian Arts & Crafts circular hammered bowl, by A. E. Jones, Birmingham, 1908, 10in. across handles, 9oz. (Woolley & Wallis) $281 £190

A 17th century two-handled silver gilt circular bowl and cover, probably Flemish, maker's mark only CD, diam. of bowl 7½in., 39oz. (Christie's) $6,264 £4,320

A footed bowl, stamped Georg Jensen 925 S 197B, 11.1cm. high, 8oz.19dwt. (Christie's) $861 £594

A Queen Anne two-handled circular Monteith, by R. Syng, 1705, 11in. diam., 69oz. (Christie's) $15,984 £10,800

An Indian circular sugar bowl and cover on four fluted lion's paw supports, by Davd. Hare, Calcutta, circa 1820, 6½in. high, 21oz. (Christie's) $3,758 £2,592

A silver mounted wood mazer, by Omar Ramsden, 1921, 8¾in. diam. (Christie's) $4,043 £2,808

A George II plain circular punch bowl, by Edward Vincent, 1730, 9½in. diam., 38oz. (Christie's) $14,774 £10,260

A George II Irish circular bowl on a rim foot, by Alexander Brown, Dublin, 1735, 6in. wide, 13oz.7dwt. (Christie's) $8,311 £5,616

BOXES

A shaped oblong silver casket by Omar Ramsden, 1921, 8¾in. long, gross 53oz. (Christie's) $4,354 £3,024

Early 19th century silver mounted coquilla nut with bird finial, 6in. high. (Christie's) $783 £540

A German oblong dressing table box with hinged cover, 7¼in. long. (Christie's) $562 £380

A Danish white metal and ivory box and cover, stamped marks W/G and CF Heise assay mark, circa 1925, 13.5cm. high. (Christie's) $600 £400

Victorian silver tobacco box, Birmingham, 1900, 3½in. high, 10oz. (Hobbs & Chambers) $446 £310

A Victorian lozenge shaped plated biscuit box, with formal engraving and panel feet. (Parsons, Welch & Cowell) $125 £85

A 17th century Dutch silver oblong marriage casket, maker's mark only PH conjoined, 2.7/8in. long. (Christie's) $2,877 £1,944

A Queen Anne oval tobacco box, Britannia Standard 1708, maker's mark rubbed, possibly AS, 10cm. long. (Lawrence Fine Art) $574 £396

A Victorian silver mounted octagonal oak jewel casket, by John S. Hunt, 1856, 10in. high. (Christie's) $1,566 £1,080

SILVER

A circular silver cosmetic box and cover, Tang Dynasty, 5.2cm. diam. (Christie's) $3,175 £2,160

A silver and silver gilt Freedom casket, 'The City of Bristol', by Walker & Hall, Sheffield, 1921, 116oz. approx. (Edgar Horn) $1,153 £799

A Charles II circular silver gilt spice box, circa 1680, maker's mark FS/S, 3¾in. wide, 4oz.13dwt. (Christie's) $11,188 £7,560

A shaped square silver casket, by Omar Ramsden, 1929, 4½in. high, 18oz.4dwt. (Christie's) $1,555 £1,080

A 17th century Dutch silver marriage casket on four ball feet, 3in. long. (Christie's) $2,877 £1,944

A George I spherical soap box, by William Fawdery, 1720, Britannia Standard, 3½in. high, 8oz.19dwt. (Christie's) $5,594 £3,780

A 17th century Dutch silver oblong marriage casket on four ball feet, 3.1/8in. long. (Christie's) $3,836 £2,592

A Liberty & Co. silver biscuit box with Birmingham hallmarks for 1902, 20oz.14dwt., 14cm. high. (Christie's) $630 £432

A silver sugar box and scoop of scuttle form, maker's mark S.D.L.D., London, 1911, 17½oz. (Parsons, Welch & Cowell) $577 £390

CANDELABRA

One of a pair of late 19th century four-light candelabra, maker MAU, Dresden, 800 standard, 154oz. (Christie's) $3,256 £2,200

One of a pair of George III style reeded two-light candelabra with inverted bell-shaped sockets, 14in. high, weight of branches 31oz. (Christie's) $666 £450

One of a pair of Empire ormolu and bronze five-light candelabra on turned engraved pedestals, 27in. high. (Christie's) $1,710 £1,296

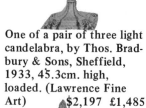

One of a pair of late Victorian table candlesticks, maker's mark J. and T., Sheffield, 1894, 46cm. overall height, loaded. (Lawrence Fine Art) $861 £594

One of a pair of Georg Jensen candelabra with five cup-shaped candle nozzles and circular drip pans supported on U-shaped branches, 27cm. high. (Christie's) $32,400 £21,600

One of a pair of three light candelabra, by Thos. Bradbury & Sons, Sheffield, 1933, 45.3cm. high, loaded. (Lawrence Fine Art) $2,197 £1,485

A George III silver gilt four-light candelabrum, by Paul Storr, 1815, 20½in. high, 143oz. (Christie's) $27,172 £18,360

A Victorian candelabrum centrepiece, by Paul Storr, 1837, 24½in. high, 297oz. (Christie's) $11,988 £8,100

One of a pair of George III three-light candelabra, by Paul Storr, 1816, 16¾in. high, 262oz. (Christie's) $135,864 £91,800

CANDELABRA

One of a pair of Victorian five-light corinthian column candelabra, dated 1886, 26½in. high, weight of branches 116oz. (Christie's) $7,516 £5,184

One of a pair of mid 18th century style three-branch candelabra, with scrolling branches, 10¾in. high, 75oz. (Christie's) $1,323 £900

A silver three-branch candelabrum, no. 159 of a limited edition of 250, London, 1977, 11in. high, 25oz. (Peter Wilson & Co.) $187 £130

One of a pair of silver gilt three-light candelabra, by The Goldsmiths & Silversmiths Co. Ltd., 1911, 33.2cm. high, 71oz. (Lawrence Fine Art) $2,392 £1,650

A Victorian six-light candelabrum centrepiece, by S. Smith and Wm. Nicholson, 1860, 26¾in. high, 201oz. (Christie's) $5,594 £3,780

One of two George IV three-light candelabra, by John Watson, Sheffield, 1823, one branch 1820, 25¼in. high, weight of branches 99oz. (Christie's) $4,698 £3,240

One of four Louis XV four-light candelabra, Paris, 1732, femier-general Hubert Louvet, 217oz. (Christie's) $71,928 £48,600

A pair of late Empire bronze and ormolu three-light candelabra, 25in. high. (Christie's) $2,138 £1,620

A George III three-light candelabra, by Digby Scott and Benjamin Smith, 1804, 17in. high, 83oz. (Christie's) $6,566 £4,320

CANDLESTICKS

Pair of table candlesticks, maker's mark of S. Dawson Ltd. overstriking another, Sheffield 1912, 30.2cm. high. (Lawrence Fine Art) $651 £440

One of a set of six candlesticks designed by H. Nielsen, stamped Dessin H.N. Georg Jensen 747B, 2cm. high, 7oz. 3dwt. (Christie's) $939 £648

A pair of George III candlesticks, by John Scofield, 1792, 11¼in. high, 41oz. (Christie's) $4,384 £3,024

Two of a set of four William IV square base candlesticks, by T. J. & N. Creswick, Sheffield, 1832, 11in. high., (loaded). (Woolley & Wallis) $1,460 £1,000

One of a set of four William III candlesticks, by Joseph Bird, 1699, 6in. high, 50oz. (Christie's) $41,469 £28,020

Pair of early George III cast table candlesticks, by Wm. Cafe, 1760, 22.6cm. high, 30oz. (Lawrence Fine Art) $1,465 £990

A pair of silver Louis XVI candlesticks by Saint-Omer, 1784, 9.3/8in. high, 31oz. (Christie's) $2,799 £1,944

One of a pair of Queen Anne candlesticks, by John Elston, Exeter, 1706, 8¾in. high, 20oz. (Christie's) $5,443 £3,780

Pair of George III table candlesticks, London marks of 1776 overstriking the original Sheffield marks, 27.9cm. high. (Lawrence Fine Art) $781 £528

CANDLESTICKS

Pair of Victorian table candlesticks embossed, on square bases, Sheffield, 1844, 9½in. high. (Hobbs & Chambers) $1,036 £720

One of a pair of Liberty & Co. three-branch silver wall sconces, with Birmingham hallmarks for 1901, 29oz., 20cm. high. (Christie's) $1,734 £1,188

Pair of George III coffee house candlesticks, by E. Coker, 1765, 28.6cm. high, 29oz. (Lawrence Fine Art) $1,628 £1,100

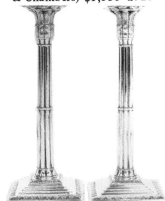

Two of a set of four George III cluster-column candlesticks, by Ebenezer Coker, 1766, 11¾in. high. (Christie's) $4,541 £3,132

One of a pair of George I candlesticks, Dublin, 1726, maker's mark presumably that of Thos. Bolton, 6in. high, 22oz. (Christie's) $4,665 £3,240

One of a pair of George II cast table candlesticks, by John Priest, 1754, 20.4cm. high, 27.3oz. (Lawrence Fine Art) $1,834 £1,265

One of a set of four George II candlesticks, by E. Wakelin, 1757, 12½in. high, 187oz. (Christie's) $80,870 £56,160

A pair of silver candlesticks with rococo and floral embossing, Edinburgh, 1893, 4½in. high. (Edgar Horn) $350 £240

One of a pair of George III silver gilt candlesticks, by John Scofield, 1796, the gilding later, 12¾in. high. (Christie's) $5,434 £3,672

CANDLESTICKS

One of a pair of Victorian candlesticks, by Elkington & Co., Birmingham, 1896 and 1899, 10½in. high. (Christie's) $1,438 £972

A pair of early George III cast table candlesticks, 1762, maker's mark DM over a star and 1763, by E. Coker, 26.1cm. high, 42oz. (Lawrence Fine Art) $1,914 £1,320

One of a pair of mid 18th century style cast baluster candlesticks, 7¼in. high, 28oz. (Christie's) $454 £320

A matched pair of George II cast table candlesticks, by Wm. Gould 1758, and 1760 maker's mark perhaps that of J. Cafe, 22.7cm. high, 34oz. (Lawrence Fine Art) $1,435 £990

One of a pair of George II candlesticks, by Thos. Heming, London, 1759, 28cm. high, 55oz. (Christie's) $2,886 £1,950

Two of four silver candlesticks, by Omar Ramsden, two 1919, two 1922, loaded, 22.5cm. high. (Phillips) $4,410 £3,000

A George II taperstick, by James Gould, London, 1737, 10.5cm. high. (Christie's) $1,140 £760

A pair of George III telescopic candlesticks, by John Roberts & Co., Sheffield, 1805, 26cm. extended, loaded. (Lawrence Fine Art) $1,148 £781

One of a pair of George II cast baluster candlesticks, with detachable nozzles, by John Priest, London, 1748, 7¾in. high, 28.75oz. (Christie's) $2,272 £1,600

One of a pair of candlesticks designed by J. Rohde, stamped Dessin JR Georg Jensen GI925S 453, circa 1920, 15cm high. (Christie's) $1,331 £918

A pair of George III bedroom candlesticks, by Thos. & James Creswick, Sheffield, 1814, 10.8cm. high. (Lawrence Fine Art) $905 £616

One of a pair of George I table candlesticks, by Matthew Cooper I, London, 1726, 16cm. high, 22oz. (Christie's) $3,108 £2,100

A pair of George I table candlesticks, by David Green, London, 1723, 16.1cm. high, 23oz. (Christie's) $3,404 £2,300

One of a pair of 18th century Sheffield candlesticks, each with a square removable nozzle, 12.3/8in. high. (Christie's) $462 £320

A pair of modern table candlesticks with detachable nozzles, by Leslie Donn Ltd., 1964, 29.5cm. high. (Lawrence Fine Art) $436 £297

One of a pair of William II candlesticks, by William Denny, 1701, 23cm. high, 23oz. (Phillips) $3,666 £2,600

Pair of candlesticks designed by S. Bernadotte, stamped Georg Jensen 355B Sigvard and London import marks, 25.9cm. high, 25oz.11dwt. (Christie's) $1,331 £918

One of a set of four George III table candlesticks, with detachable nozzles, by John Scofield, London, 1784, one nozzle 1792, 29cm. high. (Christie's) $7,200 £4,800

CASTERS

A sugar caster designed by
Harald Nielsen, stamped
Dessin H.N. 925S Georg
Jensen S Wendel A/S 645,
circa 1949, 11.4cm. high,
7oz.14dwt. (Christie's)
$626 £432

A Continental caster modelled
as a kingfisher, import hallmarks for Glasgow, 1908,
16cm. from beak to tail.
(Christie's) $262 £175

A plain cylindrical sugar
caster with domed cover,
by Goldsmiths & Silversmiths
Co., London, 1911, 7¼in.
high, 11.50oz. (Christie's)
$222 £150

A George I, West Country,
muffineer, with the mark of
Joseph Collier, circa 1725,
11cm. high. (Phillips)
$630 £420

A George II vase-shaped caster,
6¼in. high, with a pair of
matching smaller casters, 5¼in.
high, by Samuel Wood, London,
1747 and 1750, 11oz.
(Christie's) $1,278 £900

One of a pair of Charles II
cylindrical casters, by F.
Garthorne, 1683, 5in. high,
11oz.7dwt. (Christie's)
$12,441 £8,640

One of a pair of Dutch
spirally fluted pear-shaped
casters, by J. Siotteling,
Amsterdam, 1765, 8¾in.
high, 27oz. gross.(Christie's)
$7,992 £5,400

One of a pair of pounce pots,
by John McKay, Edinburgh,
1798, 3oz. (Worsfolds)
$331 £230

An Edwardian inverted
pear-shaped sugar caster,
W.F. and A.F. Sheffield,
1901, 8½in. high, 8.50oz.
(Christie's) $133 £90

SILVER

A George II epergne on four foliage, scroll and shell feet, and with four detachable scroll branches with openwork dish frames, maker's mark CM, 1759, 63oz. (Christie's) $4,795 £3,240

A George II epergne on four shell and scroll feet, by E. Wakelin, 1751, length of basket 12in., 153oz. (Christie's) $14,385 £9,720

George III silver table centrepiece, by Wm. Pitts, London, 1764, 10½in. high, 81oz. (Hobbs & Chambers) $6,048 £4,200

A Victorian table centrepiece candelabrum, by S. Hayne and D. Cater, 1845, 57.5cm. high, 66oz. (Lawrence Fine Art) $1,237 £836

A George III oval epergne, 1802, maker's mark IP, probably for Joseph Preedy, with cut glass bowl, 10in. high, 38oz. (Christie's) $2,192 £1,512

A Victorian parcel gilt centrepiece and mirror plateau, by F. Elkington, Birmingham, 1893, 27in. high, 207oz. (Christie's) $7,047 £4,860

A George III epergne and mirror plateau, by M. Boulton, Birmingham, 1810, length of plateau 26in., height of epergne 10½in. (Christie's) $14,774 £10,260

One of a pair of late 19th century repousse sterling silver compotes, by Tiffany & Co., 9.3/8in. diam., 40 troy oz. (Robt. W. Skinner Inc.) $1,258 £850

A gilt Old Sheffield plate epergne with large central glass dish and four smaller dishes on mirror plateau, by Roberts, Cadman & Co., circa 1822, 13½in. high, 24in. wide. (Christie's) $2,975 £2,052

SILVER

Late 19th century silver chamberstick by Mappin & Webb, London, 5in. high, 5oz. (Bermondsey)
$150 £100

A Hukin & Heath electro-plated chamberstick with snuffer designed by Dr. C. Dresser, stamped H & H 9658 Rd No. 228142, 12.5cm. high. (Christie's)
$1,340 £918

A George IV circular chamber candlestick with leaf-capped handle and conical snuffer, by R. Garrard, London, 1828, 5½in. diam., 14oz. (Christie's)
$444 £300

A Victorian shaped circular chamber candlestick, by Henry Wilkinson, Sheffield, 1863, 6in. diam., 11oz. (Christie's) $473 £320

A Perry Son & Co. maroon painted metal chamber candlestick, designed by Dr. C. Dresser, registration lozenge for 1883, 14.5cm. high. (Christie's)$425 £302

A George III circular chamber-stick, with detachable nozzle and snuffer, by Thos. Law, Sheffield, perhaps 1806, 15cm. high, 11oz., and a pair of plated snuffers. (Christie's)$444 £300

George III shaped circular chamberstick, by William Stroud, 1805, 13½oz. (Bermondsey)
$1,500 £1,000

George III chamber candle-stick, by John Crouch and Thos. Hannam, London, 9oz. (Bermondsey)
$600 £400

George III chamber candle-stick with removable drip tray, maker Thos. Robins, London, 1798, 4in. high, 8oz. (Capes, Dunn & Co.) $411 £280

CHOCOLATE POTS

A Queen Anne plain tapering cylindrical chocolate pot, by Nathaniel Lock, 1708, 8¾in. high, 18oz.18dwt. gross. (Christie's) $4,315 £2,916

A cylindrical chocolate pot, by S. C. S. Groth, Copenhagen, 1884, 17.5cm. high, 17oz. (Christie's) $421 £285

A George II plain tapering cylindrical chocolate pot, Exeter, 1736, 9¾in. high, gross 28oz. (Christie's) $4,795 £3,240

A George III chocolate pot, by Milne & Campbell, Glasgow, circa 1770. 36oz. (Christie's) $1,776 £1,200

Mid 18th century Flemish silver chocolate pot of baluster form, Ghent, 1200gr. (Bermondsey) $4,200 £2,750

An early 18th century silver chocolate pot, by Wm. Fawdery, London, 12oz. (Robt. W. Skinner Inc.) $450 £300

CIGARETTE BOXES

Silver cigarette box and cover, in the Art Nouveau style, by Ramsden & Carr, circa 1903, 7½in. wide. (Bermondsey) $1,125 £750

An Alfred Dunhill silver gilt and enamel cigarette box and lighter, London hallmarks for 1929. (Christie's) $1,149 £756

A Chinese wood lined oblong cigarette box ornately moulded with carp, 8¼in. long. (Christie's) $284 £200

An Austrian cigarette case applied with two-colour gold and gem set monograms and facsimile signatures, circa 1895. (Phillips) $774 £520

A Victorian cigarette case, the cover enamelled with a nude girl lying beside a stream, Birmingham, 1887. (Phillips) $588 £400

An Austrian white metal and enamel eight-sided cigarette case, the enamel by F. Zwichl, depicting a Samson car in black, red and cream. (Christie's)　$783 £540

A Continental plated cigarette case enamelled with a collie dog on a sky background, circa 1910. (Phillips) $223 £150

An Edwardian gilt lined cigarette case, polychrome-enamelled with a picture of a lady, R.C., Birmingham, 1905. (Christie's) $284 £200

A German cigarette case enamelled on cover with a spaniel carrying a dead duck in its mouth, circa 1900. (Phillips)　$367 £250

A late Victorian gilt lined cigarette case, enamelled with a scene from R. Kipling's poem 'Absent minded beggar', C.S. & F.S., Birmingham, 1899. (Christie's)　$372 £250

An Austrian enamel cigarette case, signed 'Schleiertanz', circa 1895. (Phillips) $735 £500

A white metal and enamel cigarette case, the enamel by F. Zwichl, circa 1920. (Christie's) $2,818 £1,944

CLARET JUGS

A Victorian large vase-shaped claret jug with an applied cast putto handle, by Houles & Co., London, 1841, 14½in. high, 38oz. (Christie's)
$1,837 £1,250

A George IV claret jug, maker's mark probably that of Joseph Angell, 1829, 29cm. high, 31oz. (Lawrence Fine Art)
$2,392 £1,650

A Victorian pear-shaped cut glass claret jug, hob cut, 13½in. high. (Parsons, Welch & Cowell) $214 £145

A William IV fluted, inverted pear-shaped claret jug, with presentation inscription, Messrs. Barnard, London, 1836, 12¼in. high, 29.25oz. (Christie's) $962 £650

A pair of French silver gilt mounted clear glass claret jugs, by Risler & Carre, Paris, circa 1870, 11¾in. high. (Christie's) $4,924 £3,240

A 19th century Indian silver claret jug, snake coiled around body forming handle and lid stop, 14¾in. high, 32 troy oz. (Robt. W. Skinner Inc.)
$375 £273

A Victorian claret jug, by Marshall & Sons, Edinburgh, 1865, 35cm. high, 30oz. (Christie's) $1,110 £740

A late Victorian mounted glass claret jug in the form of a cockatoo, by Alex. Crichton, 1882, 27cm. high. (Phillips)
$3,450 £2,300

A George III claret or hot water jug, by Henry Chawner, 1791, 31cm. high, 23oz. all in. (Lawrence Fine Art) $1,914 £1,320

SILVER

Pair of George III silver wine coasters in the Adam style, 5in. diam., London hallmark. (Bermondsey) $450 £300

A pair of George III circular decanter stands, by Thomas Robinson I, London, 1809. (Christie's) $1,391 £940

A pair of George III pierced silver wine coasters, by I. R. & Co., Sheffield, 1774, 5½in. diam. (Bermondsey) $900 £600

One of a pair of silver mounted Regency papier mache coasters, each with twin ring handles. (Phillips) $1,275 £850

A Sheffield plated trolley coaster, 44cm. long. (Lawrence Fine Art) $582 £396

George III circular coaster, by Jabez & Thos. Daniel, London, circa 1773. (Bermondsey) $750 £500

A pair of Old Sheffield plate 5¾in. circular wine coasters, with turned wood bases, (Parsons, Welch & Cowell) $217 £145

A superb pair of George IV brass bound mahogany wine coasters, 12½in. high. (Christie's) $3,400 £2,250

A pair of George III plain, circular wine coasters, by Solomon Hougham, London, 1802, 14.5cm. diam. (Christie's) $525 £350

COFFEE POTS

A Queen Anne plain tapering cylindrical coffee pot, by Simon Pantin, 1705, 10.3/8in. high, gross 29oz. (Christie's) $3,836 £2,592

A George IV small coffee pot, by Wm. Bateman, 1827, 19.4cm. high, 34oz. (Lawrence Fine Art) $797 £550

A George II Irish plain tapering cylindrical coffee pot, Dublin, 1734, 9in. high, gross 32oz. (Christie's) $7,672 £5,184

A George II plain tapering cylindrical coffee pot, 1727, maker's mark probably IE for John Eckfourd Jnr., 8.5/8in. high, gross 20oz. (Christie's) $2,877 £1,944

A George II pear-shaped coffee pot, by Isaac Cookson, Newcastle, 1748, 9¼in. high, gross 26oz. (Christie's) $2,035 £1,404

A George II plain tapering cylindrical coffee pot, by Thos. Farren, 1717, 9½in. high, gross 21oz. (Christie's) $2,505 £1,728

A Queen Anne plain tapering cylindrical coffee pot, by Edward Yorke, 1711, 9¼in. high, gross 20oz. (Christie's) $3,601 £2,484

A George I plain tapering octagonal coffee pot and stand, by John East, 1714, 9¾in. high, gross 33oz. (Christie's) $38,361 £25,920

A Queen Anne plain tapering cylindrical coffee pot, by A. Courtauld, 1710, 10in. high, gross 27oz. (Christie's) $5,950 £4,104

COFFEE POTS

A double pyriform coffee pot, by C. Wiltberger, Phila., circa 1785-90, 14¼in. high, gross wt. 51oz. (Christie's) $16,500 £11,619

A Continental fluted baluster coffee pot on scroll feet, with a grotesque mask spout, 9½in. high. (Christie's) $325 £220

A George III vase-shaped coffee pot, by Henry Chawner, London, 1789, 11.5in. high, 26oz. all in. (Woolley & Wallis) $1,200 £800

A Queen Anne plain tapering cylindrical coffee pot, by Robt. Timbrell, 1707, 10in. high, 23oz. gross. (Christie's) $4,315 £2,916

A George III pear-shaped coffee pot, by Francis Butty and Nicholas Dumee, London, 1765, 11½in. high, 31.75oz. gross. (Christie's) $1,136 £800

A George III gadrooned, pear-shaped coffee pot, probably by John Scofield, London, 1776, 10¾in. high, 26.25oz. (Christie's) $1,562 £1,100

A George II plain tapering cylindrical coffee pot, by John Cafe, circa 1750, 9¾in. high, gross 25oz. (Christie's) $2,349 £1,620

George III silver coffee pot, by Henry Chawner, 20oz., 11¼in. high. (Robt. W. Skinner Inc.) $1,200 £800

A George III vase-shaped coffee pot, in the Neo-Classical manner, by John Carter II, London, 1774, 29.5cm. high, 27oz. (Christie's) $1,539 £1,040

COFFEE POTS

An early George III coffee pot, by Wm. Shaw II and Wm. Priest, 1757, 29.5cm. high, 31oz. all in. (Lawrence Fine Art) $1,139 £770

Epping Forest Centenary flagon of tapering cylinder shape, London 1978, 41oz. (Peter Wilson & Co.)
     $331 £230

An early George III baluster coffee pot, by Wm. Cripps, the cover with standard mark, 27.5cm. high, 31oz. all in. (Lawrence Fine Art)
     $3,719 £2,530

A George II plain baluster coffee pot, by Wm. Shaw and Wm. Priest, London, 1753, 9in. high, 21.25oz. (Christie's) $1,349 £950

An 18th century French Provincial cafetiere, by Henry Louis Le Gaigneur, Saint-Omer, circa 1730, 29cm. high, 35oz. (Phillips) $4,512 £3,200

A George II baluster coffee pot with scalloped spout, by Whipham & Wright, 1757, 31oz. (Phillips) $1,500 £1,000

A George II baluster silver coffee pot, London, 1746, 10¼in. high, 27oz. all in. (Parsons, Welch & Cowell)
     $1,221 £825

A Liberty silver coffee pot, designed by Archibald Knox, with Birmingham hallmarks for 1906, 21.5cm. high. (Christie's) $3,040 £2,000

A George II plain, tapering coffee pot, George Hindmarsh, London, 1755, 10in. high, 27.75oz. gross. (Christie's)
     $1,215 £900

CREAM JUGS

A silver oval covered cream
jug, by Omar Ramsden, 1925,
11cm. high, 8.5oz. (Phillips)
$1,176 £800

A Continental cream jug
formed as a pug dog, wearing
a link collar and with curled
tail, 5in. long. (Christie's)
$444 £300

A George II silver gilt cast
cream jug, unmarked but
in the manner of Paul de
Lamerie, 4¾in. high, 11oz.
(Christie's)
$14,385 £9,720

A double pyriform cream
pitcher, by Cary Dunn, Newark,
circa 1780-90, 5¾in. high, 7oz.
10dwt. (Christie's)
$3,080 £2,169

A George III silver gilt vase-
shaped cream jug, maker's
mark only IS, pellet between,
4½in. high, 11oz.2dwt.
(Christie's) $3,516 £2,376

A silver cream jug of inverted
pyriform with a scroll handle,
by Wm. Hollingshead, Phila.,
circa 1760/80, 5in. high, 4oz.
(Christie's) $3,300 £2,275

A covered cream pitcher, by
Chas. Moore and J. Ferguson,
Phila., circa 1801-05, 8¼in.
high, 8oz. (Christie's)
$1,870 £1,316

Late 18th century silver
creamer, maker's mark
INR, Phila., 4½in. high, 4
troy oz. (Robt. W. Skinner
Inc.) $400 £273

A George III plain, inverted,
pear shaped cream jug,
London, 1774, 11cm. high.
(Christie's) $111 £75

CRUETS

A George III oval boat shaped condiment cruet, by Wm. Simmons, London, 1788, and a later mustard spoon, London, 1809, 29oz. (Woolley & Wallis) $1,725 £1,150

Victorian plated egg cruet, circa 1880. (British Antique Exporters) $41 £31

A boat-shaped cruet stand by Omar Ramsden, 1925, 10in. long, gross 42oz. (Christie's) $5,598 £3,888

A George III egg cruet stand with spoons, five by J. Emes, London 1804, and one by E. J. & W. Barnard, London 1837, (Christie's) $621 £420

A Victorian circular egg cruet, with a pair of casters, by John S. Hunt, 1853, 10½in. high, 76oz. (Christie's) $3,356 £2,268

A Hukin & Heath electro-plated six-sided cruet frame, designed by Dr. C. Dresser, with lozenge for 11th April 1878, 9cm. high.(Christie's) $867 £594

A plated cruet stand with eight bottles. (Worsfolds) $144 £100

A George IV egg cruet stand with revolving frame, by Robt. Hennell II, fully marked 1823, 19.5cm. high, 29oz. (Lawrence Fine Art) $732 £495

A Regency egg cruet with six matching egg cups, London, 1820, together with six George IV eggspoons, by Eley & Fearn, London, 1824, 32oz. (Woolley & Wallis) $1,197 £820

A Queen Anne two-handled cup and cover on circular fluted foot, by Lewis Mettayer, 1712, 9½in. high, 45oz. (Christie's) $6,998 £4,860

One of a pair of George III silver two-handled cups, by Thos. Whipham and Chas. Wright, 1760, 5½in. high, 35oz. (Christie's)
$1,788 £1,242

A George II silver gilt two-handled cup and cover, by B. Godfrey, 1738, 12¼in. high, 81oz. (Christie's)
$10,179 £7,020

A George III silver gilt two-handled cup and cover, by Henry Chawner, 1789, 19¼in. high, 92oz. (Christie's)
$5,909 £4,104

A George IV silver gilt racing trophy cup, by Benjamin Smith, 1824, 34cm. high, 116.5oz. (Phillips)
$3,525 £2,500

An Elizabeth I plain wine cup, engraved 'The Towne of Wollterton, 1568', by Peter Peterson, Norwich, 5¼in. high, 6oz. (Christie's)
$5,253 £3,456

A George III cup and cover, by Wm. Holmes, 1789, 32cm. high, 32oz. (Lawrence Fine Art) $669 £462

A George IV silver gilt two-handled campana-shaped cup and cover, by Wm. Burwash, 1821, 15¼in. high, 136oz. (Christie's)
$7,464 £5,184

A George III vase-shaped two-handled cup and cover, by Wm. Pitts and J. Preedy, 1794, 18½in. high, 128oz. (Christie's) $6,393 £4,320

DISHES

One of a pair of oval entree dishes, covers and detachable handles, by Walker & Hall, Sheffield, 1911, 27.7cm., 108oz. (Lawrence Fine Art) $877 £605

A silver chafing dish with a flaring brim, by Jacob Hurd, Boston, 1745, 12½in. long, gross weight 19oz.10dwt. (Christie's)$55,000 £37,931

One of a pair of George IV shaped oblong silver entree dishes and covers, by B. Smith II, 1825, 12½in. long, 146oz. (Christie's) $4,976 £3,456

One of a set of four early Victorian shell butter dishes, by Thomas James & Nathaniel Creswick, Sheffield, 1837, 23oz. (Phillips) $1,911 £1,300

One of a set of four George III meat dishes, by J. Parker and E. Wakelin, 1761, 13½in. long, 108oz. (Christie's) $8,553 £5,940

A fruit dish modelled as a shell with a seated merman, by the Goldsmiths & Silver-smiths Co., 1910, 37cm. high. (Phillips) $2,425 £1,650

A George III Irish oval butter dish with green glass liner, by Joseph Jadison, Dublin, 1779, 17.1cm. long, 14oz. (Phillips) $1,269 £900

A German parcel gilt circular dish, by Jeremias Ritter, Nuremberg, circa 1630, 7¾in. wide, 5oz.12dwt. (Christie's) $3,836 £2,592

One of a pair of George III octagonal entree dishes and covers, by Paul Storr, 1800, 12¼in. long, 104oz. (Christie's) $7,192 £4,860

DISHES

A William III large silver gilt charger, by Ralph Leeke, circa 1695, 22in. diam., 134oz. (Christie's)
$10,108 £7,020

One of a set of four silver George III shaped oblong entree dishes and covers, by Paul Storr, 1810, 11.3/8in. long, 309oz. (Christie's)
$27,993 £19,440

One of twelve George III shaped circular dinner plates, by J. Young and O. Jackson, 1774, 9.5/8in. diam., 237oz. (Christie's)
$9,270 £6,264

A silver chafing dish, by A. Hartwell, Mass., bowl 6in. diam., 27oz.10dwt. (Christie's) $1,210 £834

One of a pair of George II butter shells on three shell and rocaille feet, by Paul de Lamerie, 1746, 4¾in. wide, 10oz.6dwt. (Christie's)
$52,876 £36,720

One of a pair of silver George III entree dishes and covers, by Paul Storr, 1810, 12¾in. long, 153oz. (Christie's)
$13,996 £9,720

One of a pair of George II large shaped circular dishes, by Nicholas Sprimont, 1743, 14½in. diam, 85oz. (Christie's)
$37,324 £25,920

One of twelve George III silver gilt shaped circular dinner plates, by Wm. Stroud, 1804, the gilding later, 9¾in. wide, 231oz. (Christie's) $8,791 £5,940

A George I Irish strawberry dish with scalloped rim, by David King, Dublin, 1714. (Christie's) $6,713 £4,536

DISHES

One of twelve George II shaped circular dinner plates, by Paul De Lamerie, 1741, 9½in. diam., 233oz. (Christie's)

$44,755 £30,240

A C. R. Ashbee silver muffin dish and cover with London hallmarks for 1900, 18oz. gross weight, 22cm. high. (Christie's) $2,207 £1,512

One of four George II circular strawberry dishes, three by Chas. F. Kandler, 1747, one by S. Herbert & Co., 1753, 9.3/8in. diam., 81oz. (Christie's) $22,377 £15,120

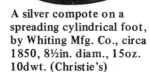

A Regency Sheffield plate oval meat dish and matching cover, 18in. diam. (Woolley & Wallis) $473 £320

A silver compote on a spreading cylindrical foot, by Whiting Mfg. Co., circa 1850, 8½in. diam., 15oz. 10dwt. (Christie's)
$440 £303

One of four George III silver gilt shell-shaped butter dishes, by J. Foskett & J. Stewart, 1810, 24oz. (Christie's) $2,818 £1,944

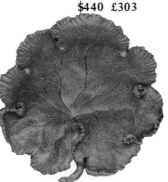

A George II silver gilt circular alms dish, by R. Beale or R. Bayley, 21.8cm. diam., 18.9oz. (Lawrence Fine Art) $3,093 £2,090

A William IV silver gilt vine leaf fruit dish, by John Watson, Sheffield 1834, 12in. wide, 29oz. (Christie's)
$3,110 £2,160

One of twelve George II shaped circular dinner plates, by Wm. Grundy, 1753, 9¾in. diam, 215oz. (Christie's)
$10,886 £7,560

SILVER

An American ovoid wine ewer, the body chased overall in the Chinese style, by S. Kirk, Baltimore, circa 1830, 16¼in. high, 48oz. (Christie's) $2,349 £1,620

A Queen Anne style ewer with caryatid handle, London, 1926, 8¾in. high, 20.25oz. (Christie's) $894 £600

A William IV Irish wine ewer, maker's mark R.S., Dublin, 1833, 12in. high, 30oz. (Christie's) $2,368 £1,600

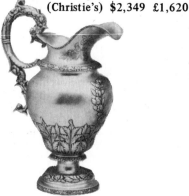

One of a pair of inverted, pyriform ewers, by F. Marquand, New York, 1826-39, 14½in. high, 38oz. 10dwt. (Christie's) $2,750 £1,936

A silver vase shaped ewer, by Jones, Ball & Poor, Boston, circa 1846, 16¼in. high, 41oz. (Christie's) $1,100 £758

Silver presentation ewer, maker's mark Shreve, Brown & Co., coin on base, 10½in. high, approx. 29 troy oz., circa 1857. (Robt. W. Skinner Inc.) $700 £472

A Victorian silver mounted claret jug, by Messrs. Barnard, 1873, 34cm. high. (Lawrence Fine Art) $1,628 £1,100

A vase shaped ewer, by B. C. Frobisher, circa 1816-25, 11.1/8in. high, 25oz. (Christie's) $935 £658

A Victorian Scottish wine jug, by Wm. Marshall, Edinburgh, 1866, 15in. high, the handle altered for hot water and reassayed H.W.C., London, 1866, 27oz. (Woolley & Wallis) $1,125 £750

FLATWARE

A George II Irish soup ladle with deep pear-shaped bowl, Dublin, circa 1745, date letter and maker's mark lacking, 15in. long, 12oz. 19dwt. on fitted wood stand. (Christie's)
$1,252 £864

A silver fish slice with a faceted handle, by Hayden & Gregg, South Carolina, 1846/52, 12in. long, 6oz.10dwt. (Christie's)$715 £493

One of a pair of jam spoons designed by Georg Jensen, the hammered and cut bowls in the form of a leaf with curving handles. (Christie's) $313 £216

A Guild of Handicraft Ltd. silver preserve spoon, stamped G. of H. Ltd. and London hallmarks for 1902. (Christie's)$406 £280

Part of a set of George IV double shell and laurel pattern table service, by Eley & Fearn, 1824, in fitted wood canteen, 235oz. (Christie's) $7,192 £4,860

A Royal silver serving spoon, Paris, circa 1815-20, 11in. long, 5 troy oz. (Robt. W. Skinner Inc.) $407 £275

Part of a silver gilt composite Kings pattern table service, 1815, 1819, etc. and modern, in fitted canteen with nine drawers, 377oz. (Christie's) $19,180 £12,960

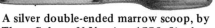

A silver double-ended marrow scoop, by Thos. Colgan, N.Y., circa 1775, 8in. long, 1oz. (Christie's) $4,400 £3,034

A William and Mary rat-tailed trefid spoon and matching three-pronged fork, by Wm. Mathew, 1689, 4oz.12dwt. (Christie's)
$74,649 £51,840

A Georg Jensen 64-piece 'chess pattern' table service stamped Georg Jensen, Sterling, Denmark, 50oz.12dwt. weight not including knives. (Christie's) $2,680 £1,836

A knife and fork designed by Henry van de Velde, the handles with curvilinear art nouveau design, circa 1900. (Christie's)
$1,252 £864

A Georg Jensen 180-piece 'acorn' pattern table service, first designed in 1915 by Johan Rohde, 181oz. weight not including knives. (Christie's) $29,959 £20,520

FLATWARE

A 106-piece 'Cypress' pattern table service designed by Tias Eckhoff, 112oz.2dwt., weight not including items that are part steel. (Christie's) $3,601 £2,484

An 89-piece 'Cactus' pattern table service, designed by Gundorph Albertus, stamped marks, 102oz., weight not including items that are part steel. (Christie's)
$3,915 £2,700

A 134-piece 'Pyramid' pattern table service designed by Harald Nielson, stamped marks, 181oz.5dwt., weight not including items that are part steel. (Christie's)
$9,396 £6,480

A set of King's pattern fish knives and forks having plated blades and embossed handles, also a matching pair of fish servers, Sheffield, 1928. (Peter Wilson & Co.) $108 £75

FLATWARE

A large part service of George III Old English and thread pattern cutlery, by various silversmiths, circa 1780, 139oz. (Lawrence Fine Art) $3,987 £2,750

A George IV service of fiddle, thread and shell pattern cutlery for twelve place settings, by Wm. Chawner, 1827, 140oz. (Lawrence Fine Art) $8,140 £5,500

A 193-piece 'Acorn' pattern table service, designed by Johan Rohde, stamped marks, 245oz., weight not including items that are part steel. (Christie's) $7,516 £5,184

A service of Hanoverian pattern cutlery for twelve place settings, maker's mark G. & H., Sheffield 1960/63, 169oz., excluding steel mounted items. (Lawrence Fine Art) $4,884 £3,300

FRAMES

A Ramsden & Carr silver picture frame, with London hallmarks for 1900, 15.5cm. high. (Christie's)
$1,425 £950

A Victorian embossed silver photograph frame, Birmingham, 1899, 8in. high. (Dacre, Son & Hartley) $187 £125

An Art Nouveau stand photograph frame, repousse with fruiting vines and panels, Birmingham 1910, 8½ x 6½in. (Capes, Dunn & Co.)
$176 £120

An embossed and pierced shaped silver photograph frame, London, 1900, 8in. high. (Dacre, Son & Hartley)
$270 £180

A WMF plated figural easel-backed mirror, stamped maker's marks, 37cm. high. (Phillips) $870 £580

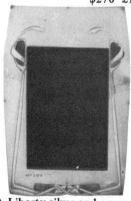

An Art Nouveau silver mounted photograph frame, by A. & J. Zimmerman, Birmingham, 1906, 28.8cm. high. (Lawrence Fine Art)
$305 £209

A Liberty silver and enamel picture frame, designed by Archibald Knox, with Birmingham hallmarks for 1904, 21.2cm. high. (Christie's) $5,909 £3,888

An Art Nouveau silver photograph frame, stamped maker's marks W.N. and Chester hallmarks for 1903, 22.3cm. high. (Christie's) $450 £300

A William III large silver gilt dressing table mirror, by Wm. Lukin, circa 1700, 32¾in. high. (Christie's)
$20,217 £14,040

GOBLETS

A 20th century enamelled and jewelled sterling silver chalice, approx. 4 troy oz. (Robt. W. Skinner Inc.)
$550 £376

One of six George IV partly fluted thistle-shaped goblets, maker's mark WE for Wm. Eaton or Wm. Elliot, 1822, 5.5/8in. high, 65oz. (Christie's) $6,713 £4,536

A Channel Islands plain wine cup, by Guillaume Henry, circa 1740, 5½in. high, 6oz. (Christie's) $1,722 £1,188

A Charles I plain wine cup on circular foot, 1640, maker's mark RW over a cinquefoil, within a dotted heart, 7in. high, 10oz. (Christie's) $7,776 £5,400

A Commonwealth wine cup on trumpet-shaped foot, 1655, maker's mark ET a crescent below, 3½in. high, 2oz.18dwt. (Christie's)
$3,421 £2,376

A 19th century Indian Colonial goblet, by Hamilton & Co., Calcutta, circa 1860, 19.6cm. high, 8.5oz. (Phillips)
$451 £320

An Arts & Crafts Movement chalice in medieval style, by Omar Ramsden & Alwin Carr, London, 1912, 5.2in. high, 10oz. all in. (Christie's)
$1,124 £760

A large goblet designed by H. Nielsen, stamped Dessin H.N. G.J. 535, circa 1928, 19.9cm. high, 25oz.15dwt. (Christie's) $2,505 £1,725

A wine cup, Guernsey, circa 1695, maker's mark RB a fleur-de-lys and coronet above, 5.5/8in. high, 7oz. 3dwt. (Christie's)
$2,114 £1,458

SILVER

A Victorian treasury inkstand on four bun feet, by Elkington & Co., Birmingham, 1900, 10¾in. long, 90oz. (Christie's) $3,036 £2,052

An Edwardian rectangular inkstand, fitted with two glass inkwells, Mappin & Webb, London, 1908, 12¼in. long, 46oz. (Christie's) $888 £600

Indian chased white metal inkstand with two glass bottles, ivory inlaid border to stand, 10½in. wide. (Hobbs & Chambers) $144 £100

A late Victorian double inkstand, by W. J. Barnard, London, 1894, 11in. long. 25oz. (Woolley & Wallis) $769 £520

A silver oblong inkstand with flat hinged lid, the interior with two glass inkwells and silver dip pen, 9in. wide, Birmingham 1918, 32oz. (Capes, Dunn & Co.) $395 £275

A George III rectangular inkstand, by Wm. Allen III, 1798, 30.3cm. long, 41oz. (Lawrence Fine Art) $1,953 £1,320

A Russian metal and marble desk set with three-quarter pierced gallery, 18½in. wide. (Christie's) $4,976 £3,456

A Guild of Handicraft white metal and enamel inkwell, attributed to C. R. Ashbee, seven sided on ball feet, 10.5cm. high. (Christie's) $2,522 £1,728

A George IV oblong inkstand, by Rebecca Emes and Edward Barnard, 1824, 25.7cm. long, 23oz. of weighable silver. (Lawrence Fine Art) $1,697 £1,155

A silver baluster ale jug, in the 18th century taste, 8in. high, 23.25oz. (Christie's) $134 £95

An English silver mounted malling-type turquoise blue tin glazed earthenware jug and cover, circa 1590, 7½in. high. (Christie's) $5,434 £3,672

A 19th century American cordial or water jug of baluster form, maker's mark of Jones, Ball & Poor, Boston, circa 1845, 28cm. high, 30oz. (Phillips) $999 £680

A George II plain silver pear-shaped beer jug, by Philip Elston, Exeter, the date letter probably for 1742, 7¾in. high, 22oz. (Christie's) $4,354 £3,024

A silver hot water jug, of oval section, by Omar Ramsden, 1930, 27cm. high, 36.5oz. (Phillips) $3,969 £2,700

A jug with ebony handle, stamped Georg Jensen 407A, 23.2cm. high, 35oz. 5dwt. gross weight. (Christie's) $2,662 £1,836

A Victorian claret jug, the oval body engraved at a later date, by Messrs. Barnard, 1867, 31.2cm. high, 21oz. (Lawrence Fine Art) $553 £374

A Victorian 'ascos' jug, by Hunt & Roskell, 1844, 33.25oz. (Phillips) $1,984 £1,350

A 17th century Rhenish stoneware baluster jug with contemporary English silver mount, 19.5cm. high. (Christie's) $766 £540

MISCELLANEOUS

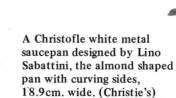

A curved shaped oblong silver spirit flask with detachable gilt lined cup and cover, by Omar Ramsden, 1924, 6½in. high, 18oz. (Christie's) $1,710 £1,188

A Christofle white metal saucepan designed by Lino Sabattini, the almond shaped pan with curving sides, 18.9cm. wide. (Christie's) $391 £270

A Hukin & Heath plated spoon-warmer with ebony handle, the design attributed to Dr. C. Dresser, stamped H & H 2857, 14.4cm. high. (Christie's) $378 £259

A French Christening set, post 1838 guarantee, with maker's mark of Veyrant, 8.8oz. of weighable silver. (Lawrence Fine Art) $510 £352

A Victorian composite silver gilt dressing table set, by various silversmiths, 1885/89, 21-pieces including Dutch silver gilt coloured metal box. (Lawrence Fine Art) $1,355 £935

A Boucheron powder compact and two lipstick holders, Made in France. (Christie's) $315 £216

A rock crystal and sterling silver crucifix, 14½in. high. (Robt. W. Skinner Inc.) $2,100 £1,438

A set of six early Victorian cast swag shape wine labels, by E. J. & W. Barnard, London, 1851, 4oz. (Woolley & Wallis) $562 £380

Victorian silver scent phial, Birmingham, 1892, 8in. long, 5oz., in case. (Hobbs & Chambers) $374 £260

A silver kojiri formed as a growling karashishi, signed Yasuyoshi (Nukagawa), early 19th century. (Christie's) $293 £216

A shallow saucepan designed by H. Nielsen, stamped Dessin H.N. Georg Jensen G.J. 925S 644, circa 1920, 5.3 cm. high, 11oz.12dwt. gross weight. (Christie's) $548 £378

A Hukin & Heath electroplated letter rack designed by Dr. C. Dresser, stamped H & H 2555 and registration lozenge for May 1881, 12.3cm. high. (Christie's) $408 £280

A Victorian electroplated meat press, by Elkington & Co., 44cm. high, excluding wood base. (Lawrence Fine Art) $2,073 £1,430

A George II triangular kettle stand, by John le Sage, 1734, 11½in. wide, 36oz. (Christie's) $4,475 £3,024

One of three George III silver gilt wine labels for Port, Claret and Champagne, by Benjamin Smith, 1808, 3in. high, 7oz.5dwt. (Christie's) $3,676 £2,484

Victorian oak hanging brush set with plated mounts, 1880. (British Antique Exporters) $40 £30

Three pieces from a dressing table set, die stamped with foliage in the Art Nouveau style, Chester 1903/04/05, by W. Neale. (Lawrence Fine Art) $112 £77

A Lacloche Freres patterned silver and red gold minaudiere set with five sapphires, stamped with import marks for 1935, 13oz.14dwt., 13 x 8.6cm. (Christie's) $1,576 £1,080

A Continental silver model of a magpie, import marks for 1899, 19½in. overall, 29oz. (Christie's) $2,177 £1,512

A late Victorian novelty port bottle carrier in the form of a donkey and cart, 13in. long, by H. T., London, 1890. (Woolley & Wallis) $1,372 £940

A 19th century Continental silver gilt model of a seated bear, 8in. high, 22oz. (Christie's) $1,805 £1,188

A Victorian model of an equestrian knight in armour, by Stephen Smith, 1870, 9in. high, 28oz. (Christie's) $1,518 £1,026

A late 19th century English silvered bronze group of a jockey on horseback, signed and dated J. Willis Good, 1875, 32.5cm. high. (Christie's) $3,000 £2,000

'Nude Girl with Shawl', a silvered bronze figure cast from a model by Lorenzl, decorated by Crejo, 37.5cm. high. (Christie's) $1,879 £1,296

'Vestal' a silvered bronze figure by Le Faguays, on stepped square shaped marble base, 14½in. high. (Christie's) $1,617 £1,100

A late 19th century English silvered bronze group of a jockey on horseback, signed and dated J. Willis Good, 1875, 27cm. high.(Christie's) $3,750 £2,500

A Victorian cigar lighter, formed as a deer-hound, by J. S. Hunt, 1851, 5¼in. high, 18oz.17dwt. (Christie's) $1,879 £1,296

MODELS

A silver cast model of a Clydesdale horse, the sculptor G. Halliday, made by Elkington & Co., Birmingham, 1911, 21in. high, 309oz. (Christie's) $14,385 £9,720

A sectional silvered model of a crayfish, unsigned, Meiji period, 43cm. long. (Christie's) $1,158 £810

A Continental silver model of a grouse, by B. Muller, import marks for 1902, 10½in. high, 26oz. (Christie's) $1,632 £1,134

MUGS

A George II plain baluster mug, by Robert Albin Cox, London, 1758, 15cm. high, 17oz. (Christie's) $651 £440

A George II beer mug, of good gauge, by John Gorham, 1759, 12cm. high, 11oz. (Phillips) $450 £300

An early George II mug, by Francis Spilsbury I, 1735, 11cm. high. (Lawrence Fine Art) $733 £506

A George II Provincial mug with leaf-capped scroll handle, by Langlands & Goodrick, Newcastle, 1756, 9cm. high, 7.25oz. (Phillips) $570 £380

A George II plain baluster mug, London, 1733, 13cm. high, 11oz. (Christie's) $407 £275

A William IV panelled campana-shaped child's mug, by Chas. Fox, London, 1831, 4oz. (Woolley & Wallis) $335 £230

MUSTARDS

George III silver mustard
pot of plain cylindrical
form with scroll handle,
3½oz. (Bermondsey)
$150 £100

A Charles Boyton hammered
silver four-piece condiments
set, London hallmarks for
1947, 11oz. (Christie's)
$882 £626

A Guild of Handicrafts silver
mustard pot, designed by C.
R. Ashbee, with London
hallmarks for 1902, 8.5cm.
high, 4oz.11dwt. gross weight.
(Christie's) $1,395 £918

One of a pair of George III
vase-shaped mustard pots,
by R. Emes and E. Barnard,
1811, 5¼in. high, 42oz.
(Christie's) $3,996 £2,700

A George III pierced and bright
cut reeded oval mustard pot,
with two matching salt cellars
and spoons, by Peter and Anne
Bateman, London, 1798.
(Christie's) $497 £350

A C. R. Ashbee silver mustard
pot, set with six turquoise
cabochons, London hallmarks
for 1900, 8cm. high.
(Christie's) $1,313 £864

George III silver mustard pot,
by Edward Capper, London,
1797, 3¾in. high.
(Bermondsey) $325 £225

A Charles Boyton hammered
silver four-piece condiments
set, the mustard pots with
spoons and glass liners, 1947,
10oz. (Christie's) $913 £648

George III oval mustard pot,
by Hester Bateman, London,
1787, 3in. high.(Bermondsey)
$325 £225

NUTMEGS

An English silver nutmeg grater, maker's marks for T. Phipps and E. Robinson, circa 1791/2, 2in. long. (Robt. W. Skinner Inc.)
$400 £281

A 19th century Continental silver nutmeg grater, with two hinged ends, 2.7/8in. long. (Robt. W. Skinner Inc.)
$250 £176

An English silver nutmeg grater, maker's marks for T. Phipps and E. Robinson, circa 1800/1, 2.3/8in. long. (Robt. W. Skinner Inc.)
$350 £246

A George III kitchen nutmeg grater of semi-circular section, with arched handle, by Phipps & Robinson, 1805. (Phillips)
$323 £220

A 20th century sterling silver nutmeg grater, Gorham Mfg. Co., in the form of a melon, 2in. long. (Robt. W. Skinner Inc.) $375 £264

A George IV kitchen nutmeg grater with tongue and dart borders, by Charles Rawlings, 1824. (Phillips) $617 £420

PORRINGERS

A Victorian two-handled porringer with leaf capped scroll handles, 19cm. high, Britannia Standard 1884, 67oz. (Phillips)
$1,386 £900

A Charles II two-handled porringer and cover, 1674, maker's mark CM, 7in. high. (Christie's)
$28,771 £19,440

A Charles II silver gilt two-handled porringer and cover, 1676, maker's mark TC, a fish above, a trefoil below, 5¾in. high, 21oz. (Christie's)
$5,594 £3,780

SALTS

Two of a set of four Hukin & Heath silver salts with salt spoons, Birmingham hallmarks for 1879, 6oz. 4dwt, each 3.4cm. high. (Christie's)$1,261 £864

One of a pair of silver octagonal salts, by Wm. Forbes for Ball, Tomkins & Black, N.Y., 1839-51, 2½in. high, 7oz. (Christie's)$605 £417

A pair of George III silver circular salts, maker possibly S. C. Young & Co., Sheffield, 1813, 3½in. diam., and a pair of salt spoons. (Edgar Horn) $452 £310

One of a pair of George IV silver gilt shell-shaped salt cellars, by Edward Farrell, 1824, 8¾in. high, 70oz. (Christie's) $16,783 £11,340

A three-piece condiment set in the Art Nouveau style, by Wm. Hutton & Sons Ltd., Birmingham, 1905. (Lawrence Fine Art) $224 £154

One of a set of six silver gilt Victorian swing handled salts, 9cm. long, 1872, by George Fox, also one of six cast gilt salt spoons, by G. Adams, 1880, 16oz. (Phillips) $2,058 £1,400

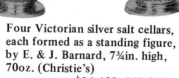

One of a set of six George III fluted circular salt cellars, by Paul Storr, four 1815, two 1818, 49oz. (Christie's) $7,992 £5,400

Four Victorian silver salt cellars, each formed as a standing figure, by E. & J. Barnard, 7¾in. high, 70oz. (Christie's) $26,438 £18,360

One of a set of four George III plain circular salt cellars, by Paul Storr, 1798, 15oz. 5dwt. (Christie's) $1,879 £1,296

SAUCEBOATS

One of a set of four George II plain shaped oval sauceboats, by John Pollock, 1752, 8½in. 60oz. (Christie's) $4,315 £2,916

One of a pair of George IV oval ogee sided sauceboats, by I. H. and G. Lias, London 1824, 28oz. (Woolley & Wallis) $1,850 £1,250

One of four George II plain sauceboats, by Edward Wakelin, 1757, 74oz. (Christie's) $6,713 £4,536

One of a pair of George II plain sauceboats with serpent scroll handle, by Robt. Brown, 1743, 24oz. (Christie's) $3,132 £2,160

One of a pair of Georgian oval sauceboats, London, 1759, 22oz. (Worsfolds) $792 £550

A George III sauceboat, makers probably WF for Wm. Fountain, 1809, 15oz. 13dwt. (Christie's) $2,488 £1,728

One of a pair of George II plain sauceboats with rising dolphin handles, by Francis Crump, 1742, 29oz. (Christie's) $6,531 £4,536

One of a pair of George III sauceboats, by Abraham Portal, 1763, 42oz. (Christie's) $5,594 £3,780

One of a pair of George II sauceboats on three rococo scroll and shell feet, by J. Kirkup, Newcastle, 1754, 46oz. (Christie's) $3,132 £2,160

SILVER

A mid 19th century Russian niello snuff box with foliate scroll decoration, maker's mark EE, Moscow, circa 1850. (Phillips) $447 £300

A Continental silver and tortoiseshell snuff box, unmarked probably French, circa 1820. (Christie's)
$170   £115

An Austro-Hungarian rectangular snuff box, Vienna, 1852, 9cm. long. (Christie's)
$125 £85

An early Victorian gilt lined, engine-turned box with applied cast floral thumbpiece, possibly by E. Edwards, London, 1839, 4¾in. long. (Christie's) $666 £450

A George IV rectangular snuff box, maker I.W.G., London, 1828, 3¼in. long. (Woolley & Wallis)
$432 £360

A Victorian silver snuff box engraved on the cover with a view of Wricklemarsh, Blackheath, Kent, by Yapp & Woodward, Birmingham, 1845, 4¾in. long.(Christie's)
$1,957 £1,350

A George III double section silver snuff box, maker's mark I.A., London, 1814, 3½ x 2½in. (Parsons, Welch & Cowell)
$301 £215

A silver mounted stag's horn snuff mull with chained pricker and perforated stopper, circa 1700, 4¾in. wide. (Christie's)
$466 £324

An early 18th century oval mounted tortoiseshell snuff box, impressed with a portrait of Queen Anne and signed 'OB' for Obrisset, circa 1710. (Phillips) $294 £200

A Scottish silver mounted cowrie shell snuff box, circa 1810. (Christie's)$162 £110

A Victorian rectangular silver snuff box, maker's mark F.M., Birmingham, 1854, 3½ x 2½in., 4½oz. (Parsons, Welch & Cowell) $287 £205

A French 19th century oblong snuff box, the base and sides nielloed with a chequered effect, 3½in. long. (Christie's)
$518 £350

SNUFF BOXES

A George IV hunting scene snuff box, by John Jones III, 1824, 8.8cm. long. (Lawrence Fine Art)
$814 £550

A late 17th/early 18th century oval tortoiseshell snuff box, the cover inlaid with chinoiserie scene. (Phillips)
$176 £120

A French 19th century oblong gilt lined snuff box, the lid finely nielloed with 18th century hunting scene, with house and trees beyond, 3½in. long. (Christie's)
$473 £320

An early Victorian castle top snuff box, by N. Mills, Birmingham, 1838, 7.2cm. long. (Lawrence Fine Art)
$574 £396

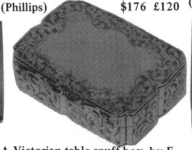

A Victorian table snuff box, by F. Clark, Birmingham, 1843, 3¾in. wide, 4½oz. (Woolley & Wallis) $414 £280

A Swiss rectangular gold musical snuff box, circa 1830, 2¾in. long. (Christie's)
$9,590 £6,480

A late 17th/early 18th century tortoiseshell snuff box inlaid in silver with a seascape, circa 1700. (Phillips) $323 £220

A George II silver gilt fox mask snuff box, by T. Phipps & E. Robinson, 1807, 3¼in., 3oz. 10dwt. (Christie's) $3,110 £2,160

An Italian rectangular silver gilt mounted hardstone snuff box, by Giacomo Sirletti, Rome, 1811-36, 3½in. long. (Christie's)
$4,510 £3,132

George IV silver snuff box, London, 1825, 3¼in. wide, 5oz. (Hobbs & Chambers)
$403 £280

A late 18th century Italian silver gilt circular snuff box, Venice, circa 1770, 5.6cm. diam. (Phillips) $372 £250

A Birmingham rectangular silver gilt snuff box, by Joseph Willmore, 1841, 3¾in. long. (Christie's)
$1,278 £864

SILVER

A William and Mary plain, slightly tapering cylindrical tankard, 1690, maker's mark FS, 6in. high, 18oz. 14dwt.(Christie's) $3,732 £2,592

A Charles II tankard and cover engraved with scenes of the Plague and Fire of London, 1675, maker's mark IN mullet below, 7¾in. high, 38oz. (Christie's)
$87,912 £59,400

A Charles II plain cylindrical tankard and cover, 1671, maker's mark EG, 6½in. high, 21oz. (Christie's)
$5,114 £3,456

A George I tankard, fully marked Britannia Standard 1719, by C. Canner II, 17.2cm. high, 22oz. (Lawrence Fine Art)
$2,073 £1,430

A George III silver baluster tankard, London, 1760, 4¼in. high, 8oz.4dwt. (Dacre, Son & Hartley)
$374 £260

A George III baluster tankard, by John Payne, 1768, the handle with maker's mark, 20cm. high, 26oz. (Lawrence Fine Art) $1,609 £1,110

A Sir Edmund Berry Godfrey flagon, maker's mark IN mullet below, 1675, with short moulded lip added, circa 1720, 12.3/8in. high, 66oz. (Christie's) $63,936 £43,200

A George IV cylindrical lidded quart tankard, by R. Emes and E. Barnard, London, 1826, 7.75in. high, 38oz. (Woolley & Wallis) $1,650 £1,100

A George III plain tapering cylindrical tankard, by Peter, Anne and William Bateman, 1800, 8in. high, 26oz. (Christie's) $1,758 £1,188

A Charles II silver gilt tankard and cover, maker's mark MK in a lozenge, mullet above and below, 1683, 7½in. high, 34oz. (Christie's) $3,676 £2,484

A German silver tankard and cover, Augsburg, circa 1690, maker's mark PS, 4½in. high, 8oz.11dwt. (Christie's) $3,732 £2,592

A William III Irish plain tapering cylindrical tankard, by Joseph Walker, Dublin, 1699, 7½in. high, 28oz. (Christie's) $3,356 £2,268

A 19th century Continental parcel gilt peg tankard and cover, 8½in. high, 38oz. (Christie's) $2,177 £1,512

A George II silver lidded tankard by James Manners, London, 1734, 7in. high, 20oz. (Chancellors Hollings-worths) $1,102 £750

A James II plain cylindrical tankard and cover, York, 1686, maker's mark IO, per-haps for John Oliver, 6¾in. high, 21oz. (Christie's) $4,795 £3,240

A Charles II plain slightly tapering cylindrical tankard, 1681, maker's mark IC, mullet below, 6¾in. high, 24oz. (Christie's) $3,996 £2,700

A George II silver baluster tankard with leaf and scroll decorated handle, London, 1759, 4¾in. high, 10oz.12dwt. (Dacre, Son & Hartley) $374 £260

An Indian tapering cylindrical tankard, by Robert Hamilton, Calcutta, circa 1812, 6in. high, 19oz.8dwt. (Christie's) $3,445 £2,376

TAZZAS

Part of a suite of Queen Anne tazze, comprising one large, 26cm. diam., and a smaller pair, 18cm. diam., by Jacob Margas, 1709, 37oz. (Phillips) $4,410 £3,000

Sterling silver covered chalice, by Georg Jensen, Denmark, circa 1923, 5¾in. high. (Robt. W. Skinner Inc.) $703 £475

A small tazza designed by G. Albertus, stamped GI 925 S 468, circa 1928, 8.9cm. high, 9oz.5dwt. (Christie's) $1,096 £756

A tazza designed by Georg Jensen, stamped G J 025S 265, circa 1940, 12.7cm. high, 7oz.5dwt.(Christie's) $939 £648

A covered tazza designed by J. Rohde, stamped Dessin J.R. Georg Jensen 43, circa 1920, 15.5cm. high, 14oz. 9dwt. (Christie's) $1,466 £1,080

A large tazza, designed by Georg Jensen, assay mark with London import mark for 1924. 26.5cm. high, 36oz. 6dwt. (Christie's) $6,000 £4,000

A tazza designed by Georg Jensen, stamped 1921, G J 830 S 263, 18.8cm. high, 16oz.5dwt. (Christie's) $1,409 £972

A Georg Jensen silver tazza, stamped with maker's marks, Georg Jensen, Denmark, Sterling, 263B and London import marks for 1928, 18.5cm. high, 18oz. (Christie's) $1,576 £1,080

A large tazza designed by G. Jensen, stamped marks Georg Jensen GI925, 264, 26.7cm. high, 35oz.12dwt.(Christie's) $6,264 £4,320

TEA & COFFEE SETS

SILVER

Three-piece silver partial teaset, America, 1870's, coffee pot 12in. high, approx. 78 troy oz. (Robt. W. Skinner Inc.) $550 £401

An early Victorian four-piece tea and coffee service, 1838 and 1839, by Wm. Eaton, the coffee pot 21.5cm. high, 75oz. (Lawrence Fine Art) $1,914 £1,320

A Victorian four-piece tea and coffee service, by John Edward Terrey, 1844, the coffee pot 26.5cm. high, 73oz. (Lawrence Fine Art) $1,850 £1,276

A Victorian four-piece tea and coffee service, by Thos. Smiley, 1865, the coffee pot 21.5cm. high, 68oz. (Lawrence Fine Art) $1,515 £1,045

Part of a William IV tea and coffee service, by Henry Wilkinson & Co., Sheffield, 1832, coffee pot 24cm. high, 62oz. (Lawrence Fine Art) $1,084 £748

SILVER

A Victorian circular three-piece tea service, Louis XV pattern, by Joseph
and Albert Savory, London, 1850. (Woolley & Wallis) $680 £460

A five-piece tea and coffee service with a tray, by Heer-Schofield Co.,
Baltimore, circa 1905/28, tray 28½in. long, coffee pot 11in. high,
gross weight 229oz. (Christie's) $6,050 £4,172

Late 19th century silver tea service, consisting of a teapot and cover, sugar
bowl and cover, milk jug and a pair of tongs, the teapot with twin dragon
pivoted handle, the others with loop handles in the form of dragons, signed
Konoike, the teapot 20cm. high. (Christie's) $1,003 £702

TEA & COFFEE SETS

An Elkington electroplated teaset, the design attributed to Dr. Christopher Dresser, with Elkington monogram, stamped Elkington & Co. plate marks and Regd. 22863, circa 1880, teapot 13.7cm. high. (Christie's) $2,049 £1,404

A Victorian four-piece tea and coffee service with circular tray en suite, by Stephen Smith, 1876, the tray 47cm. diam., 1877, the coffee pot 26.3cm. high, 140oz. (Lawrence Fine Art) $3,418 £2,310

'Como', a Christofle electroplated four-piece modernist teaset designed by Lino Sabattini, each piece stamped Gallia France Pro. Christofle, circa 1955, height of teapot 22cm. (Christie's) $5,011 £3,456

A five-piece tea service, by Joseph Lownes, Phila., circa 1815, teapot
7in. high, gross weight 115oz. (Christie's) $4,400 £3,034

Late 19th century Portuguese tea and coffee service, comprising a teapot,
coffee pot, a two-handled sugar basin and cream jug with bracket handles
and rope twist rims, coffee pot 9in. high, 175oz. (Christie's)
                                                    $2,975 £2,052

A six-piece part tea and coffee service, by various makers for Ball, Black
& Co., N.Y., circa 1851, coffee pot 11¼in. high, gross weight 162oz.
(Christie's) $2,640 £1,820

A three-piece tea service with a pair of teacups and saucers, by Gorham
Mfg. Co., Providence, 1880, teapot 4½in. high, gross weight 24oz.
(Christie's) $1,870 £1,289

An eight-piece tea and coffee service and tray, by Tiffany & Co., N.Y.,
circa 1860/70, Etruscan pattern, coffee pot 11¾in. high, tray 34in. long,
gross weight 397oz.10dwt. (Christie's) $20,350 £14,034

A six-piece tea and coffee service, the wooden handles squared and
reeded, by Fletcher & Gardiner, Phila., 1813/14, coffee pot 10in. high,
gross weight 194oz. (Christie's) $12,100 £8,344

One of a set of three George II tea caddies and sugar boxes, by Isabel Pero, 1741, the caddies each with a pewter liner, and a George III Old English pattern caddy spoon, 68oz. (Christie's) $21,772 £15,120

A George I plain, shaped oblong tea caddy with slide top, London, 1722, Britannia Standard, 4½in. high. (Christie's) $681 £480

A George III plain, oval tea caddy, by Hester Bateman, London, 1785, 12.5cm. wide, 10oz. (Christie's) $1,924 £1,300

One of a set of three George III oblong tea caddies and sugar box, by Peze Pilleau, 1743, 38oz. (Christie's)$4,071 £2,808

One of a set of three George II silver gilt, vase-shaped tea caddies, by Samuel Taylor, 1752, 31oz. (Christie's) $7,992 £5,400

A George III oval tea caddy, by Thos. Phipps and Edward Robinson II, 1784, 12.4cm. high, 12.4oz. (Lawrence Fine Art) $1,455 £990

A George III rectangular tea caddy on rim foot, with blue glass liner, unmarked, circa 1775. (Christie's) $4,795 £3,240

A George II plain, shaped rectangular tea caddy, by Edward Gibbon, London, 1721, 4¾in. high. (Christie's) $1,136 £800

A George III cylindrical tea caddy, by J. Parker and E. Wakelin, circa 1765, 5¼in. high, 19oz. (Christie's) $4,155 £2,808

Part of a silver five-piece tea and coffee service, the tea kettle on scroll pierced stand with burner, 13¾in. high. (Christie's) $681 £480

An electroplated kettle, the design attributed to Dr. Christopher Dresser, 15cm. high. (Christie's) $181 £129

A beaded and foliate chased, part fluted tea kettle with mother-of-pearl finial, on a naturalistic crossed branch stand fitted with a burner, 13¼in. high. (Christie's) $127 £90

A George II tea kettle stand and lamp, by Ayme Videau, London, 1733, 35cm. high, 70oz. (Christie's) $2,190 £1,480

An Austro-Hungarian, mid 19th century, compressed swing handled tea kettle, on a trefoil stand, fitted with a burner, 14½in. high, 55oz. free. (Christie's) $1,013 £680

George III embossed spirit kettle, London 1760, 12½in. high, 47oz. (Hobbs & Chambers) $2,400 £1,600

A Hukin & Heath electroplated picnic kettle with folding tripod stand and spirit burner, designed by Dr. C. Dresser, 14.5cm. high. (Christie's) $242 £172

A George III plain circular tea kettle, stand and burner, the kettle by H. Bateman, 1783, the stand and burner by Chas. S. Harris, 1881, 63oz. (Christie's) $1,598 £1,080

A Georgian design plated spirit kettle, the stand complete with burner, circa 1900, 12in. high. (Peter Wilson & Co.) $132 £90

TEAPOTS

A silver teapot of compressed globular shape, by Jones, Lows & Ball, Boston, 1839/40, 5¾in. high, gross weight 50oz. (Christie's) $880 £606

A George II plain bullet-shaped teapot with hinged cover, by Thos. Farren, 1727, gros 14oz.7dwt. (Christie's) $5,287 £3,672

An English silver teapot, Sheffield, maker's mark of Thos. Law, 1804/5, 4¾in. high, 15oz. (Robt. W. Skinner Inc.) $275 £193

A George III teapot with beech scroll handle and finial, by J. Emes, 1801, 27cm. across, 16.7oz. all in. (Lawrence Fine Art) $239 £165

A silver teapot, oval, with a domed hinged lid, by F. Marquand, Georgia, 1820/26, 9½in. high, gross weight 33oz. (Christie's) $660 £455

An Indian oval teapot on rim foot, by Hamilton & Co., Calcutta, circa 1822, 6¾in. high, gross 29oz. (Christie's) $2,505 £1,728

A William IV naturalistic melon-shaped teapot, by E. J. & W. Barnard, 6in. high, Port Cullus crest, London, 1835, 17oz. all in. (Christie's) $562 £380

One of a pair of early Victorian flared cylindrical teapots, by Robert Garrard, London, 1844, 46oz. all in. (Woolley & Wallis) $1,533 £1,050

An early Victorian silver bellied body teapot, by W. R. Smily, London, 1852, 6½in. high. (Edgar Horn) $248 £170

A George III oval teapot on stand, 1796, the stand 1795, by Henry Chawner, 26cm. across, 19.2oz. all in. (Lawrence Fine Art) $1,116 £770

A silver teapot with an S-shaped spout, by Samuel Williamson, Phila., 1794/1813, 7¾in. high, gross weight 28oz. (Christie's) $1,210 £834

A George II bullet shaped teapot with straight tapering hexagonal spout, by Gabriel Sleath, 1728, gross 15oz. 3dwt. (Christie's) $5,287 £3,672

TRAYS & SALVERS

A two-handled tea tray, by Walker & Hall, Sheffield, 1910, 74cm. across handles, 131oz. (Lawrence Fine Art)　　　　$1,467　£1,012

An oval tea tray with plain centre, by Walker & Hall, Sheffield, 1914, 62.3cm. wide, 92oz. (Lawrence Fine Art)　　　　$1,052　£726

One of a pair of George III oblong salvers, by Wm. Bateman, 1817, 30.5cm. wide, 52oz. (Lawrence Fine Art) $3,588　£2,475

A shaped rectangular two-handled tea tray, maker's mark JS, Sheffield, 1927, 66.2cm. across handles, 104oz. (Lawrence Fine Art)　　　　　　　　　　$1,212　£836

One of a pair of George III Irish circular salvers, by John Laughlin Jnr., Dublin, 1782, 21.6cm. diam., 26oz. (Lawrence Fine Art)　　　　　$1,052　£726

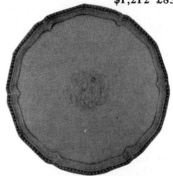

An early George III shaped circular salver, by John Crouch, 1772, 30.5cm. diam., 30oz. (Lawrence Fine Art)　　　　$957　£660

A rectangular two-handled tea tray with plain centre, maker's mark rubbed, 1906, 70.5cm. wide, 145oz. (Lawrence Fine Art)　　　　$1,674　£1,155

One of a pair of two-handled oval trays each on four feet, by J. Crouch and T. Hannam, 1791, 22¾in. long, 158oz. (Christie's)　　　　$19,699　£12,960

SILVER

A George II plain octafoil
salver, by John Robinson
II, 1738, 13½in. diam.,
30oz. (Christie's)
$3,196 £2,160

A George I silver gilt fifteen
sided salver, by A. Courtauld,
1723, 11¼in. wide, 35oz.
(Christie's) $44,755 £30,240

A George III two-handled
plain oval tray, by John
Crouch, 1807, 25¾in. long,
102oz. (Christie's)
$5,754 £3,888

One of twelve George III
plain shaped circular dinner
plates, by Robt. Calderwood,
Dublin, circa 1760, 9½in.
diam., 210oz. (Christie's)
$5,909 £4,104

A George II shaped circular
salver, by Elizabeth Buteux,
1732, 12.3/8in. diam., 33oz.
(Christie's) $4,665 £3,240

A Regency two-handled oval
tray on four shell, foliage and
lion's paw feet, by R. Sibley,
28¼in. long, 152oz.
(Christie's) $7,992 £5,400

A silver salver on four cast
foliate lion's paw feet, by
Obadiah Rich, Boston,
circa 1835, 14in. diam.,
47oz. (Christie's)
$550 £379

A Victorian large Irish silver
circular salver, by R. Sawyer,
Dublin, 1842, 25in. diam.,
215oz. (Christie's)
$5,909 £4,104

A George III shaped circular
salver, by Richard Rugg,
1775, 14in. diam., 42oz.
(Christie's) $2,349 £1,620

SILVER

A silver tazza on circular foot, by Gorham Mfg. Co., bearing the mark of Kennard & Jenks, Boston, circa 1880, 10½in. diam., 19oz. (Christie's) $13,200 £9,103

A George III circular salver, by Wm. Fountain and D. Pontifax, London 1793, 13in. diam., 30oz. (Woolley & Wallis)
$947 £640

A George II shaped circular salver, by Sarah Holaday, 1740, 16.3/8in. diam., 70oz. (Christie's) $4,635 £3,132

An English silver oval serving tray, maker's mark for J. Edward, circa 1798/9, 30¼in. long, 108oz. (Robt. W. Skinner Inc.) $3,200 £2,253

An oval silver salver, by Wm. Forbes for Ball, Tompkins & Black, N.Y., 1839/51, 13in. long, 24oz.10dwt. (Christie's)
$528 £364

A George III oval two-handled tray, by Thos. Hannam & J. Crouch, 1800, 20¾in. 53oz. (Christie's)
$2,818 £1,944

One of a pair of George I plain circular salvers, by R. Timbrell & J. Bell I, 1714, 9¾in. diam., 33oz. (Christie's) $8,791 £5,940

A George I shaped square waiter, probably by E. Cornock, 1725, 5.7/8in. square, 6oz.4dwt. (Christie's) $1,399 £972

A George III shaped circular salver, by James Ellis & Co., Sheffield, 1818, 25.8cm. diam., 23.5oz. (Lawrence Fine Art) $455 £308

One of a pair of George III shaped oval two-handled sauce tureens and covers, by D. Smith and R. Sharp, 1767, 9in. long, 41oz. (Christie's)$6,073 £4,104

One of a pair of Sheffield plated boat shape sauce tureens and covers, 23.7cm. across handles. (Lawrence Fine Art) $701 £484

A George II two-handled shaped oval soup tureen and cover, by George Methuen, 1752, with plated liner, 14in. overall, 88oz. (Christie's)
$7,992 £5,400

A George II two-handled oval bombe soup tureen and cover, by Wm. Cripps, 1751, 14½in. long, gross 117oz. (Christie's)
$11,162 £7,344

A George III circular soup tureen, stand and cover, by Paul Storr, 1805, 11¾in. high, 267oz. (Christie's)
$68,947 £45,360

A Victorian two-handled shaped oval silver soup tureen and cover, by S. Hayne and D. Cater, 1845, 14½in. long, 111oz. (Christie's) $6,531 £4,536

A two-handled shaped oval soup tureen and cover, by Elkington & Co., Birmingham, 1909, 126oz. (Christie's) $4,698 £3,240

A Regency two-handled oval soup tureen, cover and stand, by Thos. Robins, 1811, the liner 1812, 20¾in., 387oz. (Christie's) $28,771 £19,440

A Sheffield plated oval soup tureen and cover, 41cm. across handles. (Lawrence Fine Art) $1,180 £814

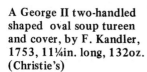

A George II two-handled shaped oval soup tureen and cover, by F. Kandler, 1753, 11¼in. long, 132oz. (Christie's)
$13,996 £9,720

A George III soup tureen, probably by Charles Hougham, 1763, together with a spare cover and plated liner, 130oz. (Phillips) $6,750 £4,500

One of a pair of George III Regency two-handled oval sauce tureens and covers, by Thos. Robins, 1810, 9in. long, 74oz. (Christie's)
$4,698 £3,240

One of a pair of Regency ormolu mounted Pontypool chestnut urns, 10½in. wide. (Christie's) $6,696 £5,400

A Victorian soup tureen and cover, by T. W. H. & H. Dobson, 1880, 30cm. across handles, 46.5oz. (Lawrence Fine Art) $1,515 £1,045

A Victorian silver two-handled shaped oval soup tureen and cover, by B. Smith II, 1838, 17½in. long, 179oz.(Christie's)
$6,220 £4,320

A Hukin & Heath electroplated soup tureen and cover, designed by Dr. C. Dresser, 31cm. diam. (Christie's)
$4,099 £2,808

One of four George III boat-shaped two-handled sauce tureens and covers, by John Emes, 1798, 9¾in. long, 72oz. (Christie's) $6,264 £4,320

A tureen and cover designed by Georg Jensen, stamped Georg Jensen 337B, 132.5cm. wide, 63oz.16dwt. (Christie's) $26,622 £18,360

A silver plated Art Nouveau covered urn, circa 1900, 16¼in. high. (Robt. W. Skinner Inc.) $200 £134

A sugar urn with a pierced gallery and a tapering conical lid with an urn finial, circa 1785-1810, 9½in. high, 15oz. (Christie's) $880 £619

A Belgian fluted, pear-shaped tea urn, on an ebonised trefoil base fitted with a burner, hallmarked in London, 1899, 14¼in. high, 53.25oz. gross. (Christie's) $2,235 £1,500

A large Victorian two-handled vase shaped tea urn in the style of Robert Adam, 22¾in. high. (Christie's) $616 £400

A Russian silver two-handled samovar, by Adolf Sper, 1847, 15¼in. high, gross 129oz. (Christie's)
$5,909 £4,104

A Victorian electroplated tea urn with domed cover, 58cm. high. (Lawrence Fine Art)
$1,034 £704

An early 19th century Sheffield plate hot water urn, complete with burner, 14in. high. (Robt. W. Skinner Inc.) $600 £400

An early 19th century silver plated samovar with campana shaped body and scroll handles, 16in. high. (Bermondsey) $270 £180

A silver George III tea urn, by J. Wakelin and R. Garrard, 1792, 18½in. high, gross 99oz. (Christie's) $4,976 £3,456

A William IV vase, by Charles Fox II, 1830, 11.7cm. high, 14.7oz. (Lawrence Fine Art) $371 £253

A William Hutton & Son silver and glass vase, stamped maker's marks, and London hallmarks for 1902, 11.2cm. high. (Phillips) $150 £100

One of a pair of reproduction Warwick vases, by the Goldsmiths & Silversmiths Co. Ltd., 1910, 29cm. diam., 245.5oz. (Phillips) $5,640 £4,000

A silver double vase on stand, by The Sweetser Co., New York, circa 1900-15, the stand of copper, 11½in. high, gross wt. of vase 20oz.10dwt. (Christie's) $1,540 £1,084

A pair of crocus-shaped embossed silver vases with leaf decoration, 6¼in. high. (Dacre, Son & Hartley) $150 £100

A Liberty silver vase, the design attributed to A. Knox, stamped Cymric. L & Co within three lozenges and with Birmingham hallmarks for 1907, 17cm. high. (Christie's) $391 £270

A silver enamelled bud base, by Tiffany & Co., N.Y., circa 1893, 5.3/8in. high, 5oz.10dwt. (Christie's) $1,210 £834

A George IV replica of the Warwick vase and cover, by The Boulton Plate Co., Birmingham, 1827, 13in. high, 163oz. (Christie's) $12,787 £8,640

A George III sugar vase with swing handle, by Robt. Hennell, 1782, 8oz. (Phillips) $661 £450

VINAIGRETTES

An oblong silver 'Castletop' vinaigrette chased on the cover with a view of Westminster Abbey, by N. Mills, Birmingham 1842, 1¾in. long. (Christie's) $959 £648

A 19th century Chinese Export oblong vinaigrette with engine-turned base, by Khecheong of Canton, circa 1850. (Phillips) $178 £120

An oblong gold vinaigrette with perforated grille, London 1818, maker's initials GL, 18ct. (Christie's) $959 £648

A George IV vinaigrette in the form of a purse, by Lawrence & Co., Birmingham, 1821, 3cm. long. (Lawrence Fine Art) $287 £198

An early Victorian castle top vinaigrette, the cover case with a view of Windsor Castle, by John Tongue, Birmingham, 1845, 4cm. long. (Lawrence Fine Art) $614 £418

A George IV rectangular vinaigrette, by Thos. Newbold, Birmingham, 1821, 3.2cm. long. (Lawrence Fine Art) $223 £154

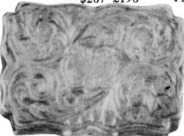

A Victorian gilt lined, bright cut, shaped oblong vinaigrette with vacant scroll cartouche, by F. Clarke, Birmingham, 1846. (Christie's) $111 £75

A William IV silver gilt vinaigrette, by Taylor & Perry, Birmingham, 1833, 2.1cm. long. (Lawrence Fine Art) $63 £44

A George IV engine-turned and gilded vinaigrette, L. & Co., Birmingham, 1822. (Christie's) $205 £140

A George III 'goldstone' mounted vinaigrette, by J. Shaw, Birmingham, 1809, 2.9cm. long. (Lawrence Fine Art) $127 £88

A William IV silver gilt engine-turned vinaigrette with reeded sides, by Thos. Shaw, Birmingham, 1830. (Christie's) $133 £90

A George III vinaigrette, by Samuel Pemberton, Birmingham, 1809. (Phillips) $205 £140

WINE COOLERS

An Old Sheffield plate wine cooler of campana shape, by Matthew Boulton & Co., 9in. high. (Capes, Dunn & Co.) $331 £230

One of a pair of wine coolers, stamped Georg Jensen GI 925S 289, 9.8cm. high, 29oz. 9dwt. (Christie's) $5,481 £3,780

One of four silver William IV two-handled vase-shaped wine coolers of krater form, by Paul Storr, 1834, 12¾in. high, 384oz. (Christie's) $116,640 £81,000

One of a pair of George III silver gilt two-handled wine coolers, by Paul Storr, 1810, the collars and liners 1809, 11¾in. high, 369oz. (Christie's) $47,952 £32,400

One of a pair of Russian silver campana-shaped two-handled wine coolers, by C. J. Tegelsten, 1849, 16in. high, 406oz. (Christie's) $23,328 £16,200

One of a pair of Old Sheffield plate two-handled campana-shaped wine coolers, by T. & J. Creswick, circa 1830, 10¼in. high. (Christie's) $3,516 £2,376

One of a pair of Sheffield plated wine coolers, by T. & J. Creswick, 23cm. high. (Lawrence Fine Art) $2,197 £1,485

One of a pair of electro-plated Victorian wine coolers, by Elkington & Co., 1873, 22cm. high. (Phillips) $1,833 £1,300

A George IV silver gilt two-handled campana-shaped wine cooler, by Paul Storr, 1825, 11¼in. high, 102oz. (Christie's) $15,552 £10,800

A plain amber flattened disc-shaped snuff bottle, with a dragon around the neck, with stopper. (Christie's) $227 £172

An agate flattened disc-shaped snuff bottle, banded with an irregular concentric panel, with stopper. (Christie's) $199 £151

A mottled apple and celadon jadeite disc-shaped snuff bottle and stopper. (Christie's) $570 £432

A red lacquer spade-shaped snuff bottle, relief carved with two pairs of figures on fenced terraces. (Christie's) $1,069 £810

An agate rounded square snuff bottled carved in intaglio from a brown inclusion on one side, with stopper. (Christie's) $683 £518

An inside painted glass disc-shaped snuff bottle, dated 1981. (Christie's) $270 £205

An inside painted rock crystal rounded rectangular snuff bottle with figures on a snowy terrace, inscribed, with stopper. (Christie's) $199 £151

An agate flattened disc-shaped snuff bottle, carved from an area of darker inclusion as a sage sitting on rockwork. (Christie's) $2,138 £1,620

An agate rounded square snuff bottle of translucent greyish tone with gilt metal collared coral stopper. (Christie's) $2,138 £1,620

An inside painted glass rectangular bottle with two equestrian archers pursuing a deer, signed Chen Zhongsan. (Christie's)$369 £280

A Beijing four-colour overlay white-ground spade-shaped snuff bottle carved with dense flowering peony sprays. (Christie's) $369 £280

An agate rounded rectangular snuff bottle carved on one side from a caramel shadow with three birds around a tree. (Christie's) $683 £518

A red lacquer spade-shaped snuff bottle, relief carved with two groups of children playing, with stopper. (Christie's) $427 £324

An inside painted glass rounded square snuff bottle painted with a leopard beneath bamboo, signed Wang Bai-chuan, dated 1982. (Christie's) $327 £248

A white jade rounded square snuff bottle and matching stopper, carved overall with bands of wicker work. (Christie's) $1,568 £1,188

An agate rounded square bottle with animal mask ring handles. (Christie's) $398 £302

A green overlay caramel-ground disc-shaped bottle carved with figures on terraces, with stopper. (Christie's) $570 £432

An agate rounded square snuff bottle carved on one side from the caramel skin with two grazing horses and a monkey. (Christie's) $512 £388

Late 17th century Buddhist stone stela of typical form, dated Genroku 5 (1692), with a later inscription and date Meiji 34 (1901), 77.5cm. high. (Christie's)
$1,389 £972

Contemporary Eskimo carving of a moustached walrus, in mottled greenish-dark grey stone, 21in. long. (Robt. W. Skinner Inc.) $450 £306

One of a pair of carved granite Foo dogs and stands; China, 19th century, 28½in. high. (Robt. W. Skinner Inc.)
$4,200 £2,818

Contemporary Eskimo carving of a wrestling man and bear in mottled greenish-grey stone, 18in. high. (Robt. W. Skinner Inc.) $700 £476

A 19th century Italian alabaster model of the Warwick Vase, after the Antique, 64cm. high. (Christie's) $2,700 £1,800

A carved limestone sculpture of Mother and Child, by W. Edmondson, circa 1934/39, 15in. high. (Christie's)
$9,900 £6,827

Contemporary Eskimo carving of a weeping woman holding a child, in greenish-grey marblised stone, 17½in. high. (Robt. W. Skinner Inc.) $850 £578

A stone horse's head, Han Dynasty, 12.9cm. high. (Christie's) $13,500 £9,000

An Egyptian alabaster ointment jar, pear shaped with short flat rimmed neck, nub handles, 5½in. high, in brocade covered box. (Robt. W. Skinner Inc.) $300 £201

STONE

A group of stone fruit in a wooden bowl, comprising fourteen pieces of various fruit, bowl 11.5/8in. diam. (Christie's) $605 £458

Contemporary Eskimo carving, Abraham, Port Harrison, of marbled green-grey stone, 23in. high. (Robt. W. Skinner Inc.) $1,600 £1,088

Contemporary Eskimo carving of three men skinning a seal, in polished medium grey soapstone, 19in. long. (Robt. W. Skinner Inc.) $1,300 £884

A James Woolford plaster figure modelled as a diving mermaid with a dolphin, circa 1930, 59cm. high. (Christie's) $315 £216

A pair of carved stone putti, the plump figures standing, one holding a bird, the other a basket of fruit, 38in. high. (Christie's) $3,300 £2,200

A greenish-grey and black stone figure of a seated roaring lion, Tang Dynasty, 13cm. high. (Christie's) $1,746 £1,188

A Northern Qi stele with two figures of Buddha seated side by side, dated Tianbao 6th year, tenth month, tenth day, corresponding to AD555, 29cm. high. (Christie's) $15,000 £10,000

A pink granite column with turned shaft and spreading base, 9¼in. diam., 46in. high. (Christie's) $1,566 £1,080

Late 17th century English stone figure of 'Prometheus Bound', in the manner of Cibber, 175cm. high. (Phillips) $15,750 £10,500

TAPESTRIES

A 17th century Brussels tapestry woven in silks and wools, 10ft.11in. x 10ft.6in. (Christie's) $8,553 £6,480

A 17th century Brussels tapestry woven in well preserved wools and silks, 8ft. x 11ft.2in. (Christie's) $14,256 £10,800

A late 17th century Brussels tapestry in well preserved silks and wools, 9ft.8in. x 7ft.10in. (Christie's) $19,245 £14,580

Mid 18th century Brussels tapestry woven in silk and wool with Jupiter and his eagle receiving thunderbolts from Vulcan, 13ft.1in. x 8ft. 4in. (Christie's)$5,909 £4,104

A 17th century Spanish or Italian tapestry woven in muted colours, 94 x 99in. (Christie's) $6,577 £4,536

An Aubusson tapestry woven with lovers and sheep in a rustic landscape, 7ft.6in. x 4ft.8in. (Christie's) $3,576 £2,484

A 17th century Flemish Verdure tapestry woven with a dog beneath a tree in a pond by a forest clearing with a palace beyond, 8ft.5in. x 9ft.7in. (Christie's) $3,421 £2,376

An 18th century Louis XV Beauvais tapestry from the Tenture des Verdures Fines, woven in silk and wool, 8ft. 7in. x 6ft.1in. (Christie's) $5,702 £4,320

A late 17th century Flemish Verdure tapestry with a shepherd and shepherdess in a forest with their flock, 9ft. 3in. x 8ft.7in. (Christie's) $4,561 £3,456

TAPESTRIES

A 17th century Flemish Verdure tapestry woven with a man with a billowing cloak and a lady in a forest clearing, 8ft.9in. x 6ft.4in. (Christie's) $2,566 £1,944

A 17th century Brussels Verdure tapestry with dancing peasants in a forest clearing, 6ft.10in. x 11ft.9in. (Christie's) $7,840 £5,940

A 16th century Flemish tapestry woven in wools and silks with a hunting scene, 7ft.8in. x 9ft.7in. (Christie's) $7,413 £5,616

An 18th century Gobelins tapestry woven in wools and silks with two Chinamen in a landscape, 9ft.6in. x 5ft. 4½in. (Christie's) $9,979 £7,560

Early 18th century Brussels tapestry woven in silk and wool with the family of Darius prostrate before Alexander the Great, 13ft.9in. x 22ft.7in. (Christie's) $6,998 £4,860

Early 18th century Brussels tapestry woven in wool and silk depicting Neptune, 13ft. 10in. x 10ft.4in.(Christie's) $4,665 £3,240

A 16th century Dutch tapestry woven in silks and wools with Christ and the woman caught in adultery, 7ft.10in. x 6ft.7in. (Christie's) $18,662 £12,960

A 17th century Brussels tapestry depicting a boar hunt, 9ft. x 6ft.1in. (Christie's) $5,702 £4,320

Late 16th century Flemish Verdure tapestry woven with various scenes in a forest, 8ft. 5in. x 21ft.11in. (Christie's) $24,883 £17,280

TAPESTRIES

A Flemish tapestry woven with a pair of partridges in a landscape, 8ft.2in. x 13ft. 8in. (Christie's) $3,421 £2,592

Late 16th century Brussels tapestry woven with the story of Tobias and the Angel in a landscape, 6ft.9in. x 14ft.4in. (Christie's)
$7,776 £5,400

Mid 18th century Brussels tapestry woven in silk and wool with the triumph of Mars, 16ft. 2in. x 12ft.11in. (Christie's) $8,553 £5,940

A Flemish tapestry, depicting Athena in three feathered helmet beside a warrior, late 17th/ early 18th century, 9ft. high x 4ft.7in. (Woolley & Wallis) $1,260 £920

A 17th century Brussels tapestry woven in silks and wools with Hercules holding the severed head of the Nemean Lion, 6ft.11½in. x 12ft.3in. (Christie's) $3,564 £2,700

Mid 18th century Brussels tapestry woven in silk and wool, with the god Apollo playing his lyre, 12ft.11in. x 9ft.6in. (Christie's)
$5,909 £4,104

'A faithful representation of Her Most Gracious Majesty, Caroline Queen of England in the House of Lords, 1820', a handkerchief on linen, 22in. wide. (Christie's) $576 £400

'A representation of the Manchester Reform Meeting dispersed by the Civil and Military Powers. August 16, 1819', handkerchief on linen, 20 x 22in. (Christie's) $504 £350

'The Reformers attack on the Old Rotten Tree — of the Foul Nests of our Morants in Danger', handkerchief printed in colour on silk, circa 1830. (Christie's) $316 £220

An early 19th century embroidered picture worked in silks and wools, 16 x 22in. (Christie's) $264 £180

A Nazca textile, comprising three bands divided into rectangular sections of motifs in pink, yellow, white and brown on a red ground, 44 x 49cm. (Phillips) $147 £100

Late 19th century embroidered picture worked in coloured silks, probably Mexican or South American, 19 x 24in. (Christie's) $382 £260

Mid 19th century needlework picture, wool, silk and metallic yarns, 8¼ x 9¼in. (Robt. W. Skinner Inc.) $20,500 £13,851

A raised work picture of an ornamental pheasant against a Berlin woolwork ground, mid 19th century, 22 x 17½in. (Christie's) $78 £54

Mid 18th century embroidered bed valance fragments, Mass., 4ft.2in. x 9½in. and 2ft.2in. x 9¼in. (Robt. W. Skinner Inc.) $3,400 £2,361

Early 19th century appliqued table mat, America. (Robt. W. Skinner Inc.) $425 £287

A circular Berlin woolwork picture of an Indian Nabob, in black glass mount framed and glazed, circa 1840, 16in. high. (Christie's) $249 £172

A needlework carpet embroidered in coloured wools, circa 1850, 43 x 82in. (Christie's) $1,146 £780

A Navajo child's blanket, woven on a white saxony ply ground, 32 x 48in. (Robt. W. Skinner Inc.) $1,550 £1,076

Probably early 19th century wide needlework border embroidered in pale coloured wools in 17th century style, 17 x 90in. (Christie's) $297 £205

One of a set of five cushions worked in coloured wools with sprays of flowers and edged with pink and yellow wool fringe, one 14 x 22in. the others smaller. (Christie's) $3,132 £2,160

Mid 18th century framed needlework panel, worked in silk and metallic thread on silk faille ground, England, 73¾in. long, 32¾in. wide. (Robt. W. Skinner Inc.) $350 £255

One of a set of four gros point borders worked in coloured wools and silks, 11in. deep, 126in. long. (Christie's) $594 £410

Plains paint decorated parfleche case, Yakima, 15 x 30in. (Robt. W. Skinner Inc.) $275 £190

A Berlin woolwork cushion, the central medallion worked with raised plush roses, circa 1860, 18in. square. (Christie's) $2,035 £1,404

Mid 19th century Berlin woolwork picture of a Turk, 29 x 25½in. (Christie's) $548 £378

A raised work applique picture of a poodle against an orange velvet ground, in gilt frame worked with cornucopiae, circa 1800. (Christie's) $594 £410

A Berlin woolwork cushion with a large central medallion and sprays of flowers, 18in. square. (Christie's) $1,409 £972

A raised work naive picture of a russet and white spotted dog, labelled Catherine Lacy, circa 1840, 9½ x 12½in.(Christie's) $861 £594

A large Berlin woolwork bag with leather clasp and brass handle, circa 1860. (Christie's) $171 £118

A naive raised work portrait of a King Charles spaniel, worked in coloured felts and long strands of wool, circa 1840, 14½ x 18in. (Christie's) $939 £648

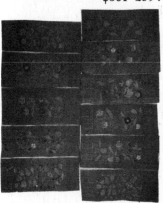

A border composed of eleven panels of green silk embroidered with spot motifs, each panel 14 x 5in. (Christie's) $4,320 £3,000

A Victorian needlework panel, possibly a stool cover, 38 x 27in., together with another. (Christie's) $861 £594

Late 19th century Indian hanging of cream velvet with a deep border worked in silver thread and sequins, 104 x 60in. (Christie's)$297 £205

Late 17th/early 18th century needlework chair back or screen cover, 29 x 22½in. (Christie's) $469 £324

One of two fine borders worked in Berlin woolwork with sprays of roses and poppies, 93 x 13in. (Christie's) $704 £486

A seat cover and chairback worked in petit point with a spray of pink and red carnations with blue stems, French, early 18th century. (Christie's) $786 £600

A needlework picture worked in silk and petit point with Susannah and the Elders, English, mid 17th century, 15 x 20in. (Christie's) $1,179 £900

A Victorian shield-shaped petit point picture worked in coloured wools with a parrot perched on a branch, 21 x 17in. (Christie's)
$391 £270

A pair of epimanikia embroidered in silver thread and red and green wool with The Annunciation, Armenian, early 17th century.
(Christie's) $655 £500

'The Garden of Adonis', a wool hanging designed and embroidered by Mary Newill, 192 x 121cm.
(Christie's) $1,576 £1,080

A large cream wool and silk shawl, circa 1860, 126 x 57in. (Christie's) $313 £216

A large wool and silk challis shawl, circa 1860, 128 x 63in.
(Christie's) $548 £378

A needlework picture worked in petit point in coloured silks with The Angel staying the hand of Abraham, English, 17th century, 11 x 12in.
(Christie's) $458 £350

One of a pair of early 19th century curtains of cotton, 75 x 64in. (Christie's)
$124 £86

A tapestry cushion cover woven with a classical scene, Dutch, 17th century, 12 x 23in. (Christie's)
$982 £750

Dinky 28M green delivery van advertising "Atco Motor Mowers'. (Christie's)
$420 £280

An early painted tinplate fish, with clockwork mechanism causing the fish to flap its fin, 8¼in. long, by Bing, circa 1910. (Christie's)
$330 £220

A Gunthermann painted and lithographed four-door limousine with clockwork mechanism, German, circa 1910, 11½in. long. (Christie's) $1,200 £800

An early printed and painted tinplate automobile, 'Tut Tut', EPL No. 490, by Lehmann, circa 1910, 6¾in. long. (Christie's) $1,350 £900

A large dappled rocking horse, on metal hinged rockers, 51½in. high. (Lawrence Fine Art)
$162 £110

'Mickey Mouse Organ Grinder', tinplate toy with clockwork and musical mechanisms, by Distler, circa 1930, 6in. long. (Christie's) $975 £650

A Triang Minic pre-war Learner's car, boxed, with key (M). (Phillips)
$441 £300

An Edwardian plush model bear on wheels, 1ft.4in. high, one ear and one eye missing. (Hobbs & Chambers) $148 £100

A Triang Minic pre-war Rolls Tourer, boxed, with key. (Phillips) $323 £220

A Jep painted tinplate 'Panhard Levassor', finished in tan with red lining, French, circa 1925, 30½in. long. (Christie's) $975 £650

An early painted metal gunboat with clockwork mechanism, by Bing, circa 1904, 10½in. long. (Christie's) $330 £220

Dinky 917, Guy van advertising 'Spratts'. (Christie's)
                    $150 £100

A dark plush teddy bear with straw stuffed body and elongated arms, back hump and felt pads, probably by Steiff, 40cm. high. (Phillips)
            $625 £420

A carved and painted rocking horse with hair mane and tail, America, circa 1880, 52in. long. (Robt. W. Skinner Inc.)
            $1,200 £810

One of three Britains' model Lifeguards and Officer, unboxed, damaged. (Hobbs & Chambers) $32 £22

A Triang Minic pre-war 59 ME Searchlight lorry, boxed (M). (Phillips) $264 £180

A dark plush teddy bear with wide apart rounded ears, black button eyes and pointed snout, probably by Steiff, 34cm. high. (Phillips) $596 £400

A Triang Minic pre-war taxi (M), boxed, with key. (Phillips) $514 £350

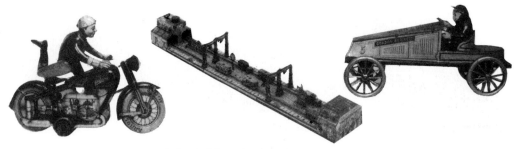

'Mac 700', a printed tinplate motorbike with rider, by Arnold, W. Germany, circa 1955, 7½in. long. (Christie's) $330 £220

A Louis Marx tinplate 'Main St.' Tramway, the loop track with overhead power pylons with trams and trucks moving between station and terminal, 24in. long. (Lawrence Fine Art) $148 £100

Gunthermann, Gordon Bennett clockwork racing car, finished in yellow with gold detail, 28cm. long. (Phillips) $5,880 £4,000

A golden plush covered teddy bear, the front unhooking to reveal a metal hot water bottle, by Steiff, 17in. high.(Christie's) $1,584 £1,100

Meccano, No. 2 Constructor Car constructed as a tourer, boxed. (Phillips) $1,764 £1,200

A Steiff pale plush teddy bear with black thread stitched nose and straw stuffed body, with button in left ear, 33cm. high. (Phillips) $745 £500

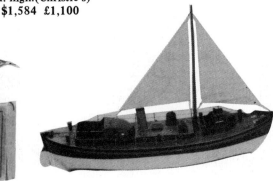

A printed and painted tinplate beetle, EPL No. 431, by Lehmann, circa 1906, 3¾in. long. (Christie's) $150 £100

A wood and metal electric powered model of a Watson Type self-righting lifeboat, circa 1925, 24in. long, by Bassett-Lowke. (Christie's) $473 £320

'New Century Cycle', EPL 345, with clockwork mechanism, by Lehmann, circa 1910, 5in. long. (Christie's) $1,275 £850

A mechanical cast iron money box, as a football player with articulated right leg, causing the player to shoot a coin into a goal and ring a bell, circa 1890, 10½in. long. (Christie's) $825 £550

A painted tinplate cat, 'Nina', EPL No. 790, by Lehmann, circa 1907, 11in. long. (Christie's) $1,500 £1,000

A hand enamelled 'New Orleans Paddle Wheeler', probably by Dent, U.S.A., circa 1903, 10½in. long. (Christie's) $600 £400

Part of a collection of five tinplate toys, comprising two prancing horses, a steam engine, a circular saw bench and another item. (Lawrence Fine Art) $14 £10

A boxed set of diecast Build-Yourself vehicles, by Solido. (Phillips) $66 £45

A Steiff blonde plush teddy bear, with metal disc in left ear, 17in. high. (Lawrence Fine Art) $1,465 £990

'Baker and Sweep', E.P.L. No. 450, by Lehmann, circa 1905, in original box. (Christie's) $2,368 £1,600

A painted wood dapple grey 'pony size' rocking horse, with horse hair mane and tail, 56in. long, British. (Christie's) $518 £350

An early Carette carpet toy tinplate sailboat, with fly-wheel mechanism, German, circa 1905, 11¾in. long. (Christie's) $270 £180

A Magic Disc phenakisticope optical toy with 8 discs, each 7in. diam., a viewing disc, 9in. diam., and a Fantascope disc, 5in. diam. (Christie's) **$595 £480**

A teddy bear of grey plush with brown button eyes, embroidered nose, hump back and long paws, 13in. high. (Christie's)**$419 £320**

A plush-covered teddy bear with round ears, button eyes, pronounced hump and long paws, probably by Steiff, 21in. high. (Christie's) **$393 £300**

'Bulky Mule, The Stubborn Donkey', EPL No. 425, by Lehmann, circa 1910, 7½in. long.(Christie's) **$217 £150**

A miniature violin in original case with mother-of-pearl inlay, the case 5in. long. (Christie's) **$340 £260**

A doll's Jacobean style chair upholstered in dark red velvet, 21in. high. (Christie's) **$917 £700**

A Crown illuminated Panorama optical toy theatre, illuminated by a candle mounted behind, 9½in. wide. (Christie's) **$223 £180**

A gauge 1 signals gantry, with four signals, oil fired lamps and ladders on both sides, by Bing, circa 1910, 21in. high. (Christie's) **$576 £440**

A clockwork automaton toy of a bisque headed doll pulling a wooden two-wheeled cart with driver, 13in. long. (Christie's) **$1,703 £1,300**

A cast iron mechanical bank, 'Trick Pony', by Shepard Hardware Co., American, circa 1890, 7in. long. (Christie's) $393 £300

A tinplate model of a fairground traction engine, with a four-wheeled car containing a carousel, by Bing, circa 1906. (Christie's) $628 £480

A golden plush-covered musical teddy bear, playing Sonny Boy by Al Jolson, 20in. high, circa 1930. (Christie's) $720 £550

A 17th century wooden skittle doll carved as a puritan woman, 6in. high. (Christie's) $262 £200

A Carette lithograph limousine, with clockwork mechanism, German, circa 1911, 8½in. long. (Christie's) $1,044 £720

Mid 19th century papier mache two-faced clockwork musical automaton figure, 18in. high. (Christie's) $550 £420

A long plush-covered teddy bear with black button eyes, with Steiff button in the ear, 25in. high. (Christie's) $1,703 £1,300

A model of a hall with marquetry floor dividing at the landing into stairs on either side going up to a galleried landing, 26in. wide. (Christie's) $393 £300

A painted tinplate toy of a monkey on a four-wheel musical carriage, German, circa 1903, 7½in. long. (Christie's) $366 £280

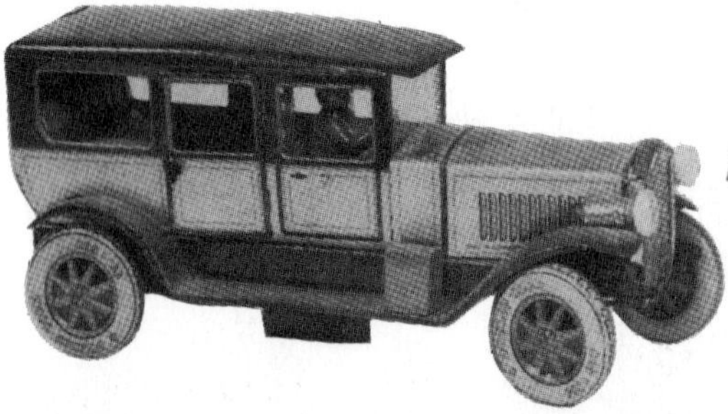

A printed and painted tinplate model of a four-door limousine with clockwork mechanism, by Tipp & Co., circa 1928, 8¼in. long. (Christie's) $628 £480

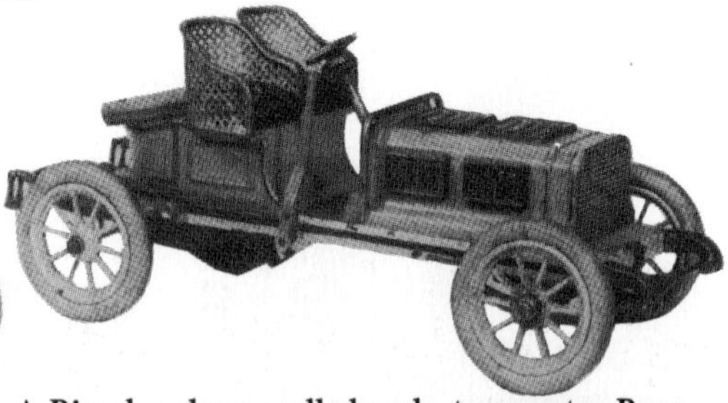

A Bing hand-enamelled early two-seater Benz racing car, with steerable front wheels, German, circa 1904, 11¼in. long. (Christie's) $12,052 £9,200

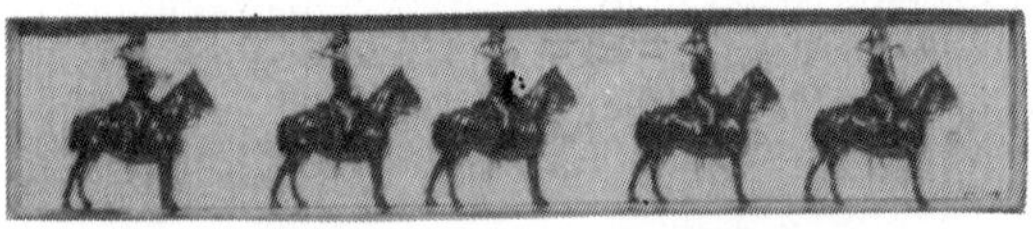

Britains' set No. 315, 10th Royal Hussars, Prince of Wales' Own, at the halt with swords, and bugler, in original box. (Christie's) $370 £250

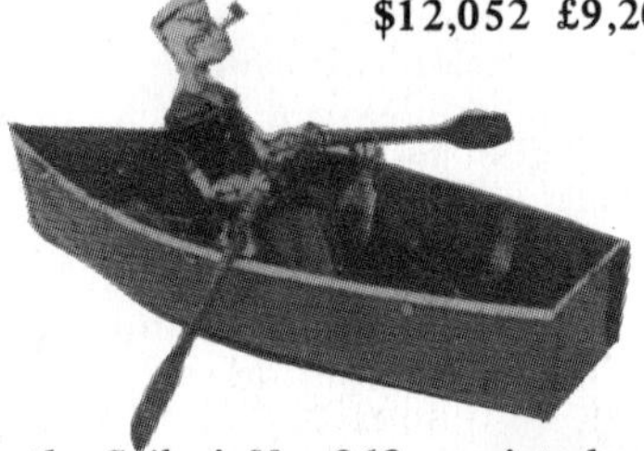

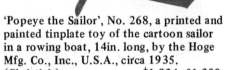

'Popeye the Sailor', No. 268, a printed and painted tinplate toy of the cartoon sailor in a rowing boat, 14in. long, by the Hoge Mfg. Co., Inc., U.S.A., circa 1935. (Christie's) $1,924 £1,300

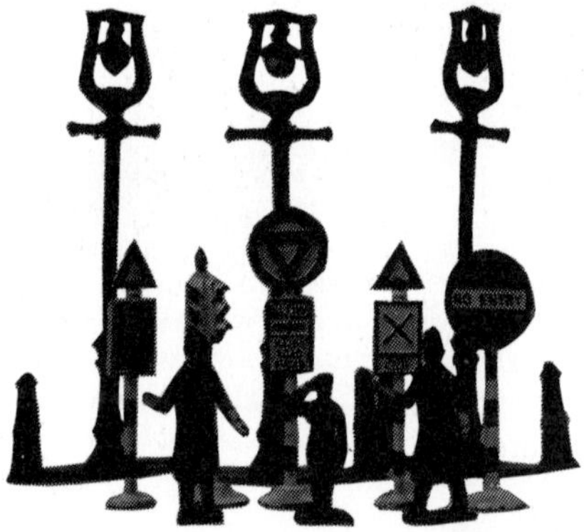

Various model road signs, nine Dinky petrol pumps, three street lamps and seven figures, unboxed. (Hobbs & Chambers) $44 £30

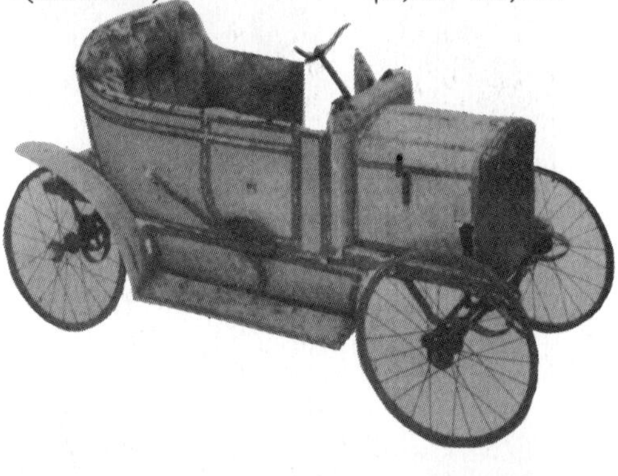

An early Lines Bros. pedal car, the wooden body painted suede grey with sprung chassis, 39in. long. (Lawrence Fine Art) $814 £550

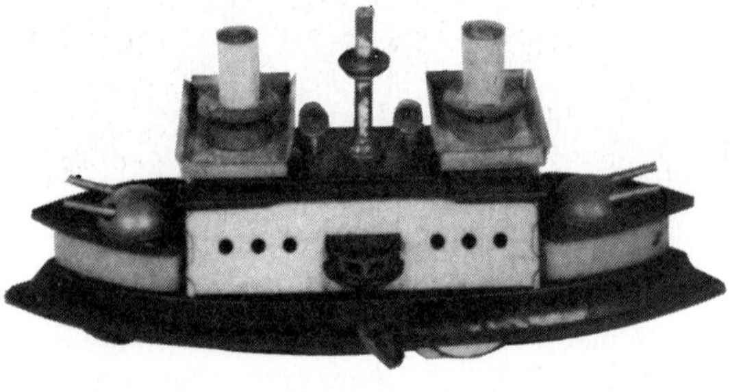

A Hess printed and painted tinplate toy of Dreadnought, with clockwork mechanism, circa 1911, 8½in. long. (Christie's) $87 £60

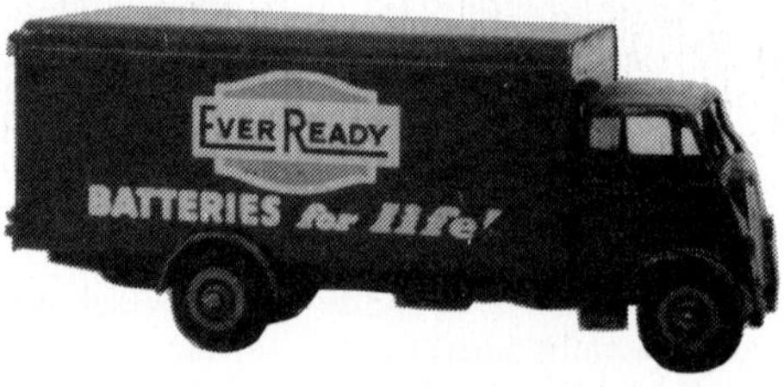

A Dinky model Guy van with upright radiator grill, unboxed. (Hobbs & Chambers) $62 £42

Lesney Yesteryear model No. 9 Fowler showman's engine, unboxed. (Hobbs & Chambers) $32 £22

A painted tinplate model of a P2 Alfa Romeo racing car, with clockwork mechanism, by C.I.G., France, circa 1926, 21½in. long. (Christie's) $1,048 £800

A Britains' farmer's gig, No. F28 with horse, together with Fordson tractor, unboxed. (Hobbs & Chambers) $44 £30

Britains' set No. 1634, The Governor-General's Foot Guards, marching at the slope arms, with officer, in original box. (Christie's) $133 £90

Part of an eighteen piece set of Britains' model hunt, unboxed. (Hobbs & Chambers) $74 £50

A tinplate toy gramophone, printed 'Made in Germany', 1930's, 8¼in. long. (Lawrence Fine Art) $88 £60

A painted metal model of an Austin J40 Roadster pedal car, 64in. long, British, circa 1950. (Christie's) $1,110 £750

A Dinky Series 28 first pattern delivery van, painted in black and red with gilt decals, 'The Manchester Guardian', circa 1935. (Lawrence Fine Art) $355 £240

1923 Rolls Royce 40/50 H.P. Silver Ghost limousine, coachwork by Maythorn, Reg. No. AA 46, Chassis No. 16NK. (Christie's) $31,680 £22,000

1933 Rolls Royce 20/25 H.P. Sports saloon, coachwork by Park Ward, Reg. No. ALD 333, Chassis No. GSY 92, Engine No. N4A. (Christie's) $12,495 £8,500

1963/4 Ferrari 250 GT Berlinetta Lusso, coachwork by Scaglietti, Reg. No. NJ KHI 791 (U.S.A.), Chassis No. 250GT/L 5851。 (Christie's) $41,160 £28,000

1954 Jaguar XK 120 Drophead Coupe, Reg. No. 664 BHX, Chassis No. 667183, Engine No. F-1935-8. (Christie's) $14,400 £10,000

C. 1904 Jackson Open two-seater, Reg. No. BM 657, Chassis No. not recorded, Engine No. 19850, De Dion Bouton two-cylinder 1141 c.c. (Christie's) $10,290 £7,000

1935 British Salmson S4C four-door saloon, coachwork by Ranalah, Reg. No. DPC 769, Chassis No. CZ 305, Engine No. CZ 305. (Christie's) $3,675 £2,500

1952 Bentley MK VI four-door 'Lightweight' Sports saloon, coachwork by H. J. Mulliner, Reg. No. CVV 62, Chassis No. B142NZ, Engine No. B307L. (Christie's) $14,700 £10,000

1935 MG NA Magnette two-seat Sports Racer, Reg. No. NJ 6218, Chassis No. NA0726, Engine No. 799A 134N. (Christie's) $11,520 £8,000

1958 BMW 507 two-seat Roadster with detachable hardtop, coachwork by Vignale, Reg. No. PPR 615W, Chassis No. 70184, Engine No. 40204. (Christie's) $69,090 £47,000

1930 Alfa Romeo 6C-1750 Fourth Series Gran Turismo four-seat Drophead Coupe, coachwork by James Young, Reg. No. GH 4124, Chassis No. 8613252, Engine No. 8613252. (Christie's) $50,400 £35,000

1969 Aston Martin DB6 Superleggera four-seat Grand Touring saloon, Reg. No. ALU 39H, Chassis No. DB64060RE, Engine No. 4004232. (Christie's) $10,080 £7,000

1935 Alva Speed Twenty four-door Sports saloon, coachwork by Charlesworth, Reg. No. WS 7223, Chassis No. 17811. (Christie's) $10,290 £7,000

1921 B.S.A. 986 c.c. Solo motorcycle, Frame No. 1296, Engine No. 1268, twin cylinder. (Christie's) $1,550 £1,100

A Morris Cowley 6 saloon, first registered 19.1.34, colour — midnight blue and black. (Reeds Rains) $2,304 £1,600

1930 MG M-Type Midget Sports two-seater, Reg. No. VR 9230, Chassis No. 2M/723, Engine No. A2685. (Christie's)
        $8,640 £6,000

1939 Packard One Twenty Drophead coupe, Reg. No. ERO 54, Chassis No. 312550, Engine No. 312550. (Christie's) $29,400 £20,000

1955 Bentley R-type Continental two-door Sports saloon, Reg. No. AHJ 448A, Chassis No. BC2E, Engine No. BC2E. (Christie's)
$32,340 £22,000

1933 Lagonda M45 4½-litre four-seat tourer, Reg. No. AMT 77, Chassis No. Z 10605, Engine No. Z 2354. (Christie's)
$26,640 £18,500

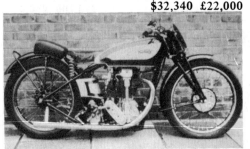

1933 Norton Racing International 500 c.c. Solo motorcycle, Reg. No. AFC 310, Frame No. 40-50946, Engine No. 2433. (Christie's)
$5,145 £3,500

1929 Riley 9 H.P. San Remo Fabric saloon, Reg. No. YC 7391, Chassis No. 606616, Engine No. 16588. (Christie's)$4,320 £3,000

1925 Lanchester Twenty-One limousine, coachwork by Penman of Dumfries, Reg. No. OSV 764, Chassis No. LVL 039 9W1 377. (Christie's) $6,468 £4,400

A sturdily constructed small full size steam timber tractor, Reg. No. 889 FUF, built by E. Bauchen, Steyning, 46 x 90in. (Christie's)
$2,940 £2,000

1938 Alvis Speed 25 four-door Sports saloon, coachwork by Charlesworth, Reg. No. EYR 219, Chassis No. 14599, Engine No. 15083. (Christie's) $8,820 £6,000

Red MGA Coupe 1960 with MOT and taxed until October. (Butler & Hatch Waterman)
$4,464 £3,100

1924 Brough Superior SS80 Solo motorcycle, Reg. No. RK3250, Frame No. 205, Engine No. KTC YM 19706/5. (Christie's)
$7,791 £5,300

1956 Ferrari 250 GT two-seat coupe, coachwork by Boano, Reg. No. XRX 507, Chassis No. 061 3GT, Engine No. 061 3GT. (Christie's)
$44,100 £30,000

1903 Miniature Velox 3½ H.P. Open two-seater, Reg. No. AY 66. (Christie's)
$13,230 £9,000

1984 Lynx Replica of Jaguar D-type with Weslake 3-litre Grand Prix engine, Reg. No. — not registered. (Christie's)
$36,750 £25,000

1908 Buick Model 10 three-seat Roadster, not registered, Chassis No. 14392, right-hand drive. (Christie's) $8,085 £5,500

1925 Fiat 501B four-seat tourer, Reg. No. TD 5457, Chassis No. 1253283, Engine No. 1153883. (Christie's) $6,912 £4,800

1969 Daimler V8 250 four-door Sports saloon, Reg. No. KUR 80G, Chassis No. PIK5278BW, Engine No. 7K5553. (Christie's)
$3,168 £2,200

1964 Rolls Royce Phantom V limousine, coachwork by H. J. Mulliner, Park Ward, Reg. No. EUC 100C, Chassis No. 5VD63, Engine No. D 31 PV. (Christie's) $294,000 £200,000

1934 Frazer-Nash TT Replica Sports two-seater, Reg. No. BMC 446, Chassis No. 2118, Engine No. 11743. (Christie's)
$20,160 £14,000

1973 Porsche 911 Carrera RS 2.7 2 + 2 Sports Coupe, Reg. No. RLX 5L, Chassis No. 9113601363, Engine No. 6631325.(Christie's)
$20,160 £14,000

1952 Bristol 401 Sports saloon, Reg. No. UMG 999, Chassis No. 1214, Engine No. 1991. (Christie's)
$5,760 £4,000

1934 British Salmson S4C four-door saloon, Reg. No. BKK 80, Chassis No. CZ 317, Engine No. CZ 317. (Christie's)
$6,912 £4,800

1922 Rolls Royce 40/50 H.P. Silver Ghost replica Open Tourer, Chassis No. 19RG, Engine No. P271H. (Christie's)
$28,800 £20,000

1970 Ferrari 365 GTB4 Daytona two-seat Berlinetta, Reg. No. PUV 100, Chassis No. 12853, Engine No. 251. (Christie's)
$46,080 £32,000

1954 Healey Tickford four-seat fixed head Coupe, Reg. No. OXU 489, Chassis No. F3094, Engine No. F8227. (Christie's) $2,736 £1,900

1952 Bentley MK VI four-door saloon, coachwork by Freestone & Webb, Reg. No. PKK 275, Chassis No. B291NY, Engine No. B395N. (Christie's)
$10,800 £7,500

1948 Lea-Francis 14 H.P. Sports open 2/4-seater, Reg. No. GJB 82, Chassis No. 7072, Engine No. S3331. (Christie's)
$8,640 £6,000

1938 Morris Ten-Four Series III four-door saloon, Reg. No. EWE 119, Chassis No. 53/7N/115599, Engine No. 7273. (Christie's)
$1,296 £900

1960 MGA 1600 Sports two-seater, Reg. No. 370 YMP, Chassis No. GHN/82765, Engine No. 14057. (Christie's) $4,896 £3,400

1921 Ford Model T four-seat Tourer, Reg. No. R 1878, Chassis No. 209225, Engine No. 209225. (Christie's) $9,360 £6,500

1926 Rolls Royce Twenty-Three-Position Drophead Coupe, coachwork by Jack Compton, Reg. No. DXR 888, Chassis No. GYK 30. (Christie's) $27,360 £19,000

1933 Rolls Royce 20/25 four-door saloon, coachwork by Park Ward, Reg. No. AKN 658, Chassis No. GYZ 20, Engine No. Y70.
(Christie's) $10,800 £7,500

Replica 1958 Maserati 450S Sports racing two-seater, Reg. No. OCN 766, Chassis No. 115140, Engine No. OA 03074. (Christie's)
$36,000 £25,000

1926 Rolls Royce Twenty Foursome Drophead Coupe, coachwork by Salmons, Reg. No. OX 20, Chassis No. GOK 64, Engine No. G 1606. (Christie's) $20,160 £14,000

A sulkie and rider with horse weathervane figure, attributed to T. W. Fiske, America, circa 1880, 36in. long. (Robt. W. Skinner Inc.) $2,500 £1,689

Late 19th century running horse with jockey weathervane figure, possibly J. L. Mott & Co., circa 1880, America, 16in. long. (Robt. W. Skinner Inc.) $2,000 £1,351

A 19th century running horse and hoop weathervane, America, 30in. long. (Robt. W. Skinner Inc.) $3,900 £2,635

Ethan Allen running horse weathervane figure, America, circa 1880, 26½in. long. (Robt. W. Skinner Inc.) $600 £405

A cast metal and copper rooster weathervane figure, American, circa 1890, 27in. high. (Robt. W. Skinner Inc.) $1,900 £1,319

A moulded copper stag weathervane, attributed to J. Harris & Co., Boston, circa 1879, 30½in. high. (Robt. W. Skinner Inc.) $28,000 £19,444

Mid 19th century American copper cow weathervane, possibly from the Howard Co., 15½in. high. (Robt. W. Skinner Inc.) $800 £555

A 19th century sheet iron silhouette weathervane, a prancing horse with military rider, 27in. long. (Robt. W. Skinner Inc.) $2,000 £1,351

An iron prospector's weathervane, Penn., circa 1900, 27½in. high. (Robt. W. Skinner Inc.)
$750   £520

Late 19th/early 20th century American gilt copper weathervane depicting a peacock, 29in. long overall. (Christie's) $3,520   £2,427

A late 19th century American carved wooden weathervane in the form of Gabriel blowing his horn, 47in. long. (Christie's)
$1,650   £1,204

A 20th century grasshopper weathervane figure, the moulded copper figure with verdigris mounted on vertical shaft, 19in. high, America. (Robt. W. Skinner Inc.)
$925   £625

A cast metal and moulded copper horse weathervane figure, attributed to J. Howard, circa 1880, 21in. high, 29in. long. (Robt. W. Skinner Inc.)
$3,300   £2,291

Mid 19th century American copper horse and groom weathervane, 20½in. high. (Robt. W. Skinner Inc.) $650   £451

Late 19th century American copper weathervane depicting a cow, 14½in. high, 24in. long. (Christie's) $440   £303

Late 19th century American copper weathervane in the form of a pig, 35in. long. (Christie's) $11,000   £7,586

A carved and painted counter top cigar store Punch figure, by Chas. Henkel, Vermont, 1870, 26in. high. (Christie's) $19,800 £13,655

A stained wood smoker's compendium in the form of a motor car, 6½ x 11½in. (Christie's) $322 £260

Early 19th century carved and gilded eagle, America, 14in. high. (Robt. W. Skinner Inc.) $525 £369

One of a pair of giltwood wall brackets, one supported on a dragon, the other on a displayed eagle, 20½in. high. (Christie's) $2,041 £1,512

A 19th century painted wood No mask of Kumasaka, signed Deme Eiman, 20.6cm. high. (Christie's) $762 £561

A 19th century American carved wooden rooster, 12½in. high. (Robt. W. Skinner Inc.) $1,500 £1,041

An engraved and painted wood pantry box, New England, circa 1800/20, 10½in. diam. (Christie's) $3,410 £2,351

A painted wooden hollow standing horse, American, circa 1850/90, 49in. long, possibly used as a harness-maker's sign. (Christie's) $3,520 £2,427

One of a pair of early George III white painted and gilded picture frames attributed to Wm. Vile and John Cobb, 75 x 59in. (Christie's) $40,176 £32,400

WOOD

A 19th century wooden model of a seated camel, 50in. wide, 27½in. high. (Christie's)
$20,358 £14,040

An African carved wood fertility god, 26in. high. (Dacre, Son & Hartley)
$6,912 £4,800

A 20th century carved and stained pine ox cart with driver and two donkeys, by Peviri, blind carver of Cape Cod, 21½in. long, together with a pitcher and six mugs. (Christie's)
$88 £60

A mahogany waste paper basket with slightly tapering octagonal body with paper lining, 13½in. diam.(Christie's)
$3,395 £2,592

Northwest coast hawk mask of polychromed alder wood, 9½in. high, 8in. wide. (Robt. W. Skinner Inc.)
$41,000 £28,472

A Gustav Stickley slat-sided wastebasket, circa 1907, no. 94, unsigned, 14in. high. (Robt. W. Skinner Inc.)
$1,000 £694

A 19th century carved head of Bodhisattva, Japan, 13½in. high overall. (Robt. W. Skinner Inc.)
$675 £462

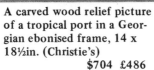

A carved wood relief picture of a tropical port in a Georgian ebonised frame, 14 x 18½in. (Christie's)
$704 £486

A wooden bust of a negress by Forrest, 18½in. high. (Christie's)
$201 £140

Late 19th/early 20th century carved wooden rooster, 31in. long overall. (Christie's) $1,650 £1,137

An 18th century Italian creche blackamoor, painted carved wood and moulded clay body, 8in. high. (Robt. W. Skinner Inc.)
$300 £205

One of a pair of Rohlfs oak and copper chambersticks, dated 1902, 5¼in. high. (Robt. W. Skinner Inc.)
$1,000 £694

An 18th century carved pine figure of Francis of Assisi, Italy, 8½in. high. (Robt. W. Skinner Inc.) $200 £140

A Momoyama period Christian folding lectern (shokendai), decorated in aogai and hiramakie, circa 1600, 50.5cm. high. (Christie's)
$38,880 £27,000

Late 19th century Oriental gong with carved teakwood stand, and wrapped leather knocker, 43in. high. (Robt. W. Skinner Inc.)
$650 £445

Victorian oak biscuit barrel with plated mounts, 1870. (British Antique Exporters)
$29 £22

Ornate carved mahogany wall bracket, 1845. (British Antique Exporters)
$194 £144

A carved gessoed and painted pine soldier, polychrome decorated, circa 1780/1815, 14in. high. (Christie's)
$6,380 £4,400

WOOD

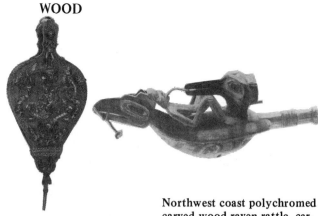

A Tapio Wirkkala laminated wood dish shaped like an oyster shell, circa 1950, 28cm. long. (Christie's) $4,099 £2,808

A 17th century pair of Italian walnut bellows, 27in. wide. (Christie's) $2,488 £1,728

Northwest coast polychromed carved wood raven rattle, carved in two sections, 12¼in. long. (Robt. W. Skinner Inc.) $4,000 £2,777

One of a pair of George III painted and gilded urns, 28in. high, 18in. wide. (Christie's) $31,320 £21,600

A carved and painted wooden zebra carousel figure, attributed to H. Speilman, circa 1880, 33in. high. (Robt. W. Skinner Inc.) $3,400 £2,361

One of a pair of giltwood wall brackets supported on scallops held by a mermaid and a merman, 20in. high. (Christie's) $1,312 £972

A carved and painted bandwagon figure of Victory, American, circa 1880, 69½in. high. (Robt. W. Skinner Inc.) $4,000 £2,777

A Biedermeier walnut cradle, the oval body with detachable tin liner, 52in. wide. (Christie's) $6,073 £4,104

An 18th century American cherry pipe box, 20½in. high. (Robt. W. Skinner Inc.) $1,500 £1,041

WOOD

A gilt bronze and carved wood figure of a Spanish flamenco dancer cast and carved from a model by Hagenauer, 23.9cm. high. (Christie's) $939 £648

A carved and painted wood figure in the form of a French Cantiniere, 39¼in. high. (Lawrence Fine Art) $703 £475

An early 18th century red lacquer and giltwood folding bible stand, 53.5cm. high.(Christie's) $1,428 £972

Eastern Plains/Wester Woodlands wood and stone pipe, 23¾in. long. (Robt. W. Skinner Inc.) $750 £520

Pair of 19th century carved and painted parcel gilt panels, one depicting St. Jerome and the other St. Catherine, 32¼in. high, 17in. wide. (Robt. W. Skinner Inc.) $1,300 £948

A carved gessoed and painted pine soldier, polychrome decorated, circa 1780/1815, 14.1/8in. high. (Christie's) $4,950 £3,413

A life size carved and painted black duck, Birchler, circa 1925, full length 18in., 19in. high. (Robt. W. Skinner Inc.) $2,700 £1,824

A George III mahogany cistern, the vase shaped body with lead lining, 17in. diam. (Christie's) $2,770 £2,052

Early 20th century American carved and painted trade sign, 39¼in. high. (Christie's) $550 £401

One of a pair of Italian parcel gilt and painted brackets with moulded D-shaped tops, 20in. wide. (Christie's) $933 £648

Early 19th century painted and carved pine hanging wall box, America, 12.5/8in. long. (Robt. W. Skinner Inc.)
$1,500 £1,013

Northwest coast portrait mask of polychrome carved and incised cedar, collected pre 1884, 10½in. high. (Robt. W. Skinner Inc.)
$25,000 £17,361

Late 18th century carved and painted tavern figure, 43in. high. (Robt. W. Skinner Inc.) $3,400 £2,297

Two carved and painted wooden figures, modelled as a rooster and chicken, American, circa 1893, 11in. and 13in. high. (Christie's)
$660 £481

Late 19th century signed heavily carved folk art scoop, West Indies, 22in. long. (Robt. W. Skinner Inc.)
$300 £202

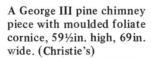

A carved wood polychrome head of Kuan Yin, 21½in. high. (Lawrence Fine Art) $414 £286

A George III pine chimney piece with moulded foliate cornice, 59½in. high, 69in. wide. (Christie's)
$3,862 £2,592

A stained wood portrait figure of a man, 11¾in. high. (Lawrence Fine Art)
$478 £330

A 16th/17th century Provincial wood sculpture of Amida, 71cm. high. (Christie's) $1,650 £1,100

A Shinto wood sculpture of a seated deity wearing Heian/Kamakura style robes and hat, Edo period, 58.8cm. high. (Christie's) $2,400 £1,600

An early wood sculpture of Buddha, late Heian period, 36.8cm. high. (Christie's) $1,275 £850

A 19th century large wood sculpture of a recumbent deer, the antlers formed from natural stag-antler, 66cm. long. (Christie's) $1,575 £1,050

A giltwood medical shop sign carved as a carp with black lacquered eyes, Meiji period, 126cm. long. (Christie's) $3,300 £2,200

A large red lacquered wood sculpture of a seated emaciated priest, early/mid Edo period, the figure 49cm. high. (Christie's) $4,500 £3,000

A 17th century Zen buddhist wood carving of a guardian figure in the style of the monk Enku, 52cm. high. (Christie's) $1,050 £700

A carved oak panel depicting the martyrdom of St. Lawrence, 1764, 96cm. high. (Phillips) $2,100 £1,400

One of a pair of gilded and green lacquered wood standing frogs, 15in. high. (Lots Road Chelsea Auction Galleries) $414 £280

INDEX

ABD Al-A-Imma 567
Absolon 286
Abuja 176, 253
Ackermann, R. 136
Acorn 715
Acteon 145
Adam 106
Adam, Robt. 604
Adams 259
Adams, George 135
Adams-Jefferson 526
Adnet, J. J. 672
Advancement of the Art of
   Navigation 135
Advertising Signs 66-69
Aeronautical 70-73
Aeronautical Paintings 73
Aircraft 72
Albertus, Gundorph 714
Alcora 193
Alcyon 72
Alden, Sally 683
Aldis 160
Aldridge, Edward 684
Alfa Romeo 769, 771
Allam, Robert 297
Allen, Ethan 776
Allen & Wheelock 101, 103,
   105
Allen, Wm. 718
Allison, M. 430
Almaric Walter 524
Alpa 161
Alva 771
Alvis 772
Ambergs 357
American China 164, 165
American Forecast 131
Amerith, R. 602
Amis, K. 135
Amours Pastorale, Les 330
Amphyrite 541
An Account of the First Aerial
   Voyage in England 135
Anagke 144
Analemmatic Dial 567
Andri, Ferdinand 660
Anfibio 438
Angell, Joseph 701
Antoniazzi, R. 624, 625

Apache 557, 559
Apollo 608
Aprey 197
Apsley Pellatt 540
Aras 544
Architect's Table 488-490
Argyll & Sutherland
   Highlanders 80, 85
Argy-Rousseau 525, 546
Arita 166
Armand 298
Armillary Sphere 567
Armoires & Wardrobes 512,
   513
Arms & Armour 74-128
Army Veterinary Dept. 93
Arnold 764
Arnold & Dent 273, 287
Arnold & Son, John 303
Arsale 547
Art Union of London 184
Arts & Crafts 313, 425, 433,
   687
Ashbee, C. R. 521, 523, 711,
   718, 724
Ashworths 172
Askey of Bedale 108
Asselin 270, 283
Aston Martin 771
Astrolabe 563, 565, 566, 567,
   568
Astronomical Dial 562
Atco Motor Mowers 762
Atkins, Lloyd 520
Atkinson, Wm. 625
Aubert & Klaftenberger 296
Audu Mugu Sokoto 253
Aug Luneburg Kile 114
Auster 72
Austin 617
Austin Roadster 769
Autissier, Louis Marie 656
Automatons 129
Avery, W. & T. 567
Ayton, R. 137

B.A. Swallow 72

Babs 616
Baccarat 521, 524, 534-539,
   540, 541, 542
Bacchus 533, 536
Backstage Ballet Girls 644
Baden Infantry 92
Badges 78-83
Bailey, I. 405
Bailey, Lebbeus 284
Baird 565
Baker, E. 108
Baker Harris 646
Baker & Sweep 765
Baker, William Robert 640
Baker's Cocoa 168
Baldwyn, C. H. C. 268
Ball, Black & Co. 736
Ball, Tomkins & Black 726,
   743
Balthazar 272
Bambocci 358
Banco Internacional 635
Banco Mercantil, EL 635
Banco Otero & Cà 635
Bank of Australasia 635
Bannister, H. 611
Bark Messenger 508
Barlow, Florence E. 253
Barlow, Hannah 190
Barlows PT. 317
Barnard, E. 684, 724, 726,
   730
Barnard, E. J. & W. 707, 720,
   740
Barnard, Messrs. 701, 712,
   719
Barnard, W. J. 718
Barners Wells 104
Barometers 130-133, 571
Barovier, Ercole 542
Barry, John 657
Barry Service, Madame Du
   241
Bartram & Co. 110
Bartram, James 400
Barye 138, 147
Barzanti, P. 592
Basket Maker 559
Baskets, Silver 684
Bassett-Lowke 608, 609, 611

Bat Dancer 151
Bate 113
Bateman 287
Bateman, Hester 724, 738, 739
Bateman, Peter & Anne 724, 730
Bateman, Wm. 703, 741
Battle Abbey 157
Bauchen, E. 772
Bauduin 661
Bavarian Infantry 90
Bavarian Jager Regt. 92
Bayes, Gilbert 144, 189
Bayley, Ed. 270
Bayley, R. 711
Bayreuth 198
Bazu-Band 74
Bazzi 450
Beakers, Glass 518
Beakers, Silver 685
Beale, R. 711
Beardmore, H. 261
Beaton, Cecil 642, 645
Beaumont Adams 102, 107
Beauvais 428
Bebe Francais 329
Becchi, Alessandro 438
Bechstein, C. 647
Beckmann, Max 666
Bedos & Cie 659
Beds 336, 337
Beilby 549
Bell, J. 743
Bella Coola 558
Belter, J. H. 383, 441
Belter, J. B. 487
Belin, Claude Alexandre 648
Bell, Glass 533
Bell, Robt. A. 588
Belleek 167
Belet 196
Benckendorff, Count A. 76
Bengal Regt. 75
Benham & Froud 314, 315
Benner Johannes 286
Bennettini 624
Bentley 770, 772, 774
Bercy 541
Beretta, P. 99
Berge 565
Beringer, D. 566, 570
Berleur 109
Berlin 168
Berliner 620
Bernadotte, S. 695
Bernard, Samuel 657
Berry, John 282
Berthoud, Ferdinand 135
Bettini 619
Bevan, Charles 487
Beyser, Jean-David 564
Bhuj 128
Bianconi, F. 546
Bichwa 87
Big Ben 621
Bigelow, Kennard & Co. 289
Bijou 554
Billings, Wm. 636

Bing 608-611, 762, 763, 766, 767, 768
Birchler 782
Bird, J. 133
Bird, Joseph 692
Bisiach, Leandro 625
Bisson De Recy, B. 334
Bizarre 183
Black Watch 78, 81, 83
Blanch & Son, J. 114
Bland & James 118
Blandford Yeomanry Cavalry 92
Blanket Chests 509-511
Blanquart-Evrard 642
Blondeau 240
Blue Band Margarine 68
Blumenfeld, E. 642
Blunderbuss 114-117
Blunt 565, 569
BMW. 771
Boa-Constrictor 616
Boardman, Thos. D. 637, 638
Boardman, Boardman & Hart 638
Boche 110
Boers, Bastiaan 530
Bogle, John 651
Bohm, Hermann 331, 332
Bolton, Thos. 693
Bolviller 274
Bombay Horse Artillery 88
Bone, William 114
Bone, Henry Pierce 652, 655
Bonheur, I. 146
Bookcases 338-340
Booker J & W 599
Books 134-137
Book Rack 486
Border Regt. 78, 81
Bordi 563
Borrell 286
Borsani, O. 374
Botas 605
Bottger 252
Bottles, Glass 519
Boucher 330, 331
Boucheron 720
Boulard, J. B. 379
Boullemier, H. 227
Boulton, M. 697
Boulton & Co, Matthew 749
Boulton Plate Co, The 747
Bourdin, Louise 655
Bourke-White, Margt. 643, 644
Bourne, Shepherd & Bourne & Shepherd 643
Bowen-Cooke 608
Bow 169
Bowie Knife 84, 85
Bowle, Lt. Col. C. W. 77
Bowls, Glass 520
Bowls, Silver 686, 687
Box, Glass 521
Boxes, Silver 688, 689
Boyd, George 323
Boyer 145
Boyton, Charles 724

Boze, Joseph 654
Bracket Clocks 270-272
Bradbury & Sons, Thos. 690
Bradford Academy 322
Bramah 447, 505
Bramah Lock 157
Brander, G. F. 570
Brandt, Bill 645
Brass & Copper 312-317
Brasso Metal Polish 68
Brau, C. 615
Breguet 287, 293, 299, 301
Breithaupt, F. W. 566
Brenneiser, S. 285
Briere A Paris 570
Bridge, John 520
Bridges, R. 135
Bristol 169, 774
Britains 763, 769
Britannia 115, 134, 611
British China 170-174
British Grenadiers 89
British Salmson 770
Brocot 288
Brodon, Nicolas 289
Brodt, Johan Georg 303
Bronze 138-152
Brooke, B. 116
Brookbank 71
Brooklands 614, 615, 617
Brooklands Aero Club 604
Brooklyn Arms Co. 104
Brooks, T. 466
Brough 773
Brown, Alexander 687
Brown Bess 113, 114
Brown, Nathaniel 282
Brown, Robt. 727
Brownfield 172, 173
Browning, F. N. 99
Bru 324, 325, 327
Bruce 498
Bruhl, Count 219, 223, 225
Brush (?) Busti, Lucretia 671
Brush Set 721
Brunswick 112
Brunswick & Balke-Collender Co. 480
Brunswick Hussars 88
Brunswick Infantry Regt. 90
Bryceson, H. 620
Brysons 280
BSA 771
Bubble Dance 150
Buckets 153
Buckingham Rifle Vol. 83
Buckle, Eliz. 174
Bugatti 601, 614
Buick 773
Build Yourself 765
Bulidon 241
Bulky Mule 766
Bull & Co., F. 319
Bullock, G. 604
Bulow-Hube, Torun 306
Bunney 108
Buquoy, Count 528
Burch, Henry 649
Burchett, P. 351, 466

Bureau Bookcases 341-343
Bureaux 344-349
Burgonet 88
Burmantofts 172
Burnett 108
Burrell 613
Bursley Ware 173
Burwash, Wm. 685, 708
Bury & Suffolk Bank 635
Busby 88, 89
Busch Rapid Aplanat 162
Bushu 125, 126
Buteux 242
Buteux, Elizabeth 742
Butter Maker 452
Butterfield 564, 568
Butty, Francis 704

Cabinets 350-358
Cactus 714
Caddies & Boxes 154-159
Cadran Universel 564
Cafe, J. 694, 704
Cafe, Wm. 692
Caiger-Smith 175
Calamanco 670
Calcanus, Bernard 624
Calder, Horatio H. 167
Calder, Wm. 639
Calderwood, Robt. 742
Caldwell & Co. E. 275
Callowhill 266
Camden, W. 134
Camera Work 641
Cameras 160-162
Cameron, Chas. Hay 643
Cameron, Julia Margt. 643-645
Caminada, P. 131
Canada Goose 323
Canal, Antonio 669
Candelabra, Silver 690, 691
Candlesticks, Glass 522
Candlesticks, Silver 692-695
Canivet 566
Canner, C. 730
Canterburys 359
Canton 175
Capper, Edward 724
Caps 89-91, 93
Carcassi, Vincenzo 623
Card & Tea Tables 458-463
Cardew, Michael 176, 177
Caressa & Francais 623
Carette 765, 767
Carlile, John Jr. 362
Carlton House 338, 505, 506
Carltonware 177
Carlu, Jean 659
Carlyle, T. 656
Carnival Girls 643
Carpenier, Wm. 283

Carr, Alwin 717
Carr Bros. 117
Carrette, G. 608, 610
Carriage Clocks 273-275
Carrier De Belleuse, Albert 229, 230
Carrington & Co. 684
Carter II, John 704
Cartier 304, 305
Cartwright 281
Cartwright, R. 606
Cary 569, 571
Cassandre, Adolphe Mouron 658-660
Cassone 509, 510
Castel 239
Casters, Silver 696
Castletop 748
Cater, D. 697, 744
Cathedral De Mayence 642
Cathedral De Mollins 642
Caughley 172
Cayette, J. 350
Cellarette 516, 517
Centrepieces, Silver 697
Centre Tables 464-467
Century of Orchidaceous Plants 135
Cetta, J. 132
Chaffer 215
Chagall, Marc 666
Chairs 360-392
Chamberlain 266, 267
Chambersticks, Silver 698
Champenoise, F. 660
Champion, Richard 169
Chandeliers 163
Chapka 88
Chavez, Raymond 557
Chawner, Henry 701, 704, 708, 740
Chawner, Wm. 715
Chelsea 178
Chelsea Keramic Art 164
Chen Zhongsan 751
Chesne, Claude Du 281
Chests of Drawers 393-399
Chests on Chests 400, 401
Chests on Stands 402, 403
Chevalier et Comp 300
Chiappa 620
Chi-Chi 673
Chiffoniers 404
Chikayoshi 576
China 164-269
Chinese China 179-182
Chiparus 143, 150, 152
Chipmunk 72
Chivers Carpet Soap 67
Chocolate Pots, Silver 699
Chohei, Jushuhan 560
Choshu 124
Choshu-Noju-Sakushinao Tomohisa 126
Christening Set 720
Christian, Philip 215
Christiansen, Hans 542
Christofferson, Gerda 558, 559

Christofle 735
Chronometer 562, 563, 569
Chuichi 633
Churchman's 'Tortoiseshell' 68
Cibber 753
Cibert & Cie 563
Cigalia 540
Cigarette Boxes, Silver 699
Cigarette Cases, Silver 700
Cigarette Lighter/Watch 302
Cinq Chevaux 615
Circumferentor 564
City of London Yeomanry 77
Civil War 74
Clan Mackinnon 80
Claret Jugs, Silver 701
Clarke, F. 748
Classic Stable Ltd. 614
Clichy 534-539, 540
Cliff, Clarice 183
Clock Sets 276, 277
Clocks & Watches 270-307
Cloisonne 308-311
Clothes Presses 405
Cloud-Band 674
Clutha 637
C.M.I. 661
Coal Box 155-157
Coalport 184
Coasters, Silver 702
Cobb, John 778
Cochin, C. N. 602
Cochiti 557
Coffee Pots, Silver 702-705
Coffers & Trunks 509-511
Cogswell & Harrison 116
Coker, E. 693, 694
Colden, Cadwallader 137
Coldstream Guards 119
Cole, T. 288, 290
Colgan Thos 713
Colin, Paul 659
Collas, A. 145
Collector, The 134
Collector's Cabinet 449
Collet, Edward-Louis 141
Collier, D. 284
Collier, Joseph 696
Collins, Samuel 653
Collis, Chas. 188
Colt 111, 113
Columbia 618
Combat, The 190
Comfort, E. 176
Commode Chests 407-409
Commodes & Pot Cupboards 406
Como 735
Compass 567
Compass/Sundial 298
Compendium 563
Compulsion 144
Compur 160
Comyns, Wm. 540
Concorde Watch Co. 305
Connaught Rangers 77
Console Tables 468, 469

Constabulary 122
Constantinidis, Joanna 251, 252
Convers, Louis 587
Conway, Richard 651
Cooke, Stenson 617
Cookson, Isaac 703
Coombe Richards 73
Cooper 104, 301
Cooper I, Matthew 695
Copeland 184
Copeland & Garrett 184
Coper, Hans 185
Copper & Brass 312-317
Coqs et Plumes 543
Coquelicot 525
Corner Cupboards 410, 411
Cornock, E. 743
Cossack's Adieu, The 148
Costume 318-322
Cosway, Richard 652, 654
Cotton, Jn. 271
Couches & Settees 436-441
Coultre Co., Le 307
County of Chester 610
County of Kent 134
Courtauld, A. 703, 742
Courvoisier Freres 302
Cox, E. 112
Cox, F. 566
Cox, Robert Albin 723
Crama, Francois 530
Crane, Walter 234
Craven & Co. 118
Crawshay, R. T. 645
Cream Jugs, Silver 706
Crejo 151
Crespin, Adolphe 658
Crespin, Paul 684
Creswick, Nathaniel 709
Creswick, Thos. & James 695, 749
Creswick, T. J. & N. 692
Criaerd, A. M. 347
Crichton, Alex. 701
Cripps, Wm. 705, 744
Crofts, Thos. 278
Crossbow 128
Crosse, Richard 648, 654
Crot 297
Crouch, Henry 563
Crouch, John 698, 741, 742, 743
Crow Bar Tobacco 69
Cruets, Silver 707
Crump, Francis 727
Crystal Set 571
Cube Dial 566, 570
Culpeper 568
Cuminoscope 565
Cumming, Alexdr. 271
Cunard 612
Cupboards 412, 413
Cups, Silver 708
Currier, N. 665, 668
Currier & Ives 664, 665, 667-669
Cursus Mathematics 136
Curtis, Lemuel 295
Cutty Sark 606
Cymric 747

Cypress 714
Cyril Ray in Islington 645

Dagenite 69
Daggers 84-87
Dagoneau, Ph. 562
Dahlia 521
Dai Nihon 213
Daihei 309
Daimler 773
Daisho 120, 126
Daisy 202
Dali, Salvador 440, 533
Dallmeyer, J. H. 161
Dalou, Aime Jules 144, 146, 147
Dalyzell 519
Dame Wiggins of Lee 137
Danaides 546
Dance of the Harlequinade 149
Dancing Girl 151
Danforth Jnr., J. 639
Danforth, Thos. 636
Daniel, H. & R. 172
Daniel, Jabez & Thos. 702
Daniell, W. 137
Daniels, Lucia A. 683
Dante Alighieri 137
Daoguang 142
Darley, M. 595
Darwin, Chas. 645
Dasson, Henry 449
Daum 533, 542, 544
Davenport China 174
Davenports 414, 415
Davey-Paxman 612
Davis 73
Davyz, I 520
Dawson, G. 99
Dawson, S. 692
Day, Thos. 650
De Havilland 72
De Morgan 188
Dean Single 611
Deane Harding 106
Decanters 523
Decca Dulcephone 619
Decorchment 520
Decoys 323
Dedham 164, 165
Deens, J. 569
Deer Dancers 558
Deerfield 394
Degani, Eugenio 622
Degani, Giulio & Eugenio 622
Degue 573
Delander, Daniel 300
Delatte 543
Delft 186, 187
Della Robbia 188, 261
Delynne, F. 300
Deme Eiman 778
Denecheau 152
Denning, S. P. 655
Dent 273-275, 765
Deptford, Thomas A. 285
Derazey, Justin 625
Derby 188
Derby & Co. 454

Derby, Lord 134, 135
Desjarlait, Patrick 559
Desk Cabinet 504
Desks & Writing Tables 504-508
Dessin 717
Devisme 106
Devonshire Regt. 81
Diana 149, 152
Diato, Albert 251
Dimple Haig 519
Dining Chairs 360-372
Dining Tables 470-473
Dinky 609, 762, 763, 768, 769
Dinky Doo 189
Dirk Set 85
Dishes, Glass 524
Dishes, Silver 709-711
Display Cabinets 416-419
Distagon 161
Distler 762
Divina Commedia 137
Dix, Otto 662
Dixon & Sons, James 110, 111
Dixon, James 636
Dixon, Miss Annie 648
Djinn Series 439
Dobson, T. W. H. & H. 745
Dod, S. 571
Dodd & Son, P. G. 285
Doisneau, Robt. 643
Dollond 130, 571
Dolls 324-329
Donald, W. 279
Donatello, F. 201
Donn Ltd., Leslie 695
Donzan Seizo 210
Doppel 160
Doreen 613
D'Orsay, Comte 140
Dorsetshire Regt. 80
Doulton 189, 190
Dower Chest 510, 511
Dr. Samuel Johnson's House 202
Draeger 659
Dragoon Guards 79, 80, 88
Draining Level 567
Drake, The Hatless 190
Dreadnought 768
Dresden 168, 191
Dresser, C. 230, 526
Dresser, Dr. C. 173, 174, 314, 315, 523, 532, 698, 707, 739, 745
Dressers 420, 421
Dressing Chest 474, 475
Dressing Tables 474, 475
Drinking Sets 525
Drocourt 273, 275
Drop-Leaf Tables 476, 477
Dry Fly Entomology 134
Dublin County Light Infantry 82
Duc D'Orleans 256
Duchess of Athol 610
Dudovich, Marcello 660
Duesbury & Co., Wm. 188
Dufrene, Maurice 508

Duke of Albany's Own Highlanders 78
Duke of Cambridge's Own Lancers 88, 91
Duke, Richard 623
Dumbwaiters 422
Dumee, Nicholas 704
Dunand, Jean 312
Dunant, Wm. 272
Dunhill 302, 554, 555
Dunhill, Alfred 699
Dunn & Co., F. 141
Dunn, Cary 706
Durer, Albrecht 222, 662
Durban Bank 634
Durham, J. 184
Dustantoy, J. P. 487
Dutton, Mattw. & Willm. 297
Duych, Edouard 658
Dyche, T. 611
Dyck, Sir Anthony Van 136
Dyer & Sons, A. R. 612
D'Ylem, Leon 658
Dyson & Sons, John 303

Eagle Dancer 557
Earl of Chester's Rifles 89
Earl of Warwick 134
Earthenware 191
Easel 451
East End Girl 645
East India Company 75, 82, 109
East, John 703
Easy Chairs 373-383
Eaton, Wm. 717, 733
Eavestaff 647
Eberlein, J. F. 219
Ebisu 142
Eckfourd Jnr., John 703
Echigo School 630
Echizen 124
Eckhoff, Tias 714
Eckmann, O. 148
Ecole Horlogerie De Paris 287
Edge, K. 609-611
Edison 618, 619
Editions Georges Visat 666
Edmondson, W. 752
Edo School 627, 628
Edward, J. 743
Edwards, A. 282
Edwards, E. 728
Edwards, W. H. 101
Edwards, Sydenham 136
E. H. 682
Eickhorn 85
Eiroku Ninen 120
Eisentrager, J. H. 200
Eishin 631
Eitoku 574
Elbow Chairs 384-392
Eley 605
Eley & Fearn 707, 713

Elkington & Co. 523, 532, 687, 694, 718, 723, 735, 744, 749
Elkington, F. 697
Elkington Mason & Co. 141
Elliot Bros. 567
Elliot, Wm. 717
Elliott, John 282
Ellis, James 743
Elmar 162
Elston, John 692
Elston, Philip 719
Elwes, Henry J. 135
Embree, E. 279, 283
Emerson, Peter Henry 644
Emes, J. 707, 740, 745
Emes, R. 724, 730
Emes, Rebecca 684, 718
Empire Clock 564
Enamel 330-333
End of the Affair, The 137
Engle, Elizabeth C. 682
Engleheart, George 650, 652, 654
Engleheart, John Cox Dillman 656
English Lakes 136
English School 650, 654
Enjyaku 667
Enku 784
Enty 108
Epping Forest Centenary 705
Equatorial Dial 565
Erfurt 199
Ernemann 160, 162
Ernoflex 160
Ernon 160
Essays on the Microscope 135
Essex Regt. 80
Etagere 483, 515
Etherington, D. 137
Etling 533
Eton Vol. Rifle Corps. 82
European China 192, 193
European Watch & Clock Co. Inc. 304
Evans 240
Ewers, Silver 712
Exotic Dancer 148

Faberge 555
Facon De Venise 519, 524
Fagnola, H. 624
Fairy III, D. 73
Fairy Firefly 73
Fairyland Lustre 258-260
Famille Rose 194, 195
Famille Verte 195
Fan Dancer, The 150
Fang 87
Fans 334, 335
Fantasque 183
Farmer 101
Farrell, Edward 726

Farren, Thos. 703, 740
Faucard 302
Faux 151
Favrile 541
Fawdery, William 689, 699
F. C. Franc JME 431
Feathers Hotel, The 202
Feibleman, D. 173
Felixmuller, Conrad 663
Fencing 428
Fenton, Roger 640, 642, 644
Ferguson 612
Ferguson, J. 706
Ferrari 770, 773, 774
Ferriere, Francois 651
Ferro Email 69
Feure, Georges De 192
Fez 91
Fiat 773
Ficker, A. 609
Field 297
Field Service Commando Knife 84
Fielding, T. H. 136
Figurines Avec Bouchon 519
Fireside 618
First Cardigan Vol. Artillery 76
Fish, Henry 270
Fish Slice 713
Fisher 132
Fisherman 139
Fiske, T. W. 776
Fitch, W. H. 135
Fladgate, John 272
Flashman, George 271
Flasks, Glass 526
Flatware, Silver 713-715
Fleming & Co., Andw. 359
Fletcher & Gardiner 737
Fleury 302
Flight, Claude 667
Flight & Barr 266
Flight, Barr & Barr 268, 269
Flower Seller 150
Fokker III 71
Foley 170, 171, 174, 288
Fonseca, Harry 558
Fontaine, J. 239
Foo Dog 151
Forbes, Wm. 726, 743
Forcker, Cristoph 290
Ford 775
Forgeron, Le 141
Formose 544, 547
Fornasetti, Piero 605
Forster, G. 278
Fortune Teller, The 190
Foskett, J. 711
Fountain, Wm. 727, 743
Fournier, Jean Baptiste 651
Fowler, Anna 683
Fowles, J. 134
Fox, Chas 723
Fox II, Charles 747
Fox, George 726
Foyne, W. 131
Frames, Silver 716
Franchini 540
Frank, Robt. 642, 643
Franklin & Co. 608

Frazer-Nash 774
Fremiet, E. 146
French Carabiniers 88
French Cavalry 123
French China 196, 197
French Dragoons 89
French School 655
Fritsch, Elizabeth 251
Frobisher, B. C. 712
Fromery, Pierre 168
Fudo Myo-o 575
Fuger, Heinrich F. 653
Fujiyuki 630
Fulda 198
Fulper 588
Funcke 168
Furber, Emily 683
Furniture 336-517
Furstenberg 200, 554

Gadoud, L. 658
Gage, Miss C. 322
Gagliano, Ferdinando 623
Gagliano, G. 624
Gagliano, Nicola 623
Gagnant, Rougier Le 73
Gaida, Giovanni 625
Gaigneur, Henry Louis Le
  705
Gallard 103
Gallaway, Alexander 648
Galle 483, 489, 519, 521, 532,
  542-547, 590, 591
Galle, Emile 448
Galner, Sara 164
Games Tables & Workboxes
  500-503
Gandhi, Mohandas 643
Gandolfi 160
Gardner, Ava 645
Gargory 132
Garnier, Paul 273
Garrard, R. 698, 740, 746
Garthorne, F. 696
Gateleg Tables 478, 479
Gebhard, M. J. 607
Gebruder-Heubach 168
Geefs, G. 593
Geib, P. & W. 647
Geill, Matthias 293
Gentso 441
Genus Lilium 135
George V 611
German China 198-200
Gerning, Johann Isaac Von 136
Gibbon Edward 738
Giles, Fayette S. 300
Giles, James 264, 265, 267
Gilfert, G. 646
Gillibaud 196
Gillman, Emily 189
Gillows 339, 340, 380, 424,
  474, 475, 481, 501, 505,
  517
Ginji 560
Gipsy Fortune Teller, The 330
Gipsy Major 72
Gipsy Minor 72
Gladstone, Margaret 318
Glashutte, H. P. 524
Glass 518-551

Globe 566, 568, 569, 571
Globe Wernicke 340
Gloucestershire Engineer Vols.
  123
Go To Sleep 184
Goblets, Glass 527-531
Goblets, Silver 717
Godard 150
Goddard, L. 610
Goddess of Sport 614
Godfrey, B. 708
Godfrey, Eliz. 684
Godfrey, Sir Edmund 730
Godwin, E. W. 351
Goffart, J. L. 661
Gold 552-555
Gold Medal 613
Golden Eye 323
Golding, W. 137
Goldscheider 201
Goldsmiths & Silversmiths
  Co. Ltd 691, 696, 709,
  747
Goltzius, Hendrik 666
Gonic 234
Goodall, T. F. 644
Goosens, J. E. 659
Gordon Highlanders 74, 77
Gore 604
Gorham, John 723
Gorham Mfg. Co. 725, 737,
  743
Gori, A. 148, 150
Gorman, Carl Nelson 559
Gornik, Friedrich 149
Gors & Kallmann, R. 646
Goshu Ju Soheishi Sei 127
Goss 202
Goto 118, 120
Gotthard Schuh 644
Gottlob, Fernand Louis 660
Gough & Bowen 113
Gould, James 694
Gould, Wm. 694
Graceful Parachute Descent
  71
Graham, Geo. 281
Graham, J. 684
Grainger & Co. 269
Gramophone & Typewriter
  Ltd. 618
Granges, David Des 653
Graphometer 566
Grasshopper 606
Gray & Reynolds 295
Great Western 611
Greek Fire 192, 193
Green Arrow 609
Green, David 695
Green, J. 280
Greene, G. 137
Greenwood, Frans 530
Grenadier Co. 83
Grendey 371
Grenouille 615
Greuter, M. 566
Greuze 197
Gricci, J. 132
Griffen, Smith & Hill 165
Grimalde 280
Grimshaw, A. 132

Grindlay, Capt. Robert
  Melville 134
Grodenthal 326, 327
Groth, S. C. S. 699
Grover & Baker 565
Grubbe 267
Grueby 203
Grun, Jules Alexandre 661
Grundy, Wm. 711
Guandi 149
Guanyin 576
Gui 543
Guild of Handicraft 521,
  713, 718, 724
Gundlach, E. 564
Gunthermann 762, 764
Gurschner, G. 139, 151
Guy 763, 768
Gyokudo 576
Gyokuzan 577
Gypsy Moth 73

Hackwood 258, 259, 261
Hadley 263, 265
Hagenauer 782
Hahn 568
Haida, Fachschule 543
Hairy Family of Mandalay,
  The 644
Hakuryu 631
Halberd 128
Halbig, S & H. 328
Halford, F. M. 134
Hall 570
Hall, R. 246
Halliday, G. 723
Hamburger & Co. 100
Hamburger Rogers 118, 123
Hamilton, Richard 669
Hamilton, Robert 731
Hamilton & Co. 299, 717, 740
Han 203, 204
Handel 588
Handschar Division 91
Hannaford 520
Hannam, T. 741, 743
Hannam, Thos. 698
Hanoverian Hussars 75
Harbeson 636
Harding & Son, J. 108
Hardy 287
Hare, Davd. 687
Harmensz, R. 666, 667
Harper, Sally 248
Harradine, L. 189
Harris 564
Harris, J. B. 613
Harris & Co., J. 776
Harris & Co., W. 130
Harris & Sons, Chas. S. 686
Harrison, M. R. 609
Harrods Ltd 616
Hart, Chas. H. 323
Hart, John 278
Hartnack. E. 571
Hartwell, A. 710
Hasegawa 561
Hassell 614
Hasted, Edward 134

Hastings Kettle 202
Hauer, B. G. 222
Hauer, Bonaventura G. 219
Hausmalerei 200, 224
Hawkes & Co 89
Hawksley, G. & J. W. 111
Hayden & Gregg 713
Hayter, Mary-Ann 682
Hayter, Sir George. 657
Hayne, S. 697, 744
Hazlehurst, Thos. 649
Healy 647
Healey 774
Hearnshaw Bros. 314
Heath, T. 570
Heath & Middleton 526
Heckel, Erich 667
Hehe Erxian 574
Hel, Joseph 623
Heller, J. H. 619
Helmets 88-93
Heming, Thos 694
Henkel, Chas. 778
Henko 67
Hennell, Robt. 747
Hennell II, Robt. 707
Henry, Guillaume 717
Herbert & Co., S. 711
Herder, F. 87
Hereford Kettle 202
Herefordshire Militia 115
Hernantis, Sebastian 123
Herold, C. F. 222
Herter Bros. 355
Hertfordshire Yeomanry 79
Hess 768
Hesse Infantry 93
Hewitt & Co., James L. 647
Higgs, Robt & Peter 272
Higo 124-126
Hilliard, J. 133
Hindmarsh, George 705
Hirato 121
Hirochika 127
Hiroshige GA. 663
His Master's Choice 66
Hisatoshi 143
History of Guy 134
History of the Apple Pie 137
History of the Birds of Ceylon, A. 136
History of the Five Indian Nations of Canada, The 137
Hitchcock, Thos 646
H. M. Reserve Regt. of Dragoon Guards 81
HMV 619, 621
Hocker, J. 303
Hockney, David 658, 663
Hodo 632
Hoffmann, J. 528, 546
Hofler, J. P. 685
Hohlwein, Ludwig 660
Hoin, Claude Jean Baptiste 653
Holaday, Sarah 743
Holder, Ernest L. 622
Holland & Sons 465
Hollingshead, Joseph & John 279
Hollingshead, Wm. 706

Holmes, Wm. 708
Holmes, L.T. 323
Holst, R. N. Roland 661
Holzl 67
Home Guard 82
Homer 589
Hone, Horace 650
Hone, Nathaniel 651
Hooker, Sir W. J. 135
Hope, Thos 600
Hopi 558, 559
Hopi Placca 165
Hopkins, O. 278
Horn 556
Horoldt 220, 223
Hoshunsai Masayuki 626
Hoskins, John 653
Hosteter, Jacob 281
Hosono Sozaemon Masamori 125
Hotchkiss & Benedict 290
Hougham, Chas. 745
Hougham, Solomon 702
Houghton 162
Houles & Co. 701
Hours of The Virgin 136
Howard, J. 777
Howard Co., The 776
Howes & Burnley 589
Hoyer, Cornelius 654
Hozan 576
Hsuan-te 148
Huber, P. 638
Huber, Patriz 525
Hughes, Thos. 270
Hukin & Heath 523, 532, 698, 707, 720, 726, 745
Humidor 155
Hunslet 609
Hunt, J. S. 722
Hunt, John S. 688. 707
Hunt & Roskell 719
Hunter, Mary Anne 682
Huntingdonshire Light Horse Volunteers 93
Hurd, Jacob 709
Hurley, F. T. 565
Hurter, Johann Heinrich 657
Hush He's Busy 68
Hussar, The 611
Hussars 74
Hutchins, A. 278
Hutton, Wm. 726
Hutton & Son, William 747

Icart, Louis 666
Iconography, The 136
Idylls of the Norfolk Broads 644
Il Torneo 136
Illinois Watch Co. 299
Illustrations to Tennyson 644
Imari 205-207
Immelmann 71
Imperial German Army 122
Imperial German Cavalry 75
Imperial German Hussars 88
Imperial Glass Co. 544
Indian Army Service Corps 80

Indian Art 557-559
Indian Craftsman Series 263, 268, 269
Inkstands, Silver 718
Inniskilling Dragoons 92
Inros 560, 561
Inspiration 183
Instruments 562-571
Intarsio 288
I. R. & Co. 702
Iron & Steel 572, 573
Isis 183
Issai 631
Italian China 208, 209
Ivory 574-579
Iwashiro School 629
Iye Mushi 89

Jackson 770
Jackson, Julia 644
Jackson, O. 710
Jacot, Henri 273, 275
Jade 580, 581
Jadison, Joseph 709
Jaeger 141
Jager, Lorenz 123
Jaguar 617, 770
Jamar, S. 356
Jambiya 84
James, Thos. 709
Japanese China 210, 211
Jaquemart 303
Jardiniere 488, 489
Jefferys 297
Jelliff, J. 382
Jenkinson, D. 610
Jenson, Georg 306, 582, 583, 686, 687, 690, 692, 695, 696, 713, 719, 721, 732, 745, 749
Jep 763
J. E. R. 154
Jeu De La Giraffe 134
Jewellery 582-585
Jinty 611
Jobbagy 141
Jogyoku 577
Johns & Pegg 119
Joi 126
Joint Chiefs of Staff 79
Jones, A. E. 687
Jones, Ball & Poor 712, 719
Jones, George 212
Jones, Hen. 270
Jones, John 729
Jones, Lows & Ball 740
Jones, Norman 73
Jones Sewing Machines 66
Joyce, Richard 234
Jugendstil 638
Jugs, Glass 532
Jugs, Silver 719
Juliet 609
Jumeau 328, 329
Jumelle 160
Juntoku 633
Jurgensen, J. 302
Jurine 605
Jurojin 577
J. V. 157

Kabotie, Fred 557
Kabuto 89
Kachina 559
Kaiguoku 632
Kaigyokusai 630
Kakosai 561
Kammer & Reinhardt 620
Kamp 662
Kamp, Willm. Hubt. Van 619
Kandinsky, Wassily 668
Kandler, Chas. F. 711
Kandler, F. 745
Kandler, J. J. 197, 219-223, 225
Kanesada 120
Kangxi 212
Kanjiro Kawai 251
Kannon 575
Kao 632, 633
Katana 120, 121
Kauba, C. 142
Kauffman, A. 657
Kayersinn 636
Kayophone 618
Kazuyoshi 119
Kazuyuki 575
Kearsar 607
Keene, Michael 650
Keiko Hasegawa 211
Kelly Boy 327
Kelpra Studio 669
Kenworthy, K. R. F. 613
Kennard & Jenks 743
Kensington Glass Works 526
Kenya Beer 66
Kern Switar 161
Kessler 144
Kestner 326
Kettle Stand 721
Khanjarli 87
Khecheong 748
Kigyoku 628
Kindjal 86
King & Co., Henry S. 644
King, David 710
King George III & Queen Caroline 140
King James I 611
King of the Herd 558
King of the Road 589
King's Own Light Infantry 82
King's Own Regt. of Norfolk Imperial Yeomanry 76, 90
King's Royal Rifle Corps. 81
Kinji 560, 561
Kinkozan zo 213
Kinsburger, S. 145
Kintozan 237
Kinzan 213
Kipling, R. 700
Kirchner, Ernst Ludwig 662, 663
Kirk, S. 712
Kirkup, J. 727
Kirschenbach, J. J. 431
Kitamura 74
Kitosai Terumitsu 121
Kiyomitsu 120
Klinger, Max 667
Kloster Veilsdorf 198-200
Kneehole Desks 423-425

Knibb, Joseph 271
Knox, Archibald 292, 636, 638, 705, 716, 747
Kodak 162
Kogo 158
Kogyoku 574
Kogyoku (Anrakusai) 629
Kogyoku, Shoryusai 561
Kogyokusai 627
Kokei 631
Komai 157
Komin 632
Konig, Anton F. 656, 657
Konig & Wernicke 324
Konoike 734
Koppel, Henning 582, 584, 585
Koraku 574
Koshare 558
Kozan 579
Kretzschmar 225
Kris 84, 86
Kromskop 569
Kruse, Kathe 328
Kutani 213
Kyoto 213
Kyoto Namikawa 310
Kyoto School 626, 628, 631, 633
Kyo-Sukashi 125
Kyusekirin 213

L. & Co, 748
L. G. of Le Guay 242
La Verite Meconnue 146
Lacloche Freres 721
Laquer 586
Lacroix, LD, 291
Lacy & Co 101
Lacy, Catherine 760
Lagonda 615, 772
Lahore 568
Lalique 520, 521, 523, 524, 525, 542-546, 615
Lamerie, Paul De 706, 710, 711
Lampi 652
Lamps 587-591
Lancaster 113
Lancaster & Sons, J. 161
Lancaster International 162
Lancere, Eugene 148
Lanchester 772
Langlands & Goodrick 723
Langley, T. 469
Lannvier, Chas. H. 458, 513
Laocoon 592
Laporte, Emile Henri 145
Large Tables 480, 481
Laughlin Jnr. John 686
Laughlin, John 741
Laurencin, Marie 659
Lautier, B. 291
Law, Thos. 698, 740
Lawrence 112
Lawrence & Co 748
Le Faguays 722
Le Forgeron 141
Le Maire 568
Le Verrier 591
Lea-Francis 774

Leach, Bernard 214
Leach, Janet 214
Leach, John 214
Lead Cutter 123
Learner's Car 762
Lederer, Hugo 145
Lee, Joseph 655
Leeke, Ralph 710
Lefevre Claude 655
Legge, Capt. W. V. 136
Legras 587
Lehmann 762, 764
Leib Regt 92
Leica 162
Lejeune 616
Leleu 588
Leleu, Jules 681
Lely 655
Lemercier 660
Lenci 209, 215, 326
Lenoir 276
Lenoir A Paris 566, 567
Lenzkirch 293
Lepine 301
Leroy 275, 283, 298, 301
Leroy, Desire 227
Les Creations 658
Lesney 769
Letter Rack 721
Levrier 615
Levy, Lucien 196
Leybourn, William 136
Leyland-Thomas 616
Lias, I. H. & G. 727
Liberty & Co 231, 292, 293, 418, 636, 638, 689, 693, 705, 747
Lieberich Fabre. C. F. Woerffel 149
Liege, B. 660
Lievres 545
Lifeguards & Officer 763
Light Company 74, 75
Lily Maid, The 189
Limbach 133
Lincoln & Lindsey Banking Co. 634
Lindenstaedt, Hans 658
Linderman, Clara C. 236
Linen Press 512, 513
Linnell, J. 378, 439
Linsey-Woolsey 670
Linthorpe 173, 174
Lip Sofa 440
Littlefield, Jane 682
Livemont, Privat 661
Liverpool 215
Lloyd George 68
Lloyd, Snr, J. 686
Lock, Nathaniel 699
Locker, J. 686
Lockey Hill 622
Lodestone 568
Loetz 542, 544
Logan, G. 170
Lohands 578
Lomax, J. 284
London Aerodrome 70
London Sporting Park Ltd 115
London Stereoscopic Co. 160, 162
London Two Gentleman 643
Long Hair Dancer 557
Longcase Clocks 278-285

Longton Hall 216
Lord of the Flies 137
Lorenzl 146, 151, 722
Loring, J. 282
Losanti 165
Lott, John 625
Louvet, Hubert 691
Lowboys 426
Lowe, Thos 612
Lowestoft 174, 216
Lownes, Joseph 736
Lucas 589
Lucky Jim 135
Lucy Anne 190
Lukin Wm. 716
Lunardi, Vincent 135
Lund & Blockley 276
Lustre 216
Lynn 548, 551
Lynx 773
Lyon, D. 641
Lyons, J.C. 135

M. G. 770-772, 775
Ma-Pe-Wi 557
Macallan Swan, J. 147
Maggiolini 407
Magic Disc 766
Magnette 770
Magnum Ruger Super 102
Mahon, C. P. 634
Mail Coach 108
Maine Flying Scoter 323
Maltese Cross 78, 81, 585
Mameluke 118, 119, 122, 123
Man Ray 645
Manchester Guardian 769
Manners, James 731
Mantegna, Andrea 668
Mantel Clocks 286-293
Manticha, P. 131
Manton, Joseph 115
Mappin & Webb 698, 718
Marble 592, 593
Marblehead 164, 165
Marc, Franz 662
Marcolini 224
Marconiphone 571
Marfurt 658
Margaine, F. A. 273
Margas, Jacob 732
Marguerit, Nicolas 555
Mariette 105
Marinot 540
Markham, J. 299
Marklin 608-610
Markwick 282
Marples, Robt. 314
Marquand, F. 712, 740
Marseille, Armand 129, 327-329
Marsh & Tatham 338
Marshall & Sons 701
Marshall, Craig, Wm. 650
Marshall, Mrs. J. Walter 670
Marshall, Wm. 253, 712
Marti & Cie 276, 277
Martin 565

Martineau 298
Martinet, Milo 660
Martinware 217, 218
Marx, Louis 764
Marville, Chas. 642
Mary, Santa Marta 641
Masakazu 629
Masamitsu 579
Masanao 630
Masatami (Shomin) 629, 631
Masatamo 630
Masatsugu 629
Masayuki 428
Maserati 775
Masileau & Co. 73
Masonic 388, 433, 526, 554
Mason's China 218
Master Mariner 307
Masters, Richard Henry 448
Mathew, Wm. 713
Matisse, Henri 667, 668
Matthsson, Bruno 438
Mauser 'Broom Handle' 103
Maws 216
Maxted, J. 609
Mayer, T. J. & J 67, 68
Maythorn 770
Mazarin 425
Meat Press 721
Meccano 764
Meckenem, Israhel Van 667
Medals 94-98
Medcat 141
Mee, Mrs, Anne 656
Mees 296
Meikei 626
Meiko, Emperor 578
Meir & Son, J. 171
Meissen 219-225, 594
Mellier & Co, C. 646
Melling, Jno. 282
Mendicant, The 189
Mene, P. J. 140
Mentor 160
Merganser 323
Merkelbach, Reinhold 199
Methuen, George 744
Mettayer, Lewis 708
Meyer 220
Meyer, F. E. 168, 221
Meyer Inc., H. S. 79
Mickey Mouse Organ Grinder 762
Microscope 562, 563, 564, 566, 570, 571
Mignon & Diana 152
Milegal Meter 615
Mills 104
Mills, N. 729, 748
Miller, B. 611
Miller Junr & Co, H. 71
Milne & Campbell 699
Minaudiere 721
Minerva 616
Ming 226, 227
Miniature Furniture 602, 603
Minko 633
Minnie 613
Mino Kanetsune 118
Minton 227-230
Miochi 125
Mirbel, A. 655
Mirrors 594-601

Miscellaneous Antiques 602-605
Miscellaneous Glass 533
Miscellaneous Silver 720, 721
Mitchells & Butlers' Ales 69
Mito Kinko 127
Miyao 142
Mode 243
Model Ships 606, 607
Model Trains 608-611
Models 612, 613
Models, M. H. C. 611
Models, Silver 722, 723
Mogan 675
Mohandas Gandhi 643
Moigniez, J. 147
Mole 123
Momoyama 159, 586
Monandrian Plants of the Order Scitamineae 134
Monarch 480, 618, 620, 621
Mondain 554, 555
Money Box 765
Monroe, Marilyn 645
Montgolfier 71
Moore & Woodward 109
Moore, Bernard 216
Moore, Chas. 706
Moorcroft 231
Moorcroft Macintyre 231
Morandi, Giorgio 662
Morane Saulnier 72
Moreau, Louis 590
Morel & Hughes 381
Morel & Seddon 370
Morey & Ober 637
Morgan & Saunders 388, 390
Morgan, Willm 272
Morning Glory 618, 621
Morris 771, 775
Morris Service 66
Morrisware 173
Mortlock 202
Moser 528
Moser, Koloman 545
Mosserine 588
Moth Minor 72
Mother 617
Motley, Jn, 280
Motor Sport 617
Motoring Items 614-617
Mott & Co, J. L. 775
Mourgue, Olivier 439
Movado 304
Mozchaeva, R. 659
Mucha, Alphonse 660, 661
Mugs, Silver 723
Muirhead, James 563
Muller 543
Muller, B. 723
Munch, Edvard 662
Murdoch of Doune 107
Murray, Keith 260, 261
Muret, Albert 661
Muroe 142
Musical Boxes 618-621
Musical Instruments 622-625
Musket 115, 116
Musketoon 114, 117
Mustards, Silver 724
Mycock, Wm. S. 234
Myochin Munenaga 88

MacDonald, Barbara 147
McInnes, Dobbie 569
McIntire, Samuel F. 393
McKay, John 696
McLaughlin, L. 165

Nagamitsu 577
Nailsea 526, 532, 533
Nakamura Haruhiro 121
Nantgarw 232
Naokazu 627
Nashiji 561
Nasson, Aldo 542
Nast 233
National Bank 635
Navajo 557, 558, 559
Nazi 74, 83, 85, 87-93, 122
Neale, W. 721
Neapolitan School 625
Neffe, Meyr's 545
Nepveu, Le 291
Netsuke 626-633
Neu, Wenzel 198, 199
New Bedford 588
New Century Cycle 764
New Flora Britannica, The
   136
New Land 109, 115
Newbold, Thos 748
Newbury, Bessie 252
Newill, Mary 761
Newman Cartwright 283
Newmarket Bank 635
Newton & Co 567
Newton, John 298
Newton, Sir William John 649
Northam, John 552
Nicholson, Wm. 691
Nicole Freres 620, 621
Nicquet 239, 240
Nielsen, H. 692, 696, 717, 721
Nielson, Harald 714
Nihon Yozan 213
Nikkormat 160
Nikkosai 561
Nikolsky 616
Nilson 200
Nina 765
Nineteen Eighty Four 134
Nipper 602
Njers, Ljerka 191, 252
Nock, H. 113
Nocturne 141
Noke 590
Noke, Chas. J. 190
Noon Cannon 567
Norfolk Champion Boots 67
Norfolk Regt. 79
Norge 71
Norman 174
Northern Bank 634
Northern British Locomotive
   Co. Ltd 641
Northumberland Artillery Vols 78
Norton 772
Norton, Eardley 271
Noshu Seki 121
Notron, Yeldrae 271
Notsjo, Nuutajarvi 545
Nottinghamshire Volunteers 113

N. P. 116, 117
Nude Girl With Shawl 722
Nutmegs 725
Nutting, Wallace 387
NYC. 1949. 643

O-Wakizashi 120
Oakley, G. 471
Oates, Captain L. E. G. 92
Oboshi-Hoshibachi 88
Obrisset 728
Occasional Tables 482-491
Occhi 547
Ochsenkopf 518
Odartchenko 239
Odundo, Magdalene A. N. 191
Ofner, J. 139
Ohr, G. E. 165
Okatomo 629, 633
Okatoto 628
Old Balloon Seller, The 189
Oliver, Isaac 653
Oliver, John 731
Ondines 524
Onin 126
Ono Ryomin 627, 631
Ontoflex 160
Orchies 193
Ordnance Survey of Jerusalem 640
Oriental China 232
Orkney Artillery Vols. 83
Orlandini, A. 624
Orrery 289, 565
Ortelli & Co., N. 133
Orton Bradshaw, Stanley 73
Orwell, G. 134
Ota Tameshiro 308
Oudry 240
Ouville, Charles D' 648
Ovaltine 66
Owari 126
Owen, George 266, 267, 269
Owl Kachina 558
Ozier 256

Pace, Thomas 272
Pacific 610
Packard 771
Paisley, Julia Matild 682
Pajou, A. 239, 242
Palais Du Louvre 643
Palais Du Tuilleries 643
Palais Royale 154-156, 158
Palethorp, Robt 639
Palethorpes 69
Paliand À Besancon 272
Palmer 130
Palmer & Co 588
Panhard Levassor 763
Pankok Bernhard 316
Pannier 610, 611
Pansy 611
Pantin, Simon 703
Panzer 82
Paper Money 634, 635
Paperweight Inkwell 533

Paperweights 534-539
Parallel Rule 571
Parang 85
Parian 232
Paris 233
Park Ward 770
Parker Field & Sons 122
Parker, J. 709, 738
Partizan 128
Pasquier, Pierre 656
Passenger, Chas 188
Pastorelli 130
Patent Steam Carpet Beating
   Co. 66
Patrick, J. 132, 133
Pattison 114
Pauly 117
Payne, John 730
Payne, W. 227
Peaslee, Judith N. 322
Pedometer 563
Peekhaus., E & H. 122
Pemberton, Samuel 748
Pembroke Tables 492, 493
Penn-Sayers, P. 613
Pennell 107
Pepys 338
Peridiez, G. 475
Perkins, Bacon & Petch 634
Perl, Karl 152
Pero, Isabel 738
Perruches 546
Perry, A. 184
Perry Son & Co. 698
Persil 69
Perthshire Regt 79
Peruvian Women 642
Pesh-Kabz 86
Pet, Joh 566
Peterson, Abraham 684
Peterson, Peter 708
Petitot, L. 292
Peviri 779
Pewter 636-639
Peynot, E. 152
Pezzato 546
Pfranger, Snr. 199
Philippe & Co., P. 298, 301, 303,
   307
Philippe, R. 174
Philippes, Henry 135
Phipps, T. 725, 729, 738
Photographs 640-645
Photographs From Abyssinia 645
Pianos 646, 647
Picard, M 660
Picasso, Pablo 666, 668
Pick Plate Note 634
Pickelhaube 91-93
Picturesque Tour, A. 136
Pier Table 496, 497
Pierre Le Doux, Jean 241
Piguet, Audemars 307
Pike & Son 133
Pilgrim Century 386
Pilkington 234
Pillar Dial 570
Pilleau, Peze 738
Pinet, Nicolas 656
Piranesi. G. B. 140
Pistofilo (Bonaventura) 136

Pistols 99-109
Pith Helmet 88
Pitts, Wm. 684, 697, 708
Planche, Andrew 188
Players Please 67, 68
Pleydell-Bouverie, Katharine 253
Plimer, Andrew 651, 653, 655
Pliny's Doves 604
Plummer, John F. 70
Pobjoy Cataract 72
Pogliani 351
Poivre 545
Polearm 128
Poliarkova, K. 659
Polito 246
Pollock, John 727
Polyphones & Musical Boxes
  618-621
Poncelet, Jacqueline 251
Pontifax, D. 743
Pool Table 480
Pope, Francis C. 190
Popeye 768
Porringers 725
Porsche 774
Portal, Abraham 727
Portet, Jean 649
Portland 524
Portrait Miniatures 648-657
Poschinger, Ferdinand 547
Posters 658-661
Potez 72
Potschappel 199
Pouss-Nouk-Nouk 613
Powder Flasks 110,111
Power, Tho. 283
Praha, M. 659
Pratt & Whitney 72
Prattware 234
Precursor Tank 608
Preedy, J. 684, 708
Preedy, Joseph 697
Preiss, F. 151, 289, 579
Pressnitz, F. F. Mayer Von 224
Priest, John 693, 694
Priest, Wm 705
Priestess 152
Prime of Miss Jean Brodie, The
  135
Primitive Brant 323
Prince Albert 644
Prince of Wales's Own Royal
  Wiltshire Yeomanry 76
Princs of Wales's Own West
  Yorkshire Regt 78
Princess Alice 640
Princess Royal & Prince
  Arthur As Summer 642
Prints 662-669
Prof. Highschool Daguer-
  reotype Institution 645
Protractor 566, 569
Provender for the Monastery
  198
Provincial Bank 634
Prussian Artillery 92, 93
Prussian Infantry 91, 93
Prussian Line Cuirassier Regt.
  90, 92
Prussian Regt. of Garde Du
  Corps. 75, 88, 89

Pub Table 485
Punch Magazine 71
Puritan Soap 68
Puttnam, James, H. 638
Pyramid 714

Quare, Daniel 281
Queen's Lancers 75
Queen's Own Regt. 83
Queensland Scottish 81
Questura, R. 660
Quilts 670, 671

Raby, E. 268
Radford 299
Raingo Fres. 290, 291
Rakan 579
Raleigh 66
Ramage, John 649
Ramsden, A. 646
Ramsden & Carr 699, 716
Ramsden, Omar 687-689, 694,
  706, 707, 717, 719, 720
Ramsey Robt 270
Rantei 626
Ratseys & Lapthorn 604
Rattle For Germination 557
Ravenel 330, 333
Rawlings, Chas. 220
Ray, Man 645
Reckitt's Blue 67
Red Ashay 617
Red Gem 619
Redding's Luzo 161, 162
Redier A Paris 568
Redoubtable 606
Redware 234
Reed, Olga G. 236
Refrigerator 605
Regiment of Life Guards
  109
Rehwald, J. D. 685
Reily, James 652
Reinalda, Agge Jelles 685
Reinicke, P. 223
Rejlander, O. G. 642
Revenue, Police 122
Rey, Margaret 252
Rhodes, David 259
Rich, Mary 174
Rich, Obadiah 742
Richard 542
Richards, T. 100
Richardson, Arthur 622
Richthofen, Manfred Von 70
Rie, Lucy 235
Riemerschmid, R. 199
Riessner, Stretmacher & Kessel 192
Rifles 112-117
Rikouku Nokami Fujiwara
  Kanenobu 121
Riley 772
Risler & Carre 701
Ritter, Jeremias 709
Riviere, G. 193
Riviere, M. Giraud 143

Robart 530
Robert, L. V. E. 147
Roberte, Jane 247
Roberts 378
Roberts & Co., John 694
Roberts, Cadman & Co. 697
Robin Starch 69
Robins, Thos. 698, 744, 745
Robinson I, Thomas 702
Robinson & Leadbetter 232
Robinson, E. 725, 729, 738
Robinson, John 742
Rocca, Joseph 622, 623
Rochard 143
Rochard, Simon J. 650
Roche, Sampson T. 651
Rockstuhl, Alois G. 652
Rodgers Joseph 85
Roe, N. 71
Roger Et Gallet 540
Rohde, J. 686, 695
Rohde, Johan 713, 715
Rohilkund Vol. Rifle Corps 78
Rohlfs 780
Rolleiflex 161
Rolex 304, 307
Rolls, Royce 770, 773-775
Rolls Tourer 762
Rookwood 236
Roscoe, William 134
Rose, John 184
Rosenthal 199, 200
Roseville Pottery 188
Ross 162
Ross, Sir Wm, Charles 657
Rossay, J. A. 300
Rossetti 209
Roswell Gleason 637, 638
Rotali, Frateli 378
Rothenbush F. D. H. 236
Rouff 321
Roux, Alex 505
Rowland's Aqua D'oro 69
Rowland's Macassar Oil 67
Rowntree 66
Roy Charles Le 295
Royal Army Medical Corps 77
Royal Artillery 90, 122
Royal Dockyard Bn. 92
Royal Dux 236
Royal East India Vol. 75
Royal Fusiliers 83
Royal Horse Guards, (The Blues)
  91, 93
Royal Irish Dragoon Guards
  83, 91
Royal Lanark Militia 82
Royal Lancashire Militia 90
Royal Mail Stereolette 162
Royal Military Academy 90
Royal North British Fusiliers 79
Royal Polytechnic 131
Royal Scots 74, 81
Royal Tank Regt. 83
Royal Tyrone Fusiliers 79
Royal Warwickshire Regt. 82
Rozane Ware 188
Rozenburg 192
Rubberoid Roofing 68
Rubicon Twist 69
Rugg, Richard 742

ANTIQUES REVIEW

Rugs 672- 681
Rushton, J. 263
Ruskin 237
Russell, G. 188
Ryozan 211
Ryukai 574
Ryuko 633
Ryukosai 632

S. F. B. J. 327, 329
Sabattini, Lino 720, 735
Sado 124
Safavid 232
Sage, John Le 721
Saint-Omer 692, 705
Saint Vincent 520
Sakes, Paulus 685
Salazar, Fiona 170
Salem's (?), Phebeann H. 671
Salmone, M. 131
Salmson 770, 774
Salome & Herodias 152
Salts, Silver 726
Samplers 682, 683
Samson 196, 197
San Ildefonso 559
Sandoz 197
Sandwich 589
Sandwich Clambroth 522
Sang, Jacob 527, 530, 531, 549
Sang, Simon J. 530
Sancai 254, 255
Santa Ana 164
Santa Clare 164
Santa Clause 189
Sare, A. 613
Sari 629
Sashu No Ju Toshioki 124
Satsuma 237, 238
Saturday Evening Girls 164
Sauceboats 727
Saviouress 148
Savoye Freres & Cie 302
Savory, J. & A. 734
Savy 197
Sawyer, R. 742
Scenery Costumes & Architecture 134
Scent Bottles 540, 541
Sceptre 610
Schieland 550
Schleiertanz 700
Schliepstein 199, 200
Schmidt, Franz 327
Schneider 161
Schofield, Heer 734
School of Daubigny 652
School of Koloman Moser 192
Schott, N. 441
Schubert, Carl G. 200
Schwarzlot 257
Scofield, John 692, 693, 695, 704
Scott, Digby 691
Scowen 641
Screens 427-429
Sea Coast 132

Secretaire Bookcases 432-435
Secretaires 430, 431
Sector 570
Seguso 545
Seidel 223
Seignior, R. 281
Seiso 577
Seiya 144
Sekiran 626
Selchow, J. H. C. v. 200
Sellers, J. Henry 389
Semah, M. 567
Senefelder 658
Senzan 213
Serrurier-Bovy 371
Servia 612
Settees & Couches 436-441
Settles 436-438, 440
Seven Provinces 528
Severini, Gino 669
Sevres 239-242
Sewill 295
Sewing Machine 565, 570
Sextant 565
Seymour, Thos. 502
Shades 541
Shakespeare's Cottage 202
Shako 90, 92
Shand-Mason 612
Sharp 112
Sharp, R. 744
Shaw II, Wm. 705
Shaw, J. 748
Shaw, Thos. 748
Shelley 243
Shelley, Samuel 649
Shelton, Peter 558
Shepherd, G. 643
Sherratt, Obadiah 246, 250
Shibayama 631
Shichifukujin 577
Shields, Micha. 283
Shigemasa 627, 628
Shije, Velino 557
Shinko 428
Shinmei 575
Shinsai 575
Shirreff, Charles 649
Shizan 428
Shoji 211
Shoko 627
Short Solent 73
Shosai 143, 575
Shourds, Samuel 279
Showato 121
Shreve, Brown & Co. 712
Shrewsbury Service 172
Shufflebottoms, Elizabeth 682
Shuho 667
Shuji 632
Shunjuken Tadaomi 575
Shunpu 578
Shunsen 663
Shunyosai Nobuyuki 575
Sibley, R. 685, 742
Side Tables 494-497
Sideboards 442-445
Siebe, Gorman & Co. 315
Sika, Jutta 192
Silex 371

Silhouette 605
Silver 684-749
Silver Ghost 770
Simon & Halbig 129
Simmons 114
Simmons, Wm. 707
Simpoles 340
Sinclair, John 69
Singer Sewing Machines 66
Singleton, Wm. 654
Siotteling, J. 696
Sioux Maiden 559
Sirene 524
Sirletti, Giacomo 729
Skates 319
Skean Dhu 86
Skeen & Co., W. L. H. 641
Skeleton Clocks 294
Skinner's Horse 119
Slater, Eric 243
Sleath, Gabriel 740
Slessor, Hannah L. 682
Slessor, Jane 683
Slessor, Phebe L. 683
Sloane, Hans 178
Slocum 104
Slodtz 147
Sluiter, Willy 658
Smiley, Thos. 733
Smily, W & R 740
Smith II, B. 709, 745
Smith & Beck 571
Smith, Benjamin 691, 708, 721
Smith, D. 744
Smith, S. 691
Smith, Stephen 722, 735
Smith, Steven 423
Snake Tree 183
Snowdon, R. 499
Snuff Bottles 750, 751
Snuff Box 552-554, 728, 729
Sofa Tables 498, 499
Sohlingen, J. J. R. 118
Soiron 333
Somalvico & Son, J. 133
Somersetshire Regt. 82
Song 244
Sonnar 161
Sonor 661
Soten 127
Sousy Ricketts, Charles De 152
South Australia Militia Lancers 77
South Lancashire Regt. 80
South Staffordshire Regt. 81
South Wales Borderers 79
Southwell, Wm. 647
Spark, M. 135
Spavento, Capitano 198
Speedometer Co. Ltd., A. T. 616
Speilman, H. 781
Spencer, Gervase 648, 650
Sper, Adolf 746
Spicer, Henry 654
Spilsbury, Francis 723
Spirit Flask 720
Spirit of Triumph, The 614

796

Spitfire 73
Spode 245
Spoon Warmer 720
Spratt's 69, 763
Sprimont, Nicholas 710
Spring Morning, Busbridge 644
Springbok 611
St. Andrew 86
St. George 190
St. Louis 534, 536, 537, 538
St. Michael 146
Staffordshire China 246-250
Stands 446-452
Stanley 162, 562
Starr Arms Co. 102
Stauffer 303
Steel 230
Steiff 763-767
Steiner 324, 325, 327
Steinheil 562
Steinway, T. H. 647
Steinway & Sons 646
Stella 621
Stephen, Pierre 660
Stephens Inks 69
Stephens, Wm. 285
Steps 446, 447
Stereographoscope 564
Stereoscope 562, 564
Steuben 520
Stevengraph 70
Stevens, Samuel 278
Stevens, T. 70
Stewart, J. 711
Stewart Jr., Joseph 513
Stickley, Gustav 284, 346, 353, 383, 417, 448, 473, 496, 589, 779
Stickley, L. & J. G. 440
Stieglitz, Alfred 641
Stinton 263, 264, 268, 269
Stirling Single 611
Stirn's Waistcoat Detective Camera 161
Stoak, Gab 562
Stone 752, 753
Stoneware 251-253
Stools 453-455
Storr, Paul 555, 690, 709, 710, 726, 744, 749
Stourbridge 547
Strachan, A. J. 555
Straeton, Van Der 138
Stralsund 199
Strasbourg 193, 196
Stratford, W. 404
Strathspey Highlanders 83
Street, R. 279
Streeter, E. W. 287
Stroud, William 698, 710
Stroudley 611
Stubborn Donkey 766
Stubbs, J. 249
Sturm, F. 168
Sublime Harmony 621
Sucher 161
Sue Et Mare 351
Suffolk Dredging Tractor 612
Suites 456, 457
Sundial 565

Sunshade Girl 151
Suzuribako 158
Swan Ink 68
Swedish Livregementel 89
Sweetser Co., The 747
Swords 118-123
Sykes 110, 111
Sylvester 300
Symphonion 284, 285, 620, 621
Syng, R. 687
Systeme Campiche De Metz 296

Tabako-Bon 159
Table A Ecrire 487
Table Bureau 159
Tables 458-508
Tachi 120, 121
Tadamitsu 120
Tadaomi 577
Tahoma, Quincy 558
Takarabune 577
Tamahide 578
Tamayuki 574
Tamba School 630
Tamenuri 560
Tang 254, 255
Tangermann, Christian 652
Tankards 730, 731
Tantallon Castle 184
Tanto 118, 120, 121
Tapestries 754-756
Tapio Wirkkala 253
Tassie 604
Taylor & Perry 748
Taylor, E. A. 419
Taylor, H. A. 613
Taylor, Henry 644
Taylor, John 271, 279
Taylor, Samuel 738
Tazzas 732
Tea & Coffee Sets 733-737
Tea Caddies 738
Tea Kettles 739
Tea Tables 458-463
Teapots, Silver 740
Tecno 'P45' 374
Tegelsten, C. J. 749
Telescope 562, 567, 571
Televisor 565
Temple of Vesta 603
Temple, Shirley 329
Terracotta 256
Terrey, John Edward 733
Terroux, Madame 656
Tessar 160, 161
Tetes-De-Boule 155
Textiles 757-761
Thibault, Aimee 650
Thomas, F. B. 686
Thomas, Parry 616
Thorn, C. E. 612
Thornhill & Co., W. 274
Thornton-Pickard 162
Thoughts 143
Three Dahlias 521
Thuillier 287
Thunder House 568
Tiepolo, Giovanni Domenico 137

Tiffany 541, 555, 587, 591, 737, 747
Tiffany & Co. 299, 301, 697
Tiger Moth 72
Timbrell, R. 743
Timbrell, Robt. 704
Timeche, Bruce 557
Tinworth, G. 190
Tipp & Co. 768
Tohekido 577
Toilette Pastorale, La 331
Tolly, Jean 272
Tom 138
Tomochika 627
Tomoyuki 632
Tompion, Thos. 291
Tongue, John 748
Tonnel 554
Tools 314
Toshimasa 576
Toshitsugu 627
Touchon & Co. 298
Toullet Decamps 328
Toulouse-Lautrec, Henri De 663
Tournai 256
Tower, James 253
Toyomasa 630
Toys 762-769
Traffic Warner 562, 563
Transport 770-775
Tranter 103, 106
Trask, Israel 639
Trays & Salvers 741-743
Triang Minic 762, 763
Trick Pony 767
Trigg 131
Trivulzio, Count 257
Tropical Goertz Tenax 160
Tropical Model Improved Artist 160
Troughton & Simms 563
Trunks & Coffers 509-511
Tsu School 631
Tsubas 124-127
Tsuguji Foujita 669
Tsunemitsu 138
Tuck, Raphael 660, 661
Tudric 292, 293, 637, 638
Tumblers, Glass 541
Tureens, Silver 744, 745
Turn Teplitz, R. St. K. 193
Tut Tut 762
Tutt, Hannah 165
Typewriter 564, 570

U. S. Army 74
Ullmann, Th. 149
Ulster Bank 634
Underhill, H. A. 607
Union 184
Union Castle Line 68
Unite, George 686
United Kingdom Tea Company 67
Universal Dial 564, 568, 569, 570
Urns, Silver 746
Use of Chartres 136
Utamaro 666
Utamaro Hitsu 662

V. P. 161
Vacheron & Constantin 304
Vajradhara 142
Van Cleef & Arpels 583
Vase-Kraft 588
Vases, Glass 542-547
Vases, Silver 747
Vaso 545
Vedar 529
Velazquez 652
Velde, Henry Van De 713
Velox 773
Venini 542, 546, 547
Ver Centre 545
Vercassou 658
Verde Di Prato 592
Verga 304
Verneau, Ch. 661
Verre Francais, Le 541
Vestal 722
Veyrant 720
Vichy, G. 129
Videau, Ayme 739
Viel-O-Phone 619
Vienna 257
Vile, Wm. 778
Villanis, E. 152
Vinaigrettes, Silver 748
Vincent, Edward 687
Vincent, Rene 659
Virginia 610
Voille, Jean Marie 651
Volkstedt 198
Voyage Round Great Britain, 137
Vuillaume, Jean-Baptiste 622, 623, 625
Vulliamy 301
Vyse, Charles 257

Waals, P. 351, 466
Wackerle, Prof, J. 198
Waffen S. S. 91
Wagner 168
Wain, Louis 173
Wakelin, E. 693, 697, 727, 738
Wakelin, Edward 684, 709
Wakelin, J. 746
Wakizashi 119
Walker & Hall 689, 709, 741
Walker, Joseph 731
Wall Clocks 295-297
Waller, Edmund 135
Walley 164
Wallis, R. 116
Wallpaper 602,605
Walmore 571
Walrath 164
Walton, J. 136
Ward, Benj. 271
Ward Bros., L. T. 323
Ward, John 251
Ward, Richd 270
Wardrobes & Armoires 512, 513
Warhol, Andy 663
Warren 297
Warrior 557
Wartenberg, S. 277
Washstands 514
Wasp 72
Watches 298-303
Watchmakers Lathe 569

Waterloo Tree 554
Watkins. J. 130
Watson Type 764
Watt, Wm. 351
Watts Gun, The 115
Watts, Jas. 288
Watson, J. 567
Watson, John 691, 711
Way, Charlotte 683
Weapons 128
Weathervanes 776, 777
Webley 99
Webster 272, 292, 298
Wedgwood 258-261
Wedgwood & Bentley 258, 260, 261
Weekes, James 636
Weeks 141
Weeks, Fredricks e. 640, 641
Weeks Museum 290
Weigall, H. 141
Weisweiler 446, 449, 452
Weller Dickensware 165
Wellington 140, 141, 145
Wendel, S. 696
Wenford Bridge 176, 177
Werkstatte Wiener 546
Wesson's & Leavitt's 107
West, F. 610
West Norfolk Regt 74
West Yorkshire Regt 78
Westerwald 170, 252
Westward Ho Smoking Mixture 66
Weston Of Brighton 107
Weyersberg, Paul 86, 122
Whatnots 515
Wheeler 648
Whieldon 259, 261, 262
Whipham & Wright 705
Whipham, Thos 708
White Glass Works 526
Whitefriars 533
Whitelaw, David 299
Whiting Mfg., Co. 711
Whiting, Riley 292
Whitney 105
Wilkes, John 188
Wilkie, I. H. 606
Wilkinson, Bradbury 635
Wilkinson, Henry 698, 733
Wilkinson Sword 84
Will, Henry 637
Willard, Aaron 280, 281, 295
Willard, Alex. J. 279
Willard, B. 285
William Dean, The 610
Williams 112
Williams, T. R. 640
Williamson, Samuel 740
Willings & Co 68
Willis Good, J. 722
Willmore, J. 554
Willmore, Joseph 729
Wills, W. D. & H. O. 66, 67
Wilson, Capt. Charles W. 640
Wilson, 'Gus' Aaron 323
Wilson, Margaret 300
Willson, T. 505
Wiltberger, C. 704
Winchester 112

Winchcombe Pottery 176
Windmills 282
Wine Coolers, Silver 749
Wine Coolers 516, 517
Wine Glasses 548-551
Wine Label 720, 721
Winter, James 436
Winters, Christian 278
Wisker 133
Wittelsbach 239
Wittingham, R. 313
Wolfers, P. 583
Wolfers Freres 583
Wolff David 530, 548, 594
Worcester 263-269
Workboxes & Games 500-503
Worth 541
Wood 778-784
Wood, David 286
Wood, Enoch 262
Wood, H. J. 173
Wood Ralph 262
Wood, Samuel 696
Woodhead, G. 85
Wricklemarsh 728
Wright 71
Wright, Chas 708
Wristwatches 304-307
Writing Tables & Desks 504-508
Wucai 227
Wye Level 566
Wyland, N. 284
Wylie & Lochhead 419
Wyon, E. W. 173

Xenar 160
Xpres 162

Yamada School 629, 631
Yamahiko 629
Yamashiro 121
Yapp & Woodward 728
Yasuyoshi 721
Yavapai 557
Yazan 628
Yokhi 578
York & Lancaster Regt. 79
Yorke, Edward 703
Young, Grace 236
Young, J. 710
Young, S. C. 726
Yoshitada (?) 630
Yoshitomo 628
Ysart, Paul 534-536
Yukimune 121
Yuma 559
Yun Wenming 313
Yvelines 546

Zappler 296
Zeiss 161
Zeiss, Carl 588
Zeshin 159
Zettel, J. 236
Zia 559
Zimmerman, A & J 716
Zinke, Christian F. 648, 651, 652, 654-656
Zoetrope 565
Zoffany, Johann 335
Zuccani 131
Zwichl, F. 700